World Yearbook of
Education 2010

World Yearbook of Education Series

Series editors: Terri Seddon, Jenny Ozga, Gita Steiner-Khamsi and Agnes van Zantén

World Yearbook of Education 1989
HEALTH EDUCATION
Edited by Chris James, John Balding and Duncan Harris

World Yearbook of Education 1990
ASSESSMENT AND EVALUATION
Edited by Chris Bell and Duncan Harris

World Yearbook of Education 1991
INTERNATIONAL SCHOOLS AND INTERNATIONAL EDUCATION
Edited by Patricia L. Jonietz and Duncan Harris

World Yearbook of Education 1992
URBAN EDUCATION
Edited by David Coulby, Crispin Jones and Duncan Harris

World Yearbook of Education 1993
SPECIAL NEEDS EDUCATION
Edited by Peter Mittler, Ron Brouilette and Duncan Harris

World Yearbook of Education 1994
THE GENDER GAP IN HIGHER EDUCATION
Edited by Suzanne Stiver Lie, Lynda Malik and Duncan Harris

World Yearbook of Education 1995
YOUTH, EDUCATION AND WORK
Edited by Leslie Bash and Andy Green

World Yearbook of Education 1996
THE EVALUATION OF HIGHER EDUCATION SYSTEMS
Edited by Robert Cowen

World Yearbook of Education 1997
INTERCULTURAL EDUCATION
Edited by David Coulby, Jagdish Gundara and Crispin Jones

World Yearbook of Education 1998
FUTURES EDUCATION
Edited by David Hicks and Richard Slaughter

World Yearbook of Education 1999
INCLUSIVE EDUCATION
Edited by Harry Daniels and Philip Garner

World Yearbook of Education 2000
EDUCATION IN TIMES OF TRANSITION
Edited by David Coulby, Robert Cowen and Crispin Jones

World Yearbook of Education 2001
VALUES, CULTURE AND EDUCATION
Edited by Roy Gardner, Jo Cairns and Denis Lawton

World Yearbook of Education 2002
TEACHER EDUCATION: DILEMMAS AND PROSPECTS
Edited by Elwyn Thomas

World Yearbook of Education 2003
LANGUAGE EDUCATION
Edited by Jill Bourne and Euan Reid

World Yearbook of Education 2004
DIGITAL TECHNOLOGY, COMMUNITIES AND EDUCATION
Edited by Andrew Brown and Niki Davis

World Yearbook of Education 2005
GLOBALIZATION AND NATIONALISM IN EDUCATION
Edited by David Coulby and Evie Zambeta

World Yearbook of Education 2010

Education and the Arab 'World':
Political Projects, Struggles, and
Geometries of Power

Edited by
André E. Mazawi and Ronald G. Sultana

Routledge
Taylor & Francis Group

NEW YORK AND LONDON

First published 2010
by Routledge
270 Madison Avenue, New York, NY 10016

Simultaneously published in the UK
by Routledge
2 Park Square, Milton Park, Abingdon, Oxon OX14 4RN

Routledge is an imprint of the Taylor & Francis Group, an informa business

© 2010 Taylor & Francis

Typeset in Minion by
HWA Text and Data Management, London
Printed and bound in the United States of America on acid-free paper by
Sheridan Books, Inc.

Library of Congress Cataloging-in-Publication Data
World yearbook of education 2010 : education and the 'Arab' world :
    political projects, struggles, and geometries of power / edited by
    André E. Mazawi and Ronald G. Sultana.
        p. cm.
    Includes bibliographical references and index.
    1. Education – Arab countries. 2. Education – Middle East. 3. Education
    and state – Arab countries. 4. Education and state – Middle East.
    I. Mazawi, André Elias. II. Sultana, Ronald G. III. Title: Education
    and the Arab world.
    LA1491.W67 2009
    370.17'4927–dc22   2009024568

ISBN 10: 0-415-80034-X (hbk)
ISBN 10: 0-203-86359-3 (ebk)

ISBN 13: 978-0-415-80034-1 (hbk)
ISBN 13: 978-0-203-86359-6 (ebk)

In honour of the many educators across the Arab region and beyond, who toil under difficult and often oppressive conditions; who seek, through their work, to promote social justice, equity, and emancipation, and a better world for those in their care.

In memory of
Jihan Nagib Mazzawi, née Srouji
(Nazareth, 1935–Jaffa, 2008)

Contents

Tables

Contributors

Fida Adely is an Assistant Professor at the Center for Contemporary Arab Studies in the School of Foreign Service at Georgetown University. She is also the holder of the Clovis and Hala Maksoud Chair in Arab Studies. Dr Adely's research and teaching interests include education in the Middle East and North Africa, development in the Arab world and specifically socio-cultural approaches to the study of development, issues related to women and gender in the Arab World; gender and development more broadly, and Arab society and culture. Her most recent article, 'Educating women for development: the Arab Human Development Report 2005 and the problem with women's choices', appeared in the *International Journal for Middle East Studies* in 2009. She earned her PhD in Comparative Education and Anthropology from Teachers College, Columbia University in February 2007.

Nabil Al-Tikriti is Assistant Professor of Middle East History, University of Mary Washington, Fredericksburg, Virginia. He was a member of the team that operated the Catholic Relief Services humanitarian assistance project in Iraq in 1991–1992, and later served with Médecins Sans Frontières as a relief worker in Somalia, Iran, Albania, Turkey, and Jordan. After serving as a field administrator and election monitor in various program assignments, he joined the Department of History at the University of Mary Washington in 2004. He has been awarded a U.S. Institute of Peace Senior Fellowship, two Fulbright grants, and research support from both the University of Chicago and the University of Mary Washington.

Abdeljalil Akkari is Associate Professor in the Department of Education, Geneva University. He is also consultant for the International Bureau of Education (UNESCO) and other international organizations. He was the Dean for Research at the Higher Pedagogical Institute HEP-BEJUNE (Bienne, Switzerland). His major publications include studies on educational planning, multicultural education, teacher training and educational inequalities. His main research interests now focus on teacher education and reforms of educational systems in a comparative perspective.

Sara Ashencaen Crabtree is a Senior Academic in the School of Health and Social Care at Bournemouth University, where she is also Deputy Director of the Centre of Social Work and Social Policy. Her research interests include international social work and education, disability, mental health and gender, together with social work and faith/spirituality issues; she has published widely in all these areas. Recent publications include *Islam and social work: debating values, transforming practice* (co-authored with F. Husain and B. Spalek, and published by Policy Press in 2008); 'Dilemmas in international social work education in the United Arab Emirates: Islam, localization and social need', in *Social Work Education*, 27(5), 2008, and 'Maternal perceptions of care-giving of children with developmental disabilities in the United Arab Emirates', in *Journal of Applied Research in Intellectual Disabilities*, 20, 2007. She is currently working on a new book on colonial psychiatry in Malaysia.

Orit Bashkin works as an Assistant Professor in the department of Near Eastern Languages and Civilizations at the University of Chicago. Her publications include *The Other Iraq—Intellectuals and Culture in Hashemite Iraq, 1921–1958* (Stanford University Press, 2009), articles on the history of Arab-Jews in Iraq, on Iraqi history and on Arabic literature.

Borhène Chakroun is Senior VET Expert at the European Training Foundation (ETF). He is team leader of the EU-funded regional project Education and Training for Employment (MEDA-ETE) and Coordinator of the ETF's community of practices on qualifications frameworks and recognition of qualifications. Before joining ETF, Chakroun worked as advisor to the Tunisian Minister of Vocational Training and Employment and as consultant for several international organizations in the Middle East and North Africa. His work covered operational and strategic activities in the field of skills development including design and implementation of VET reforms and development programmes. Chakroun's publications focus on policy learning and education policies development and the role played by international organizations in this field.

Louise Chircop has recently completed a post-graduate degree with the Euro-Mediterranean Centre of Educational Research at the University of Malta. Her dissertation, titled *Maltese Muslims and Education*, critiques the ideals of Maltese identity and citizenship as portrayed in Malta's National Curriculum. She is a teacher in a state school in Malta.

Matthew Clarke is Senior Lecturer in the School of Education within the Faculty of Arts and Social Sciences at the University of New South Wales. He has also worked in teacher education in Hong Kong and the United Arab Emirates. His research interests include issues of identity and ethics in teacher education and his work has been published in various international journals, including *Educational Philosophy and Theory, Teaching Education, The Journal of Pragmatics*, and *TESOL Quarterly*. His recent book, *Language teacher identities: co-constructing discourse and community* (Multilingual Matters, 2008), was based on his research in the United Arab Emirates.

Steven C. Dinero is Associate Professor of Human Geography at Philadelphia University, Philadelphia, PA. He received his doctorate from Rutgers University in Urban and Regional Planning, with a minor in Middle Eastern Regional

Development, in 1995. Dr Dinero is a Fulbright Scholar whose primary areas of research center upon the study of post-nomadic communities in transition. Much of his work concerns the social and economic consequences of the resettlement of the Negev Bedouin community in Israel. He has published on such topics as gender/women, identity formation, religion (Islam), education, and tourism. All of these topics, among others, are addressed in his first monograph, *Settling for less: the planned resettlement of Israel's Negev Bedouin community* (Oxford/Milford, CT: Berghahn Publishers, forthcoming).

Iman Farag is Senior Researcher at CEDEJ (Centre d'études et de documentation économique, juridique et sociale), in Cairo, Egypt. She holds a doctorate in political sociology from the EHESS (Ecole des Hautes Études en Sciences Sociales), Paris. Recent publications include *Jeunesses des sociétés arabes. Par delà les menaces et les promesses* (edited with Mounia Bennani-Chraïbi, Le Caire/Paris, Cedej/Aux lieux d'être, 2007), 'Higher Education in Egypt' (in P.G. Altbach and J.J.F. Forest (eds.), *International Handbook of Higher Education*, 2006); 'A great vocation, a modest profession: teachers' paths and practices' (in L. Herrera and C.A. Torres (eds.), *Cultures of Arab Schooling: Critical Ethnographies from Egypt*, 2006).

Nemer Frayha was the President of the Educational Center for Research and Development (ECRD) in Beirut, Lebanon from 1999 to 2002 during the implementation of the new curricula. The ECRD was responsible for articulating a plan for Educational Reform in 1994, following the end of the civil war in 1989. Dr Frayha also served as a professor in the Faculty of Pedagogy at the Lebanese University. His publications, which focus mainly on citizenship education and basic education, include *The school's effect on citizenship education* (2002, in Arabic), *Global education and the Lebanese experience* (2003, in Arabic), *Civics education: curriculum and teaching methods* (2006, in Arabic); *Citizenship education in the thinking of Sultan Qaboos* (2007, in English), and *Holistic education for basic education* (2008, in Arabic).

Linda Herrera is a Senior Lecturer in International Development Studies at the Institute of Social Studies, The Hague, and Convenor of the Children and Youth Studies MA specialization. Her research interests lie at the intersection of critical pedagogy, the social history of education in the Middle East and North Africa, and youth and international development. Her publications include the co-edited volumes, *Cultures of Arab schooling: critical ethnographies from Egypt* (State University of New York Press, 2006), and *Being young and Muslim: new cultural politics in the global south and north* (Oxford University Press, 2010).

Eva Jimeno Sicilia is the Deputy Head of the Operations Department at the European Training Foundation (ETF), overseeing projects and activities in the field of education, training and employment in North Africa, the Middle East, Eastern Europe and Southern Caucasus. She has served as ETF Country Manager for Syria, Jordan, Palestine and Lebanon, and as Head of the Mediterranean Unit. Before joining the ETF, Eva worked in the field of higher education, and in trans-European cooperation projects supporting tertiary education reforms in Central and Eastern Europe.

Imad N. K. Karam received his schooling in Palestine, where he worked as a journalist before undertaking postgraduate studies. He graduated from Al-Azhar University in Gaza, and received an MA in Media and Communications from Goldsmiths College, University of London. He is a Visiting Lecturer in the Department of Sociology at City University London, where he teaches international communications and media studies. He is also affiliated to the Centre for International Communications and Society at City University. His research interests include globalization, media audiences, and youth cultural studies. His doctoral thesis was on *Identity construction among youth audiences of Arab satellite television*. Imad is also a documentary film-maker focusing on intercultural encounters and peace initiatives. He co-produced the award-winning film, *The imam and the pastor* (2007).

Omar El-Khairy is a playwright and PhD candidate in political sociology at the London School of Economics and Political Science. He was part of the Young Writer's Programme at the Royal Court Theatre (London) and is currently completing his first full-length play, *Boom Bap Babylon: a heart's metronome*, at Soho Theatre (London). The working title of his thesis is *'Freedom's a lifestyle choice': a sociology of globalisation for a segregated world, Americanisation and the travels of African American popular culture*. His research interests include the aesthetics of committed art, political economies of popular culture(s) and socio-political histories of technological innovation.

Hocine Khelfaoui is a sociologist and Associate Professor in the Interuniversity Center for Research on Science and Technology (University of Québec at Montréal). His research focuses on scientific professions, higher education, scientific research and innovation systems in North and West Africa. Recent publications include 'L'enseignement professionnel en Algérie: contraintes institutionnelles et réponses sociales' (*Sociologie et Sociétés*, XL:1, 2008), and 'Ingénieurs de recherche en Algérie: affirmation, professionnalité, identité' (*Savoir, Travail et Société*, 5:1, 2008). In 2006 he edited *L'intégration de la science au developpement: expériences Maghrébines* (Paris: Publisud).

Abdelouahad Mabrour is Professor of Linguistics at the University Chouaïb Doukkali El Jadida, Morocco. He is Director of Studies and Research in the Laboratoire d'Etudes et de Recherches sur l'Interculturel (LERIC)—a cross-cultural laboratory—and member of the Inter-Network Collective in Language Didactics (CIRDL) and of the Francophone Network of Sociolinguistics (RFS). He has published scholarly articles in Moroccan and international journals. With Danielle Bajomée, he has co-edited (in French): *Trajectoires interculturelles. Représentation et image de l'autre dans le domaine francophone* (El-Jadida); *Exils imaginaires et exils réels dans le domaine francophone (théorie, histoire, figures, pratiques)* (El-Jadida).

André Elias Mazawi is Associate Professor, Department of Educational Studies, Faculty of Education, University of British Columbia (Vancouver, BC, Canada) and Associate Fellow at the Euro-Mediterranean Centre for Educational Research, University of Malta. A sociologist of education, he is interested in the impacts of geopolitics on schooling and educational policies, governance, and school/higher education restructuring in Arab and Muslim societies.

Golnar Mehran is Associate Professor of Education at Al-Zahra University in Tehran, Iran, and has acted as education consultant to UNICEF (Iran, Jordan, Oman), UNESCO, and the World Bank. Her research interests include ideology and education in post-revolutionary Iran; political socialization of Iranian schoolchildren; female education in Iran and the Middle East; presentation of the 'self' and the 'other' in Iranian education; political reform and schooling in Iran; and religious education in the Islamic Republic of Iran. Her most recent publications are 'Iran: A Shi'ite curriculum to serve the Islamic state', in E. A. Doumato and G. Starrett (eds.), *Teaching Islam* (Boulder: Lynne Rienner, 2007); and 'Religious education of Muslim and non-Muslim schoolchildren in the Islamic Republic of Iran', in C. Brock and L.Z. Levers (eds.), *Aspects of education in the Middle East and North Africa* (Oxford: Symposium Books, 2007).

Khalil Mgharfaoui has served as Professor of Language Sciences in the Faculties of Arts of the University of Marrakech and the University of El Jadida in Morocco. He has published widely in the field of education in such areas as aesthetics, e-learning and language teaching, pedagogical innovations in the teaching of French, ICT in language teaching, and intercultural didactics and the issue of identity. He is a member of the Laboratoire d'Etudes et de Recherches sur l'Interculturel (LERIC). He is responsible for editing *Economix*, an encyclopaedia on human and societal development.

Fatma H. Sayed is a Specialist in development assistance, policy analysis, governance in the Euro-Mediterranean region and welfare and social policies. She teaches and carries out research at the European University Institute in Florence/Italy, and is professor of Comparative Middle East Politics at Gonzaga University in Florence. Dr Sayed is also an international consultant to UNDESA (United Nations' Department of Economic and Social Affairs) on governance and innovation in public administration in the Euro-Mediterranean region. Dr Sayed obtained her PhD in Political and Social Sciences in June 2004 from the European University Institute; her BA in Mass Communication from the American University in Cairo (1989); and a Master in Public Administration MPA from the same University in February 1999. She has authored several publications on governance, education reform, development assistance, public policy reforms, and innovation in public administration.

Nadera Shalhoub-Kevorkian is a scholar at the Faculty of Law, Institute of Criminology and School of Social Work and Public Welfare at the Hebrew University in Israel. Her main theoretical and research interest focuses on the study of women in conflict zones, mainly in Palestine. She has worked on examining the limits and the power of the law in conflict zones from a critical race theory perspective, while also looking at the obstacles facing local social policies, international law and international humanitarian law when addressing violence against women and children. In doing so, she also studied the juxtaposition between race, class and gender issues and their interactions with the formal and informal legal system during nation-building periods. She just published *Militarization and violence against women in conflict zones in the Middle East: A Palestinian case study* (Cambridge University Press, 2009). Together with other scholars and feminist activists, Dr Nadera Shalhoub-Kevorkian won the Women's Rights Prize by Peter and Patricia Gruber on Human Rights and the Phenomenal Woman for 2008—California State University, Northridge.

Ronald G. Sultana is Professor of Comparative Education and Educational Sociology at the University of Malta, where he is Founding Director of the Euro-Mediterranean Centre for Educational Research, and Founding Editor of the *Mediterranean Journal of Educational Studies*. He has published widely on education, social justice and development, and he has carried out several qualitative research studies in the region, including Egypt (on girls' education), Jordan (on early childhood education), Lebanon (on the education of Palestinian refugees), Syria (on global education), Tunisia (on competence-based learning), and Palestine (on education planning, on career guidance, and on the impact of the Intifada on education). Research interests and publications are available at: http://www.um.edu.mt/emcer.

Richard Williams is a Senior Lecturer in the School of Health and Social Care at Bournemouth University. His research interests are in educational exclusion, infant mortality and restorative practices. He has recently co-authored, with C. Pritchard, *'Liking school'—Breaking the cycle of educational alienation* (Open University Press, 2008).

Sawsan Zaher is an Attorney at Adalah—the Legal Center for Arab Minority Rights in Israel, and specializes in social and economic rights. As an active legal professional, she provided expert opinion on minority education for the UN Minority Forum held in December 2008 in Geneva. She further established and coordinated the legal Department for Arab Women's Rights in Kayan—Feminist Organization (2004–2005). She has also been an Assistant Instructor at Tel Aviv University for a course on Legal Status of the Arab Minority Rights in Israel (2007, 2009), and is a member of the Gender Working Group at the Euro-Med Human Rights Network.

Rukhsana Zia has multi-disciplinary experience. In government service since 1975, she taught at undergraduate and post-graduate levels in Pakistan. She completed her doctoral degree in Education from University College of Swansea Wales in 1994, on a merit scholarship awarded by her government. Since then she has published nationally and internationally, and she edited *Globalization, modernization and education in Muslim countries* (Nova Science Publishers, 2006). Her research interests have centred on gender, education and development, and values in education. She had the honour to represent Punjab at the newly established National Commission on Status of Women in 2000. She represented Pakistan at various UN forums, and between 2001 and 2004 was posted in Paris as Pakistan's Deputy Delegate to UNESCO. In her previous position (2004–2008), as the head of the organization responsible for professional development of public school teachers of Punjab, she was instrumental in large-scale policy development and implementation.

Series Editors' Introduction

This 2010 volume of the *Routledge World Yearbook of Education* takes up the question of Education in relation to the Arab world. It extends the work of the *World Yearbook of Education* series that, since 2005, has been interrogating the effects and implications of globalisation: for education; for education policy, practice and research; and for the world.

The 2010 volume editors, André Elias Mazawi and Ronald G. Sultana, have broken new ground in the *Routledge World Yearbook of Education* by tackling a topic, 'Arab education', which can be linked to a distinct geographic region of the world. This breaks with tradition because the World Yearbook has always strived for a 'world perspective'. Historically this 'world-ness' was achieved through country-based studies; a chapter from here, another from there. Since 2005, as series editors, we have moved on from this notion of 'the world' as a collection of countries to consider world-ness as a global space, within which agencies interact and relationships between agencies support flows of people, knowledge, money, goods and services, symbols, meanings. This way of understanding the world indicates that in addition to fixed spaces, like countries or regions, there are also movements of things and ideas, which connect up and influence spaces. These movements, and the reach of different agencies, extend across space and time, not just at one scale (ie. global, regional, national, local, individual) but also within and between many scales.

This volume on Arab education continues this work by considering the significance of Education in the making of the Arab world. This work opens up fundamental questions about the notion of an 'Arab world' and how it might be named. It also explores what is involved in 'Education' when it is influenced, understood and represented by diverse agencies and flows that are located not only within the particular geographic space but also through relationships at and between different scales.

The practicalities of these conceptual issues become apparent as soon as you start to think about what is represented by the term 'Arab world'. Mazawi and Sultana acknowledge that in simple physical terms, the Arab world can be seen as a distinct geographic region comprising 22 countries and a population of 325 million living in North Africa, the Middle East, and the Arabian Peninsula including Yemen, the Gulf States, and Iraq. It is a region that is widely seen to have a certain cultural consistency. For instance, there is pervasive use of the Arabic language, making the Arab world one of the largest global language units in the world. There is often seen to be associations with faith, although even schoolbook history tells us that this geographical region was the birthplace for many religions. Yet economic development and restructuring, expanding tourist industries, wars and political conflicts, refugees and displaced persons and groups, as well as wider cultural flows across the region, have created multiple forms of engagement between the Arab world and other world regions. It means that ethnic, cultural and linguistic groups who reside and live in the Arab region are also located as diasporic communities in many other regions of the world, including Europe and North America. Alongside this physical movement of people is the movement of ideas, goods and services, policy frameworks, money and media images. It all adds up to a furious traffic that conveys meanings, values and expectations.

These practical questions about the Arab world have been focused in this volume through the lens of Education. Thinking about the relationships that make up geographic and cultural spaces shows that they are ordered by the naming of space and boundaries, centres and peripheries, mainstream and marginal voices. The volume offers insights into this complexity by selecting chapter authors who are differently positioned within this world-space. There are chapters about policies, the dominant voices backed by governments or global governance agencies, and about the way these policies are received by particular ethnic, cultural, linguistic groups: young people, women, Iraqi-Jews, children with disabilities. The chapters represent mainstream views of Education in the Arab world, and also perspectives from the margins – from insiders and outsiders, those who write from and about diasporic communities, and those who take a more distanced view seeing Arab education in the context of wider geopolitical considerations.

These issues of conceptualisation have even emerged as practical challenges for us in relation to the title of this *World Yearbook of Education*. We, as volume editors, series editors and publisher, have been involved in discussions about how to represent the core theme of this volume. Different options have been explored: '*Education and the Arab World*', '*The Naming of Arab Education*', and '*The Worlds of Arab Education*'. Each of these creates problems for at least one of us involved in the discussion. The reason is that time–space compression, our greater awareness of global interconnectedness and interests that intersect across many scales make a simple consensus decision almost impossible. There are different but legitimate stakes at play. In the rush to produce the volume these difficulties can be frustrating for all concerned. Yet they are a salutary reminder that in a globally connected world having different but legitimate stakes in play is commonplace. It happens to all of us, every day and at every scale. It is the challenge of our time to find ways of working and living together that acknowledge and respect these differences but also to develop practices and mindsets that permit give-and-take resolution of intractable but legitimate issues. Education has a significant part to play in this negotiation of global processes and the development of capacities for civil living.

As series editors, we are delighted that André and Ronald have brought the WYB 2010 to publication. We acknowledge and celebrate their detailed and scholarly engagement over two and a half years with chapter authors from around the world. We thank them all for their efforts, for the chapters in this volume offer great insight in the state of play within and around Arab education. More importantly, they create a space for dialogue, understanding and more respectful engagement between the different and legitimate concerns of Arab educators and scholars and those of us, in and beyond Education, who are located in other parts of the world.

Terri Seddon, Jenny Ozga, Gita Steiner-Khamsi, Agnes van Zantén
Melbourne, Edinburgh, New York, Paris, 2010

Acknowledgements

This volume is the outcome of the labour of many people. We would first of all like to thank Professor Terri Seddon (Monash University, Australia) and Professor Jenny Ozga (Edinburgh University, UK), for inviting us to submit a proposal, and for their faith in our ability to carry the project through to the end. Their enthusiasm and guidance sustained us through the ups and downs that mark any publishing endeavour on this scale. The Euro-Mediterranean Centre for Educational Research at the University of Malta provided both of us a welcome haven for quiet reflection, supporting intense periods of editing and writing at key points throughout the project. Thanks are also due to the Routledge editorial team in New York—and especially to Sarah Burrows and Alexandra Sharp—who carefully and painstakingly followed the manuscript through its various stages, and who were understanding enough to concede a much-needed extension which enabled us to tie up all the loose ends prior to submission of the volume for publication. We are also indebted to Suher Zaher for her careful, painstaking and professional work in providing a detailed index for the volume. We thank John Hodgson and his team for their hard work in the editing and production of the final version.

This collection of chapters is, over and above all else, a testimony to the contributors, who showed a remarkable degree of perseverance, patience and professionalism as they worked and re-worked drafts in our collective efforts to capture the resonances and intersections between local, regional, and global dynamics and the complex and multifaceted ways in which these shape the field of education. To all the authors in the volume, therefore, we owe a major debt of gratitude for their trust and scholarly engagement. We hope that this journey we commenced together, however arduous it was at times, will not deter them from joining us in future reflections on education in its diverse articulations across the Arab region and beyond.

Thanks are due to the American University in Cairo Press for permitting the use of material published in 2006, authored by Fatma Sayed and titled *The transformation of education in Egypt: Western influence and domestic policy reform*, which appears in Chapter 4 of this World Yearbook. Similarly, we acknowledge the kind copyright release of Fida Adely's contribution in Chapter 7, aspects of which previously appeared in *Teachers' College Record*, Vol. 109(7), 2007.

To Suher and Roseline we owe more than we can ever possibly repay: for two and a half years they have had to bear with often-absent partners, who inevitably gravitated towards their computers to edit and re-edit texts, to provide feedback and encouragement, and to e-mail, skype and chat to/with authors spread over five continents. They will be relieved to see this book in print.

A final word of thanks to the Bella Vista Hotel staff in Malta, who kept the coffee cups filled and our laptops linked to the world-wide web while we struggled to bring the volume together and to complete the editorial introduction, even when it was long past their bedtime, and ours.

This book has provided us with opportunities to open conversations with so many different people that we had never met before. This augurs well for the kinds of conversations that we hope the volume will trigger, as it leaves our desks and takes on a life of its own across space and time.

A.E.M. & R.G.S., Buġibba
June 2009

1 Editorial Introduction

Situating the 'Worlds' of Arab Education: Critical Engagements

André Elias Mazawi and Ronald G. Sultana

1. Presentations and Representations

When the Series Editors of the *Routledge World Yearbook of Education* invited us to submit a proposal to edit a volume on education in the Arab region, we felt that this was an honour and an opportunity—but above all else, a responsibility. Probably never more than in the last decade has Western interest in all things 'Arab' and 'Muslim' been as searching, and as insistent. The gaze on the 'orient' (whose orient?, and where does this lie?—the dis-oriented might well ask), with all the complex issues that this raises, and which have been so well articulated by Edward Said (1978), is a double-edged sword. For, on the one hand, it invites knowledge and understanding of the 'Other', but also the distancing and objectification of this same 'Other' as a subaltern through/in academic discourses and methodological articulations. It also runs the risk of thinking of the 'Arab World' as somehow distinct, a world apart, a space of exceptionalism, lying somewhere 'out there', forgetting the great lessons of history that teach us that cultures are part of the great web of competing meanings—and of 'modes of being' (Mouffe, 2005)—that constitute intimately and inextricably linked human societies. And linked this world certainly is, and has been well before the concept of 'globalization' became the catchword that seeks to describe—but perhaps more insidiously to justify—the flows of trade, of people, of ideas around the globe. Insidious, because like tides, the terms we use can serve to both mask and reveal the ebb and flow of ascendant and falling powers, and the flotsam and jetsam they leave behind. Equally, as Brighenti (2007), to whom we return later, has suggested, we are cognizant that the terms we use can also serve to delimit the 'features of visibility' that allow or prevent the voice of the 'Other' from being heard and seen, in brief, from 'manifesting' itself. Thus, we realize that the making of our disciplinary fields and methodological approaches, as well as our locations as authors and editors, can lead us to view the 'Arab region' as a set of geographically delimited spaces which negate the complex processes and dynamics which underpin the field of education in a wide range of contexts of practice, whether those located within the region proper or those which emerge as part of its interactions and convergences beyond it. This has been a major priority for us to attend to, in terms of capturing these imbricated realities that form and inform in many ways the field of education in its local, regional, geopolitical and global engagements and resonances.

Our approach to the shaping of this volume has been intensely personal, and as intensely political and collective. It is profoundly shaped by two and a half years of engagement with initially over eighty potential contributors, living across five continents. They all enabled our initial framings and their underlying assumptions to shift as the project of the volume gradually materialized and the final list of authors determined. We can now state that this edited collection has opened for us all multifaceted conversations and new conceptual and empirical horizons of engagement that touch on some of the neglected questions regarding education in the Arab region, the projects it serves, the equity with which it is accessible, and its relations to broader issues of social justice and political inclusion.

In diverse ways, we are both 'of/in' the region, and yet 'outside' of it. Our personal and larger histories are powerfully intertwined with its ever-shifting and mutating borders and borderlines, whether political or cultural; those imposed, negotiated or which crystallized and built up in fluid forms of construction.

André was born in Jaffa, an ancient harbour town on the shores of the Mediterranean, part of the state of Israel following the 1948 Palestinian Nakba. A Palestinian Arab, his family originates from the city of Nazareth in Galilee, and from there, over two centuries backward in time, his ancestral genealogy stretches to Al-Mazzeh, now incorporated as part of Syria's capital, Damascus, and to Duma, a locality to its north-east. For him, the engagement with this volume is an attempt to reflect on a history of colonization and political fragmentation; a history that radically transformed the institutional, social, political and economic underpinnings of education across the region and its intersections with constructions of citizenship and of nation-states.

Ronald was born in Malta, an ancient harbour island 1900 kilometres west of Jaffa, independent of British colonial rule since 1964, and previously subject to layers of European powers which, since 1090, had wrested what has come to be perceived as the 'bulwark of Christianity' from Arab and Muslim hands. An island, therefore, at the geographical crossroads of history, whose hybrid ancestry reveals itself in a local patois, half Arabic, half Italian—a member of the European Union, yet classified as one of the Arab states by UNESCO. For Ronald, this volume is part of his personal, professional and political engagement in the search for roots, and the cultivation of a sense of self within broadening circles of overlapping communities. Writing about this odyssean journey, Ronald recently recalled how he had been schooled by a British colonial education into thinking of himself "as white, as European, as Christian, and indeed as almost English ... though not quite" (Sultana, 2008, p.15), only to experience a splintering of identity when, travelling through the region, he discovered that Tunisians and Moroccans could understand most of what he told them when he spoke Maltese and that there were areas in Jerba, Rabat, Beirut, Jaffa, Naples, Valencia, Alexandria or Tripoli which evoked his own childhood in villages in Malta and Gozo: "those smells, those colours, those flat-roofed houses, those women talking to each other as they hung the family clothes to dry on rooftops, the sprawl of bodies, those hot nights with windows and doors ajar at cleverly calculated angles to catch the remotest of cool breezes, those scrawny cats running down dark, winding yet comforting alleyways ..." (Sultana, 2008, p. 16). Another story, then, that speaks about bordered/bothered identities, difficult to pin down, gifted with the burden of multiperspectival uncertainties that makes its bearers ever without a home, always 'out of place'.

Shifting sands, therefore ... and one can hardly be blamed for wondering whether an edifice can be soundly built on a foundation such as this. And yet this is an appropriate metaphor for our project, which we took in hand not as rock-solid 'experts' but rather as keen students of a field that needs to be cautiously, carefully and tentatively approached, not to ring it round with defining boundaries and to stake a claim to it as much as to appreciate its contours, its valleys, hills and ravines, building on the efforts of other scholars—located in different times and spaces—who have engaged with this task before us. Our desire, therefore, was to facilitate sensitive, multifaceted portrayals by authors who knew well the lie of the land, and who could write passionately, sincerely and even lovingly about it, but who never lost that critical edge of discernment and analysis that comes from a deep-seated discomfort with final, finished and totalized narratives that purport to know it all, and to frame it all.

Such portrayals—at least from our perspectives as editors—were not meant to constitute the object of a 'western' gaze, a window on the potentially exotic. Elements of that are certainly there, and unavoidably so, partly due to our own geo-cultural locations, but also to those of the publishing vehicle that brings this collection of chapters to readers. The volume is, after all, written in English, and produced and marketed by an international publishing house based in the UK, with offices in the US, Australia and Singapore, and for whom the term 'Arab World'—as a geographic space/gaze of recognized reference—absolutely needed to figure in the main title of the book, despite our position to the contrary. As editors, however, we were clear from the start that one of our major aspirations was to put together a volume that would also be read by educators in the very spaces that are the focus of our collective attention. Authors were therefore encouraged to write their chapters keeping in mind that every effort would be made to translate the volume into Arabic, following the English version. In many cases, this, in itself, served to introduce an interesting tension in the way issues were articulated, as authors grappled with the challenge of how to present thoughts, viewpoints and evaluations which could be meaningful to, and resonate with, diversely located readers. At the same time, neither did we avoid the complexities, tensions, and difficulties associated with engaging authors operating in diverse geographical locations, cultural frameworks, political régimes, institutional settings, and academic and linguistic traditions. Navigating the intricacies associated with such a diverse congregation of academics, researchers and policy makers meant engaging not only the linguistic diversity of the region, but also having some authors initially engage the project in the language they felt most comfortable writing in. This offered us the opportunity to problematize questions discussed by Paul Ricoeur (2006a) in *On Translation*. Ricoeur observes that the problem of translation is one of interpretation, a hermeneutic question in the most fundamental sense of the word. As such, it cannot be reduced exclusively to challenges facing translation from one language to the other. What he calls 'internal translation', that is, "translation within the same linguistic community" (p. 24), also raises equally considerable methodological and epistemic challenges in terms of how 'explanations' or 'reformulations' "try to say the same thing in another way" (p. 25). In line with Ricoeur, as editors, the fundamental issue at stake in this project is not one of translation *strictu sensu*. Rather, it is one of generating 'understandings' into 'foreign' or 'Other' texts-in-contexts, in ways which, in the words of Richard Kearney's (2006) introduction to Ricoeur's book, "translate our own wounds into the language of strangers and retranslate the wounds of strangers into our own language [so] that healing and reconciliation can take place" (p. xx).

Taken from this perspective, our ambitions and hopes for the volume are not to put together a collection of chapters that claim comprehensive thematic coverage as much as to make forays into areas in ways that generate new insights and new understandings, helping to render their complexities in engaging and theoretically sophisticated ways. A major challenge was therefore to identify authors who would engage with the task as we had articulated it. In the majority of cases, the papers presented here have been especially written for the volume, with original research, in English. Two chapters were ultimately translated from French, once written. A few authors have drawn on previously published material, reworking this, however, into a new chapter that fitted within the underpinning rationale of the project.

Our choices were guided by a desire for contributions that, by all means, showed mastery over the content area covered, but also a probing and restless intellect that asked new questions—or at least revisited old questions in ways that troubled and unsettled received wisdom. This partly explains why, while we have some of the leading and established scholars in the area, we also feature newer names, young researchers who are considering their academic débuts, and who are doing exciting, cutting-edge and engaged work in/on the region within different contexts of practice.

Some of the questions raised in the chapters are being asked by academics, researchers and policy makers living and working in the region, but who have not let familiarity numb them into intellectual comfort zones that, from our point of view, is a contradiction in terms. Others, while being from the region, are, for a range of different reasons, living outside of it— permanently, intermittently or provisionally. For many of them, now working in North America or Europe, the exercise of reflecting on home truths in 'exile', as it were, provides them with an opportunity to refract phenomena through complex, multilayered lenses, where distance not only makes the heart grow fonder, but also makes the insights potentially sharper and keener. Yet others travelled to the region, for whatever reason, allowing themselves to be unsettled and decentred, but not deterred from their quest to understand the meaning-making efforts of fellow humans in different parts of the land, teetering uneasily between the need to make the strange familiar, and the familiar strange.

Voice, therefore, was important to us in making our final selection of authors, not only in terms of gendered, located identities, but also in terms of the perspectives and frames through which topics were apprehended. Rather than thematic coverage, what we hoped for—and to an extent succeeded in obtaining—was a range of theoretical and methodological tools that serve to provoke thought, open a field up to fresh insights and new conversations, and generate novel research questions. There is, of course, an engagement with some of the key themes that one would expect to be addressed in a volume such as this, themes that are approached with an eye on the simultaneity, interconnectedness and interpenetration of what has come to be called the 'global' and the 'local'. Such themes not only provide us with the substantive knowledge that we need to make inroads in better understanding the dynamics of educational policy and practice in the region, but also indicate how particular aspects of this knowledge lend themselves to being uncovered through the use of particular research methodologies.

Voice was also important for another reason. We wished to avoid closed and mono-vocal narratives, which would essentialize representations of education, trapping them in homogeneous discourses that reproduce the positions of power, and which are already in effect. Here, the choice of voices allowed us to include narratives related to educational policies and practices that make it difficult for issues to be defined by a 'single-valence reference' recognizing, along with Jacques Derrida, and in the words of Bleich (2008), "the immovable embeddedness of language in the total political context" (p. 512).

Many of the chapters rely on qualitative data—in itself quite unusual in a region where education often tends to be represented and analysed in quantitative terms, with number toting often reinforcing a sense of 'deficit' in terms of such 'indicators' as the number of girls without access to schooling, the performance of students in international assessment exercises, the number of Nobel prize winners based in the region's universities, and so on. Some of the chapters take us into schools and classrooms, providing rare ethnographic insights into the interactional dynamics that both reflect and shape social relations in the wider context. Many chapters make good use of interview material—and in one case, online discussion forums—in order to reveal perspectives and to give voice to social actors whose views are not often heard in the region, let alone beyond. Teachers, children and young people feature particularly prominently in this collection.

The representation and analysis of a range of textual materials is also used to good effect by several authors in this collection. This includes the use of autobiographies and diaries—which provide us with striking and original insights into a range of issues—and of newspapers, which capture the way some of these issues are articulated and fought over in the public sphere. It also includes in-depth and close analyses of policy and legal documents, as well as of school textbooks— their contents, design, and the annotations left on the margins by students. Some of the authors in this collection use case studies to good effect, especially when the focus on the particular opens up a door to a deeper understanding of the broader societal dynamics in which the local is inextricably enmeshed. Similar insights are sometimes generated through a careful use of comparative methods, which are particularly apt at showing how what seems to be particularly contingent in spatial and temporal terms is in fact a regional—or even global—phenomenon, indicative of wider and deeper and interlocked patterns that reveal the inexorable ubiquity of power. This wide-ranging use of research methods resonates with Sholkamy's (2006) call "for a critical consideration of the relations of knowledge production in the Arab world" by creatively exploring ways which boost "the viability of multi-disciplinary research" in the social sciences (p. 21). The methodological spectrum present in the book is therefore indicative of the authors' creativity in reflecting on their multiple and often contradictory locations, as researchers, in relation to social and political action and to pedagogic practice, identifying new sites of research, and engaging new ways through which data collection and analysis could be undertaken. From our point of view as editors, we believe that this methodological spectrum helps readers better understand how texts—and their performative articulations—give form not only to consciousness, but also to the contexts in which such consciousness of self and others is developed.

What brings all these contributions together is the operative word 'critical': authors in this volume write from a variety of disciplinary and/or professional backgrounds, as anthropologists, sociologists, media and cultural studies scholars, educators, lawyers, playwrights, policy researchers and policy makers; a gamut indicative of the epistemic standpoints involved in articulating interdisciplinary explorations of 'education'. The authors do not shy away from the arduous, uncomfortable—and in this region as much as (if not more than) elsewhere, often perilous—task of 'speaking truth to power'. Using a range of theoretical approaches, they strive to live up to a tradition in scholarly work that sees intellectual activity not as value-free or distant, but rather as a way of engaging with the world as it is, in order to imagine—and strive for—a world as it could and 'should' be.

Theoretical lenses, therefore, help the authors negotiate the challenging task of apprehending phenomena from both an 'insider's' and an 'outsider's' point of view, and to occupy that liminal/luminal space reserved for those who are 'in' the world, but not 'of' it, 'insiders–outsiders' (Banks, 1998). Intellectual activity, therefore, becomes the preserve not of 'academics' as much as of those who have the courage to stand both within and outside of society and its institutions, to actively disturb a status quo that works against the principle of social justice. Critical theory, critical hermeneutics, discourse analysis, comparative studies, policy sociology, critical multiculturalism, postcolonial studies, post-structuralism, social anthropology, historical and critical ethnography, political economy, cultural studies, critical legal studies … one and all provide the sharp conceptual and methodological tools that prise open a range of educational phenomena in the region, in the hope that a deeper understanding of issues leads to the reconstruction of educational structures and practices.

2. The Arab 'Region' as a 'Spatial Analytic'

The 'shifting sands' of identities, cultures, belongings and locations outlined above are indicative of the difficulties to capture the varied ways in which the Arab region is referred to from the standpoint of competing narrational locations by the authors of the various chapters. These difficulties also impel us, inevitably, to clarify how we imagine the global–local intersections and resonances and their effects on the organization of educational opportunities in the Arab region. In the present section we problematize and unpack, first, spatial representations of the Arab 'region', as spaces of historically-situated political, cultural and economic flows; and second, the global–local dynamics within which we seek to shed some light on the forces that shape the spaces of educational action.

'The Politics of Space', the Space of (Educational) Politics

The nomenclature that refers to the 'Arab region', and which one finds in the literature, offers an impressive array of crisscrossing appellations, articulating historically and politically situated frames of reference, narratives, and modes of representation. While a discussion of the genealogies underpinning these appellations lies clearly beyond the scope of this editorial introduction, it is nonetheless worthy to reflect on its implications for our endeavour, that is, if one is to capture the intensity of the struggles and conflicts over the naming— or construction—of the region as a space of politics. Naming is, after all, part of controlling a space, giving it shape, labelling it, and placing it under a particular political, economic and cultural gaze that determines its location within a broader worldview and world order.

One can think, of course, of an 'Orient', a 'Middle East', a 'Middle East and North Africa (MENA)', a 'Greater Middle East', an 'Arab World', an 'Arab region', or an 'Arab–Islamic World'. As one invokes these names, among others, one can see the 'region' stretch or contract, shift or tilt, to include or exclude from its geographic, cultural and political contours and delimitations entire groups, countries and sub-regions. Nor does the list of appellations stop there. 'Sub-regional' appellations abound too. Whether one refers to the 'Arabian Peninsula' or the 'Gulf' (and as part of that, either to the 'Arab Gulf states' or to the 'Gulf Arab states' or still, to the 'Persian Gulf'), 'Arabia', the 'Levant' or 'West Asia', or, to add quite a different dimension, the 'Holy Land'; or still, whether one invokes sub-regional Arabic terms such as 'Machreq' (East) and 'Maghreb' (West); one is bound to recognize the intersecting dimensions—both cultural, economic and political—which dramatically enter into play when naming 'the region' and its sub-components.

To complicate matters further, some appellations reconfigure the Arab region— in whole or in part—within larger regional or geopolitical units, imagining it, for instance, centred around the Mediterranean Sea, which is, for Chambers (2008), "not so much a frontier and barrier between the North and the South, or the East and the West, as an intricate site of encounters and currents" (p. 32). In contradistinction, in Arabic, the Arab World (*al-ālam al-'arabi*) is probably the most prevalent term in use when referring to the Arab region, often further subsumed within larger civilizational configurations, such as the Islamic World (*al-ālam al-islāmi*). For many Arabic speakers, while opting for either one of these two terms, or for both, invoking the 'Mediterranean' setting is often perceived as expressing a 'western' designation that downplays the Arab and Islamic heritage of a region stretching 'from the [Atlantic] Ocean to the Gulf' or, as some would emphasize, 'from the [Atlantic] Ocean to the [Indian] Ocean', thus offering two other bracketing seas instead of the Mediterranean one. These interplays between water and land are metaphorically indicative in terms of how they situate and foreground regional identity constructs and modes of being in relation to naturalized settings, for instance, 'nestled around' an oval Mediterranean Sea, or 'stretching outwards' to be stopped only by mighty 'natural' barriers such as oceans.

Not least, some countries, which may be classified under some of the appellations listed above (e.g. Middle East), are considered under other respects and for other purposes to be part of Europe (e.g. Turkey) or effectively of the European Union (EU), even if they lie much 'closer', or at the very doorsteps of other continents.[1] Thus, 'borders' and 'frontiers', aspects we return to, emerge as engulfed in multilayered spatial imaginings, which bear testimony to overlapping modes of souvenir and recalling. Clearly, then, while names differ in what they capture, and they do capture different 'things', which names are used does matter in creating a gaze that objectifies a 'region' in particularly loaded ways.

What the above cursory overview highlights is the plasticity and considerable overlap of appellations through which the Arab region, as a space of action and as object of study, can be known by different people and by different regional and international institutions creating their own spatial systems of classification. This plasticity—or should we rather say 'fluidity'?—is indicative of the epistemic difficulties to capture—in scholarly discourses—not only a geographic space, but also its peoples, communities, and the complex realms of connotations and meanings which shape people's worldviews, consciousness, cultures, politics and modes of social and political organization. This plasticity is particularly indicative of the power relations and struggles that take place over the naming of a region; struggles—often violent—which seek to shape it within particular socio-cultural, political, economic, and civilizational moulds. Thus, we acknowledge that names and their discursive articulations are deployed as part of strategic political ends, creating an 'order of discourse' (Foucault, 1984) within which phenomena, such as education, acquire their familiarity and legitimacy.

The spatial terms listed above should not be conflated in terms of their underlying discursive and semiotic underpinnings. Some seek to represent political configurations, and as such they revolve around the articulation of political borders or, in other words, the geographic delimitation of nation-states. Others seek to capture cultural, civilizational or economic landscapes that often cut across continents, capturing diasporic and trans-national modes of being and social organization (Mediterranean; Islamic World). The latter represent shifting 'frontiers', articulated by human flows seeking a better future; or by modes of social and political organization associated with settlement and colonization, sustained by 'cultural logics' which ultimately create what Ong (1999) refers to as 'cultural régimes'. Thus, 'borders' and 'frontiers' do not necessarily overlap, even though they feed on each other in terms of maintaining ever-present dynamics and tensions that inform their political articulations and spatial configurations. Their interplay, however, is indicative of the way a 'region' can be done and undone, at least in the scholarly and political imaginaries, between interlocking forces and overlapping dynamics.

As editors, we sought to remain sensitive to these varied spatial intersections and the dynamics and power struggles they capture, either those operating within the bounds of a given nation-state; or those operating within wider spatial contexts, whether regional-geopolitical, diasporic or trans-national. We attempt to understand how these spatial tensions and contradictory dynamics—within, between, and across borders and frontiers—shape and impact the deployment of educational opportunities and practices, as contested political projects and as sites of struggle, in ways that articulate, or capture, the multifaceted and multilayered 'worlds' of Arab education as a horizon of possibility and action. This is well reflected in the present volume. We include contributions by authors who locate their analyses of educational processes within the borders of a specific Arab nation-state—such as Algeria, Egypt, Jordan, Iraq, Lebanon, and the UAE. At the same time, we include chapters which capture spatial configurations of 'frontiers'—either civilizational (e.g. representations of Arabs in Iranian textbooks) or diasporic (the schooling of Imazighen children and youth in a former colonial power, such as France; or the schooling of Arab and Muslim children in Malta). We also include geopolitical spatial articulations which reflect the standpoint of 'world powers', such as the United States of America (USA) and the European Union (EU), and representational enactment of a 'region' as part of geopolitically strategic frames of reference.

In bringing together these multifaceted spatial contexts of education, we have in mind Doreen Massey's (1999) emphasis on the importance of understanding 'spatiality' as the acknowledgment of "a genuinely co-existing multiplicity—a different kind of difference from any which can be compressed into a supposed temporal sequence" (p. 281). This implies, according to Massey, the co-existence of 'a multiplicity of narratives' and "entails the recognition that there is much more than one story going on in the world and that these stories have, at least, a relative autonomy" (p. 281). This recognition of spatiality, Massey further adds, "is particularly adequate for—indeed necessary for—some contemporary changes in the way in which 'politics' itself is imagined" (p. 286). It is the recognition of the power relations embedded in imagining and naming a space of possibilities which provides us with the opportunity to understand the multifaceted 'politics of space' which shape education and its institutional and politico-cultural articulations across the Arab region. For Massey, "it is that recognition of the 'maps of power', or the power geometries, within which and through which we are all constructed that opens up the possibility of a politics of renegotiating those identities" (p. 289).

Within this framework, throughout the editing of the volume, we kept our approach open not only on the cultural ebb and flows which underpin the movements of human communities, but also on the spatial meanings and significations that the 'Arab region'—as a space always-already configured and re-configured by borders and frontiers—gathers in the minds of the contributors to this volume, in terms of how *they* approach education from within differentially located geographic and socio-cultural contexts of practice. In brief, we consciously avoided a reifying spatial perspective that would erect the Arab region into a homogeneous and harmonious ethnic, national, or linguistic geographic space, and one where the Arab nation-state would be our exclusive frame of analysis (on this point, see Ayubi, 1995). This would have reduced the multifaceted spectrum of potentialities within which the shaping of minds and identities takes place through education, simultaneously in the form of an ever-contested political project and site of struggle. Rather, we consciously sought to keep our choices, editorial decisions, and our engagement with contributors sensitive to, and open on the multiplicity of contemporaneously intersecting dynamics of power and cultures within which the educational phenomenon—in its manifold spatial articulations—could be captured within and in relation to 'geometries of power' that enact and constitute the Arab region, as an object of politics, constructed at distinct levels of action and within distinct contexts of practice.

Multifaceted and Multilayered Engagements and Resonances

In Pierre Bourdieu's sense, the chapters in this volume examine the interplays of the 'field' of education and the broader fields of politics, economy, and culture of the Arab region. Along with Marginson and Rhoades (2002) we recognize that the field of education operates under the impact of "increasingly integrated systems and relationships beyond the nation" (p. 288), "systems and relationships which are more than just economic: they are also technological, cultural and political" (p. 288). According to them, this "requires a new analytic framework, one that can take us beyond the hitherto almost exclusive reliance on national policy and national markets as the horizon of possibility" for understanding educational policies and their institutional articulations (p. 305). This specific concern stands out as a foundational thread that cuts across all contributions in this volume. Each chapter shows how the field of 'education', within particular contexts of practice, is shaped by dynamics and tensions operating at the intersections of local, regional, and global dynamics, capturing what Susan L. Robertson (2006) refers to as "the social relations of space and scale" within which educational policies, educational institutions and practices translate into "political projects and struggles" (p. 313). While the various chapters approach the manifestations of globalization as local and distinctive, at the same time they show the myriad interpretations and constructions put forward by social actors involved in their enactment. This analytic remains sensitive to the wider debates and controversies around the geopolitics of Arab education and its intersection with globalization. Many writers located within the region perceive 'globalization' ('awlama) as a threat to Arab culture, identity, and to the viability of an Arab educational project. For instance, Labyadh (2004), referring to US-initiated foreign polices with regard to the Arab states, argues that calls to "reform education and the tools of knowledge and information" in the Arab region seek "to alter the components of the Arab and Islamic culture and identity" and "organize the markets in favor of trans-national corporations, completely disregarding a genuine economic development of the countries, their industrialization and agriculture while providing priority to the freeing of trade and the limiting of the role of the state" (p. 140). Controversies and debates around the 'impacts' of globalization on Arab education have not remained confined to rhetorical formulations. They rather powerfully shape the prospects and feasibility of development policies, policy formulation and policy implementation in the various contexts of educational practice (Mazawi, 2009).

Robertson's (2006) identifies "three [substantive] absences" in our current knowledge of the intersection between globalization and education. These are central to this volume and the articulation of its sections:

first, the absence of critical spatial analytic in research on globalization and education; second, the absence of subaltern and alternative knowledges in our understanding of globalization and education; and third, the absence of a sustained engagement with the implications for education systems in nation states of the altered spaces for political engagement and representation resulting from neoliberal governance at multiple scales. (p. 304)

First, Robertson's call to adopt a "spatial analytic" leads us to shift the analysis of the field of education in the Arab region, from a 'horizontal' focus on nation-states (as has been customarily the case with regard to studies of Arab education), to a set of vertical analyses, which "reveal an emerging functional and scalar division of the labour of education between global, regional, national and local scales" (p. 308). In the present volume, this scalar dimension reveals the imbrications of national and international policy-making networks in the form of policy initiatives which involve Arab, international, European Union and American governmental agencies (USAID). This leads to what Carnoy and Castells (2001) call "the network state", or a state marked by intricate and intertwined networks of policy making and implementation, where power is iterative and negotiated at every stage and level of action, shared by intertwined configurations of state and non-state actors. Within this context, the modalities through which policy initiatives are deployed across the 'field of power' (Bourdieu), how they are mobilized, configured and operationalized within different spaces of practice are indicative of the hierarchical locations of power and how these determine policy directions and policy emphases in the field of education. Part I and Part V of the volume engage this aspect of the intersection between globalization and education, namely 'Contested policyscapes' and 'Geopolitical predicaments'. These sections offer contrasting lenses on the dynamics of reform and policy initiatives within the broader contexts of structural adjustment policies with regard to the former, and within the contexts of geopolitics and militarism with regard to the latter.

Secondly, Robertson's call to interrogate "whose knowledge is being globalized" and how knowledge is "instrumentalized" in particular contexts of practice, allows for a deeper examination of the modalities through which educational agendas, including educational research agendas, are set and reproduced over time and space. This interrogation also allows for a critical unpacking of the modalities through which hegemonic social science discourses in the field of education determine what education should stand for, as a political project, while excluding and silencing context-specific voices and the political experiences they are associated with. Part II and Part IV of the volume engage this aspect of the intersection of globalization and education, namely 'Re-calling voices' and 'Knowledge imaginaries'. These sections delve on the tensions and contradictions that underpin education as a political project, through which the different 'Other' and the Arab nation are narrated, articulated, and represented. They also show how power relations shape subaltern and marginalized identities and voices as part of this process.

Thirdly, how does the intersection between globalization and the field of education shape the "structure of justice and the means for contesting [the] forces" that determine political engagement, legitimation, and representation (Robertson, 2006, p. 311)? This specific concern stands at the centre of the Part III, entitled 'Suspended visibilities'. The section unpacks the "architecture[s] of power" (p. 311) that function as gatekeepers, determining access to the public space of politics and to political legitimacy across the region. The section interrogates the modalities through which narrow visions of the political community are constructed, through exclusive educational discourses that effectively marginalize and subordinate entire publics, be they defined along gender, class, ethnicity, religion, disability or civic status. The section also identifies new ways to approach the field of education, as political engagements grounded in notions of human rights and struggles for inclusive citizenship.

By delving on Robertson's (2006) scalar, epistemic, and political facets underpinning the intersection of globalization and education, the five parts along which the volume is organized open up new spaces of understanding the predicament of education in the Arab region, within the broader contexts of the cultural politics of space and the effects of neoliberal economic policies. This framework situates the analyses presented in the various chapters not only in relation to the geometries of power which shape education, but also in relation to the scalar divisions of labour that such geometries sustain, while being involved in the reconfiguration of the purposes of education and its re-articulation along market-driven rationalities.

3. Thematic Organization of the Volume

The contributions to this volume have been clustered around five main parts. In this section, we briefly foreground the key themes addressed by each author. Our aspiration here is not only to briefly introduce the parts of the volume and their respective chapters, but also to open up conversations between them, as well as with the broader literature. This ensures that each chapter is not read in isolation but rather in relation to a whole field of research. Our thematic approach, refracted through the lenses of the social sciences, builds on previous attempts to construct the field of regional education studies (Matthews & Akrawi, 1949; Massialas & Jarrar, 1983, 1991). Yet, our approach significantly differs from these in that an important leitmotif in the presentation and analyses is the critical highlighting of the imbrications of the global in what, at first sight, might appear to be narrowly local, or even merely regional or national in scope. Not least, the spatial analytic discussed above clearly means that we do not conflate education in the Arab 'World' with the worlds of Arab education. We rather consider the tensions between both 'fields' as a productive space of contradictions where global and trans-national articulations of education can be more fully explored.

Part I: Contested Policyscapes

In Part I, the focus on policy contexts and dynamics highlights the centrality that "[t]he image, the imagined, [and] the imaginary" have come to play in determining, according to Appadurai (1996), the "organization of social practices, as a form of work (in the sense of both labor and culturally organized practice), and a form of negotiation between sites of agency (individuals) and globally defined fields of possibility" (p. 31). The chapters in this section explore, more particularly, how policy formulation and implementation in the field of education represent not only a contested space, within the wider context of politics, geopolitics, and international relations; but also venues which effect epistemic and ontological disruptions in the way education in the Arab region, as a political project, comes to be imagined and pursued in diverse contexts of practice. Policy initiatives are conceived of as 'scapes', 'imagined worlds' which serve as 'building blocks' in the construction of 'master narratives', and which frame the relationship between education and social and economic development and mobility. How these master narratives are regionally and trans-nationally deployed, how they are situated in relation to different centres of power, and how they imagine and invoke 'education' as a normative political project within and for Arab societies, all these aspects are central to this section.

While several of the contributions in the volume as a whole refer to educational policies, often within the larger canvas of nation-state policy-making initiatives, the four chapters in this part deal more specifically with the policy process itself. Thus, they provide us with a useful backdrop that puts some of the issues addressed by subsequent authors in better relief. Abdeljalil Akkari raises the issue of the neo-liberal framing of the education project across a number of Arab states, focusing particularly on his native Tunisia and on the other two countries in the Maghreb, namely Algeria and Morocco. He provides us with an overview of the impact of economistic discourses that have taken root across the region. He shows how neo-liberalism finds expression in the privatization of several educational sectors not only thanks to the impact of hegemonic ideas promoted by such agencies as the World Bank, but also because global economic and ideological interests intersect in complex ways with those of local policy-making elites. Akkari sees here major tensions and challenges for the post-colonial state. The latter finds itself torn between two key options: living up to the challenge of acting as the provident state, thus striving to cater for the interests of all citizens; or becoming the market state, facilitating the privatization of services and the inevitable deepening of the divide between social groups, under the banner of 'free choice', to ensure the support of regulative international financial institutions. While many Arab states remain keen to regulate schooling, privatization creeps in by default, as states fail to generate sufficient revenue to meet the demand for educational services.

Such privatization presents a number of challenges to the state, not least in terms of regulating what goes on in the non-state sector. The opportunities offered by the marketization of educational services are not escaping the attention of a range of social actors, both local (e.g. through Qur'anic schools) and international (e.g. through European or American religious or diplomatic schools, and increasingly, outreach campuses of European or American universities), who capitalize on the vacuum left by the state. This, they not only (or necessarily) undertake for financial gain, but also to inculcate specific ideologies, religious or other. Schools privatized through a range of policies and practices may be perceived as subverting the 'national project' of the Arab nation-state in a whole host of ways, whether by the retrenching state, or by interest groups who seek to assert a specific construct of national identity—often expressed through an insistence on Arabic as the language of instruction. Some forms of privatization, however, fall well below the radar of the regulative state. Key among these is a phenomenon that has received scant research attention in the region: private tuition. The latter is not only deleterious to the quality of education offered within the state educational sector, but also serves to reproduce and accentuate class, gender, and urban–rural inequalities.

Akkari thus introduces some important themes that are central to this volume. Key among these is the role of the state and the complex interplays between the global and the local in establishing educational policies. Both themes feature prominently in the next two chapters in this part. The impact of globalization, expressed in the way educational 'policy solutions' are produced, packaged and marketed internationally is at the heart of the chapter written by Borhène Chakroun and Eva Jimeno Sicilia. The authors consider the 'push' and 'pull' factors that shape the dynamics of policy borrowing and policy lending in the region. Their focus is on the Technical and Vocational Education and Training (TVET) sector, and especially on the introduction of National Qualifications Frameworks (NQFs). The latter are increasingly taking on the dimensions of a 'policy epidemic' worldwide. The authors' reflections, however, are broader in scope, not only because they review region-wide dynamics, but also because they consider the intricate inter-relationships between this region and the political and economic construction of the 'Euro-Mediterranean' space by the European Union, as a space of policy initiatives and as a space of political and economic action. While the TVET sector is often shunned by parents and students in the region, since it is seen to be a dead-end destiny/destination for the low-achieving from less economically established social backgrounds, TVET 'policy busy-ness' features prominently both in state and international agency interventions in the Arab states. The economic agendas here are clear. They are also linked to the increasing importance accorded to NQFs, encapsulating as they do aspirations for development of appropriately skilled labour that can circulate freely within and beyond the region in search for employment opportunities that serve personal— and by extension, state—prosperity. NQFs have a major role to play in signalling skills that are made 'readable' across enterprises and sectors within national borders, and even more, across nation-state and geographic borders. They are therefore seen to be of value to national governments, to international capital that seeks guarantees in terms of the availability of skills, and to EU political and economic interests that seek to pace and systematize the flow of labour from the economic south in ways that can be more easily and more advantageously absorbed in the economic north. The authors thus highlight another key thematic in this volume, namely the complex imbrications of the global and the local, where the 'push' and 'pull' of policy solutions interact together in multifaceted ways, thus defining what is implemented within the prevalent geometry of power dynamics. As with Akkari's contribution, here as well, we see the long shadow cast by neo-liberal ideologies, in this case articulated through the legitimizing power of a human capital discourse that gestures towards the reified 'needs' of an imagined, immanent knowledge-based economy—a discourse that Arab states seem only too eager to buy into. Chakroun and Jimeno Sicilia explore the mechanisms by means of which policy 'solutions' circulate—even when there is very little evidence regarding their effectiveness. They make a case for other forms of policy learning interactions between the global and the local, ones that put players on a footing approximating more closely to equality and to mutually beneficial cooperation where the coherence and integrity of national education systems are more likely to be safeguarded.

The next two chapters in this part consider the theme of global/local dynamics and resonances in educational policy making from other levels and perspectives. They focus on the meso/institutional and even the micro/personal, respectively. Fatma Sayed thus provides us with a riveting account of the political contestation over educational policies, this time in relation to the reforms being implemented in Egypt. Here, various sections of the public are particularly sensitive to efforts by the state to reform core aspects of education, such as curricula and textbooks, convinced, as they are, that the local governing elites are in collusion with global players, including agencies such as the World Bank and USAID. Rife with accusations of conspiracy, policy making and policy implementation are marred by controversies and power struggles. Suspicions abound that educational reform is driven by agendas set elsewhere, outside the Arab region, and which could therefore represent a deepening of dependency and a threat to national identity and security, rather than offer an opportunity to respond to and fulfil national needs, interests and emancipation.

Through her analysis of the Egyptian experience—and especially through her focus on what she calls the curricular 'identity triangle'—composed of history, language and religious instruction, and on the role played by the Centre of Curriculum and Instructional Materials Development—Sayed shows how social, cultural and political contexts at the local level influence and determine the articulation, implementation and sustainability of educational reforms supported by international development assistance. In this case, frustrations about a régime's authoritarian rule, seen to be overly sympathetic to 'western' ideologies and interests for strategic and geopolitical reasons, are vigorously expressed through strong public opinion campaigns in the press, effectively stalling the collaboration between local and international actors in addressing key aspects of educational reforms. Local experts engaged by international agencies are dubbed 'traitors' who are prepared to sell their country down the river, while aid and donor agencies invest in less sensitive—and hence often less crucial—areas of educational reform. One is therefore left wondering about the extent to which the dynamics of the global and the local playing themselves out in Egypt lead to educational development— or to paralysis. Sayed is careful to show how local tensions and resistance, even if not solidly founded on evidence, are not without their own 'logic of practice' within the Egyptian political field of power (see Bourdieu, 1990). Rather, they reflect concerns and anxieties that are fuelled by serious challenges to democratic processes that lead most to feel that they cannot participate in the shaping of the destiny of their own country, particularly in the context of deepening globalization processes and persisting demands by international agencies and regulative bodies for structural adjustments and re-alignments in the economy and labour market.

The concluding chapter in this part takes us to yet another level of policy making, one that is hardly ever addressed in policy research, especially with regard to Arab education, where public revelations of insider knowledge about policy making within government or government-dependent departments and units can be foolhardy, if not perilous. We are thus particularly pleased to feature a chapter by Nemer Frayha, who provides us with unique insights into the hazards of policy making in political régimes common across the region, this time seen from the perspective of the policy maker in person. This candid, introspective and reflexive account, which tells us how the macro-level is experienced at the micro-level, speaks volumes about the way in which power works in Lebanon, and how religious and secular pressure groups jostle with each other in the political arena, cutting deals with political elites in order to establish dominant educational agendas and practices. Here, Frayha comes across as an academic who crosses over to the 'other side', and who commits the understandable yet somewhat fatal leap of faith of thinking that the rules (presumably) governing scholarly work will also apply to the policy-making field. Instead, he quickly realizes that education is not an endeavour guided by objectively identified quality standards and protocols, by means of which the greatest good for the greatest number of people can be easily defined, articulated and implemented. Rather, the education arena represents another vehicle for the scramble for hearts and minds, where other epistemologies and 'régimes of truth' (see Foucault, 1979) prevail, and where there are hidden—and at times not so hidden—linkages to the larger configurations of national and regional geometries of power operating within Lebanese society. Like Sayed, Frayha highlights how the issue of 'narrating the nation' through the curriculum—and especially through such subjects as history, religion and language—is fraught with complexity, especially in a context where social groups are burdened with a history of civil strife based on claims to precedence on the basis of ethnic origin or religious affiliation. In this scenario, the notion of 'Arabness', its political conflation with Islam, and the efforts of some to ensure the curricular representation of Lebanese society in ways that give some groups more 'legitimacy' than others, feeds into old anxieties and fears so that competing 'imagined communities' (Anderson, 1983) vie for recognition and legitimacy in the public sphere, simultaneously. Education thus becomes a card in a game where the stakes are high, the rules difficult to pin down, and the policy outcomes predicated not on forms of technical or emancipatory rationality, but rather on the power of diversely located groups to use their guile, grit and gumption to ensure that their interests win the day. This is perhaps not so different from the educational policy-making field elsewhere, which has been famously characterized as typically being a 'messy', 'hit-and-miss' affair (Ball, 1998, p. 126), where policies are closely related to politics, and as such embody normative stances "that cannot be readily, fully or permanently resolved through rational deliberations or unanimous agreements. As a result, these policies tend to be adopted and implemented through political processes that reflect the relative power of contending groups more than the relative merits of policy options" (Malen, 2006, p. 83). What is specific to the Lebanese scene—and here there are both similarities and differences with other political contexts in the region—is that the protocols that in some polities regulate the influence of the different 'contending groups' are either missing, or too amorphous, or insufficiently formalized and embedded in institutional ways as to permit enforcement. In Lebanon too—as in the USA (Apple, 2000), for instance— religious and conservative groups have been particularly successful in establishing their agendas, sometimes even overcoming denominational differences in order to form alliances that powerfully define what is educationally legitimate, appropriate and acceptable in such areas as the representation of sexuality and gender relations in the curriculum, as well as the nature and extent of religious instruction. Indeed, their power to mobilize and organize positional resources is nothing short of impressive when it comes to influencing the framing of educational policies in Lebanon.

Taken together, the chapters in this section suggest that the very notion of the post-colonial Arab nation-state is shifting in terms of its bureaucratic and ideological roles in the field of educational policy. The growing role of international organizations in determining educational policies points to displacements and disruptions of established notions of sovereignty and the articulation of new forms of political legitimacy, partly grounded in market ideologies and international relations and partly in rentier forms of political sponsorship. While this clearly suggests the emergence of complex spatial networks and hierarchies of power that shape educational policy making, the resulting policy disjunctures are also intensifying inward, with myriad ideological, opposition and class-based groups becoming increasingly more active and vocal in contesting or bypassing the policy-making process using different strategies. At this juncture, the resulting cultural politics of education is indicative of the larger crisis underpinning the political legitimacy of the contemporary Arab state and the central role debates around educational policy play in attempting to reclaim it.

Part II: Re-calling Voices

Part II proceeds by 'displacement' and 'reversal' in relation to the first. The contributions 'displace' the focus from policy concerns, to students and teachers as social and political actors located within the 'frontline' of classrooms and schools. Here, authors explore how educational policies and governance structures are experienced within the daily experiential realities of schooling, in diverse contexts. The chapters in this section also 'inverse' the questions raised in the previous section, from those pertaining to policies as 'imaginary worlds' to those which seek to understand, through critical ethnographic work, how social actors within classrooms and schools, including educational researchers, make sense of their selves, of the different 'Other', and of what is valued as education, in ways which "bear the seeds of an alternative future grounded in participatory democracy and economic and social justice" (Lipman, 2005, p. 326). Central to this section is therefore a concern for voices and how they respond to 'exclusionary discourses and practices', re-claiming their sense of community and belonging in multiple ways.

Part II clusters together four chapters—those of Linda Herrera, Fida Adely, Matthew Clarke and Orit Bashkin. Linda Herrera's contribution introduces the ethnographic ethos in her qualitative capture of life in classrooms in Cairo, Egypt. There are few ethnographers of school life in the Arab region, where structural and policy analysis on the one hand, and quantitative, often positivistic studies on the other, have tended to form much of the staple of educational research. Herrera and Adely are notable exceptions. The former employs 'critical ethnography' not only as a research methodology (Carspecken, 1996), but also as an epistemological and political tool to prise open spaces where issues of social justice and the promotion of democratic forms of life are foregrounded (Madison, 2005)—in stark contrast to neoliberal concerns that would have us 'see' education almost entirely in human capital terms. Herrera's case for an ethnography of Arab schooling, therefore, is not merely about the use of yet another form of research—which in itself is not necessarily progressive, especially given the close historical and genealogical associations between ethnography and empire (Lipman, 2005)—but rather it is about embedding forms of participatory research where voices, especially subaltern ones, matter (Abu El-Haj, 2009). And this is precisely why ethnographic work is a difficult endeavour in the region, given that it has the power to reveal that which authority desires to conceal, to unsettle hierarchies, and to give voice to those whose point of view is not often heard. Herrera's depiction of both the research process itself, and the insights generated by extended observations of classroom life in a girls' school, forcefully capture the different layers of authority and power as they operate at different levels of institutional life, and the extent to which bodies and minds are disciplined into submission. 'Pain and shame' is the syntax employed by the school and its teachers in its effort to speak to the students … a syntax that is differentially employed according to the social class backgrounds of those to whom it is addressed. Students do not often 'speak back', but if given the chance they do so—and ethnography provides relatively safe opportunities for this to happen. Then we become aware of the extent to which they can transcend their daily experience of authoritative restraints in order to express their desire for fairness, respect, and joyful forms of pedagogical interaction. As an interruption in the established narrative of everyday routines, 'ethnographic seeing' also places a mirror in front of teachers, challenging them to rethink habitual practices that have been too often and too unreflectively adopted as part of the legitimate repertoire of classroom management.

The value of ethnography in reconstructing our understanding of everyday life in classrooms and schools also comes through powerfully in the chapter by Fida Adely, who takes us into another girls' school—this time in the Hashemite Kingdom of Jordan. Adely skilfully portrays the daily rituals and the raft of symbols that permeate everyday life in the school, and shows how they serve to socialize female students into assenting to the legitimacy of the overarching authority structure inspired by Arab nationalism, religious beliefs, patriarchy, and loyalty to the Hashemite monarchy. In finely textured ethnographic detail, Adely shows how the performance of these rituals, meant to publicly solidify state ideology and consolidate patriotic sentiments, clashes with notions of piety, propriety and morality embraced by some students, thus prising open a space for resistance, producing new ways of reading patriotic performances and their contested symbolism.

Where others might have seen—or assumed—a confluence of 'régimes of truth', therefore, where patriotism and morality work hand in hand to socialize the 'modern' Jordanian woman into a specific form, Adely discerns an active re-articulation by some students of this intended construct. These young women are thus far from being the 'docile bodies' and 'docile minds' that the 'script' embedded in the ritual demands them to be. Rather, they draw on other value systems—in this case constructions of Islamic notions of modesty—in order to resist the muscular invitations to loudly and publicly express their patriotic allegiance to the monarch during the daily *tāboor*, or morning assembly queue. Music, clothing, headdress—one and all position girls at the centre of contested interpretations of what is appropriate as a display of patriotism, and what is commendable in terms of living up to perceived standards of modesty. The outcome of this contested meaning is not predictable, however: while the state/religion binary is questioned by some, others draw moral legitimacy from it, thus recognizing the power of the state to define what is appropriate, and in that very process legitimizing the régime. In this, Adely opens up new ways of unpacking semiotic *and* performative constructions of gendered spaces that operate within schools, classrooms, and community settings. These spaces, located at the intersections of contradictory political projects, are underpinned by notions of women's 'modesty' that operate as regulative devices of power agendas located at different levels of action, and extending far beyond the school.

With regard to the search for meaning, Matthew Clarke provides us with important insights into identity constructions through a focus on teachers in the United Arab Emirates (UAE), a confederacy of seven emirates. Clarke works with a notion of identity as 'difference'—a particularly generative theme in the context of the UAE which he speaks of as a 'willed nation', one that has constructed itself through differentiation, both with those Arab states outside its borders, and those confederated emirates that constitute it from within. Clarke notes "identity's paradoxical reliance on difference for its self-constitution often takes the form of antagonism towards those same constitutive differences". Clarke takes us to the micro/person level where the work of identity building is carried out, focusing on how a teacher goes 'against the grain' by critically reframing available discourses on what it means to be a teacher in a context powerfully impacted by the flow of global capital, shifting oil markets and labour markets dominated by migrant labour.

In order to do this, Clarke uses data from focus groups and online asynchronous discussion forums. He skilfully draws on Foucauldian notions of a 'historical ontology' of the self to show how one pre-service teacher attempts to cultivate an ethos of critical responsiveness, constructing a professional identity that parted ways from the 'norm' by adopting progressive pedagogy. This teacher thus attempts to define herself and her work differently from the way it is set out in the prevalent social discourses that produce available understandings of what it means to be a teacher and what the activity of teaching entails. Her efforts represent a labour of ethical self-formation, sustained, in this case, within an evolving community of practice that defines itself in contrast to prevalent practices by teachers in mainstream government schools. Such teachers, however, are thought of in pathological terms, echoing similar representations that often appear in the international literature on educators in the Arab region, who are generally described as being authoritarian in attitude, conventional in pedagogy, and as distant and disengaged. The 'Othering' of 'traditional teachers' in the UAE case was particularly fraught given that the target of their critique was often expatriates which they, as UAE nationals, were destined to replace given the evolving policies regarding foreign workers in the country.

Clarke suggests, however, that identity is 'fugitive' rather than 'fixed', a 'work in progress' that is constantly shaped by the discourses and practices that prevail in the social contexts we participate in. It is through such 'conversations'—both with self and others—that 'conversions' can occur, with certainties and fixities becoming unsettled with deepening realizations about the complexities that shape consciousness. It is through such ethical work on—and care of—the self that the ground is prepared for the 'care of the other', where difference opens the door to conversations, rather than to dismissive prejudice.

The concluding chapter in this cluster is a contribution by Orit Bashkin, who also takes us into schools and classrooms. Bashkin, however, does so from the perspective of the memories of Arab Jews, who recall their childhood, as Iraqi citizens, attending religious and secular schools prior to their exodus in the aftermath of the establishment of the state of Israel in 1948. Bashkin's historical ethnography creatively, and with great sensitivity, draws on autobiographies from which the educational experiences of members of the Jewish community in Iraq can be reconstructed, focusing on the pre-1948 period when the notion of an 'Arab Jew'—in itself a hegemony-shattering term if ever there was one—was actively inculcated. Bashkin—through her reading of fourteen of these autobiographies—gives testimony to a time when Iraqi children and youth, whether Shi'a, Sunnis, Christians or Jews, were socialized into nationalist ideologies and a love for country and nation that were meant to transcend ethnic and faith-based differences. She captures the accommodations to and appropriations of—but also the tensions and resistances around—Iraq Hashemites' call to patriotism, with Jewish students sometimes joining forces with other Arab activists to take a stand vis-à-vis the state's social policies. Bashkin also builds on these autobiographies to illustrate the many ways in which the encounter between Jews and Muslims in Baghdad, Basra, Hilla, and Mosul was as playful and positive as it was profound: some felt emancipated when they moved from the dark, often unsanitary confines of their community's religious schools to the more congenial and open-minded learning spaces found in some state schools; many were enamoured of the beauty of the Arabic language, showing familiarity with both contemporary and medieval literature; others felt at home in mosque and synagogue alike, cheered at stories of Arab conquest in the Middle East, identified with Arab national heroes, and took part in plays written by Arabs, or in Jewish plays translated into Arabic.

What Bashkin succeeds in capturing is the way schools—especially until the anti-monarchist coup in 1941, which led to the British invasion and occupation of Iraq—provided effective environments for crossing religious and ethnic boundaries, with fast friendships being formed that spilled outside school walls into everyday life. The identification of the Arab Jew with the Iraqi nation—so strongly promoted through the secular schools by very much the same rituals that Adely describes in her account of a Jordanian school—was not always accepted by Arab Muslim colleagues or teachers. The autobiographies recount stories of aggression, prejudice, and rejection as well, but they also bear testimony to conviviality and solidarity in the face of diversity, with some students joining the Communist Party, marching arm in arm in causes they shared a passionate commitment to, identifying with the same nation but standing against a state which they considered corrupt and autocratic. Such school and classroom ethnographies, recaptured through autobiographic memories, are extremely powerful in contesting and subverting univocal—and therefore less real—accounts, providing a range much wider than prevalent representations of Arab–Jewish relations, which are, as Bashkin writes, "mediated solely through the lenses of the conflict".

Part II sheds light on the multifaceted discursive and semiotic intersections between power and knowledge, unpacking their representational and performative articulations within classrooms, schools and communities across the Arab region, and at different points in time. By undertaking critical ethnographies into diverse sites of practice, the chapters further our "understanding [of] the relationship between power and thought and power and truth claims" (Carspecken, 1996, p. 10). They thus lead us to better grasp, not only how these relationships unfold within classrooms and schools, but also which larger political projects of nation, country, and community they seek to legitimate, and at what toll and loss.

Part III: Suspended Visibilities

In constructing their gaze on the Arab region, many writers point to the centrality of the Arabic language, as a medium of communication, and of Islam, as the dominant religion. Language and religion are viewed as foundational pillars of a shared regional culture; for many, they capture the quintessential manifestations through which Arab societies can be known. The Arab region is thus presented as exhibiting culturally homogeneous traits, despite other aspects of diversity, with local dialects and cultural variations expressing, so the argument goes, a range of localized functional accommodations. Some have identified an 'Arab mind', that can be studied and understood in terms of its underlying phenomenology, ontology, and socio-cultural manifestations (Patai, 1973). In *Orientalism*, Edward W. Said (1978) has critiqued other objectifications of this type, locating them within the domain of imperialist and colonial encounters. Others, however, focus on the wide diversity of ethnic, social, cultural, religious, and linguistic traditions prevalent across the Arab region. For them, as they see it, the question of 'minorities', and its political articulations within the frame of the Arab nation-state, emphasizes instead the centrality of sectarian identities as a landscape over which the cultural politics of the Arab region plays out. Still, for others, the question of culture and its ramifications is avoided altogether by focusing on the 'modernizing' effects of the state, and how by constructing and narrating the nation, ruling elites carve for themselves the foundations of power—rentier, patriarchal, ideological—on which their legitimacy relies (Beblawi, 1987; Sharabi, 1988; Ayubi, 1995, respectively).

For these writers, cultural configurations and their articulations reflect larger identity politics understood over the backdrop of the economic and political contradictions that underpin the Arab nation-state, as a postcolonial phenomenon, and its political contestation by different power groups.

At the juncture of these competing approaches, the question of social diversity, how it intersects with education, and how it informs or shapes the bounds of the political community, has been explored from different conceptual and methodological standpoints. For some, the intersection of social diversity and education is addressed as part of the question of development and modernization, in which the expansion of schooling mediates the formation of human capital, while mediating the tensions between "forces of tradition" and "forces of change" (Massialas and Jarrar, 1987); "examining whether the unique mix of traditional and modern institutions structures educational opportunity" (Wiseman & Alromi, 2003, p. 208) in Arab societies. For others, human capital delimits the bounds of the 'healthy' and 'legitimate' polity (see the chapters in Part IV in Laabas, 2002). Groups that are perceived as located outside what stands for a 'modern' society—such as Bedouin, pastoralist or rural communities, to name but a few— are perceived by policy makers as redeemable through schooling more specifically (Chatty, 2006). Others, still, perceive education in its social reproductive capacity, accounting for the various ways in which schools are engaged in the reproduction of symbolic and effective power within diverse contexts across the Arab region (Herrera & Torres, 2006). Notwithstanding the commendable contributions that these approaches have made, each in their respective disciplinary framework, the bulk of the discussion in the field has not *yet* clarified how the institutionalization of schooling—as *the* privileged socio-political and cultural ritual—effectively shapes notions of citizenship, a sense of belonging and civic and political rights, beyond the rhetorical statements of constitutions and ideological platforms, and beyond the question of mobility opportunities.

From this point of view, then, we consider the question of social diversity as tied to the question of social justice and belonging, in relation to which the role of education should be also discussed. In this regard, social science studies of education in the Arab region need to address what Brighenti (2007) refers to as an "epistemology of seeing", in terms of clarifying how education and schooling in the Arab region take part in delimiting "the field of visibility" which renders certain social groups "visible" or "invisible" in the public sphere. Such a focus— and the conceptual framework that underpins it—opens up new horizons for research. It conceives of educational settings as "sites of visibility" (pp. 331–334), actively implicated in processes of political recognition and/or misrecognition; and actively involved in the constitution of educators, students and communities, as both objects and subjects of the politics of schooling. Equally, how marginalized social groups struggle to become visible and 'be seen' in the public sphere, by engaging the educational project in its varied articulations and sites, acquires particular importance in understanding shifting articulations of citizenship. Thus, examining how educational settings shape, through their organization, the 'features of visibility' in the Arab region provides valuable opportunities to consider their "relational, strategic and processual" (p. 339) articulations and socio-political deployments. Such an examination also sheds light on the classificatory schemes through which educational settings delimit the public and private domains by determining what stands for a 'legitimate' participation in the public sphere and what belongs to the realm of the private.

The five contributors in Part III critically engage these issues. They interrogate how educational institutions, through their legal and symbolic articulations, mediate the 'field of visibility' in relation to imagined constructions of the political community. Sawsan Zaher heads this section with a chapter that approaches education as a human right from an international law perspective. Her analysis of international legal instruments, and their implementation in the Arab region, reveals a significant discrepancy between rhetoric and effective policy in terms of the state's obligation to secure an equitable and universal access to education. Zaher shows how narrow interpretations of citizenship status build classificatory schemes which render 'invisible' vulnerable social groups in Arab societies— women, children in rural areas, stateless individuals, refugees and displaced persons, to name but a few—effectively excluding them from participating in and accessing education. Zaher's analysis advances some suggestions for the articulation of an alternative 'field of visibility' to the one offered, for instance, by neo-liberal conceptions of education, and which approach education "as a sub-set of economic policy" (Peters & Besley, 2006). Her chapter shifts the discussion on education in the Arab region from the customary emphasis on human capital, mobility, and socio-economic returns and development, to a critical interrogation of the ethical ends of schooling. By decentring the notion of citizenship, and by redefining education as an inalienable human right, Zaher lays the foundation for postnational—or rather post-national?—constructions of the polity. She makes the case for inclusion and justice in ways that engage, not only the socio-cultural diversity prevalent in Arab societies, but also the social and symbolic realms within which a sense of belonging can be fostered through education, independent of citizenship status.

With regard to human rights, Sarah Ashencaen Crabtree and Richard Williams push a step further. They provide a richly detailed overview of inclusive education of students with disability in the Arab region, and particularly in the Gulf Cooperation Council states. Their chapter highlights some of the attitudes towards persons with disability prevalent in Arab societies, which dismiss them as legitimate members of the wider political community. Ashencaen Crabtree and Williams also show how elements of cultural and religious traditions can bolster empowering models of education, ones that are more intimately linked to the discourse of human rights and entitlements. Thus, effectively, their chapter expands the scope of Zaher's chapter by delving on the intersections of disability, culture, and inclusive citizenship in contemporary Arab societies and their legal and institutional articulations. By critically unpacking the political, culturally-embedded and historically-situated discourses that classify disability and the dis/abled in Arab societies, the authors interrogate the nexus of individual rights and state responsibilities within the framework of political and civic participation. They also convincingly show how, in some cases, geopolitical conflicts, and the establishment of state boundaries, affect the prevalence and distribution of disability. Zaher and Ashencaen Crabtree and Williams agree on the foundational contribution of a philosophy of rights in articulating an ethically defensible approach to an inclusive education. Yet, they develop their arguments in relation to different approaches, relying, respectively, on international instruments of enforcement, and on the unpacking of dominant discourses and the encouragement of advocacy groups.

Abdelouahad Mabrour and Khalil Mgharfaoui adopt a different entry point to the discussion on social diversity and education. They undertake a comparative examination of language policies in Morocco and France. They consider their differential impacts on the status of Amazigh, languages spoken in various dialects across the Maghreb states (Algeria, Morocco and Tunisia) and among some Maghrebi diasporic communities in France. The authors unpack the homogenizing and assimilationist effects of language policies in the Maghreb states, contrasting their rationale to language policies prevalent in Europe. They then offer a critical reading of the struggles of Amazigh-speaking communities (Imazighen or 'Berbers') in the Maghreb for the recognition of their multi-dialectical linguistic heritage and identities, in states defined around Arabness and the Arabic language. Mabrour and Mgharfaoui's discussion sheds light on the cultural and identity politics surrounding the efforts deployed by politically subordinate communities to mobilize symbolic forms of capital, such as language, as part of articulating alternative educational horizons. Such movements are part of attempts to reconfigure the 'field of visibility' through which more inclusive articulations of citizenship can be pursued and decentred narrational representations of the nation rendered 'legitimate'. Notwithstanding, it would be misleading to consider this chapter under the exclusive prism of multicultural citizenship. In fact, Mabrour and Mgharfaoui's chapter offers a valuable opportunity to reflect on the tensions and contradictions that underpin the Arab nation-state, as a post-colonial phenomenon, yet itself involved in internal colonialism. Reading this chapter one cannot avoid the conclusion that education in the Arab nation-state remains trapped on two fronts simultaneously: at the domestic level, sustaining modes of 'internal colonialism' vis-à-vis the different 'Other'; and at the geopolitical level, in terms of the continued subservience of the field of education—as part of the field of power—to priorities and strategic aims determined by geopolitical and global contingencies.

Yet, if the manifestations of diversity prompted authors in the previous chapters to focus on institutional politics, in this section Steven Dinero allows us to engage the theme by exploring the challenges and contradictions framing the schooling of pastoralist communities. The chapter shows how the pastoralist way of life is construed as a 'problem' by governments—one that can be overcome through formal education, which will 'modernize' and 'develop' nomadic and semi-nomadic communities, integrating them into a redeeming modern civitas. Dinero shows, however, how seemingly benign and benevolent education programmes serve the state's interest to control, assimilate, encapsulate and, ultimately, sedentarize pastoralist communities—thus paving the way to state requisition of their lands. Such programmes also implicitly delegitimize indigenous ways of knowing, disorienting communities in terms of their ways of life.

Dinero's chapter leads us to reflect on two major consequences of education, and more specifically of schooling. First, the chapter captures the powerful ways through which schooling violently disrupts and alters the modes of ownership and attachment of pastoralist communities and their individual members to the land, transforming their spatio-cultural articulations. Here, one can readily observe the power of schooling to disorient pastoralist communities in terms of relocating them across the physical space, reconfiguring its experienced spatial dimensions. This has been the case of nomadic and semi-nomadic communities, as Chatty (2006) clearly shows, for instance, with regard to the Harasiis tribe in the Sultanate of Oman. As such, schooling emerges as a political project of modernity, grounded in a spatial rationality that considers urbanity, ultimately and over time, as its hegemonic mode of social organization (Yiftachel, 2006, pp. 188–189). This process also alters the mode of production of pastoralist communities and institutionalizes their marginal location within the broader labour market (Krätli & Dyer, 2006, pp. 15–16), as has been, for instance, the case of Bedouin Arab communities in the Negev Desert in Israel (Yiftachel, 2006, pp. 188–210). These observations underline the role schooling actively plays in enacting and re-enacting the territorial contours of the nation-state. Yet, they also show how schooling institutionalizes territorial enclaves and modes of social organization within the nation-state, thus constructing spatial hierarchical trappings that subordinate particular communities, politically and economically. Secondly, Dinero's chapter points to deeper levels of transformation, those associated with the consciousness and perceptions of younger generations and the multifaceted ways through which schooling imputes 'new' 'modes of being', particularly among the younger generations. In many ways, Dinero's chapter resonates with Zaher's chapter in its interrogation of current educational policies and practices and how they negatively affect the human rights of pastoralist communities. Dinero's chapter also resonates with the basic problematics discussed by Mabrour and Mgharfaoui in their chapter on the struggle of the Imazighen communities in the Maghreb for the recognition of their heritage, language and modes of being, within an inclusive polity. Taken together, these three chapters—Zaher's, Mabrour and Mgharfaoui's, and Dinero's—critically interrogate the 'logics of practice' that underpin current educational policies, particularly those that target the education of indigenous communities.

As we have seen so far, the question of citizenship is central to the discussion of multicultural citizenship and its intersection with education. This issue is taken up audaciously by Louise Chircop, in a study concerned with the schooling of Muslim children and youth living in Malta, a European Union member state. Hers is a study of the role played by a hegemonic educational system—premised on a fervently Catholic identity—and how it determines the "features of visibility" of Muslim children and youth (including Arab Muslims), not only within Maltese schools but also within the larger society. Chircop's study is important for two key reasons. First, it is a reminder that political and geographic boundaries represent delimitations that do not necessarily overlap with the complexity of diasporic engagements of individuals and communities. Thus, diasporic communities— whether one refers to Imazighen living in France (Mabrour and Mgharfaoui), or to Muslims and Arabs living in Malta (Chircop), offer vivid examples of the multifaceted ways through which cultures play out within educational institutions, and how, as part of that, cultures and particularly "youth cultures leap geographical scales in the search for influences and references to tap into" (Massey, 1998, p. 123). These leaps underpin not only the construction of hyphenated identities, but also the articulation of new modes of civic engagement and new modalities of exercising citizenship (Soysal, 2000). 'Leaps' are also indicative of trans-national or trans-cultural articulations of difference. Secondly, the study offers rare insights into the educational activism of diasporic communities, for instance, through the foundation of schools. By exploring the Mariam Albatool School, the only Muslim school currently operating in Malta, Chircop not only sheds new light on the multifaceted roles played by the school in sustaining the diasporic experience; she also shows that diasporic institutions offer the first articulations of new modes of civic engagement.

Two aspects of Part III deserve particular attention. First, the authors of the various chapters conceive of the intersection between social diversity and education as an important dimension through which the larger question of an inclusive citizenship can be raised, unpacked and critiqued. This is a crucial point that allows us to transcend the question on the social reproductive role of education, towards an examination of the modalities through which educational systems throughout the Arab region and beyond are implicated in the construction, reproduction and dissemination of the imagined foundations of the state, as 'nation-state', and of the boundaries of the 'legitimate' political community it refers to. In doing so, the chapters open up new conceptual and empirical spaces of investigation through which the voices of marginalized, oppressed and discriminated communities and groups can be heard. Secondly, the chapters capture the identity politics involved in the educational process, and their relation to movements of resistance and struggle for social justice in diverse contexts of practice. Yet, as the chapters also show, the educational articulations of diversity are powerfully intertwined with local, regional, geopolitical, trans-cultural and global processes.

Part IV: Knowledge Imaginaries

The complex relationships between knowledge and power are the focus of the four chapters in Part IV. Some aspects of this relationship have already been addressed in earlier sections of the volume: Chakroun and Jimeno Sicilia, for instance, as well as Akkari, Sayed and Clarke, all noted the global reach of power that is exercised through the production, circulation, and legitimation of specific kinds of knowledge and understandings of the world. In line with Robertson's (2006) call, the chapters in Part IV look more closely at other questions related to the exercise of power through knowledge, questions that are equally central to the region and beyond, such as: Whose knowledge counts? Whose knowledge has been subjugated, and why? Whose knowledge is globalized? How is access to socially valued knowledge controlled? By who, and for what ends? How is knowledge represented in formal and informal learning programmes? Such questions are particularly timely given the intensification of discourse around the notions of a 'knowledge society' that is so perceptible in the region (Mazawi, 2007).

In the first chapter, Rukhsana Zia considers Islamic education in the Arab region and beyond, paying particular attention to how it features in the curriculum. She explores how the articulation of religious knowledge in public and non-public educational settings plays out against the backdrop of competing political agendas, those grounded in Arab and pan-Arab movements and worldviews, as well as those grounded in pan-Islamic philosophies. Along with Apple (1990), Zia approaches curricular and textbook spaces as contentious and contested which cannot be understood outside the context of the shifting terrain of colliding political ideologies and political movements. Her argument regarding religious education in the Arab states resonates with Said's (1997) observation that texts, and curricular texts pertaining to religious education more particularly, represent "acts of will and interpretation that take place in history, and can be dealt with in history as acts of will and interpretation" (p. 41). In that, Zia breaks with the invoked duality between 'modernity' and 'traditionalism' so often found in accounts of education in the Arab region. She rather places her analysis within a wider frame of reference, which sees the space of religious education within the context of competing worldviews operating at the national, regional and global levels. She also shows that even for those Arab states upholding secular or secularized ideologies—whether nationalist, socialist, pan-Arabist or a combination thereof, religious education remains a space that is not (and perhaps cannot be) relinquished by ruling elites. Its centrality—in relation to broader articulations of legitimacy—clearly positions it within the realm of a political philosophy that transcends the distinctions between the secular and the religious realms as fixed antinomies. Rather, her analyses and conclusions coincide with those of recent and more detailed studies of religious curricula in the Arab and Muslim states. These indicate that how Islam is taught, and how it is choreographed within textbooks cannot be detached from the broader struggles over political power and their ideological articulations. In that sense, the crucial point here is not so much that religious education operates as the 'integrative' and 'distinctive' force within Arab school systems, than it should rather be approached and understood over the backdrop of the wider politics in relation to which claims to morality and ethical supremacy are put forward. This has been well captured and expressed by Starrett (2007) who pointed out that:

> Moral, religious, and political education may be less the causal force of national unity and progress than they are a band-aid to cover the social wounds gouged by the everyday operation of other institutions: the rational brutalities of the market, the stifling influence of patriarchy, the casual violence of power politics. (p. 227)

And he therefore concludes, "If we wish to understand the politics of inclusion and exclusion, it's that wide world, rather than the restricted universe of the textbooks, to which we need to direct our attention" (p. 230). Shifting her attention to the wider socio-political contexts in which religious education in the Arab states takes place, Zia shows how competing religious worldviews play out differentially, within and across different types of institutional settings, such as the *madrasa* and the more recent public school.

Two chapters address the power–knowledge relationship as this has played itself out in higher education in Algeria and in Egypt, respectively. In Algeria, according to Hocine Khelfaoui, political elites—in collusion with the interests of global capital linked to the petroleum industry—maintain their grip over power, obstructing the university from fulfilling its role in supporting the democratization of knowledge and the construction of a merit-based society. As a result, the promise of education—as a project that facilitates personal mobility and the installation of democratic relations—is thwarted by a totalitarian State that does not let go its stranglehold over power. If anything, and as Foucault has taught us, this same power recreates its own fields of exercise through knowledge. Firmly locating himself within the work of Pierre Bourdieu, and drawing on his political economy of symbolic power (Swartz, 1997, pp. 65–94), Khelfaoui offers a penetrating set of insights into "the generative anthropology of power" (Wacquant, 1993, p. 1) in contemporary Algeria, through which political labour, associated with resistance to colonialism, is abstracted and mobilized, to be recast in the public sphere as a symbolic form of capital which overrides and marginalizes other forms of capital, such as education and scholarly merit. This process underpins what Bourdieu calls a "chiasmatic" social structure, that is, the operation of differential hierarchies of situated economic, political and cultural forms of capital in relation to which social stratification and differentiation play out within the broader field of power. Khelfaoui uses this conceptualization to show how within Algeria's national, regional (Euro-Mediterranean) and global articulations of power collisions, academic work and the governance structures of universities are subdued, creating not only lines of subordination of the academic to the political, but further reinforcing the power of the State over the means and trajectories along which knowledge production, social mobility and respectability can take place. This analysis resonates powerfully with a metaphor coined by M'hammed Sabour (2001), in his pioneering work on Arab academics, and which likens the latter to "*a matador without a muleta*" (p. 143; italics in the original). Khelfaoui therefore allows new perspectives to emerge regarding the political sociology within which one can account for the effects of geopolitics and globalization on the articulation of epistemic frameworks within academe. In this, Khelfaoui joins Bishara Doumani (2006) who wrote on academic freedom in American universities after September 11, showing how commercialism and privatization are but some of the aspects underpinning the larger reconfiguration of higher education institutions. As both Khelfaoui and Doumani show, each drawing on different bodies of work, academic freedom and the ability of academics to 'speak truth to power' are situated within the web of cultural, political and institutional practices that enact them. Khelfaoui's analysis also offers a refreshing contribution to the broader literatures on the internationalization and globalization of higher education institutions. It transcends the quasi-exclusive emphases placed on the neo-liberal political economy and its managerialist articulations. Khelfaoui thus approaches the State both as the Power (*Pouvoir*) and as part of the 'field of power'.

His analysis remains sensitive to the historical, cultural, class, and linguistic dynamics which underpin the higher education system and its operation.

Iman Farag, on her part, pushes ahead as she considers the way the 'internationalization' of higher education in Egypt has similarly jeopardized the mission of the university. The latter has allowed itself to be colonized by the global speak relating to managerialism and quality assurance. New discourses—which mediate the relationships between the state and the citizen—emerge as part of this process. Free higher education, once a fundamental political tenet of the 1952 anti-monarchist revolution and its agenda for social change, is now being "transformed into a negotiable relationship between the student and the State; it is no longer a systematic commitment of public institutions towards students". Previously, free higher education was also seen as a social and political right. The knowledge transmitted through higher education institutions was perceived as serving the private and public good through the alleviation of class differences and by addressing social injustices inherited from the past. Such a mission for the university has been superimposed by an international 'script' that has penetrated and permeated the debates on the university in Egypt, where the notions of global ranking and league tables introduce a whole set of complex dynamics between the local and the global, determining what a university stands for. While Sayed— who also speaks of educational reform in Egypt—considered the way subordinate groups react to the perceived imposition of agendas worked out in complicit agreement between local and foreign elites, Farag, echoing Chakroun and Jimeno Sicilia, locates her analysis in relation to the impact of an international language and recipes of reform that, while shaped by the local and the particular, serves to stabilize and normalize "a kit of ready-made solutions, where 'evaluation' occupies the central place." The technology of ranking universities, therefore, serves to implicitly organize the world of higher education and to make sense of it, in terms of what should be valued and aspired to.

In a way, Farag's approach also engages the cultural praxis analysis undertaken by Khelfaoui with regard to Algeria. She shows how new 'scripts' that underpin higher education reform initiatives operate as symbolic forms of capital which signify the emergence of new modes of legitimacy, and shifting power structures, either in relation to the state or in relation to the institution of external bodies and agencies which become part and parcel of the reproduction of a new cultural prism of sorts perceived as universal in its articulation. In that sense, Farag's contribution is valuable in terms of the insights it offers into the cultural praxis that underpin higher education reforms, and their discursive, symbolic, and political manifestations. For instance, her analysis of international university rankings shows social actors involved in locally enacting the global and, at the same time, performing the global in relation to other sites of actions. This imbrication, one could argue, is fundamental for our understanding of the intersections between globalization and education. First, as Farag's discussion of the Shanghai international university ranking suggests, the 'scripts' that shape higher education reforms have become more diffuse, horizontally, operating in a more autonomous fashion outside state control in terms of their rationalities. Secondly, and as a corollary of the first point, Farag approaches 'globalization' and its impact on knowledge production within a wider range of cultural praxes, in relation to which both 'locality' and 'globality' are enacted simultaneously, within dynamic and relational power configurations that determine their meanings.

Yet, if higher education institutions remain central in the reproduction of state power, or its reconfiguration, as Khelfaoui and Farag show, higher education institutions are far from operating as the exclusive fields of power in relation to which these processes take place. Shifting to the study of satellite broadcasting, Imad Karam explores the impact that media in all its forms has on Arab youth and how they situate themselves in relation to the political. His analysis challenges the widely held notion in the region that the new information and communications technologies have a corrupting, anti-educational influence on young people. Karam disagrees with those who dismiss the media, and satellite broadcasting more particularly, as sources of knowledge. He unpacks the assumptions of those who contribute to a 'moral panic', instigated in part by fears that the media are a conduit for western hegemony over the Arab world, and that Arab identity, culture and value systems are therefore under threat. Karam, however, has a different understanding of how the global and the local interact with each other. He conceives of culture not in essentialist or static terms but rather as an on-going precipitate of diverse influences and confluences. He thus adopts a constructivist perspective that stresses the fact that young people are active negotiators of meanings, rather than mere passive recipients of manipulated media messages. Based on empirical fieldwork, he shows that youths draw upon, integrate, but also contest and rework the myriad meaning- and value-systems they encounter in their everyday lives, using this as material to construct their own lifestyles, modes of being and identities. Karam also contests the way the older generations draw the boundaries between what is 'educational' and what is not, and their framing of 'entertainment', 'learning', 'formal', and 'informal' education in oppositional, mutually exclusive terms. In making his point, Karam privileges the voices of youth from Egypt, Jordan, the UAE and Palestine—young people whose enthusiasm for civic engagement is often dampened by the silencing, authoritative voice of the elders, as of the state, who crowd them out from the public sphere. For this up-and-coming generation—whose demographic ascendancy has enormous implications for the Arab region and world-wide—it is perhaps the media and popular culture that resonate with and respond to their concerns, providing opportunities for meaningful self-learning that are sometimes absent in the spaces formally dedicated to education, schools.

An interesting aspect of Karam's narrative pertains to the way satellite broadcasting is viewed by youth in relation to other institutions—political (the government), economic (labour market opportunities) or social (the school). It is by framing their consumption of different types of mediatized contents— such as news, entertainment, and political broadcasts—as disappointing, frustrating or boring, that youth operate a "generative" (Appadurai, 1996, pp. 183–187) contextualization of the larger inequities operated by hegemonic power structures that inhibit prospects for political engagement, breeding alienation and disillusionment. Here, their testimonies operate as potent 'rhetorical spaces', which make manifest "an expectation of being heard, understood, taken seriously" (Code,

1995, pp. ix–x). These 'rhetorical spaces' are underpinned by an "epistemology of everyday life" (p. xi) through which youth in the Arab region come to know the context-specific and inter-contextual forces that shape their destinies. Their testimonies express, ultimately, an "acknowledgment" (p. xii) of failed political and social projects—either personal or collective that may have carried the seeds of an imagined dawn.

The chapters in Part IV illustrate the multiple ways through which Arab education drains around it 'aborted' political projects, located at different levels of action. Whether one engages Zia's chapter on religious education in schools, Khelfaoui's contribution on Algerian higher education, Farag's critique of Egypt's higher education internationalization, or Karam's fieldwork on youth and satellite broadcasting, one is bound to acknowledge the effects the "architecture of power" (Robertson, 2006, p. 311) exerts on the viability of educational projects, as political projects.

Part V: Geopolitical Predicaments

Part V of this volume addresses the intersection between militarization and education. Needless to say, all the previous chapters have already highlighted some of the ways in which education operates as a site for contestation over a whole host of issues. At the macro level, there is, for instance, a struggle over how to define the nation (Frayha, Adely, Clarke), who to include within its borders and how (Zaher, Mabrour & Mgharfaoui, Dinero, Ashencaen Crabtree & Williams, Chircop), and the extent to which international agencies are allowed to intervene in the local, and if so, within the frame of which modalities (Chakroun & Jimeno Sicilia, Sayed, Mehran, Farag, Khelfaoui). At the meso or institutional level too, there are struggles over the linkages between the educational system, particularly in relation to the intervening and regulatory roles of the state vis-à-vis private provision (Akkari) as well as in relation to informal modes of engaging with learning (Karam), and to struggles between differentially located pressure groups that seek to impact educational policies (Frayha, Zia). At the micro level, there is resistance to—and rearticulations of—the pedagogic relationship (Herrera, Clarke), as well as of symbolic discourses and ritual enactments that would conflate state power with moral power (Adely). These contestations, struggles, resistances, accommodations to, around and in power are crucially important if we are to capture the dynamics that shape the field of education in the Arab region—and indeed, anywhere else for that matter. However, it is equally important to go beyond this level of generality to address the specificity of context. For 'raw power' has also defined it. We are here referring to the ways in which 'education'—defined both as schooling and more broadly as 'culture'—has been part of the terrain of geopolitical struggles that have not only regional, but also planetary ramifications.

Four chapters address this thematic in the final cluster of the volume. Omar El-Khairy sets the scene by reminding us that while the very mention of the 'Middle East' conjures up bellicose images, raw power has in fact been expressed through 'soft' as much as through 'hard wars'. El-Khairy is referring to non-militaristic and diplomatic techniques that seek to shape the cultures and societies in the Arab region, techniques that have tended to be overshadowed by a focus on the more dramatic flare-ups that lit the skies in the orient over the past several decades. Indeed, for El-Khairy, the distinction between 'soft' and 'hard' wars is unsatisfactory: he thus refers to the notion of 'smart' power that is increasingly used in US foreign policy circles, a term which more successfully captures the 'synergetic interaction' between ideological and armed combat and its interface with broad notions of education, as identities and modes of being. Such a relationship suggests that while "there can ultimately be no military solutions to political wars", violence is nevertheless "not only still a viable option, but also a necessary one".

In the tradition of Edward Said and *contra* Huntington—El-Khairy shows how the post-9/11 era has led to an increasing reification of culture that feeds into the notion of a 'clash of civilizations' between a 'West' and its construct of the 'Orient'—between 'mullahs and malls', and between 'religious absolutism and market determinism'. Such thinking serves the purpose of maintaining a wartime frame of mind, distilled in and through such 'jihadist' battle cries as 'the war on terror'. While the world has witnessed the military might that the US and its allies have been able and willing to deploy in and across the region, El-Khairy focuses on the use of education as part of the arsenal of cultural weaponry at the service of the neo-colonial pursuit for hegemony through policies of modernization and development. The global flows in and through education that Akkari, Sayed, Chakroun and Jimeno Sicilia, Farag, and Khelfaoui have described in earlier chapters in this volume, become, when seen through the lens proposed by El-Khairy, the most recent expression of a predatory capitalism that has productively combined the 'welfare state' and the 'warfare state' in an effort to attain 'benevolent supremacy' through global economic integration. Cultural globalization—now finding fast and fluid world-wide conduits through digital networks—is nothing less than war parading under another name, effectively "submerging the effects of imperialism into cultural ecumenism or economic fatalism", and serving to make "transnational relationships of power appear both neutral and necessary; in other words the naturalization of the schemata of neo-liberal thought". It is this incisive and provocative analytic capture of the synergy between geopolitical, pedagogic and economic interests, and their spatial deployments, that qualifies El-Khairy's contribution to feature in this cluster: education as a project at the service of human dignity, democracy and social justice can only be articulated if there is a sharp recognition of the global confluent conduits of power.

Conflict, war, democracy, social justice: all are powerful words that, when placed against the backdrop of the Arab region, instantly call to mind one of the key hotspots—Palestine. In her contribution, Nadera Shalhoub-Kevorkian constructs her understanding of the conflict between Israel and Palestine, and the impact this has on delivering education in militarized zones, from the perspective of the dominated and the displaced, who experience enormous difficulties in attaining their right to a safe and secure education. Under such conditions, it cannot be considered a neutral haven in the midst of conflict: quite the contrary, education becomes a highly politicized political project, one that provides fodder for the creation of an 'industry of fear' and 'terror', racializing Palestinians as people to be feared. Such constructs generate modes of racism that effectively exclude access to schooling in the interests of 'security considerations'. The 'war on terror' that Israel wages is, from Shalhoub-Kevorkian's point of view, a convenient umbrella that obfuscates and camouflages atrocities, including the obstruction of access to education precisely because education grants Palestinians the intellectual tools required to liberate themselves from oppression. In the face of the loss of land and the cumulative loss of rights and dignity, education becomes a central factor in shaping, reproducing and representing Palestinian identity, as well as a key source of hope for the future, both individually and collectively. Curfews, however, lead to the loss of a considerable number of school days; check points and the Wall of Separation, illegally built by Israel on Palestinian lands, snakes through Palestinian communities, rendering access to schools tortuous, if not impossible. Skirmishes with the Israeli military and settlers result in loss of life and limb for students and teachers alike; mobility restrictions make it impossible for highly achieving students to take up scholarships in the region and beyond, leading to serious skills shortages in critical areas such as health care; educational institutions are immediately targeted and even closed down at the first sign of organized resistance to the occupation. The impact of all this on access to education is dramatic and consequential, especially so for women—and not just in terms of knowledge acquisition, but also in terms of the forms of sociability and support that it provides and that help individuals cope with the deprivation, stress and trauma of everyday life.

In making her case, Shalhoub-Kevorkian refuses to engage in what seems to her the pointless project of 'discovering' or 'uncovering' the ultimate, invincible, inviolate 'truth' about the Israeli–Palestinian conflict. Rather, she is interested in upholding the mechanisms within which multiple versions of truth may be allowed to reside and circulate. Her chapter is one such portrayal, its power emanating from her political commitment to privileging the voices of those children and youths who are directly affected by the prevailing ideology of militarism and the various manifestations of oppression, in a situation where a whole people is dehumanized, and demonized, in ways that insidiously serve to justify their silencing and dispossession. Even the Israeli law courts are complicit in this silencing, using a permanently enacted 'state of exception' to justify the state's power to operate outside the law. Shalhoub-Kevorkian's chapter therefore serves to counteract this silencing, and to fulfil the duty impressed upon her by her young interviewees, who are only too aware of the difficulties they face in getting their story out there, to the rest of the world, in becoming visible: "They fear educated people that can speak English and tell the world about their crimes", says one of the interviewed girls. In her own way, therefore, Shalhoub-Kevorkian has made the commitment to mediate between the local and the global political form of engagement, in which the question of voice is first and foremost a question not of representation, but that of justice.

The two concluding chapters in this cluster—and in the volume—focus on two other hotspots in the region, Iraq and Iran, both of whose education systems have been greatly impacted by conflict and wars between them in the recent past. The two contributions—that of Nabil Al-Tikriti on Iraq and of Golnar Mehran on Iran—analyse school textbooks. They show how textual and pictorial constructions of nationhood and its history are central to the socialization of whole generations into frames of mind that, to a greater or lesser extent, determine future relations with neighbouring countries and the international community. For Nabil Al-Tikriti, post-2003 Iraq has seen an unprecedented level of intervention under the watchful eye of officials affiliated with the US-created Coalition Provisional Authority (CPA), where the hope "to shepherd a new and more amenable Iraq out of the shell of the old" has led to the targeting of educational curricula to render them more in line with 'international standards'. This concern has been translated into efforts to re-present Iraq to young generations of Iraqis in ways that dismantle the personality cult towards Saddam Hussein, remove all references to the Ba'th Party and its political ideology, as well as any references considered hostile to the United States, Israel, or gender equality. New textbooks have thus been published, presumably mirroring 'UNESCO principles of universal values', with a mixed commission—made up of American, UNESCO and Iraqi officials as well as international consultants—ensuring that the texts were 'free of bias' and of discriminatory statements against ethnic, religious and other groups, or that might be construed as inciting violence. What Al-Tikriti shows is that such interventions—clearly civilizational in scope and purpose—were leveraged by USAID as the donor institution, recalling the points made in an earlier chapter by El-Khairy regarding the diplomatic techniques that are marshalled to shape cultures and societies in the region, techniques that, in Iraq perhaps more than anywhere else, lay bare the synergy between 'soft' and 'hard' power.

Al-Tikriti's account, however, is noteworthy for at least two other reasons: first, it shows historical continuities—where one would have expected ruptures—in the way central powers have shaped textbook representations in Iraq in the pre- and post-occupation period. Textbooks in Iraq have therefore served to buttress Hashemite legitimacy (as Bashkin's chapter shows); they have fanned support for the ruling Ba'thist Party following the 1958 revolution; they have, in the mid-1970s, facilitated the shaping of a 'new Arab' who, in the image of Saddam Hussein, would protect the ideals of the revolution throughout a unitary society that brooked no divisions or dissent, and which ensured the forceful melding into one Iraq of 'minorities' such as the Kurds. In the course of the Iran–Iraq war (1980–1988), textbooks also served central powers in portraying Iran as a long-standing enemy. In short, Al-Tikriti goes to some lengths to show how the use of textbooks by those in power, before, during and after the Saddam Hussein régime, has been remarkably stable in form, if not in content, serving to define the 'them' and 'us' in ways that are often overt, if not brutal. However, the author also brings in another dimension, which resonates with a point made earlier by Bashkin on Iraqi attempts to socialize Iraqi children and youth of different religious traditions into a secularized national identity. As with Bashkin, Al-Tikriti shows how outcomes are not necessarily a mirror image of intentionalities: in a remarkable analysis of used textbooks purchased at the al-Mutanabi book market in Baghdad, Al-Tikriti successfully shows how students (and teachers) resist, re-write and deface power through the subversive comments they write in the textbooks in reaction to the systematic attempts by the state to inculcate its values.

Like Al-Tikriti in this cluster, and like Adely in an earlier one, Golnar Mehran addresses the role that schools have in nation/identity building. Mehran focuses on the overt curriculum by analysing the 'representations of the Arab' in the 2008 elementary school textbooks in the Islamic Republic of Iran. She approaches these themes from a macro-perspective, reading 'against the text' in order to problematize and make visible the intentional imperatives embedded in texts, disclose their ideological underpinnings and analyse their discursive articulations. This leads her to identify the messages relayed to young people that serve to situate converging and diverging aspects of 'Iranian' and 'Arab' identities in relation to a Muslim *umma*, or community of believers. Such tensions between the different layers of history that have contributed to a nation's identity—tensions that we have already seen expressed in similar ways but with diverse outcomes in the case of Lebanon—have been managed in different ways by textbook writers in Iran, depending on the régime in power. These authors—especially those responsible for language, social studies (a subject that includes history and geography besides civic education) and religious instruction, have had to tread carefully in the way they represent such themes as identity, gender roles, nationalism, and ideology more generally, given contrasting approaches to such issues in the pre- and post-1979 revolution which overthrew the Shah's régime.

Mehran focuses on the ways through which the 'self' and the 'Other' are portrayed both textually and pictorially, and the extent to which such representations lead to openness on the 'Other'. Her key argument, echoing that made by Clarke earlier on, is that the drawing of borders, between 'self' and 'Other', between one's own nation and that of others—paradoxically—entails a process whereby the 'Other' can only be identified in relation to the self, not in isolation. To speak of the 'Other' as such requires an appreciation of the distinguishing qualities that make a distinction possible, leading to a deeper knowledge of the 'self'. That 'self'—and its distinction from the 'Other'—are not to be seen as immutable essences but can rather be shaped in ways that encourage and make possible the interplay of differences. Such playfulness is of course difficult to maintain when the State's major concern is legitimation, a need that expresses itself in an emphasis on external foes that may have historically been diverse in origin, but who nevertheless represent a similar set of threats to the nation's core beliefs, not to mention its territorial integrity. Often, the 'spatial' encapsulation of national, religious, ethnic and gender identities in the textbooks reveals a hierarchical construction achieved through rendering the 'Other' invisible, principally by adopting a policy of silence on potentially controversial issues.

Central to Mehran's endeavour is the intertextual—or perhaps, intercontextual—dynamics operating between textbooks and the wider domains of national, geopolitical, and global power politics. Based on a meticulous and detailed analysis, Mehran shows how textbook writers constantly shift their representations of 'self' and 'Other' as geopolitical alliances, military conflicts, and international politics shift as well, minutely constructing and re-constructing frames of reference that seek to capture an Iranian identity in relation to an Arab one, while Iranian–Arab relations over the centuries are trapped in complex and multifaceted historical layers. Reading Mehran's study one acknowledges that, in many ways, social studies and history textbooks operate as sites of remembrance and re-calling, where time is incessantly invoked, as part of a Sisyphian enactment and re-enactment of an essence which escapes any attempt to stabilize it through a textual narrative. Textbooks can offer not more than provisional syntaxes, which shadow an unfathomable past, while the present keeps shifting beneath. In that sense, Mehran's explorations resonate well with Ricoeur's (2006b) question: "must we not ask whether the writing of history, too, is remedy or poison?" (p. 141). To which Mehran replies with regard to Iranian textbooks and their representation of Arabs, "it is both a blessing and a wound". Through their respective contributions, Mehran, Al-Tikriti, and Bashkin, delve into the hitherto unexplored workings of historical time and temporality, examining how their choreographing is irremediably intertwined with the articulation of political projects through education. In this, they foreground the tensions and contradictions that underpin the invocation and mobilization of an always-already elusive present past.

In concluding our editorial introduction we acknowledge the many aspects of education in the Arab region that this volume has not engaged with. We remain hopeful, however, that the insights generated by the various chapters open up new spaces for reflection and research. We recognize absences that need to be attended. Yet, we hope that the analytic along which we organized this volume offers readers what Mikhail Bakhtin (1984) refers to as "polyphonic" insights, allowing them "hearing and understanding all voices immediately and simultaneously" (p. 30), as a vibrant testimony to the complex profusion of human and political interactions involved in and around the worlds of Arab education and their multifaceted spatial articulations.

Note

1 For example, Cyprus is considered as part of the Middle East while being an EU member; furthermore UNESCO classifies Malta as part of the Arab region.

References

Abu El-Haj, Th.R. (2009). Imagining postnationalism: Arts, citizenship education, and Arab American youth. *Anthropology and Education Quarterly*, 40(1), 1–19.

Anderson, B. (1983). *Imagined communities: Reflections on the origins and spread of nationalism*. London: Verso.

Appadurai, A. (1996). *Modernity at large: Cultural dimensions of globalization*. Minneapolis, MN and London: University of Minnesota Press.

Apple, M.W. (1990). *Ideology and curriculum*. Second Edition. New York and London: Routledge.

Apple, M.W. (2000). *Official knowledge: Democratic education in a conservative age*. Second Edition. New York & London: Routledge.

Ayubi, N.N. (1995). *Over-stating the Arab state: Politics and society in the Middle East*. London: I.B. Tauris.

Bakhtin, M. (1984). *Problems of Dostoevsky's poetics*. Edited and translated by C. Emmerson. Minneapolis, MN & London: University of Minnesota Press.

Ball, S. (1998). Big policies/small world: An introduction to international perspectives in education policy. *Comparative Education, 34*(2), 119–130.

Banks, J. (1998). The lives and values of researchers: implications for educating citizens in a multicultural society. *Educational Researcher, 27*(7), 4–17.

Beblawi, H. (1987). The rentier state in the Arab world. In H. Beblawi & G. Luciani (Eds.), *The rentier state* (pp. 49–62). London: Routledge.

Bleich, D. (2008). Globalization, translation, and the university tradition. *New Literary History, 39*, 497–517.

Bourdieu, P. (1990). *The logic of practice*. Translated by R. Nice. Stanford, CA: Stanford University Press.

Brighenti, A. (2007). Visibility: A category for the social sciences. *Current Sociology, 55*(3), 323–342.

Carnoy, M., & M. Castells (2001). Globalization, the knowledge society, and the network state: Poulantzas at the millennium. *Global Networks, 1*(1), 1–18.

Carspecken, Ph.F. (1996). *Critical ethnography in educational research: A theoretical and practical guide*. London: Routledge.

Chambers, I. (2008). *Mediterranean crossings: The politics of interrupted modernity*. Durham, NC & London: Duke University.

Chatty, D. (2006). Boarding schools for mobile people: The Harasiis in the Sultanate of Oman. In C. Dyer (Ed.), *The education of nomadic peoples: Current issues, future prospects* (pp. 212–230). New York and Oxford: Berghahn Books.

Code, L. (1995). *Rhetorical spaces: Essays on gendered locations*. London and New York: Routledge.

Doumani, B. (Ed.) (2006). *Academic freedom after September 11*. New York: Zone Books.

Foucault, M. (1979). *Discipline and punish: The birth of the prison*. New York: Vintage Books.

Foucault, M. (1984). Order of discourse. In M. Shapiro (Ed.), *Language and politics* (pp. 108–138). New York: New York University Press.

Herrera, L., & C.A. Torres (Eds.) (2006). *Cultures of schooling: Critical ethnographies from Egypt*. Albany, NY: State University of New York Press.

Kearney, R. (2006). Introduction: Ricoeur's philosophy of translation. In P. Ricoeur, *On translation* (pp. vii–xx). London and New York: Routledge.

Krätli, S., & C. Dyer (2006). Education and development for nomads: The issues and the evidence. In C. Dyer (Ed.), *The education of nomadic peoples: Current issues, future prospects* (pp. 8–34). New York and Oxford: Berghahn Books.

Laabas, B. (Ed.) (2002). *Arab development challenges of the new millennium*. Burlington, VT: Ashgate.

Labyadh, S. (2004). What role for globalization in the events of September 11 and the occupation of Iraq? *Shu'un 'Arabiya [Arab Affairs]*, 120, 122–141. (In Arabic.)

Lipman, P. (2005). Educational ethnography and the politics of globalization, war, and resistance. *Anthropology and Education Quarterly, 36*(4), 315–328.

Madison, S. (2005). *Critical ethnography: Method, ethics, and performance*. London: Sage.

Malen, B. (2006). Revisiting policy implementation as a political phenomenon: The case of reconstitution policies. In M.I. Honig (Ed.), *New directions in education policy implementation: Confronting complexity* (pp. 83–104). Albany, NY: SUNY Press.

Marginson, S., & G. Rhoades (2002). Beyond national states, markets, and systems of higher education: A glonacal agency heuristic. *Higher Education, 43*, 281–309.

Massey, D. (1998). The spatial construction of youth cultures. In T. Skelton & G. Valentine (Eds.), *Cool places: Geographies of youth cultures* (pp. 121–129). London: Routledge.

Massey, D. (1999). Spaces of politics. In D. Massey, J. Allen, & Ph. Sarre (Eds.), *Human geography today* (pp. 279–294). London: Wiley-Blackwell.

Massialas, B.G., & S.A. Jarrar (1983). *Education in the Arab world.* New York: Praeger.

Massialas, B.G., & S.A. Jarrar (1987). Conflicts in education in the Arab world: The present challenge. *Arab Studies Quarterly, 9,* 35–53.

Massialas, B.G., & S.A. Jarrar (1991). *Arab education in transition.* New York: Garland Publishing.

Matthews, R.D., & M. Akrawi (1949). *Education in Arab countries of the Near East: Egypt, Iraq, Palestine, Transjordan, Syria, Lebanon.* Washington, DC: American Council of Education.

Mazawi, A.E. (2007). 'Knowledge society' or work as 'spectacle'? Education for work and the prospects of social transformation in Arab societies. In L. Farrell & T. Fenwick (Eds.), *Educating the global workforce: Knowledge, knowledge work and knowledge workers* (pp. 251–267). London: Routledge.

Mazawi, A.E. (2009). Naming the imaginary: 'Building an Arab knowledge society' and the contested terrain of educational reforms for development. In O. Abi-Mershed (Ed.), *Trajectories of education in the Arab world: Legacies and challenges* (pp. 201–225). London: Routledge.

Mouffe, C. (2005). *The return of the political.* London and New York: Verso.

Ong, A. (1999). *Flexible citizenship: The cultural logics of transnationality.* Durham, NC and London: Duke University Press.

Patai, R. (1973). *The Arab mind.* New York: Scribner.

Peters, M.A., with A.C. Besley (2006). *Building knowledge cultures: Education and development in the age of knowledge capitalism.* Lanham, MD: Rowman & Littlefield.

Ricoeur, P. (2006a). *On translation.* Translated by E. Brennan. London and New York: Routledge.

Ricoeur, P. (2006b). *History, memory, forgetting.* Translated by K. Blamey & D. Pellauer. Chicago, IL: University of Chicago Press.

Robertson, S.L. (2006). Absences and imaginings: The production of knowledge on globalisation and education. *Globalisation, Societies and Education, 4*(2), 303–318.

Sabour, M. (2001). *The ontology and status of intellectuals in Arab academia and society.* Aldershot: Ashgate.

Said, E.W. (1978). *Orientalism.* New York: Pantheon Books.

Said, E.W. (1997). *Covering Islam: How the media and the experts determine how we see the rest of the world.* New York: Vintage Books.

Sharabi, H. (1988). *Neopatriarchy: A theory of distorted change in Arab society.* New York: Oxford University Press.

Sholkamy, H. (2006). The frustrations and future of teaching qualitative methods in the Arab world. *Anthropology of the Middle East, 1*(2), 20–34.

Soysal, Y.N. (2000). Citizenship and identity: Living in diasporas in postwar Europe? *Ethnic and Racial Studies, 23*(1), 1–15.

Starrett, G. (2007). Textbook meanings and the power of interpretation. In E.A. Doumato & G. Starrett (Eds.), *Teaching Islam: Textbooks and religion in the Middle East* (pp. 215–231). Boulder, CO: Lynne Rienner.

Sultana, R.G. (2008). Looking back before moving forwards: Building on 15 years of comparative education research in the Mediterranean. *Mediterranean Journal of Educational Studies, 13*(2), 9–25.

Swartz, D. (1997). *Culture & power: The sociology of Pierre Bourdieu.* Chicago, IL and London: University of Chicago Press.

Wacquant, L. (1993). On the tracks of symbolic power: Prefatory notes to Bourdieu's 'State Nobility.' *Theory, Culture & Society*, 10, 1–17.

Wiseman, A.W., & N.H. Alromi (2003). The intersection of traditional and modern institutions in Gulf states: A contextual analysis of educational opportunities and outcomes in Iran and Kuwait. *Compare: A Journal of Comparative Education*, 33(2), 207–234.

Yiftachel, O. (2006). *Ethnocracy: Land and identity politics in Israel/Palestine*. Philadelphia, PA: University of Pennsylvania Press.

Part I

Contested Policyscapes

2 Privatizing Education in the Maghreb

A Path for a Two-Tiered Education System

Abdeljalil Akkari

Introduction

The development of the education systems in the Maghreb (Algeria, Tunisia, Morocco) has been heavily dominated by the public sector, in line with French colonial traditions (Lelièvre, 1999; Leon, 1991; Sraïeb, 1974).[1] Since the early 1990s, however, the Maghreb has been marked by a strong tendency towards privatization of education. Privatization means an increase in the availability of private education, including a greater choice of certain families who can afford to pay for private schools or/and private tutoring in order to provide an academic advantage to their children, especially at the secondary level (Ball & Youdell, 2007; Bray, 2003).

By analyzing this budding privatization of Maghrebi education systems, the present chapter focuses on the diversification of educational provision in postcolonial contexts. In this chapter I argue that in the Maghrebi context, privatization is underpinned by two tensions. On the one hand, it signals the emergence of a private marketplace in which education is perceived as a service like any other in the perspective of economic globalization. On the other hand, it reflects the growing centrality of a discourse around education as a social right of all social groups and a pillar of the welfare state. Within the context of the construction of the postcolonial state, these tensions operate a crisis of legitimacy that reconfigures the role of the state and transforms the relationships between different social groups in relation to schooling.

Neoliberal reforms around the world promote the centrality of market mechanisms such as choice, competition, accountability and deregulation in order to improve educational services. These mechanisms have been implemented in a number of fields where the government plays a dominant role such as health care and education (Lubienski, 2005). The extent to which public education is suited for market-style organization is highly debatable. The very idea of "a market" is particularly contested in education (Henig, 1994; Margonis & Parker, 1995). Some analysts argue that essential aspects of public education make it unique and therefore inappropriate for direct control by market forces (Belfield & Levin, 2005). Others advocate the subordination of education to economic principles in order to improve educational provision and synchronize it with occupational outlets of graduates (Walberg & Bast, 2003). Apple (2001) pointed out that privatization reforms have been underpinned by contradictions. On the one hand, the discourse of competition, markets and choice encourages schools to be free agents. On the other hand, accountability, performance objectives, standards, national testing, and national curriculum have stressed accountability to government policies.

As this policy trend is largely implicit and not well documented, the debate on privatization of education in the Maghreb countries takes place mainly in the press and revolves around three axes. First, some writers are concerned about the widespread private pre-schooling sector as a result of the development of private and Qur'anic schools and the attempt of the state to regulate it (Samira, 2008; Bouzoubaa, 1998). Others protest against the burden that private tutoring inflicts on families (Yahya, 2009). Still others are alarmed by the prevalence of private education provided by schools related to European embassies among established social classes. For them, this type of education represents a risk to national identity and to the status of Arabic as the language of instruction (Benzakour, 2007; Dakhlia, 2004; Lacoste, 2001).

There are a range of educational policies that can be clearly understood as forms of privatization. They originate from both national governments across the Maghreb and from international agencies actively involved in the region. Notwithstanding, in many cases privatization remains a hidden agenda, as is the case in the development of private tutoring, which is discussed in greater detail below. As pointed out by Bray (2007), private tutoring consumes massive amounts of money and demands huge amounts of time from both students and tutors.

National Development and Postcolonial Dependence

Educational systems in the Maghreb under French domination were characterized by a strong duality in which distinct schooling systems coexisted. European children were educated in line with European standards while North African children were schooled in a separate, qualitatively inferior and much less accessible system. When the Maghreb countries – Algeria, Morocco and Tunisia – gained their independence between 1955 and 1962, the gross rate of primary schooling was around 10 percent of the primary school age group (Lacoste, 2001; Lezé, 2001; Kateb, 2006). The quality of education was poor for children who were lucky enough to enroll in school. The under-schooling of Maghrebi children was not solely linked to the dominating policies of the colonizers and their desire to leave the indigenous population in ignorance. It also reflected a form of resistance to cultural assimilation on the part of North Africans; a resistance to the school as an institution closely connected with colonization. It was also a linguistic and religious resistance. Parents were hesitant to send their children to modern schools because colonial instruction was primarily administered in the French language (Sraïeb, 1974).

Yet, as the Tunisian case[2] shows, colonization opened the door to schooling for Maghrebi girls. According to Clancy Smith (2000), the imposition of the French Protectorate in 1881 brought major changes to the two existing education systems in Tunisia: the old Islamic system exclusively for boys and the European system primarily made up of missionary schools. In addition to hundreds of Qur'anic schools, Tunisia had roughly twenty-three private institutions offering primary education, essentially in French or Italian, even if Arabic was occasionally used.

The schooling histories and trajectories of Maghrebi political elites are crucial to our understanding of the power struggles that occurred following independence. North African nationalists, who took part in liberating the Maghreb from the colonial yoke, had an ambivalent relationship with the colonial school system. Some elite members were schooled partly in traditional Islamic schools (such as Al-Zeitouna in Tunisia and Al-Qarawiyyine and Kutubia in Morroco) while others were schooled in colonial schools. Following the independence of Algeria and Tunisia, it was the modernist tide favoring the nationalization of the colonial school that won out over nationalists who had Islamic or Arabic leanings. In Morocco, the power struggle was rather more equal in that Qur'anic schools were continued and supported by the Sharifian monarchy.[3] Notwithstanding, following independence the structure and orientation of the colonial education systems were maintained in the Maghreb with one important change: the progressive rehabilitation of Arabic as main language of instruction (Kateb, 2006; Sraïeb, 2003; Storm, 2007).

The setting up of public education systems played a crucial role in the construction of the North African postcolonial states. First, these systems were considered strategic in cementing national unity and in constructing a political citizenship that transcended the deeply-rooted regional or tribal divides (Zidan, 2007). Secondly, public education systems were perceived as crucial in the replacement of French colonial professionals (Sraïeb, 1974). Additionally, it should be remembered that during the 1950s and 1960s this perception was strengthened by human capital theory, which stipulated the vital importance of education for economic development (see Schultz, 1963). Thus, the three Maghrebi countries have invested in all levels of education, particularly in scientific and professional streams of study (Allman, 1979; Tiano, 1968).

Following independence, the French language continued to play an important role as a second language of instruction in spite of rhetoric and policies that emphasized the importance of the Arabic language (Moatassime, 1992). Moreover, pedagogical orientations and school reforms were greatly influenced by educational transformations taking place in France. The flow of North African students to France ensured a cultural and educational kinship with the French educational model when these students returned to their country of origin. French aid workers, who were very present in North African schools during the 1950s–1970s, ensured a continued French influence on education (Geisser, 2000; Vermeren, 2002). Finally, while independence allowed a certain diversification of economic partners, the majority of economic exchanges across the Maghreb continued to involve France. As Santucci (1993) correctly states, decolonization in conjunction with national movements, through the combined effects of the contradictory objectives underpinning nation-building, contributed to making the independent state a catalyst of social processes and the geometric center of all social hopes.

Civil society deserves special attention beyond a description of the real expansion of education systems in the Arab world (Mazawi, 1999). It can be argued that it is this fundamental connection between the construction of the postcolonial nation-state and of the education system that is being questioned by the current wave of educational reforms. This questioning is reflected in policies of decentralization, an emphasis placed on achievement, school choice, privatization, and curricular reforms (Cowen, 1996). These new policies, which for the most part diminish the role of the "state-teacher", are pushing North African education systems towards a new configuration.

Mapping Educational Privatization

Compared to other Arab nations or developing nations, private sector participation remains generally small at different levels of educational systems in the Maghreb (see Table 2.1). The only exception is pre-schooling and early childhood education where the majority of children attend private institutions. Even if these are under the jurisdiction of the state, pre-school funding is largely assumed by parents and local communities (Bouzoubaa and Benghabrit-Remaoun, 2004; Chedati and Faiq, 2003; UNICEF, 2004). In the Arab region, early childhood education is predominantly private,[4] with provision largely in the hands of for-profit entities, and to a lesser extent NGO and religious organizations. In 2004, only 15.7 percent of the total number of eligible children in the Arab region had access to pre-primary education and 67 percent of those children were enrolled in private institutions (UNESCO Institute for Statistics, 2006).

At the level of primary education, the number of children in the private sector is marginal in Tunisia (1 percent) and small in Morocco (7 percent). Only in the latter does there seem to be a regular increase since the 1990s. In Algeria, in spite of the emergence of the private sector, few official statistics are available.[5] In secondary education, the private sector's share is 5 percent in Tunisia and Morocco. This percentage is lower compared with other Arab countries, such as Egypt, Jordan and particularly Lebanon. In tertiary education, despite an increase over the past few years, the number of students in private institutions remains equally small, with the notable exception of Morocco.

How can we explain the low enrollment in private education in the Maghreb? We can invoke two main explanations. First, the few private schools connected with foreign diplomatic and religious missions or with Muslim organizations are

Table 2.1   Private enrollment share as a percentage of total enrollment

	1990			2003			2005		
	Primary	Secondary	Tertiary	Primary	Secondary	Tertiary	Primary	Secondary	Tertiary
Algeria	–	–	–	–	–	–	–	–	–
Egypt	5.8	3.8	12.5	8.0	16.5	16.5	7.0	4.0	4.0
Lebanon	68.3	57.8		64.7	49.3	49.3	66.0	53.0	53.0
Morocco	3.6	2.7	1.5	5.5	5.1	5.1	7.0	5.0	5.0
Tunisia	0.5	12	–	1.0	0.4	0.4	1.0	5.0	5.0

Sources: UNESCO Institute for Statistics (2007); World Bank (2008)

rigorously supervised by the Maghrebi states, as is the case in the Arab region. Secondly, as stated by Dillman (2001), the emerging elites organize democratization through a selective commitment to global markets that maintains distributional coalitions and co-opts a domestic private sector largely dependent on political authority. Dillman notes that the more régimes "deregulate", the more they "re-regulate" by precisely determining who would gain the most from the change and by rejoining the distributional coalitions that profit from the market. Privatization remains rather limited in the Arab region and does not signify the withdrawal of the state from the economy or from the education sector. Privatization is fundamentally a public order that is reluctantly pursued by the state only under certain internal or external pressures, coming especially from international organizations such as the International Monetary Fund (IMF) or the World Bank. As a result, privatization has not become a dynamic process where the initiative comes from private sector participants. If the private sector is gaining ground it is primarily because the state can no longer continue to finance existing social and educational policies, thus letting the private sector grow "by default" (Kohstall, 2007; Younis, 1996).

In the 1980s and 1990s the Maghreb witnessed a succession of social crises and administrative changes revolving around the disengagement of the state in order to meet the directives of the IMF and the World Bank and the demands by civil society for greater liberalization. Notwithstanding, in spite of recommendations by international organizations, the Maghreb resisted a large-scale privatization of the education sector. Since their foundation, the Maghrebi states reserved the privilege of organizing education. Lessening their control over education would endanger their historically-construed legitimacy. The example of Algeria is instructive in this respect. The importance of the private sector in the Algerian economy was affirmed by the constitution, which also recognizes political liberties and free trade. The development of private initiatives in many sectors allows for the emergence of a private education sector. Yet, the latter remains dependent on legislation that is frequently changing and on strict bureaucratic control (Delhaye & Le Pape, 2004; Benachenhou, 1992).

Some international organizations support the idea of increased participation of the private sector in the education market in the Maghreb and elsewhere. The World Bank is the leader among international organizations which advocates the opening of the education market. Analyzing the development of the private sector in the Arab region, the World Bank observes that the region is based more and more on the private sector at every level of the educational system. According to the World Bank (2008), while this tendency may increase inequality in educational distribution, the results depend on the strategy adopted by governments, especially in terms of the educational level entrusted to the private sector and the nature of public financing. According to this line of thought, a strategy where the private sector supplies higher education and the government supplies basic education is likely to be more egalitarian than one allowing the private sector greater participation in basic education. In addition, a strategy that allocates public financing to poor students, even if they are enrolled in private schools, is likely more egalitarian than one where the students in all households, independent of their ability to pay, were to receive financing. On both accounts, the strategy adopted in the Arab region is less efficient than the one adopted in Southeast Asia and to a lesser degree than the one chosen in Latin America (World Bank, 2008).[6]

The World Bank (2008) suggests that countries in the Arab region have increased participation by the private sector in providing education at all levels, but especially at the level of basic education. Other regions have decreased their share of private education enrollment in secondary education. The priority for the World Bank would seem to be privatization at the tertiary level. In both Southeast Asia and Latin America, there are very few private schools at the elementary level, slightly more at the secondary level, and a very high percentage at the tertiary level. In these regions it is more and more up to the family to pay the costs associated with higher education. According to the World Bank (2008), "private education is used as a strategy to mobilize private resources and also to socially stratify educational access" (p. 28). The general argument underlying the development of private higher education is that fully funding public universities may be sustainable only when a small percentage of each age group desire to access and de facto accesses higher education (Sultana, 2001).

Hence, the development of private education in the Maghreb seems to be governed by a logic that differs not only from other southern countries but also from Arab countries in the Middle East. The number of students in the private sector remains small. According to the World Bank (2008):

> The nongovernment financial contribution to education is difficult to discern in MENA [Middle East and North Africa], as few data are available. However, there is a widespread belief that this contribution is modest. In part, this is because enrollment in private education tends to be very low in some countries, for example, in Tunisia, Algeria, Yemen, and Libya. Although this pattern is changing and some countries have traditionally had large private enrollment (e.g., Lebanon), low private enrollment suggests that governments carry most of the financial burden of education. (p. 105)

Lessard, Brassard and Lusignan (2002) observe that the transformation of the role of the state in the education sector relays international trends that consist in abandoning certain prerogatives and acquiring others, especially in terms of regulation. The state is not withdrawing from education. It has found a new role, that of regulator and evaluator defining the large orientations and targets to reach by setting educational policy. It puts in place a system of monitoring and evaluation of students' achievement. While the state continues to invest a large part of its budget in education, it partially disengages from the organization and daily management of the system, leaving these functions to intermediate and local levels both in partnership and in competition with the private sector that hopes to take a significant share of the education market. Thus a new governance of education is emerging (Ball & Youdell, 2007). In spite of the small number of children and youth enrolled in private schools in the Maghreb, this tendency towards privatization, supported by governments,[7] signals a new epoch in the organization of education systems in the region and in the role of the state in the way it regulates the educational system.

A Multifaceted and Untamed Privatization

What dynamics underpin the privatization of educational services across the Maghreb? How do these dynamics fare when compared with what is happening internationally?

The first form of privatization concerns the increasing participation of the private sector in determining educational offer, even if, as we have seen, this remains modest. Three observations are called for regarding this aspect: (1) the regulatory[8] power of the state and its importance in maintaining control on the private sector, (2) the share of the private sector between different operators (NGOs, private companies, religious organizations, foreign missions etc.) and (3) the educational levels that are particularly affected by privatization.

Discussing privatization cannot be disconnected from the broader structural characteristics of private schools. Four principal networks of private schools are identifiable: (a) Qur'anic, (b) For-profit, (c) Foreign diplomatic and religious and (d) Foreign universities.

(a) Qur'anic

This network, connected with the tradition of the Islamic education, has developed to a great extent in the preschool sector. In the case of Morocco this has to do with a community-based offer that makes up for the underdevelopment of public education in remote regions (Tawil, 2006).

(b) For-profit

This network concerns small and medium private, for-profit institutions usually founded by former public school teachers or by entrepreneurs. This network started to develop in the Maghreb at the secondary level in order to offer an option to students who were excluded by the very selective public schools. More recently local private higher education institutions have been expanding. The main courses offered by local private universities are linked to economic sectors related to international trade and exchange (finance, tourism, ICT and textile industry).

(c) Foreign diplomatic and religious schools

This network includes schools connected to diplomatic and foreign religious missions, especially French and other European countries. These institutions are particularly valued by the socio-economically established upper classes. French establishments in the Maghreb are in high demand. According to the latest numbers published for the 2008 school year, French schools in Tunisia have distinguished themselves by an increase in enrollment that totals 5,500 students from thirty different nationalities, of which 36 percent are Tunisian. The latter chose French schooling in order to obtain an international diploma and for the quality of instruction delivered by the 360 teachers who work in these schools. The results, especially concerning the French baccalaureate, demonstrate the high interest in enrolling in these schools. The rate of success is around 92 percent for the general diploma and 97.5 percent for the technology diploma. The increase in the number of French businesses in Tunisia combined with the return of many Franco-Tunisian citizens has led to an increase in the demand for these schools at the primary level (*Le Temps* newspaper, September 20, 2008). In Morocco, the 23 French schools enrolled in 2009 about 22,000 students, with about two-thirds being Moroccans (Marmié, 2009).

(d) Foreign universities

This network, still at the early stages of development, includes foreign university campuses. This nascent network, which initially developed in Morocco, is now expanding in Tunisia as higher education is considered as a resource of the world market (Mazzella, 2008). As pointed out by Rikowski (2001), such a process of commercializing higher education took place under the General Agreement on Trades and Services (GATS) requirements. This process can be achieved by different modes of educational provision such as "cross-border" supply.

As presented in Table 2.2, two private education networks (Qur'anic and for-profit) emerged in the Maghreb as a consequence of underprivileged and middle class families' strategies[9] to compensate the failure of public mass schooling to address the needs of their children. Two other networks (foreign diplomatic and religious, as well as foreign universities) developed as result of both upper class strategies to equip their children with knowledge and diplomas needed in a global world and the policies of foreign actors, particularly the French mission in Morocco.

The second form of educational privatization in the Maghreb concerns private tutoring, a private service paid for by families whose children are enrolled in both private and public schools as a complement for the education of their children.

Table 2.2   Private education networks in the Maghreb

	(a) Qur'anic	*(b) For-profit*	*(c) Foreign diplomatic and religious*	*(d)Foreign universities*
School level	Mainly preschool	All levels	All levels	Higher education
Students' economic background	Underprivileged classes	Middle classes	Upper classes	Upper classes
State regulation[1]	Medium	Medium	Strong	Strong

1   Tunisian law 2008-59, relative to private higher education, modifying and complementing law 73, stipulates in article 4 that the capital of a private institution cannot be less than two million dinars (1.4 million USD). The authorization is granted in accordance with the objectives of the state in the domain of higher education and those defined in the economic and social development plans.

Private lessons in a particular subject usually take place once or twice a week. They are provided for a fee, closely following and oriented towards the school syllabus, with the goal of improving the students' performance at exams. This phenomenon has reached all spheres of the education system in the Maghreb from the first year of elementary school to higher education, especially during the middle school years and transition years between the different educational levels. Faced with this phenomenon, educational administrators adopt a policy of *fait accompli* and react only to flagrant and proven excesses where public school teachers propose hours of private tutoring. Responsibility for this form of privatization falls on parents seeking to boost the achievement of their children, on teachers hoping to improve their income, and on a passive administration that allows it. This form of privatization also implies the responsibility of the state, which neither pays teachers adequately, nor provides different regions and social classes with equitable educational opportunities (Dang & Rogers, 2008; Elbadawy, Levison, Ahlburg, & Assaad, 2009; Popa & Acedo, 2006).

The majority of private tutors are public school teachers. Sometimes, in addition to the lessons they teach in the public school, they deliver private lessons to their own students.[10] It is difficult to estimate the size of this phenomenon in the Maghreb. A recent study in Tunisia, undertaken by the Association for the Protection of Consumers (*Al Anwar*, August 2, 2008), suggests that of the 250 households polled, 73.2 percent reported that their children receive private tutoring and 90.2 percent asserted that tutoring is a strain on the family budget. The majority of the households agreed that the parents are the main culprits in the explosion of private tutoring, which in turn keeps students from taking responsibility for their own education. Finally, 90 percent of the households indicated that private tutoring lacks transparency in price, location and content. Because of the absence of a private sector able to respond to familial education strategies, a largely underground tutoring sector, escaping any regulation, is quickly prevalent across the region.

A third form of privatization is linked to public/private partnerships. Private for-profit institutions are especially active in the areas of professional training and ICT (Abbate, 2002). In Morocco, 521 vocational private schools enroll 30 percent of students in professional training. The number of trainees rose by 12 percent from 2003 to 2006 (Conseil Supérieur de l'Enseignement, 2008). To develop the off-shoring sector and the position of Morocco as a premier destination for foreign businesses have contributed to the development of professional private training to provide a ready supply of workers.

A fourth form of privatization concerns the strategies of distinction that the elites use in order to reserve a part of the education system for their own use. This can be done through the construction of reputed public establishments whose access is reserved for the best students. In Tunisia this phenomenon took place through the building of model secondary schools reserved for the highest achieving students. School inequalities may also be observed within cities. At the national level in Tunisia, 39 percent of students succeeded in passing the secondary school entrance exam in June 1991. Yet, large regional differences in success rates persist. From the region (*gouvernorat*) of Sousse, 46.8 percent of the students succeeded and four schools from the city of Sousse were ranked in the top five of the whole region, with a success rate of over 80 percent. However, a careful inspection of a map of Sousse shows deviations of over 50 points in the success rate between city-center schools and schools on the outskirts (Vermeren, 2002). Private education is not available equally to all social groups in the Maghreb. We observe inequalities among regions, gender groups and language communities. Private schools are concentrated in urban areas and major cities[11] of the Maghreb. It is difficult to find a private school in rural areas (except Qur'anic schools). In Morocco, in the southern region of Ktaoua, Oudada (2007) points out that in 2006 only 2,217 students were enrolled in secondary school while potentially three times this number are interested by secondary education. If public schools are insufficient in many rural areas, it is difficult to imagine an emerging private sector in rural regions. In Morocco, 47 percent of private schools are concentrated in the Atlantic urbanized coast between Kenitra and Casablanca (Slimani, 2009).

In his study in one of the most disadvantaged provinces in Morocco located in the impoverished northwestern region of the country (Chefchaouen), Tawil (2006) examined patterns of take-up of Qur'anic education. He pointed to the disarticulation of the traditional system of Islamic education. He observed that a population of learners (7+ years of age) participating in traditional "*kuttāb*" remains statistically "invisible" and consequently excluded from conventional analyses. According to Tawil (2006), Qur'anic education functions as an alternative to public schooling, satisfying the demand of poorer rural households, which cannot bear the direct and indirect costs of schooling or whose children are pulled out of the schooling system as a result of academic failure.

Despite the increasing enrollment of girls, some families invest more in the schooling of boys, particularly in rural areas (Gastineau, 2003). However, gender inequalities are decreasing in the Maghreb, despite persistent and significant inequities. Currently, one out of two women has been or is in school and 30 to 50 percent of students are women (Daoud, 1996).

At the level of inequalities linked to linguistic competencies, we observe that institutions using French as the language of instruction offer the best private education in the Maghreb. Similarly, scientific and prestigious courses at the university level are also taught in French (Moatassime, 1992; Azouzi, 2008).

In sum, the privatization of education results both from a limited disengagement of the state from public education and private sector initiatives in order to respond to the demands of families for specific private schooling for their children. This situation occurs in the Maghreb as it is the case in many other countries. What is specific to the Maghreb compared with other developing countries is the relatively late growth of the private sector and the fact that privatization remains hidden by including a largely uncontrolled and informal private tutoring sector. The massification of education has caused a decline in the quality of public education in the Maghreb. Families of middle and upper social classes resort to private schooling as a strategy for distinguishing themselves from the lower social classes that have gradually gained access to public schools.

The full impact of privatization in the Maghreb is still difficult to analyze. At the international level we notice that educational privatization can be articulated differently, depending on national traditions and education policies (Carnoy, 2000; Maroy, 2006). For instance, privatization could be a constitutional right consecrating a political or religious heritage, as is the case in North America and in most Anglo-Saxon countries. Alternatively, the education market develops through a voluntary action of the state which organizes and stimulates competition between educational networks in order to improve their performance. In the case of developing countries, this action by the state is a result of pressures exerted by international organizations, especially the World Bank. Still, privatization can also emerge as an opaque and informal market, the fruit of a hijacking of the public system (Van Zanten & Obin, 2008) or as a result of the blurring of the frontiers between what represents and is constructed as public and private spheres, as is the case with private tutoring. The present preliminary analysis of educational privatization in the Maghreb leads us to locate it somewhere between competition between educational networks and the opacity of the informal market. Private tutoring and foreign institutions escape any regulation. This is indicative of an untamed privatization of schooling in the Maghreb. The nonexistence of public policies providing subsidies to private schools or educational vouchers exacerbates this dynamic.

Some Reflections on the Future

Because of the importance of schooling in modern society, the quality of educational services will always be of concern in discussing the equity issues underpinning educational provision. Clearly, the modes of educational provision are highly debated and contested. On the one hand, there are those who believe that parents, rather than the state, should be the decision-makers over educational issues. They feel that the only answer to current 'problems' in education is to encourage private-sector involvement and to ensure flexibility for families through choice and competition among providers. On the other hand, there are those who contend that universal public education is an inalienable right in a democracy and that privatization leads to economic and social segregation, repression and marginalization.

In the Maghreb, the private education sector is developing even if it is still marginal in terms of enrollment compared with the public education system at all levels except pre-schooling. The state remains the principal agent in the education system and controls its structure. Even when the state agrees to open up the education sector, it retains a regulatory power over its modalities of development. However, responding to both parents seeking better educational opportunities for their children and the injunctions of international organizations encouraging privatization policies, Maghrebi countries are undergoing important changes in terms of the social distribution of equitable opportunities.

One reflection that is unavoidable has to do with the consequences that educational privatization has on how Maghrebi citizens perceive the role of the state in relation to educational policy making. Until recently, the nation-state has been the sole guarantor of national unity and of the public services for which it is responsible, such as education, health and social security. In a context marked by a crisis of legitimacy on the part of the nation-state, a debate on the privatization of public services means decentering the role of the state and accommodating additional, if not new, ways through which social and economic resources are distributed. As stated by Mons (2004), what characterizes contemporary education is that the system was created or financed by state authorities and served to convey a common culture around which a national identity was formed. The state ensured the control of education either directly, since it is responsible for the education structure, or indirectly, since it is the principal financer.

Maghrebi societies are experiencing multiple social and political tensions. Islamic activism continues to trigger political debates on social cohesion, identity and citizenship. The lack of prospects for young people fuels both illegal immigration to Europe and local radical groups. In such contexts, the development of private education may be associated with two contradictory scenarios of future development. In the first scenario, the rise of private education underscores the vitality of Maghrebi societies becoming more open, more diverse and more entrepreneurial. The advantage of geographical and cultural proximity reinforces the existing ties with Europe and the middle classes' seeking of diversified venues of educational provision. In the second and less desirable scenario, private education exacerbates social tensions and divisions within the Maghreb. The propensity of upper class families to use foreign organized instruction weakens national consensus and opens the way for the construction of a two-tiered and stratified education system. The first tier will attend the more affluent, who enjoy the privileges of a relatively healthy educational environment in private institutions where foreign languages are intensively used. The second tier will cater for the least privileged, who suffer an educational environment that, in many cases, virtually forecloses their chance of learning.[12] Overcrowded classrooms, fewer textbooks or other teaching materials and unqualified teachers are common in this second education system. Even if it is developed outside the education system, the development of private tutoring is speeding up the construction of a two-tiered education system.

Four relevant research priorities need to be followed up on in order to better understand educational privatization in the Maghreb. First, this chapter did not compare the privatization processes across the three Maghrebi countries. Undertaking a comparative study would be crucial in the future because Morocco and Tunisia took different paths to privatization as compared with Algeria. Secondly, research on private tutoring is of particular relevance. The strategies that lead certain families to turn to private tutoring need to be analyzed and better understood, within the diverse regional, gender, and linguistic contexts of the Maghreb. Thirdly, private tutoring has emerged as an instrument that maintains or increases social and geographic inequalities. Assessing the impact of private tutoring on family budgets is important in order to analyze the new forms of social inequality associated with these newly emerging educational structures. A fourth focus for researchers would be to compare the quality of education in the private and public sector in terms of its institutional articulations and its impact on the redistribution of social goods and political power and opportunities in Maghrebi societies.

Notes

1 See the work of Lelièvre (1999) on the predominance of State control of education in the French tradition.
2 In Algeria, the access of Algerian women to schooling was developed through the creation of schools for girls (Lemdani-Belkaid, 2000).
3 The political and religious power of the Moroccan monarch is based on Sharifism which considers the king as a descendent of the Prophet Muhammad.
4 In Tunisia one can see a decrease in the number of municipal kindergartens (250 in 1990 versus 155 in 2000) and a clear increase in the number of private ones (262 in 1990 versus 1,168 in 2000). This comes from a public policy favorable to private initiative, from the many encouragements and advantages in current legislation for investments, and also from the increasing demand for early education (Bureau International d'Education, 2006).
5 According to Samira (2008), the private sector accounts for only 0.54% of the global enrollment in Algeria.
6 In the Maghreb, most students in higher education are enrolled in public universities.
7 In Morocco, the Charter of Education enacted in 2000 predicts 20% of total enrollment in the private sector by 2015 (Slimani, 2009).
8 In the Maghreb, the state has always exerted a strict control over private education, whether this has to do with the use of the Arabic language or curricular contents.
9 According to Allman (1979), a private education sector began to develop in the late 1960s. Run primarily by Tunisians, these institutions cater to the needs of the ever-increasing numbers of Tunisians forced out of government schools. Parents see these schools as a second chance for education, which is increasingly viewed as a prerequisite for their children's success.
10 The existence of directives banning this type of practice and trying to channel tutoring by teachers underlines the scope of this largely underground phenomenon.
11 In Algeria, 65% of private schools recognized by the state are located in Algiers (Samira, 2008).
12 In Tunisia, students often use the following slogan to express their scepticism regarding schooling outcomes: You study or you don't, there is no future for you.

References

Abbate, F. (2002). *L'intégration de la Tunisie dans l'économie mondiale: Opportunités et défis.* Geneva: CNUCED/PNUD.
Allman, J. (1979). *Social mobility, education, and development in Tunisia.* Leiden: Brill.
Apple, M.W. (2001). Comparing neo-liberal projects and inequality in education. *Comparative Education,* 37(4), 409–423.
Azouzi, A. (2008). Le français au Maghreb: Statut ambivalent d'une langue. *Synergies Europe,* 3, 37–50.
Ball, J., & D. Youdell (2007). *La privatisation déguisée dans le secteur éducatif public.* Brussels: Internationale de l'Education.
Belfield, C.R., & H.M. Levin (2005). *Privatizing educational choice: Consequences for parents, schools, and public policy.* Boulder, CO: Paradigm.
Benachenhou, A. (1992). L'aventure de la désétatisation en Algérie. *Revue des mondes musulmans et de la méditerranée,* 65, 175–185.
Benzakour, F. (2007). Langue française et langues locales en terre marocaine: Rapports de force et reconstructions identitaires, *Hérodote,* 3(126), 45–56.
Bouzoubaa, K. (1998). *An innovation in Morocco's Koranic pre-schools.* The Hague: Bernard van Leer Foundation.

Bouzoubaa, K., & N. Benghabrit-Remaoun (2004). L'éducation préscolaire au Maroc et en Algérie. *Perspectives*, XXXIV(4), 471–480.

Bray, M. (2003). *Adverse effects of private supplementary tutoring: Dimensions, implications and government responses*. Paris: International Institute for Educational Planning.

Bray, M. (2007). *The shadow education system: Private tutoring and its implications for planners*. Paris: International Institute for Educational Planning

Bureau International d'Education de l'UNESCO. (2006). *Tunisie: Programmes de protection et d'éducation de la petite enfance (PEPE)*. Geneva: BIE.

Carnoy, M. (2000). School choice? Or is it privatization? *Educational Researcher*, 29(7), 15–20.

Chedati, B. & M. Faiq (2003). *L'enseignement préscolaire: Etat des lieux et propositions. Rapport réalisé pour la Commission spéciale éducation formation (COSEF)*. Rabat: Ministère de l'Education.

Clancy Smith, J. (2000). L'École Rue du Pacha, Tunis: L'enseignement de la femme arabe et 'la Plus Grande France' (1900–1914). *Clio*, 12, *Le genre de la nation*. Retrieved December 15, 2008, from http://clio.revues.org/document186.html.

Conseil Supérieur de l'Enseignement (2008). *Rapport annuel 2008*. Rabat: Conseil Supérieur de l'Enseignement.

Cowen, R. (1996). Last past the post: Comparative education, modernity and perhaps post-modernity. *Comparative Education*, 32(2), 151–170.

Dakhlia, J. (Ed.) (2004). *Trames de langues: Usages et métissages linguistiques dans l'histoire du Maghreb*. Paris: Maisonneuve et Larose.

Dang, H.-A., & F.H. Rogers (2008). The growing phenomenon of private tutoring: Does it deepen human capital, widen inequalities, or waste resources? *World Bank Research Observer*, 23(2), 161–200.

Daoud, Z. (1996). *Féminisme et politique au Maghreb: Soixante ans de lutte*. Paris: Maisonneuve Larose.

Delhaye, G., & L. Le Pape (2004). Les transformations économiques en Algérie: Privatisation ou prédation de l'État? *Journal des Anthropologues*, 96–97, 177–194.

Dillman, B. (2001). Facing the market in North Africa. *Middle East Journal*, 55(2), 198–215.

Elbadawy, A., D. Levison, D. Ahlburg & R. Assaad (2009). Private and group tutoring in Egypt: Where is the gender inequality? Union internationale pour l'étude scientifique de la population. XXVIe Congrès international de la population, Marrakech, 27 September–2 October. Retrieved from http://iussp2009.princeton.edu/download.aspx?submissionId=91279.

Gastineau, B. (2003). Les facteurs de la déscolarisation en milieu rural tunisien – L'exemple de deux zones rurales tunisiennes: la Kroumirie et El Faouar. In M. Cosio, R. Marcoux, M. Pilon, & A. Quesnel (Eds.), *Education, family and population dynamics/Education, famille et dynamiques démographiques* (pp. 103–123). París: Cicred.

Geisser, V. (Ed.) (2000). *Diplômés maghrébins d'ici et d'ailleurs: Trajectoires sociales et itinéraires migratoires*. Paris: CNRS-Editions.

Henig, J. (1994). *Rethinking school choice: Limits of the market metaphor*. Princeton, NJ: Princeton University Press.

Kateb, K. (2006). *École, population et société en Algérie*. Paris: Harmattan.

Kohstall, F. (2007). Morocco/Egypt: Educational reform's selective benefits. *Arab Reform Bulletin*, 5(2), 1–2.

Lacoste, Y. (2001). Enjeux politiques et géopolitiques de la langue française en Algérie: Contradictions coloniales et postcoloniales. *Hérodote*, 126. Retrieved December 15, 2008, from http://www.herodote.org/article.php3?id_article=288

Lelièvre, C. (1999). *Jules Ferry: La république éducatrice*. Paris: Hachette.

Lemdani-Belkaid, M. (2000). *Normaliennes en Algérie*. Paris: Harmattan.

Leon, A. (1991). *Colonisation, enseignement, éducation: Étude historique et comparative*. Paris: Harmattan.

Lessard, C., A. Brassard, & J. Lusignan (2002). *Les tendances évolutives des politiques éducatives en matière de structures et de régulation, d'imputabilité et de reddition de comptes: Le cas du Canada (Ontario et Colombie-Britannique), des États-Unis (Californie), de la France et du Royaume-Uni*. Montreal: Université de Montréal-LABRIPROF-CRIPFE.

Lezé, G. (December 2001). La généralisation de l'enseignement primaire au Maghreb: Correspondances. *Bulletin scientifique de l'IRMC*. Retrieved June 20, 2005, from http://www.irmcmaghreb.org/corres/textes/leze.htm

Lubienski, C. (2005). Public schools in marketized environments: Shifting incentives and unintended consequences of competition-based educational reforms. *American Journal of Education*, 111(4), 464–486.

Margonis, F., & L. Parker (1995). Choice, privatization, and unspoken strategies of containment. *Educational Policy*, 9(4), 375–403.

Marmié, N. (2009). La 'mission', une tradition d'excellence. *Jeune Afrique*, 2519, 43–44.

Maroy, C. (2006). *Ecole, régulation, marché: Une comparaison de six espaces scolaires locaux en Europe*. Paris: PUF.

Mazawi, A.E. (1999). The contested terrains of education in the Arab States: An appraisal of major research trends. *Comparative Education Review*, 43(3), 332–352.

Mazzella, S. (2008). *L'enseignement supérieur dans la globalisation libérale: Une comparaison Maghreb, Afrique, Canada et France*. Paris: Maisonneuve et Larose.

Moatassime, A. (1992). *Arabisation et langue française au Maghreb: Un aspect sociolinguistique des dilemmes du développement*. Paris: PUF.

Mons, N. (2004). De l'école unifiée aux écoles plurielles: Evaluation internationale des politiques de différenciation et de diversification de l'offre éducative. Doctorat en Sciences de l'Education. Dijon: Université de Bourgogne.

Oudada, M. (2007). The school in the oasis. *Les Cahiers pédagogiques*, 458, 57–59.

Popa, S., & C. Acedo (2006). Redefining professionalism: Romanian secondary education teachers and the private tutoring system. *International Journal of Educational Development*, 26(1), 98–110.

Rikowski, G. (2001). *The battle in Seattle: Its significance for education*. London: Tufnell Press.

Samira, H. (2008). La liste de 119 écoles privées agréées par l'Etat rendue publique. *Le Maghreb: Le quotidien de l'économie*. Retrieved July 13, 2008 from http://www.lemaghrebdz.com/

Santucci, J.-C. (1993). Etat, légitimité et identité au Maghreb: Les dilemmes de la modernité. *Confluences méditerranée*, 6, 65–78.

Schultz, T.W. (1963). *The economic value of education*. New York: Columbia University Press.

Slimani, L. (2009). Education: Le privé à la rescousse du public. *Jeune Afrique*, 2519, 43–44.

Sraïeb, N. (1974). *Colonisation, décolonisation et enseignement*. Tunis: Institut National des Sciences de l'Education.

Sraïeb, N. (2003). *Anciennes et nouvelles élites du Maghreb*. Tunis and Aix-en-Provence: Inas-Cérès-Édisud.

Storm, L. (2007). *Democratization in Morocco: The political elite and struggles for power in the post-independence state*. London: Routledge.

Sultana, R. (2001). Le défi de l'enseignement supérieur dans les pays méditerranéens. *Monde Arabe-Maghreb-Machrek*, 171–172, 26–41.

Tawil, S. (2006). Qur'anic education and social change in northern Morocco: Perspectives from Chefchaouen. *Comparative Education Review*, 50(3), 496–517.

Tiano, A. (1968). *Le développement économique au Maghreb.* Paris: PUF.

UNESCO Institute for Statistics (2006). *Global education digest 2006.* Montreal: UNESCO Institute for Statistics.

UNESCO Institute for Statistics (2007). *Global education digest 2007: Comparing education statistics across the world.* Montreal: UNESCO Institute for Statistics.

UNICEF. (2004). *La situation des enfants en Tunisie: Analyse et recommandations.* Tunis: UNICEF.

Van Zanten, A., & J.-P. Obin (2008). *La carte scolaire.* Paris: PUF.

Vermeren, P. (2002). *La formation des élites marocaines et tunisiennes: Des nationalistes aux islamistes, 1920–2000.* Paris: La Découverte.

Walberg, H.J., & J.L. Bast (2003). *Education and capitalism: How overcoming our fear of markets and economics can improve America's schools.* Stanford, CA: Hoover Institution Press.

World Bank. (2008). *The road not traveled: Education reform in the Middle East and North Africa.* Washington, DC: The World Bank.

Yahya, M. (2009). Baccalauréat: Les cours particuliers accablent les parents tunisiens. *Magharebia.* Retrieved April 22, 2005, from http://www.magharebia.com/

Younis, T. (1996). Privatization: A review of policy and implementation in selected Arab countries. *International Journal of Public Sector Management, 9*(3), 18–25.

Zidan, M. (2007). *Etat et tribu dans le monde arabe: Deux systèmes pour une seule société.* Paris: Harmattan.

3   TVET Reforms in the Arab Region

The 'Push' and 'Pull' in Policy Development

Borhène Chakroun and Eva Jimeno Sicilia[1]

Introduction

There is a growing concern about the autonomy of national policy making and implementation within the turbulent global context. Globalisation, it is argued, reinforces the tendency for national economies to be increasingly interconnected, and for national policies to be shaped not only by national actors but also by global dynamics. The effects of globalisation hold true not only for economic relations but also for contemporary educational systems (Schriewer & Martinez, 2004), and the dialectic of the global and the local in education has been the focus of much research and debate in recent years (Steiner-Khamsi, 2004; Zajda, 2005; Rust, 2000; Sahlberg, 2008). At the heart of this debate are the complex issues of policy borrowing and policy lending (Phillips, 2005), which are of particular relevance to the educational reform movements that we see taking place across the Arab region.

Several authors have proposed different models to describe and analyse processes of educational policy borrowing, with the focus typically being on cross-national attraction in education, the distinctive stages of policy borrowing, and the spectrum of policies and practices that are subject to educational transfers (Ochs & Phillips, 2004; Steiner-Khamsi, 2004). These models help us understand why some countries are more likely than others to be 'policy makers' rather than 'policy takers', identify patterns in the international flows of educational policies and practices, and decode the motivations behind a country's or a region's ambition to export (or import) policies, as well as the mechanisms that are usually used in order to facilitate the circulation of 'solutions' to perceived educational challenges. In this chapter, we will draw on some of this extensive literature in order to offer some reflections about the way such global forces have an impact on educational policy making in a number of Arab states. Our purview will necessarily have to be limited, and we will adopt a case-study approach, focusing on one education sector – Technical and Vocational Education and Training (TVET) – and on one dimension of that sector – National Qualifications Frameworks (NQFs) – in an effort to illustrate some of the dynamic interactions between the global and the local in educational policy development in the Arab region.

The Arab region is in a state of flux: population growth, urbanisation, industrialisation, growing graduate unemployment, and inward and outward migration, are some of the more immediately visible trends that have a major impact on most if not all the social institutions, not least the education system. As the different Arab countries engage reforms, they have major options to consider and choices to make, in an effort to safeguard identity and culture within an ever more tightly interlinked world. While there seems to be well-nigh consensus about the need to build knowledge-based economies and societies, a key debate is the manner in which the local and the global are to interact. The authors of the *Arab Human Development Report*, for instance, emphasise that lasting reform "must come from within", but also argue that the "Arab World must turn outwards and immerse itself in the global knowledge stream" and that "Arabs need to drive the process themselves: promoting local innovation as a necessary complement to harnessing knowledge and technology from abroad" (UNDP, 2004, pp. i–ii). Similar views have been expressed by other agencies (inter alia, ETF and World Bank, 2006; World Bank, 2008).

The Interplay Between the Local and the Global

Despite awareness of the need for wholesale transformation of education systems, and for that change to "come from within", reform of education generally, and of the TVET sub-sector specifically, are more often than not driven, designed and funded by international donors. Indeed, much of the assistance supporting TVET reform in Arab countries, as in most transition countries, has hitherto been guided by principles of policy borrowing and policy lending (King & McGrath, 2004; Grootings, 2004; Ellerman, 2004) – and the outcomes have not been particularly successful. Such failure of policy transfer to Arab countries provokes critical reflections on the whole notion of policy borrowing from abroad, which is often resorted to in the desire of policy makers to find quick and tried solutions to urgent problems (see Phillips, 1989, and Steiner-Khamsi, 2004, for a broad discussion).

This chapter engages such critical reflection by focusing on one area of educational reform which has entailed a high degree of policy influence, namely NQFs. We will draw on our experiences as 'boundary' or 'mediating' persons engaged with an institution – the European Training Foundation (ETF) – to co-ordinate a European Union (EU)-funded project whose overall objective is to create opportunities for TVET policy learning between EU member states and a number of Arab states in the south and east Mediterranean. While the project had several sub-components,[2] our focus will be on NQFs which, as Young (2003a) noted, have become increasingly popular internationally as a policy tool for TVET reform, itself seen in the context of the broader transformation that, it is argued, the educational system as a whole must engage in order to deliver the skills needed by the labour market (OECD, 2007). NQFs are therefore closely associated with the whole rhetorical discourse surrounding 'lifelong learning' for a 'knowledge-based economy' – which has become the mantra of developed and developing countries the world over.

We will therefore consider NQFs as an example of the globalisation and internationalisation of an educational agenda: their growing importance internationally, and more specifically in the Arab region, provides us with a good opportunity to examine the complex interactions that occur within and across local and global levels. These interactions are complex because they can take different forms. Phillips and Ochs (2004, p. 8), for instance, note a continuum in the dynamics of education transfer processes ranging from reforms that are 'imposed' ('policy lending') to those that are more 'voluntarily' sought or accepted ('policy borrowing'). This continuum, in fact, functions as a heuristic, for in reality the 'push' and 'pull' are not independent of each other: rather, they interact together in complex ways, so that the synergy between global and local interests define what becomes policy within the prevalent matrix of power dynamics. Furthermore, this complex and situated or 'territorialized' (Sultana, 2009) interaction between the local and the global is neither one-dimensional nor linear, but typically goes through diverse phases and trajectories, which could include, for instance, cross-national attraction, adoption, adaptation, internalisation and 'indigenisation'.

The rationale underpinning policy attraction, and the motives behind policy borrowing, can be equally diverse and complex. Phillips (2000), for instance, identifies four such reasons and motives, including serious scientific/academic investigation of the situation in a foreign environment; popular conceptions of the superiority of other approaches to educational questions; politically motivated endeavours to seek reform of provision by identifying clear contrasts with the situation elsewhere; and distortion (exaggeration), whether or not deliberate, of evidence from abroad to highlight perceived deficiencies at home. Phillips (2004, p. 54) also helpfully considers several types of stimuli that spark off such 'cross-national attraction', including, among others, a negative external evaluation (such as the ones associated with the Programme for International Student Assessment, or PISA and Trends in International Mathematics and Science Study, or TIMSS) and new configurations and alliances between potential policy players in a given region.

In this chapter we argue that recent reforms of TVET systems undertaken in some Arab countries, and particularly the discussion among national stakeholders on the development of NQFs, reflect a convergence of *both* national and international interests, and a response to *both* local and global agendas. On the one hand, national governments want to ensure that nationally based qualifications are useful and coherent, that they facilitate economic development, and that they are recognised and accredited beyond national boundaries. On the other hand, NQFs also hold the promise of regulating and guaranteeing the availability of skills for international capital that invests in Arab states, as well as of pacing and systematising the flow of labour from the economic south in ways that can be more easily and more advantageously absorbed in the economic north.

Our overall aspirations for this chapter are therefore to generate knowledge about – as well as critical reflections on – the issues of policy travel and policy making in Arab countries, by extrapolating on the NQF as a case in point. A related aspiration is to investigate the extent to which 'policy learning' (Raffe & Spours, 2007; ETF, 2008) – as distinct from 'policy borrowing' and 'policy lending'

– can potentially help overcome some of the pitfalls that are usually associated with the latter models of policy influence, since they enable participating countries to engage in policy development, formulation and implementation processes that are based on broad ownership and embeddedness in existing institutions.

We will first focus on NQFs and their rise as a 'policy solution' on the world scene, examining in particular the part played by international organisations and their mediating role in the Arab region.

Introducing National Qualification Frameworks

NQFs can be understood as classifiers that specify the relationship and the continuum – horizontally and vertically – between different forms of qualifications (Coles, 2006). The main features that distinguish NQFs from existing qualification systems can be summarised as follows: all qualifications are described according to a single set of criteria, ranked on a single hierarchy of levels and described in terms of learning outcomes (Grootings, 2007). As already noted above, NQFs are increasingly linked to lifelong learning strategies (OECD, 2007) and as such are also generally open to the learning taking place outside formal education settings. In most cases, they go beyond the role of classifiers ('qualification grids') and aim at a redefinition of the way qualifications are related to each other, how they are valued and eventually put into use in societies. As noted by Bjørnavold and Coles (2009) modern NQFs are 'instruments with a vision', designed to be overarching frameworks that incorporate qualifications from different education and training sectors (general, vocational and academic). Designing an NQF therefore entails going beyond reaching national agreement on a set of technical features: rather, it is about creating a platform for national (and hence cross-institutional and cross-sectoral) dialogue and mutual trust among different stakeholders including governments, social partners, as well as education and training providers.

International experience in designing and implementing an NQF emphasises the need that the system developed is fit for both purpose and context. Fitness of purpose is ensured by constructing the framework on the basis of a careful analysis of the needs and aspirations of the societies in question, and in ways that encourage ownership by national stakeholders. Raffe (2003) and Young (2003b) suggest that context relevance be viewed from the perspective of what they refer to as "intrinsic" and "institutional" logics. The first refers to the broad educational goals of an NQF, while the second comprises the opportunities, incentives and constraints arising from such factors as the labour market and the social structure.

This distinction between intrinsic and institutional logics is important when it comes to understanding how policies travel between countries. According to Young (2003b), when it comes to intrinsic logic, broad NQF goals related to lifelong learning and the learning society are widely shared across a range of different countries, and indeed are to be found in almost every national and international policy document. Problems arise, however, when we consider institutional logics, whereby "qualifications, like so much in social life, depend on trust, not just rules, laws and criteria … in other words, the context in which they work and gain acceptability and establish their credibility" (Young, 2003b, p.

235). Young concludes that countries which have looked overseas for models for implementing an NQF have tended to look only at the intrinsic logic underpinning other frameworks, ignoring the dynamics of the institutional matrix in which they are expected to be implemented.

The tensions between the intrinsic and institutional logics of qualifications – in other words, the dynamics that arise out of the attempt to adopt broad educational goals within a context that is necessarily marked by economic, social and cultural specificities – reflects the wider debate on policy borrowing and lending in the field of education and training. As such, the rise of NQFs can be seen as an increasingly global phenomenon which, however, is incarnated in particular ways when the global and the local meet. It is instructive to consider such global/local dynamics and resonances, by focusing on the key elements of the debates around policy borrowing, and the nature of the 'push' and 'pull' factors in the process.

Policy Borrowing and the International 'Push' for Qualifications Frameworks

The justification for NQFs seems increasingly to be "because everyone else is doing it" (Allais, 2007, p. 61). Bjørnavold and Coles (2009) see in it an international "snowball-effect": from just a handful of countries in 2004 with qualification frameworks,[3] there are currently more than 50 countries around the world[4] that have adopted such frameworks. At least 20 more countries are considering their implementation.[5] This expansion reflects both a global 'epidemic' of NQFs, and considerable 'borrowing' and 'lending' of structures and design principles that were originally formulated in the UK (Young, 2005). It also reflects the effect of the adoption of the logic underpinning NQFs, and extending it at a regional level through the elaboration of nothing less than a European Qualifications Framework (EQF), applicable to EU Member States and seen as a reference point for their neighbourhood countries (ETF, forthcoming).

Policy trends, however, do not simply 'happen'. As several authors have noted, the international popularity of NQFs needs to be seen in relation to the hegemonic hold exercised by neoliberalism and market-based economic reforms. Phillips (2003), for instance, considers that qualification reform in New Zealand had an economic focus from the start, resulting directly from the public sector reforms that emphasised a market-based economy. Young (2003b, p. 232), on his part, observes that NQFs illustrate an "almost paradigm case of government intervention in a neoliberal economy", while Allais (2007), in her critical analysis of the development of an NQF in South Africa, shows that neoliberal trends in thinking about education and public sector reform, together with social constructivist ideas about knowledge, made the development of a qualifications framework seem an attractive policy option.

Much of the international 'push' in favour of NQFs, therefore, relates directly to the 'need' – by an imagined, immanent knowledge-based economy – for mobile, flexible and adaptable workers, and in response to the aspirations of mobile, global capital (OECD, 2007). The 'need' for cross-border recognition of qualifications, therefore, is constructed in relation to the discourse around –

and reality of – global labour markets and the massive migration movement of people. Governments keen to attract foreign capital, and to assure international investors that they have the required skills base, are increasingly concerned about the transparency and comparability of their national qualifications in relation to those that are produced, allocated and used elsewhere (Grootings, 2007). While of course the dynamics in the Arab region can be quite different, it can be argued that neoliberalism, the rise of a rhetoric around the development of a knowledge-based economy, and arguments favouring the mobility of labour both in the region and beyond have laid the foundations for a policy context that is sympathetic to the notion of an NQF (Leney, 2009).

The rise of NQFs – for reasons such as those suggested above – does not necessarily mean that they are indeed useful in satisfying the policy aspirations for which they were adopted in the first place. Quite the contrary: several scholars have in fact argued that, irrespective of their increasing appeal, NQFs are not necessarily good policy practice, especially in the context of developing countries (Young, 2004, 2005; Allais, 2007). Internationally, there does not seem to be much information available about the extent to which existing NQFs have actually attained the objectives for which they were developed; there is little evidence, for instance, that NQFs promote lifelong learning (OECD, 2007). None of the NQFs that are in place are without problems, whether political, administrative or educational (Young, 2004), with Grootings (2007) and Castejon (2007) highlighting the risks that NQFs represent, given their preoccupation with learning outcomes at the expense of the learning process itself. Other researchers have furthermore noted that NQFs are inadequate policy instruments since they fail to address TVET reform in a systemic and comprehensive manner. They thus tend to lack what Raffe (2003) refers to as 'policy breadth', and are insufficiently linked with other policy measures that need to be addressed in the process of reform, such as funding, teacher training, and the autonomy of education institutions. It is therefore not particularly surprising that Allais (2007), in her evaluation of the introduction of an NQF in South Africa, speaks of their "rise and fall", thus signalling the extensive problems encountered at the implementation stage.

This effectively means that many countries could well be investing considerable resources in a policy mechanism which is untested, under-researched, and unproven. This is important for our discussion of policy lending and policy borrowing, since it helps drive home the point that 'policy solutions' can become popular and even endemic despite the lack of any clear evidence as to their effectiveness in addressing the problems they are presumed to 'solve'. Why then, one might ask, are NQFs being seen as a policy solution in several countries across the Arab region? It is to an exploration of why and how NQFs are travelling to this part of the world that we now turn.

The 'Pull' of NQFs in the Arab Region

The NQF 'policy bandwagon' has 'travelled' to the Arab region for different reasons and in different ways – with such diversity of motives and mechanisms only partly accounted for by the very diversity of countries within the region itself.

As has already been noted, there is a growing interest in Arab states in ensuring that different aspects of nationally based qualifications are useful and coherent with one another, and that they are recognised and respected beyond national boundaries, thus taking into account migration trends and the globalisation of labour markets. Given the importance of the informal sector in most if not all the Arab labour markets, where young people learn skills through informal apprenticeships with members of their own family, NQFs also hold the promise of recognising learning gained through such experience, besides improving linkages between education institutions and evolving labour markets. The increasing concern with outputs of – rather than inputs to – national education systems finds a ready echo in the NQF focus on describing qualifications according to outcomes, thus encouraging the implementation of quality assurance systems and the valuing of more transparency, partly through the involvement of users of 'outputs' – such as employers – in designing new qualifications (Seyfried, 2008). Leney (2009), in a study that focused specifically on qualification frameworks in some countries in the Middle East and North Africa, reports a range of reasons that render NQFs attractive as a policy solution to four Arab countries, namely Egypt, Jordan, Morocco and Tunisia:

> Egypt needs to update its qualifications system to keep up with the fast pace of change in the Egyptian labour market and the wider economy. The country aims to use the NQF as a way of moving from a traditional input-based model of education to something better able to cope with changing skill needs.

> Jordan wishes to make its workforce more competitive and is striving to boost the quality and relevance of its outputs to the labour market with this aim in mind.

> Morocco sees building an NQF as a way of revamping its entire education system. It is hoped that it will bring greater coherence to the system by establishing pathways between the three sub-systems and increase the readability of Moroccan qualifications nationally, through the region and further afield.

> Tunisia sees the NQF as a means of increasing the coherence, readability and quality of its human resources system and encouraging lifelong learning. These objectives are at the heart of the reforms currently under way in TVET. The growing mobility of labour as a result of free trade agreements between Tunisia and the EU has provided a second, more pressing reason for the mutual recognition of qualifications.

Such varying if converging motives help us understand how global factors interact with national priorities, and that globalising policy practices can have multiple trajectories. For the four countries referred to above, there is a mix of purposes linked to the market-based economy reforms resulting from the free trade zone with Europe, international competitiveness, the preparation of individuals for the international labour market and the recognition of national qualifications. While there may be common ground, there are also necessarily specificities in the way a particular policy is considered and taken up. The Tunisian vision for NQF, for instance, indicates a shift in the policy vision for TVET: here, social promotion and individual well-being through lifelong learning appear together with economic arguments. Furthermore, the opening up of this 'black box of qualifications' and the introduction of a Tunisia-wide, coherent approach to certification is viewed in relation to its potential to reduce uncertainties as regards the relative value of different certificates and diplomas in the labour market (Feutrie & Mghirbi, 2007; Consultation nationale sur l'emploi, 2008).

For Morocco, a key motive in considering an NQF as a policy option was the relevant Ministry's interest in ensuring that EU Member States understood and recognised the range of qualifications that the country produces. In fact, as Morocco's negotiations with the European Commission on advanced status entered their final phase in the spring of 2008, the NQF project gathered new momentum by virtue of its contribution to a wider understanding of the Moroccan education and training system, and players whose commitment had hitherto been limited have become more strongly motivated (Feutrie & Bouhafa, 2008). Thus, the NQF concept became attractive to politicians and policy makers at the moment they saw its relevance for their EU negotiation agenda.

As these examples show, it is difficult – if not impossible – to separate national and global factors that render a policy option attractive to a particular country. The free trade zone with Europe, market-based economies, national labour markets, international competition, the national and international debate on certification and the recognition of qualifications – one and all find a way into the policy discourse potpourri and are used as drivers for introducing an NQF. As such, the purposes and strategies surrounding the borrowing of NQF policy reflect a 'voluntary' rather than an 'imposed' amalgam of global and national factors (Phillips, 2005).

NQFs also prove attractive to countries in the Arab region due to what has earlier been referred to as 'international pressure'. We can here refer to three such key elements that have played an important role in making some policy options more attractive than others in the region. First are broader socio-economic regional policies and processes, key among which is the Barcelona Process. Second are more specific 'socialisation' processes reflecting EU developments in the field of education, and which have an impact on the region. Third, and linked to the second, are regional cooperation and regional initiatives in the education generally, and in TVET specifically. We will briefly consider all three pressures and influences in the next section, noting how they have had a regional impact on TVET generally, and NQF more specifically.

'Push' Forces Promoting NQFs in the Arab Region

An important source of policy influence leading some Arab countries to consider NQFs as a 'solution' to challenges in the TVET area is the EU – particularly so within the framework of the so-called 'Barcelona Process'.[6] This process entailed the adoption of the Barcelona Declaration in 1995, which launched the Euro-Mediterranean Partnership (EMP), the European Neighbourhood Policy in 2003, and the Union for the Mediterranean in 2008. Fundamental to all three phases of the Process is the interest of the EU in surrounding itself by a ring of prosperous and stable friendly nations, where peace and security is ensured through such countries having a stake in the EU's internal market. This is in part attained through the promotion of the free movement of people, goods, services and capital, as well as through preferential trading relations – all of which are expected to add value to domestic reforms (Euromed, 2007).

There have been a number of critiques of this 'partnership' – Amin and El Kenz (2005), for instance, raise several issues regarding the way the economically negative impact of globalised capitalism overrides the intention of the EU to put Arab countries of the Mediterranean and Gulf region on a new footing of equality and mutually beneficial cooperation. In as far as this chapter is concerned, however, it is important to highlight the fact that from its launch in 1995, right through 2008, when the EMP shifted gear to strengthen cooperation under the guise of the Union for the Mediterranean, and on to 2010, the EU, via its external assistance programmes, will have invested as much as 500 million euros in TVET reforms in several Arab countries in the Middle East and North Africa. Needless to say, given the volume of this support, TVET reform goals in the different parts of the Arab region have been influenced, to a greater or lesser extent, by EU developments in the field, with EU experiences in the TVET sector shaping the flows of ideas north–south. NQFs are central to such EU experience, thereby featuring highly on the agenda in the relations between Europe and the region, whether mediated by single country input, or by such agencies as the ETF.

EU policy influence works its way into different countries and across the region in a number of ways. As Emerson and Noutcheva (2004, p. 13) have noted in regard to European international cooperation approaches, one such form or mechanism of influence is 'socialisation', which they define as "a process of inducing behavioural and identity change through interaction with the partners at any or all levels which results in social learning model emulation, lessons drawn, and so on". The impact of this 'socialisation' process is even greater when a similar set of messages reach target countries from a whole range of international or regional policy actors. In the case of NQFs, for instance, Young (2003b) has highlighted an overlap of discourse around NQFs as articulated not only by the EU, but also by such international agencies as the World Bank, the International Labour Organisation, and the OECD. In many ways, through the convergence of opinion – which is relayed via international and regional projects, research, publications, conferences, virtual communities, and so on – a set of policy solutions is legitimised, other options are disregarded or eclipsed, with the international community guiding or promoting the development of a domestic debate that can lead to policy change. Several questions can of course be raised in relation to the positive consequences of such 'socialisation', and the extent to which it reflects the ideological, economic and political interests of the international agencies involved rather than those of the so-called 'beneficiaries'.

While the convergent agenda and policy advice of several international agencies has had an impact on a range of countries in the Arab region, the fact that the establishment of a European Qualifications Framework (EQF) is a policy priority in the EU has been particularly influential. The EQF – which is a meta-framework that, like NQFs, is based on learning outcomes aiming to facilitate the transparency and portability of qualifications and to support lifelong learning – is one of the central planks in the EU's effort to attain a set of social and economic goals for Europe. These goals, known as the 'Lisbon Agenda',[7] aim to achieve a highly competitive economy for Europe, social inclusion for groups at risk and promote socially cohesive societies, more and better jobs in the labour market, and environmental sustainability. The EQF – discussions around which began in 2004, with consensus around a framework being reached four years later – is one of the more tangible outcomes that facilitate the EU's lifelong learning agenda, and its aspirations to become "the most dynamic and competitive knowledge-based economy in the world".[8] The establishment of a Europe-wide qualifications framework is considered to be particularly useful in facilitating mobility of students and workers across borders, an agenda that also has implications for countries that, while not members of the EU, have special ties to it. As the European Commission (2008, p. 4) points out, "The adoption of a common reference framework based on learning outcomes will facilitate the comparison and (potential) linking together of traditional qualifications awarded by national authorities and qualifications awarded by other stakeholders. The EQF will thus help sectors and individuals take advantage of this growing internationalisation of qualifications."

In terms of the Barcelona Process, and in relation to the goal of strengthening economic links between the Arab states of the Mediterranean and the EU, the EQF is seen as a way of facilitating skills mobility. A meeting of Euro-Mediterranean employment and labour ministers in Marrakech in November 2008, for instance, highlighted the need for regional cooperation both in ensuring improved TVET in response to labour market needs, as well as the establishment of qualification frameworks that support the match between the supply and demand for skills (EU French Presidency, 2008, p. 2). Mediterranean countries that engage in this process will, it is argued, have the advantage of having their national qualifications more easily recognised, rendering them more transferable between regions. This would – in principle – facilitate and support smoother and more dignified migrations of labour. Indeed, one of the initiatives that have been agreed to between Mediterranean partners in the Union for the Mediterranean and the EU is the development of a blue card scheme that will enable highly skilled immigrants to take jobs in skills-shortage sectors in the EU labour market.

Several questions can be asked here, echoing those raised earlier. One can wonder, for instance, about the impact of this transferability on what the qualifications stand for, and whose point of view or priorities they will engage. Such agreements, for instance, can easily be seen to contribute to the brain drain problem, with the EU poaching the best available skilled workers in the Arab Mediterranean, whose contribution is sorely needed in their home countries. The Arab region's aspirations for development could very well be undermined, given the fact that the typical profile of Arab migrants towards Europe, the USA and

Canada is changing from a low-skilled to a more highly skilled one. The French National Centre for Scientific Research, for instance, now includes no less than 700 Moroccan, 500 Algerian and 450 Tunisian researchers (Bardak, 2006).

Other EU initiatives in the region have also served to steer policies in a specific direction. A key mechanism here is regional cooperation, which is implemented and sustained through comparative research, networking and regional forums, and where a key goal is the stimulation of national reforms. The EU funded MEDA-ETE[9] project, co-ordinated by the ETF, is an example of such regional cooperation, and has relevance to this chapter because it helps us understand some of the mechanisms that can facilitate education policy lending and borrowing, as well as how such mechanisms have been used to vehicle EU experiences regarding the implementation of NQFs to Arab countries. It also helps us understand how other mechanisms, such as policy learning, can overcome some of the pitfalls of policy borrowing and lending.

The guiding rationale behind this regional project was that rather than 'policy lending' and 'policy borrowing', participating countries would remain free to develop their coherent and comprehensive strategies by designing and managing their own systems – on the basis, however, of an agreement around an ultimate goal and direction, towards which they would all move given a shared vision and common guidelines. This entailed a process of 'peer policy learning' between eight Arab countries – namely Algeria, Egypt, Jordan, Lebanon, Morocco, Palestine, Syria and Tunisia – who constituted the NQF project partners in 2005, with inputs from EU Member States that had already benefited from experience and expertise in the design and implementation of NQFs. The goal was therefore to facilitate reflection on TVET reform using national qualifications as a strategic framework for discussion, and to encourage policy learning about both opportunities and risks related to the development of NQFs.

Participating countries agreed about the value of qualification frameworks for the region, in terms of their usefulness in developing progression routes, in improving access to learning opportunities and skills recognition, in creating more flexibility, in ensuring transparency, in quality assurance and in increasing the relevance of qualifications for employment (Gordon, 2006). The countries that made most headway in developing an NQF approach – namely Egypt, Jordan, Morocco and Tunisia – played an important role in south–south exchange of learning and experiences, so that peer policy learning in some ways overcame the one-way, north–south flows that characterise much interaction in development projects. It also meant that, to use the terms suggested by Phillips and Ochs (2004) in their overview of educational policy transfer, what is at hand is not policy lending but rather policy influence, with a common goal and purpose generated on the basis of a concern for embedded and territorialised interest, reflected upon in the light of international experience. In this case, the transparency of qualifications responds to a common interest in mobility and migration, both inside and outside regional borders.

In the next section we will reflect on the value of peer policy learning, again focusing on NQFs to illustrate the points that we wish to make. Our argument will be that an emphasis on policy *learning* contributes to increased context relevance and ownership of reform policies.

From Policy Lending and Borrowing to Policy Learning

Concerns with policy lending and policy borrowing have led some agencies to focus rather more on peer policy learning as a development strategy. Some of these concerns are political, in terms of the underlying and vested interests often underpinning the interchange between countries in the economic north and south. While such concerns are very important, in this case we would like to stress that even from the perspective of the technical exchange of knowledge and expertise, peer policy learning seems to us to be a more effective manner by means of which governments or systems of governance inform policy development by drawing lessons from available evidence and experience (Grootings, 2004; Raffe & Spours, 2007; Chakroun, 2008). Peer policy learning therefore highlights the capacity of policy makers in specific countries to learn from their own experience and from that of other countries, in ways that strive for a deeper understanding of policy problems and processes than what is provided by simple search for – and implementation of – so-called 'best practice'.

Recent work (e.g. ETF, 2007, 2008), suggests that policy learning – as distinct from policy borrowing and lending – encourages *situated* problem solving and reflection. If we again focus on NQFs to illustrate what is at stake here, a national qualification framework is not something that can easily be copied from other countries and then quickly implemented at home – it is strategically linked to goals and outcomes for national education systems, and thus is perforce firmly related to the specific institutional context of the country – a point that we tried to highlight earlier when we followed Young (2003b) in drawing a distinction between 'intrinsic' and 'institutional' logic. For this and other reasons, an NQF that fits all countries does not exist (Grootings, 2007), since like any other national institution, qualification frameworks are a social construct put together by people who are themselves caught up in the nexus of global and local demands, opportunities and constraints.

It is in recognition of the interplay of the local and the global when it comes to policy making that the value of policy learning becomes most evident. In the case of NQFs as a potentially relevant policy option for the Arab countries engaged in the ETF-led project, policy learning involves a number of activities and initiatives. First, it requires the building of a knowledge base on national and EU experiences in developing qualification frameworks, and the dissemination of this knowledge with national policy makers. It also involves the organisation of regional cooperation to facilitate the making of sustainable policy decisions through peer learning processes. Finally, it leads to interventions at national levels to facilitate reform processes and actions. The assumption underpinning this approach is that such learning may be more effective than policy recommendations, with the key objective being that of strengthening the capacity of policy makers to develop and implement context-relevant policies (Nikolovska & Vos, 2008; Sultana, 2008; ETF, 2008). It is also more up-front in recognising that while NQF holds many promises, there is scant evidence that such promise is easily fulfilled, or that it can be a panacea for the many ills that beset TVET in the region.

The context-specificity encouraged by peer policy learning comes across very powerfully when we consider the issue of the participation of social partners in the development of NQFs. As we had noted earlier, this is one of the key building blocks – and indeed justifications – in the design of an NQF in a number of industrially advanced economies. In the EU, where social partner representation is quite common in the organisation and even delivery of TVET, it is clear that any NQF has to have the support and input of employers and workers' representatives, besides the state. In Arab countries, however, the limited development of TVET is generally mirrored in very weak structures supporting the involvement by employers and unions in advising on the system or in helping to manage it (Sweet, 2009). This leads to a paradoxical situation when it comes to considering NQFs: whereas private sector or social partner involvement is presented internationally as *sine qua non* for NQF development (Bjørnavold & Coles, 2009), in the Arab countries involved in the NQF peer learning project, governments were at times reluctant to involve social partners. At other times social partners were not at all interested in invitations to make an input. In the report on NQF peer learning activities in the region, Feutrie and Mghirbi (2007) highlighted the difficulties encountered in this regard, noting that

> In Tunisia the social partners have been involved at an early stage of the project, although for the moment they are adopting a wait-and-see attitude. The others have not yet reached this point. The social partners are not involved at present in Jordan, and planned participation is restricted to the economic stakeholders. In Egypt, the plan is to involve the social partners at the start and end of the process of implementing the project. In Morocco, their participation is currently regarded as premature (p. 13).

One explanation for this state of affairs would be the lack of representative organisations at national and sectoral levels. Another is the absence of much in the way of professional capacity among social partners to deal with vocational education and training matters in a reform context. In a situation such as this, public education authorities are obliged to remain the driving force behind vocational education and training reform. Such embedded insights are crucial to policy learning processes, whereby specificities of context are identified and acknowledged. This leads away from a deficit discourse which typically blames implementation problems on lack of local capacity or 'backwardness', to a critical consideration of the contextual factors and 'institutional logic' that serve to shape policy 'solutions' in particular ways.

Thus, while the different Arab countries, for their own good reasons, and in their own way, remained committed to the 'intrinsic logic' underpinning the NQF approach – such as its value in re-visioning TVET, its articulation of a qualification grid using learning outcomes descriptors, and its usefulness in providing new pathways for learners to obtain qualifications – each participating country established its own agenda when it came to formulating policy options, to determining policy choices, and to implementing change.

It follows from this that the achievements of the project are varied: Tunisia, for instance, has included the NQF in the new TVET law of 2008. Jordan found it more appropriate to include the NQF as part of its national Employment and TVET strategy, which will receive EU support as from 2010. Morocco, as noted earlier, sees the NQF as a link in the chain that ties the country more closely to the EU, thus serving its own strategic interests. Egypt, on its part, is engaged in an ongoing and vigorous policy debate regarding the scope of an NQF, and its potential contribution to education system reform. It has followed up this debate by issuing a new decree (no. 288/2009), which establishes a cross-ministerial committee for TVET development, with an explicit reference to NQF as a tool for linking a modern TVET system to both the labour market and other education sectors in a lifelong learning perspective.

Each country is thus giving a specific shape to its own NQF, and doing so for its own reasons, in its own way, and at its own pace. This specificity and embeddedness is reflected in the NQF construct itself: thus, what is called an 'NQF' has different configurations in the different Arab countries concerned: in Jordan we find sectoral frameworks covering only vocational qualifications; in Morocco the focus has been on national frameworks; in Tunisia the preference has been to develop a classification of qualifications; while in Egypt the commitment is to come up with a framework for integrating professional and scientific qualifications. Each country is also taking into account its institutional traditions when it comes to establishing the institutional settings that are expected to manage the NQF. Thus, the two countries mostly (though not exclusively) influenced by Anglo-Saxon traditions – namely Egypt and Jordan – are envisaging the setting up of new institutions that will be in charge of developing and implementing the NQF (Egypt) and for quality assurance and accreditation (Jordan). On their part, the francophone countries – namely Morocco and Tunisia – are marked by a traditional institutional inertia, and are consequently less eager to set up an overarching entity which would be responsible for regulating all qualifications.

Looking Forward, Inwards and Ahead

This chapter attempted to identify and explore some of the 'push' and 'pull' factors that influence the policy-making process in a number of Arab states. It did so by focusing on NQFs, and the way in which the EU, via projects related to the Euro-Med Partnership, encourages a particular approach to qualification frameworks and promotes reflection on particular policy options through policy learning activities. Care has been taken to highlight the fact that the interaction between national and international levels is complex. In the case of national qualifications in particular, not only do qualifications need to fit in a country's own context, but they also need to be recognised abroad and trusted by neighbours and international investors entering the country. As such, NQFs cannot be developed in isolation from those in other countries. The intended transparency and underlying trust also have to serve the international mobility of students and workers and, indeed, the globalised labour market and international mobility of capital investments.

The interaction between local 'pull' and global 'push' also obliges Arab countries to carefully consider the extent to which they succeed in preserving the coherence and integrity of their national education systems in a globalising world (Holmes, 2003), thus seeing the local wood from the trees of foreign constructs (Klenha *et al.*, 2008). The challenge to balance global pressures with national interest is a common concern for all Arab countries, especially when, as in the case of NQFs and the related rhetoric of the lifelong learning global gospel, there seems to be an international consensus as to the way forward in relation to reforming TVET systems. The words of the authors of the *Arab Human Development Report* (UNDP, 2004, p. ii) seem to be particularly apropos in this context: "Immersion, yes, but swamped or drowned, no".

This is why policy learning – rather than policy lending or policy borrowing – seems to be a more suitable metaphor for the interaction between the local and the global. Peer learning processes facilitate not only north–south, but also south–south dialogue, providing opportunities for Arab countries to learn from each other. Certainly, an 'external eye' can help to introduce new points of view and alternative policy options as national discussions very often become 'locked' in old habits and traditional ways of looking at issues (Grootings, 2007). The experience from abroad can be a useful eye-opener and help to redirect national discussions into hitherto unknown policy territory. However, there is much that to be gained by fostering cooperation and mutual understanding among Arab countries. The NQF projects briefly documented above have fostered the emergence of a regional perspective on qualifications, which is likely to encourage both multi-lateral and bilateral approaches to the recognition of qualifications. On a more fundamental level, it helps build trust among Arab countries, providing the basis for future regional developments.

Notes

1 This chapter reflects the views of the authors and not necessarily those of the European Training Foundation, the European Commission Agency with which they are employed.
2 This project initially involved eight Arab countries that participate in the Euromed partnership process, namely Algeria, Egypt, Jordan, Lebanon, Morocco, Palestine, Syria and Tunisia.
3 These included the UK, Ireland, France, South Africa, Australia and New Zealand.
4 This estimate is based on an ETF mapping exercise carried out in early 2009.
5 These countries are to be found in all regions of the world, and range from the most industrially and economically developed in Europe to fast-developing countries in Asia and developing countries in Africa. Not all of these countries try to cover all the sectors of an education and training system, and not all of them are developing overreaching frameworks. In Europe, apart from Norway, Sweden and Greece – which have not yet decided – all the 32 countries that are part of the Education & Training 2010 process (EU Member States, the European Free Trade Area countries and the Candidate Countries) have decided to develop qualification frameworks that should be compatible with the European Qualifications Framework. In Africa the South African Qualification Framework has been functioning since the early 1990s.

Apart from South Africa, smaller countries such as Gambia, Botswana, Namibia and Mauritius have also developed frameworks recently. In Asia, India has developed its VET framework; Singapore, Malaysia and the Philippines have also established National Qualification Frameworks.

6 This process initially involved eight Arab countries, namely Algeria, Egypt, Jordan, Lebanon, Morocco, Palestine, Syria and Tunisia. Since 2008, Mauritania has joined the process. The other Arab countries are represented in the process through the Arab League.

7 These goals were agreed to by the EU prime ministers at a conference in Lisbon, Portugal, in 2000. Hence they are known as the 'Lisbon goals'. The Lisbon process is the agreed strategy of voluntary collaboration between Member States in areas such as education, where it is the Member States themselves, not the European Commission, that have powers under the principle of 'subsidiarity'. In 2000 the EU had 15 Member States. It enlarged to 25 in 2004 and to 27 in 2007, with Turkey and Croatia currently having the status of 'Candidate Countries'.

8 Lisbon European Council 23 and 24 March 2000, Presidency Conclusion available at http://www.europarl.europa.eu/summits/lis1_en.htm

9 MEDA-ETE is a regional project, funded by the European Commission and implemented by the European Training Foundation, which aims at supporting Arab countries from the Middle East and North Africa to design relevant TVET policies that can contribute to promote employment through a regional approach. The project encompasses four components, namely a Euro-Med Annual Forum on TVET for employment; a Euro-Med Network on TVET for employment; support for young unemployed people in the areas of self-employment and the creation of micro-enterprises; and the development of e-learning for training in Information and Communication Technologies and TVET. Further information about the regional project can be accessed at: http://www.meda-ete.net

References

Allais, S. (2007). The rise and fall of NQF: A critical analysis of the South African National Qualifications Framework. Doctoral thesis, University of Witwatersrand.

Amin, S., & A. El Kenz (2005). *Europe and the Arab World: Patterns and prospects for the new relationship*. London: Zed Books.

Bardak, U. (2006). Understanding the dynamics between migration, skills and poverty reduction in the Mediterranean Region. *ETF yearbook 2006: Skills development for poverty reduction* (pp. 39–54). Turin: European Training Foundation.

Bjørnavold, J., & M. Coles (2009) (unpublished). The added value of national qualifications frameworks in implementing the EQF. European Qualifications Framework Explanatory note 2.

Castejon, J.M. (2007). National Qualifications Frameworks: Tools for relating learning and employability in North Africa and the Middle East. *ETF yearbook 2007: Quality in vocational education and training* (pp. 75–84). Turin: European Training Foundation.

Chakroun, B. (2008). What can we learn from policy learning? *ETF yearbook 2008: Policy learning in action* (pp. 11–18). Turin: European Training Foundation.

Coles, M. (2006). *A review of international and national developments in the use of qualifications frameworks*. Turin: European Training Foundation.

Consultation Nationale sur l'Emploi (2008) (unpublished). Rapport intermédiaire, version 2. 'Compétitivité et Croissance: Le défi de l'emploi aux multiples dimensions. Diagnostic'.

Ellerman, D. (2004). Autonomy in education and development. *Journal of International Co-operation in Education*, 7(1), 3–14.

Emerson, M., & G. Noutcheva (March 2004). *From Barcelona Process to neighbourhood policy: assessments and open issues.* CEPS Working Document No. 220, CEPS. Retrieved January 15, 2009, from http://www.ceps.be

EU French Presidency (2008). *Conclusions of the first Euro-Mediterranean Employment and Labour Ministers' Conference,* November 9–10, 2008, Marrakech.

Euromed (2007). *European neighbourhood and partnership instrument.* Regional Strategy Paper 2007–2013. Retrieved January 20, 2009, from http://ec.europa.eu

European Commission (2008). *The European Qualifications Framework for Lifelong Learning (EQF).* Luxembourg: European Commission

ETF (2007). *ETF yearbook 2007: Quality in vocational education and training.* Turin: European Training Foundation.

ETF (2008). *ETF yearbook 2008: Policy learning in action.* Turin: European Training Foundation.

ETF (forthcoming). *Qualifications systems: Tools for modernising education and training.* Turin: European Training Foundation.

ETF and World Bank (2006). *Reforming technical vocational education and training in the Middle East and North Africa.* Turin: European Training Foundation.

Feutrie, M., & F. Bouhafa (2008). *Peer review, national qualifications framework development in Morocco.* Turin: European Training Foundation.

Feutrie, M., & M. Mghirbi (2007). *Peer review, national qualifications framework development in Tunisia.* Turin: European Training Foundation.

Gordon, J. (2006) (unpublished). National qualifications frameworks and recognition of qualifications in the MENA region. Synthesis Report. Turin: European Training Foundation.

Grootings, P. (Ed.) (2004). *ETF yearbook 2004: Learning matters.* Turin: European Training Foundation.

Grootings, P. (2007). Discussing national qualification frameworks: Facilitating policy learning in practice. *ETF yearbook 2007. Quality in vocational education and training* (pp. 17–40). Turin: European Training Foundation.

Holmes, K. (2003). Qualifications frameworks: Issues, problems and possibilities for small states. In G. Donn & T. Davies (Eds.), *Promises and problems for Commonwealth qualifications frameworks* (pp. 94–106). London: Commonwealth Secretariat and Wellington, New Zealand Qualifications Authority.

King, K., & S. McGrath (2004). *Knowledge for development? Comparing British, Japanese, Swedish and World Bank aid.* London: Zed Books.

Klenha, V. *et al.* (2008). Developing Kyrgyz TVET policy and strategy: The challenge of facilitating policy learning processes. *ETF yearbook 2008: Policy learning in action* (pp. 53–64). Turin: European Training Foundation.

Leney, T. (2009). *Qualifications that count: Strengthening the recognition of qualifications in the Mediterranean Area.* Turin: European Training Foundation.

Nikolovska, M., & A. Vos (2008). ETF peer learning: From policy learning to policy change in partner countries. *ETF yearbook 2008: Policy learning in action* (pp. 39–52). Turin: European Training Foundation.

Ochs, K., & D. Phillips (2004). Processes of educational borrowing in historical context. In D. Phillips & K. Ochs (Eds.), *Educational policy borrowing: Historical perspectives* (pp. 7–23). Oxford: Symposium Books.

OECD (2007). *Qualifications systems: Bridges to lifelong learning, education and training policy.* Paris: OECD.

Phillips, D. (1989). Neither a borrower nor a lender be? The problems of cross-national attraction in education. *Comparative Education,* 25(3), 267–274.

Phillips, D. (2000). Learning from elsewhere in education: Some perennial problems revisited with reference to British interest in Germany. *Comparative Education*, 36(3), 297–307.

Phillips, D. (2003). Lessons from New Zealand's National Qualifications Framework. *Journal of Education and Work*, 16(3), 289–304.

Phillips, D. (2004). Toward a theory of policy attraction in education. In G. Steiner-Khamsi (Ed.), *The global politics of educational borrowing and lending*. New York: Teachers College Press.

Phillips, D. (2005). Borrowing in education: Frameworks for analysis. In J. Zajda (Ed.), *International handbook on globalisation, education and policy research: Global pedagogies and policies*. Dordecht: Springer.

Phillips, D., & K. Ochs (Eds.) (2004). *Educational policy borrowing: historical perspectives*. Oxford: Symposium Books.

Raffe, D. (2003). Simplicity itself: The creation of the Scottish Credit and Qualifications Framework. *Journal of Education and Work*, 16(3), 239–258.

Raffe, D., & K. Spours (Eds.) (2007). *Policy-making and policy learning in 14–19 education*. London: Bedford Way Papers.

Rust, V.D. (2000). Education policy studies and comparative education. In R. Alexander, M. Osborn & D. Phillips (Eds.), *Learning from comparing: New directions in comparative educational research*, Vol. 2. Oxford: Symposium Books.

Sahlberg, P. (2008). Letter to a new Education Minister. *ETF yearbook 2008: Policy learning in action* (pp. 119–124). Turin: European Training Foundation.

Schriewer, J., and C. Martinez (2004). Constructions of internationality in education. In G. Steiner-Khamsi (Ed.), *The global politics of educational borrowing and lending*. New York: Teachers College Press.

Seyfried, E. (2008). *Quality and quality assurance in technical and vocational education and training*. Turin: European Training Foundation.

Steiner-Khamsi, G. (Ed.) (2004). *The global politics of educational borrowing and lending*. New York: Teachers College Press.

Sultana, R.G. (2008). The promises and pitfalls of peer learning. *ETF yearbook 2008: Policy learning in action* (pp. 95–100). Turin: European Training Foundation.

Sultana, R.G. (2009). Career guidance policies: Global dynamics, local resonances. 11th Annual International Centre for Guidance Studies (iCeGS), University of Derby.

Sweet, R. (2009). *Work-based learning programmes for young people in the Mediterranean region: A comparative analysis*. Turin: European Training Foundation.

UNDP (2004). *Arab Human Development Report:Towards freedom in the Arab world*. New York: UNDP.

World Bank (2008). *The road not traveled: Education reform in the Middle East and North Africa*. MENA Development Report. Washington DC: World Bank.

Young, M. (2003a). National qualifications frameworks as global phenomenon. In G. Donn & T. Davies (Eds.), *Promises and problems for Commonwealth qualifications frameworks* (pp. 94–106). London: Commonwealth Secretariat and Wellington, New Zealand Qualifications Authority.

Young, M. (2003b). National qualifications frameworks as a global phenomenon: A comparative perspective. *Journal of Education and Work*, 16(3), 239–258.

Young, M. (2004). *Towards a European Qualifications Framework: Some cautionary observations*. Strasbourg: Symposium on European Qualifications, 30 September–1 October 2004.

Young, M. (2005). *National qualifications frameworks: Their feasibility for effective implementation in developing countries*. Geneva: ILO.

Zajda, J. (Ed.) (2005). *International handbook on globalisation, education and policy research*. Dordecht: Springer.

4   The Contested Terrain of Educational Reform in Egypt

Fatma Sayed

Introduction

The events that have been shaping the world since 9/11/2001 have brought into sharp focus democratization and governance issues in the Middle East, issues which are themselves critically intertwined with questions of culture. International aid is highly controversial. It is already deemed by supporters to be a means for positive transformation, while opponents view it as a source of increased foreign control and domination. These controversies increasingly occupy centre stage of domestic politics in Egypt. Nowhere are the debates around culture more heated, however, than in the domain of education. In fact education has been recognized as a fundamental agent of social and economic development and poverty alleviation in developing countries and has attracted increased attention from the Bretton Woods[1] institutions (the World Bank and Intentional Monetary Fund) as well as international development assistance agencies since the 1990s. The international commitment for the Education For All (EFA) objectives was first launched in Jomtien, Thailand in 1990 'to bring the benefits of education to every citizen in every society.' International consensus for the EFA objectives was re-confirmed in Dakar, Senegal in April 2000 and again in September 2000 (World Bank, 2009).

Egypt has been among the countries that receive significant amounts of international development assistance throughout the past three decades and has evidently been affected by international development assistance trends. Along the general trends, focusing on issues of social welfare and sustainable development and placing education as a corner-stone for achieving the United Nations' unanimously agreed upon 'Millennium Development Goals,' basic education attracted significant attention from the donor community in Egypt. Various programs addressing educational reform in Egypt have been planned and implemented by several international assistance agencies, both bilaterally and multilaterally, during the past two decades (EU Commission in Egypt and World Bank internal document, 2002).

The failure or success of international development assistance (in its multilateral and/or bilateral forms) has engaged public discourse in Egypt for many years and the debate was often oriented towards the conspiracy theory, claims regarding the corruption of the government and/or development agencies, or local cultural values that get in the way of reforms. In this chapter, I argue that the successful implementation, internalization and sustainability of education reforms supported by international development assistance is highly conditioned by the social, cultural and political contexts. I briefly review the provision of development assistance to Egypt during the past two decades, its political motives, and how conspiracy theories originate and spread in the context of educational policies. I also more specifically examine how conspiracy theories played out in the case of the Center of Curriculum and Instructional Materials Development funded by the United States Agency for International Development (USAID) in the 1990s. This chapter capitalizes on a comprehensive research exploring the impact of international development assistance on education policy making in Egypt discussed extensively in my book, *Transforming Education in Egypt: Western Influence and Domestic Policy Reform* (Sayed, 2006).

The main argument in this chapter is that education reform programs operate in a climate of tangible cultural and political sensitivity and fear of the implications of potential foreign interference in education policy making. This hinders not only the implementation and internalization of programs but also the flow of potential bilateral assistance that otherwise could have been allocated to basic education. Lack of political participation as well as various political and economic frustrations tend to be projected on the public debate on education that is often used as the safety valve to release the dissatisfaction created by other public policy issues.

International Development Assistance to Egypt: Trends and Motivations

Since the signing of the Camp David Accords in 1978, Egypt has been second only to Israel in receiving development assistance from the United States (USAID) in addition to receiving international development assistance from other Western/industrialized countries. International assistance to Egypt is provided at different levels: multilateral, bilateral, and special agreements. The volume and the sources of foreign donations to Egypt have varied during the past three decades and significantly expanded after the 1991 Gulf War to reward the Egyptian role in the war. According to a report published by the Danish Ministry of Foreign Affairs, overall international development assistance provided to Egypt in 1991 amounted to US$4.6 billion, or approximately 10 percent of total world development assistance (DANIDA, 1996). The United States is Egypt's largest donor in addition to thirty-five other bilateral and multilateral organizations working in the country (USAID Congress Presentation, 1999).

Area specialists link Egypt's position as a major recipient of development assistance in the Mediterranean and Middle East region to its strategic importance, geopolitical position, its key role in the Arab–Israeli peace process, its massive population, and its cultural influence in the region. All these factors render Egypt a central agent in determining the stability of the Middle East and the Southern Mediterranean area (Sharp, 2007; Parfitt, 1997). Egypt is a key ally of the United States and Western European countries. The Egyptian régime also maintains cordial relations with other key powers in Southeast Asian and Eastern European countries. Therefore, providing development assistance and improving the living conditions of Egyptians has been of major importance in maintaining a degree of political and economic stability in the volatile region of the Middle East and North Africa. Besides its political influence, Egypt also controls the Suez Canal, the strategic sea route transferring oil from the Arabian Gulf and peninsula to the Mediterranean region, in addition to the Suez–Mediterranean (SUMED) pipeline of oil and natural gas.[2]

Another important strategic motive for providing development assistance to Egypt is the American and West European desire to contain militant Islamic fundamentalist movements, perceived as a major strategic threat to the interests of the West in the region. Such fears originated with the Iranian revolution of 1979 and were reinforced by the Algerian crisis in 1991. They gained ground following September 11, 2001. Various studies have argued that among the internal problems stimulating militant fundamentalism in Egypt are slow democratization and the failure to promote sound economic growth with equity, as well as poor prospects for social mobility, which demoralize and frustrate young people (Ibrahim, 2002). Along these lines, Washington File Staff Writer, Michael O'Toole, cites Foreign Relations Committee Chairman Richard Lugar at a U.S. Senate hearing in April 2005 on "Combating Terrorism through Education," who states that the education gap caused by poor funding of education systems all over the Middle East and South Asia "'has contributed to the rise of extremist ideologies that have provided fertile ground for terrorist recruitment in the last decade.'" (O'Toole, 2005). In fact, Edwin Hullander, senior policy adviser at the USAID bureau for policy and program coordination, stated that the Agency has tripled its basic education programs addressing poorer areas in Egypt under the Egypt counter-terrorism integrated programs to diminish conditions for terrorism (Hullander, 2004).

The Conspiracy Theory: Origins and Propagators

The 'conspiracy theory' is a coined term that refers to any presupposition that explains political, economic, social and historical events or phenomena in the light of hypothetical secret plots schemed by some underground influential and scheming conspirators. The term 'conspiracy theory' is often used with a high degree of skepticism in social science literature (especially in social and political psychology), since such presuppositions frequently lack empirical evidence and are often in contrast with institutional analysis (Domhoff, 2005).

The conspiracy theory in Egypt is the legacy of more than 150 years of Western colonialism, which began with the French invasion of Egypt in 1798. In 1882, the British took complete control of Egypt and later in the 1920s the British and French colonies and League of Nations' mandates extended over strategic regions in the Middle East, leading to the creation of the state of Israel in 1948. Ever since ancient times, colonialism has often been analogous with underground pacts and power struggles that reinforced the idea of the behind-the-scenes politics that historically have dominated political decision-making in Egypt. Even though the conspiracy theory is not particular to Egyptian political culture, it finds fertile grounds there in which to flourish. The conspiracy theory, as applied to national politics in Egypt, is the conviction that foreign or local agents are engineering episodes, events, and public or foreign policies to advance their own strategic interests against those of the country in question. The theory flourishes during times of war, cold war or 'cold peace',[3] and produces general skepticism regarding the purposes and schemes of 'the Other.' The definition of 'the Other' differs over time and is usually determined by an influential domestic elite or opinion leaders. The presumed agents of 'the plot' are not only foreigners but also sometimes nationals who act as cognizant or incognizant clients of the conspiracy. In some cases they can be minority or sub-groups from within the society itself. Such a belief can either be a genuine conviction promoted by a state of war or unarmed conflict, or mere political propaganda to justify some extreme security measures on ideological or practical grounds. The conspiracy theory is not a distinctive feature of Third World countries, who tend to see themselves as vulnerable victims of historic and modern forms of colonialism. It has also emerged in the industrialized world, sometimes in association with racism and xenophobia.

In fact, the dependency theory, upon which capitalizes the rationale of the conspiracy theory, is not a notion devised in the Middle East; rather, it matured during the 1970s to describe the state of economic and political dependency of Latin American countries on the Western industrialized world, particularly the USA. "Dependency is concerned with the influence of external forces on a network of internal relationships, structures, political and economic decisions in individual third world countries" (Watson, 1982, p. 181). Dependency theorists as well as many developmentalists often denounce the concept of conditionality of aid that links the provision and disbursement of financial and/or technical development assistance (in the form of grants or soft loans) to the recipients' adherence to the specific internal or external, formal or informal policies proposed by donors or funding institutions. In effect, the supporters of the conspiracy theory weave many of their allegations around the terms of conditionality and tied aid[4] that are imposed by donors on aid recipients and the clientelism it generates among the ruling elites of developing nations.

The climax of the Arab–Israeli war in the early 1970s provoked a huge intensification of the conspiracy rationale linked to the threat of military conflict. Ever since the peace treaty signed with Israel in 1978, Egypt has been living in a state of 'cold peace' with Israel, which Egyptians identify as an aggressive neighbor intent on enlarging its national boarders at the expense of Palestine, Lebanon, and Syria. The conspiracy rationale prevails most heavily during periods of increased tension in the Arab–Israeli conflict, and is reinforced by the belief that the world powers, led by the USA, give unconditional support to Israeli actions and veto all United Nations declarations that condemn Israeli aggression. The situation is exacerbated by Huntington's famous theory, expressed in his *The Clash of Civilizations* (Huntington, 1996), and the declaration of the war on terrorism after the terrorist attacks of September 11, 2001 followed by the war in Iraq in 2003. Advocates of the conspiracy theory use the Arab–Israeli conflict as a source of evidence regarding a '*Western plot*' against the Arabs and the continuous deterioration of the six-decades-long Middle Eastern crisis has further complicated matters. Another concern for the adherents of the conspiracy theory is neocolonialism represented by the West's economic and cultural hegemony, particularly the USA. According to John Esposito, an excessive dependence on the West at the political, economic, military and socio-cultural levels is criticized by national intellectuals as a form of neocolonialism that is exported by the West and imposed by local elites (Esposito, 2000).

If we agree that the conspiracy theory emphasizes the struggle of one's identity against the 'Other,' we can comprehend that national or group identity is always a presumed target of the plot. Education is not simply the transfer of information to new generations—it is the transfer of knowledge, which makes up the foundation of cultures, religions, as well as political, economic, and social paradigms. Educational systems provide predetermined definitions of identity (individual and collective) and distinct definitions of the 'Other.' Self-knowledge and the crystallization of one's identity are formed during early childhood, when human beings are more receptive to external influences and have fewer faculties to reflect on the information and concepts transferred to them. Accordingly, the basic education years represent the most critical formation period for new generations, and are thus – according to the adherents of conspiracy theories – the natural target, of any outside plots aimed at transforming national identity.

The Impact of Conspiracy Theory on Development Assistance and Education in Egypt

What is 'the conspiracy'? This question is addressed by Neamat Fouad's in *What is Wanted for Egypt?! The Issue of Education* (Fouad, 2001). Fouad, a university professor and columnist for the national daily newspaper *al-Ahram*, is an influential opinion leader, who has influenced the public standpoint on various environmental issues and changed the state's position with respect to certain public policies. An ardent defender of national values and traditions, she defines herself as being in the tradition of the enlightened intellectuals who came to maturity during the second half of the twentieth century, and not as an Islamist or a leftist writer. Fouad agrees with several Egyptian writers, education specialists, and others in regarding the targets of the 'plot' on education as the teaching of the Arabic language, history, and Islam. Language, history, and religion are recognized by the nation's intellectuals as the main components of national identity and pride. It is interesting to note again that British Prime Minister Margaret Thatcher's Conservative government education reforms during the 1980s identified exactly these three subjects as targets of change, aimed at increasing levels of patriotism among new generations in the United Kingdom. Similarly, following the terrorist attacks of September 11, 2001 conservative voices in the US have called for a renewed emphasis on American history and English language instruction in school curricula in order to ensure the complete assimilation of second-generation immigrants. This illustrates how history, language, and religion tend to be widely regarded as making up a triangle of national identity. Consequently, any attempt to undermine these three components of national collective identity would be to produce a vulnerable society, one that is easily dominated by stronger cultures and identities. After all, the long experience of colonialism shows that the first educational policies adopted by colonial powers were to make the colonizer's language the official language of instruction in public and missionary schools. National students were taught the history of the colonial power in order to create a fascination for the colonial power's legacy and to remind them of the colonizer's tight grip on the colony (Mitchell, 1991). As Spring (1998) observes, "Westerners imposed their forms of education as part of a conscious attempt to impose Western culture and languages. As a result, European technology, concepts of economic growth, and languages spread around the world. That English became the language of the global economy symbolizes the powerful effect of colonial education and trade" (Spring, 1998, p. 9). Hence, an education policy that forges compliance among colonized subjects by assimilating them into the colonizer's culture has been an important feature of the colonial legacy. Therefore, we cannot simply discard as paranoid the national intelligentsia's concern about the content of Arabic language, history, and religious instruction curricula. However, it is important to examine why and how they consider this identity triangle to be the target of a conspiracy.

The Arabic language, its curricula and teaching, are particularly susceptible to the effects of the controversies regarding foreign influences. The Arabic language is not simply an element of a single religious or cultural identity. For many, it is perceived as the lifeblood that circulates in the hearts and minds of the peoples of twenty-five nations and carries with it the blueprint of a whole civilization. Still, in a region wracked by conflict and war, the Arabic language remains a unifying element. For instance, a claimed target of the *imperialistic conspiracy plan* is to cripple the Arabic language or at least marginalize it in relation to English. The claimed plots aim at reducing the emphasis on Arabic, and improving the quality of instruction and increasing the importance of the English language, using it for instruction in the sciences and mathematics, thus paving the way for the hegemony of English in the name of globalization and development. The evidence put forward for this is a Ministry of Education 1994 decree that reduced the weighting given to the Arabic language in the second and third year of the secondary school exams (the tight bottleneck of the Egyptian schooling system). As a result, Arabic was placed on an equal footing with the English language in the final secondary school grades. In reaction, Moustafa Mahmoud, a renowned Egyptian intellectual, criticized the decree by writing in an *al-Ahram* daily that "Israel brought education ministers to revive the dead Hebrew language, so how come we brought an education minister to kill our language?" (Mahmoud, 1994). Meanwhile, leading Islamist thinker Mohamed Al-Ghazali reminded his readers of Egypt's experience with British colonialism and how the instruction of Arabic language was an element of resistance. In a piece published in *al-Ahram*, Al-Ghazali maintained that the Arabic language is in danger and that if it dies the Holy Qur'ān would be relegated to museums and Arab nations would lose their scientific and literary patrimony (Al-Ghazali, 1994). Other prominent and influential Egyptian writers concerned with the fate of the Arabic language resulting from the Ministry of Education decree joined in, such as Ahmad Bahgat (1994), Farouk Gouayda (1995), and Fathi Salama (1994). They criticized the minister and expressed their alarm against the deteriorating command of the Arabic language among young university graduates and even some government officials. While these writers did not mention the concept of conspiracy and blamed the Ministry of Education, Neamat Fouad pointed directly to the former Minister of Education, Hussein Kamel Bahaaeddin, whom she accused of being an agent of a conspiracy led by USAID. The second alleged target of the conspiracy is the teaching of Egypt's history, a discipline perceived as one of the most important components of national and collective identity.[5] Egyptians are immensely proud of their mosaic-like history which reconstructs a broad panorama of several civilizations. In times of political, and economic distress they appeal to history in order to derive some encouragement to go on. As a subject of study, over the last two decades, history has been taught in primary schools from the fourth grade (changed to the second grade in 2002). It is an optional subject of study in secondary schools. The history curriculum has been revised and condensed to exclude what the Ministry of Education deemed to be excessive and superfluous information that confuses students. The national debate about the history curriculum is replete with accusations to government officials claiming that they are trying to rewrite Egypt's history and render new generations more vulnerable to the influence of other cultures (Howeidy, 1999; Ammar, 1996). History is a complementary part of the social science curriculum at primary education level in Egypt, where maps of the Arab world (often poorly depicted as black and white small images) avoid indicating the location of either the Palestinian territories or Israel. This ambiguous position reflects the delicate balance that the Egyptian government is striving to maintain in order to honor the Arab–Israeli peace agreement of 1978 without turning its back on its citizens, who are enraged by the desperate fate of the Palestinians in the Occupied Territories. Fouad (2001) maintains that the Ministry of Education is deliberately rewriting and revising the history curriculum in order to marginalize the role of Islamic civilization and the contemporary history of the period surrounding the 1952 revolution period and 1967 Arab–Israeli war, when Israel occupied Egyptian, Palestinian, and Syrian land. The Ministry of Education has been accused of sacrificing the Arab and Islamic identity of Egypt in favor of its ancient one, thus diminishing national and cultural identity in favor of the neocolonial project.

Religion is a major ingredient of collective identity, especially in the Middle East. Egyptian national movements drew upon Islam and Islamic civilization as a source of national and cultural pride, and in resisting British colonialism. This was particularly true since religious education was associated more with traditional culture, while secular education was modeled after Western education systems and served to help reproduce a local elite collaborating with British institutions and less likely to contest them. Consequently, religion is arguably the third and most important target of the conspiracy. Islam is widely believed to have represented an important source of resistance to colonialism in many nations during the past three centuries. It would be logical for colonial powers to plan to marginalize it in order to weaken the spiritual reference-points of local populations. The common claim of both leftist and Islamist opposition groups is that among the conditions of the Camp David Accords of 1978 was a requirement that the Egyptian Ministry of Education excludes from the religious curriculum those verses of the Holy Qur'ān that narrate any history of discord with the Jews or the descendants of Israel. The ultimate concern is that while in the past, colonial powers employed their immediate administrations and military powers to directly and openly control their colonies, neocolonialism aims at diminishing national cultural and religious identities. In connection with this line of thought, prominent Islamist thinker Yusef al-Qaradāwi maintains that "cultural colonialism does not take over lands, but minds and souls in order to influence ideas, concepts, values, standards, tastes, tendencies, ethics and attitudes thus swaying legislation, traditions and the general morale of the whole nation" (al-Qaradāwi, 2000). Elaborating on the issue of education and national identity, Cook (2000) holds that recent education policies have raised controversies about the issues of national identity and character leading many parents to resort to private Islamic schools and free private lessons provided by Islamic charitable organizations. A general discontent with the public educational system, writes Cook, has led to a questioning of the state's ability to promote and nurture the integrity of Egypt's Islamic heritage. Regarding the concern about national identity in the face of a cultural invasion, Cook quotes Egyptian educator, Sayyid A. Bahwashi as saying, "the last and only hope for the Egyptian national character in facing future challenges is through Islamic upbringing.... It is the only safeguard from the dangers of the future.... The Egyptian national character is surrounded by global dangers that are trying to destroy it, and only Islamic instruction can save it" (Cook, 2000, p. 487).

Since it is perceived as the heart of the Arab world and the role model that shapes the life-styles of other Arabs, Egypt is deemed an important target of cultural colonialism. Neocolonialist aspirations are seen as aiming to bring about a total economic and political dependence on the West and most importantly, promote Arab passivity in the face of Israeli hunger for Arab land. Accordingly, as part of this neocolonial conspiracy, Egypt should continue to be a dependent developing country with an unstable political system that receives instructions from the West for foreign and internal policies. Moreover, Egyptians' fascination with Western cultural symbols and consumer goods should be such that it amplifies their demand for Western consumer and cultural goods and closes their eyes to Israeli aggression. This will be achieved when the Arabic language becomes second to English among the elite, Egyptian history is referred to only in the catalogues of tour operators, and religious occasions become opportunities for multinationals to launch more consumer products that continue to alienate Egyptians from their roots and assimilate them to a West that scorns them. With Egypt having reached such a stage of mediocrity and vulnerability, Israel would claim not only more Arab and Egyptian territories but also ancient Egyptian history and pride in order to forge an Israeli national identity for its flow of migrants from various parts of the world and from various ethnic and racial origins, based on a hypothetical collective history and not simply a single religion.

Several Egyptian writers claim (conscious or unconscious) state compliance with this presumed conspiracy. However, Neamat Fouad directly accused Farouk Hosni, the Egyptian Minister of Culture (and Egypt's candidate for the role of UNESCO's Director General for the October 2009 elections), together with former Minister of Education (Hussein Kamel Bahaaeddin) of being conscious agents of the conspiracy, accepting developmental aid, mainly USAID, in order to trivialize Egyptian culture and history. Fouad echoes the opinions of several leftists (mainly Nasserist) and Islamist Members of Parliament (MPs), as well as columnists in the national and opposition press who denounce the conspiracy and accuse the ruling elite of being its mediators. Islamists represented by the Muslim Brotherhood movement in the Egyptian parliament (formally elected as independent MPs) adopt a particularly critical position against the involvement of USAID in education development programs. Brotherhood MP Ali Laban was quoted by Gamal Essam El-Din in *Al-Ahram Weekly* of 30 November 2006, as demanding the execution of the Egyptian Minister of Education (Yusri El Gamal) for allowing an American expert to work on an education curriculum reform project: "'The appointment of an American expert to take responsibility for modernizing education in Egypt is an act of treason for which the Minister of Education should be executed'" (Essam El-Din, 2006). Many of the allegations cite the views expressed by Elizabeth Cheney (daughter of former US Vice President Dick Cheney and the Principal Deputy Assistant Secretary of State in the World Economic Forum in Jordan in June 2003), who stated that USAID should sponsor a new education curriculum promoting religious tolerance and boosting democratization. Her position was interpreted by critics as an American project aiming at removing educational material which Washington believes is promoting hatred against Israel (Dawoud, 2003).

The Case of the Center of Curriculum and Instructional Materials Development (1990s)

The core of the conspiracy theory in the context of education is based on arguments related to national, religious, and cultural identity. The issue of history, Arabic language, and religious education curricula has been the main concern of those writers who speak out against an intentional blurring of the teaching of these three subjects. Accordingly, the Center of Curriculum and Instructional Materials Development, CCIMD, funded by USAID and set up within the Ministry of Education in 1989, has been a regular target of criticism and skepticism. The functions of the CCIMD are, first, "to design, develop, improve, modify, test, evaluate, and revise curricula and instructional materials in all subject fields for all levels of pre-university education; and second to train leaders and counselors in newly developed curriculum and instructional materials to enable them in turn to train teachers on nation wide basis."

The CCIMD has been plagued by bureaucratic and public dissent ever since its creation. Set up by USAID within the Ministry of Education, by virtue of ministerial decree number 192/1989 as part of the Basic Education Agreement, the CCIMD was superimposed on already existent units that performed the same functions, such as the Curriculum Development Unit (CDU) and the National Center for Educational Research and Development (NCERD). The new unit duplicates the work of two others. It reports directly to the Minister of Education, and enjoys superior facilities, remuneration schemes, professional development plans, and administrative flexibility. In that sense, bureaucratic resistance was predictable. The functions of the CCIMD drew even more opposition from the intellectual elite and journalists of diverse political persuasions and stimulated intense sessions of the People's Assembly in the early 1990s. Many influential writers refer to the CCIMD as the invisible hand of USAID that aims at muddying Egyptian national identity in the minds of young generations. The main allegations have been that the CCIMD is a tool used by USAID to mislead Egyptian children on the Palestinian issue and influence their religious position on specific questions relevant to the Arab–Israeli conflict.

Egyptian researcher Sahar Ramy cites Sydney Chamber, the Vice President of Education Aid Program in USAID, regarding the objectives of USAID. These are "to help the Government improve educational methods, upgrade the educational system in Egypt, broaden the perception of students and create an international orientation for the curriculum" (Ramy, 1993). In fact, the "international orientation for the curriculum" is the element that is most contested and gives weight to conspiracy theory arguments. A fierce press campaign in the opposition newspapers, representing leftists and Islamists (*al-Ahaly*, *Misr-al-Fatah*, and *al-Sha'b*),[6] accused the CCIMD of collaborating with American experts to favor the international orientation of curricula at the expense of national identity, reducing the presence of geopolitical and historic maps and Arab–Islamic history. The CCIMD and USAID received laudatory coverage from *al-Wafd* daily newspaper (the paper of the right-wing opposition party by the same name) together with the two major official papers *al-Ahram* and *al-Akhbar*. However, the loudest voices were the disapproving ones. The CCIMD was also attacked by some of the state-aligned columnists in the national semi-official press. Criticism was often directed at the CCIMD director, Kouthar Koutchok, accusing her and CCIMD staff (including Egyptian education experts) of submitting to the will of USAID officials, enticed by lucrative salaries and stipends.

In response to such allegations, Koutchok answered that "the foreigners" have helped a lot in training and capacity-building on how to develop school curricula and enhance teaching methods, and that their assistance is evident in these fields. During an in-depth personal interview conducted with Kouthar Koutchok in March 2001, she stated that

> the interference of the USAID experts in any other subject that they are not invited to is entirely refused. If they want to help, they have to listen to our needs and not dictate their own agenda.

Koutchok added that:

> The sad event in the history of the unit, was the story of the general and comprehensive textbook for basic education classes that was meant to give an integrated curriculum that encompasses knowledge and positive behavior, and simplifies the learning process for school children at the primary stages of education. An Egyptian team of educators with the guidance of an American expert carefully developed the comprehensive textbook (a textbook that contains all subjects of study). The team conducted the field testing through focus groups with school children, guided by Egyptian and American education experts in bilingual sessions with the help of simultaneous

interpreters. The textbooks were ingeniously developed and printed and were ready for distribution. Somehow some drafts (of the translations) were stolen from the CCIMD and published in the press. The purpose was to make it seem that the textbook was originally an American textbook imposed by the USAID and translated by Egyptian workers as an episode of the presumed cultural conspiracy against the minds of Egyptian children. A ferocious press campaign was launched to attack the textbook, the CCIMD, and the director, accusing them of clientelism and a lack of national pride and loyalty. Public opinion believed the claims of those writers and no journalist took the time or made the effort to verify the story. It reached the stage that some academics published books on the issue, incriminating the work of the center. As a result, the new innovative textbooks were never used and were withdrawn from the curriculum!

(In-depth personal interview, March 2001)

Koutchok described this episode as a sabotage of the hard work, creativity, and thought of innovation in the education process. "It is mental terrorism against intellectual innovation and creativity," said Koutchok bitterly. The CCIMD director's affirmations clarifying the issue, which were often communicated through press releases or personal contacts did not persuade the critics of the CCIMD or the proponents of the conspiracy. Answering a question regarding the USAID interference in school curriculum development in Egypt, USAID mission director in 2003, Kenneth Ellis, said "the allegation that we are trying to change the education curricula is more a fear than a reality; it is entirely unfounded ... As a matter of fact, we have increased our funding to education sector (by USD 200 million by 2009) in Egypt because the government asked us to" (Essam El-Din, 2003).

The CCIMD program is also criticized by some international education experts, who blame the Ministry of Education for using American education consultants instead of investing in capacity building of national experts. They argue that the issue of curriculum reform should not be dealt with by foreign experts but by national ones. The claim is that the CCIMD is not an outcome of organizational development in the Ministry of Education but a superimposed unit that is carrying out the functions of an already existing one, resulting in internal organizational conflicts. Press campaigns in the early 1990s claimed that Koutchok was highly compensated with a lucrative monthly salary of 5,000 Egyptian Pounds (equivalent to the sum of US$ 1,500 at the time). She, however, rejected this, stating that her gross monthly salary was around half that amount. Koutchok maintained that her stipend as the director of the CCIMD unit never matched the salary of a secretary in USAID (in-depth personal interview, March 2001). Even though USAID has discontinued its direct involvement in the curriculum reform project, many critical pens in the opposition and national press have traced USAID influence on the history and Islamic religion curricula, suggesting that English language instruction is given priority over Arabic language instruction. In fact, USAID's involvement in educational development programs still attracts criticism from opposition groups on the grounds that American experts intervene in the content of school syllabi. On this issue, Hilda M. Arellano (head of USAID Egypt's mission in 2008) commented that 95 percent of the experts employed in educational projects are Egyptian and that American experts are only involved in technical assistance in areas of methodology of teacher training, use of information technologies in classrooms, production of pedagogical material and planning curricula (El-Sayed, 2008).

The Impact of Conspiracy Theory on International Assistance to Basic Education

Perceiving a foreign plot behind every decision or opinion proposed by national education experts, in or out of the Ministry of Education, risks paralyzing education reform efforts. National education reform policy makers and collaborating development agency representatives operate in a climate of acute cultural sensitivity and heed the opinions of those decrying conspiracy. The common accusation leveled against national experts or staff is that they are disloyal and unpatriotic agents of foreign powers. The deep-seated belief in a conspiracy influences the daily decisions of government and development agency officials who design programs around those concerns. Even though all funded development assistance programs take into account potential confrontation with conspiracy allegations and cultural sensitivities, bilateral development assistance programs continue to be in a more delicate position than multilateral efforts due to the political nature of bilateral assistance and the political and economic interests of individual donors. The bilateral US assistance provided to Egypt for the past three decades has been the most heavily debated source of funding for education in Egypt. On the other hand, the least controversial assistance so far has been in the form of multilateral forms of development assistance provided by the European Union and United Nations organizations, such as the United Nations International Children's Emergency Fund (UNICEF) and the United Nations Educational, Scientific and Cultural Organization (UNESCO). Yet, many voices often contest the assistance also provided by the World Bank, considering it a US-controlled institution. In the face of public skepticism aroused by strong public opinion campaigns, some projects were cancelled, as in the case of primary school comprehensive textbooks. Other bilateral donors have limited their activities in basic education to avoid being involved in such sensitive areas. Bilateral donors, such as the Japanese International Cooperation Agency (JICA), the (German) Deutsche Gesellschaft für Technische Zusammenarbeit GmbH (GTZ), the Danish International Development Agency (DANIDA), the British government, and others have dedicated most of their assistance to higher or technical education, or to subjects of study that are not related to the identity-triangle. For example, JICA assisted technical cooperation for the development of lessons in creativity in mathematics for primary education in Egypt during 1997–2000 in cooperation with the NCERD (Miyashita, 1998).Most of the above-mentioned agencies have either minimized their direct involvement in basic education programs or directed their assistance through multilateral organizations, such as UNICEF, UNESCO, the World Bank, or international non-governmental organizations, as in the case of the Canadian International Development Agency (CIDA). Answering the question about World Bank involvement in basic education curriculum reform, Mahmoud Gamal El-Din, senior operations officer for education in the World Bank Cairo Office, said that the World Bank does not participate in curriculum reform, especially after the unfavorable USAID experience in the field during the 1990s. Gamal El-Din added that USAID was attacked largely on the political and cultural levels because of the CCIMD, which he described as a successful unit that managed to produce a lot of reforms, until its activities were hijacked by press campaigns. He also said that such episodes discourage donors from working on curriculum reform and that even though the World Bank is a multilateral organization, it is too closely associated with the US, and therefore carries the same stigma (in-depth personal interview, August 2002).

Interestingly, USAID reports point out that USAID/Cairo funded a program soliciting "Increased Use of Egyptian Universities in Quality, Demand-Driven Applied Research." It was a program designed in collaboration with Egyptian universities and it achieved its predetermined targets for 1999, contrary to the case of USAID programs targeting basic education. USAID provided funds to support several small linkage grants for applied research in Egyptian universities in association with US universities that also include historically Afro-American colleges. According to the same USAID report, such grants illustrated that academic research that is aligned with developmental priorities attracts sustained support from the national private sector and increases the research and the instructional awareness and involvement of students and faculty members (USAID, 1999). While the reasons for success or failure may be related only to intrinsic program designs or administrative problems, the fact of the matter is that joint research programs did not have media coverage and have not been received with the same skepticism by the adherents of the conspiracy theory. This same fear of press coverage was shared by Malak Zaalouk, a UNICEF program officer in Cairo, who preferred to maintain a low media profile during the early years of her project to avoid stimulating the 'conspiracy' ideology that could have been detrimental to it (in-depth personal interview, summer 2000).

Conclusion

The skeptical intellectual elite supports the dependency theory view that foreign powers control local policies in coordination and cooperation with the local elite. However, before dismissing the views of national intellectuals, who belong to diverse schools of thought ranging from leftist to Islamist as unverifiable, we need to understand their rationale. The reservations of the domestic intelligentsia toward education reforms could be partially related to a historically constructed domestic identity that erects a barrier to change, especially when mediated by foreign donors. However, another important factor is the lack of communication with key local actors (such as education experts, legislators, teachers' union, political parties, technocracy, civil society and parents' associations as well as private education institutions), as well as the inability to make strong enough arguments in favor of the reform process that would persuade these actors to come on board. This process alienates them and increases their distrust and resistance to change. Exclusion from the decision-making process and a lack of formal and informal communication is one reason for the resistance to the change introduced by foreign development agencies through state institutions.

The Egyptian intellectual elite is to a large extent distant from the decision-making process, and their participation in official conferences and workshops launching reform programs often turns out to be purely ceremonial. For example, commenting on the case of the CCIMD unit, the Head of the Education Committee in the Shura Council (Upper House), Mahmoud Mahfouz said, "The CCIMD did not sufficiently consult the numerous national intellectuals, artists, and scientists, and this is why it failed, and received heavy criticism. The lack of support to several programs is due to the poor participation of Egyptian intellectuals as well as many other institutions" (in-depth personal interview, 2001). Indeed, complaints of exclusion from participation in the general process of decision-making are not only limited to national experts with Islamist or leftist inclinations, but also extend to others who are distant from the centers of power. A director of a civil society association that operates in the field of basic education, with an evident liberal ideological tendency, complained of this lack of participation. The director of the association criticized the CCIMD for being "a rigid and undemocratic Ministry of Education unit that does not consult experts and civil society associations directly involved in the field, thus reflecting the general disease of the absence of democracy in the rest of the Ministry of Education and the rigid and centralized structure of decision-making even in the most trivial of decisions" (in-depth personal interview, August 2001).

Participation in the decision-making process may be one of the keys to explaining the dominance of the conspiracy theory. In the absence of overall organizational and political democracy and given the poor opportunities for participation (usually reserved to those who agree with the state), various political and economic frustrations tend to be projected onto the public educational debate, an issue that enjoys relative freedom and openness. The fervent debate surrounding education, which is unparalleled compared to other policy issues, reveals that public discourse on education is often used as a safety valve to release dissatisfaction created by other public issues as well.

Notes

1 Bretton Woods was the site of the United Nations Monetary and Financial Conference in 1944 resulting in the Bretton Woods system of monetary management and leading to the establishment of both the World Bank and the International Monetary Fund in 1945.

2 SUMED is a 320 km long oil pipeline in Egypt, which runs from 'Ain-Sukhna on the Gulf of Suez to Sidi Kerir on the Mediterranean and provides an alternative to the Suez Canal for transporting oil from the Persian Gulf region to the Mediterranean.

3 'Cold peace' is a phrase coined by the international media and some academic works to characterize the relations between Egypt and Israel. The phrase seeks to convey the idea of a ceasefire/peace without settlement/normalization. During the past three decades Egypt adhered to the Camp David Accords of 1978 while being reluctant to totally normalize relations with Israel.

4 Tied aid requires that the funds received by a recipient country are spent on the procurement of goods and technical assistance from donor countries.

5 Egypt's peculiarity is its assimilation of its remarkable rulers of non-Egyptian origin, who all ruled in its name and ingrained the spirit of its civilization, wrote prominent Egyptian social scientist and geographer Gamal Hemdan in *The Personality of Egypt, a Study in the Genius of Place, 1975–1984* (Hemdan, 1994). Egyptians refer to Cleopatra *69BC–30BC*, Ahmad Ibn Tulun *835–884*, and Salah al-Din 'Saladin' *1138–1193* as Egyptians and not as Hellenic, Turk or Kurd.

6 *al-Ahaly newspaper:* organ of the 'leftist–socialist' National Progressive Unionist Party. *Misr-al-Fatah newspaper:* organ of the 'Socialist–Islamist' Misr El-Fatah (Young Egypt) Party. *al-Sha'b newpaper:* organ of the 'Islamist' Socialist Labour Party (The newspaper and the party were under suspension at the time of writing).

References

Al-Ghazali, M. (1994). Lughatuna al-Arabiya fi khatar. *al-Ahram*, October 1. p. 11. (In Arabic.)

Al-Qaradāwi, Y. (2000). *Thaqāfatunā bayn al-infitāh wa-l inghilāq [Our culture between openness and closing up]*. Cairo: Dār al-Shuruk. (In Arabic.)

Ammar, H. (1996). *Dirāsāt fi-l tarbiya wa-l thaqāfa 2: Mushkilat al-'amaliya al-ta'limiyya.* Cairo: Maktabat Dar al-Rabi' lil-Kitāb. (In Arabic.)

Bahgat, A. (1994). Sandouk el-dounia. *al-Ahram*, August 16. p. 14. (In Arabic.)

Cook, B.J. (2000). Egypt's national education debate. *Comparative Education*, 36(4), 477–90.

DANIDA (1996). Egypt-strategy for Danish-Egypt development cooperation. April. Retrieved March, 2000 from http://www.danida.gov.

Dawoud, K. (2003). Pushing regional reform. *Al-Ahram Weekly*, August 21–27. Retrieved February 11, 2009 from https://weekly.ahram.org.eg/2003/652/re11.htm.

Domhoff, W. (2005). Theories of power: There are no conspiracies. March. Retrieved April 6, 2009 from http://sociology.ucsc.edu/whorulesamerica/theory/conspiracy.html

El-Sayed, M. (2008). The job down south. *Al-Ahram Weekly*, May 29–June 4. Retrieved January 28, 2009 from http://weekly.ahram.org.eg/2008/899/ec3.htm.

Esposito, J.L. (2000). Political Islam: Radicalism, revolution or reform? Paper presented as part of the European University Institute's Mediterranean Seminar Series, October 20.

Essam El-Din, G. (2006). One more episode. *Al-Ahram Weekly*, November 30–December 6. Retrieved January 17, 2009 from http://weekly.ahram.org.eg/2006/822/eg7.htm

Essam El-Din, G. (2003). With the government's blessings. *Al-Ahram Weekly*, October 30–November 5. Retrieved January 17, 2009 from http://weekly.ahram.org.eg/2003/662/ec3.htm.

EU Commission in Egypt and World Bank (2002). EEP Internal Document: Memorandum of Understanding/Annex: Technical Papers. Arab Republic of Egypt, Education Enhancement Programme, European Commission/World Bank Joint Supervision Mission, February 8–20.

Fouad, N.A. (2001). *Matha yurad bi Misr? Qadiyyat al-ta'lim*. Cairo: Dar al-Fikr al-'Arabi. (In Arabic.)

Gouayda, Farouk. (1995). Qadāya wa-ārā'. *al-Ahram*, October 8, p. 14. (In Arabic.)

Hemdan, G. (1994). *Shakhsiyat Masr. (The personality of Egypt, a study in the genius of place, 1975–1984)* Cairo: Madbouli Bookshop. (In Arabic.)

Howeidy, A. (1999). New history for new millennium. *Al-Ahram Weekly*, April 29–May 5. Retrieved January 17, 2009 from http://weekly.ahram.org.eg/1999/427/eg8.htm

Hullander, E. (2004). USAID's role in combating terrorism. USAID Bureau for Policy and Program Coordination. August. Retrieved January 19, 2009 from http://www.usaid.gov/policy/cdie/8-10.pdf

Huntington, S.P. (1996). *The clash of civilizations and the remaking of world order*. New York: Simon and Schuster.

Ibrahim, S.E. (2002). *Egypt Islam and democracy: Twelve critical essays*. Cairo: American University in Cairo Press.

Mahmoud, M. (1994). Qadāya wa-ārā'. *al-Ahram*, November 12, p. 12. (In Arabic).

Mitchell, T. (1991). *Colonising Egypt*. New York: University of California Press.

Miyashita, H. (1998). *Technical cooperation for the development of creativity lessons of mathematics for primary education in Egypt from (1997–2000)*. Cairo: JICA-Egypt.

O'Toole, M. (2005). Jordan hosts conference on Arab education development: education critical for jobs, stability, prosperity. *The Washington File*. Bureau of International Information Programs. U.S. Department of State. May. Retrieved February 13, 2009 from https://www.america.gov/st/washfile-english/2005/May/20050517160312mgelooto0.6

Parfitt, T. (1997). Europe's Mediterranean designs: An analysis of the Euromed relationship with special reference to Egypt. Special Issue, *Third World Quarterly*, 18(5), 865–81.

Ramy, S.M. (1993). Impact of US assistance on educational policy in Egypt: A case study on the Center of Curriculum and Instructional Materials Development (1989–1992). MA thesis, American University in Cairo.

Salama, F. (1994). Qadāya wa-ārā'. *al-Ahram*, October 11, p. 11. (In Arabic.)

Sayed, F.H. (2006). *Transforming education in Egypt: Western influence and domestic policy reform*. Cairo: American University in Cairo Press.

Sharp, J.M. (2007). *CRS report for Congress: Egypt – Background and U.S. relations*. Washington, DC: Congressional Research Service.

Spring, J. (1998). *Education and the rise of the global economy*. New York: SUNY Press.

USAID (1999). Annual performance plan FY 2000. Bureau for Policy and Program Coordination, by Creative Associates International, Inc. for USAID, Cairo, February 28. USAID Congress Presentation 1999 on Egypt, www.info.usaid.gov.

Watson, K. (Ed.) (1982). *Education in the Third World*. London: Croom Helm.

World Bank (1996). Staff Appraisal Report: The Arab Republic of Egypt – Education Enhancement Program. Internal Document, Report No. 15750-EGT, Human Development Group, Middle-East and North Africa Region, October 21.

World Bank (2009). Education for all (EFA). Retrieved February 11, 2009 from http://web.worldbank.org/WBSITE/EXTERNAL/TOPICS/EXTEDUCATION/

5   Pressure Groups, Education Policy, and Curriculum Development in Lebanon

A Policy Maker's Retrospective and Introspective Standpoint

Nemer Frayha

Introduction

Societies differ in the ways they engage the process of policy making in the field of education. Indeed, pressure groups, which operate within any society, monitor and influence the education policy-making arena as part of negotiating and engaging the broader politics of power. These groups (be they political, religious, societal, economic, or gender-based) are concerned with the kind of education provided to the country's citizens. Each group likes to see its ideology present in the school curriculum. Thus, education policy making is influenced by competing claims to knowledge, values, interests, and the manipulation of resources and of the decision-making process. Within this context, education policy remains subject to media and public scrutiny. As a result, policy makers act within a constantly contested terrain, particularly in deeply divided societies in which ethnic-cultural identities, religious conflict, and class stratification come into play in a significant way and the question of a 'unified' curriculum emerges as a central yet contested concern.

As one of these societies, Lebanon has faced internal strife because of its religious structure which led to four civil wars between 1840 and 1975. The 1975–1989 war was the most recent and destructive since it claimed the lives of 100,000 people and left state institutions paralyzed and inefficient. Many educators, politicians, and ordinary citizens blamed the education system for being unable to form citizens who believe in their country's common identity and unity, since a large number of combatants were high school and university students.

The members of the Lebanese parliament, who met in Al-Taef, Saudi Arabia, in 1989, signed a peace agreement to stop the fighting and reform the political, social, economic, judicial and education systems. Many measures were taken gradually to reform education by adopting a 'Plan for an Educational Renaissance' in 1995, a 'New Structure of Instruction' in 1996, and by developing a new curriculum in 1995–1997 which then became the focus of concern for pressure groups keen to assert their interests and agendas. The strife between the secular and religious groups was particularly tense around the issue of religious instruction. Also, the new history curriculum and textbooks, as can well be imagined, became another target for acrimonious and lasting debates, with much pressure being exerted on education decision makers, particularly by a single-issue interest group.

It was within this very challenging socio-political context that I was appointed head of the Educational Center for Research and Development (ECRD, or CERD in French), affiliated to the Ministry of Education of Lebanon. The ECRD is in charge of education planning, curriculum development, writing school textbooks, training in-service teachers, carrying out education research and compiling statistics about students, teachers, and schools. The timing was critical since the country was trying to recover from the effects of civil war. Each group used to look at any decision taken by the government with suspicion, wary of any decision that would serve the interests of its opponent/s. Needless to say, this wariness was also present in the field of education, leading various groups to articulate their own perspectives and to promote their own interests and agendas whenever possible.

The present chapter focuses on the case of pressure groups operating in Lebanon and their involvement in education policy making. Even though the focus will largely be on development since the Al-Taef Accord, an account of what had taken place during the development of 1946 and 1968 curricula will be covered briefly as well. My aim is to address the following question: How do pressure groups in Lebanon engage with the policy-making process in order to affect education policies and curriculum development within the context of competing sectarian and political agendas and a deeply divided polity?

As an educationist, I was involved indirectly in educational policy making in Lebanon for two years, first, in 1996, as member of the Higher Planning Committee at ECRD—a position I left since I was critical of the Committee's work—and then of the Lebanese University Council, a position I took up in 1997. My direct involvement in educational policy making was between 1999 and 2002, when I was appointed head of ECRD. I have come to experience the pressure exerted by interest groups and bear the consequences of the politics of educational policy making in a direct and personal way. In what follows, I reflect on this experience.

Pressure Groups: A Policy Maker's Standpoint

Broadly speaking, a pressure group is a collection of individuals sharing common values and interests based on religious, ethnic, or political backgrounds who try to affect the decision-making process in order to have their views taken into consideration. An effective pressure group requires a well-organized, knowledgeable, and assertive membership if its lobbying efforts are to have any significant effects. Three types of pressure groups are considered in this chapter: religious, secular, and a single-issue group. We will also consider the tactics and strategies that pressure groups use in their attempts to advance their agendas with decision makers.

In Western countries, pressure groups play their role in the educational arena within a framework of rights and freedoms guaranteed by constitutions and laws. They can thus have an impact on several aspects of social and political life, including education policy and curriculum as well (Grace, 1995; Hirshberg, 2001; Ravitch, 2003; Edmondson, 2005). To a certain degree, this is the case with Lebanon where, despite a number of democratic deficits, various groups can nevertheless make their voices heard in education matters—indeed, they have no hesitation to do so even in those cases where the law does not encourage civilians to air their views.

I start by outlining how I experienced the 'political labour' of pressure groups during my tenure as head of the ECRD from 1999 till 2002.[1] As a Stanford University graduate in Curriculum and Teacher Education, I was teaching at the Faculty of Pedagogy of the Lebanese University when I was asked by government to head the ECRD. The task I was assigned involved the continuation of the curriculum development and education reform which was already under way. This reform was launched in 1994 when the government developed an economic plan and asked the Ministry of Education to work on reforming the educational system in response to this plan on the one hand, and to the Taef Accord on the other hand. Since ECRD is the technical arm of the Ministry of Education in charge of educational planning, it had the lead role in this task and developed 'The Plan for Educational Renaissance', the 'New Structure for Instruction', and the new curricula as mentioned earlier. My predecessor's term was to end in 2000, but the government relieved him of the post in early January of 1999, presumably for 'administrative reasons'. At that time, the new curriculum was being implemented in four grades out of twelve—without there being, however, an evaluation system in place, and without the implementation of the new religious education and history curricula.

Obviously, my appointment cannot be detached from the larger configurations of power operating within Lebanese society. While my specialization in the field was widely recognized, I also needed to have a member of government who was willing to recommend me. My profile corresponded to what was needed, in terms of the leadership of the ECRD and the development of a curriculum that purported to serve the country's school system in socializing a new generation of citizens for a new Lebanon. I applied for the post and competed with other professors by presenting not only my technical credentials, but also my determination to act as a specialized scholar rather than a public relations figure. My critical views about the curriculum were well known, since I had written articles to that effect in such newspapers as *Assafir* and *Annahar*, and had moreover participated in panel discussions and been interviewed on radio and television.

I came to this post with a vision of introducing a range of quality education criteria to the reform process underway. I thus focused on the training of in-service teachers, on the introduction of a new evaluation system based on competency, and a holistic approach to basic education (Frayha, 2003a). Among the projects I gave my support to was one that encouraged the principles and practice of conflict resolution (Frayha, 2003b). I was firmly convinced that this initiative was badly needed in a country like Lebanon, which had to constantly deal with internal strife. Both the holistic education and the conflict resolution projects were stopped after I was relieved from my post.

Policy and the (Missing) Question of Accountability

Controlling education is an aspect of government policy, or public policy which, as some have correctly observed, touches on all aspects of our lives in ways we sometimes appreciate and other times do not (Edmondson, 2005). Government considers education as a means to foster the orientations, values, and knowledge of future generations in ways that lead them to accept the legitimacy of the state's political system and the authority of its rulers. It is also understood that the major role of school is to form future citizens who believe in the unity of their state, participate in its affairs, and work towards its development.

It was within this frame of reference that I wanted to carry out my duties. I also expected that the Ministry of Education responsible for a whole range of tasks— including the development of educational policies and strategies as well as the hiring of teachers to implement the prescribed curricula—was also working within the same frame of reference. Needless to say, I was alert to the fact that some civil society groups would want to have their say whenever the opportunity arose, keen as they always are to assert their points of view. The work I was entrusted to do represented such an opportunity, for there is hardly anything more political than the development of curricula and the writing of textbooks (Apple, 2004).

There are several approaches conceptualizing the role and function of pressure groups in a polity. A pluralist approach to policy making, for instance, argues that policy is the outcome of struggles among groups in a social formation. Within a society, various social, economic, ethnic, and religious groups put pressure on the government to produce policy which is favorable to them, so that the policy arena is in fact a site for contestation (Edmonson, 2005). Policies are therefore the articulation, by an individual or a group, of a vision for the way something should be or should not be done. Such visions are communicated through texts, practices, and discourses that define and express these values (Schneider & Ingram, 1997). From such a pluralist perspective, then, education policy refers to rules and laws which govern the operation of an education system, but these same rules and laws are the outcome of democratic processes which ensure that various voices are heard, leading to a policy position that can be implemented by a legitimately appointed authority. This democratic process is of course deeply flawed, given that not all individuals, and not all groups, have the same access to power to affect policy.

The process of policy making is not quite the same in many developing states, including most states in the Arab region. Here, and to put it somewhat crudely, the final word is left to the highest political figure, a king, prince or president, who does not intervene in the details of the process, but who is mainly concerned with ensuring that each generation is socialized in ways that do not contradict the underpinnings of the state's political system, society's traditions and established religious beliefs. In contexts such as these, the Minister of Education typically and unquestioningly follows the policy set down in writing, and as approved by government.

Lebanon shares some of these dynamics, but it is also different in that some of the highest figures in the State do not interfere in education affairs, leaving the forum open to the minister in charge. Lebanese ministers of education therefore tend to have quite a lot of discretion, and enough autonomy to not only change basic policies according to their personal attitudes and beliefs, but also to breach laws as well. The fact that Lebanon does not have a formally articulated and written education policy gives the Minister of Education even more leeway to exercise personal judgment.

While in Lebanon the power to make educational decisions is ultimately invested in the government, the Minister is the 'real' policy maker. Given the prevailing situation in the country, then, the Minister's power is often neither curtailed from the top, nor accountable to citizens. Parents, students, and other stakeholders are rarely given the opportunity to monitor, question and challenge the performance of the Ministry of Education, despite the fact that such a right is embedded in the country's constitution. This lack of accountability leaves the door open not only for personal rather than public interests to prevail, but also for pressure groups to assume a central and largely unchecked role in policy making, whether in education or other domains. What follows is an attempt to reflect on my own experience, as a policy maker, in that very context.

The Politics of Policy Making

In hindsight, it is now clear to me that, as ECRD director, I really had little room to maneuver given the power wielded by pressure groups. Under the prevailing situation as briefly described above, there was little chance for me to stand my ground, given that groups affiliated with the religious establishment and with political parties had the power to lobby and influence official politicians in high positions. The latter were ever ready to compromise and to reach an agreement in order to avoid damaging confrontations, or, worse still, in order to exchange services and defend mutual interests. Education officials and experts are ultimately outranked by politicians, and their word is never the last one. This naturally leads to situations where partisan politics rather than educational considerations determine which policy direction is adopted.

Civil society in Lebanon is very active and exerts an important influence on many political, economic and social aspects of life, including on such sensitive areas as education policies and curricular objectives. Both religious and secular pressure groups, understandably, consider education and curricula as important sites where their beliefs and interests should be expressed and guaranteed, and indeed one way they have historically achieved this is by developing their own school systems. There are in fact—and as I note in greater detail below—more community-run than state-run public schools in Lebanon. The government school system is poorly established (Akl, 2007). The challenge that arises here is to ensure that minorities are protected from the prejudices of the majority, while the majority is, in turn, protected from any undue influence on the part of a minority. Most democratic societies have learnt to place checks and balances to ensure fair outcomes, but this kind of balance has proved elusive in conflict-ridden Lebanon.

Much of this conflict is expressed through groups affiliated with the religious establishment of the various communities. These groups effectively represent the most influential pressure groups in the country. Often, they are led by clergymen who enjoy support among the general public. They scrutinize not only the curricula but any publication in the field of literature, social sciences, education, and the arts, evaluate their potential relevance and impact in terms of their own world views and interests, and then take action. They carefully examine the contents of curricula and voice their opposition to anything which, in their views, challenges or questions religious beliefs or traditions. Religious leaders consider that they have the responsibility to watch over what 'fellow believers' learn and do. In this way, they justify their interference, not only in education, but also in every aspect of people's life and society's affairs, whether this be the mass media, politics, the economy—or education. Religious leaders and their acolytes therefore constitute influential and highly active pressure groups, who tend to consider education as a particularly sensitive area worthy of their attention, especially since they run a large number of private schools and universities.

The lobbying strategies of these denominational pressure groups typically follow four steps:

- They first scrutinize any publication and gather data about the subject of interest to them.
- They then contact the decision-maker(s) and ask for either a 'correction' or for the inclusion of a particular issue or topic.
- Thirdly, and in the event that their request fails to receive a positive response, they voice their opposition openly, indicating where they think the authorities are in the wrong.
- Finally, if this open contestation fails to work, they up the ante by using places of worship to appeal for support from believers, who are encouraged to take a stand. They make effective use of religious platforms, especially in their Friday (for Muslims) or Sunday sermons (for Christians) to deliver their message and instructions to their followers. The latter usually respond positively to the appeals of their leaders.

The religious establishment, therefore, is a key sphere of influence in Lebanese policy development. Religious leaders have access to the grass roots, and the ability to mobilize the masses in favor or against a particular policy initiative. It is important to reflect on why the religious establishment has such a hold on Lebanese politics, and it is to this that I now turn.

Why is the Religious Establishment so Effective in Impacting Lebanese State Affairs?

Lebanese society embraces more than five different ethnic groups: Phoenician, Arab, Armenian, Assyrian, and Kurd. They either follow Christianity, Islam or Judaism, but these religions include a whole panoply of denominations, numbering eighteen in all. Thus, Christians include, among others, Maronites, Greek Catholics, Greek Orthodox, Protestants, Assyrians, Chaldeans, Copts,

Armenian Orthodox, and Armenian Catholics. Muslims include Sunnis, Shi'a, Alawits and Druze.[2]

Judaism now includes only one denomination, since most Lebanese Jews have left the country. Religious affiliation, not ethnicity, plays a major role in people's identification, loyalty, stands, and activities. As one commentator pointed out,

> Lebanon is dominated by its religions. Religion is not only part of the Lebanese culture, it is the catalyst that binds the individual subcultures internally. Casual or professional encounters between Lebanese people often entail indirect questions, with the intention of finding out the religion of the other person.
>
> (Akl, 2007, p. 100)

It is understandable, therefore, that Lebanese governments solicit the support of religious leaders, groups and associations—particularly given the fact that their own standing has historically tended to be weak.

Throughout most of its history, Lebanon has been occupied by foreign powers. While these have tended to both persecute and exploit the local population, it also needs to be said that many times, such persecution was also exercised by the various religious communities. Suspicion, caution, distrust and hatred became embedded in the different denominational groups, with each religious community looking for an external protector. This led to a further disintegration of Lebanese society, with little evidence of elements that could help 'bind' the different groups together and ensure social cohesion. When the Ottomans were defeated in World War I, they withdrew from Lebanon after 400 years of occupation. The Lebanese political and religious leaders agreed to have France as the mandatory power over their country as arranged at the Paris Conference. Then the mandate statute adopted by the League of Nations required France to help with establishing State institutions and training people to carry out their national affairs. Thus, Lebanon was established as a state in 1920, the various religious communities came together in a reconciliatory approach to allow what I like to refer to as its 'caesarean birth'. Therefore, each denomination considers itself as a major contributor to the foundation of the 'State of Greater Lebanon', and claims status, influence and power in the political sphere on account of that.

The government, on its part, is often ill-placed to resist the pressures of religious groups, whether Christian or Muslim, and often gives in to their claims. The weakness of the state apparatus and its vulnerability to the pressures exerted by religious groups is attributable to a number of reasons. When the State was established in 1920, political groups and parties played a very limited role in national affairs. Furthermore, legislators have further eclipsed and muted the role of the State by making the civil affairs of citizens the prerogative of religious rather than of State institutions. Public offices are shared among the country's religious factions, and assigned according to religious affiliation of their incumbents, and not according to their political or partisan affiliations.

Lebanon's political system allows groups a great deal of freedom to express their views and exercise their rights, to the extent that some political and religious factions actually state that Lebanon, as an independent country, should not even exist. Examples of these include the Syrian Nationalist Party (which wants Lebanon incorporated into Greater Syria along with Iraq, Jordan, and Palestine), and the Islamic Liberation Party (whose founding principles state that Lebanon cannot be an independent state, but rather a part of the Islamic nation—a program which was publicly declared on television in 2008). Such political programs strip the Lebanese government of its power and credibility, rendering it inordinately susceptible to internal and external pressures. It is easy to see how education becomes a highly contentious sphere where extremely diverse political visions vigorously jostle with each other, with a view to ensuring that their interests are not only protected, but also furthered.

Civil Society and the Influence of Religious Communities

Lebanese civil society enjoys a great deal of freedom. It has a large number of NGOs, charitable and voluntary organizations, professional associations and unions, private schools and universities. However, when it comes to decisions in critical and central areas of Lebanese life, none of these civil organizations can tilt the balance in their favor. Neither can they successfully challenge the entrenched power of religious groups. Religion plays a more powerful role in determining policy issues. This explains why, for example, the attempt to introduce civil marriage in 1998 had to be aborted. Religious leaders were determined to fight the proposed bill, since this would have freed up an important area in one's personal life that was no longer susceptible to the clergy's direct control. It is the clergy that gives its blessing for marriages to be celebrated, and for children to be baptized. It is the clergy that leads prayers over the deceased, teaches children religious creeds and rituals, and mediates among people in towns and villages in order to bring about reconciliation between families and groups that have fallen out with each other. This multiplicity of roles played by clergymen in Lebanon makes them local leaders and gives them a special social status, deserving of respect and obedience.

When it comes to education, Article 10 of the Lebanese constitution of 1926 states that: "Education is free in so far as it is not contrary to public order and good morals and does not affect the dignity of the various faiths. There shall be no violation of the rights of the communities to have their own schools, subject to the general regulations concerning public education as decreed by the State" (Lebanese Republic, 2000). This remains the only article dealing with education. It has never been changed or modified, even though the constitution has been amended nine times over the past eight decades.

Based on this Article, religious groups have been able to establish and operate schools that bring up children according to their parents' wishes and religious beliefs, with little concern for a 'national' conception of citizenship—Lebanese citizenship. For instance, the Maronites have set up many schools since the eighteenth century, and so have the Catholics, Greek Orthodox, Protestants, Armenians, and Assyrians. The Sunnis, on their part, established the Makassed schools in 1878, while the Shi'a recently founded Mabarrat and Al-Mustapha schools, and the Druzes the Al-'Ourfan schools. The latter are established in areas where Druze communities live such as Al-Shouf, Alay, and Maten in Mount Lebanon, and in the Beka' and South Lebanon. All these different schools bring up students in accordance with their religious 'ideologies', especially when it comes to interpreting the country's history and identity. Some have promoted the idea of 'Phoenician Lebanon', or 'Lebanism'; others support the notion of an 'Arab identity', and yet others believe in the country's 'Mediterranean' cultural identity, even though the constitution of 1990 states clearly that "Lebanon is Arabic in its belonging and identity" (Lebanese Republic, 2000). As a result, this complex, multi-ethnic and multi-faith society of almost four million people has been vulnerable to direct or indirect cultural and political 'interference' from both internal and external powers. Moreover, all of its groups intervene at different levels in each aspect of education, especially in matters related to curricula. They are determined to have their say in what schoolchildren learn and how they are formed as citizens.

It is instructive to explore the dynamics and processes that such groups engage in when it comes to exerting their agenda. In the sections that follow, I reflect on four examples of such influence, all of which I had to deal with during my term as head of ECRD. The first concerns a chapter on 'reproduction' in one of the textbooks, the second concerns the language of instruction, the third religious instruction, and the fourth the teaching of history.

Teaching About 'Reproduction'

One of the cases that I had to deal with as ECRD director concerned a chapter on 'reproduction' in a Grade 8 biology textbook. One religious-political party objected to the inclusion of this chapter, believing it to be related to sex education. The 'offending' chapter was, in fact, merely a continuation of 'plant reproduction', and 'animal reproduction' that appeared in previous textbooks. Notwithstanding, the party insisted that it would not be satisfied until the topic was removed from the textbook altogether. It felt that such a subject should be taught from a religious perspective, at least to those students from its own religious background. As far as they were concerned, any topic related to sexuality could not be discussed in co-educational settings. ECRD curriculum planners, however, felt they had to resist this point of view. After lengthy discussions, a compromise was reached: the chapter would be moved from Grade 8 to Grade 11. Why Grade 11, one might ask? In Lebanon, the secondary school system, which includes Grades 10, 11 and 12, is not co-educational in most parts of the country, so girls taking these lessons would not be in the same classroom with boys.

Clearly, other curricular initiatives in other countries have had to deal with similar challenges. Topics related to sex education, evolution, and creationism are still contested in some states in the USA, where the production of educational materials is governed by an intricate set of rules to screen out language and topics that might be considered controversial or offensive to minority groups. Ravitch (2003), for instance, refers to "forbidden topics, forbidden words" in her documentation of the role of pressure groups like the 'Bias and Sensitivity Review Panel' in censoring social studies and literature textbooks. Many societies, however, have developed protocols which, once again, ensure that minority and majority rights and interests are kept in balance. Such protocols, however, are generally missing in Lebanon.

A Lobbying Alliance

There is a frequent conflict between the various religious groups, and sometimes among the denominations of the same religion. However, on some occasions they form an alliance to lobby for a common cause, such as to voice their opposition to civil marriage, or in order to support compulsory religious instruction, or to challenge the authority of the State over the education provided in their private schools.

Christian and Muslim denominations thus sometimes find that it is in their interest to put aside their differences in order to create a cooperative advocacy that helps them reach mutually agreed-upon goals. This kind of cooperation was less visible among the secular pressure groups, rendering the latter less powerful and influential when it came to asserting agendas in the public sphere.

In this complicated and complex context, educational policy and curriculum development have to face many challenges before they even reach the implementation stage. Such controversies and obstacles have endured over the years, and have in fact been particularly acrimonious whenever the State, in an effort to assert a notion of independence and of 'national unity', tried to introduce national curricula. In what follows I discuss the 1946 and 1997 curricula, highlighting some of the more important issues to illustrate the points at stake.

The 1946 Curriculum and the Language of Instruction

During the period of the French mandate over Lebanon (1919–1943), the school curriculum was very similar to that of France. At that time, most Christians did not object to this because they felt close to 'Western' culture and because French schools had been established in their areas for a long time. On their part, the majority of Muslims, who opposed French influence, preferred to run their schools in their own way. They had a different curriculum and different textbooks. Even the language of instruction was not the same. In the Muslim schools, all subjects other than French were taught in Arabic. Conversely, in Christian schools, all subjects other than Arabic were taught in French.

This difference between the two communities touched on the whole issue of the country's identity. Prior to independence, Christians promoted the idea of a 'Mediterranean culture' by advocating that "Lebanon should not be swayed too far to the East, to the point of losing its identity to an Arab–Muslim ideology. On the contrary, we should take care to maintain a close relationship with the West, the Christian Catholic West in particular" (Matthews & Akrawi, 1949, pp. 505–506). Muslims opposed this view, declaring that, "What is called Mediterranean culture is nothing more than a thinly veiled attempt to preserve French Catholic influence and education in Lebanon" (Matthews & Akrawi, 1949, p. 206). However, as a compromise between the views of these two communities, the Lebanese government stated in its declaration of the country's independence (1943) that

"Lebanon is a sovereign state with an Arab face" (Lebanese Republic, 1943). The idea of reconciliation is always present in the government's action regardless of the prime minister, cabinet members, and the president.

The first post-independence government declared that, "The time of national awakening in Lebanon's history shall be when we can abolish Taifiyah [sectarianism] ... From now on, the government will offer Lebanese youth an appropriate citizenship education and orient them toward freedom, independence and national pride ... Our schools should graduate a generation unified in aims and national feelings".[3]

The Lebanese government then started to develop new curricula. It tried to create a sense of nationhood among the Lebanese based on 'Lebanism', rather than on Christianity or Islam. In this way, curricular objectives and content centered on the notion of citizenship education (see Lebanese Republic, Ministry of Education, 1946). These curricula were to be adopted by the private schools, whether native or foreign, according to Article 13 of Decree 7000, 1946. In the curriculum rationale, the government indicated that it was very interested in "forming the Lebanese citizen as a participating and knowledgeable member of his society ... who would know his country's history, making him proud of its past, understand its present, and be ready for the future" (Lebanese Republic, Ministry of Education, 1946, p. 3). Curricular objectives reflected this rationale by emphasizing the national affiliation of students and being tolerant and open-minded towards each other. This is what the country needed at that time: a unified generation for a unified country, one that had more than its fair share of disagreements about its identity and affiliation.

The government also enacted a series of laws regulating and supervising the use of textbooks. The private sector, however, did not abide by these laws. Christian schools continued teaching most subjects in French, especially in the case of mathematics and the sciences. Some of these schools imported textbooks from overseas. Muslim schools—represented mainly by Al-Makassed—insisted that Arabic should be the language of instruction and communication.[4] This stand is well understood since the Makassed association is based on Islamic-pan-Arab principles. Terc (2006) concludes that, "despite a change in what aspects of its identity have been highlighted, the Makassed discourse has always incorporated both religious and national aspects" (p. 439).

Moreover, private schools did not always follow the government's regulations regarding the language and textbooks to be used. The government proved to be unable and unwilling to enforce its policy on the private sector, which enrolled more than 60 percent of all Lebanese students. Personal 'loyalty' must also have played a role, given that parliament and cabinet members were themselves graduates of private schools and private universities, since public schools only catered for primary education, and no public university existed at that time. Furthermore, the government failed to persuade private schools to adopt and advocate its vision for Lebanon, and therefore its understanding of what Lebanese citizenship meant and entailed. As a result, community schools strongly influenced their students' views and attitudes regarding the country's history, international relations, and identity in ways that were not consonant with the views and attitudes that the State hoped to get national agreement over.

The government's failure to extend its agendas to the community-based private education sector, except when it came to official examinations, reflects the power exercised by the clergy. The latter group's legitimacy seemed to be rock solid, compared with that of the government. Would such a state of affairs change over time, or would the balance of power remain tilted in favor of religious and other pressure groups? I try to address this question by considering the evolution of the new curriculum, a project that kicked off in 1997.

The New Curriculum of 1997 and the Teaching of Religion

When the revision of the curriculum was undertaken between 1968 and 1971, the internal balance of power had already shifted to one of the religious groups, i.e., Muslims. This can at least partly be explained by referring to the emergence of the Palestine Liberation Organization (PLO), and to the steady rise of Nasserism (1952–1970).[5] The Muslim community came together in its internal struggle over power with the Christian one. The result, on the educational front, was a basic change in curricular objectives. As I mentioned earlier, in the 1946 curriculum, the focus was on promoting the idea of a Lebanese 'nation', identity and citizenship. This vision, which was also vehicled through textbooks (see *Manāhij al-Ta'lim*, 1968–1971; Frayha, 1985), no longer seemed acceptable, given that many political figures openly showed their contempt to the idea of a "Lebanese nation". Just a few years after the curriculum was revised, a civil war erupted in 1975, which only came to an end with the signing of the Al-Taef Accord in 1989—reference to which was made earlier. The task now was clearly one of rebuilding Lebanon out of the ashes of internecine conflict, with education being roped in to facilitate such a rebirth. The development of new curricula which presented a unified history—as well as the writing of civics textbooks—became, as already noted earlier in this chapter, a focus of concern for pressure groups.

Religious Education and Pressure Groups

Secular pressure groups comprising scholars, lawyers, writers, artists, and professionals were keen to have a new curriculum which did not include religious instruction, as this subject had always been presented in a divisive way. The common denominator of these groups is a commitment to secularism and an opposition to the prevalent, ever-present sectarianism which, so they believed, would take Lebanon down the road to further civil wars and destruction. For these secularists—and I count myself among them—the fight against sectarianism is a duty of every citizen, and a key to avoiding future conflicts. They were therefore understandably concerned about the effects of religious instruction on the young generations, especially in a situation where inter-faith dialogue seemed well-nigh impossible. Suffice it to point out that, according to the official regulation supervising the teaching of religion, when the subject teacher, affiliated either with the Muslim or Christian clergy, steps into the classroom, students of other religions should leave the classroom, as the purpose of the session is to give their classmates instruction in their own religion. Many Lebanese believe that this practice not only reinforces students' sectarian identification, but also creates negative attitudes among students towards each other.

At first, the secular pressure groups were supported in their demands by a majority of politicians and educational decision-makers, including myself. When the new curriculum was published by the government in 1997, religious instruction was not included as a subject matter as it used to be. However, religious groups did not follow the official curriculum in their schools. Instead, they scheduled two sessions per week for religious instruction. The government did not intervene, despite the fact that its directives were being flaunted. An alliance of religious groups then tried to force state schools to adopt religious instruction too, expressing their united opposition to the government for removing religion from the curriculum. They exerted continuous pressure on the government, both through direct representation and through the media, to the extent that the government issued Decision 73, dated 10 October 1998, asking the ECRD to study the religious alliance's request and to propose a solution. This was the first sign of the government yielding to the alliance's pressure, which then resumed its campaign after the election of a new President of the Republic in November 1998, and following my appointment as new head of ECRD in 1999.[6]

No sooner had I been appointed that representatives of religious groups contacted me inquiring about the government's decision of October 1998. These representatives were invariably well-educated Christian and Muslim clergymen of various denominations, holding important posts in the hierarchy of their respective religious institutions. I had no other option, given the seriousness of the issues at stake, but to take the matter in person to the Minister of Education, the Prime Minister, and the President of the Republic. In my talks with them, I argued that the religious instruction proposed by the members of the clergy would impact negatively on students' citizenship education, and that schools would revert indirectly to discrimination between students based on their religious affiliation. The three leaders agreed that these negative outcomes were likely to occur, and privately expressed support for the position I was prepared to take. Given what I considered such high-level backing, I proposed that a course in religious studies and the common values of Christianity and Islam would be offered to all students, instead of the re-introduction of a segregated and separate religious instruction.

The clergymen were determined to fight against this proposal, which had been tabled through the ECRD. They considered it as a threat to their prerogatives in the field of education. Indeed, what they were after was the deepening and broadening of their influence. In addition to teaching religion to students at their schools, they also wanted to reclaim their roles in public schools. They saw this as a 'religious duty' they had to fulfill, namely taking whatever measure necessary in order to bring up the younger generation in ways that ensured a religious following, whether Muslim or Christian. Their resistance to the ECRD proposal was efficacious: I soon received an official request from the government asking me to take the necessary measures to develop, within one year, a curriculum and textbooks for religious instruction—and not religious studies as I proposed.

I conveyed this request to the ECRD's Specialists' Council[7] which made efforts to avoid introducing this subject in the way suggested by the members of the clergy and supported by the government. Instead, this council submitted to the government a counter-proposal, expressing its views about religious education in the curriculum, and arguing that if the subject were to be introduced, it would need to have the following main objectives:

- To enhance national unity among students;
- To focus on the common values shared by all religions;
- To emphasize the value of human beings as enshrined in these religions;
- To strengthen the ideas of love, tolerance, fraternity, and respect for the Other;
- To live in peace and harmony [*Ta'ayosh*] in all aspects of life

(Frayha, 2003b, pp. 233–234).

In order to achieve these objectives, three steps were suggested as for any subject, namely developing a curriculum for this subject matter, writing textbooks, and training teachers to carry out the teaching of this sensitive subject.

Once the government agreed to this format, a committee consisting of lay persons (chosen by ECRD) and of members of the clergy (chosen by religious leaders) was set up and mandated with developing the proposed curriculum. When the committee started meeting, a controversy immediately arose over the name of this subject matter: should it be 'religious education' or 'religious instruction'? The ECRD group advocated the term 'education', given that this oriented the subject in ways that provided all students a chance to learn about other religions in addition to their own, without the need for more than one teacher per classroom. In this way, students would not be required to leave the classroom as they do. The members of the clergy—both Christian and Muslim—rejected the concept of religious education and insisted on 'instruction', with its connotations of reproducing knowledge and value systems rather than opening them up for discussion and debate.

The ECRD and the members of the clergy both took the issue back to the government trying to justify their respective points of view. Talking on behalf of the ECRD, I was certain of the government's support because I had all along been coordinating my work with the concerned ministerial and governmental authorities, who had earlier assured me of their support on this issue. However, in the end, the government took the side of the clergy, though without actually being convinced by their arguments—it only did so in order to avoid more pressure and criticism by the powerful religious alliance.

As a result of this showdown, a new request came from the government based on its Decision 5, dated 10 November 1999, which was issued as Presidential Decree 1847, dated 12 December 1999. It once again requested me to take the necessary measures in order to have 'religious instruction' in place at the beginning of the 2000–2001 school year. Government instructions also specified that the ECRD should prepare the relevant textbooks. Those to be used by Christian students throughout their Basic Education (Grades 1–9) had to include a chapter on Islam in order to introduce them to a religion other than their own. A chapter on

Christianity should also be introduced in the textbooks used by Muslim students. Moreover, the textbooks for Grades 10 and 11 had to be divided into three parts: one for all Christian denominatons, one for all Muslim denominations, and a third having a common text about values shared by both religions.

Only the Druze representative agreed to this. Neither the Muslim nor the Christian members of the clergy could bring themselves to accept the directive. Instead, they insisted on having separate textbooks for Christians and Muslims containing nothing about the other religion except in Grades 10 and 11. The government neither rejected nor accepted their latest proposal, preferring instead to ignore the issue in order to extricate itself out of this dilemma.[8]

Many observers were surprised to see the government's response to this religious alliance which then pushed forward yet another demand: that the clergy should be given the role of preparing teachers to teach this subject matter in state schools, with the government having no role at all except paying the teachers' salaries. Each victory chalked up by the religious alliance consolidated the previous one, and prepared the ground for the next. This multi-faith group ended up making its way directly into state schools with the permission of the Minister, even though such permission was not his to give, requiring as it does the approval of the whole cabinet. The religious alliance representatives busily selected teachers, supplying them with the very same textbooks used in private schools. Their victory was complete. Government, only too sensitive to its electoral interests and the powerbase enjoyed by the representatives of the religious establishments, lost face yet again, impotently looking on without expressing a clear policy or taking a clear stand. The secularists, on their part, not only failed to remove what they considered to be a divisive subject from the curriculum; they ended up losing whatever they had previously achieved. One could not blame the clergy for their achievement; rather, their victory was at least partly due to the inability of the secularists to assert their agenda, leaving the arena open to their opponents.

The History Curriculum and the Single-Subject Pressure Group

History as a school subject has always been a controversial issue among the Lebanese. Since independence, schools have used various textbooks with different interpretations of events according to the writers' religious or ideological affiliation. As a result, students ended up learning 'different histories' of their country, which led them to have different conceptions of their national identity with a more obvious attachment to their religious groups (Jabra, 1970; Wehbe & Al-Amine, 1980; Frayha, 1985). Other studies, conducted within the same context between 1998 and 2008, show similar results concerning students' orientations. When it comes to national identity and religious attitudes, students tend to be affected by their religious affiliations and to have a weak sense of common national memory and interest (Al-Amine & Faour, 1998; Frayha, 2002; UNDP, 2008). The history subject cannot be the only one to blame for this situation in the Lebanese schools, but it is still a major factor in 'developing' or 'forging' a common national memory and identity among students. I believe that misusing the history subject-matter in schools leads to very negative consequences at the national level.

While the new school curriculum was developed within two years (1995–1997), it took three more years to complete the history curriculum: it was finally issued by Presidential Decree 3175, dated 8 June 2000. When the history curriculum was first published, no objections were made. The ECRD therefore set up writing committees for eleven textbooks, covering Grades 2 to 12. Each committee consisted of one historian, or at least a specialist in history; a school teacher currently teaching the relevant grade; another teacher or university professor specialized in the methodology of teaching social studies; and a fourth member with an experience in writing history textbooks. The religious affiliation of members was taken into consideration just as in any other curriculum committee. As a result, all religious communities were effectively represented by qualified scholars. This policy tried to circumvent and short-circuit objections from any religious groups who could put the new curriculum in jeopardy on the grounds that their faith was not represented on the committee. Every effort was made to exclude individuals who were openly ideological in ways that could harm the credibility of the project. The plan was to finish writing the textbooks for Grades 2 to 6 by the start of the 2001–2002 school year, and the remaining textbooks by the start of the following school year.

After more than a year's work, printed copies of the textbooks for Grades 2 and 3 were ready for distribution to schools in September 2001 (Educational Center for Research and Development, 2001). At that time, and in accordance with the rules, I sent a memo, with copies attached, to the Ministry informing it that the two history textbooks were ready for schools and students. Before formally approving this request, the Minister sent copies of the textbooks to some people close to him, who together formed an interest group which monitored all the details of the writing and publishing of history textbooks. It needs to be pointed out that I had already used my discretion and excluded some of them from membership in the curriculum committees due to what I considered their openly ideological positions. I viewed such positions as a 'threat' to the project's credibility. The Ministry's action was neither required nor sanctioned by any Lebanese laws. In fact, the production of textbooks, and the approval of any textbooks produced by anybody else, is the prerogative of the ECRD (Article 4 of Presidential Decree 2356, dated 10 December 1971).

Thus, two different points of view with their own standards of evaluation emerged regarding the up-coming textbooks: one reflected the view of the authoring committee and ECRD in general, while the other represented what I characterize as an intense 'Pan-Arab' and 'anti-Western' ideology. The latter is difficult to account for, given that the Lebanese constitution of 1990 states clearly that "Lebanon is an Arab state in its identity and affiliation". However, given the intricate political situation prevailing at that time—particularly with regard to the Syrian army presence in Lebanon—it was common for individuals and groups to be charged with 'anti-Arabism', a charge that often discredited them publicly. The Minister's group used this tactic in order to discredit the third grade textbook and then to rewrite a new one. They built their argument on the book content which had the temerity to claim that Lebanon was not an Arab entity prior to the Arab conquest in 636 AD. Other reasons cited by the reviewers were that the book was replete with 'historical errors'.

The Minister of Education summoned a meeting, inviting me as ECRD Head, together with the 'Consulting Committee', made up of scholars charged by the ECRD with reviewing the history and civics textbooks. To my surprise, the Minister also called in three leaders of the teachers' unions—a high school English teacher, a physics teacher, and an intermediate teacher. None of them could stake any claim to expertise in history, and yet they started pointing out 'errors' in the textbook, such as the fact that the wife of Taha Hussein (the reknowned Arab writer) was French; that the Ottomans drafted Kamel Al-Sabbah (the Lebanese scientist) into the army during World War I; that the French presented Prince Abd Al-Kader Al-Jazairi with a medal because he had protected the Syrian Christians in 1860 when they were attacked, and so on and so forth.

Arguably, the claim made was not that these well-documented events presented Arabs in a bad light and should perhaps not be included in the textbooks. Rather, the claim was that these facts were wrong. Clearly, the motive behind these objections echoed the views of some influential Lebanese groups who insisted on the portrayal of the West as a conglomerate of colonial powers ever keen to oppress Arabs; a view with which I disagree. Any mention of the West in Lebanese textbooks had, according to them, either to be avoided, or if that was not possible, to be accompanied by a negative remark. On the other hand, according to this view, even though the Ottomans had oppressed the Lebanese for 400 years, no negative reference should ever be made in their regard.

The conflict over the history textbooks—which ultimately cost me my position as ECRD Head—included the rejection of a unit titled "They have gone, and Lebanon remained: the independence of a country". This title is underpinned by a 'chain' of events showing what I believe are the cornerstones of Lebanon's history. The 'chain' includes the Arab conquest in 636 of the common era. The Minister's group wanted to exclude this event from the 'chain', claiming that Lebanon was not conquered by the Arabs, rather it was already an Arab area. Such a claim contradicts my understanding that Lebanon or Phoenicia was under the Byzantines' control, and it was a Christian society speaking the Syriac/Aramaic language.[9]

I reckon that the above conflict with the Minister's group was not so much on how to look at historical facts, but how to interpret them and what to include as part of historical 'chains'. It was also not about 'facts' or 'errors' as much as it was about specific 'constructions' and competing imagined conceptions of identity, and 'national' identity at that. The Minister's group wanted to construct and represent Lebanon's history as a collection of events played out within the larger theatre of the region's history. Lebanon would thus appear as a peripheral entity, with the Middle East and Arab world being the protagonist on center stage. The ECRD, and I on my part, wanted to represent Lebanon's history and culture in a way that safeguarded its distinctiveness and uniqueness. Indeed, my conviction was that if students were presented with a history book that marginalized their country's culture and role throughout history, they would not be proud of it, or love it and protect it. History, for us, was at the heart of our goals for citizenship education.

It is important to point out that I did not question Lebanon's Arab identity or that of any textbook writer, especially given that the constitution already identifies Lebanon as an "Arab state". In other words, the debates, including my position as

ECRD Head, were political in nature, and could only be 'decided' in the broader field of political power—something that effectively and ultimately did take place.

I was in fact summarily dismissed from my post, accused by the Minister of "writing textbooks full of mistakes" (*Annahar* newspaper, 14 December 2001). Another person was appointed in my place. A new history curriculum and new textbooks were written. Those textbooks I had been responsible for were discarded while the newer textbooks have not been distributed to schools because a large group of citizens would not accept Lebanon's history presented to students as written by that pressure group. Thus, these textbooks have been stored away for years waiting till an expedient Minister feels there is a suitable 'political opportunity' for distributing them.

A political culture that expects no politician or deputy to interfere with what his colleagues have done means that nobody challenges the Minister of Education, whose support for a strong ideological view of history went against the "unified history textbooks" mandated by the Al-Taef Accord. Such are the ways of raw power.

Reflections

Lebanon seems to be quite a unique case when it comes to the development of its education sector. As I have noted in the sections above, it has been religious groups, rather than civil or secular society, that have contributed most effectively to founding the State, and they still play a major role in its affairs. As a consequence, religious pressure groups outweigh secular groups in influencing the state's politics in general, and education policy in particular.

The members of religious pressure groups, both Christians and Muslims, are organized, knowledgeable, and assertive. They have proved able and willing to use these qualities efficiently, and to achieve their goals. In contrast, while being knowledgeable, secular pressure groups have tended to lack sound organization, possibly because their members are a motley group, with very diverse professional, ideological and cultural backgrounds. They have also proved to be less assertive, failing to intervene in any effective manner when the decision to reinstall religious instruction was made.

The religious alliance, on its part, proved remarkably strategic, making good use of its links with the grass roots in order to mobilize 'believers' behind them. They calculated their odds carefully, and planned to take action knowing well who they should contact and when. They made alliances, patiently and consistently built up their connections and networks where it mattered, and followed up one victory with another, thus ensuring a deepening hold on the apparatus of power.

The balance of power is such in Lebanon that single-issue interest groups have a good chance of success. Ministers tend to cooperate with pressure made in an organized manner, as the case of the history interest group shows. They were not only able to stop the adoption of the new textbooks, but also managed to persuade the Minister to commission the development of a new curriculum and the writing of new textbooks. Here, we have a good example of a pressure group that, despite being small in number, was effective: it was well organized, knew what it wanted, and was assertive. It had no qualms in manipulating information in ways that served to convince others about their own ideological position. A minority group, without formal legitimacy, was nevertheless capable of transforming its vision into policy.

Pressure groups in education—as much in the wider public sphere—can be a sign of democracy, but can equally be a threat to democracy. When pressure groups can insinuate themselves within ministries and impact the policy-making process in ways which are not open to scrutiny and accountability, then serious governance issues arise. That seriousness is heightened when there is a lack of a policy framework and a vacuum in governance protocols, leading to situations where those in authority can make decisions without bearing any responsibility for the consequences or outcomes. It is even more serious when pressure groups serve narrow interests, without consideration to what might be called the 'greater good' of the polity. And that is exactly what I have tried to suggest in this chapter, namely, that a sound curriculum and educational practice have been jeopardized by powerful groups that fail to subsume their sectarian interests for a greater sense of the public good.

Notes

1 I remained in this post until January 2002 when the Minister of Education relieved me of my duties.
2 Demographic statistics are a sensitive matter in Lebanon, something of a taboo, the belief being that denominational groups might use this information to wrest greater shares of political power (Akl, 2007). While some claim that Muslims comprise 70% of the total resident population of the country, with the remaining 30% being Christian, it is actually difficult to know the exact percentages. The UNDP, for instance, avoids giving a breakdown by religious affiliation, reporting only that the total Lebanese population was 3.5 million in 2003.
3 As cited in Abou Haidar (1979, p. 115), personal translation.
4 Makassed schools kept using Arabic to teach math and sciences up to 1999, when a written request reached ECRD asking for textbooks to be provided in English or French rather than in Arabic. It transpired that parents had lobbied for this change, given the difficulties their children were encountering when pursuing their higher education, which is mostly private, and where English or French are often used. While the school administration had initially resisted parents' demands, it quickly gave in when parents indirectly 'threatened' to withdraw their children and to place them in other schools.
5 Gamal 'Abd Al-Nasser assumed Egypt's presidency following a military coup in 1952. After a two-year interim rule by his colleague, M. Najih, Nasser took charge of the country from 1954 until his death in 1970. He was a charismatic leader and ardent advocate of Pan-Arabism. People of most Arab countries looked up to him as their champion and were strongly affected by his policy towards the West. Since Pan-Arabism was very strong among Lebanese, especially among Muslim groups, Nasser supported them vis-à-vis other groups, including Christians, who were 'labeled' as pro-West. The Palestine Liberation Organization (PLO) in Lebanon followed the same line.
6 Even though I opposed the way the curriculum was developed as a 'subject-matter curriculum', I strongly supported the policy of having religious teaching out of it. It is worth mentioning that I never had any confrontation with religious groups over this

issue. I considered the curriculum as a main component of educational reform and as a means to shape students' personalities.

7   The ECRD has a Council that comprises four 'specialists' and is headed by the ECRD Head. It operates as the administrative body of the ECRD.

8   Clearly, the alliance between the various religious groups carried a lot of weight. It shows, once again, where the power truly lies. Interestingly enough, such power has different aspects to it. The Druze representative, for instance, felt outmaneuvered by his 'colleagues', and ended up withdrawing from the committee. He objected to the idea of having a special textbook for each religion, preferring instead a unified textbook for students of different religious backgrounds. The Druze, considering themselves a Muslim denomination, do not have a publicly visible and accessible holy scripture, as is the case with majoritarian Christians and Muslims with their Holy Books, the Bible and Qur'ān, respectively. In their case, the Druze selectively introduce followers to the study of the Al-Hikmah, their holy book only when they are mature. The Druze are therefore open to the idea that their children are exposed to knowledge about religions in general, but do not want them to be instructed in the creed of any single faith.

9   This view is expressed by the most renowned historians of the Middle East, such as Philip Hitti, Jawad Boulos, Kamal al-Salibi, Costantine Zureik, Assad Ristom, Fouad Ifram al-Boustani, and Sabatino Moscati. Lebanon was part of the Byzantine Empire from the fourth century until 636 AD, and its people consisted of Christians speaking the Syriac/Aramic language. "Lebanon", says Hitti (1957, p. 257) "remained Christian in faith and Syriac in speech for centuries after the Islamization and Arabization of the entire area."

References

Abou Haidar, Sh. (1979). Siyasat Lubnān fi al-Hakl al-Tarbawi Ibbān al-'Ahd al-Istiqlāli [Lebanese policy in the field of education during the independence era]. Dissertation, St. Joseph University, Beirut . (In Arabic.)

Akl, L. (2007). The implicaions of Lebanese cultural complexities for education. *Mediterranean Journal of Educational Studies*, 12(2), 91–113.

Al-Amine, A., & M. Faour (1998). *Al-Jami'yun fi Lubnan Watijāhātihim: Irth al-Inkisāmāt [Academics in Lebanon and Their Orientations: The Heritage of Divisions]*. Beirut: Lebanese Association for Educational Studies. (In Arabic.)

Apple, M. (2004*). Ideology and the Curriculum*. 3rd Edition. New York: Routledge.

Edmondson, J. (2004). *Understanding and Applying Critical Policy Study: Reading Educators Advocating for Change*. Newark, DE: International Reading Association.

Edmondson, J. (2005). Policymaking in education: Understanding influences on the Reading Excellence Act. *Education Policy Analysis Archives*, 13(11). Retrieved 20 August 2009, from http://epaa.asu.edu/epaa/v13n11/.

Educational Center for Research and Development (2001). *Nāfizah 'Ala Al-Mādi, 2 [Window on the past]*. Beirut: ECRD. [Third grade history textbook] (In Arabic.)

Frayha, N. (1985). Religious conflict and the role of social studies for citizenship education in the Lebanese schools between 1920 and 1983. Doctoral Dissertation, Stanford University, School of Education.

Frayha, N. (2002). *Fa'iliyat al-Madrasa fi Al-tarbiya Al-muwātiniya [School's Effect on Citizenship Education]*. Beirut: Sharikat Al-Matbou'at. (In Arabic.)

Frayha, N. (2003b). *Al-Markaz Al-Tarbawi fi 1017 Yawm [The Educational Center in 1017 Days]*. Beirut: Dar Al-Ibdā'. (In Arabic.)

Frayha, N. (2003a). *Al-tarbiya al-shumuliya wal-tajriba al-Lubnāniya [Global Education and the Lebanese Experience]*. Beirut: Dar Al-Ibdā'. (In Arabic.)

Grace, G. (1995). School leadership: Beyond education policy borrowing. *Comparative Education*, 31, 303–310.

Hirshberg, D.B. (2001). Northern exploring: A case study of non-Native Alaskan education policymakers' social constructions of Alaska Natives as target populations. Doctoral Dissertation, University of California, Los Angeles.

Hitti, Ph. (1957). *Lebanon in History*. London: Macmillan.

Jabra, J. (1970). Political orientation of Lebanese college freshmen: A survey. Dissertation, Catholic University of America.

Lebanese Republic (1943). *Lebanese Constitution.*

Lebanese Republic (2000). *Lebanese Constitution: Its History, Amendments and Current Text (1926–1991).* Chafic Jiha (Ed.). Beirut: Dar Al-'Ilm Lilmalāyin.

Lebanese Republic, Ministry of Education (1946). *Manāhij al-Ta'lim* [*The Curricula*]. Beirut: Matba't Majallat al-Thaqāfa. (In Arabic.)

Lebanese Republic, Ministry of Education (1968–1971). *Manāhij al-Tal'im* [*The Curricula*]. Beirut: Matba't Majallat al-Thaqāfa. (In Arabic.)

Matthews, R., & M. Akrawi (1949). *Education in Arab countries of the Near East.* Washington, DC: American Council on Education.

Ravitch, D. (2003). *The Language Police: How Pressure Groups Restrict What Students Learn.* New York: A. Knopf.

Schneider, A., & H. Ingram (1997). *Policy Design for Democracy.* Lawrenceville, KS: University of Kansas Press.

Terc, M. (2006). "A modern integral, and open understanding": Sunni Islam and Lebanese identity. *Comparative Education Review*, 50(3), 431–445.

UNDP (2008). *Al-Tarbiya wal Muwatana* [*Education and Citizenship*]. Research Study. Beirut: UNDP.

Wehbe, N., & A. Al-Amine (1980). *System d'Enseignement et Division Sociale au Liban.* Paris: Le Sycomore.

Part II
Re-calling Voices

6   Education and Ethnography

Insiders, Outsiders, and Gatekeepers

Linda Herrera

Introduction

This chapter deals with critical ethnography as a research approach to interrogate and intervene into the practice of schooling. It is divided into three sections: part one deals with the question of why ethnographies of Arab schooling are so rare; part two makes a case for the efficacy of ethnographic research to inform educational practitioners, policy makers, and academics; and part three provides some snapshots of schooling by probing the everyday life of a girls' school in Cairo with emphasis on how the ethnographic ethos can play a part in raising consciousness for a schooling grounded in principles of equity and justice.

Where is the Ethnography of Arab Schooling?

Schooling plays a vital role in the lives of millions of youths in the Arab states who constitute the most schooled generation in history. Yet little is known about the everyday functioning of schooling in the region and the ways it prepares (or fails to prepare) the young for participation in economic, socio-cultural, and political life. This gap in understanding about schooling and society in the Arab states can in part be attributed to the type of research that informs our knowledge of educational processes and the scarcity of independent qualitative and critical ethnographic accounts of school life (see Herrera & Torres, 2006a). Some excellent works, many of which deal with Islam and education, draw on interviews, life histories, individual school histories, limited classroom observation and other qualitative methods (see Eickelman, 1985; Fortna, 2002; Hamouda & Clement, 2002; Ichilov & Mazawi, 1996; Messick, 1993; Starrett, 1998; Zeghal, 1996; Hefner & Zaman, 2006). In addition, a number of insightful large-scale studies from international development organizations and NGOs combine quantitative analysis with a qualitative component (see El Tawila *et al.*, 1999, 2000; Awartani *et al.*, 2007). But in-depth, independent, ethnographic studies of the life world of schools remain a rarity.

The ethnographic lacuna can be explained in part by the limitations of the method. National school systems are vast and varied. Egypt, for instance, which boasts by far the largest pre-university education sector in the region in terms of sheer numbers, contains some 37,000 schools, 15.5 million pupils, and 1.5 million staff of whom 807,000 are teachers (UNESCO, 2006, p. 9). An ethnographic study might include as few as one and as many as a handful of schools. By its very nature, ethnographic research deals with a small and statistically insignificant sample size and, as such, cannot claim to be representative. Indeed the method does not attempt representativeness but in-depth insights that cannot be garnered through surveys or questionnaires alone. Many researchers and organizations involved in commissioning or undertaking educational research design large-scale surveys to be able to make statistically convincing generalizations about school systems. Even with the emphasis in recent years on "evidence-based research" and "child-centered approaches" much of the research commissioned, for example, by UNICEF, UNDP, or the World Bank, takes a normative approach to schooling and development that supports the prevailing human capital and economic development models; they offer little scope to question, reject, or offer alternative visions, demands and arrangements for societal, economic and political justice.

A second and perhaps more fundamental reason why so few ethnographic accounts of schooling in Arab states exist is due to the problem of access: it is incredibly difficult—though not impossible—to gain access to institutions such as schools that are considered part of the security apparatus.[1] Put differently, there are barriers to carrying out ethnographic and other forms of qualitative research in authoritarian régimes where control over information and information gathering is subject to censorship and regulated by the state (Shami & Herrera, 1999).

As a researcher who has been involved in conducting and coordinating ethnographic research in schools in Egypt for two decades, this chapter provides an opportunity to reflect on the practice of ethnographic research, its limitations, and the role it can play in contributing to a richer epistemic landscape of schooling and society in the Arab states. More specifically, it aims to serve three general purposes: to advocate for the need for critical ethnographic research that can lead to a more empirically grounded and evidence-based understanding of the life world of schooling for the purpose of improving it towards more equity and democracy; to reflect as an educational ethnographer on the challenges and misconceptions about carrying out ethnographies of schools in Arab states; and to provide some vignettes of classroom life in Egypt as a way to raise some of the ethical concerns that the ethnographer invariably will encounter.

Why Critical Ethnography?

The ethnographic method is a means for both studying *and* engaging in a dialogue with children, teens, teachers, and other groups whose voices may be underrepresented or entirely neglected in mainstream narratives about schooling. In the words of renowned educational ethnographers George and Louise Spindler, ethnography is essentially about studying the "culturally constructed dialogue," the process of "action and interaction" that takes place between social actors (1997, p. 51). The school, seen as a microcosm of society, can serve as a window into understanding how a range of social relationships take shape and how they are resisted, negotiated, and, potentially transformed (Carspecken, 1996; Levinson,

Foley, & Holland, 1996; Morrow & Brown, 1994; Spradley & McCurdy, 1972; Torres, 2006). The ethnography of schooling is also valuable because of the different audiences it can reach; it can potentially inform policy makers, educators, public intellectuals, social scientists, political scientists, government officials, international development practitioners, and youths, all of whom have tremendous stakes, collectively and individually, in the quality of education systems.

A simultaneous strength and weakness of the ethnographic method is that it is flexible and open-ended. This does not mean that the researcher should enter the field unprepared with the hope of finding direction and inspiration somewhere along the way. The ethnographer should prepare by identifying what Bronislaw Malinowski calls, "foreshadowed problems" which are "revealed to the observer by his theoretical studies" (Malinowski, 1922 cited in Hammersley & Atkinson, 1983). The approaches, or foreshadowed problems raised here derive from a proclivity towards critical theory and critical pedagogy. When *critical* is used in the context of critical theory, it contains three distinct yet interrelated meanings. The first meaning relates to "unveiling ideological mystifications in social relations." The second "even more fundamental connotation is methodological, given a concern with critique as involving establishing the presuppositions of approaches to the nature of reality, knowledge, and explanation." The third dimension "is associated with the self-reflexivity of the investigator and the linguistic basis of representation" (Morrow & Brown, 1994, p. 7).[2]

On this last point, the ethnographer will confront a host of challenges about identity, representation, and audience which can seriously test the ethnographic enterprise. Ethnographic research requires reflexivity, a conscious awareness of the researcher's place in the construction of knowledge, and recognition of how we are all embroiled in relations of power whether we like it or not. As Hammersley and Atkinson assert in their important work on ethnography, every researcher is "part of the social world we study … This is not a matter of methodological commitment, it is an existential fact. There is no way in which we can escape the social world in order to study it" (1983, pp. 14–15). The critical researcher must acknowledge her biases and theoretical positions, must reflect on her self-identity and the ways other perceive her, and be prepared to negotiate with the many gatekeepers whom she will meet throughout the journey.

Moving from the Outside to the Inside

The practice of ethnography can be likened to a series of encounters with gatekeepers who have firm ideas about who should be allowed in, who needs to be kept out, and, in the case of uncertainty, who should sit on the fence and wait. The very first gate one encounters is the actual gate that protects the entrance to a school. The researcher can face a difficult, sometimes insurmountable problem, of how to gain access to the physical space of the school. Schools in Egypt as in many Arab states, especially public sector schools, are highly restricted zones that are designed to keep outsiders at bay (which is a sensible policy given that schools act *in loco parentis*).

My first experience with a security gatekeeper arose in relation to research I planned to conduct on an Egyptian girls' school for an MA thesis in anthropology at the American University in Cairo (AUC). It took nearly two years from the time of getting the first letter of introduction from the University to actually walking through the school (see Herrera, 1992). As a US national and foreign resident in Egypt, the permission process entailed getting clearance from both the Ministry of Education security office and the state security office. When I asked an officer why so much caution was being exerted for a simple research, he explained that they had to ensure that I did not want to get into a school for purposes of spying, or, I later found out, proselytizing. When asked why a spy would want to study a school, he said that as a foreigner I might see some bad things and they wanted to make sure that I was not someone who wanted to harm Egypt. I remembered these words about causing harm to Egypt when it became time to make decisions about how to write up the study and make choices about how to represent school life in a way that would be fair but hopefully not damaging.

After passing the security check, the next hurdle was to get approval from the Ministry for my research proposal. The research office of the Ministry of Education required that I submit a concise research proposal with the presumed questionnaire. I prepared a proposal but explained that I did not intend to administer a questionnaire, for I was doing a qualitative study (*dirassa kayfiyya*), an ethnography (*ethnographia*), based on participant observation interviews (including life-history interviews), focus group discussions and discourse analysis. The research officer explained that these were not valid terms to use in a formal written research request to the Ministry. He insisted, "what you mean to say is you want to do a *survey*. Here in Egypt we call research 'survey' (*istimāra*). Where's your questionnaire?" I eventually relented and drafted a questionnaire which I eventually ended up using to determine the socio-economic background of students. My file was dispatched to a special office of research and training and sometime thereafter I received a letter, to my immense surprise, granting me permission to carry out a research in the said school for the entirety of the academic year.

In another experience of obtaining research clearance, the process was somewhat different. From 2001–2003 I coordinated an education working group at the International NGO, the Population Council. The group consisted of ten Egyptian scholars who worked in the critical tradition and who did not have experience carrying out qualitative ethnographic research, but were keen to experiment with it.[3] On behalf of the group I directly approached the Undersecretary to the Minister who, in his former position as a university professor, had written about the benefits of critical ethnography and had even led a discussion on the topic with the group. He graciously, though not without some reservations, accepted to push through the research request which was granted in less than two months.[4] Gaining permission to access schools is generally much faster the higher the connection (*wāsta*).

Once the research permit is in hand, the next challenge is how to present oneself to the school community in a way that will inspire trust and legitimacy. This process can be as tricky—or as smooth, as the case may be—for the foreigner as for the Egyptian, the Christian as for the Muslim, the woman as for the man, the young as for the older. I remember worrying as I made my way to the school for my first day of research in 1990 that I might face hostility because of political tensions during that period with the US, and never be welcomed by the school community, but my fears were soon quelled. As long as I was willing to address the many questions directed at me in an open and honest way, show interest and respect in the opinions and lives of the members of the school community, accept the light teasing that was directed at me with good humor, and behave with the male teachers in a professional manner, I found myself for the most part in a welcoming environment.

Being in my mid-20s at the time, female, and a western foreigner could have posed complications, especially with regards to dealing with unmarried male teachers. In my first week at the school I greeted a (single) teacher who had introduced himself to me earlier in the week, Mr. Mahmood, as he was sitting around a table with his fellow math teachers. His colleague, a buxom woman in her 40s, eyed me slyly and then shouted out, "Mahmood, I think Linda's trying to flirt with you. I can tell she likes you a lot! What do you think?" She let out a cynical laugh as I stood there mortified. A more senior math teacher whose class I had attended the previous day, came to my defense and said, "No! She's married and has a daughter." The mood instantly changed and the woman abruptly stopped laughing, became curious, and continued with a flurry of questions that would be posed numerous times by other teachers, pupils and parents. My answers went something like this:

"How old am I? I'm 26 years old. My daughter? Her name is Shiva, she's almost two years old. What kind of name is that? It's Persian. No, my husband's not American, he's Iranian. Yes, he's Muslim. Yes, he's Shi'i. No, I haven't converted to Islam. My religion? I'm Christian. Why haven't I converted? Because I'm not convinced and only God knows if and when I will be convinced. Why don't I look American? Because my mother's family was originally from Lebanon and my father's from Spain. What does my husband do? He's a professor at the American University in Cairo. How long have I been living in Egypt? For four years. Yes, I really love Egypt a lot, it has the best people (*ahsan nās*). Which country is better? Well, I prefer some things about Egypt and other things about America. Each place has its strong points." And so the basic details of my life became known and spread throughout the school community.

Over the months many teachers pressed me for more personal information, sought out my views on a range of social and political issues, and, above all, initiated conversations about religion. The Christian teachers wanted to understand how my family could have accepted that I marry a Muslim man and were curious to know how I was dealing with a mixed religious marriage. The Christian teachers invited me to their churches and sometimes initiated discussions about religious discrimination in the school and often sought my ear to complain about what they perceived as unfair treatment of Christian staff and students.[5] Some of the female Muslim teachers held regular conversations with me about why I should convert to Islam, invited me to religious events, and expressed concerns about the religious education of my daughter. Whereas I was expecting my identity as a woman and foreigner to outweigh other identities, instead it was my mixed-religious family life that became the main object of curiosity.

The pupils, for their part, considered it a matter of amusement to have a non-authority adult in their midst, a foreigner who showed interest in their lives and wanted to spend time with them and converse about their opinions about school life. They showered me with affection and exuberance. They invited me to cookies and chips at break time, crowded around me and spoke over each other when I had questions, and followed me halfway home to continue chattering about school matters. In the first weeks I was worried about being a disruptive presence in the classroom as girls would sometimes pass me notes, crowd around to kiss me before the class started, turn around to smile at me and wave during the lesson, or jostle to sit next to me. (When a single chair was available I would sit in the front corner of the room, but if not I would sit in the back of the room at a bench-style desk with one or two of the students.) With time I was less of a disturbance though I was never a fly on the wall.

After the initial curiosity wore off, I moved more unobtrusively through the school grounds and my relationship with the teachers shifted to a state of more normalcy as we learned that we shared many common points of interest. We related to each other as parents, age cohorts, women, peers, and Cairenes.[6] But most of all we were joined by a common interest and commitment to educational justice which connected us in ways that transcended nationality, religion, gender, age, class and other marks of identity. We engaged in numerous discussion and debates about a range of issues pertaining to education and the organization and practice of schooling. Teachers were especially concerned with labor issues since they earned what was essentially an unlivable wage and struggled with a number of unfavorable conditions such as over-crowding of classrooms, excessive inspection and surveillance, and sometimes incapacitating bureaucratization. Teachers often asked me to record their grievances in the hope that my research would play some role in informing policy change to their advantage. I did not make promises that what I wrote would make a difference, but I assured them that I would do my best to ensure that their grievances would be heard.[7]

Egyptian colleagues who took part in the above-mentioned education working group at the Population Council, mid-career men and women from both the Christian and Muslim faiths, noted similar kinds of early cautionary interactions with school staff when they started their ethnographic journeys. Some related how teachers avoided them in the early days for fear that they were spying for the Ministry of Education, or trying to find out about who was giving private lessons (an illegal but widely practiced extracurricular activity), or working undercover for state security trying to find out if anyone was spreading militant Islamic messages. But once they established their identities as critical education researchers, teachers opened up to them and placed great hopes on them to do something about the unfavorable conditions. One researcher who conducted her study in rural schools in Upper Egypt, described her experience as follows:

> For the record, I would like to state that a spirit of goodwill and cooperation existed between members of the local district education office, school

principals, deputies, and teachers during the course of this study. The school community welcomed me warmly throughout the entire four-month research period in 2003. At first I attributed this warm reception to the legendary hospitality of Egyptian rural society. But it became clear that the community was eager to participate because they regarded it as a way to reach education officials. There was an overwhelming desire on the part of most participants to work towards improving both the education system and the conditions under which they worked. By sharing aspects of their work and lives with me, these teachers, even those whose words ring with hostility and anger, hoped that their participation would lead to a greater awareness of their struggles and situations. The female teachers who cooperated with me were seriously interested in benefiting from the experience. They asked me many questions about how to provide their daughters with a future that will ensure the rights to which they are entitled.

(Maugith, 2006, pp. 137–138)

Ethics of Doing and Writing Ethnography

The first and enduring ethical principle of any researcher, critical or otherwise, remains "do no harm." A researcher must enter the field with humility in the knowledge of her own ignorance, with a spirit of respect, honesty and good will towards the community in which she is entering, and an understanding that her presence, questions, and intentions—good as they may be—may not be greeted with overwhelming enthusiasm. The ethnographer, like any researcher, is faced with how to make sense of and explain the social world under study and convey it in a way that is responsible and adheres to ethnical principles. But at the same time, it remains imperative that the researcher not compromise on quality and "the rigors of scientific inquiry," a point eloquently elaborated by Van Heertum who states:

> Research can still start from a standpoint with a particular ethical and political project in mind, but it should adhere to the rigors of scientific inquiry and ensure that it is not skewed to a given end. Through a balanced and reflexive approach, a science could be implemented that is verifiable, open to critique, and that looks for evidence that does not simply produce the results that comport with researchers' desires. In this vision, practitioners would scrutinize research methods and theory for their limitations, lacunas, and underlying biases, as they work sedulously to engage disconfirming evidence and alternative narratives. At the same time, they should work to avoid dogmatism and exaggerated claims about the significance of their research at all costs.

(Van Heertum, 2005, p. 13)

In addition to avoiding dogmatism, the researcher should avoid being an apologist or resort to cultural relativism to explain away any practice. Instead, the ethnographer, through a process of consultation, open inquiry, and empathy, must try to find ways to deal with all the shades of social practice in a balanced and fair way. How to deal with information that is less than flattering, what to include in a study, how to address questions of language and audience, raise important ethical issues which require deep introspection on the part of the researcher and have no easy answers.

To address some of these issues of ethics, I will return to the first study I carried out in 1990–91 in a girls' preparatory school in Cairo and reflect on difficult encounters and choices I grappled with as a foreign ethnographer (Herrera, 1992). The research was carried out in a preparatory school in Cairo (*madrasa i'dādiyya*), which in other school systems carries the designation, middle school or junior high school (grades 6–8). The study was meant to address gaps in educational policy and anthropology. As it was about a public sector girls' school that catered to pupils from the urban poor to the lower middle class, it had a gender and class component. As an Egyptian preparatory school for girls between roughly 11–13 years of age, it was also concerned with the life stage of adolescence and the type of gender and citizenship socialization, or put differently, the "upbringing" that was taking place at the school through rules, rituals, and formal and informal practices.[8] Adolescence is an especially important transitional life marker in Arab society, and a period when gendered policies become more pronounced in schools.[9] Finally, it sought to understand if the young themselves acquiesced to or resisted these normative frameworks of what it meant to be an Egyptian/ Arab adolescent schoolgirl. In short, my main interest was to study schooling and the overlapping processes of nation building, upbringing, political (i.e. citizen) socialization, and agency as they pertain to urban adolescent girls. As I came to know and better understand teachers, it also evolved into a study that addressed teachers' perspectives and work conditions. It did not take long for me to realize that it would be difficult to write about school life. To illustrate tensions between learning, interpreting, interacting and representing, we will now turn to vignettes dealing with gender policy and classroom practice.

In an all-girls public sector school, "Tawfiq Public School for Girls" in a bustling part of downtown Cairo, adult authorities in the school—from senior administrators and teachers, guards, and custodians—all expressed firm and relatively corresponding ideas about the education and upbringing of their female pupils. The headmistress of the school, Abla Amira, who had worked in girls' schools throughout her three-decade career, set the standards and translated her ideas into school practice. She explained that it was incumbent upon teachers to prepare girls for roles that accompanied educated womanhood:

> My most important priority is to raise the level of the girls scientifically, intellectually, morally; the whole being of the girl. To implant values and morals in them. To teach them to follow the correct rules of society so that she, the female student, grows correctly and doesn't become unstable. It is important for her to learn how to respect and deal, how to maintain cleanliness, these are the very basics … She must be decent, not vulgar.
>
> (cited in Herrera 1992, p. 28)

Within the first week of the academic year, the headmistress stood sternly and erect at the top of a platform facing the 1,066 pupils lined up in the courtyard for the *tāboor*, or morning "lining-up" assembly. She announced that she would be leading a campaign against vulgarity. She warned that girls with dyed hair, gold jewelry, decorative hair accessories, nail polish, high heels, short skirts, long nails, and make-up would suffer serious consequences. She made a point of spending a portion of each morning assembly on bodily inspection. Certain mornings she would simply scan the sea of white blouses, grey skirts and black shoes for any signs of deviance. When spotting an anomaly she would point forcefully and shout in the microphone, "You, year 3A [third preparatory year, class A], you with the red hair band, I want to see you after the *tāboor*. And you, year 2C, with that filthy shirt and no socks, I want to see you too!"

Other times she would descend her perch and pace the lines slowly, stopping before an offender. A girl wearing a dangling necklace risked having the chain wrenched off her neck. Rings or bracelets were confiscated and returned only after a parent made a personal visit to the school to pick up the jewelry. Some girls got off with a public rebuke, while others had to face the stick and the headmistress's scorn after the *tāboor*.

Most girls abided by the rules and respected the authority of the headmistress whom they found to be stern but fair. Others lived dangerously. Certain girls continued wearing jewelry as an act of subversion to authority; they concealed gold necklaces under high lace collars and laughed among each other about how they outsmarted their teachers. Others wore clunky rings and showed them off to their peers, only to swiftly take them off and hide them in their pockets at the sign of an approaching authority figure. Whereas some girls chose to break the rules in a deliberate act of defiance, something that is to be expected among at least some adolescents, others, by virtue of having a disheveled or unkempt appearance, also suffered consequences. These girls did not defy uniform codes out of a sense of rebellion or as a way to test authority, but simply because they did not have support at home to keep a tidy uniform, or the means to purchase a new and well-fitted uniform. Some of them wore a sibling's skirt that was too large, an old skirt that they had outgrown, a brother's white shirt that had the wrong kind of collar, all of which could and did earn them hits and insults. The school, in its attempt to "raise the girl's level" sometimes lost the battle by bringing down her morale. One girl, who lived in a home with no electricity and limited running water which made it difficult to wash and iron her uniform, left the school halfway into the first year since she was so tired of getting punished and insulted for her appearance.

Inside the classroom there was a high degree of consensus about norms of behavior, rewards, and punishment. Teachers used a combination of pain and shame as their preferred modes of disciplining. Physical punishment usually took the form of caning the palms. Though caning is formally forbidden, it was a widely practiced and accepted mode of punishment. With only one exception, all the teachers carried and used, though with different degrees of frequency and force, their own personal stick. A student could expect praise for obtaining high exam results, keeping a tidy notebook, being punctual with homework, correctly answering a question in class, and coming to class prepared. She could expect censure for incorrectly answering a question, not completing homework, talking in class, sleeping in class, arriving late, forgetting her notebook, or showing disrespect to a teacher by, for example, not standing up as the teacher entered and exited the room, or not addressing a female teacher with the honorary "*abla*" or a male teacher with "*ustāz*."

Teachers expressed definite views regarding the differences between disciplining girls and boys. A male math teacher with experience in both girls' and boys' schools explained: "The major difference between teaching boys and girls is the way in which they are punished. Girls can be punished more verbally. A teacher basically just needs to embarrass her in front of her colleagues. This cannot work with a boy. He has to be beaten, and beaten harshly. The boy feels that he's grown up and on the same level as the teacher so he won't respond to a slight punishment. As the boys get older and stronger, however, the teacher begins to worry that they might hit back so he must change tactics."

A female Arabic teacher reinforced this position and said, "The best punishment for girls, which differs from that for boys, is to attack them psychologically. Maybe I'll say something that will upset her, make her feel like she's not good. This would be an instant punishment. This also serves as a warning for the better students to stay away from such a girl."

The pupils aired contrary opinions about corporal and verbal punishment. One 12-year-old girl argued, "Parents should decide on their daughter's punishment, not the teachers. Anyway, when done at the school hitting always gives the opposite result." Another girl, the top student in her year, disagreed and said, "Sometimes hitting works for students who will only work if punished first. If it brings results then it's worth it." Whatever their opinion about hitting, most girls agreed it was wrong to punish a slow learner or someone who was making an effort to learn but answered a question incorrectly.

Some of the mechanisms of discrimination were not easily apparent to the observer. The girls drew my attention to how private lessons, a widespread practice that some call a shadow education system,[10] were distorting relations between teachers and pupils. They pointed out how some pupils who took after-hours private lessons from a class teacher enjoyed preferential treatment in the classroom and those who did not sometimes suffered harsh mistreatment. (I came to know who took lessons in what and with whom and detected some patterns of favouritism and abuse.)

When asked about their favorite teachers, girls commonly responded that they liked teachers with a good sense of humor who made them laugh, or teachers who showed them kindness, or those who were able to explain the material so clearly that they did not need to depend on private lessons. They offered several names, but the teacher who consistently landed at the top of the list was Abla Safaa, a senior female science teacher, because, "she's the only one in the school who never hits us or shouts at us, and she is an excellent teacher. She doesn't give private lessons so she really teaches us what we need to know in the classroom." In fact Abla Safaa was the sole teacher who did not carry a stick. She was also one of the few teachers who believed that her pupils, even the ones from the poorest households, could aspire to professional careers and use their education for more than being a good mother and wife.

The students, though they discussed unjust practices among themselves, rarely confronted authority figures directly, openly questioned a policy, or tried to formally change it. They tried collectively to mitigate the injustices they and their colleagues suffered by officering each other support, and engaging in long conversations about right and wrong, justice and corruption, kindness and cruelty. But they more or less accepted the system and placed a high value on completing their basic education and receiving a certificate confirming their status as an educated person.

Opening the Gates for Critical Consciousness

These very cursory glimpses into the life of a school are presented for the purpose of raising some of the dilemmas involved in the ethnographic enterprise. I focus here on gendered policies, class biases, and ubiquitous punitive practices of individual actors. Due to lack of space, I have not been able to elaborate on the range of social relations and hierarchies, or the complex set of structural forces that shape institutional practices and norms. When it came time to write up the ethnography, I grappled with how to describe and explain what I understood as repressive, discriminatory practices in a way that would not be misconstrued as Orientalist or western-centric (with the problems of cultural superiority and otherizing that underpin these approaches), but as a humanist. I should note, however, that the Egyptian ethnographers referred to above were not concerned in the same way about coming across as overly-critical. Their identification as Egyptian and Arab intellectuals, they explained in our meetings, compelled them to expose and take a harsh and uncompromising stand on the oppressive and unjust educational practices which they linked to the authoritarian political order, even at the cost of possible retribution to themselves.

For my part, I looked for guidance in the community, in the literature, and in the theory. I consulted with the group of teachers who had been involved in many aspects of the research. From the beginning I strove, with mixed success, to employ participatory methodological approaches so that members of the school community would shape key aspects of the research questions and analysis.[11] When the study was published, I returned to the school and gave copies of it to several of the key participants. We discussed the book in detail and they assessed it to be a fair and accurate rendering of the school community. One math teacher, however, raised a strong objection to my calculation about the amount of money a teacher could make in private tutoring and chided me, "Who are you working for, the tax office? Do you want to get us in trouble?" I had not seen that coming and learned to be more discreet when dealing with monetary matters.

I turned to critical theory for explanations as to why, in an ordinary school run for the most part by caring and committed teachers, punitive practices and discriminatory class behavior permeated the schooling experience. The repressive and authoritarian Egyptian state, colonial school model, and poor salaries, structural adjustment policies and other external pressures, could all provide plausible structural explanations. But at the level of human agency and behavior I looked to the aspect of consciousness. The teachers for the most part considered their practices of "pain and shame" normal, the correct way to maintain control and to ensure high academic performance. They did not think that a practice of humiliation and shaming would serve to perpetuate an oppressive order in which fear and dehumanizing practices would be reproduced.

Ethnography can be viewed as a knowledge product and as a series of interactions and human engagements. As a source of knowledge it can play a role in informing policy makers from national governments and international development organization, scholars, and practitioners about the social relations and structures influencing school practices. Policies intended to improve equity, democracy, and participation, for instance, should not be based solely on ideological or theoretical suppositions about what schooling is and should be, but on evidence based research about what it actually is in practice. As a series of interactions, ethnography is ideally suited for facilitating open and critical conversations between educators, youth, parents, reformers and researchers about how to arrive at a schooling grounded in ideals of excellence, fairness, quality, and joy. I believe the ethnographic enterprise, with its principles of inclusion, participation, critical inquiry, empirical rigor and reflexivity, can aid in these endeavors for realizing more inclusive and democratic education systems in the Arab states.

Notes

1 For a more in-depth discussion about schooling and its relation to national and international security see Herrera (2006, 2008).
2 For additional reading on questions of methodology, representation and power, see Clifford & Marcus (1986), Asad (1995), Smith (1999).
3 The group was the Culture and Education in Egypt Working Group (CEEWG) based in the Population Council's Cairo office.
4 The person I refer to is Dr Hassan El Bialawi who not only helped us in obtaining research permits, but read and approved the edited Arabic book that was produced from that critical ethnographic research (Herrera, 2003a). Even though he, as a high ranking representative of the Ministry of Education, endorsed the book, the powers that be at the Council found it too critical and ceased its distribution. An English volume with some of that research is also available (Herrera & Torres, 2006).
5 The Christian minority make up somewhere between 10–15% of the population. I did not write up and publish these conversations about religious discrimination partly because I had no valid way to check them. I knew of the great sensitivity surrounding Christian minorities, the sectarian violence that periodically erupted, especially in Upper Egypt, and did not think it prudent to pursue this line of inquiry at the school. I felt it would lead me into a territory which I was not equipped to deal with and could put the Christian staff at risk.
6 Some of us visited each others' homes, partook in each others' family celebrations, called to check on one another after absences. I was especially close to a group of teachers of about my age who guided me through the school and provided me with insights and shared resources such as ministerial orders, textbooks, work schedules, evaluations, things of that nature. We stayed in touch long after the period of research ended.
7 Along these lines in the late 1980s and 1990s I wrote articles about education in newspapers, *Al-Ahram Weekly, The Middle East Times, The Cairo Times, The Egyptian*

    Gazette and *Al-Akhbar* and have shared my academic writings with Ministry of Education officials and people in key education policy positions in international development agencies such as USAID and UNICEF.

8 Egypt's Ministry of Education, in literal translation, is the Ministry of Upbringing and Education (*Wizārat al-Tarbiyya wal-Ta'lim*). The word *"tarbiyya"* is derived from the root *"rbb"* and the verb *"rabba"*, which literally means to grow up, rear, raise, bring up, educate or teach. That the word "upbringing" appears before "instruction" in the title of the Ministry is not by chance. The state's emphasis on the "upbringing" and moral formation of the young is a hallmark of its educational history. As Gregory Starrett asserts, "Muslim states have followed a different course to modernity, insisting explicitly that progress requires a centrally administered emphasis upon moral as well as economic development" (1998, p. 10).

9 There are different words in Arabic to denote adolescence. The term used in the Egyptian constitution to describe the period between childhood and young adulthood is *"al-nash'a"* ("to rise," "emerge," "come into being") (El Tawila *et al.* 1999, p. 2). Another widely used term, *murāhaqa*, literally means "to reach" or "overtake," and designates a life stage beyond childhood due, in large measure, to sexual maturity (Booth, 2002, p. 210). In her analysis of adolescence in the Arab world, Marilyn Booth posits, "Whether Muslims or Christians, Arabs consider adolescence to be a time particularly fraught with sexual temptations, and both draw on religious authority to regulate children's lives during this period" (Booth, 2002, p. 211). Adolescence, therefore, represents a critical juncture in young people's lives since it is a time when they are considered in need of intensified adult supervision and surveillance.

10 A nationwide survey of 6006 households in Egypt found that children in 64% of urban households and 54% of rural homes attending both public and private schools took private lessons (Egypt Human Development Report, 2005, pp. 55–56). According to a 2002 World Bank report, nearly 9% of the total GDP goes towards education, 60% of which is publicly financed and a substantial 40% of which is privately financed. Households spend the equivalent of an extra 1.6% of the GDP, or LE4.81 million, on tutoring at the pre-university level. But it is likely that these figures do not even begin to measure the extent of private educational services provided, particularly at the level of secondary education, when lessons for exam preparation which determine entry to the university are rampant.

11 However well intentioned the researcher, genuine participatory research may not materialize and in worse case scenarios it can put members of the school community at risk (see Carr & Kemmis, 1986; Cooke & Kothari, 2001; Herrera, 2003b; Whitehead & Lomax, 1987).

References

Awartani, M., Whitman, C.V., & Gordon, J. (2007) *The Voice of Children: Student Well-Being and the School Environment, Middle East Pilot*. Ramallah, Palestine: Universal Education Foundation. https://sccurc.cdc.org/publications/prodview.asp?1,865 (accessed 16 December 2008).

Booth, M. (2002) Arab Adolescents Facing the Future: Enduring Ideals and Pressures to Change. In B. Bradford Brown, R.W. Larson & T.S. Saraswathi (Eds).*The World's Youth: Adolescence in Eight Regions of the Globe* (pp. 207–242). Cambridge: Cambridge University Press.

Carr, W., & Kemmis, S. (1986) *Becoming Critical: Education, Knowledge and Action Research*. New York: RoutledgeFarmer.

Carspecken, P.F. (1996) *Critical Ethnography in Educational Research: A Theoretical and Practical Guide*. New York and London: Routledge.

Clifford, J., & Marcus, G. (Eds) (1986) *Writing Culture: The Poetics and Politics of Ethnography*. Berkeley, CA: University of California Press.

Cooke, B., & Kothari, U. (2001) *Participation: the New Tyranny?* London: Zed Books.

Egypt Human Development Report (2005) *Choosing our Future: Towards a New Social Contract*. Cairo: UNDP and Institute of National Planning, Egypt.

Eickelman, D.F. (1985) *Knowledge and Power in Morocco: The Education of a Twentieth-Century Notable*. Princeton, NJ: Princeton University Press.

El Tawila, S., *et al.* (1999) *Transitions to Adulthood: A National Survey of Egyptian Adolescents*. Cairo: Population Council.

El Tawila, S., *et al.* (2000) *The School Environment in Egypt: A Situational Analysis of Public Preparatory Schools*. New York: The Population Council.

Fortna, B.C. (2002) *Imperial Classroom: Islam, The State, and Education in the Late Ottoman Empire*. Oxford: Oxford University Press.

Freire, P. (1998) *Pedagogy of Freedom*. Lanham, MD: Rowman & Littlefield.

Hammersley, M., & Atkinson, P. (1983) *Ethnography: Principles in Practice*. London and New York: Tavistock Publications.

Hamouda, S., & Clement, C. (Eds.) (2002) *Victoria College: A History Revealed*. Cairo and New York: American University in Cairo Press.

Hefner, R.W., & Zaman, M.Q. (2006) *Schooling Islam: The Culture and Politics of Modern Muslim Education*. Princeton, NJ: Princeton University Press.

Herrera, L. (1992) Scenes of Schooling: Inside a Girls' School in Cairo. *Cairo Papers in Social Science*, 15(1): 1–89.

Herrera, L. (Ed.) (2003a). *Qiyām! Julus! Thaqāfāt al-Ta'lim fi Misr* ["*Stand-up! Sit Down!" Cultures of Schooling in Egypt*]. Cairo: Population Council. (In Arabic.)

Herrera, L. (2003b) Participation in School Upgrading: Gender, Class and (in)Action in Egypt. *International Journal of Educational Development*, 23(2): 187–199.

Herrera, L. (2006) Islamization and Education: Between Politics, Profit, and Pluralism. In L. Herrera and C.A. Torres (Eds.) *Cultures of Arab Schooling: Critical Ethnographies from Egypt* (pp. 25–52). New York: State University of New York Press.

Herrera, L. (2008) Education and Empire: Democratic Reform in the Arab World? *International Journal of Educational Reform*, 17(4): 355–574.

Herrera, L., & Torres, C.A. (2006a) Introduction: Possibilities for Critical Education in the Arab World. In L. Herrera & C.A. Torres (Eds) *Cultures of Arab Schooling: Critical Ethnographies from Egypt* (pp. 1–24). New York: State University of New York Press.

Herrera, L., & Torres, C. A. (Eds.) (2006b) *Cultures of Arab Schooling: Critical Ethnographies from Egypt*. New York: State University of New York Press.

Ichilov, O., & Mazawi, A.E. (1996) *Between Church and State: Life-History of a French-Catholic School in Jaffa*. Frankfurt am Main: Peter Lang.

Levinson, B., Foley, D., & Holland, D. (1996) *The Cultural Production of the Educated Person: Critical Ethnographies of Schooling and Local Practice*. New York: State University of New York Press.

Maugith, F. (2006) What are Teachers Transmitting? Pedagogic Culture in Rural Egypt. In L. Herrera & C.A. Torres (Eds.) *Cultures of Arab Schooling: Critical Ethnographies from Egypt* (pp. 135–151). New York: State University of New York Press.

Messick, B. (1993) *The Calligraphic State: Textual Domination and History in a Muslim Society*. Berkeley, CA: University of California Press.

Morrow, R., & Brown, D. (1994) *Critical Theory and Methodology*. Thousand Oaks, CA: Sage Publications.

Shami, S., & Herrera L. (Eds.) (1999) *Between Field and Text: Emerging Voices in Egyptian Social Science*. Cairo: American University in Cairo Press.

Smith, L.T. (1999) *Decolonizing Methodologies: Research and Indigenous Peoples*. London and New York: Zed Books.

Spindler, G., & Spindler, L. (1997 [1985]) Ethnography: An Anthropological View. In G.D. Spindler, (Ed.) *Education and Cultural Process: Anthropological Approaches*, 3rd edition. Prospect Heights, IL: Waveland Press.

Spradley, J.P., & McCurdy, D.W. (1972) *The Cultural Experience Ethnography in Complex Society*. Prospect Heights, IL: Waveland Press.

Starrett, G. (1998) *Putting Islam to Work: Education, Politics, and Religious Transformation in Egypt*. Berkeley, CA: University of California Press.

Torres, C.A. (2006) Conclusion: The Struggle for Education in the Arab World. In L. Herrera & C.A. Torres (Eds) *Cultures of Arab Schooling: Critical Ethnographies from Egypt* (pp. 179–196). New York: State University of New York Press.

UNESCO Institute for Statistics (2006) http://www.uis.unesco.org/profiles/EN/EDU/countryProfile_en.aspx?code=2,200 (accessed 26 May 2007).

Van Heertum, R. (2005) How Objective is Objectivity? A Critique of Current Trends in Educational Research. *InterActions: UCLA Journal of Education and Information Studies*, 1(2): 1–21. http://repositories.cdlib.org/gseis/interactions/vol1/iss2/art5 (accessed 20 February 2009).

Whitehead, J., & Lomax, P. (1987) Action Research and the Politics of Educational Knowledge. *British Educational Research Journal*, 13(2): 175–190.

World Bank & Arab Republic of Egypt (2002) *Education Sector Review: Progress and Priorities for the Future*. Volume 1, Report No. 24905-EGT. Washington, DC: World Bank.

Zeghal, M. (1996) *Gardiens de l'Islam. Les Oulémas d'al-Azhar dans l'Egypte Contemporaine*. Paris: Presses de Sciences Po.

7 Performing Patriotism

Rituals and Moral Authority in a Jordanian High School[1]

Fida Adely

Introduction

Upon first entering the al-Khatwa Secondary School for Girls[2] in Bawadi al-Naseem, in 2005, seemingly unambiguous national symbols met my eye. The halls were decorated with pictures of King Abdullah II, his father the late King Hussein, and at times his great-grandfather King Abdullah I. Pictures of King Hussein who ruled for over 45 years before his death in 1999 were just as numerous as those of the current King. In the photos, the royal attire varied from Western business suits, to military attire, to more "traditional" dress, namely the male head cover – the *hatta* and the *'aqāl* – each form of dress conveying a particular image of leadership. The photos of the two kings – father and son – were often hung together, conveying an image of continuity between the two. Also prominent throughout the school were signs and symbols of King Abdullah's "Jordan First" campaign, a campaign launched in 2002 whose stated intention was to put Jordan's priorities first in a time of escalating regional crises (Greenwood, 2003a, 2003b; Jordan First National Commission, 2002; Ryan, 2004).

The deployment of such national symbols is particularly strong in schools as they are considered crucial sites for inculcating national loyalties. Yet, the symbols are not without ambiguity, as the terms of Jordanian national identity continue to be contested, a reality that leads to persistent efforts, through rituals and performances in schools, to solidify, constitute and at times reconstitute what it means to be Jordanian. Paradoxically, however, these efforts can serve to challenge the dominant national narrative of legitimacy. Specifically, the regular and very public participation of young women in patriotic performances that I observed in the course of my research served to highlight competing moral projects and to challenge a narrative of régime legitimacy which rests on both its ability to deliver on the promises of modernity and on its political and moral authority.

Women have been at the center of the Jordanian régime's public discourse about development, with very public displays of what the "modern" Jordanian woman could or should be. Among them the venues are official speeches and platforms, TV public service announcements, high-profile workshops sponsored by international development organizations and the almost daily media coverage of the very public activities of women in the royal family. All are meant to educate the Jordanian public about forms of citizenship, participation in the nation's development, and the particular role women should play in these processes. Yet, the role that women should have in Jordan today is one that continues to be a source of much debate and official policies vis-à-vis women have been inconsistent (Amawi, 2000; Brand, 1998). In many respects, debates about women in Jordan continue to be central to debates about what is Islamic, authentic and legitimate, as they have throughout the region (Abu-Lughod, 1998; Ahmed, 1992; Kandiyoti, 1991). Yet, their "uplift" has been consistently underlined as central to progress or development.[3] The intersection of these two discourses, as well as the constraints – material and ideological – that limit their actualization, present strong contradictions for many young women and fuel struggles surrounding moral legitimacy and authority in Jordan today.

This chapter examines state efforts to teach young women in a Jordanian school about national identity through daily school rituals and extracurricular activities. First, I look at the daily school assembly in which young people participated each day. This assembly was rife with the national symbols upon which the régime has built its legitimacy (Arab Nationalism, Islam, and loyalty to the King) for decades. From the start, the Hashemites were tasked with establishing a state and creating a national identity where none had existed, and establishing themselves as the legitimate rulers of this state and nation. This process has not gone unchallenged. One powerful force that the régime has had to contend with in the past 25 years has been the prominence of Islamist movements and the growth in religious sentiment among the population, which challenge the régime's attempts to shape religious discourse and define the terms of Jordanian national identity. The other major challenge in the construction of a distinctly Jordanian national identity has been the large influx of Palestinian refugees in 1948 and 1967. Today Jordanian citizens of Palestinian origin make up a majority of Jordan's population (Brand, 1995; Massad, 2001).

Second, I discuss student participation in musical performances at patriotic events, showing how such events highlight tensions in the relationship between patriotism and morality, potentially challenging the régime's legitimacy as moral guide. Through these ethnographic examples, I demonstrate that despite efforts to solidify a state ideology that serves to reinforce the legitimacy of the régime in schools, the patriotic rituals performed by students may indeed serve to rupture rather than embolden the symbolic content they are intended to convey.

This article draws on ethnographic research conducted in Jordan over a period of 13 months in 2002 and 2005 in Bawadi al-Naseem, a city in northern Jordan. My research consisted of interviews, classroom observation and observation of daily interactions in the schoolyard, teachers' room, principal's office, and other spaces within and around the school. During this time I also attended numerous patriotic celebrations held in the school and events at government venues throughout the city arranged by and for students and education officials.

Enforcing Patriotism

In Jordan, students throughout the country are reminded of their duty as loyal citizens through the daily performance of the morning assembly, or *tāboor* (literally "line up" or line). This ritual serves as a reminder of the need for loyalty to the King, the Hashemite family and Jordan, as well as the importance of the Islamic faith and the Arab Nation.[4] Such a morning ritual is not unique to Jordan; it is part and parcel of states' efforts to build patriotism and loyalty throughout school systems around the world (e.g., Herrera, 2000; Levinson, 2001). In the al-Khatwa Secondary School, the morning assembly began with the *fātiha* (the opening verse of the Qur'ān), followed by a student raising the Jordanian flag and chanting "Long Live Jordan" with students repeating after her. The students finished by singing "Long Live the King" and another patriotic song, "*Mawtini*" or "My Homeland", a reference to the Arab nation and a link to the Arab Revolution that the Hashemites have relied upon heavily to develop an image as leaders of the Arab nation (Anderson, 2001 & 2005; Brand, 1995; Layne, 1994).[5]

These rituals seek to reinforce national symbols that have been the bedrock of the Hashemite claim to legitimacy from the start. However, the symbols embedded in this performance have been altered to respond to new realities. One of my informants who had been an educator in the region for over 25 years was surprised to hear that the *fātiha* was read during the daily *tāboor* as this had not been the case previously. Several others whom I spoke with, who had gone to school in the late 1970s and early 1980s, also reported that as far as they recalled the *tāboor* did not include the *fātiha*. According to one employee of the Ministry of Education, the official expectation was that the *tāboor* would begin with the singing of "Long Live the King" and the salute to the flag, and this would be followed by a reading from the Qur'ān. According to this source, these were not explicit policies per se but rather expectations. The relatively recent incorporation of the *fātiha* into the morning ritual reflects the régime's efforts to strengthen its religious credentials and to co-opt religious symbols and discourse as a counterweight to the many non-governmental religious organizations or movements vying for the loyalty of the students.

An important part of creating Jordan and making the Hashemites synonymous with Jordan has been the creation and performance of such rituals. Schools have historically been a central arena for such performances, for the construction of a shared history and identity and for the socialization of the young to these new attachments. For adolescent girls in al-Khatwa Secondary School, the school was in large part the only arena in which engagement with such patriotic endeavors was likely. However, even the most mundane and long-standing forms of instilling patriotism and loyalty, such as the *tāboor*, do not rest on firm ground, as I discovered one morning at al-Khatwa.

On that particular morning, I was surprised to find two men standing near the podium for the morning *tāboor*. I soon discovered that they were supervisors from the local office of the Ministry of Education on a surprise inspection of the *tāboor*.[6] One of these men went to the podium and admonished the girls for their lack of enthusiasm during the singing of "Long Live the King" and "My Homeland." He grabbed the microphone angrily and shouted: "Girls your voices are low. You are singing the anthem of your country. You should sing with feeling." Ironically, the very explicit efforts of these state monitors to enforce the patriotic performance served both to highlight the wavering ground on which the legitimacy narrative being enacted stood and to index competing moral discourses.

In her analysis of state rituals in Bolivian educational institutions, Luykx (1999) discusses the intended effects of such rituals:

> Schools often operate under the implicit assumption that habituation to a ritual will lead to the absorption of its symbolic content ... Though the link between practice and ideology is rarely so direct as such rituals might imply, the *existence* of such a link is the basis of many disciplinary practices ... "Docile bodies" are molded in the hopes that docile minds will follow. (p. 101)

The appearance of the monitors at the morning assembly shows us the régime's desire to mold young bodies in the hope that minds will follow. According to the régime's rules, the girls should sing with feeling; they should make their loyalty manifest. However, by reminding everyone at al-Khatwa of the links between these daily practices and the state's attempts to reinforce a national ideology, they were also reminded of the weakness of such links. The fact that Ministry of Education inspectors had to come to enforce the morning *tāboor* both highlighted the state's power, and the state's need to regularly protect it. The expectation of the régime and its emissaries may be that patriotic ideals will flow from these performances; however, rather than create patriotism, the need to enforce patriotism inadvertently reinforces the tenuous nature of the legitimacy narrative on which this patriotism rests, even as it acts as show of state power.[7] Yet the potential rupture or dissonance of the intended symbolic content extends beyond the need for enforcement. The content is further challenged in this instance by the exhortation that the girls raise their voices and sing with feeling.

For some of the students at al-Khatwa, the command to raise their voices posed a moral predicament for it offended the beliefs of some citizens in this particular community about modesty, gender and acceptable interactions between males and females. On several occasions, I heard students at al-Khatwa say that a woman should not raise her voice, particularly in the presence of men, because her voice is "*awrāt*." '*Awrāt* literally means "private parts" or "that which is indecent to reveal" (Berkey, 1992). With reference to a woman's voice, its use is metaphorical implying that a woman's voice should not be revealed.[8] The students who expressed this sentiment were those who self-identified as more religious or committed than their peers, and who were labeled as such by others. Sometimes this label was negative when they were considered by others to be too extreme. The majority of teachers and students I spoke with did not accept or give sufficient weight to these assertions about the female voice. Suffice it to say, however, in this context, with a male education official at the podium, a few of the girls and some parents would have found the demand that they raise their voices immoral and even un-Islamic.

The ambiguities produced by the need to enforce patriotism are not merely about half-hearted performances but the contested meaning of its symbols. In this case, the coherence of the state ideology is also challenged by competing moral projects. The objection to the form of the ritual – raised voices – is itself a critique of the intended meaning of the symbols enacted and specifically the moral authority of the régime, for the régime seeks to be the primary arbitrator of that which is right, good and Islamic. Enforcing "singing with feeling" elicits morally-based objections to patriotic performances and to the moral legitimacy of the institutions that enable them. At al-Khatwa such objections were also regularly raised about the performances of the "music girls" at patriotic events, as I will discuss in the next section.

Singing and Dancing for the Nation

Throughout the course of my research, girls were typically the only performers at public celebrations of national holidays.[9] In a region of Jordan where public space was male-dominated and most events were sex-segregated, female students were at the forefront of public events held at the school and in the surrounding community, organized to show support for the régime. At al-Khatwa the music program was the key conduit for such performances. The school music group involved anywhere from 20 to 40 students at a given time and participation was voluntary. Their activities centered largely on preparing for events organized around national holidays. The "music girls" took a prominent place in public national performances, singing patriotic songs, dancing folkdances and reciting poetry. On several occasions, both teachers and fellow students questioned the participation of the music girls in these performances on moral grounds.[10] Specifically these objections focused on notions of appropriate gendered modesty and beliefs about religious prohibitions on music. The girls in turn justified their participation through an emphasis on the patriotic nature of their performances. They also regularly distinguished between their performances and popular musical performances on satellite television that many found morally objectionable.

The music girls' performances were consistent with the régime's efforts to create and display an image of a "modern" Jordan, one with a particular place for Jordanian women. Yet because the role of women in Jordanian society continues to be at the crux of debates and struggles surrounding political and moral legitimacy, the performances also served to highlight the contested nature of such images and conflicts among competing forms of religiosity, calling into question the acceptability of the form and, implicitly, the content of these patriotic performances. A glimpse of one such performance will better illuminate my argument. In May of 2005, I attended the celebration of Independence Day and Armed Services Day at the Municipal Hall in Bawadi al-Naseem.[11] The hall was filled with educators and students (male and female) who sat and waited for the dignitaries to arrive. The honored guests were the Head of the Municipality, the Head of Education for the governornate and a number of education officials, all but one of whom were men. All of the students who participated in this performance, in celebration of the nation's independence and the armed forces, were girls. The girls wore "traditional" ankle-length embroidered dresses[12] with the exception of one girl who wore a *jelbāb*, an overcoat or robe worn over one's clothes. With the exception of the girl in the *jelbāb* and two of her peers, all of the girls performed without covering their hair.

The event began as all such events do, with the singing of "Long Live the King," in this case to the accompaniment of live music. The Director of Education talked about history, the Arab Revolution and Jordanian independence. He also praised the King and his support for education and reform. The master of ceremonies, a student, gave her own speech praising the "miraculous accomplishments" of Jordan in education and development. She also talked about the importance of being "moderate" and moral students.[13] The group sang several patriotic and national folksongs.[14] Interspersed with their singing was the recitation of a poem called "Oh My Country" read by an al-Khatwa student and a speech by a student from another school about the need to defend the homeland.

This brief glimpse at a patriotic event in which the performance of schoolgirls figured centrally, reveals the obvious ways in which the dominant national symbols are incorporated into such events. The main speakers acknowledged Jordan's progress – the "miraculous" achievements of the Jordanian state – and expressed gratitude to the King for this progress.[15] The standard references to the Arab Revolution and Jordan's independence were included. Finally, the girls displayed and performed the symbols of Jordan's history – the folk dress and songs which stood for this history, both rural and tribal. However, a more subtle meaning was also conveyed in this performance via the primary role of girls; namely, the central place of women in the narrative of Jordanian progress and development.

When I inquired about the lack of boys' participation, parents and staff usually said that boys did not like such activities, and had many more activities to which they were interested, mostly because they were permitted greater mobility than their female peers. Thus, the dominant role that girls held in such performances did not appear to be an explicit policy and was understood to be a matter of boys' preferences. Of course such preferences could clearly be constructed as music was not even offered as an option for high school boys in Bawadi al-Naseem, assumptions having already been made about their preferences. However unintended, the fact that some girls play a very central and public role in national performances fits decidedly into the image of Jordan that the régime is struggling to portray, namely the image of a modern nation with women at its center. However, such images are not uncontested; as such, the symbolic meaning conveyed through music performances for patriotic events cannot be taken for granted. While the participation of these young women in these public events helps project the image of a "modern" Jordanian woman who is a full participant in her society, they also served to highlight the tensions in the narrative of national legitimacy.

Although I never heard of any official objections to girls' participation in public events (in fact the administration fully supported and facilitated their participation and the Ministry needed schools to participate in such events), teachers and peers at al-Khatwa regularly raised objections to the participation of the music girls in such events; objections focused on issues of female modesty and proper comportment, as well as the permissibility of music in Islam. As already mentioned, during their performances the girls wore "traditional" embroidered dresses that were full length with long sleeves. Many of the girls did not cover their hair for these performances, although the large majority of females in this community covered their hair with a head scarf or *ishār*, a phenomenon that has become widespread in the past two decades in Jordan, as elsewhere in the region. In addition to covering their hair, for many girls there were other means of covering up or dressing more modestly. One common form in this community was the donning of a *jelbāb*, an ankle-length robe which was worn over one's clothing. It is a decidedly modern form of Islamic dress worn by many young women in the region today. Some of the music girls, responding to such criticism, defended their "costumes" as sufficiently modest. As Mahmood (2005) has argued, although modesty as a widely held norm is not new historically speaking, the ways in which the norm is meant to be "inhabited" is fiercely contested (pp. 23–24).

Dia, a 10th grader, discussed concerns about modesty and dress in defending her participation in music. Specifically, she differentiated their performances from musical performances which were found on TV in music videos:[16]

> We are not doing anything wrong. We don't get up there like the people who sing on TV, wearing things that are not good. There is nothing *harām*[17] [in our music activities]. On TV the singers, they sing and get dressed in this [objectionable] way. But we all wear the same thing and our sleeves are to here (she pointed to her wrist).

Music videos were frequently the target of criticism by teachers and some students. The objections to music videos were not about the music per se (although for some families this was part of the problem); rather, the most prominent objections had to do with the way in which women dressed in these videos, their appearance with men, and the sexual suggestiveness of many of these videos (Armbrust, 2005).

The second major moral objection to the activities of the music group had to do with religious prohibitions on music. Without delving into the details of doctrinal exegesis on music in Islam, I wish to mention only that on some issues debates about what is acceptable in Islam remain pertinent questions in everyday life, and the subject of music is one that has entered religious discourse in new ways in the past two decades – with some Muslims identifying a greater religiosity with, among other things, a prohibition on music or particular forms of music (Herrera, 2000).[18] Nevertheless, most people still listen to music in Jordan and many young people expressed ambivalence toward the music prohibition. In fact watching music videos was a favorite student pastime. Furthermore, music was part of the formal curriculum in elementary school and optional in high school. However, some of the students at al-Khatwa, particularly those who were involved in local "piety movements,"[19] were adamant about music being *harām* and preached to their peers regularly about the dangers of music. Some teachers also believed that music was *harām* and conveyed this sentiment to the students.

The following conversation with two 11th graders who were active participants in music is indicative of how the girls understood the prohibition on music, and how they attempted to rationalize their own participation.

FIDA: *Do you face any problems because people have the opinion that music is immoral?*

HANAN: We hear this kind of talk a lot. For example, the other day the computer teacher got a hold of me and said "Don't you cover your hair? So why music?"

HANAN CONTINUES: But I am not that committed (i.e., religiously). Should I tell her I am free to do what I want? That would be rude. She will say, "Why do you go to music? Music is *harām*."

FIDA: *How do you react to her?*

HANAN: I try to take it lightly and joke so as to pull myself out of the discussion.

FARIAL: So that there won't be problems between you and the teacher.

HANAN: Then we go and tell our music teacher, "This teacher said this, this and that."

FARIAL: We just ignore it. We know what we are doing and music is fine. We listen to music at home.

FIDA: *In religion there seems to be a difference of opinion. Do most Muslims consider music to be harām?*

HANAN: Everyone knows music is *harām* but there are some who don't pay attention like us and others who do.

FIDA: *You mean it is harām in religion?*

FARIAL: Musical instruments are *harām*. Only the *def* is not *harām*. But these are [national] anthems? Everything that we do is not *harām*. I just recite [poetry] and Hanan plays the *def*.

HANAN: Look. It's like [wearing] the *jelbāb*. It is not required but there are some people who say if you wear a headscarf that you must wear a *jelbāb*.

Here, Hanan's teacher, as Hanan recalls it, implies that if she covers her hair she must be religious and if she is religious she should not participate in music. In fact Hanan did not normally cover her hair in school (although on at least one occasion I saw her cover her hair in school), although she may have outside of school. During her music performances she did not cover her hair. In their conversation with me, Farial and Hanan rationalized their participation in music by distinguishing it from other modes of music which were *harām*. Farial argued that because their role in the music performances was limited to recitation in her own case, and playing the *def* in the case of Hanan, that their participation was religiously acceptable. She specifically pointed out that they did not play instruments (ignoring the fact that they were participating in a performance while accompanied by people playing on instruments). Thus, Farial did not deny that some music was *harām* but tried to separate her own form of participation from that which would be considered prohibited by some. Hanan too seemed to accept the premise that some forms of music were *harām*, but she related the prohibitions and her willingness to participate in music activities, to different degrees of religiosity – how "committed" she was. The parallel that Hanan made with the *jelbāb* here was a pointed one. She used this analogy to emphasize that people have different interpretations and expectations about how a Muslim should dress, act and behave. Both girls appeared little concerned about the objections to their participation. They rationalized their participation in similar ways, although

Farial invoked distinctions based on religious teachings, while Hanan emphasized different degrees of being "religious."

Girls who participated in music also regularly defended their activities in terms of patriotic duty. Performing at such events, they argued, could not be "wrong" as they were events in celebration of the nation and king. Objections to music participation could be read as serious challenges to official attempts to instill national values in young Jordanian citizens, as such performances were almost always in celebration of some national event. A music teacher from another school shared this perspective. When I asked her about parental objections to their daughters' participation she argued that since participation in music was not required and the music events were nationalistic events it would be difficult for parents to complain as they would appear unpatriotic. In a number of instances I observed or heard about, such objections appeared to be expressly that – a challenge to the régime's attempts to define the terms of religious life and practice, for by sanctioning that which is considered to be *harām* by some, the state can be viewed as ipso facto illegitimate or at least an unqualified arbitrator of that which is *halāl* or *harām*.[20] Hanan argued that as a sanctioned school activity of a national and cultural nature – it must be viewed as legitimate:

HANAN: When there is a music event in the municipal hall you find the whole school there. Isn't it supposed to be *harām*? So why does the whole school come then?

FARIAL: This is something different. This music is national music. It's not something loose (immoral) ... that which is in their minds ... that which is *harām*. About love and things like that.

FIDA: *Are all music activities nationalistic?*

HANAN: Not necessarily. They could be folklore too ... from Jordanian culture. It has to be that way because we are under the supervision of the Ministry of Education.

Note that Hanan did not draw on nationalist sentiment per se, but rather on official power to designate some activities legitimate, and others not. The state not only sanctions their activities but defines the parameters of acceptable content according to Hanan. The music girls I spoke with also regularly emphasized the legitimacy granted by the patriotic content, by distinguishing between music about the nation and music which evokes morally questionable sentiments about love and longing (Abu-Lughod, 1998). Like the discussion about dress and modesty, such distinctions were typically made by contrasting with the pop music of video clips.

Music performances positioned these girls at the center of struggles over proper displays of patriotism, appropriate forms of modesty, and accepted religious teaching and practices. The girls grappled with music prohibitions that seemed to clash with a nationalism that is also explicitly Islamic. For some observers, the patriotic performances called into question the "Islamicness" of such state-sanctioned practices. For others it was the state and patriotism which made their activities legitimate. The music girls persisted in an activity they enjoyed even if they were at times forced to justify their participation. Regardless of whether they were committed to the patriotic sentiments on which they sometimes drew, the fact that these were state-sponsored patriotic events helped legitimize their participation in their own eyes. However, for those who held serious objections to such performances, these events exemplified the very crisis of legitimacy that these performances served to forestall.

Conclusion

McLaren (1999) has argued that "rituals do more than simply inscribe or display symbolic meanings or states of affairs but *instrumentally bring states of affairs into being*" (p. 41). In this chapter, I have shown how patriotic rituals designed to display the power of the régime and to build loyalty, potentially create a "state of affairs" that serves to undermine this ritual intent. Yet, as with any ritual performance, the meaning produced is unpredictable, and the "interpretations of ritual infinitely extendable" (McLaren, 1999, p. 129). Thus, while I have highlighted the unexpected interpretations that flow from patriotic rituals, the perspective of the music girls reminds us of the contested nature of legitimacy and the power of the state. Cognizant of that power, the music girls draw on it for moral legitimacy; as such, they recognize that power and in the process legitimize the régime.

Drawing on ethnographic research and an analysis of schooling as a set of everyday actions and rituals, which are far more contingent than state control of education might lead us to believe, I have shown how national ideals as they unfold in schools, through rituals and performance often do as much to unbalance legitimacy as to produce it. As Mazawi (2002) has argued, "the expansion of schooling is closely associated with a rise in political contestation of the established order" (p. 60), a reality he argues has been often neglected in the scholarship on the Arab world. Schools continue to be arenas in this contest, providing both the space and the material (symbols and signs, civic and national education curricula, a music program, extra-curricular events) that draw attention to conflicts surrounding national identity. With their regular performance of symbol-laden ritual, schools also habitually create opportunities for engagement with such conflicts and for the possibility of constructing new symbols with new meaning. Exploring the gendered dimensions of patriotic performances in schools is productive of new ways of reading patriotic performances and their contested symbolism.

Notes

1 I would like to thank Betty Anderson for invaluable feedback on this chapter. The research for this chapter was made possible through a Fulbright Islamic Civilization Grant. Some of the research presented here was previously published in Adely (2007).
2 All names of people and places have been changed to preserve anonymity.
3 Although the discourse about women's uplift has taken on a new form in a relatively recent era of development, a focus on "modernizing" women has existed in the region since at least the mid-nineteenth century (Abu-Lughod, 1998).

4   It also functions as a time for school-wide announcements and admonition (about school cleanliness, tardiness, etc.), as well as an opportunity for staff to inspect students to ensure they heed regulations about dress and appearance.

5   Even today the régime's legitimacy narrative still rests on this pillar of the "Arab Nation." For example, the Ministry of Education's 2006 "National Education Strategy" lists the Great Arab Revolt as a key principle upon which the "philosophy of the Jordanian education system is based."

6   It became clear after speaking to several teachers that some teachers, including at least one from al-Khatwa, had made comments at a staff development workshop about the sorry state of the *tāboor* in schools. It was assumed that this is what prompted the inspection.

7   Wedeen (1999), in her analysis of the cult of Hafiz al-Asad, Syria's late leader, argues that the need to enforce national rituals has contradictory effects. She argues that by forcing citizens to publically avow the terms which constitute the cult (however outlandish), the régime conveys its power; however, the need to deploy this force is also evidence of the state's weakness.

8   The belief that women's voices should be concealed stems from a particular interpretation of a *hadith*, a saying of the Prophet, regarding the response of worshipers in the mosque when an imam or prayer leader has made a mistake. According to the *hadith*, women worshipers should clap (as opposed to the men who should speak) to bring the imam's attention to the mistake. Thus, some have interpreted this *hadith* to mean that a woman's voice is *'awrāt*. Those who oppose this interpretation refer to another *hadith* about slave women singing in the Prophet Muhammad's home.

9   The one exception I observed was a co-ed chorus, which performed on the King's birthday in 2002.

10 Many also had academically-based objections as they saw such activities as detracting from students' studies.

11 I attended the same event – a celebration in honor of Independence and Armed Services Day – at the Municipal Hall in 2002, along with a similar event in a soccer field in the neighboring town. In 2005, I attended four additional celebrations and performances on national holidays, two of which were held at the al-Khatwa School. I also talked with some of the girls about events I was not able to attend, in particular two events that were held in honor of the King's birthday.

12 Layne (1994) discusses the importance of "traditional" dress in the repertoire of national symbols in Jordan. Massad (2001) also discusses the creation of folklore or tradition in Jordan, in part through selective adaptation of particular symbols and their construction as authentically Jordanian, forms of dress being one important symbolic tool.

13 Moderation in religion has been a key theme of King Abdullah II's régime. In November 2004, the King delivered a speech entitled the "Amman Message," which emphasized that Islam is a religion of moderation, peace, tolerance, and progress. Although the King's message was in many respects for external consumption, is can also be seen as a response to internal concerns about the growing strength of more militant Islamic groups which threaten the régime (International Conflict Group, 2005; Wiktorowicz, 2001).

14 Two of the songs sung on this occasion were patriotic songs: *Rayeti takhfiqu bil majd, Rayeti anti howai* (My flag fluttering with glory, My flag you are my love) and *Itha shtadu al laylu, ughaniki 'ammān* (If the night gets darker, I sing for you Amman). In addition three folk songs were sung: *Wayli mahlaha bint al rifiyye* (Oh how beautiful she is the rural girl), *Balla ya ghāli salim 'ala wālifi* (Please my dear, give my greetings to my love), and *Yuma andahalu, shogi marag kheyāl* (Oh mother call him to stop in, my love is passing by on his horse).

15 At such events there would often be an accounting of these achievements such as a quick overview on the number of schools that had been built, the number of computer labs recently installed or the number of new teachers hired.

16 As in many parts of the world, there has been a mushrooming of satellite TV access in Jordan. Just 15 years ago the only programming on TV was provided by two state channels that only broadcast for part of the day. Today many Jordanians have access to programming from around the Arab world and beyond. Among the most popular channels for young people were music video channels. These channels, as well as other programs, were frequent targets of criticism by teachers who argued that satellite TV was a corrupting influence.

17 *Harām* literally means forbidden, prohibited, or sin. In religious terms then it means that which has been prohibited by religion. In colloquial form it is also used to convey pity as in "too bad" or "what a shame".

18 Music, and specifically music videos, is also a focus of intense scrutiny by adults because of its perceived influence on youth and adult fears about losing control.

19 Mahmood (2005) describes piety activists as those who "seek to imbue each of the various spheres of contemporary life with a regulative sensibility that takes its cue from the Islamic theological corpus rather than from modern secular ethics" (p. 47). This is consistent with what I observed among those who considered themselves part of various *da'wā* organizations in Jordan, although clearly some *da'wā* missionaries were more well-versed in this corpus than others.

20 I am very grateful to Abdellatif Cristillo for pointing to these potential implications.

References

Abu-Lughod, L. (Ed.) (1998). *Remaking Women: Feminism and Modernity in the Middle East.* Princeton, NJ: Princeton University Press.

Adely, F. (2007). "Is music harām?" Jordanian girls educating each other about nation, faith and gender. *Teachers College Record*, 109(7), 1663–1681.

Ahmed, L. (1992). *Women and Gender in Islam: Historical Roots of a Modern Debate.* New Haven, CT: Yale University Press.

Amawi, A. (2000). Gender and citizenship in Jordan. In S. Joseph (Ed.) *Gender and Citizenship in the Middle East* (pp. 158–184). Syracuse, NY: Syracuse University Press.

Anderson, B. (2001). Writing the nation: Textbooks of the Hashemite Kingdom of Jordan. *Comparative Studies of South Asia, Africa and the Middle East*, XXI(1), 5–11.

Armbrust, W. (2005). What would Sayyid Qutb say? Some reflections on video clips *Transnational Broadcasting Studies*, 14, 18–29.

Berkey, J. (1992). *The Transmission of Knowledge in Medieval Cairo: A Social History of Islamic Education.* Princeton, NJ: Princeton University Press.

Brand, L. (1995). Palestinians and Jordanians: A crisis of identity. *Journal of Palestine Studies*, 24(4), 46–61.

Brand, L. (1998). *Women, the State and Political Liberalization: Middle Eastern and North African Experiences.* New York: Columbia University Press.

Greenwood, S. (2003a). Jordan, the Al-Aqsa Intifada and America's War on Terror. *Middle East Policy*, X(3), 90–111.

Greenwood, S. (2003b). Jordan's "New Bargain": The political economy of regime security. *Middle East Journal*, 57(2), 248–268.

Herrera, L.A. (2000). The sanctity of the school: New Islamic education and modern Egypt. Doctoral dissertation, Columbia University.

Herrera, L. (2006). Islamization and education: Between politics, profit, and pluralism. In L. Herrera & C.A. Torres (Eds.) *Cultures of Arab Schooling: Critical Ethnographies from Egypt* (pp. 25–52). Albany, NY: State University of New York Press.

International Conflict Group (2005). Jordan's 9/11: Dealing with *Jihadi* Islamism. Middle East Report No.47.

Jordan First National Commission (2002). Jordan First Document. http://www. kingabdullah.jo/main.php?main_page=0&lang_hmka1= 1FirefoxHTML\Shell \Open\ Command (accessed November 15, 2008).

Kandiyoti, D. (1991). *Women, Islam and the State*. Philadelphia, PA: Temple University Press.

Layne, L. (1994). *Home and Homeland: The Dialogics of Tribal and National Identities in Jordan*. Princeton, NJ: Princeton University Press.

Levinson, B. (2001). *We Are All Equal: Student Culture and Identity in a Mexican Secondary School*. Durham, NC: Duke University Press.

Luykx, A. (1999). *The Citizen Factory: Schooling and Cultural Production in Bolivia*. Albany, NY: State University of New York Press.

Mahmood, S. (2005). *Politics of Piety: The Islamic Revival and the Feminist Subject*. Princeton, NJ and Oxford: Princeton University Press.

Massad, J. (2001). *Colonial Effects: The Making of National Identity in Jordan*. New York: Columbia University Press.

Mazawi, A.E. (2002). Educational expansion and the mediation of discontent: The cultural politics of schooling in the Arab states. *Discourse: Studies in the Cultural Politics of Education*, 23(1), 59–74.

McLaren, P. (1999). *Schooling as Ritual Performance: Toward a Political Economy of Educational Symbols and Gestures*. 3rd edn. Lanham, MD: Rowman & Littlefield.

Ryan, C. (2004). "Jordan First": Jordan's inter-Arab relations and foreign policy under King Abdullah II. *Arab Studies Quarterly*, 26(3), 43–62.

Wedeen, L. (1999). *Ambiguities of Domination: Politics, Rhetoric, and Symbols in Contemporary Syria*. Chicago, IL: University of Chicago Press.

Wiktorowicz, Q. (2001). *The Management of Islamic Activism: Salafis, the Muslim Brotherhood, and State Power in Jordan*. Albany, NY: State University of New York Press.

8 Doing 'Identity Work' in Teacher Education

The Case of a UAE Teacher

Matthew Clarke

Introduction

> The functionality of identity. Reassurance in identity. Habituation to identity. Resentment and violence through identity. How could one become responsive to all these elements?
>
> (Connolly, 2002, p. 158)

The juxtapositions of modernity and tradition, the global and the local, extreme wealth and poverty, which comprise the United Arab Emirates (UAE) offers a vivid example of the notion that identity relies on difference. A paradigm case of what Findlow (2000) calls a 'willed nation', since its inception as a modern nation-state in 1971 the UAE has established a range of practices and codes that serve at once to provide a sense of national identity, and to identify differences between the local and non-local populations, as well as within the local population, for example in terms of gender. However, identity's paradoxical reliance on difference for its self-constitution often takes the form of antagonism towards those same constitutive differences. In this chapter, issues arising from constructions of identity and difference are examined in relation to teacher formation in the context of a new Bachelor of Education program, designed to prepare UAE female nationals for English teaching positions, working alongside non-UAE nationals, in UAE government schools. The notion of engaging in ongoing 'identity work' is explored as one approach to managing these issues.

The past decade has seen a steady rise in research in teacher education employing identity as an 'analytic lens' (Gee, 2000), including research that uses identity as a conceptual tool to investigate the development of teachers' professional knowledge (Alsup, 2006; Britzman, 1991, 1994; Clarke, 2008; Danielewicz, 2001; Geijsel & Meijers, 2005; Miller Marsh, 2003; Phillips, 2002; Santoro, 1997; Tsui, 2007), to explore their emotions (Evans, 2002; Zembylas, 2003a, 2003b), as well as to examine the relationship between their personal and professional lives (Day, Kington, Stobart, & Sammons, 2006; Goodson & Sikes, 2001; MacLure, 1993; Mitchell & Weber, 1999; Reid & Santoro, 2006; Søreide, 2006). Reflecting this conceptual approach that sees personal and professional knowledge as unfolding within wider socially, culturally, historically and politically shaped discursive contexts, Varghese, Morgan, Johnston, and Johnson argue that "in order to understand [language] teaching and learning we need to understand teachers: the professional, cultural, political and individual identities which they claim or which are assigned to them" (2005, p. 22). But what particular advantages does identity offer in thinking about teaching and how people learn to teach? Here I argue that identity, through the way it embodies and reflects the paradoxical and contradictory nature of socially organized human life, assists us in making explicit, and potentially working productively with, the 'heteroglossic' tensions and contradictions that construct the teacher (Britzman, 1991, p. 111). My aim in this chapter is to explore how these complexities might be productively leveraged through the notion of doing 'identity work' in teacher education. In order to do this, the following discussion presents an initial exploration of identity, drawing on poststructuralist theorizations that have been particularly influential in thinking about the complexities of identity in recent years.

The Indispensability and Impossibility of Identity

Identity is indispensable for its role in self-definition; and yet at the same time, a full or pure identity is made impossible by its reliance on that which exceeds its scope. Identity, then, is replete with paradox and tension: a complex matter of the social and the individual, of discourse and practice, of similarity and difference, of reification and participation, of the rational and the emotional, and of the symbolic and the 'real'. Far from the mere donning of a pre-determined set of characteristics, identity is a never-completed 'work-in-progress', a project of personal formation through active participation in the living communities where practices and meanings are established, affirmed, or contested across time and space, reflecting the interplay of the past, present and future and interconnections between the global and the local. But what does this paradoxical complexity imply in relation to teaching and the process of becoming a teacher? Is recognition of the complexities through which our identities are constructed as much as we can expect to achieve? Or is it possible, despite the paradoxes discussed above, to go beyond understanding and engage in work by the self on the self? And how might teacher educators and pre-service teachers do such 'identity work'? What I want to argue here is that these very aspects of tension and paradox are sources of creative potential in our identities. This notion has affinities to what Alsup describes as 'borderland discourses', or uncomfortable, disturbing, edgy zones where disparate discourses collide, and in the process open windows onto "an enhanced consciousness, a meta-awareness of thought and action that can incorporate the personal as well as the professional, and multifaceted, contextual, and sometimes contradictory ideologies and situated identities" (2006, p. 125).

Identity is about the 'I'; it is deeply personal. But 'I' only exists in relation to 'you', just as 'self' only exists in relation to 'others' who populate my/our/the world. Indeed, the initial term and the second term in each of the pairs, 'I' and 'you', 'self' and 'other', are mutually dependent upon each other's existence in order to be meaningful. So identity is at once individual and personal yet also social and relational, with language as discourse providing the link between these domains

(Weedon, 1997). In this sense my identity as a teacher is dependent upon social discourses that produce available understandings of teachers and teaching, and if I am to be recognized as a teacher, I cannot construct an identity that ignores these discourses. As Denise Riley puts it, "a category has its political life long before I sidle up to wrap myself in it, and whether my advance is made in a spirit of glad militancy or in a spirit of dejected resignation isn't material to that" (2000, p. 132). Since discourse mediates, and is mediated within and through, contingent socio-historical contexts and contested socio-political worldviews, identity becomes an unfinalizable site of tension and struggle.

This becomes far more than an abstract theoretical nicety when we relate it to concrete historical practices. For example, as a teacher, do I identify with economic rationalist discourses that view teaching as preparing students to succeed in the competitive global market, or do I retain my identification with earlier 'progressive' discourses of teaching as fostering students' personal growth and development? This dependence upon historically sedimented discourses is at once a source of constraint but also – once we recognize the contingent and contestable aspects of identity that were previously read as 'natural' or inevitable – a source of potential liberation. Returning to Riley once again, "there may be a measure of relief in tracing the extent of your own historical dispersal, rather than struggling to be able to cup some newly consolidated and satisfyingly fully rounded identity in your hands" (2000, p. 136).

Identity is about identifications and differentiations, as we define who and what we are in terms of who and what we are not; identity is always built on systems of equivalences and differentiations involving relations of similarity and difference. For example, if I say, "I am a responsible teacher who believes in standards, not an anything-goes, 'progressive' teacher", there is a paradox at work here; for while my identity defines itself in relation to what it is not, at the same time, it relies on this difference in order to be what it is. All too often, this difference, converted into 'otherness', is perceived as a threat to identity's integrity:

> Identity is always connected to a series of differences that help it to be what it is ... there is a drive to diminish difference and to complete itself inside the pursuit of identity ... a pressure to make space for the fullness of self-identity for one constituency by marginalizing, demeaning, or excluding the differences on which it depends to specify itself.
>
> (Connolly, 2002, pp. xiv–xv)

Through this process of identifications and differentiations – by which I identify who and what I am in contradistinction to who and what I am not – identity becomes implicated in ethical and political issues of power, since "every relationship of power puts into operation differentiations which are at the same time its conditions and its results" (Foucault, 1983b, p. 223). In this sense, identity does work; the differences on which identity relies not only help it to be what it is but also enable it to do what it does, for example, indicating solidarity or opposition. As a young, newly qualified teacher joining the older and more experienced staff at the school where I commence my teaching career, I am positioned in particular ways through the differences between me and my more established colleagues ("When you've been teaching as long as we have you'll understand …"). If I want to challenge this positioning there are likely to be consequences in terms of interpersonal conflict. Again, we are confronted by paradox in that the very possibility of our freedom is dependent upon the existence of such power relations: "in order for power relations to come into play, there must be at least a certain degree of freedom on both sides … If there are relations of power in every social field, this is because there is freedom everywhere" (Foucault, 2003).

Identity's relations of equivalence and difference are not established and settled once and for all; identity has a dynamic, ever-changing temporal dimension, as we constantly integrate remembered pasts and imagined futures into the relentlessly moving target of our present selves. I see my older colleague slip deeper into cynicism and, glimpsing what I might become, whilst recalling the idealism of my early teaching days, I resolve to retain at least some of my optimistic and enthusiastic outlook. Even though the meanings of identity are temporarily fixed, or 'reified', in order that we and others can talk about ourselves and present a sort of synopsis of who we are, these identities are not static but involve a constant process of becoming shaped through our participation in the multiple and evolving discourses and practices that comprise social contexts of our lives (Wenger, 1998).

In addition to comprising aspects of self and other, similarity and difference, past and future, identity also involves thought and emotion. Of particular significance here is the influential work of Antonio Damasio, who challenges the Platonic–Cartesian mind–body dualism in which emotion is the enemy of reason (Damasio, 1994, 2000). He talks instead of "the feeling brain" (Damasio, 2003). As I begin to teach a new unit that I haven't adequately prepared, I feel a rising tide of anxiety and prompted by this feeling decide to change tack and spend this Friday lesson reviewing the previous unit, which in turn brings a discomforting mixture of guilt and relief. Teaching involves engaging in and managing this sort of intensive emotional work on a daily basis (Day, 2004, p. 49) and the cumulative effects of this labor comprise our identities just as much as do our beliefs.

A further source of tension and paradox results from the always ambiguous and incomplete relationship between the discursive definitions and social meanings that we and others assign to ourselves and the 'real', i.e. the non-symbolic order of "a pure, unspeakable, pre-representational plenitude" (Grosz, 1990, p. 71). In other words, the meaning of our identities will always exceed our capacity to 'capture' them in representational systems such as language:

> There is more in my life than any official definition of identity can express. I am not exhausted by my identity. I am not entirely captured by it, even though it is stamped upon me – and even though it enables me. This fugitive difference between my identity and that in me which slips through its conceptual net is to be prized; it forms a pool from which creativity can flow and attentiveness to the claims of other identities might be drawn.
>
> (Connolly, 2002, p. 120)

We encounter this 'fugitive difference' repeatedly in our lives, for example, in instances where we carry out a rapid assessment of an-other only to discover on deeper acquaintance that the person we had initially written-off as a typical sports-obsessed, techno-geek, also harbors passions for late-romantic symphonies and magical-realist literature and turns out to be great company. Life continuously blurs and disrupts the settled categories and conceptual nets – including our prejudices – with which we seek to grasp and capture it. If we can remain open to this un-settling, our identities may sometimes find sources of freedom and creation in this susceptibility to that which lies beyond them.

I want to think further about the possibility of doing 'identity work' (Clarke, 2009) using Foucault's notion of a 'historical ontology' of ourselves, as a basis for conducting a micropolitics of the self, or work *by* the self *on* the self, in order to cultivate what political theorist William Connolly (1995) calls an ethos of critical responsiveness that might assist in ameliorating some of the adverse effects of identity's tendency to marginalize difference. My case for 'identity work' draws on Foucault's (1983a, p. 237) argument that we can conduct such an ontological inquiry on three domains: first, a historical ontology of ourselves in relation to truth through which we constitute ourselves as subjects of knowledge; second, a historical ontology of ourselves in relation to a field of power through which we constitute ourselves as subjects acting on others; third, a historical ontology in relation to ethics through which we constitute ourselves as moral agents.

These three domains of historical ontology, i.e, knowledge, power, and ethics correspond to the three aspects of discursive construction in critical discourse analysis, i.e. systems of knowledge and belief; interpersonal relations; and intrapersonal identities (Fairclough, 1992). And while Foucault's notion of a historical ontology of ourselves is particularly valuable since it allows us to bring together the political and ethical aspects of teaching as a socio-historical practice as these converge in the identity of the teacher, critical discourse analysis offers specific tools with which to engage in this task. Moreover, in considering identity in relation to ethics as self-constitution, we can frame our thinking in terms of four aspects or axes of this ethical relationship to oneself (Foucault, 1983a, 1985). In brief, these four axes include: the aspects or domains of the self that is problematized; the source of authority drawn on in managing these parts of the self; the techniques or practices of self-formation utilized; and the telos, or endpoint, of ethical self-formation (May, 2006, pp. 121–153; O'Leary, 2002, Chapters 7 and 8).

In the following section I explain the research context within which I apply these notions of 'identity work' to discursive identity negotiations of pre-service teachers.

The Research

The research in question is situated in an English language teacher education program in the United Arab Emirates (UAE). The UAE is a rapidly changing society whose phenomenal growth since the country's establishment as a modern nation state in the 1970s has been largely fuelled by the development of its oil reserves, although tourism and trade have been increasingly significant sectors of the economy in recent years (Davidson, 2005; Kazim, 2000). The contemporary UAE has been described as 'schizophrenic' in its dual allegiance to the discourses of 'traditional' 'Arab-Islamic' values, alongside its eager embrace of the economic opportunities offered by globalization (Findlow, 2005, p. 287). Reflecting this somewhat bifurcated outlook, is an unofficial policy of linguistic dualism, whereby Arabic is associated with religion, tradition, and localism and English is associated with business, modernity, and internationalism (Findlow, 2006; Karmani, 2005).

The data discussed here is taken from a two-year study with the first cohort of pre-service teachers to complete a new Bachelor of Education program, designed to prepare Emirati women as English teachers for UAE schools. The country's education system has experienced rapid expansion since independence in 1971 in order to support the country's dramatic economic and social development. The lack of a comprehensive education system prior to 1971, and hence the absence of an indigenous pool of available teachers, has meant that the majority of the teaching force in UAE schools has traditionally been drawn from other Arabic-speaking nations, such as Egypt, Jordan, and Palestine. The rationale for the establishment of the Higher Colleges of Technology[1] (HCT) Bachelor of Education program is to decrease this proportion, as part of Emiratization, or nationalization of the workforce. It also aims to expand the culturally acceptable work options for women and to further consolidate, through the education system, the UAE's national identity – an identity that has had to be consciously constructed since 1971 and that is actively nurtured by the government in a context where UAE nationals are a minority, comprising only 20 percent of the population (Kazim, 2000; Khalaf, 2000). However, this has inadvertently created a potential source of tensions, as the expatriate teachers are supervising the teaching placements of the very students who will eventually replace them. These potential tensions are exacerbated by a number of factors, such as the unequal conditions between local and non-local teachers, with the former enjoying superior job security, salaries, and conditions; the lack of an established culture of mentoring and teacher preparation, and hence the inexperience of many teachers in supervising pre-service teachers, which means that the HCT students are unlikely to receive the levels of expert support from schools and teachers that might well be taken for granted elsewhere; and the fact that many non-local English teachers are graduates of literature or linguistics, rather than education.

The study theorized learning to teach in terms of the development of a discursively constructed teacher identity and sought to explore the ways in which this discursive construction was being accomplished: in other words, to investigate the social and educational discourses that pre-service teachers were utilizing in constructing their evolving teacher identities. Consonant with the notion of language-as-discourse as a key site of identity construction, the research involved discursive data gathered through focus group interviews and online asynchronous discussions, in which the 75 pre-service teachers discussed topics such as teaching beliefs, critical incidents, and moral and cultural issues in English language teaching in the UAE. The data was initially analyzed in terms of the ideational, relational and identity functions of discourse, reading the pre-service teachers' discursive comments as constitutive at the three levels of systems of knowledge and belief, interpersonal relations, and intrapersonal identities noted above (Fairclough, 1992; Phillips & Jørgensen, 2002).

I have described other findings from the UAE study elsewhere, noting in particular the tendency of the pre-service teachers to construct their identities around a series of discursively constructed oppositions, such as 'traditional' versus 'progressive' education, 'teacher-centered' versus 'student-centered' teaching, 'active' versus 'passive' learning and 'hierarchical' versus 'democratic' classrooms (Clarke, 2006, 2008). Through these discursively constructed oppositions, the pre-service teachers positioned themselves in an antagonistic 'us' / 'them' relation vis-à-vis the existing generation of school teachers in ways that are captured in the following statement from one student teacher, Nabila, during a focus group discussion: "We thought that we would be as our teachers but thanks, no. Thanks to God we are not like them". It was this pervasive tendency emerging in the UAE study – corroborated by research elsewhere on pedagogical over-zealousness and utopian tendencies in pre-service teachers (Eilam, 2003; Hinchman & Oyler, 2000) – that prompted me to think about the notion of doing identity work in teacher education.

In particular, the 'antagonism' noted in the UAE study reflects the relational nature of identities as necessarily constructed through a series of equivalences and differences, such as those seen above. As Connolly notes, "identities, in the ordinary course of events, tend to congeal of their own accord into hard doctrines of truth and falsity, self and otherness, good and evil, rational and irrational, commonsense and absurdity" (2002, p. 173). Here, using data from the online discussion forum, my focus is on the ways in which one of the pre-service teachers, Aisha (a pseudonym), while partly conforming to the antagonistic teacher identity constructed in the dominant discourse of the pre-service teachers' community, at the same time demonstrated critical tendencies that correspond to Foucauldian historico-ontological, ethico-political identity work.

However, before discussing the data I need to briefly discuss my use of notions of 'self', 'identity' and 'care of the self' in a context that culturally, and in other ways, seems so distant from the origins of these terms, deriving as they do from the Western academy. Indeed, at first glance, to analyze the reflections of Emirati women through a conceptual framework derived from such a quintessential European thinker as Foucault may seem culturally insensitive or inappropriate. However, I would like to problematize this reaction, as well as the potentially essentialist reading of 'culture' underpinning it, by offering a 'genealogy' of my own use of Foucault's later work. My interest in the potential of Foucault's ethics for thinking about teacher identity generally, and the notion of doing identity work in particular, was inspired by reading Saba Mahmood's (2005) depiction of women in the pietist movement in Cairo. In a work rich in insights, that deconstructs contemporary Western dichotomies, such as feminism/Islam, and challenges dominant stereotypes, Mahmood draws attention to the shared origins of both Foucault's ethics and Islamic piety (as well as certain Christian traditions) in Aristotelian notions of habitus and ethical pedagogy, involving the cultivation of virtue through engagement in particular practices. For my interest in the notion of doing identity work, as with Mahmood's examination of the agency of women in the mosque movement, "the importance of these [ethical] practices does not reside in the meanings they signify to their practitioners but in the *work they do* in constituting the individual" (2005, p. 29, emphasis in original). My hope is that the following discussion of the constitution of one individual teacher might, in the spirit of Mahmood's work, unsettle certainties by providing a sense of the complexities that shape consciousness.

Aisha's Evolving Teacher Identity: Knowledge and Beliefs

The pre-service teachers' community in the UAE study was characterized by a system of knowledge and beliefs about teaching that produced a dichotomous divide between what the students saw as 'traditional' teaching approaches, embodied by past and current generations of (largely expatriate) government school teachers, and the 'new' or 'progressive' approaches that they saw themselves as embodying. Not surprisingly then, on a number of occasions, Aisha outlined beliefs about education and teaching that aligned with this dominant 'progressive' discourse. Typical is the following statement, written in response to another student teacher's posting entitled 'Different learning styles': "I believe that children do have different learning styles and multiple intelligences. Therefore, teachers should respect each child as an individual with his/her own learning abilities". Similar themes are evident in the following extract from a posting appropriately called 'My beliefs about teaching and learning', which employs a discursive strategy that became a genre with the pre-service teachers, that of contrasting the 'traditional' beliefs of their past with those they had since embraced: "When I was still a student at school, I did not know that the teaching strategies and methods used by my teachers were outdated. I know the difference now. I know that their teaching methods were so traditional. They did not introduce activities that met different needs, intelligences and learning styles". This discursive strategy of metaphorically drawing a line in the sand between past and present served to distance the pre-service teachers from what they saw as undesirable 'traditional' practices. However, in the process of consolidating their identities as 'new' teachers embodying 'progressive' pedagogical approaches, the community members inadvertently worked to marginalize, demean and pathologize the government school teachers, against whom they defined themselves, in ways that have unsettling echoes of colonial discourses (Shields, Bishop, & Mazawi, 2005, p. 2). What's more, this discursive practice was all the more pervasive and potent because, as we will see below, the construction of particular ideational meanings was reinforced through a specific set of discursive strategies operating at the interpersonal level.

Aisha's Evolving Teacher Identity: Interpersonal Relations

The strongly held beliefs that characterized the pre-service teachers' community required constant maintenance and monitoring if they were to be sustained by the community members. This requirement was reflected in a number of strategies employed by the pre-service teachers in their interpersonal communication, including: statements of strong agreement with messages espousing the community's beliefs; the confessional nature of many postings, particularly when reporting on experiencing difficulties in the classroom, and the evaluations of these confessions against the standard of their progressive tenets; and agenda-setting statements to rally and inspire the community members with regard to their future mission of spreading progressive teaching practices to English teaching in UAE government schools and classrooms.

In her correspondence with other community members Aisha often positioned herself as someone capable of giving advice and commentary to her peers. We see this in the following response to a fellow student teacher's posting 'Difficulties dealing with challenging behaviour': "As you stated, shouting at students or beating them is not the solution. Try not to let your SST's (supervising school teacher, i.e. mentor teacher) attitude influence you in a negative way. If you believe there are other ways to manage the students' behaviour then you should look for them." The sequence of declarative statements implying universal truth ("is not the solution"), followed by two pieces of advice, one using the imperative ("try not"), and the other implying obligation ("should"), combine to position her peer as requiring moral bolstering and support in order to maintain the community's mission. In other postings, Aisha adopted a distinctly evaluative role vis-à-vis her peers' performance as agents of change:

> I find the fact that you identified some of the areas (communication skills and your use of the English language) that you still need to improve for your professional life quite good. It means you are reflecting on your professional development as a teacher ... Moreover, I liked what you said about wanting to improve your English so you can model its use in a good way to your students. What you said reflects that you really understand your role as a teacher and illustrates clearly that the students' learning and progress is your main concern.

In this response to a fellow student teacher's reply to her posting, in which her peer 'confessed' to a number of challenges she was still experiencing in the classroom ('a positive change'), Aisha assumes the higher ground. Her chosen combination of first person voice ("I find"; "I liked"), judgment ("quite good") and explication ("It means you are reflecting"; "What you said reflects that you really understand") serves to construct a mentor–mentee relationship that individuates her respondent ("*you identified*", "*you responded*"; "*you said*"; "*you really* understand") and measures her against aspects of the community's knowledge and belief system ("students' learning and progress is your main concern"). Discursive 'truths', interpersonal power relations, and social identities are thus simultaneously established and maintained through reinforcement, reiteration and evaluation strategies that combine to support the normalizing judgment of disciplinary power.

Aisha's Evolving Teacher Identity: Ethical Self-Formation

In the above excerpts we see the co-construction of discourse and community as Aisha constitutes herself as a subject of knowledge, and as a subject of power acting on (and being acted upon by) others, in conformity with the dominant ideology of the pre-service teachers' evolving community of practice. This process involved the community constructing itself and its members' teacher identities as agents of educational change and reform, whose mission was to supplant the 'traditional' teaching approaches represented by past and existing government schoolteachers. Yet the strength of the pre-service teachers' discursively constructed community was only possible through an equally strong 'otherization' of these 'traditional' teachers, who were viewed antagonistically as blocking the full fruition of the community's 'progressive' identities.

However, we will gain a different perspective by exploring Aisha's identity construction in relation to the third dimension of Foucault's historical ontology, involving the practices of ethical self-formation through which we constitute ourselves as moral agents. We can think of this third dimension in terms of Foucault's notion of 'the care of the self' (1986), which at the same time encourages an ethos of care for others: "The care of the self, then, is always at the same time concerned with care for others" (Olssen, 2006, p. 166). As Gore notes, 'care of the self' is not about self-absorption but rather, "suggests an ethic of self-disengagement and self-invention" (1993, p. 129). There are a number of instances where Aisha focuses explicitly on her own self-formation as a teacher, yet at the same time links this to her capacity to work with others. The following extended excerpt from her posting, 'A positive change', is one such instance:

> Teaching has changed my life in so many ways. It made me more professional in the way I deal with different people and different personalities and contributed to developing my communication skills. Five years ago, I would have avoided working or interacting with people whose opinions and ideas were different to mine. However, since I joined the B.Ed program and started going out to schools (especially in the last two years), I have begun to discuss different issues and ideas with my SSTs, principals, other teachers and sometimes my peers. I am more willing now to share my ideas and point of view with them even if they do not agree with me (which is the case most of the time). In fact, having a good understanding of educational theories and putting them into practice encourages me to negotiate things with different people from different backgrounds and with different perspectives. I try to let them understand that my beliefs about teaching and teaching strategies might be different to theirs but that does not mean that they are meaningless or not as effective as theirs. I have also learned that the way we discuss subjects plays a role in persuading others of our point of view. Moreover, I believe that teaching reinforced my sense of responsibility and punctuality positively. I feel responsible for each child in the classroom and I try as much as I can to respond to the students' individual differences. I like the fact that I make the children my main concern and think of their learning as a priority ... Teaching

helped me work on fostering my creativity. I am not a very creative person but teaching motivated me to surf the net, read books or even ask for other peers' support so I can use good teaching strategies and resources that get the students interested and motivated. Teaching enhanced my critical thinking skills. It made me a reflective person who reflects constantly on everything, not only on the incidents that take place in school but also on every article I read or program I watch. I just feel that reflection deepens my understanding of certain things and strengthens my beliefs about teaching. I know that what I am going to say might seem odd to some of you, but I feel that reflection, somehow, makes me a better person! Yes, teaching has changed my life and when I look back on the things I have learned in the last four years, I realize it's been a positive change.

In discussing this posting, I will use Foucault's four axes of ethical self-formation as a matrix for analysis (Foucault, 1983a). The first ethical axis refers to the 'substance' of ethics, or what part of teacher identity is problematized. Aisha highlights her growing professionalism, and in turn relates this to her developing interpersonal communication skills in handling difference with other educators in a constructive manner, and also to her sense of responsibility, which encourages her to focus on the learning of her students. She also highlights her developing creative skills, which enable her to develop more effective teaching resources, and her critical thinking and reflective skills, which, she says, "deepens my understanding of certain things and strengthens my beliefs about teaching ... reflection somehow makes me a better person".

The second axis concerns what Foucault calls the mode of subjection, involving the sources of authority I recognize and am guided by in my life. Here Aisha refers to the significance of her experiences of learning, both in college and in schools, and also to the educational theories that she has been able to put into practice and that have increased her confidence in discussing educational issues with other educators.

The third axis concerns the techniques and practices I use to fashion and shape myself. Aisha's reference to her practice of discussing different issues with her mentor teachers and school principals, as well as with other teachers and her peers, is clearly a self-practice that has had an educative effect ("I have also learned that *the way* we discuss subjects plays a role in persuading others of our point of view") and occupies a significant role in shaping the teacher she is becoming. Another self-practice has been working "on fostering my creativity" which, as we have seen, she feels has helped her develop a more effective learning environment for her students. And clearly, her self-practices of critical thinking and reflection – she describes herself as "a reflective person who reflects constantly on everything" – have been significant self-shaping practices.

The fourth axis concerns our telos, or ultimate endpoint, goal, or purpose. In the context of teacher identities, we can think of our telos in terms of the question: What is my ultimate guiding purpose as a teacher? Aisha's statement that "I like the fact that I make the children my main concern and think of their learning as a priority" is indicative of one such guiding purpose for her as a teacher. She also talks about the value of fostering her creativity in terms of developing "good teaching strategies and resources that get the students interested and motivated". Implicit in the importance she attaches to critical thinking and reflection as sources of deepening understanding, strengthened beliefs, and becoming "a better person", is the ultimate value she places on her own ongoing self-development as a teacher, both personally and professionally.

Looking at this posting in terms of these four axes we can get a strong sense of Aisha's concern for her evolving teacher identity. Yet at the same time, she seems to be aware that her engagement in practices of 'care of the self' may have paradoxically distanced her from the pre-service teachers' community, whilst simultaneously nurturing a critical and ethical responsiveness to the contingent differences upon which the community's identity has been built. This is implicit in the preface, "I know that what I am going to say might seem odd to some of you", that she provides for her comments on the changes brought about by reflection.

'Identity Work' as Care of the Self and Care for 'Others'

I noted above that my interest in considering the notion of doing 'identity work' was prompted by the powerful identities the pre-service teachers' community constructed upon a foundation of differences between themselves and the otherized UAE government schoolteachers and the pervasive antagonism that was manifested by the pre-service teachers towards the schoolteachers as a result. In particular, I am interested in the extent to which an explicit focus on identity, conceived as a practice of care of the self, might lead towards a heightened sense of care for others and so diminish the tendency for identities to congeal and harden around established 'true' beliefs, whilst treating difference with circumspection and resentment: "To possess a true identity is to be false to difference, while to be true to difference is to sacrifice the promise of a true identity" (Connolly, 2002, p. 67). My hope is that critical encounters with the self might foster a sense of contingency and fragility in our identities, leading to the possibility of our being more open to encounters with others, to exploration of others' ideas and to the unsettling of our pedagogical certainties. In this way, critique becomes linked to self-transformation:

> Critique, I believe, is most powerful when it leaves open the possibility that we might also be remade in the process of engaging another's worldview, that we might come to learn things that we did not already know before we undertook the engagement. This requires that we occasionally turn the critical gaze upon ourselves, to leave open the possibility that we may be remade through an encounter with the other.
>
> (Mahmood, 2005, pp. 36–37)

This statement reflects Foucault's notion of the care of the self being linked to care of others, as part of a critical ethos involving the self in "the endeavor to know how and to what extent it might be possible to think differently, instead of legitimating what is already known ... to explore what might be changed, in its own thought, through the practice of a knowledge that is foreign to it" (Foucault, 1985, p. 9). We have seen that Aisha engages in practices of active encounters with others' ideas through discussions and negotiations with mentor teachers, principals and other teachers in her teaching placement schools and that she also engages in self-practices of ongoing reflection on whatever ideas or practices she encounters. To what extent did these self-practices of 'care of the self' translate into care for others? We have seen that Aisha placed great emphasis on the care of her students. But what about care for others in terms of a softening of the antagonistic stance the community members generally adopted vis-à-vis past and current UAE teachers? Consider the following excerpt from one of her postings:

> You asked what we think an effective learning environment is. I think an effective learning environment is an environment that encourages interaction and fosters the students' skills not only linguistically but also interpersonally … On the other hand, I want to draw your attention to another issue. We were taught how to create a positive learning environment and we got the chance to see the effectiveness of using child-centered activities through going out to schools and teaching. We were introduced to many educational theories and got the opportunities to put them into practice. Government school teachers did not get that chance though. If we did not join the B.Ed program, do you think we would have had these strong beliefs about teaching? Maybe we would have taught our students the same way we were taught.

Aisha's views as to what comprises an effective learning environment (and some of the details are elided here for the sake of space) are aligned with key tenets of the community's 'progressive' educational belief system. Aisha pauses and metaphorically steps into an-'other' space, as she empathetically places herself in the position of the government teachers. In response to Nabila's comment, noted earlier, thanking God that "we are not like them", Aisha reflects on the fragility and contingency of that fate that could so easily have turned out 'other'-wise. In so doing she takes a crucial step towards, to cite Mahmood again, "the possibility that we may be remade through an encounter with the other" (2005, p. 37). This leads her, in the same posting, to think beyond the celebration of a pure identity that, in Connolly's words cited above, "is false to difference", and to consider the real challenges of working through future encounters with difference as the community members try to implement their vision of an effective learning environment:

> We can always start with our own classrooms and then try to help other teachers in the school to see our point of view, but what is next? How will we change a procedure that has been followed step by step for so many years? And what if our ideas were completely rejected and we were put under pressure to change our beliefs about teaching when we start working as full-time teachers? I am not saying that I will throw what I learned away. I am only thinking ahead and trying to find ways to deal with the challenges that we surely are going to face once we start working as English teachers! Let me know what you think.

Aisha's remarks demonstrate a willingness to think beyond the rhetorical statements of antagonistic opposition to 'traditional' teaching approaches that characterized so many of the pre-service teachers' comments. She steps back and thus moves away from the community's stance in order to gain a new perspective and, in doing so, possibly risks her relationship to and membership in the community. For her questions push the community out of its preferred pedagogically 'fundamentalist' comfort zone (and as Connolly, 1995, p. 106, notes, "all of us have strains of fundamentalism flowing through us"), within which its identity is seemingly secure, and evince a will to engage with thorny issues of managing, rather than marginalizing and demeaning, difference. In a later posting in the same discussion thread, Aisha elaborated on this same theme:

> If you graduated from an art college with a degree in English literature and were placed as a teacher in a school, would your beliefs about teaching have been the same? If you were not a B.Ed student, would you TRULY have had the knowledge you have now about teaching and learning? Most of the English teachers in our government schools graduated with degrees in English literature. They were not introduced to the same kind of information and theories we were introduced to. Most of the feedback they get on their teaching is from principals and Zone Supervisors [school inspectors] who are (generally speaking) very traditional. If we put ourselves in their positions for a minute we might understand why they are very reluctant to change their teaching styles even if they had professional development sessions.

Aisha uses rhetorical questions, followed by detailed explications which address them, in order to dislodge the sedimented assumptions of the community regarding the naturalness of their knowledge and their identities. In delineating the constructed nature of both the pre-service teachers' and the government schoolteachers' knowledge and understanding and tracing these back to particular discrete and contingent experiences out of which they have been constructed, Aisha is in effect conducting a genealogical inquiry. In the process, she unsettles and contests the community's congealed identities in relation to each of the three ontological domains of knowledge, power relations, and ethics, and she evidences two key ingredients required if we are to resist normalization and engage in ethical self-formation, namely critical reflection and intersubjective engagement (Gunzenhauser, 2008, p. 2234). Her acknowledging the validity – in the sense of their legitimate right to exist, which is not the same as their correctness – and the historical reasonableness of different perspectives, illustrates how "new possibilities for the negotiation of difference are created by identifying traces in the other of the sensibility one identifies in oneself and locating in the self elements of the sensibility attributed to the other" (Connolly, 1993, p. 382). In this way, "an element of care is built into contestation and of contestation into care" (Connolly, 1993, p. 382).

Conclusion

Identity is an indispensable resource for teachers in thinking about what they believe, what they stand for and what they do: in short how they define who they are. Yet identity is replete with tension and paradox, stemming from its dependence on relations of similarity and difference, its individual and personal yet simultaneously social and relational character, its ever-frustrated efforts to capture and define the plenitude of life that always exceeds these attempts, as well as its intermingling of elements of past and future, thought and emotion, actuality and desire. However rather than proving an insurmountable obstacle to ethical agency, I have argued in this chapter that by drawing on Foucault's notion of a 'historical ontology' of ourselves, these tensions can be seen as offering potential points of focus for conducting work *by* the self *on* the self, or a micropolitics of the self. This possibility has been considered via an exploration of the case of one UAE pre-service teacher, Aisha, and her efforts to cultivate an ethos of critical responsiveness.

The evolving community of practice that the UAE pre-service teachers established was one of hegemonic 'progressive' teacher identities. These nascent teacher identities were constructed through the strategy of affirming their difference from, and opposition to, the 'traditional' identities that were simultaneously attributed to the existing UAE schoolteachers, and reinforced through particular social maintenance and monitoring strategies, such as bolstering, evaluation and reinforcement, as part of the discursively constructed system of interpersonal relations. We have seen how Aisha's system of knowledge and belief in many ways conformed to the key tenets of this discursively constructed 'progressive' identity. However, we have also seen how the resulting antagonistic relations vis-à-vis the government schoolteachers was undermined and mitigated to at least some degree by Aisha's identity work of ethical self-formation, and in particular how her micropolitical practices of 'care of the self' may have prepared the ground for the 'care for the other' she evinced in a number of her postings:

> When the self makes itself an explicit site of micropolitics, it becomes a domain to be worked on cautiously and experimentally *by* the self in response to the identifications and performances through which it has acquired its current shape. By working patiently on specific contingencies on oneself, one may become more appreciative of the crucial role of contingency in identity and desire. And this in turn opens up new possibilities of ethical responsiveness to difference.
>
> (Connolly, 1995, p. 69)

There is no guarantee that such critical responsiveness will result from such micropolitical identity work on the self, but that is no reason not to pursue it, for as Connolly notes, "reflection on the contingencies of identity does not provide a key to the resolution of every ethical paradox and dilemma. Since no other ethical orientation has passed such a test, this orientation need not achieve such purity either" (Connolly, 2002, p. 183). What I have tried to outline here is how one pre-service teacher engaged in such identity work and how, within the context of a remarkably coherent community with a passionately held set of pedagogical beliefs, this micropolitical identity work may well have contributed to the ethos of critical responsiveness to difference she demonstrated. Whether such outcomes can result from more deliberate attempts to foster this sort of critical responsiveness through doing identity work in teacher education is surely a worthwhile topic for further research.

Notes

1   The Higher Colleges of Technology is one of three government-funded providers of tertiary education in the UAE, along with the United Arab Emirates University and Zayed University.

References

Alsup, J. (2006). *Teacher identity discourses: Negotiating personal and professional spaces.* Mahwah, NJ: Lawrence Erlbaum Associates.

Britzman, D. (1991). *Practice makes practice: A critical study of learning to teach.* Albany, NY: SUNY.

Britzman, D. (1994). Is there a problem with knowing thyself? Towards a poststructuralist view of teacher identity. In T. Shanahan (Ed.), *Teachers thinking, teachers knowing: Reflections on literacy and language education* (pp. 53–75). Urbana, IL: National Council of Teachers of English Press.

Clarke, M. (2006). Beyond antagonism? The discursive construction of 'new' teachers in the United Arab Emirates. *Teaching Education, 17*(3), 225–237.

Clarke, M. (2008). *Language teacher identities: Co-constructing discourse and community.* Clevedon: Multilingual Matters.

Clarke, M. (2009). The ethico-politics of teacher identity. *Educational Philosophy & Theory, 41*(2), 185–200.

Connolly, W. (1993). Beyond good and evil: The ethical sensibility of Michel Foucault. *Political Theory, 21*(3), 365–389.

Connolly, W. (1995). *The ethos of pluralization.* Minneapolis, MN: University of Minnesota Press.

Connolly, W. (2002). *Identity\difference: Democratic negotiations of political paradox* (2nd edn). Minneapolis, MN: University of Minnesota Press.

Damasio, A. (1994). *Descartes' error: Emotion, reason, and the human brain.* New York: Putnam.

Damasio, A. (2000). *The feeling of what happens.* London: Vintage.

Damasio, A. (2003). *Looking for Spinoza: Joy, sorrow, and the feeling brain.* Orlando, FL: Harcourt.

Danielewicz, J. (2001). *Teaching selves: Identity, pedagogy and teacher education.* Albany, NY: SUNY University Press

Davidson, C. (2005). *The United Arab Emirates: A study in survival.* Boulder, CO: Lynne Rennier.

Day, C. (2004). *A passion for teaching.* London: RoutledgeFalmer.

Day, C., Kington, A., Stobart, G., & Sammons, P. (2006). The personal and professional selves of teachers: Stable and unstable identities. *British Educational Research Journal, 32*(4), 601–616.

Eilam, B. (2003). Jewish and Arab teacher trainees' orientations toward teaching–learning processes. *Teaching Education, 14*(2), 169–186.

Evans, K. (2002). *Negotiating the self: Identity, sexuality, and emotions in learning to teach.* New York: Routledge.

Fairclough, N. (1992). *Discourse and social change.* Cambridge, UK: Polity Press.

Findlow, S. (2000). *The United Arab Emirates: Nationalism and Arab-Islamic identity.* Abu Dhabi: Emirates Center for Strategic Studies and Research.

Findlow, S. (2005). International networking in the United Arab Emirates higher education system: Global–local tensions. *Compare, 35*(3), 285–302.

Findlow, S. (2006). Higher education and linguistic dualism in the Arab Gulf. *British Journal of Sociology of Education, 27*(1), 19–36.

Foucault, M. (1983a). On the genealogy of ethics: An overview of work in progress. In H. Dreyfus & P. Rabinow (Eds.), *Michel Foucault: Beyond structuralism and hermeneutics* (2nd edn). Chicago, IL: University of Chicago Press.

Foucault, M. (1983b). The subject and power. In H. Dreyfus & P. Rabinow (Eds.), *Michel Foucault: Beyond structuralism and hermeneutics* (2nd edn). Chicago, IL: University of Chicago Press.

Foucault, M. (1985). *The use of pleasure: The history of sexuality, Vol. 2* (R. Hurley, Trans.). New York: Pantheon Books.

Foucault, M. (1986). *The care of the self: The history of sexuality, Vol. 3* (R. Hurley, Trans.). London: Penguin.

Foucault, M. (2003). The ethics of the concern of the self as a practice of freedom. In P. Rabinow & N. Rose (Eds.), *The essential Foucault: Selections from the works of Foucault, 1954–1984.* New York: New Press.

Gee, J.P. (2000). Identity as an analytic lens for research in education. *Review of Research in Education, 25,* 99–125.

Geijsel, F., & Meijers, F. (2005). Identity learning: The core process of educational change. *Educational Studies, 31*(4), 419–430.

Goodson, I., & Sikes, P. (2001). *Life history research in educational settings.* Buckingham: Open University Press.

Gore, J. (1993). *The struggle for pedagogies: Critical and feminist discourses as regimes of truth.* New York, London: Routledge.

Grosz, E. (1990). *Lacan: A feminist introduction.* London: Routledge.

Gunzenhauser, M.G. (2008). Care of the self in a context of accountability. *Teachers College Record, 110*(10), 2224–2244.

Hinchman, K., & Oyler, C. (2000). Us and Them: Finding irony in our teaching methods. *Journal of Curriculum Studies, 32*(4), 495–508.

Karmani, S. (2005). Petro-linguistics: The emerging nexus between oil, English, and Islam. *Journal of Language, Identity and Education, 4*(2), 87–102.

Kazim, A. (2000). *The United Arab Emirates A.D. 600 to the present: A sociodiscursive transformation in the Arabian Gulf.* Dubai: Gulf Book Center.

Khalaf, S. (2000). Poetics and politics of newly invented traditions in the Gulf: Camel racing in the United Arab Emirates. *Ethnology, 39*(3), 243–262.

MacLure, M. (1993). Arguing for your self: Identity as an organising principle in teachers' jobs and lives. *British Educational Research Journal, 19*(4), 311–322.

Mahmood, S. (2005). *Politics of piety: The Islamic revival and the feminist subject.* Princeton, NJ: Princeton University Press.

May, T. (2006). *The philosophy of Foucault.* Chesham: Acumen Publishing.

Miller Marsh, M. (2003). *The social fashioning of teacher identities.* New York: Peter Lang Publishing.

Mitchell, C., & Weber, S. (1999). *Reinventing ourselves as teachers: Beyond nostalgia.* London: Falmer Press.

O'Leary, T. (2002). *Foucault and the art of ethics.* London: Continuum.

Olssen, M. (2006). *Michel Foucault: Materialism and education* (updated edn). Boulder, CO: Paradigm Publishers.

Phillips, D.K. (2002). Female preservice teachers' talk: Illustrations of subjectivity, visions of 'nomadic' space. *Teachers and Teaching: Theory and Practice, 8*(1), 9–27.

Phillips, L., & Jørgensen, M. (2002). *Discourse analysis as theory and method.* Thousand Oaks, CA: Sage.

Reid, J.A., & Santoro, N. (2006). Cinders in snow? Indigenous teacher identities in formation. *Asia–Pacific Journal of Teacher Education, 34*(2), 143–160.

Riley, D. (2000). *The words of selves: Identification, solidarity, irony.* Stanford, CA: Stanford University Press.

Santoro, N. (1997). The construction of teacher identity: An analysis of school practicum discourse. *Asia–Pacific Journal of Teacher Education, 25*(1), 91–99.

Shields, C.M., Bishop, R., & Mazawi, A.E. (2005). *Pathologizing practices: The impact of deficit thinking on education.* New York: Peter Lang.

Søreide, G.E. (2006). Narrative construction of teacher identity: Positioning and negotiation. *Teachers and Teaching: Theory and Practice, 12*(5), 527–547.

Tsui, A. (2007). Complexities of identity formation: A narrative inquiry of an EFL teacher. *TESOL Quarterly, 41*(4), 657–680.

Varghese, M., Morgan, B., Johnston, B., & Johnson, K.A. (2005). Theorizing language teacher identity: Three perspectives and beyond. *Journal of Language Identity & Education, 4*(1), 21–44.

Weedon, C. (1997). *Feminist practice and poststructuralist theory* (2nd edn). London: Blackwell.

Wenger, E. (1998). *Communities of practice: Learning, meaning and identity.* Cambridge: Cambridge University Press.

Zembylas, M. (2003a). Emotions and teacher identity: A poststructural perspective. *Teachers and Teaching: Theory and Practice, 9*(3), 213–238.

Zembylas, M. (2003b). Interrogating "teacher identity": Emotion, resistance, and self-formation. *Educational Theory, 53*(1), 107.

9 To Educate an Iraqi-Jew

Or, What Can We Learn from Hebrew Autobiographies about Arab Nationalism and the Iraqi Education System (1921–1952)

Orit Bashkin

Autobiographies, Arab-Jews and Iraqi Education

Historians tend to work within the national languages of the communities they study. In the Iraqi case, Arabic source material is often used to explore Iraq's modern history. However, the existence of Iraqi diasporic and exilic communities means that Iraqi history is mediated in other languages as well. In this chapter, I discuss Hebrew autobiographies as a way of illuminating the manners in which Iraqi education had instilled a sense of Iraqi patriotism and Arab nationalism amongst its young members. I likewise explore the modes in which such narratives expose the limits of the state's power.

Seemingly, the educational experiences of Iraqi Jews appear far from an ideal prism through which we might examine the relationship between Iraqi education and Iraqi-Arab nationalism, because the Iraqi Jewish community, almost in its entirety, had left Iraq in the early 1950s, propelled by the circumstances created after the 1948 War in Palestine. Moreover, both Arab and Jewish nationalists understood this mass migration as a failure of the Iraqi nation-state to inculcate a true sense of nationalism within this minority community (Moreh & Yehudah 1992; Cohen 1969; Barrak 1985; Fawzi 1988). Nonetheless, members of the Jewish community in Iraq had left a large body of texts from which their educational experiences can be reconstructed, including newspapers produced by students, teachers' accounts, reports in the local press, and works of poetry and narrative-prose. In recent years, following the recognition that national and colonial historiographies have often sought to appropriate and silence subaltern voices, historians reassessed their archival practices and engaged in innovative reading techniques (of the colonial archive, national historiographies, and ethnographies) in order to reconstruct such voices. Gayatri Spivak (1988), however, criticized the presumptions of scholars to represent themselves as part of a subaltern group whom they historicize and study. Historians could, however hear indirectly subaltern voices and challenge nationalist and colonial representations, while being aware of the partiality of their reconstruction and the problematic mediums they employ.

When writing about the history of education, the question of "voice" becomes immensely important. How can we hear the voices of Jewish children from the accounts of their teachers? Can we think of children as a subaltern group? How can we learn about what transpired in the classrooms, or about the children's reception of their educational curricula? More broadly, how are we to identify zones of agreement, mediation and interpretation between children, teachers and the state?

An important channel through which we can hear the students' voices is autobiographies. Outwardly, autobiographies silence the child's voice. As a grownup, now speaking in the child's name, the author's representation of his or her past addresses contemporary audiences, whose perceptions of the past shape the biography narrated in the text. Autobiographies, moreover, are not only a historical genre, but also a literary one, subscribing to particular sets of norms and expectations. Nonetheless, Peter Wien (2006) has demonstrated that the comparative reading of autobiographies written by individuals belonging to the same age-group and depicting the same historical moment can provide historians with indispensable insights on their authors' collective perceptions of nationalism. Similarly, Iraqi Jews produced a large number of autobiographies, whose reading, following Wien's model, illuminates how members of a minority community responded to the national visions of the state.

Our understanding of Iraqi Jewish education is intimately connected to the concept of the "Arab-Jew." This concept was recently evoked by critics Yehouda Shenhav (2006) and Ella Shohat (1988, 1999, 2006) in order to signify the identity of Jews living in Arab countries who saw themselves as part of Arab society. Being fully aware of the meaning of affixing the words "Arab" and "Jew" within the context of the Arab–Israeli conflict, Shohat and Shenhav not only utilized the term in order to recapture the identity of Middle Eastern Jews prior to 1948, but also employed it as a critical way to think about Israel's discriminatory practices with respect to its non-European Jewish populations.

The role that the Iraqi education system played in the formation of this Arab-Jewish identity was of extreme importance. To illustrate this point, I have considered fourteen autobiographies written by Iraqi Jews. All were written in Hebrew and published in Israel during the last fifteen years (mostly in the last decade) and all address an Israeli audience. Some of their authors were members of the Zionist underground and some, despite being highly critical of Zionism at the time, came to identify with the Israeli state and its goals in later years. For example, Tikva Agasi (née Amal Salih, 1928) includes in her autobiography photos of her children in IDF (Israel Defense Forces) uniforms, while Avner-Ya'qov Yaron's (2004) text includes praise for former US presidents George Bush senior and George W. Bush for their actions against Saddam's régime, which Yaron interprets as divine punishments for the ways in which Iraq had treated its Jews. These are not the sole autobiographies of Iraqi Jews. Many others were written in Hebrew, Arabic, English and French. Some of their authors, like Mir Basri (1991) (writing in Arabic) or Nissim Rejwan (2004) (writing in English) emphasize the Arab dimensions of their Judeo-Iraqi culture and the vital connections they maintained with several Arab and Iraqi public spheres. Other autobiographies, in Hebrew, like Sasson Somekh's (2007), intentionally reflect on the concept of the Arab-Jew within the Iraqi and Israeli contexts. Moreover, Somekh, a scholar of Arabic literature, reflects in his text on the intertextuality of his own autobiography and the problematic nature of his reconstruction of his childhood's memories. The autobiographies I study are different. Their authors are neither literary scholars nor historians. Some published their books at their own expense. While Somekh or Rejwan constructed their memoirs as "vernacular memories," positioned against the official readings of the state (Bodnar 1992; Gillis 1994), the authors of these autobiographies see their books as memory-sites (Nora 1984–86) which authenticate the national Zionist narrative rather than challenge it.

Writing on the meanings of trauma and memory, Dominique LaCapra highlighted the ways in which the differences between past and present collapse in Holocaust survivors' testimonies. No matter whether the accounts of the past produced by the survivors are accurate or not, such persons sense that they are living the past in the present (LaCapra 2001). LaCapra's comments (although taken from an entirely different context) seem to be useful to the case study I describe. While the transformation from Iraq to Israel is depicted in many autobiographies as a redemption story, namely, as a move from an oppressive exile to a new home, at certain moments when these adults describe their childhood, their friends, or their families, the Israeli present seems to disappear and be taken over by the voices of the past, and by the national narratives of this Iraqi Arab past. In other words, deconstructing each *auto-bio-graphy*, reveals important tensions between the *auto* (self) and the *graphia* (writing), namely, the representation of the self by writing, on the one hand, and the *bio* (life), the life-story of the biography's writer, on the other. At times, emotionality, longing and affection color the experiences narrated in such texts. These autobiographies, despite their authors' intentions, thus express nostalgia for Iraq, reflect on texts written in Arabic that their authors read and loved, appropriate narratives and symbols emblematic of the Iraqi national discourse, and celebrate affection and love for Iraq. These ostensibly Zionist narratives, then, tell us much about Arab-Iraqi nationalism, since (to the delight of the somewhat critical historian), these most committed Zionist adults attended Iraqi schools as children. Thus, instead of reading these autobiographies with the purpose of learning about Zionism in Iraq, I look for moments in which the authors' reflections on the urban Baghdadi space celebrate the cultural hybridity and the linguistic tolerance emblematic of the Iraqi Hashemite milieu. I therefore illustrate how historians are able to hear the voices of these children, socializing and playing with their Iraqi friends (Shi'a, Sunnis, Christians and Jews). Moreover, such narratives also enable us to detect another voice, that of the adult author, a voice that is nostalgic too, and appreciative of the Iraqi landscape in which he or she was raised.

The autobiographies analyzed in the present chapter reflect a few classes and locations; most are from Baghdad, but three narrate the experiences of students from Basra, Hilla and Mosul. Some represent the upper echelons of Iraqi society, yet many were written by members of lower middle class and poor Jewish families. Most texts were written by men and only three were composed by women. The texts convey the experiences of Jews who studied in both private Jewish schools and public schools in which Jews were the minority. My historical ethnography based on these texts uncovers the ways in which the Iraqi education system has been successful in generating a sense of a secularized national identity amongst its students and the means it employed in achieving such aims, whilst also recognizing the limits of these nationalization processes. Iraqi schools, in other words, were not simply social laboratories in which the state's national visions were experimented with and implemented, but rather the spaces in which both teachers and students called these experiments into question.

Becoming an Iraqi Arab

Represented as a hotbed of ultranationalists, desiring to mold the minds and bodies of their students, scholars underlined the Iraqi education system's contribution to the emergence of nationalist discourses. Religious divisions between Sunnis and Shi'a as well as between the nation's various other religious communities were thus to be obliterated by a national Arab education and the students' awareness of their nation's glorious history (Simona 1986; Dawn 1988; Cleveland 1971). Nonetheless, the Iraqi education system was far from monolithic. Students and teachers had the power to challenge curricula and alter official state planning. As early as the 1930s, a minority group of social-democratic and left-leaning teachers offered alternative educational visions. From the mid-1940s onwards, schools became important centers for radical activities. In middle schools and high schools, young activists – especially the communists – attempted to convince fellow students that the state's misguided social policies, its land régime, fraudulent electoral system, and comprador ruling elites halted Iraq's progress and imperiled its geo-strategic interests (Bashkin 2009, pp. 229–265).

Jews in Iraq attended various schools. Religious instruction was provided either in a private school, which was usually held at the teacher's home (*ustāz*), or in a larger religious school (*Midrash Talmud Torah*). In the Hashemite period (1921–1958), private religious schooling nearly disappeared because of the spread of secular education, although religious preschools, in which children from the ages of five to eight were taught, were still active. Since the mid-19th century, Jews enjoyed secular private education. The *Alliance israélite universelle* was established in Baghdad in 1864 and was sponsored by a French Jewish organization which aimed at improving the conditions of Middle Eastern Jewry through education. The dominance of Francophile education was challenged in 1928, when the Jewish high school, *Shammash*, opened its gates and offered bilingual instruction in English and Arabic. Female education started at an early period as well. The first Jewish school for girls was opened in 1893 and attracted the Jewish members of the upper and middle classes. In the 1930s, upper and middle class Jewish women began working as teachers in the community's schools. During the 1940s and early 1950s, lower middle class and poor Jewish families increasingly sent their children to government schools. Some of these schools included mostly Jewish students, whilst in others, Jews were the minority. Jewish students, both in private and public schools, took the government matriculation exams due to an Iraqi military service law from the mid-1930s that exempted secondary school graduates from military service under certain conditions. Since the mid-1940s, Iraqi Jewish students, like their Muslim peers, became radicalized and many turned to communism. After 1945 the Zionist movement began spreading in Iraq, although participation in

Zionist activities was illegal and extremely dangerous. The movement, however, was challenged by two powers: Jewish intellectuals who were affiliated with the state and Iraqi communists who saw the implementation of a revolution in Iraq as *an Iraqi* patriotic solution to the Jewish question (Me'ir 1989; Meir-Gitzenstein 2004; Bashkin 2009, pp. 185–190, 254–264).

The secular ideology of the Iraqi education system affected Jewish students. In their memoirs, authors recall how they moved from a dark, isolated, and violent religious preschool, which they attended at the kindergarten stage, to the spacious, and illuminated secular school. Ezra Drori (b. 1934) describes the religious school in Basra as a room in a narrow street, lacking in sanitation and hygiene (Drori, 2005, pp. 29–31). The teachers in David Naggar's Baghdadi preschool taught pupils that whoever fails to put on his *Tefillin* (phylacteries) would be tortured after death, as angels would come and place nails on the sinner's forehead and left arm. In his new school, *al-Wataniyya* ("Patriotism," established 1923), the geography teacher taught the class about the movement of the earth and the solar system. Comparing the information provided in the book of Genesis with his geography classes, David reached the conclusion that while the movement of sun and the moon could be scientifically authenticated, the stories he heard from his religious teachers were "nothing but superstitions and figments of the imagination" (Naggar 2007, pp. 61–65). Shoshana Levi (b. 1938), also from Baghdad, was relieved to change teaching environments. "I cannot remember learning a single character [of the Hebrew alphabet] in my first class, which was more like a jail to me." The *Alliance* school for girls, which she started attending in 1945, was a different experience altogether; she was thrilled about the new school uniform, the well-lit classrooms, and the Arabic and French classes (Levi 2001, p. 36).

In the autobiographies, the secularization of Jewish students is represented as an enlightenment process. It is a spatial transformation from sealed and dark spaces to orderly and illuminated places. It is also a mental transformation from an education system based on violence, religious superstitions and memorization to scientific and modern instruction. Such comparisons between old and new schools were seen also in the writings of Muslim pedagogues and poets of the time that were highly critical of Iraq's religious education, which they saw as a sectarian and parochial structure propagating sectarianism and standing in the way of scientific progress (Zubaida 2002; Bashkin 2009, pp. 229–230). The autobiographies reproduce such narratives, though now in Hebrew, and highlight the importance of the process within the Jewish context. The national narratives concerning the necessity of secular education, however, acquire a personal meaning as the former students depict the effects of religious and secular education on their bodies, their state of mind, and their perceptions of the world. The fact that David went to a school named *al-Wataniyya* echoes the desire of the school's management, and not only of its students, to integrate into the larger Iraqi community and become part of the nation. Noticeably, the school's principal, Ezra Haddad, was one of the community's leading intellectuals who had contributed much to the field of Arab journalism and Arabic literature.

Jewish students felt they were a part of an Iraqi and Arab nation. In many memoirs, authors report being mesmerized by the beauty of the Arabic language.

Mastering the Arabic language offered alluring cultural possibilities, as it opened up a whole world of translated and popular literature, films and plays. Jewish students could now read translated children books, Arabic newspapers, Arabic novels like *al-Ayyam* ("The Days") by Taha Husayn, Arabic renditions of European texts, and they could also compose poetry and prose in Arabic. Kamil Kahila, for example, used to borrow from the school's library books detailing the adventures of *Arsène Lupin* (written by Maurice Leblanc) and later became interested in the works of Naguib Mahfouz (Kahila 2007, p. 61). In the years 1929–1952, Jewish schools, like the *Alliance* schools in Baghdad and Basra, and *Shammash*, published students' newspapers; some were in Hebrew but most were in Arabic. Significantly, the reading-habits of the autobiographies' authors were shaped by an Iraqi, and indeed by an Arab, textual universe of original and translated novels that dominated the contemporary Arabic print market (Sagiv 2004, pp. 109, 145; Barshan, 1997, pp. 121–122). Students, however, also relate to the rich medieval Arabic literary tradition. Amal Salih, for example, recalls that she loved the Arabic language and Arabic literature, and read at home books about Arabic rhetoric and prosody (Agasi, 2004, p. 79).

The relationship between learning Arabic and living in an Arab city (Baghdad) is also reflected in the autobiography of Shoshana Levi: "when I learned to read Arabic, my father used to stop by the signs above the shops, asking me to read them" (Levi 2001, p. 47). The textual city – its posters, street signs, and commercials – thus become decipherable to the child who studies Arabic in school, as she, and her father, are able to name things in the city and make them their own. The Islamic nature of Baghdad was also intertwined with the social practices related to education. Upon going to school, Emile Murad used to stop by the mosque. The keeper would always offer him a glass of water, taken from the taps with which worshippers cleansed their hands before prayer (Murad 1972, p. 13). In all likelihood, the keeper did not know the child's Jewish identity. Significant, however, is the fact that in Emile's mind, walking in the city's streets, stopping by the mosque, and appreciating the keeper's kindness, became part of the daily ceremonies that made up his road to school. His schooling, in a way, began at the mosque.

Iraqi and Arab history also fascinated the Jewish students. Jonah Cohen (b. 1931), whose family lived in Hilla, first studied in a Jewish school that belonged to the Daniel family. David Mu'allim's Bible teacher also taught the students national songs, history and geography and told them stories about the heroism of Arab commanders who conquered the Middle East. The class would cheer, with utmost excitement, after listening to such tales (Cohen 2004, p. 92). The stories about Arab national heroes, offering a nationalized and secularized view of the Islamic conquest of the Middle East in the seventh century, were common in Iraqi schools (Simon, 1986b). In Jonah's school they appealed to Iraqi Jews, who heard about them from their Bible teacher.

National commitment was also publicly performed. Schools introduced plays, concerts and public ceremonies, and conducted secular pilgrimages to national memory sites. A key moment in the schools' calendar was the visits of important dignitaries, especially members of the royal household. In 1925, Judah Asia (b.

1917), then a student in the Jewish private school *Rachel Shahmon* (*al-Ta'awwun*, established 1909), was highly impressed by the visit of King Faysal to his school, which Judah understood as reflective of Faysal's "progressive views, his liberal mentality and the recognition Jews received from the royal court" (Asia 2005, p. 34). The ceremony of the raising of the nation's flag was also important in many schools. It was a great honor for an upper classmate to raise the flag in the morning, whilst the rest of the students sang the national anthem. Amal Salih argues that the ceremony of raising the flag and the passionate speeches she delivered on such an occasion during the 1940s turned her into a fervent patriot (Agasi 2004, p. 4). In handicraft classes of the first and second grades, students created the Iraqi flag out of pieces of paper (Cohen 2004, p. 94).

The public performance of national sentiments meant that Jewish schools became a public institution for the entire community, which offered a secular option to the community's synagogues. Grownups attended schools to watch their children perform skits, plays and theatrical productions, as well as sports competitions. As the national discourse often posited that the nation was the larger family of the individual, the schools materialized this goal by bringing students and their parents together. Amal Salih played Qays, the quintessential tormented Arab lover, in the play *Majnun Layla*, which was performed by the *Frank 'Eyni* school for girls (established 1941) and attended by leading members of the Jewish community (Agasi 2004, pp. 55–57). The students in the [non-Jewish] middle school in Hilla designed the sets for, and played in, *Cleopatra*, a play written by Egyptian neoclassical poet Ahmad Shawqi (1868–1932) (Cohen 2004, p. 194). In the Jewish schools, the performance of Arabic plays served to illustrate the schools' commitment to the national language. Translated plays, moreover, demonstrated the schools' modernizing agenda, which exposed the students to the best European masterpieces. In public schools where Jews were not the majority, the arrival of Jewish parents to watch their son's play meant further interaction with the non-Jewish parents of fellow students.

Alliance and *Shammash* had sports facilities in their schoolyards, where students played ball-games and exercised (Shammash 1946, 1947). The Baghdadi *Alliance* was the first to have such public sports competitions, but other schools of the Jewish community followed its example (Barshan 1997, p. 35). In such events, students performed physical exercises, especially acrobatics, and introduced plays and skits in between acts. At times, different teams played various ball-games, such as basketball and volleyball. These events correlated with the state's agenda, whose demographic and militaristic anxieties pushed it to invest in the cultivation of its students' physique (Bashkin 2009, pp. 229–265). Jewish schools contributed to these national efforts.

During the mid-1930s, Jewish students participated in the state-promoted paramilitary youth organization, *al-Futuwwa* ("Chivalry," "manliness") (Wild, 1985). The students did not necessarily feel that *al-Futuwwa* was a militaristic organization based on fascist models; some expressed unhappiness with the physical chores, others liked it. David Naggar was in charge of a small unit of eight high school students in his Baghdadi *Futuwwa* group. He was irritated, however, by the group's leader, a physical education teacher, who boasted of his military training in Germany (Naggar 2007, pp. 76–78). In *Shammash*, Anver Sha'shua' enjoyed singing the *Futuwwa* anthem, a song calling for *jihād*. "I admit that I, like many others, was very much attracted to the words of the song, although we did not understand its meaning in our youth" (Sha'shua' 1999, pp. 41–42).

As students, then, children often did not realize the devastating effects of the militarist Iraqi nationalism of the 1930s upon their lives. A few even failed to understand the disastrous meanings of the nationalist coup (April–May 1941) led by Rashid 'Ali al-Kaylani and his radical pan-Arab and nationalist supporters within Iraq's military and political circles. The coup ousted Iraq's pro-British leadership, causing some of them to leave the country, in favor of a more nationalistic and radical one, and consequently much enthusiasm arose amongst the Iraqi public. The British, who suspected the pro-German sympathies of Kaylani and some of his nationalist supporters, reoccupied Iraq in response. In the aftermath of the revolt, during the first days of the month of June, as Kaylani's forces left Baghdad but prior to the entry of Britain, over 150 Jews were killed in a series of riots in Baghdad's poor Jewish neighborhood, an event marked by the word "*Farhud*" (literally meaning "looting", "robbing").

Nonetheless, during the coup, students were not fully aware of its meanings. The class of Avner Sha'shua' sang nationalist songs, guided by their teacher, Husayn Muruwah, a Shi'i teacher who taught Arabic literature in the school. Regrettably, a carpentry-owner who lived by the school reported to the authorities that the students were chanting the British anthem. Avner relates that although there was much sympathy for Great Britain, no student would have endangered himself by singing such an anthem. Muruwah, however, came to their rescue and testified that the class was singing national songs (Sha'shua', 1999, pp. 41–42). Shmuel Aviezer's autobiographical novel recalls how in al-'Ashshar public high school in Basra "a wave of nationalism took over all reason." Students of the upper classes demanded to be enlisted in the army and fight the colonizers, while the blackboards were filled with passionate letters dispatched to the authorities from the students and citing national poets. Students delivered fervent speeches to encourage the revolt and in adulation of its leaders. The Jewish student in the class wanted to write a national poem as well, but he did not dare read it in class (Aviezer 1996, p. 38).

Clearly, Iraqi Jews feared the 1941 coup. They were worried about the pro-German inclinations of its leadership, and they ultimately paid a horrific price for its failure. My aim here, however, is to underline the processes of meaning-making, namely, the claims made by autobiographies' authors that they, as children, were able to imagine themselves as part of the anti-British movement, even at a time when their parents feared the movement, and suffered from its consequences. Noticeably, the students wish to be Iraqi patriots, yet such patriotism is rejected. In the first account, a neighbor is suspicious of the authenticity of their singing voices, and in the second, the fears of disbelief from his fellow students force a Jewish student to censor his voice, which desired to articulate his national sympathies.

Finally, schools were effective environments for crossing religious boundaries. This was particularly true for Jews who attended schools in which the majority of the students were Muslims. Avner-Ya'qov Yaron recalls that after the breakout of World War II, his school *Ra's al-qariya* (established 1929), which was previously populated by Jews, turned into a public school in which students came from diverse backgrounds. His class included Sunnis, Shi'a, Christians (Catholics, Protestants, Assyrians), and Kurds. Every student brought with him his cultural and religious stereotypes regarding the other groups, but such prejudice disappeared owing to the shared experience of studying together. Living in a mixed neighborhood, Avner-Ya'qov did not speak the dialect that was unique to the Jews of Baghdad, but rather used the dialect spoken by the city's Muslims. He now remembers "the profound feelings of friendship" that marked his interactions with fellow students (Yaron 2004, p. 22). Shoshana Arbeli Almozlino who studied at a public school in Mosul describes similar experiences. In the first grade she was the only Jewish student in a class of forty girls. During the first few days the girls did not play with her, but quite soon she made new friends and joined their games (Almozlino 1998, pp. 15–16).

The bonds cemented in the school prevailed outside its walls. Badri Pattal, a high school student in the 1940s, came from a poor family. As his home was crowded and dark, he met with his fellow students in coffee-shops in Baghdad that had electricity and were open most of the night (Pattal 2005, p. 87). Schoolwork thus forced him outside of his home and encouraged socialization with Muslim students. Avner-Ya'qov Yaron frequently visited his Muslim friends:

> When I visited them in their homes, they knew full well that I was proud of being Jewish, and did not touch their food. They respected this ... although they would always tell me: "come, convert, be a Muslim like us." When they came to my home, we enjoyed (my) mother Na'ima's Kosher food.
>
> (Yaron 2004, pp. 94–97)

Despite the recognition of religious differences by the students (marked by the words "I" and "them" in Yaron's narration), these do not stand in the way of mutual visits and closeness.

Much has been written about the role of Arabic in the formation of Arab nationalism in Iraq. The autobiographies imply that the introduction of Arabic into schools was not merely an imposition by a policing state that anticipated that Arabic monolingualism replace various sorts of bilingualisms. Rather, Arabic offered alluring possibilities; it introduced students to an Arab print market, constructed new conversations with Muslim children, and facilitated the integration in the dominant culture. Curiosity, love and affect are the terms used by the authors to depict their relationship to Arabic. The autobiographies also explore the variety of techniques through which nationalism was cultivated, such as the secular rituals promoted by the state and their acceptance by the state's clients, namely, the students themselves. The schools promoted intra-sectarian dialogues between students of different religions. While full integration in the nation was not always possible, the *desire* to be part of the nation is seen in many texts, and is understood as originating from the education received in secular and national schools.

Becoming a Radical – Limits of State Power

The relationships between Jewish students, their teachers, and their state, were not always harmonious. Autobiographers report discriminatory practices based on race and religion in their schools. During the 1930s, Jurji Barshan detested his high school secretary in *al-Kharakhiyya* high school, who believed that all Jewish students belonged to rich families. He was likewise deeply insulted when a skit performed in his high school mocked poor Iraqi Jews (Barshan 1997, pp. 82–87). David Naggar, a student in the middle-school *al-Thānawiyya al-mutawasita*, was displeased with his geography teacher, Muhammad Fityan, who, in 1939, wrongly accused a Jewish student of being a Zionist and humiliated him in front of the class. Although an anonymous complaint was sent to the headmaster, the teacher remained in his post (Naggar 2005, p. 72). In April 1939, on the day that King Ghazi died in a car accident, rumors in Mosul spread, claiming that the British assassinated the King and were aided by Jews. In the high school where Shoshana Arbeli Almozlino and a few dozens Jewish girls studied, a woman stood in the school's court and preached against the Jews who were responsible for Ghazi's death. A Christian teacher helped the girls escape (Almozlino 1998, p. 20).

During the mid-1940s, Amal Salih moved from the Jewish school system to the central Baghdadi high school for girls (*al-Thānawiya al-markaziyya lil banāt*), where Jews were the minority. When she wanted to deliver a speech at the weekly ceremony for the raising of the flag, she was refused. She realized, she writes, that her Iraqi-ness and her love of the flag which she had sanctified from girlhood were being rejected (Agasi 2004, p. 5). In the late 1940s, Badri Pattal regretted the fact that he could not get into the high school he desired because he was Jewish and was forced to go to a night school (Pattal 2005, pp. 88–89). Most severely, after 1948 limitations on university entrance were imposed on Jews, which affected their commitment to the state (Shiblak 2005, pp. 79–132). The autobiographies, significantly, still articulate a desire to be part of the surrounding society. The students' attempts, however, were discarded.

Nevertheless, the Jewish students found useful means to cope with these mechanisms of discrimination. One such means was the positioning of the students as a unified body *against* the state. Jurji Barshan's history teacher was the famous Palestinian intellectual Akram Zu'aytar. The relationship between the two was far from cordial:

> He entered the class, and began discussing some historical matter. … Later he asked me directly: Are you Jewish? I replied: Yes, I am Jewish. To my surprise, a Muslim student sitting next to me stood up and said: *ustāz, maku huna farak bein yahudi wa-muslim*, Sir, there is no difference here between a Jew and the Muslim.
>
> (Barshan 1997, p. 92; Arabic colloquial in the original)

Zu'aytar is credited as being one of the intellectuals designing Iraqi national education, especially its history classes (Dawn 1988; Zu'aytar 1994). In Jurji's narration, however, he is positioned against both his Jewish and his Muslim students. The teacher sent by the state is thus rejected because his perception of the Iraqi community differs from the more tolerant view of his Iraqi students.

The Jewish students also realized that they were not the only minority that suffered because of its religion, as they comprehended that fellow classmates faced similar problems. In this respect, schools were not only a place where students learned about the unity of the nation, but also the location where the fragments within the nation itself became visible. Emile Murad, who went to the American School for Boys in Baghdad, had a Kurdish friend, Baban 'Ali Baban, whose family lived in Sulimaniya. Baban informed Emile about the hardships of the Kurds and their national desires. An Armenian friend from the same school taught Emile about the Armenian people and their troubled history (Murad 1972, pp. 15–17). Jonah Cohen who studied in a high school in which the majority of the students were Shi'a reports that the teaching of Iraqi history, especially 'Abbasid, inspired much pride amongst the students, as well as "longing for those glorious days, when the land of the two rivers controlled all nations in the Middle East." However, in classes where the early history of Islam was taught, a period "in which 'Ali, the Prophet's cousin and son in law, was killed" and "his sons rebelled against the state and found their death in battle," Shi'a students, who found the depiction of Shi'i history offensive, "would bite their teeth in anger, cursing the King (Yazid ibn Mu'awiya) whose armies killed the sons of 'Ali" (Cohen 2004, p. 198). Official Iraqi history, and the historiography that perpetuated it, pointed to the centrality of the tales about the early Islamic conquests as encouraged by the Ministry of Education. Jonah's accounts, however, detail the resistance with which these narratives were received. The sympathy the Jewish student felt towards the pains of his Shi'a classmates epitomizes a type of communalism from below which is not fostered by the state, but rather conceptualized against it.

Schools were also spaces in which students learned how to be political activists, and were informed, by fellow students and teachers, about the state's failed social and foreign policies. This was particularly true for the period of the late 1940s, when young students became exposed to a host of new ideologies: communism, socialism, and radical nationalism. The illegal Iraqi Communist Party (ICP) became an influential factor in Iraq's cultural and political life after World War II, especially around 1948, when grassroots demonstrations against the state, known as the *Wathba*, shocked Baghdad. The ICP's secularism and vision of social justice and Iraqi patriotism appealed to many Jewish students. Kamil Kahila testifies that the militant Jewish communist youth demanded that all pupils in his high school participate in the *Wathba* and confronted the schoolmaster, who finally capitulated, and let the students demonstrate.

> I was amongst the hundreds of students who marched towards the center of the demonstrations in Baghdad. We carried posters and cried against the [Portsmouth] Agreement and British imperialism. The communists led the rally, whereas the Zionists left on the first occasion.

"These demonstrations," writes Kamil, "were the most meaningful memory in my political and public consciousness" (Kahila 2007, p. 65).

Salim Pattal, who attended a Baghdadi night school, *al-Ma'had al-'ilmi*, ("The Scientific Institute") was similarly influenced by the radical politics of his school and became a communist. His communist Muslim friend, Muhammad Janabi, "was the first to tell me: you are my brother" (Pattal 2003, p. 293). During the *Wathba*, Muhammad organized a demonstration in the school and convinced other students to come and protect the Iraqi nation. The 1948 *Wathba*, and, moreover, the activities of the communists in the schools, enabled Jewish students to position themselves with the nation and against the state. They learned in their schools about brotherhood and equality, about their role in history, and the ways in which history will judge them. Yet such lessons were not the product of their teachers' labor, but rather of their fellow students. While the teachers often evoked the past and the present, the communist students spoke of the future; they spoke of revolution.

Nonetheless, the state's inability to control its rebellious youth affected the teachers' positions. During the 1940s, generous government stipends allowed poor and lower middle class youngsters to acquire teaching certificates in the state's teacher training colleges. These new teachers were highly radical, and they accordingly radicalized their students. Communist Muslim teachers, like Muhammad Sharara, preached against the state in their classrooms, and offered alternatives to its fraudulent social and political agendas. The phenomenon started in the early 1930s. David Naggar respected his communist Algebra teacher, Dhu Nun Ayyub, a man who held progressive ideas and called for social justice. His students purchased his books, knowing full well that Ayyub's stories critiqued the Ministry of Education for its paramilitary education, "reeking of Nazism," and the Ministry's racist and ultranationalist administrators. In the class, moreover, Ayyub preached against discrimination between citizens (Naggar 2007, p. 70). The students, however, loved their teacher because of his other qualities as well:

> Ayyub was red-headed, tall and towering ... Sometimes he would physically confront his violent adversaries, and occasionally we would see the "effects" of such encounters, like a shiny eye or a swollen lip. When we saw him this way, our esteem of him grew considerably.
>
> (Naggar 2007, p. 80)

Dhu Nun Ayyub was indeed a famous communist writer during the 1930s and 1940s (Hajj 1990). In Naggar's autobiography, Ayyub becomes a role model to his students because of his critique of the state and his publications, which stimulated the students' curiosity and shaped their political consciousness. The Jewish students also liked him because of his abhorrence for Nazi sympathizers in the Ministry of Education. Whilst the state encouraged the cultivation of the body in physical education classes and sporting events, Ayyub's masculinity is connected to the corruption of his own body (being beaten up), and to his willingness to fight for his ideals, not only with the power of the pen, but also with that of the fist. The teacher is thus detached from the state's bureaucracy, and is connected more to the public sphere (publishing books) and the Iraqi street.

Jonah Cohen reports that the high school in Hilla included both poor and rich students, since poor children could ask to be exempted from paying tuition fees. During the late 1940s, the communists in the city appealed to both teachers and students, Jews and Muslims alike. "It was not the communist ideology that attracted students, but rather the desire to overthrow the corrupt régime, a régime of bribery that cared for the landowners and the capitalists." Jews thus joined the ICP, seeking "to be liberated from discrimination and fear, and to attain equality" (Cohen 2004, pp. 192–193).

For the Jewish students, the learning experience reflected not only the state's successful management of the nation's ethnic groups, but also the manners in which the state failed to address the needs of the nation's minorities. Jewish students have learned this from their personal experience, in which their Jewish-ness was seen as incompatible with their patriotism and nationalism. They have likewise learned it from the experience of fellow students, belonging to different religious and ethnic groups, whose relationships to the state were equally problematic. In the 1940s, and especially after 1948, the ability of the state to effectively police what transpired in the classrooms subsided. The gap between the state's goals and its radicalized youth engendered a new affiliation between teachers and students. The teachers, according to the narratives of their Jewish students, were not simply agents mediating between the state and its young subject-citizens. Rather, the inability of powerless administrators to act against their rebellious students, and, moreover, the aptitude of teachers to challenge the state's instruction, signify an important gap between the state's desired order and its problematic execution. For communist teachers and students, as well as for their Jewish friends, identifying with the nation meant standing out against the state.

Conclusions

Scholars engaged with the study of education in the Arab world usually turn to the documents produced by the state, namely, textbooks, instruction of state officials and theories produced by leading national pedagogues. While these documents could prove extremely illuminating as to the ways in which the state imagined its relationship to the nation, a need arises to write a history from below that studies the reception of such texts by the students themselves and the meanings they ascribed to the state's secularized rituals, its perception of history, and its notions of time and space. Such a history may help produce a postcolonial understanding of Arab education, that is, a reading that does not assume that national elites managed to instill notions of prosperity, nationalism, and obedience without modifications, resistance or questioning. Thus, the linearity which takes for granted the process – state, education, production of loyal national subjects – ought to be complicated and problematized.

Autobiographies can play an important part in this process, because they often depict things that the state is silent about. Whilst problematic, and always understood through the lenses of the present, such texts articulate the experience of the individual student in his or her classroom. They uncover what the state found embarrassing, for example, the fact that students were more affected by their communist classmates than by their nationalist teachers. The postcolonial aspects relating to the re-reading of these very complex personal narratives about their authors' schooldays are threefold. First, they challenge the view of Arab nationalist educators from the Hashemite period itself who celebrated the ability of schools to form loyal national subjects. Second, they challenge *contemporary* nationalist Arab readings of the Iraqi past in which the Jews are presented as traitors who left their Arab homeland, by emphasizing the degree to which Jews were affected by Arab culture and by celebrating their nostalgia to Iraq. Thirdly, and perhaps most importantly, they subvert Israeli discourses that emphasize victimization and persecution of Iraqi Jews, by accentuating the pluralism and reciprocity that typified the Hashemite cultural and educational milieu, despite the policing nature of the state. In addition, we often need to read beyond, and against, the intentions of the authors of the autobiographies themselves, who frequently subscribe to these Israeli national narratives. A careful reading beyond the organizing narrative of each autobiography and a careful search for moments which commemorate friendship, coexistence and tolerance could expose us to a cultural and educational universe which is very different from the present representations of Arab–Jewish relations, mediated solely through the lenses of the conflict.

The autobiographies of Iraqi Jews living in Israel demonstrate that the schools were important sites of interaction between students and teachers. Schools were nationalist spaces which helped dissipate notions of religious difference and dissolve relations of kin and sect in favor of a nation state whose Arab culture united students of various social, religious and ethnic backgrounds. Nonetheless, the school was an institution in which the state's power was broken, as schools became spaces in which students were exposed to various political options, learned about social justice and social injustice, and challenged the state's policies. Although perceived as locations enabling teachers to shape the bodies and mentalities of the state's youngest subjects, schools were pluralistic settings, where the meanings of religiosity, citizenship and nationalism were negotiated. Such negotiations did not necessarily occur within the classroom itself, yet the bonds created amongst the students within the classroom were maintained in the schoolyard, in the local coffee-shop, in the communist cell, and in the public demonstration. Having said that, as any institution in Iraq, schools were also institutions that were under surveillance and were habitually monitored, and thus students also observed the violent nature of the state, in which classmates often paid a heavy price for their willingness to challenge the state.

The autobiographies, then, reveal the efficacy of the national language, considering the degree to which Jewish students identified with the majority language and enjoyed the fruits of the Iraqi and Arab print markets, as well as their enthusiastic participation in the secularized rituals with which the state, as mediated by its schooling system, sought to discipline the nation. On the other hand, the national education system also exposed the fragments within the nation. Each public school, and indeed, each classroom within the school, was a microcosm of Iraqi society, and thus often reflected the nation's ethno-religious makeup and the sociopolitical inequalities which characterized Hashemite society. However, the elements which protected students from ultra-militarism, chauvinism and the discriminatory policies of the state, were to be found *within* the community itself. Coexistence in mixed neighborhoods, sympathetic teachers (themselves critical of the state), and fellow Muslim students whom Jews befriended, represent a different type of nationalism, distinct from the realm of the state. And it is this type of communalism from below, in which Shi'a, Sunni and Christian students participated, that is celebrated in the autobiographies. With the recent civil war and ethnic clashes that followed the American occupation (starting in March 2003), these commemorative acts acquire important contemporary meanings.

As noted, these autobiographies unsettle the dominance of a Zionist hegemonic narrative, despite their authors' Zionism and support for the Israeli state. The autobiographies, akin to ones written in Arabic, English and French by non-Zionist Jews, evoke moments of nostalgia to Iraq, its peoples, Muslim and Jewish alike, and to a certain pluralistic, albeit extremely tenuous, social milieu. Reading such texts, we hear the voices of Arabic-speaking Jews, who cite poems, texts, and proverbs from their Arab-Iraqi childhood. Such readings, in other words, undermine a temporal position that reflects Israeli anxieties, in favor of a period-specific narrative which unpacks the Iraqi Jewish past – its troubled and traumatic moments, but also its moments of joy. This contemporary Hebrew–Arabic bilingualism and the Arabic culture mediated by Hebrew texts is rooted in the past, that is, in the efforts of the Iraqi state to utilize Arabic as a language that would unite children of varying religious and ethnic backgrounds. Nonetheless, it also offers us some hope for the future.

Acknowledgements

I would like to thank James Chandler and my fellows at the Franke Institute for their insightful critiques and kind assistance.

References

Agasi, Tikva (née Amal Salih) (2004) *Mi-Baghdad le-Israel [From Baghdad to Israel]*, Ramat-Gan: Kolgraph. (In Hebrew.)

Almozlino, Shoshana Arbeli (1998) *Me-Hamahteret be-Bavel le-memshlet Israel [From the underground in Babylon to the government of Israel]*, Tel Aviv: Ha-Kibbutz Ha-me'uhad. (In Hebrew.)

Asia, Judah (2005) *Ha-gsharim shel hayay [The bridges of my life]*, Tel Aviv: Dahlia Assia Pelled. (In Hebrew.)

Aviezer, Shmuel (1996) *Mey ha-vradim [Rose waters]*, Tel Aviv: Gevanim. (In Hebrew.)

al-Barrak, Fadhil (1985) *al-Madāris al-Yahudiyya wal Irāniyya fil 'Irāq: dirāsa muqārana [Jewish and Iranian schools in Iraq, a comparative study]*, Baghdad: s.n. (In Arabic.)

Barshan, Judah (Jurji) (1997) *Yehudi be-tzel ha-Islam, pirkey zikhronot mi-Baghdad, [A Jew in the shadow of Islam, memories from Baghdad]*, Ramat-Gan: Y. Barshan. (In Hebrew.)

Bashkin, Orit (2009) *The other Iraq: Pluralism and culture in Hashemite Iraq*, Stanford, CA: Stanford University Press.

Basri, Mir (1991) *Rihlat al-'umr [Journey of my Life]*, Jerusalem: Rabitat al-Jami'iyin al-Yahud al-Nāzihin min al-'Irāq fi Israil. (In Arabic)

Ben Ya'qov, Avraham (1965) *Yehudey Bavel mi-sof tekufat ha-ge'onim ve-'ad yemeynu* [*Babylonian Jews from the end of the ge'onim period until our days*], Jerusalem: Yad Ben Zvi. (In Hebrew.)

Bodnar, John (1992) *Remaking America: Public memory, commemoration, and patriotism in the twentieth century*, Princeton, NJ: Princeton University Press.

Chatterjee, Partha (1993) *The Nation and its fragments: Colonial and postcolonial histories*, Princeton, NJ: Princeton University Press.

Cleveland, William L. (1971) *The making of an Arab nationalist: Ottomanism and Arabism in the life and thought of Sati'al-Husri*, Princeton, NJ: Princeton University Press.

Cohen, Haim (1969) *Ha-pe'ilut ha-zionit be-'Irāq* [*Zionist activities in Iraq*], Jerusalem: Ha-sifriya Ha-zionit. (In Hebrew.)

Cohen, Jonah (2004) *Hilla 'al gedot ha-Perat* [*Hilla on the banks of Euphrates*], Carmiel: Jonah Cohen. (In Hebrew.)

Dawn, Ernest C. (2001) "The formation of pan-Arab ideology in the inter-war years," *International Journal of Middle East Studies*, 20(1), 67–91.

Drori, Ezra (2005) *Mi-Bavel la-Carmel* [*From Babylon to [Mount] Carmel*], Haifa: Carmel. (In Hebrew.)

Fawzi, Hisham 'Abd al-'Aziz (1988) "al-Nashāt al-sahyuni fil 'Irāq fi dhill al-intidāb al-Baritāni" ["Zionist activities in Iraq under the British mandate"], *Shu'un Filastiniyya* 180 (March), 41–60. (In Arabic.)

Gillis, John R. (ed.) (1994) *Commemorations: The politics of national identity*, Princeton, NJ: Princeton University Press.

Guha, Ranjit (1988) "The Prose of Counter-Insurgency," in Ranajit Guha & Gayatri Spivak (eds.), *Selected subaltern studies*, New York: Oxford University Press.

al-Hajj, 'Aziz (1990) *Abu Hurayra al-mawsili*, London: Riyad al-Rayyis. (In Arabic.)

Jum'a al-Ma'didi, Isām Ahmad (2001) *al-Sahafa al-yahudiyya fil 'Iraq* [*Jewish press in Iraq*], Cairo: al-dar al-dawliyya lil istithmārāt al-thaqāfiyya. (In Arabic.)

Kahila, Avraham (2007) *Hayinu ke-holmim* [*We were as dreamers*], Jerusalem: Research Institute of the Zionist-Pioneer Underground in Iraq. (In Hebrew.)

Kazzaz, Nissim (1991) *Ha-Yehudim be-'Iraq ba-me'a ha-'esrim* [*Iraqi Jews in the twentieth century*], Jerusalem: Yad Ben Zvi. (In Hebrew.)

LaCapra, Dominick (2001) *Writing history, writing trauma*, Baltimore, MD: Johns Hopkins University Press.

Levi, Shoshana (2001) *'Al em ha-derekh* [*At the crossroad*], Tel Aviv: Sh. Levi. (In Hebrew.)

Madrasat Shammash (1945) *Minhāj al-hafla al-riyādiyya al-sanawiyya li-madrasat Shammash al-thānawiyya*, Baghdad: al-matba'a al-sharqiyya. (In Arabic.)

Madrasat Shammash (1947) *Minhāj al-hafla al-riyādiyya al-sanawiyya li-madrasat Shammash al-thānawiyya*, Baghdad: al-matba'a al-sharqiyya. (In Arabic.)

Meir-Glitzenstein, Esther (2004) *Zionism in an Arab country: Jews in Iraq in the 1940s*, London and New York: Routledge.

Me'ir, Yosef (1989) *Hitpathut tarbutit hevratit shel Yehudey 'Iraq me'az 1,830 ve 'ad yemeynu* [*Cultural and social developments amongst Iraqi Jews since 1830 until the present*], Tel Aviv: Naharayim. (In Hebrew.)

Moreh, Shemu'el and Yehudah, Zvi (eds.) (1992) *Sin'at Yehudim u-pra'ot be-'Iraq* [*Hatred of Jews and riots in Iraq*], Or-Yehudah: Merkaz moreshet Yahadut Bavel, ha-Makhon le-heker Yahadut Bavel. (In Hebrew.)

Murad, Emile (1972) *Mi-Bavel ba-mahteret* [*From Babylon in the underground*], Tel Aviv: 'Am 'Oved. (In Hebrew.)

Naggar, David (2007) *Bab al- Sheikh*, Tel Aviv: Kobbi Ran. (In Hebrew.)

Nora, Pierre *et al.* (1984–1992) *Les lieux de mémoire*, Paris: Gallimard.

Pattal, Badri (2005) *Halomot be-Tatran, Baghdad* [*Dreams in Tatran, Baghdad*], Jerusalem: Carmel. (In Hebrew.)

Pattal, Salim (2003) *Be Simtaòt Baghdad* [*In the alleys of Baghdad*], Jerusalem: Carmel. (In Hebrew.)

Rejwan, Nissim (1985) *The Jews of Iraq: 3,000 years of history and culture*, Boulder, CO: Westview Press.

Rejwan, Nissim (2004) *The last Jews in Baghdad: Remembering a lost homeland*, Austin, TX: University of Texas Press.

Sagiv, David (2004) *Yahadut be-mifgash ha-nahariyim, kehilat Yehudey Basra* [*Judaism at the meeting of the two rivers: The Jewish community of Basra*], Jerusalem: Markaz Moreshet. (In Hebrew.)

Sha'shua' Avner (1999) *Yemi Baghdad – me'eretz ha-naharyim le-ertz Israel – sippur ma'vakah la-'aliyya shel-mishpaha mi-Bavel* [*Baghdad days: From the Land of the Two Rivers to Israel – The story of a Jewish Babylonian family's struggle for aliya*], Tel Aviv. (In Hebrew.)

Shenhav, Yehouda (2006) *The Arab Jews: A postcolonial reading of nationalism, religion, and ethnicity*, Stanford, CA: Stanford University Press.

Shiblak, Abbas (1986) *The lure of Zion: The case of Iraqi Jews*. London: Al-Saqi Books.

Shohat, Ella (1988) "Sephardim in Israel: Zionism from the standpoint of its Jewish victims," *Social Text* 19/20: 1–35.

Shohat, Ella (1999) "The invention of the Mizrahim," *Journal of Palestine Studies* 29(1): 5–20.

Shohat, Ella (2006) *Taboo memories, diasporic voices*, Durham, NC: Duke University Press.

Simon, Reeva (1986a) *Iraq between the two World Wars: The creation and implementation of a nationalist ideology*, New York: Columbia University Press.

Simon, Reeva (1986b) "The teaching of history in Iraq before the Rashid 'Ali coup of 1941," *Middle Eastern Studies*, 22(1): 37–51.

Somekh, Sasson (2007) *Baghdad, yesterday, the making of an Arab-Jew*, Jerusalem: Ibis Editions.

Spivak, Gayatry (1988) "Can the subaltern speak," in Cornel West, Cary Nelson & Lawrence Grossberg (eds.) *Marxism and the interpretation of culture*, Chicago, IL: University of Illinois Press, pp. 271–313.

Wien, Peter (2006) *Iraqi Arab nationalism: Authoritarian, totalitarian and pro-Fascist inclinations, 1932–1941*, New York: Routledge.

Wild, Stefan (1985) "National Socialism in the Arab Near East between 1933 and 1939," *Die Welt des Islams*, 1/4, 136–137.

Yaron, Avner-Ya'qov (2004) *Shalom lakh Baghdad* [*Farewell Baghdad*], Jerusalem: Research Institute of the Zionist-Pioneer Underground in Iraq. (In Hebrew.)

Zu'aytar, Akram (1994) *Bawākir al-nidāl, min mudhakkirāt Akram Zu'aytar, 1909–1935* [*My struggle: The memoirs of Akram Zu'aytar, 1909–1935*], Beirut: al-mu'assasa al-'arabiyya lil-dirāsāt wal-nashr (In Arabic.)

Zubaida, Sami (2002) "The fragments imagine the nation: The case of Iraq," *International Journal of Middle East Studies* 34(2): 205–215.

Part III
Suspended Visibilities

10 The Human Right to Education in Arab Countries

An International Law Perspective

Sawsan Zaher

Introduction

Until the formulation of international human rights law, which followed the grave violations and genocidal policies committed during World War II, 'education' was recognized only as a duty of parents.[1] Initially, the 1945 Charter of the United Nations did not recognize the right to education as such. Subsequently, major international legal instruments recognized and affirmed the right to education. Article 26 of the UN Declaration of Human Rights (UNDHR) of 1948 recognized that "Everyone has the right to education." According to Hodgson, setting elementary and fundamental education as a compulsory obligation on state members through Article 26 "appears to be based on the notion that every person has an irrevocable entitlement to a period of education at public expense."[2] Hodgson further argues that "the apparent inconsistency between the right to education and the compulsory nature of elementary education can be accommodated if the term 'compulsory' is intended to imply that no person or body can prevent children from receiving a basic education", thus imposing a minimum obligation on the state to ensure that children receive elementary education in circumstances of parental neglect or ignorance.[3] Nevertheless, Article 26 lacks full recognition of the state's obligation to all components of the right to education. As such, it stipulates that elementary and fundamental education should be compulsory. Secondary and tertiary education were not mentioned explicitly, nor were they recognized by Article 26. However, the latter did recognize that technical and professional education should be generally available, but not necessarily compulsory, and higher education should be equally accessible to all.

The UNESCO Convention against Discrimination in Education of 1960 was the first international instrument after the UNDHR to detail the international standards for public education.[4] Nevertheless, its major aim was to eliminate discrimination and ensure equality of opportunities of public education at all levels and for all.[5] This is also the case in the International Convention on the Elimination of All Kinds of Discrimination Against Women (CEDAW) in which Article 10 stipulates that States "shall take all appropriate measures to eliminate discrimination against women in order to ensure to them equal rights with men in the field of education ...".[6]

The scope of the right to education was further detailed in 1966, when the International Convention on Economic, Social and Cultural Rights (ICESCR) was adopted.[7] In its Article 13 the scope of the right to education reaffirms that everyone has the right to education for the "full development of the human personality and the sense of dignity", in ways that "strengthen the respect for human rights and fundamental freedoms." In addition, this article defines the scope of the right to education to include primary education as compulsory and free for all; secondary education in its different forms "shall be made generally available and accessible to all"; higher education "shall be equally accessible to all" and basic education "shall be encouraged or intensified as far as possible for those persons who have not received or completed the whole periods of their primary education." Thus, Article 13 expands the scope of the right to education addressed in Article 26 of the UNDHR. It is considered as the most detailed provision of the right to education enshrined in international legal instruments. It not only expands the scope of elementary public education to include compulsory education but it also calls for the progressive introduction of free education, and recognizes secondary education as well. According to Article 2 of the ICESCR, the implementation of the right to education contained in Article 13 imposes positive action on state members to take steps in order to implement the right to education.[8] Article 13 is even stronger and wider than the scope of the right to education as addressed in the Convention on the Rights of the Child (CRC).[9] Whereas Article 13 of the ICESCR sets a State's obligation to provide compulsory and free primary education, Article 28 of the CRC asserts that States should "*make* primary education compulsory and available free to all". It hence enables States to provide primary education progressively and not immediately. In addition, the CRC provides a weaker frame for State obligation regarding secondary education. While according to the ICESCR States should make secondary education available in its different forms, the CRC provides that States must *encourage* the development of different forms of secondary education. In addition the CRC does not mandate the progressive introduction of free secondary and higher education, as is the case with the ICESCR.[10]

Failure to fulfill the right to education will be considered as a violation of the ICESCR by the State party. The 1986 Limburg Principles on the Implementation of the ICESCR defined as a "violation" of the Covenant a "failure by State party to comply with an obligation contained in the Covenant," either by commission or omission. Later on, the Maastricht Guidelines, adopted in 1997 to elaborate on the Limburg Principles, have defined violations of ICESCR in relation to the obligations of states as failure of the member State to "respect, protect and fulfill" the rights set out in the ICESCR.

The Philosophical Foundations of the Right to Education

Katarina Tomasevski, the Special Rapporteur on the right to education for the United Nations Commission on Human Rights, observes that "rights-based education necessitates two changes: human rights ought to be moved from the margins to the core of the many policies that shape education, and the universality of the right to education ought to be translated into universal human rights obligations" in the field of education.[11] By not adopting education as a human right, core benefits which arise from respecting and fulfilling the right to education will remain ignored.

The most important foundation of the human right to education is a person's "inherent dignity".[12] According to Beiter, "education should be seen as a requirement of human dignity and should, therefore, be recognized as a human right".[13] This foundation can be based on the language of the UNDHR and on Article 13 of the ICESCR, which clearly establish the connection between education and human dignity. Secondly, the "social utilitarian argument" emphasizes the important role of education in exercising citizenship and public responsibilities and in exercising basic political rights, such as the right to vote and to actively participate in political life in a meaningful way. This aspect of the right to education is important in order to maintain democratic social structures and values.[14] Thirdly, education is a 'prerequisite for individual development', thus illustrating the importance of education for the development of the individual and realizing his/her own potential.[15] Such an approach is grounded in international legal instruments, especially CEDAW, which focuses on enabling all individuals, especially women and children, to develop their "abilities, individual judgment and sense of moral and social responsibility".[16] Fourth, the 'individual welfare argument', emphasizes the right of the individual for such a welfare necessity which he/she cannot provide by him/herself, and thus he/she is entitled to receive their basic needs.[17] Thus, realizing the human right to education encompasses an inclusive approach to the role of a person, either citizen or non-citizen. Fulfilling the right to education to all enables all persons to undertake an active role both at the level of their personal lives and at the public and political levels.

Right to Education in the Arab States

International institutions, such as the United Nations Development Program (UNDP) and the World Bank, have adopted an approach in the Arab states which articulates education within the context of economic policy. 'Knowledge' is defined as the 'road to development and liberation'.[18] Recently, the World Bank (2008) issued a report, *The Road Not Traveled*, which focuses on economic growth as an ultimate benefit from education. The report focuses on the economic dimensions of education rather than on the rights-based dimension. The report explores whether past investments in education in the Middle East and North Africa (MENA) region have generated their maximum economic returns. It concludes that despite improvements the MENA region "has not capitalized fully on past investments in education, let alone developed education systems capable of meeting new challenges. The education systems did not produce what the markets needed, and the markets were not sufficiently developed to absorb the educated labor force into the most efficient uses" (p. 2).

In this chapter, I argue that adopting an education as a right-based approach – which binds the state to respect, protect and fulfill the right to education – should be considered as an alternative approach in Arab countries which currently situate education almost exclusively within the context of economic policy.

Education as a Human Right in Arab Legal Instruments

It is important to start by addressing the status of the right to education and its scope as articulated in the Arab Charter on Human Rights. The Charter, whose 1994 version was revised, was adopted by the League of Arab States in May 2004 and entered into effect in March 2008.[19] The Charter imposes an obligation on States to "provide education directed to the full development of the human person and to strengthen respect for human rights and fundamental freedoms." Article 41(1) of the Arab Charter sets an obligation on the States to eradicate illiteracy and stipulates that "everybody has the right to education." Article 41(2) of the Charter asserts that free education should at least be applicable at the primary and basic level and education shall be compulsory and accessible to all without discrimination of any kind. Despite the universal application of Article 41(1) to 'everyone', Article 41(2) limits the applicability of free and compulsory education to 'citizens' only. The distinction between citizens and non-citizens is illustrated in Article 41(6) of the Charter which stipulates that "States parties shall guarantee the establishment of the mechanisms necessary to provide ongoing education for every citizen and shall develop national plans for adult education." Thus, while the Charter is a revised version of, and seemingly is largely consistent with international law, it still does not totally comply with the provisions of international law and universal human rights, including Article 13 of the ICESCR, which refers to the right of 'everyone' to education.[20] It should be noted that Article 43 of the Charter provides that, "Nothing in this Charter may be construed or interpreted as impairing the rights and freedoms protected by the domestic laws of the States parties or those set in force in the international and regional human rights instruments which the states parties have adopted or ratified, including the rights of women, the rights of the child and the rights of persons belonging to minorities." According to Rishmawi, this latter provision does not resolve the incompatibility of the Charter with the international instruments mentioned in the introduction to this chapter. Rishmawi asserts that reference to Article 43 might be provided in order to strengthen the weak protection of the Charter to the rights of groups mentioned in Article 43 even though it remains unclear how Article 43 would practically protect these groups, especially when many national laws in most Arab countries do not comply with international law (see note 20).

Compliance of Arab States with the International Human Right to Education

This section examines the compliance of Arab countries with the international human rights to education. It discusses the cases of Arab States that have signed and ratified the ICESCR and have already reported to the Committee on Economic, Social and Cultural Rights (CESCR).[21] It is worth noting that the right to education is regarded as part of the customary international law which binds

States that have never signed or ratified the Covenant; thus it is applicable to non-member states as well.[22]

Among the 22 member states affiliated with the League of Arab States,[23] only 14 have signed and ratified the ICESCR: Algeria, Djibouti, Egypt, Iraq, Jordan, Kuwait, Lebanon, Libya, Morocco, Somalia, Sudan, Syria, Tunisia and Yemen.[24] Among these States, only 11 have submitted their reports to the CESCR, leaving out Djibouti, Somalia and Lebanon. Out of the 11 States mentioned above, only nine have submitted their reports within the last decade (1997–2007) and only five (Algeria, Jordan, Morocco, Syria and Libya) have submitted an additional report since their initial one.[25]

The reports submitted by the different Arab States convey the impression that they comply with their international obligation to respect, protect and fulfill the right to education. For example, Arab States examined in this chapter have included compulsory and free elementary or basic education stipulations in their Constitutions. The Egyptian Constitution of 1971 acknowledges compulsory and free primary education for all male and female children above the age of six for eight academic years without discrimination. In addition, since 1990 governmental plans have been authorized to expand educational infrastructure and buildings paralleled by an increase in student enrollment in schools. In Kuwait, the right to free primary education is guaranteed in Article 40 of the Kuwaiti Constitution for both males and females. Such is also the case in Yemen, Syria, Morocco, Jordan and Algeria. As for Sudan, specific legislations exist to the effect of providing every citizen with the right to public basic education for eight years. Primary education has been explicitly recognized as free and compulsory in Article 13 of the Interim National Constitution of the Sudan (2005), while secondary and tertiary education have not. However, no specific legislation exists to ensure education for those who are not enrolled in schools.

According to the States' reports, the majority of Arab States have reported about the availability of secondary, high school and higher education. For example, in Egypt, Kuwait, Syria, Morocco, Jordan and Algeria, secondary education is free, as is higher education in each of Kuwait, Syria and Morocco. In Yemen, no specific legislation exists to ensure the availability of equal and free secondary education to all. However, plans have been adopted to ensure its availability. As for Sudan, secondary and higher education are not guaranteed by law. However, a government plan was adopted in 1998 in order to guarantee general availability of education followed by compulsory education. Still, according to Sudan's report, secondary education is not yet available to all and higher education is available with charge. Exemptions from fees are provided to those who are unable to meet the costs.

According to the States' reports, all States have either adopted plans to eradicate illiteracy or passed specific legislation to that end. In Egypt, the Constitution establishes a national obligation for eradicating illiteracy. Kuwait has passed specific legislation setting compulsory enrollment in illiteracy programs for all males between 14 and 40 years and for females from 14 to 35. Sudan and Syria have passed specific laws aiming to eradicate illiteracy as well. In Yemen, despite the absence of specific legislation ensuring the eradication of illiteracy, plans have been adopted for such purposes. In Morocco, the National Charter for Education and Training of 2000 was formally adopted by the government as a frame of reference for educational policy. It aims to ensure access to primary education and secondary education; the creation of a teacher organization; the improvement of the quality of education, human resources and governance, as well as the elimination of illiteracy by 2015. Algeria, however, did not report on steps and measures taken to eradicate illiteracy. Moreover, almost all countries claimed that they allow the establishment of private education institutions, alongside the public ones. As for the rights of parents to enroll their children in educational institution of their choice, only Egypt and Kuwait have reported that they ensure the realization of such a right.

A closer look reveals a different and much more complex reality, however.

A. Indicators Reveal Low Level of Access to Education

First, despite the fact that the right to education is included in State constitutions (except Sudan until 2005), access to primary education is not guaranteed to all children. According to the World Bank (2008), the Net Enrollment Rate (NER) in each State is measured as "the percentage of number of pupils who are of the official age group for a given level of education in that age group". In this regard, the average NER in the Arab States is still low as well as the percentage of children reaching grade 5. The World Bank's report of 2008 reveals that, for example, in Yemen the NER of children who reached grade 5 in 2005 was only 67.3 percent and in Morocco it only reached 75.6 percent.[26] The World Bank (2008) compared these rates with NER rates in East Asia and Latin America where the average NER in East Asia was 78 percent and 90 percent respectively.

Secondly, the enrollment rate of students in secondary and tertiary education is equally low as illustrated in Table 10.1. These percentages explain the low average of schooling of the total population above the age of 15. For example in 2000, the average years of schooling in Algeria was 5.37; in Egypt 5.51; in Jordan 6.91; in Kuwait 7.05; in Syria 5.77, and in Yemen 2.91.[27]

Thirdly, despite specific legislation and governmental plans adopted to eliminate illiteracy, illiteracy rates in most of the Arab States remain high, especially among females, while only few States have signaled lower illiteracy rates (see Table 10.2).

As for private school enrollment, the World Bank report (2008) reveals that in most of the Arab States examined in this chapter, the percentage of private enrollment in primary, secondary and tertiary education rose during the past years.[28] A few examples are provided in Table 10.3. This trend shows the positive steps undertaken by States to encourage the establishment and operation of private schools. However, it also sheds light on the inequality of the distribution of education such as budget allocation and State funding for private and public schools. Most importantly it sheds light on inequality in access to education since access to private education is available mostly to students from more established economic social backgrounds and it is also more accessible to boys than girls.

Table 10.1   Percentage of Gross Enrollment Rate (GER) of overall students in secondary and tertiary education (2003)*

Country	Secondary	Tertiary
Algeria	80.7	19.6
Egypt	87.1	32.6
Jordan	87.4	39.3
Kuwait	89.9	22.3
Morocco	47.6	10.6
Syria	63.2	45.9
Yemen	45.9	13.2

* The UNDP defines GER as the number of students enrolled in secondary and tertiary education, regardless of age, as a percentage of the population in the relevant age-groups for this level. World Bank (2008): Table 1.4.

Table 10.2   Percentage of illiteracy in the population aged 15+ (2003)

Country	Out of Total Population	Among Females
Algeria	30.1	39.3
Egypt	28.6	40.6
Morocco	47.7	60.4
Syria	20.4	26.4
Yemen	51.0	71.5
Jordan	9.7	15.3
Kuwait	6.7	9.0

* World Bank (2008): Table 1.9.

Table 10.3   Percentage of student enrollment in private schools (1990, 2003)

Country	Primary		Secondary		Tertiary	
	1990	2003	1990	2003	1990	2003
Egypt	5.8	8	3.8	5.5	12.5	16.5
Jordan	22.9	29.9	6.1	16.6	–	24.7
Morocco	3.6	5.5	2.7	4.6	1.5	5.1

* World Bank (2008): Table 1.12

B. Partial Realization of the Right to Compulsory and Free Education

In response to the States' reports, the CESCR acknowledged the progress made by several States in fulfilling the right to education. However, it expressed concern over several components of the right to education that have not been fulfilled, and particularly regarding the fact that compulsory education has not been ensured. For example, in its concluding observation on Egypt's report, the CESCR expressed its 'deep concern' over the schooling of children under 12 years of age who work more than six hours daily in the agricultural sector, an activity which deprives them of their right to education. The Committee added that "reports also claim that children between 8 and 15 years of age work in cotton gins in the Nile Delta under unfavourable conditions without lunch or rest breaks, and have no protection under Egyptian law, particularly with regard to work-related injuries and diseases." According to a report published by Human Rights Watch (2001) titled *Underage and Unprotected: Child Labor in Egypt's Cotton Field*, each year "over one million children between the ages of seven and twelve are hired by Egypt's agricultural cooperatives to take part in cotton pest management ... they work eleven hours a day, including a one to two hour break, seven days a week – far in excess of limits set by the Egyptian Child Law."[29] In addition, according to a UNICEF report of 2005 titled *State of World's Children 2005* the percentage of children aged 5 to 14 involved in child labor activities in Egypt between the years 1999–2003 was 6 percent.[30] A similar concern was expressed in the Committee's concluding observation with regard to Syria's report. According to a UNICEF report (2005), the percentage of children between the ages 5 to 14 involved in child labor in Syria was 8 percent. With regard to Algeria, the CESCR was "deeply concerned about the high drop-out rates, which was acknowledged by the delegation during the dialogue with the Committee" as well as about the decrease in public spending on education. As for Yemen, the CESCR noted that the policy of compulsory education has not yet been fully implemented. It further noted with concern the high drop-out rates, especially among girls in rural areas and the inadequate training of teachers. In its concluding observation on Morocco's report, the CESCR expressed its 'deep concern' about the low level of primary school attendance of both sexes. According to the Committee, 50 percent of children of both sexes are being regularly educated. Access to education remains limited in rural areas, especially for young girls. Thus, clearly, obstacles to education as a right is impacted by a variety of contextual barriers related to economic, labor market, social and political, and gendered social opportunities and practices.

C. Unequal Access to Education

The Committee has also discussed inequality in the implementation and fulfillment of the right to education between diverse socio-cultural groups. For example, the Committee noted with concern the existence of unequal access to education between boys and girls in Egypt as well as the high drop-out rates for boys and high illiteracy rates among adults, particularly women. Regarding Syria's report the Committee expressed, "its concern about the persisting discrimination in the political, social and economic spheres of life against women in Syrian society", especially those practices which result in the low age of marriage of women that prevents them from pursuing their education. In addition, the Committee was "concerned about discrimination against certain minority groups in Syria on the basis of their non-Arab heritage, including those groups that have been living in the territory of the State party for many generations." Moreover, in its concluding observation on Kuwait's report the CESCR expressed its concern over the fact that "ages for admission and completion of free compulsory primary to intermediate education have not been clearly set." The CESCR was concerned over Kuwait's failure to provide free compulsory education to 'non-Kuwaiti' children as well. According to Kuwait's report the Kuwaiti Constitution stipulates that every 'Kuwaiti' has the right to education; it thus excludes non-citizens from the scope of the State's obligation to fulfill their right to education. Hence, the CESCR urged Kuwait to "adopt the necessary measures to ensure that non-Kuwaiti children living in Kuwait have access to free compulsory education."

Moreover the CESCR expressed its concern that, in Morocco, the access of young girls to education is limited, particularly in the rural areas, which leads to high rates of illiteracy especially among adult women. In a country where private education has grown significantly faster compared with other countries in the Maghreb, the Committee noted with concern the "striking difference in level between public and private education which denies equal opportunities to low-income sectors of society." The Committee also expressed concern over the fact that primary and secondary education is given in Arabic whereas higher education in scientific subjects is available only in French, "making it difficult for students from the public sector to enroll." Clearly, then, the structure of educational provision is associated with significant inequities in the fulfillment of the right to education.

In some cases, the Committee urged States to undertake steps and enact legal measures to eliminate discrimination against marginalized groups. For instance, the Committee urged Jordan to take effective legal measures to prohibit discrimination on grounds of sex in all fields, including the field of education. It also requested Sudan to address the root causes of the problem of internally displaced persons in order to provide for adequate measures ensuring their basic needs, such as the continuation of education for children and adequate basic shelter, employment, food and health care.

Two important observations ought to be made in relation to the Committee's concluding observations. First, despite the fact that the Committee touched on issues of inequality between citizens and non-citizens (Kuwait) or between citizens and internally displaced persons (Sudan), it did not clarify to which specific group it is referring, that is, the Committee did not specify whether it was referring to aliens, ethnic, national or other minorities, refugees, stateless persons, indigenous people or some other social group. For instance, according to a Human Rights Watch report from 2000 titled, *Promises Betrayed: Denial of Rights of Bidun, Women and Freedom of Expression*, there were more than 120,000 'Biduns', who reside or were born in Kuwait for decades or generations, but do not hold Kuwaiti citizenship. According to Human Rights Watch (2000), "Bidun in Kuwait face widespread and systematic discrimination on the basis of their origin and status … government policies discriminating against the Bidun are also responsible for serious violations of economic and social rights, such as the right to work, the right to education, and the right to health." In a previous Human Rights Watch (1995) report titled *The Bedoons of Kuwait 'Citizens without Citizenship'*, it was observed that since the 1980s the Kuwaiti government has reversed the practice of granting the Biduns Kuwaiti citizenship. According to the same report, this policy was justified on the theory that the Biduns "are illegal aliens and therefore are not entitled to live in Kuwait or enjoy the basic rights to which citizens and lawful residents are entitled." It should be noted that, occasionally, the Biduns are referred to as an indigenous population residing in most of the Gulf States, including Kuwait.[31] This being mentioned, it should be noted that as an indigenous population they are entitled to all levels of education. The UN Declaration on the Rights of Indigenous Peoples (2007) stipulates in Article 14(2) that "Indigenous individuals, particularly children, have the right to all levels and forms of education of the State without discrimination." Notwithstanding the question of whether or not the Biduns define themselves as 'indigenous', they are still entitled to the protection of other international legal instruments such as the Convention Relating to the Status of Stateless Persons of 1954; the Declaration on the Rights of Persons Belonging to National or Ethnic, Religious or Linguistic Minorities of 1992; and the Declaration on the Human Rights of Individuals Who are not Nationals of the Country in Which They Live of 1985.

In any case it is not clear whether the CESCR relates to the Bidun or to other 'non-citizens' residing in Kuwait. This is the case with other indigenous populations in the Arab States examined in this chapter. It seems that the Committee still needs to be more specific in its approach to indigenous and marginalized communities in order to enable a more effective and efficient enforcement of it recommendations.

Second, the Committee does not specify the measures to be adopted by the States to remediate discrimination. Thus, one might question the weight given to such concluding observations and the extent of their enforcement by State members. The observations presented in this section raise several questions regarding the power of the Committee to enforce its approach to education as an inalienable right. Most importantly, these observations raise crucial questions regarding the philosophical, conceptual and legal bases which frame the right to education for it to be crucially realized and fulfilled for all people.

Conclusion

A substantial involvement of the judiciary is needed in order to ensure the full realization of the right to education. General Comment No. 9 set by the CESCR states that "whenever a Covenant right cannot be made fully effective without some role for the judiciary, judicial remedies are necessary." Without securing the right to education, vulnerable and powerless people remain excluded from the enjoyment of their essential human entitlements.[32] However, enforcement of the right to education through the judiciary in domestic courts in Arab States, including those examined in this chapter, cannot provide a sufficient solution. One of the bases for successful adjudication is preservation of the separation of powers principle between State authorities which includes the independence of the judiciary. This latter principle is lacking in most of the Arab States. The results manifest themselves in the form of social pressures put on judges; restrictions on the jurisdictions of the judiciary; existing provisions for special courts that do not comply with international standards for fair procedures and inadequate allocation of resources to most of the judiciaries in Arab countries.[33] Sherif and Brown observe that "no country in the Arab world lives up to domestic or international standards for independence of the judiciary."[34] The absence of judiciary independence sheds light on the absence of the rule of law in Arab countries. This chapter does not discuss the major role courts can have in implementing and enforcing the right to education. Such reflection should be a matter for a separate chapter, as it raises crucial questions around issues of sovereignty, jurisdiction, and the incorporation of international law within national legislations.

Human rights activists and organizations have a major role in translating the standards of international human rights to the local and national levels. International standards, both in terms of the individual's rights and the State's obligations, should be incorporated at the local level in all relevant institutions. Only then will international human rights law be enforceable nationally. Harold Koh suggests that international human rights law is enforced "through a transnational legal process of institutional interaction, interpretation of legal norms, and attempts to internalize those norms into domestic legal systems."[35] Such a theory "seeks to enforce international norms by motivating nation-states to *obey* international human rights law – out of sense of internal acceptance of international law – as opposed to merely conforming to or complying with specific international legal rules when the state finds it convenient."[36] The process of internalization is accomplished through acquiring public legitimacy and the adoption of international norms by political elites and government policies. Finally, the legal incorporation of international standards into domestic legislation, through the executive, legislative and judicial branches represents an important step.[37]

This chapter suggests that compliance of the Arab States with the international human right to education is partial. The present discussion should provide an incentive for future research into the diverse and contradictory processes which prevent social groups from accessing education as a matter of a human right. Research should also focus on the right of all persons across the Arab region to education, without distinction based on ethnicity, nationality, citizenship, gender, socio-economic status, rural or urban residence, and so on. Here, it would be important to clarify the challenges facing processes of internalization of the international standard regarding access to education as a human right in different parts of the Arab region. Finally, research should examine the steps that need to be taken in the various contexts of the Arab region in order to render the Arab Charter on Human Rights more inclusive and compatible with international standards on the right to education, with the aim of providing 'everyone' with free and compulsory education.

Adopting a universal human rights approach to education shifts the focus from the exclusive focus on education as a market-driven good, to an approach that does not neglect to consider the development of individuals and groups in an inclusive way which leads them to fully exercise their membership in society. Most importantly, it shifts attention from an amorphous conception of education as human capital, driven by 'what the market needs' to an understanding of education as inherently related to an individual's and a community's right to live and fulfill their potential without discrimination and hindrance.

Notes

1 Klaus Beiter, *The Protection of the Right to Education by International Law*, Martinus Nijhoff, 2005 (Chapter 2); and also Douglas Hodgson, *The Human Right to Education*, Dartmouth Publishing Company, 1998.
2 Hodgson, page 41.
3 Hodgson, page 41.
4 http://www.unhchr.ch/html/menu3/b/d_c_educ.htm
5 For the definition of discrimination in education see, Article 1 of the UNESCO Convention.
6 http://www.un.org/womenwatch/daw/cedaw/text/econvention.htm#article10
7 http://www.unhchr.ch/html/menu3/b/a_cescr.htm
8 Beiter, page 96.
9 http://www.unhchr.ch/html/menu3/b/k2crc.htm
10 To compare the two Articles, see Beiter, pages 118–120. In addition, other international instruments address the right to education for specific groups, such as: the Convention Relating to the Status of Refugees of 1951; the Convention Relating to the Status of Stateless Persons of 1954; the Guiding Principles on Internal Displacement of 1998; the Geneva Convention Relative to the Treatment of Prisoners of War of 1949; the Geneva Convention Relative to the Protection of Civilian Persons in Time of War of 1949; the Declaration on the Human Rights of Individuals Who are not Nationals of the Country in Which They Live of 1985; the International Convention on the Protection of the Rights of All Migrant Workers and Members of their Families of 1990; the Declaration on the Rights of Indigenous Peoples of 2007, the Declaration on the Rights of Disabled Persons of 1975; the Declaration on the Rights of Persons Belonging to National or Ethnic, Religious or Linguistic Minorities adopted in 1992.
11 Katarina Tomasevski, *Education Denied: Costs and Remedies*, Zed Books, 2004.
12 Beiter, page 27 and Lonbay, 1988 from Beiter, footnote 35.
13 Beiter, page 26 and Hodgson, pages 18–19.
14 Beiter, page 26 and Hodgson, pages 18–19.
15 Beiter, page 26 and Hodgson, pages 18–19.
16 Hodgson, page 19.
17 Beiter, page 26 and Hodgson, pages 18–19.
18 UNDP, Arab Human Development Report, *Creating Opportunities for Future Generations*, 2002, page 19. See also UNDP, *The Arab Human Development Report, Building a Knowledge Society*, 2003.
19 For the full text of the revised Arab Charter on Human Rights, see: http://www1.umn.edu/humanrts/instree/loas2005.html?msource=UNWDEC19001&tr=y&auid=3337655
20 Mervat Rishmawi, 'The revised Arab Charter on Human Rights: a step forward?', *Human Rights Law Review*, 5(2) 361–376, 2005.
21 Initially and according to the ICESCR, States should have reported to the CESCR every two years. However in its decision from 25 May 1988, the UN Economic and Social Council (ECOSOC) extended the reporting cycle to five years (ECOSOC Resolution 1988/4).
22 Stephen Knight, 'Proposition187 and international human rights law: illegal discrimination in the right to education', *Hastings International and Comparative Law Review*, 19(1) 88, 1995.
23 The States which are members in the League of Arab States are: Jordan, United Arab Emirates, Bahrain, Tunisia, Algeria, Djibouti, Saudi Arabia, Sudan, Syria, Somalia, Iraq, Oman, Qatar, Kuwait, Lebanon, Libya, Egypt, Morocco, Mauritania, Yemen and Comoros. It should be noted that Palestine is also a member in the League of Arab States, however this chapter will not examine its compliance with the international right to education since reports on its behalf have been submitted to the CESCR by the State of Israel. However, due to the fact that Israel is an occupying power over

Palestine, its reports cannot and have not been reflecting appropriately or at all the compliance of Palestine with the right to education. http://www.arableagueonline.org/las/arabic/categoryList.jsp?next−20&level_id−61&image.x−23&image.y=9

24 http://www.unhchr.ch/pdf/report.pdf

25 The Arab States that have reported to the CESCR are: Algeria submitted its initial report in 1994 and its periodic report in 2000; Iraq submitted its second and third periodic reports in 1993 and 1996 respectively; Egypt submitted its initial report in 1998 and has not submitted any periodic report; Jordan submitted its second periodic report in 1998 and has not submitted its third report yet; Morocco submitted its initial and second periodic report in 1999 and its third periodic report in 2005; Yemen submitted its initial report in 2002; Syria submitted its third periodic report in 1999 and has not submitted its fourth report yet; Sudan submitted its initial report in 1998 and has not submitted its second periodic report; Tunisia submitted its second periodic report in 1996; Libya submitted its initial report in 1996 and its second periodic report in 2005 and Kuwait submitted its initial report in 2003. As for Libya, despite having submitted its periodic report in 2005, in the chapter related to its compliance with Article 13, Libya referred back to the initial report it submitted in 1996. Thus, since this chapter deals only with State reports submissions within the last ten years, an analysis of Libya's compliance with Article 13 will not be examined.

26 World Bank, *The Road Not Traveled: Education Reform in the Middle East and North Africa*, Washington, DC: The World Bank, 2008. The data cited is from Table 1.3.

27 World Bank (2008, Table 1.5).

28 World Bank (2008, Table 1.12).

29 For the full report see: http://www.hrw.org/legacy/reports/2001/egypt/Egypt01-03.htm#P143_21787

30 For the full report see: http://www.unicef.org/publications/files/SOWC_2005_(English).pdf

31 Abeer Etefa and Astrid Van Genderen Stort, 'The Excluded: The strange hidden world of the stateless – The Bidoon', *Refugees Magazine*, Issue 147, 2007. Available at: http://www.unchr.org/46dbcdbd2.html

32 Lord Lester of Herne Hill & Colm O'Cinneide "The Effective Protection of Socio-Economic Right" in Yash Ghai & Jill Cottrell, eds., *Economic, Social and Cultural Rights in Practice: The Role of Judges in Implementing Economic, Social and Cultural Rights*, Interights, 2004. Cited on page 17.

33 Adel Omar Sherif and Nathan Brown, 'Judicial Independence in the Arab World' (A study presented to the program of Arab governance of the UNDP), September 2002. Available at: http://www.pogar.org/publications/judiciary/sherif/jud-independence.pdf

34 Ibid.

35 Harold Koh, 'How is International Human Rights Law Enforced? *Indiana Law Journal 74* (January) 1397-1417, 1998, page 1399.

36 Koh page 1408.

37 Koh page 1413.

11 Inclusive Education and Children with Disabilities in the Gulf Cooperation Council Member States

Sara Ashencaen Crabtree and Richard Williams

Introduction

The argument for inclusive education of children with disabilities is one that has been embraced by developing nations in theory, if not always in practice. It is claimed that this is becoming a global movement (Leyser and Romi, 2008). However, little is known about how far the principles underpinning integration in mainstream education for historically excluded groups have been accepted in various world regions, particularly in the Gulf Cooperation Council (GCC) member states. Yet, the GCC region is a particularly interesting one to explore in relation to disability due to the raised awareness of this issue, together with the rapid development of the social infrastructure taking place. So poor is our knowledge of this issue that we remain heavily reliant for information based on a limited body of research that has been used to construe some broad generalisations about disabilities across the Arab region.

It has been estimated that 85 per cent of children with disabilities are located in developing regions, including in GCC countries (Milaat *et al.*, 2001). Yet, although the majority of people with disabilities live in the world's poorer regions there is correspondingly less recognition of what constitutes disability, compared with the higher rates of reported incidence among affluent nations (Barnes and Mercer, 2007). Explanations for this discrepancy refer to the improved survival rate of people with disabilities living in wealthier regions, together with the greater longevity of the general population resulting in disability at a later point in the lifespan. A further explanation could lie in the weaker educational infrastructure in many poor countries preventing schools from being sufficiently equipped to accommodate the needs of pupils with disabilities. A final and cogent point considers the issue of normative behaviour and expectations, where dyslexia, for example, is considered to be a notable handicap for individuals living in societies that depend highly upon literacy skills. However, in the Arab States, traditionally, illiteracy has been widespread in the population, particularly among women, and until recently disability has not been viewed as especially disadvantageous to their prospects in life (Ashencaen Crabtree, 2007a; Haw, 1998). However, the contemporary social agenda of many countries, including the Arab States, is focusing ever more closely on the issues of disability and access to education. The ideologies that underpin more inclusive models of education depend upon particular social constructions of disability; these in turn conform to normative beliefs regarding the roles of individuals within society. Thus, quite different connotations may be given towards the whole conceptualisation of disability in the various parts of the Arab region and their associated life prospects, compared with those found in other regions.

Arguably, there is an urgent need to begin a more systematic scoping of educational inclusion within the geographical boundaries of the GCC. Such an enterprise unfortunately lies beyond the scope of a single chapter, particularly as this information remains difficult to access. Instead, we offer a condensed review of the educational opportunities available to children with disabilities in the GCC states. Over and above the mapping of inclusive education in this region, we offer an analysis of contextual knowledge regarding the social construction of disability in Arab societies.

The Context of Disability and Inclusive Education

Inclusive education is inherently an ideological position, as is the value of education for all and the right to it; all of which are grounded in the conceptualisation of citizenship for all. This said, citizenship is a problematic issue in terms of disenfranchisement where some children experience severe disabilities that render education difficult to achieve. This point notwithstanding, a genuine commitment to inclusive education demands an overhaul of the mainstream school system towards complete restructuring, involving large-scale revisions of pedagogical approaches and curriculum design (Mittler, 1999).

The historical foundation for the principles of a more inclusive education can be traced back to the 1948 Universal Declaration of Human Rights, where Article 26 states that,

> Everyone has the right to education ... [and that] Education shall be directed to the full development of the human personality and to the strengthening of respect for human rights and fundamental freedoms.
>
> (UN, 1948)

Some decades later the 1989 UN Convention on the Rights of the Child acknowledged the vulnerability of children and their need for protection. In addition, the Convention recognised the special needs of children with disabilities and their right to access education, as well as rehabilitative services. This was followed by the World Conference on Education in 1990, which sought to universalise primary education. In 1992, two pioneering countries took the first steps to ensure the full inclusion of children with disabilities. Accordingly, in Italy and Lesotho special schools were abolished, enabling disabled children to be educated in mainstream systems (Mittler, 1999). Although this was experimental and therefore subject to adjustments, these social experiments proved that cautious, lengthy strategies (typical of the approach in the UK, for example) or a large budget were not necessary to embrace the principles of inclusive education. In the same year, the Alliance for Inclusive Education in the UK produced 'The

Inclusive Education System – A National Policy for Fully Integrated Education' (Centre for Studies of Inclusive Education, 2009; Williams and Pritchard, 2006). The following year the UN Standard Rules on the Equalisation of Opportunities for Persons with Disabilities promoted a strong moral and political commitment on the part of governments, in order to achieve equality of opportunities for people with disabilities, commensurate with recognition of their human rights. Inclusive education may form part of such equality, but does not in itself guarantee that other opportunities across the lifespan of individuals will automatically follow.

UNESCO is the primary UN agency focusing on special needs and inclusive education (Mittler, 1999). In 1994 UNESCO's Salamanca Statement asserted that mainstream education provided the most effective means of combating discriminatory attitudes (Centre for Studies of Inclusive Education, 2009). Here it is assumed that early exposure to diversity in classroom settings helps to create a society that is more accepting towards difference. Indeed, a further crucial issue for inclusion in mainstream schools concerns the quality of education provided for children with disabilities in segregated facilities. For example, children who attend 'special schools' are more than twice as likely to leave school with no formal qualifications compared with non-disabled counterparts (Barnes and Mercer, 2007). This in turn will almost inevitably lead to higher rates of unemployment among those with disabilities, with accompanying high rates of poverty and deprivation. Nonetheless, some, including policy makers, educators and parents themselves, to name but a few, have not wholeheartedly embraced the concept of inclusive education, but continue to regard the 'rough-and-tumble' of mainstream education as too challenging an environment for many children with disabilities.

Although the philosophy behind inclusive education has obviously been subject to critique, the momentum towards its social acceptance has been relatively steady. A driving force behind the acceptance of inclusive education is the Education for All (EFA) Global Action Plan, as endorsed at Dakar in 2000 by a host of powerful international bodies, including UNESCO, UNICEF and the World Bank. The six goals include universal primary education and gender equality, and although they do not specifically mention disability by name, referring instead to 'vulnerable and disadvantaged children' (UNESCO, 2009). Although intuitively this definition would appear to include disability, drawing such an inference is problematic. This is owing to conflation of socioeconomic disadvantage with disability. Although it is true that many people with disabilities live in poverty, the application of this definition fails to address many of the unique disadvantages experienced by such groups, in terms of both physical infirmity as well as social attitudes towards disability.

Since 2000 it has become evident that certain regions (sub-Saharan Africa, South and West Asia and the Arab States) will fail to achieve the EFA goals by the deadline of 2005, which has now been extended by another decade (UNESCO, 2009). It is evident therefore that the powerful combination of the UN and the EFA movement combine to form a formidable dynamic that is placing pressure on nations globally to put into place educational targets that overtly accommodate the needs of the most underprivileged children in each society.

To give some indication of the current circumstances affecting the education of children in Arab societies, according to Richards (2003), within the GCC region (at the time of writing) it was estimated that only 75 per cent of girls attended primary school in Saudi Arabia, compared with full attendance by boys. This situation was asserted to be comparable in Oman. Moreover, it is claimed that beyond the GCC region over a third of Moroccan girls did not attend primary school, while in the Yemen, primary school attendance of girls was said to stand at a mere 40 per cent (Richards, 2003). Given these figures the author's point regarding the waste of human potential is well taken. The overall loss must be accounted for not only in terms of human wastage in terms of life opportunities and skilled labour, but also in relation to human dignity and emancipation. This loss could therefore be estimated to be very much higher, if it were possible to factor in the number of children with disabilities who have been excluded from education altogether.

Disability and Inclusive Education in the Arab World

Research is at its early stages in the GCC states. Consequently although inclusive education is evidently on the GCC agenda, a paucity of research literature prevents us from articulating more critical insights into how inclusive education is being interpreted and constructed in the region. Moreover, although there may well be a valuable research canon on disability issues in Arabic, this unfortunately is not accessible to non-Arabic speaking readers. For example, some epidemiological studies into disability in Saudi Arabia help to inform our impressions of the context of disability in that country, but do not provide a great deal of information on social inclusion (Al-Shehri *et al.*, 2008; Al-Asmari *et al.*, 2006; Milaat *et al.*, 2001). Nevertheless highly intriguing snippets of research data can be gathered from across the GCC states that help to inform our understanding of how inclusive education is construed in terms of policies and what the potential issues are.

To-date one of the most informative pieces of data on contemporary social policy in the GCC region comes from the UNESCO–International Bureau of Education (IBE) Preparatory Report (2007) on inclusive education in Gulf Arab States. From this we learn that there is no universally accepted concept of inclusion across the GCC and that each country is at a different location in terms of articulating inclusive strategies (UNESCO–IBE, 2007).

The Kingdom of Saudi Arabia, for example, has a long history in terms of the education of children with disabilities, whereby forty years ago children with disabilities were accommodated in mainstream schools. Later, an interesting *volte face* occurred, whereby once special schools were established separately from mainstream education (although the exact reasons for this are unclear), regular schools declined to admit children with disabilities. However, since 1984 such children have once more been admitted to mainstream education and follow the same curriculum with due adjustments to their learning needs where necessary (UNESCO–IBE, 2007). Inclusive education facilities in the Kingdom appear to be comparatively advanced in offering the supplementary assistance of boarding schools, specially equipped resource rooms and specialist, peripatetic teachers. Moreover, it would appear that the general social attitudes towards inclusive education are reasonably progressive, which could well be a logical consequence of long public exposure to inclusive educational trends in this country.

Commensurate with these educational and social developments, legislation in Saudi Arabia has kept abreast, where in 2009 the Kingdom ratified the UN Convention on the Rights of Persons with Disabilities. The Convention includes a number of Articles referring to the preservation of rights, such as the elimination of obstacles and barriers that create 'disabling environments' in limiting access to public services and resources (Oliver, 1993). Among others, it also includes the commitment in Article 24 that people with disabilities enjoy equal access to primary and secondary education, as well as adult education (UN, 2006).

Apart from ratifying the Convention, Saudi Arabia has also accepted the Optional Protocol, enabling individuals to bring violations of these rights to the International Committee on the Rights of Persons with Disabilities (Shettle, 2008). The Kingdom of Bahrain has also signed the Convention, but has yet to ratify it, as has the UAE. Of the GCC states that have both signed and ratified the Convention, apart from Saudi Arabia, these include both the Sultanate of Oman and the State of Qatar. An interesting observation is that the UK has merely signed the Convention, but has yet to ratify it; and the USA has yet to sign the Convention.

The UNESCO–IBE (2007) report informs us that despite Bahrain's omission in terms of ratification, it is considered by UNESCO to have excellent integrative policies. Here the rights of children with disabilities to education represent a distinct criterion of social development in this society, in keeping with equal opportunities. A concerted attempt is made to offer equitable learning environments to all children regardless of need. That said, some children with serious and complex needs are unlikely to have their learning needs met on an equal basis to other children with disabilities. Nonetheless, special education for both children and adults in Bahrain encompasses a wide variety of special needs, including sensory disabilities, physical and mild to moderate learning disabilities, including children with Down's syndrome.

The State of Kuwait offers an interesting example of commitment to basic education for children in that families are subject to a level of surveillance, whereby children are tracked from birth onwards, ensuring that they are given the opportunity to receive education, and where omission or neglect by parents in this regard is subject to legal sanctions (UNESCO–IBE, 2007). However, Kuwait has not yet moved from a 'special school' model to that of inclusive education in mainstream school systems, although how these special schools operate remains as yet obscure. However, the Kuwaiti 'law of the disabled' (13/96) is said to protect the inclusion rights of people with disabilities in relation to various social settings, including schools and the workplace (Salih and Al-Kandari, 2007: 13). Unfortunately, once again, little more is known of how this particular law operates in practice.

The educational starting point in Oman has lagged behind many of the other GCC states, where the educational system for non-disabled children only commenced in 1970 and that for male children only. Therefore, Oman has a steeper curve to negotiate in relation to the EFA goals towards meeting the educational needs of children with disabilities and the overlapping issue of gender discrimination. Consequently, although the State recognises that much is needed to create a more inclusive model of education, progress is hindered by a lack of specialist knowledge (UNESCO–IBE, 2007). In the meantime there has been notable improvement of school facilities for children in general, but social awareness of disability issues and inclusive education remains at a weak level. It is interesting therefore to speculate whether Oman will actually reach the EFA goals by the new target date of 2015, which under the circumstances looks overly ambitious for this particular country.

In contrast with Oman, Qatar started to promote gender parity through widened access to schools for girls in 1957. From 1972 onwards teacher training programmes were well established, including special needs training. In addition, the Higher Council of Education in Qatar, which has responsibility for the overall education of all children, is engaged in the task of creating an educational terrain built on the principles of 'independence, accountability, diversity and (parental) selection' (UNESCO–IBE, 2007: 28). There are already nine schools practising inclusion in Qatar that accommodate a wide range of disabilities, except for children with severe learning disabilities. Practical steps forward remain at an early stage, with interruptions to an otherwise possible smooth process of integration due to closures of certain designated inclusive schools. Nonetheless a few privately run institutions have been established and are enrolling a number of children with learning disabilities (Al Attiyah and Lazarus, 2007). For example, in 2001, a Qatari government project was set up to undertake the educational inclusion of children with physical disabilities. The evaluation of the success of this programme indicates that bullying has been a problem, underlining the perception in schools of basic differences between children with disabilities and the non-disabled. In addition, the authors indicate that improved preparation for inclusive strategies and the training of teachers needs to be addressed (Al Attiyah and Lazarus, 2007).

Finally, with regards to the UAE, educational issues form a main agenda for the government (UNESCO–IBE, 2007). Although the idea of inclusion is embraced in principle, policy-driven practice has yet to be fully realised. Full inclusion of children with disabilities has some way to go before being fully established. Yet, it is notable that in many mainstream schools such children are provided with learning environments within the school institution itself, in relation to special educational classrooms and resource rooms. Children may access these resources for sessions or spend the entire day in these specialised classrooms. In addition, however, the same curriculum is provided to children with special needs, with additional supported programmes, if required. It is interesting to note that according to UNESCO–IBE (2007) by the year 2006–07, 1709 children had benefited from these educational facilities.

Much of our knowledge regarding the development of inclusion strategies in the UAE has been gained from the work of Arab-British researcher Eman Gaad, who has written extensively on this subject (Alghazo and Gaad, 2004; Gaad, 2001; 2004). Gaad (2004) offers a critique that counterbalances the UNESCO reports, where she claims that although parents in the UAE are largely unaware of inclusion issues, teachers by contrast are well informed. Nevertheless this has yet to translate into fully inclusive practices. Although children holding UAE citizenship are entitled to state-funded education, a two-tier delivery operates. Those children with an IQ of less than 75 (including all children with Down's syndrome) are excluded from mainstream education, to be designated instead for support at 'local centres for preparation and Rehabilitation of the Handicapped' (Gaad, 2001: 195). These centres, although caring and well run, are not always able to entertain ambitious educational goals for many of their students. A curious feature, noted by Gaad (2001), is that these children's services may remain accessible to adult learners well past childhood years; although according to Gaad, without a visible increase in the learning goals offered.

By and large, the legislative framework in the UAE supports the broader educational developments taking place there by acknowledging the rights of people with disabilities to equal status, as well as being entitled to care (Section 25 of the UAE Constitution) (Ashencaen Crabtree, 2007b). In addition, the Disability Act (Federal Law No.29/2006) was passed in 2006 with a view to protecting the rights of children with disabilities in terms of equal physical access to buildings and resources (Emirates Special Needs, 2007).

Implications for Inclusive Education in the GCC

Aside from inclusive educational issues, general and tertiary education in the GCC states have increasingly come to the fore with regards to the question of how far they equip citizens to participate more fully in the global economy. For example, the UAE is highly dependent upon expatriate workers who form 70 per cent of the labour force (Al-Sulayti, 1999). In fact, one of the significant anomalies of the GCC states is that, with the exception of Saudi Arabia, nationals form a minority population in comparison with a majority and diverse population of expatriates. Thus, although the predominance of such workers in the UAE represents a very high figure, it reflects a general problem in the GCC region, and arguably, particularly in terms of highly qualified or skilled labour.

It has also been noted that religious instruction forms a main item in the curriculum in some GCC countries (Gaad, 2001), to the extent that in Saudi Arabia it is claimed that '30 or 40% percent of all course hours are devoted to the study of scripture' (Richards, 2003: 12). In addition to this, across several GCC states, including the UAE, there has been a heavy reliance on rote learning and memorisation, rather than analysis and critical thinking, which tends to encourage surface learning, as opposed to the deep learning processes that are critical to successful tertiary level education (Al-Sulayti, 1999; Richards, 2003). Nevertheless the caveat proffered by Clarke (2008) warns against the static essentialising of both the dynamic culture and those presumed cultural and religious values that underpin education in the given national context.

Boud and Walker (1990) argue that the 'learning milieu' involves a number of interconnected factors relating to the social, cultural, institutional and material environment. The student's motivation to learn, as a personal and intentional endeavour, differs from the imposition of learning goals by instructors. For the student, a sense of purpose needs to be developed for success. However, in educational milieus that rely heavily on student compliance and learning dependency, such as in the case of rote learning strategies, learning becomes a series of futile obstacles to overcome, but without much accompanying sense of self-actualisation or personal development. It is questionable how this kind of pedagogy impacts upon the learning needs of children with disabilities, since to our best knowledge there is no research data emerging from the GCC to enlighten us on this subject. Nonetheless any desirable revisions to educational curricula in mainstream education will have some positive impact on curriculum development for special needs.

What is known is that inclusive education is forming a strand in emerging debates about education in general, but is not yet viewed as a priority issue in the GCC states (UNESCO–IBE, 2007). The accelerated pace of development characteristic of many GCC states may mean that the goal of 'Education for All' could in theory be achieved within a reasonably rapid time span. This is dependent upon the political and professional commitment to an overhaul of current educational systems where these militate against inclusivity. In the meantime, free state-run education and many special services can be accessed, in many instances, only by nationals. Where such policies exist there is a conspicuous failure to accommodate the needs of those dependent families of migrant labourers who are permitted to enter the GCC states with the main breadwinner. This in turn cuts across the intersections of class, ethnicity and gender, in that skilled workers (the vast majority of whom are male) are more likely to be permitted to bring in their spouses and children than manual labourers.

An important implication for rehabilitative services working in alliance with educational services is that a large number of these employ skilled expatriate labour. It is as yet unknown how many of such services have widened access to include expatriate service users, as opposed to those primarily run by nationals. Nonetheless the issue of social justice and equal access of opportunity in relation to the needs of people with disabilities across diverse ethnic groups must be addressed to fall within the letter and spirit of Education for All. Across most of the GCC region this is a particularly pertinent issue, in relation to the mass of expatriate workers who have made a huge contribution to the wealth of the GCC, but may be forever barred from achieving citizenship and all those benefits associated with that status.

As has been noted in a number of studies, the attitude of the teaching profession towards inclusion is critical to the success and maintenance of inclusive strategies (Alghazo and Gaad, 2004; Opdal *et al.*, 2001; Leyser and Romi, 2008; Salih and Al-Kandari, 2007). In this vein, a study by Alghazo and Gaad (2004) indicates that the attitudes of UAE teachers towards inclusion of children with disabilities are heavily weighed against the inclusion of children with learning disabilities, in favour of those with physical disabilities or visual impairments. However, in opposition to this stance Clarke (2008: 184) argues that in fact there is a 'wholehearted engagement' by UAE national teachers with the complex modalities of emerging pedagogical philosophy that is in turn transforming the educational scene in the State. Despite this confident and positive assertion by Clarke, other research findings referring to the GCC states indicate that, for example, in Kuwait, astonishingly, despite studying social work at tertiary level, future educators retain highly discriminatory attitudes towards people with learning disabilities (Salih and Al-Kandari, 2007). Among other oppressive responses noted, the authors state that '65.6% of the students reported their disagreement to renting an apartment to a family who has a person with MR [mental retardation]' (Salih and Al-Kandari, 2007: 24).

Finally, the aforementioned inclusion project in Qatar was only made available to children with physical disabilities in an educational environment that was totally reliant on families to attend to the physical needs of their disabled child, as well as to provide special transport. Such heavy dependency on family caregivers on a daily basis can hardly represent a sustainable model for inclusion, over and above the demoralising educational prospects for those with other forms of disability (Al Attiyah and Lazarus, 2007).

Notwithstanding the evidence of patchy provision of education for children with disabilities, this is clearly a task that the GCC states are engaging with, although at variable rates of progress. At a regional conference on inclusive education in the Gulf Arab States (including the countries of the GCC), Bubshait (2007), a representative of the Gulf Arab States Educational Research Centre, outlined the conceptual framework for inclusion, where it was stated that mainstream school *is* the normal environment for the education of children with disabilities, with the associated goal of 'Education for All'. Encouragingly, both children with Down's syndrome and learning disabilities (mild to moderate) are included in this group, although autistic children and those with severe learning disabilities remain excluded, even though autism, as is well known, covers a wide spectrum of abilities. Bubshait (2007) also identifies several strategic needs, including a requirement to redesign the educational curriculum to be more adaptive. This is a very important consideration, as exclusion of children, other than those with physical disabilities, has to a large extent been caused by the need for greater flexibility of mainstream curricula in some GCC countries. In this respect there is a need to take greater account of the alternative learning needs of some children who could otherwise succeed in mainstream schools (Al Attiyah and Lazarus, 2007).

Despite the paucity of data, the Middle East nonetheless offers some interesting comparisons in relation to the attitudes and practices by teachers towards the implementation of inclusive education. Egypt, for instance, is one of the less affluent Arab countries, along with Syria, Jordan and Tunisia, whose wealth partially lies in the exporting of professional expertise in various skilled capacities. The UAE, in particular is a major importer of these peripatetic professionals recruited to meet the needs created by the national current skills deficit in several essential areas. One irony therefore is that while educational inclusion is beginning to gain a foothold in the UAE, Egypt has failed to keep pace in this respect (Gaad, 2004). Gaad (2004) further reports that, to date, Egyptian children with disabilities have been subject to so much overt discrimination and social exclusion that their parents express gratitude for any services they can access that will assist their child at all.

In comparison, in the Palestinian context, despite the tremendous fragmentation of the social infrastructure due to continued conflict, this has become a promising arena for educational inclusion. Opdal *et al.* (2001) note that after 1994, when the Palestinians were permitted by Israel to run their own education system, they chose to deal with the issues of disability and education through a combination of rehabilitation services, together with inclusive education approaches. Not only had there been very little investment in the Palestinian teaching profession under Israeli occupation, but classrooms were extremely overcrowded and operated under dire conditions without basic amenities, such as water and electricity (Opdal *et al.*, 2001). The implications of a weakened infrastructure, whether due to general poverty or civil strife, clearly are that children with disabilities are once again even more disadvantaged than their non-disabled peers. This situation, however, has yet to be critically examined and resolved. Although arguably in their official capacity the International Monetary Fund and World Bank are in a good position to promote policies towards greater inclusion, alongside that of underpinning economic stability in the poorer regions of the world. Yet, as the Lesotho and Italian experiments amply demonstrate, successful inclusion does not primarily hinge upon fiscal resources but upon the intangible factor of the commitment to the cause of inclusion (Mittler, 1999).

In their study, Opdal *et al.* (2001) report that despite the repercussions of civil conflict that have in turn impacted on education in Palestine, 87 per cent of the participating teachers (of a total of 90 respondents interviewed) were currently dealing with children with disability/special needs in their classrooms. The high percentage of disability, in what could be considered mainstream education, is due to a number of factors, some of which can be viewed as a consequence of often extreme conflict-ridden local conditions. In the main, however, regardless of the singularity of the Palestinian example, poverty and malnutrition are the main cause of disability globally (Barnes and Mercer, 2007). To return to the Palestinian situation, children with physical disabilities, visual and speech/language impairments, psychological problems and learning disabilities are all seen within the school system. In this vein Punamäki *et al.* (2001: 256) discuss the effects of trauma in Palestinian children exposed to political and military violence leading to 'high levels of anxiety, emotional and behavioural symptoms, and post-traumatic stress disorder (PTSD) among children and adolescents ...'. Although it is recognised that trauma is connected to a number of psychological and learning difficulties in children (as well as adults), how such needs are actively accommodated within the ideological framework and pedagogical strategies of inclusive education in Palestine requires further illumination.

Finally, of these respondents 60 per cent of Palestinian teachers are said to have supported mainstreaming inclusion policies, with no particular differences based on the gender of the teachers, unlike in the UAE study, where female teachers were more supportive of inclusive policies than their male counterparts (Alghazo and Gaad, 2004). In relation to the Palestinian study, Opdal *et al.* (2001) point out that given the extremely poor infrastructure for effective teaching, as well as presumably the continued challenges for teachers in a conflict zone, this is a surprising and indeed encouragingly high figure (Opdal *et al.*, 2001). This level of acceptance among teachers may reflect the changing attitudes towards disability in Palestinian society, where disability in youths has come to be associated with civil resistance to Israeli occupation (Atshan, 2007).

The Social Construction of Disability in Arab Societies

Disability has been subject to a considerable amount of theorising, leading to the establishment of a new area of academic inquiry, notably disability studies. Theoretical debates have clarified how disability is socially constructed. These perspectives serve to inform our understanding of similar phenomena cross-culturally, such as in GCC societies, where although the nuances may differ, these are equally subject to socially constructed norms and interpretations. Foucault's conceptualisation of 'régimes of truth' reminds us that the 'truths' inherent in social constructions cannot be separated from ideology, which is itself embedded in the social and historical context (Alvesson, 2002; Cohen, 2008). It behoves us therefore to seek to understand how 'disablement', to borrow Oliver's (1996) term, is shaped and mediated by the 'vectors of power' in society (Narayan, 1997).

Accordingly, Oliver (1996), writing from the context of the UK, examined prevalent but transitional models of disability, commencing with the individual model of disability, where the problem is perceived to lie with the individual. Connected with this model is that of the 'personal tragedy of disability', where disability is seen as catastrophic and virtually irredeemably negative (Oliver, 1996). The so-called 'social model of disability' challenges the tragedy model, which includes the less radical interpretation by Barnes and Mercer (2007: 9) in noting that people with disabilities are seen as 'unfortunate' and excluded from participating in normal interactions and rewards in society. Again, connected with the social model is an overlapping conceptualisation of the 'social death' model, as articulated by Finkelstein (1993), which emphasises the expected withdrawal of the individual from mainstream society due to disability.

A second body of critique deconstructs this assumed withdrawal in relation to the social barriers that people with disability must negotiate in order to participate in a society that is oppressive (Mittler, 1999). These barriers encompass the issues of equal access to education, together with those that disadvantage people with disabilities in exploiting essential resources like education, transport, appropriate housing and employment. Theorisation therefore revolves around environments that are viewed as disabling, rather than on the deficiencies of individuals with disabilities (Oliver, 1993). Moreover, as Oliver (1996) later argues, the concept of integration has undergone revision, in that it is now viewed as an aspect of social diversity and hence to be celebrated, rather than premised on the 'personal tragedy' perspective. The view of disability as a form of diversity has close links to that of citizenship in terms of the extent of how far people with disabilities can participate equally in society, which has become a marker by which to measure social progress (Oliver, 1996). Citizenship is fundamentally linked to the relationship between the citizen and the State, informed by a historical discourse that has long explored the contentious issues of individual rights and State responsibilities.

Molloy and Vasil (2002) locate disability critiques, like Oliver's, as co-emerging with social activism and advocacy movements, which view the prevailing social construction of disability as essentially hostile towards people with disabilities. However, although this is not the case in Lebanon where people with disabilities and their advocates have formed effective pressure groups (Lakkis, 2007), within GCC societies vigorous social activism against the disenfranchisement of such individuals would sit uneasily in Arab states where democratic models of governance are not practised. Therefore, while the negative connotations of disability are being reconstructed in these societies, it may not be via the form of highly politicised citizenship agenda that has shaped disability discourses and social activism in the West. Instead, there is an uneasy tension between culturally-based attitudes towards the issue of disability and that of Islamic frames of reference aimed at enhancing social equity and welfare (Ashencaen Crabtree *et al.*, 2008). For example, discrimination towards people with disabilities is not condoned by Islam; instead Muslims are exhorted to extend care to vulnerable individuals (Ashencaen Crabtree *et al.*, 2008; Bywaters *et al.*, 2003). Many welfare and rehabilitation centres in the GCC do appear to be premised on Oliver's (1996) 'personal tragedy' perspective towards disability; and this view is compatible with the Islamic perspective. Historically, however, such individuals have sometimes successfully occupied socially valuable roles, such as the example of blind reciters of the Holy Qur'ān, who were able to traverse the segregated worlds of the sexes without causing offence (Ashencaen Crabtree *et al.*, 2008). That said, Morad *et al.* (2001: 65) also note that intellectual disability in Islam is viewed as relegating the individual to a non-competent status in the Qur'ān and the Hadith. The ramifications of this status may well have coloured both historical and contemporary attitudes towards people with disabilities, leading to more paternalistic paradigms of care, which may not fit well with modern inclusive ideologies.

It is also recognised that religion tends to determine social attitudes in non-Western societies. Barnes and Mercer (2007) argue that a closer engagement with material oppressions affecting minority groups is often lacking, thereby serving vested interests within the prevailing status quo. This same concern would also apply when considering disability in Arab (and predominantly Muslim) societies: clearly the danger for people with disabilities lies in creating paternalistic, charitable service provision that effectively obscures a service user, rights- and empowerment-based discourse.

With regards to how disability is perceived, it has often been stated that Arab communities, whether based in the Middle East or as part of a global diaspora, regard disability as a stigmatising condition that affects the entire family (Ashencaen Crabtree, 2007c; Atshan, 2007; Boukhari, 2007; Sharifzadeh, 2004; Westbrook and Legge, 1993). Despite some changing attitudes and positive developments towards disability in the GCC and the wider Middle East, stigmatisation of people with disabilities remains a serious issue. However, it should be noted that following the Second World War, in the West there was a widespread professional assumption that guilt was a normal reaction of parents of disabled children (Read, 2000). Consequently we should be wary of wholesale generalisations of negative responses towards disability, for a small body of research indicates that certain Arab families consciously extend acceptance towards their own disabled child based on religious piety, as well as normal parental love (Ashencaen Crabtree 2007b; Ashencaen Crabtree *et al.* 2007).

However, there is also evidence to show that a high level of stigma towards disability features in societal attitudes among Arab groups. Westbrook and Legge

(1993: 179) argue that ethnic groups from collectivist cultures, such as Arabs, primarily view the value of children in economic terms; hence due to patriarchal notions, disability in sons is considered 'particularly tragic'. Ashencaen Crabtree *et al.* (2007) note that in their study of family perceptions in the UAE, disability in sons was often viewed as more disappointing to fathers than that in daughters, as economic hopes tended to rest upon the birth of sons due to prevailing gender norms. Other studies confirm that the birth of disabled children is considered shameful and stigmatising (Boukhari, 2007; Khamis, 2007; Sharifzadeh, 2004). Even the very term 'disability' can be overtly rejected in some quarters as unacceptably demeaning: 'If you call someone disabled, it is as if you are insulting them' a member of the Federal National Council in Abu Dhabi, UAE is quoted as saying in response to the replacement of the term 'special needs' (bin Huwaidi, 2008). This apparent idiosyncrasy is also noted by Ashencaen Crabtree (2007b), where in her study a mother of a wheelchair-bound teenager with complex needs denies that he is actually disabled.

It is, however, interesting to reflect upon this mother's response in the light of the previously discussed dichotomy between disparaging social attitudes informing the concept of disability and the lived experience. On the one hand such a response by this parent may be construed as resistance towards the stigmatisation of disability, while not denying the impairment. However, findings from the same study indicate that in fact parental attitudes towards disability in offspring tend to revolve around attempts to normalise impairment, with the aim of meeting general expectations governing gender norms within society, such as that adult children will marry and produce families of their own (Ashencaen Crabtree, 2007a, 2007b).

The foundation of such disparaging attitudes may possibly derive in some small part from religious interpretation, but it is also probable that the source lies in cultural beliefs. One antiquated but interesting paper offers an intriguing clue to this question in noting that

> the Jews from Iraq (and possibly other Middle-Eastern countries) regard physical disability in the child as a punishment from heaven, and the owner of the defect is expected to be 'kept in' at the home of the family.
>
> (Chigier and Chigier, 1968: 314)

Commensurate with this observation, confinement within the family setting has been a common feature of life for many Arabs with disabilities (Ashencaen Crabtree, 2007b; Gaad, 2001; Westbrook and Legge, 1993). Cloistering practices like these, despite taking place in the home, rather than in Western institutional care, conform to Finkelstein's (1993) notion of 'social death'. In this vein Siminski (2003), citing Oliver (1996), echoes the dichotomised discourse revolving around physical impairment and social experience in terms of the imposition of restrictions towards people with disabilities, and their removal from productivity and participation in civic society.

Disability in Arab societies, as elsewhere, intersects across gender, ethnicity and class, militating against a disabled equality of oppression. This holds a particular significance in relation to inclusive education, as gender equality forms a main item on the EFA agenda. Critically, impoverished girls and women with disabilities are the most oppressed group in predominantly patrilineal societies. The repercussions of sexist devaluation of females, in terms of social and health inequities in Arab societies, are an important area of concern, but one where data is scant. Inferences may be obliquely drawn from observations like that of Shawky *et al.* (2002) who note that in Saudi Arabia high levels of illiteracy in mothers is correlated with childhood disability. Additionally, Khandekar and Al Khabori (2004) comment that girls and women in Oman demonstrated higher rates of visual and aural disability than among males.

Abu-Habib (2007) in turn expresses that in her study of women's experiences of disability in the Middle East, many girls were found to be deprived of opportunities, including basic education. A tiny minority, however, had been granted more autonomy and freedom of movement than their non-disabled sisters, as they were not perceived as meriting the greater protection and surveillance that patriarchal gender norms extend to women.

It is apparent that the social attitudes that have disempowered people with disabilities are changing in Arab states, with associated improvements towards equal access to resources, such as education. In certain societies, such as Israel and the UK, for instance, Muslims have been viewed as partially culpable for the reported high rates of disability that can affect these minority communities in majority cultures (Ashencaen Crabtree *et al*, 2008; Ahmad, 1994; Dinero, 2002). Studies of Arabs in the Israeli context refer to a dominant group subtext: namely, that minority Arab groups are viewed as being reproducers of disability through traditional practices, such as consanguinity (first cousin marital unions), and the early and prolonged fertility patterns among Arab women (Abu-Rabia and Maroun, 2004; Dinero, 2002). Kenan and Burck (2002: 404) offer some useful insights into the increase of such unions among Muslims in Israel, whereby they argue that this has become a necessity due to the national borders having closed, preventing 'bride-trading' practices among neighbouring tribal groups. The issue of consanguinity as the main cause of disability among Muslim minority communities has additionally been raised as a social issue in Western countries. It has in turn been challenged as racist and Islamophobic, rather than being based on incontrovertible scientific evidence (Ashencaen Crabtree *et al.*, 2008). Nonetheless a combination of factors, including political ones, are liable to lead to increased rates of disability in Muslim populations, including underprivileged conditions, the disinclination of Muslims to abort abnormal foetuses and the potential effects of consanguineous unions.

In conclusion, while it is clear that international and local socio-political forces are driving an inclusion agenda in the countries of the GCC, albeit unevenly, a number of issues need to be addressed to enable a smoother transition from segregation to inclusion of children with disabilities. These may be summarised in the following way: firstly, disempowering social constructions of disability need to be challenged, not only by professionals and parents, but also through the encouraged development of self-advocacy disability groups that are active in the political field of power. Linked to the issue of discrimination, gender inequalities in relation to access to education must be a recognised priority across all sectors of society. Thirdly, traditional and inflexible teaching styles that serve to inhibit educational inclusion need to be replaced by more effective forms of pedagogy. Fourthly, and connected with the former point, suitable and progressive curriculum development forms a vital component in this endeavour. Fifthly, teachers need to be adequately supported to adopt inclusive strategies through not only additional training locally, but also where appropriate exposure to environments where they may witness this being successfully implemented.

Developing inclusive education for children with disabilities is, as we have seen, a global issue. The concern that disability is linked to educational under-achievement can be best understood and thereby rectified as an issue that relates to inadequate educational opportunities, rather than being one caused by disability (Peters, 2003). Inclusive practices are committed to the ideal of all children and young people achieving their potential. In addition to this is a need to ensure that all children can experience success and, regardless of disability, will be welcomed and valued in schools. In turn, schools must focus upon the strengths of individuals, rather than continue to defend a deficit model, which seeks to define a person by their disability and thereby undermines their intrinsic value as a human being.

The process of including children with disabilities in education entails a long-term commitment from across the multi-faceted layers within any given society; layers that essentially include both the political spectrum and professional bodies. While there is evidence that inclusive provision leads to improvements for all at the individual school level (Williams and Pritchard, 2006), and that such outcomes can be influenced by individual practitioners and managers, the macro level of practice development requires more strategic action.

UNESCO's commitment to support universal primary education for all by 2015 will be crucial in securing the provision to include children with disability in manageable, all-ability groups. These need to offer a formative, inclusive experience to all children within the normative, mainstream school setting as early as possible; and thereby erect a barrier against socially and educationally excluding experiences.

Teacher training plays an essential role. For example the Brazilian government has legislated to improve the provision for students with profound hearing impairment. This has led to new teacher training programmes to improve the outcomes for school-aged students; and has increased access to higher education for these people as mature students (Ferreira, 2005).

Finally, inclusion is more likely to be successful and sustainable where material resources and facilities are carefully planned to meet the needs of diverse groups of children with disabilities within a larger framework of social justice and equity. Furthermore, although research in this area has been scant in the GCC to date, charting the momentum of the adoption and adaptive indigenisation of inclusion strategies within the region would provide fascinating material for future research. This is likely to be of enormous benefit to local educators and practitioners, as well as making a valuable contribution to the international knowledge base.

Acknowledgements

The authors would like to thank the following participating Centres for offering valuable insights into inclusion and children with disabilities: the Sharjah City for Humanitarian Services and the Dubai Center for Special Needs in the UAE; and finally, the Association of Early Intervention for Children with Special Needs in Oman. We would also like to thank Nahida Seifert for her assistance in the completion of this chapter.

References

Abu-Habib, L. (2007) Working with disabled women: reviewing our approach. In L. Abu-Habib (Ed.) *Gender and Disability: Women's Experiences in the Middle East* (pp. 1–26). Oxford: Oxfam.

Abu-Rabia, S., & Maroun, L. (2005) The effect of consanguineous marriage on reading disability in the Arab community. *Dyslexia, 11*, 1–21.

Ahmad, W. I. U. (1994) Reflections on the consanguinity and birth outcome debate. *Journal of Public Health Medicine, 16*(4), 423–28.

Al-Asmari, A., Al Moutaery, K., Akhdar, F., and Al Jadid, M. (2006) Cerebral palsy: Incidence and clinical features in Saudi Arabia. *Disability and Rehabilitation, 28*(22), 1373–1377.

Al Attiyah, A., and Lazarus, B. (2007) 'Hope in the life': the children of Qatar speak about inclusion. *Childhood Education,* Retrieved Jan 20, 2009, from http://www.articlearchives. com/medicine-health/diseases-disorders/518385-1.html

Alghazo, E.M., and Gaad, E.E.N. (2004) General education teachers in the United Arab Emirates and their acceptance of the inclusion of students with disabilities. *British Journal of Special Education, 31*(2), 94–99.

Al-Shehri, A.-S., Farahat, F.M., Hassan, M.H., and Abdel-Fattah, M.M. (2008) Pattern of disability among patients attending Taif rehabilitation center, Saudi Arabia. *Disability & Rehabilitation, 30*(11), 884–890.

Al-Sulayti, H. (1999) Education and training in GCC countries: Some issues of concern. In *Education and the Arab World: Challenges of the New Millennium* (pp. 271–278). UAE: Emirates Center for Strategic Studies and Research.

Alvesson, M. (2002) *Postmodernism and Social Research.* Buckingham: Open University Press.

Ashencaen Crabtree, S. (2007a) Culture, gender and the influence of social change among Emirati families in the United Arab Emirates. *Journal of Comparative Family Studies, XXXVII*(4), 575–587.

Ashencaen Crabtree, S. (2007b) Family responses to the social inclusion of children with developmental disabilities in the United Arab Emirates. *Disability & Society, 22*(1), 49–62.

Ashencaen Crabtree, S. *et al.* (2007) Maternal perceptions of care-giving of children with developmental disabilities in the United Arab Emirates. *Journal of Applied Research in Intellectual Disabilities, 20*, 247–255.

Ashencaen Crabtree, S., Husain, F. and Spalek, B. (2008) *Islam and Social Work: Debating Values, Transforming Practice.* Bristol: Policy Press.

Atshan, L. (2007) Disability and gender at a cross-roads: A Palestinian perspective. In L. Abu-Habib (Ed.) *Gender and Disability: Women's Experiences in the Middle East* (pp. 53–59). Oxford: Oxfam.

Barnes, C. and Mercer, G. (2007) *Disability.* Cambridge: Polity Press.

bin Huwaidi, K. (2008) Proposal to term 'special needs' people as 'disabled' sparks debate. *Khaleej Times Online*. Retrieved Feb 3, 2009, from http://www.donateabrick.org/pdf/Press_release-'special_needs'_people_as_'disabled'_sparks_debate.pdf

Boud, D., and Walker, D. (1990) Making the most of experience. *Studies in Continued Education, 12* (2), 61–80.

Boukhari, H. (2007) Invisible victims: Working with mothers of children with learning disabilities. In L. Abu-Habib (Ed.) *Gender and Disability: Women's Experiences in the Middle East* (pp. 36–45). Oxford: Oxfam.

Bubshait, A. (2007) Regional Preparatory Workshop on Inclusive education for the 48th Session of the ICE 2008. Retrieved, Jan 21, 2009, from http://www.udesa.edu.ar/files/EscEdu/Inclusi%C3%B3n%20Educativa/11%20Ali%20Bubshait%20(GAS).pdf

Bywaters, P., Ali, Z., Fazil, Q., Wallace, L.M., and Singh, G. (2003) Attitudes towards disability amongst Pakistani and Bangladeshi parents of disabled children in the UK: Considerations for service providers and the disability movement. *Health and Social Care in the Community, 11*(6), 502–509.

Centre for Studies of Inclusive Education (2009) Retrieved Jan 20, 2009, from http://www.csie.org.uk/inclusion/

Chigier, E., and Chigier, M. (1968) Attitudes to disability of children in the multi-cultural society of Israel. *Journal of Health & Social Behavior, 9*(4), 310–317.

Clarke, M. (2008) *Language Teacher Identities*. Clevedon: Multilingual Matters.

Cohen, L.E. (2008) Foucault and the early childhood classroom. *Educational Studies, 44*, 7–21.

Dinero, S.C. (2002) Special education use among the Negev Bedouin Arabs of Israel: A case of minority *under*representation? *Race Ethnicity and Education, 5*(4), 377–396.

Emirates Special Needs (2007) Retrieved Jan 21, 2009, from http://www.disabledaccess.ae/news/single/article/uae-disability-act-activated-federal-law-no292006/

Ferreira, W. (2005) Developments towards inclusive education in Brazil. Retrieved April 20, 2009, from http://portal.unesco.org/ci/en/files/21013/11380091751windzyferreira.doc/windzyferreira.doc

Finkelstein, V. (1993) Disability: An administrative challenge? In M. Oliver (Ed.). *Social Work: Disabled People and Disabling Environments* (pp. 19–39). London: Jessica Kingsley.

Gaad, E. (2004) Cross-cultural perspectives on the effect of cultural attitudes towards inclusion for children with intellectual disabilities. *International Journal of Inclusive Education, 8*(3), 311–328.

Gaad, E.E.N. (2001) Educating children with Down's syndrome in the United Arab Emirates. *British Journal of Special Education, 28*(4), 195–203.

Haw, K. (1998) *Educating Muslim Girls: Shifting Discourses*. Buckingham: Open University.

Kenan, G., and Burck, L. (2002) Trends in patrilineal parallel first cousin marriages among Israeli Arabs: 1949–1995. *Annals of Human Biology, 29*(4), 398–413.

Khamis, V. (2007) Psychological distress among parents of children with mental retardation in the United Arab Emirates. *Social Science & Medicine, 64*(4), 850–857.

Khandekar, R., and Al Khabori, M. (2004) Double disability: The hearing-impaired blind in the Sultanate of Oman. *International Journal of Audiology, 43*, 172–176.

Lakkis, S. (2007) Mobilising women with physical disabilities: The Lebanese Sitting Handicapped Association. In L. Abu-Habib (Ed.) *Gender and Disability: Women's Experiences in the Middle East* (pp. 28–35). Oxford: Oxfam.

Leyser, Y., and Romi, S. (2008) Religion and attitudes of college preservice teachers towards students with disabilities: Implications for higher education. *Higher Education, 55*, 703–717.

Milaat, W.A., Ghabrah, T.M., Al-Bar, H.M.S., Abalkhail, B.A., and Kordy, M.N. (2001) Population-based survey of childhood disability in Eastern Jeddah using the ten questions tool. *Disability and Rehabilitation, 23*(5), 199–203.

Mittler, P. (1999) *Working Towards Inclusive Education*. London: David Fulton.

Molloy, H., and Vasil, L. (2002) The social construction of Asperger Syndrome: The pathologising of difference? *Disability & Society, 17*(6), 659–669.

Morad, M., Nasri, Y., and Merrick, J. (2001) Islam and the person with intellectual disability. *Religion, Disability and Health, 5*(2/3), 65–71.

Narayan, K. (1997) How native is a 'native' anthropologist. In L. Lamphere, H. Ragoné and P. Zavella (Eds.) *Situated Lives: Gender and Culture in Everyday Life.* London/New York: Routledge.

Oliver, M. (1993) From disabling to supportive environments. In M. Oliver (Ed.) *Social Work: Disabled People and Disabling Environments* (pp. 13–18). London: Jessica Kingsley.

Oliver, M. (1996) *Understanding Disability.* Basingstoke: Macmillan Press.

Opdal, L.R., Wormnæs, S., and Habayeb, A. (2001) Teachers' opinions about inclusion: A pilot study in a Palestinian context. *International Journal of Disability, Development and Education, 48*(2), 143–162.

Peters, S. (2003) Education for All: Including Children with Disabilities. Retrieved April 20, 2009, from http://siteresources.worldbank.org/DISABILITY/Resources/280658-1172610312075/EFAIncluding.pdf

Punamäki, R.-L., Qouta, S., and El-Sarraj, E. (2001) Resiliency factors predicting psychological adjustment after political violence among Palestinian children. *International Journal of Behavioral Development, 25*(3), 256–267.

Read, J. (2000) *Disability, the Family and Society.* Buckingham: Open University Press.

Richards, A. (2003) *Socio-economic Roots of Radicalism? Towards Explaining the Appeal of Islamic Radicals.* Retrieved Jan 19, 2009, from http://www.strategicstudiesinstitute.army.mil/pubs/display.cfm?pubID=105 The Strategic Studies Institute, United States Army War College.

Salih, F.A., and Al-Kandari, H.Y. (2007) Effect of a disability course on prospective educators' attitudes toward individuals with mental retardation. *Digest of Middle East Studies, 16*(1), 2–29.

Sharifzadeh, V.-S.(2004) Families with Middle Eastern roots. In E.W. Lynch and M.J. Hanson (Eds.) *Developing Cross-cultural Competence*, 2nd edn (pp. 441–482). Baltimore, MD: Paul H. Brookes.

Shawky, S., Abalkhail, B., and Soliman, N. (2002) An epidemiological study of childhood disability in Jeddah, Saudi Arabia. *Paediatric and Perinatal Epidemiology, 16*, 61–66.

Shettle, A. (2008) Saudi Arabia ratifies the International Disability Treaty. Retrieved Jan 20, 2009, from http://ratifynow.org/2008/07/14/saudi-arabia-ratifies-international-disability-treaty/ CRPD RatifyNow.

Siminski, P. (2003) Patterns of disability and norms of participation through the life course: Empirical support for a social model of disability. *Disability & Society, 18*(6), 707–718.

UN (1948) The Universal Declaration of Human Rights. Retrieved March 19, 2009, from http://www.un.org/Overview/rights.html#a26

UN (2006) Convention on the Rights of Persons with Disabilities. Retrieved Jan 20, 2009, from http://www.un.org/disabilities/default.asp?id=284

UNESCO (2009) Education for All (EFA) International Coordination. Retrieved March 17, 2009, from http://portal.unesco.org/education/en/ev.php-URL_ID=53844&URL_DO=DO_TOPIC&URL_SECTION=201.html

UNESCO–IBE (2007) Preparatory Report for the 48th ICE on Inclusive Education. Regional Preparatory Work on Inclusive Education – the Gulf Arab States. Dubai, United Arab Emirates, 27–29 August.

Westbrook, M.T. and Legge, V. (1993) Health practitioners' perceptions of family attitudes toward children with disabilities: A comparison of six communities in a multicultural society. *Rehabilitation Psychology, 38*(3), 177–185.

Williams, R., and Pritchard, C. (2006) *Breaking the Cycle of Educational Alienation.* Maidenhead: Open University Press.

12 The Teaching of Amazigh in France and Morocco

Language Policies and Citizenship Between Pedagogy and Power Politics

Abdelouahad Mabrour and Khalil Mgharfaoui

Introduction

In any bilingual or multilingual context, policy makers are called upon to manage the ensuing political, social and institutional tensions. They thus have to consider the nature, status and function of these languages, the co-existence of language varieties, the type of contact between the different languages, their relationship to internal and external dimensions of identity, and the part they play in giving access to information. They are also faced with different institutional arrangements (legislation, policies, recommendations, and circulars) or practices (imposed by usage) undertaken on a daily basis in the areas of administration, economy, education, media and the construction of the public space.

In this chapter, we will investigate the sociolinguistic situation of the Amazigh ('Berber') language[1] in the Maghreb, especially in Morocco and Algeria. It appears that the teaching of the Amazigh language does not merely respond to didactic needs. Rather, the decision to teach this language, as well as its legitimacy in the public arena through its introduction in the media, cannot be disconnected from its political and cultural dimensions. It is well known that what leads to linguistic and 'ethnic' conflicts is the idea that the central government, namely, the State, serves only the interests of the dominant group by imposing a unifying policy based on the assumption that a nation must speak exclusively one language in order to ensure its survival. This ideological position defines the social space made available for languages and their identity correlates. This position also impacts the viability of democratic arrangements in a pluralist and multicultural society.

Contrary to the situation in the Maghreb, where the Amazigh language is perceived as competing with the primacy of the national language, Arabic; in France, where the Amazigh language is also present, one would expect things to be different. The teaching of this language, spoken by quite a large minority of French of Maghrebi descent, should benefit from the democratic environment supported by the recognition of linguistic diversity. Theoretically, the Amazigh language does not face the question of legitimacy in France, as it does in the Maghreb, because it does not compete with a national language as a symbol of identity. However, despite the apparent dissimilarity between the situation of Amazigh in France and the Maghreb, the promotion of the language will only be successful if the question of its legitimacy is considered, not from the point of view of the nation-state but from that of citizenship.

In this chapter, we investigate two institutions dedicated to the teaching of the Amazigh language: The National Institute of Oriental Languages and Civilizations (INALCO) in France and the Royal Institute for Amazigh Culture (IRCAM) in Morocco. The relevance of both institutions for this chapter lies in the fact that, while they both share the same objective, they differ on several points given the specific geopolitical space in which they operate. In the French case, this involves policies and practices that relate primarily to the teaching and learning of the Amazigh language and research carried out on it. In the Maghreb case, the introduction of the Amazigh language is part of an ongoing language development course, endorsed by institutional and operational measures aiming to support the position of this language in the linguistic market, both in the education sector (teaching) and the broader national linguistic landscape (media). In this chapter we suggest that the introduction of the Amazigh language in the linguistic landscapes of France and Morocco is related to political reasons, and in particular to the legitimacy and location granted to the different 'Other' within an imagined conception of the nation. The role of education in mediating language policies in this context is fundamental. The accommodation of the Amazigh language into the educational systems of France and Morocco serves as an illustration of these processes.

The Amazigh Language

Amazigh is the oldest language attested in North Africa. Yet, Amazigh includes several regional dialects spread over a wide geographic area: from the Egyptian border with Libya in the east, to the Atlantic coast of North Africa in the west, to Sub-Saharan Africa in the south. Amazigh extends over Morocco, Algeria, Tunisia, Libya, Egypt, Niger, Mali, Burkina Faso, and Mauritania (Boukous, 1979; Chaker, 2007). It is estimated that around one million Amazigh-speaking Tuareg[2] are scattered over several areas (Sahara, Sahel): around 50,000 in Tunisia and a few thousands in Mauritania (Chaker, 2007). The socio-linguistic question is especially sensitive when it comes to countries with the largest Amazigh-speaking groups: Morocco and Algeria where, according to Chaker (2007), the number of Amazigh-speakers "is itself a major political issue … [having also been] the subject of strong controversies and divergent estimates" (p. 2). Amazigh-speakers are estimated at about 20 to 25 percent of the population in Algeria (Chaker, 2007), and 35 to 45 percent in Morocco (Chaker, 2007; Boukous 1995). Obviously, it is in these two countries that the linguistic and cultural tensions arise more visibly. They have weighed very heavily on the social, educational, and current cultural scene, especially during the last three decades.

In Morocco, three main Amazigh dialects exist: Tarifit, Tamazight and Tashelhit. These three dialects are characterized by both complementarity and linguistic particularism. The differences between the three major dialects concern primarily phonetic, morphological and lexical aspects. The Arabic dialect is often used as a means of communication among Amazigh speakers of the different areas.

In Algeria, the Kabyl region is by far the largest Amazigh-speaking area. It accounts for some 70 percent of all Amazigh-speakers in Algeria, or about 5 million people. Other Algerian regions with a strong concentration of Amazigh-speakers are Chaouia of the Aures, Ouarrgla-Ngouça, Gouara, Chenoua, and Mzab-Ghardaïa, to name but some.

It is true that the Amazigh language has experienced a slow but persisting decline over several centuries, yielding the ground to Arabic. The process was exacerbated by a gradual assimilation of Berbers into Arab-Muslim societies, mainly through massive ethnic Islamization. Arabization has also gained terrain with the establishment of the first language policies introduced by the successive governments in power since the independence of Morocco (1956) and Algeria (1962). It should be noted that the political and ideological context of the 1960s and 1970s was facilitated by the emergence of liberation movements, a widespread pan-Arab ideology and deeply rooted class preferences among intellectuals (even among some Amazigh-speakers). These factors led to the articulation of a centralist and assimilationist ideology, inspired by the French approach to language policies. Moreover, many Maghrebi policy makers at the time were trained in France or in the French language. Notwithstanding, as a language, Amazigh continues to enjoy a persisting vitality.

Political Issues

It is very difficult to speak of the Amazigh language in the Maghreb countries without relating it to 'national' (Arabic and its varieties) and European languages (French, Spanish), with which it enters into relations of complementarity, conflict or competition.

'Classical Arabic' plays the role of official language in the Maghreb states, with all that this status implies in terms of privileges. It remains, however, cut off from everyday reality since it is not natively spoken by Maghrebis. In contradistinction, Amazigh and Arabic dialects, through their various regional varieties, are languages used in daily life. They derive great vitality from their users. French, introduced and imposed by France's colonial enterprise in the Maghreb countries,[3] occupies a very important place in almost all sectors: education, administration, and media. It therefore competes with the official (Arabic) language and has a high added value in the language market: a language of work and a guarantee for personal success.

In both Morocco and Algeria, Arabization policies implemented after independence represent a political reaction to the former colonial power, and a nationalist assertion following independence. For the political class of that period, the preservation of the French language in the period following independence was perceived as prolonging foreign occupation and consolidating France's grip on the educational and administrative systems. At that time, 'national unity' was deemed essential to 'weld' the parts of a young emerging nation. Within this context of nation-building, Amazigh was excluded as a component of Maghrebi identity.

An official attitude of hostility towards Amazigh and its identity correlates prevailed. The successive versions of the constitutions of Algeria and Morocco have failed to recognize this language. It was not until 2001 that the IRCAM was created in Morocco. Several months later Amazigh was recognized as a national language by the Algerian constitution. Such a breakthrough would not have occurred without the convergence of a number of political, economic and cultural factors. These include an international context more and more attentive to voices calling for greater democracy in the treatment of public affairs, a dying Arab nationalism, a persistent economic crisis, and a very dynamic and politically active Amazigh movement. The claim to restore the national identity heritage covers both the Amazigh language and culture and the Arabic dialects in their linguistic and cultural dimensions, including popular traditional musical genres (Elmedlaoui, 2007). But it is around the Amazigh question that these issues acquire a particular importance. The sense of belonging to this community, if only during recent years, witnessed the birth of the Amazigh movement and strengthened it.

Cultural and Educational Issues

Non-government organizations have taken center stage to advocate reforms concerning the status of the Amazigh language and culture in the Maghreb. Their aim is to rehabilitate Amazigh identity as a fundamental component of the North African identity, accommodating it into the education systems of Morocco and Algeria. And yet, the context of Amazigh in these two countries offers some important contrasts. Relations between Amazigh NGOs and the government in Algeria are increasingly strained and very often lead to open conflicts which manifested themselves in the Berber Spring of 1980, in repeated and long-term strikes in 1994–1995, in clashes following the murder of Lounès Matoub,[4] and in what is known as the 'Black Spring'[5] of 2001 (Chaker, 2007).

In Morocco, the Amazigh NGO tradition dates back to the late 1960s. Of particular interest here is the Moroccan Association for Research and Cultural Exchange (AMREC), regarded as the first Moroccan Amazigh movement. But the literature in this field of activism cites 5 August 1991, as a landmark in the history of the movement, referred to as the Agadir Charter where six associations representing different regions of Morocco signed a manifesto articulating the main demands of the Amazigh movement. In 1994, during a national holiday,[6] King Hassan II of Morocco delivered a speech in which he announced some measures to rehabilitate the Amazigh language and culture,[7] mainly in primary education[8] and the media. On 1 March 2000, a few months after the succession of Mohammed VI to power, 229 Moroccan intellectuals signed and published the 'Berber Manifesto' which "explains how the Amazigh culture is part of the Moroccan identity and that there is no democracy in Morocco without the effective participation of Imazighen" people (Ruiter, 2006: 24).

The local political context was particularly favorable to such a development with the accession to the throne of a young king, the formation of a government of alternation,[9] and the publication of the Education and Training Charter in 2000. The Charter officially refers to the introduction of the Amazigh language into the national education system. It aims "[to] improve the teaching and the use of the Arabic language, master foreign languages and open up to Tamazight". In spite of the hierarchy the Charter establishes between languages at the national level (with Arabic at the top), it nonetheless represents the first official text that explicitly mentions the introduction of Amazigh into the Moroccan national school system.

With regard to the introduction of the Amazigh language into primary school, the Charter states:

> educational authorities may, as part of the curriculum share left to their initiative, choose the use of the Amazigh language or any local dialect with the aim of facilitating the learning the official language at the preschool and the first cycle of the primary school.

The Charter also calls for the creation of specialized "structures for the researching and development of the Amazigh language and culture, as well as for the training of teacher educators and the development of school programs and curricula" (Commission Spéciale Education-Formation, 2000, pp. 66–68).[10] It is worth mentioning that the introduction of the Amazigh language into the Moroccan school system represents a crucial turn in the field of language policies. The rehabilitation of the Amazigh language and culture remained a matter of taboo up to the 1980s. It is also worth adding that the decision to give regional educational authorities the right to choose which Amazigh language to include in school curricula aims to accommodate the different dialects we signaled above.

Language, Democracy and Citizenship

The intersections between language, democracy and citizenship offer an important backdrop to understand the current debates over the Amazigh language. In this regard, the case of Europe remains emblematic. The European Union is conceivable only in terms of a fundamental and founding plurality. Europe has substituted the notion of heterogeneity to a presumed national unity in the different nation states. Currently, the Common European Framework of Reference for Languages (CEFR), enacted in 2001, emphasizes the virtues of multilingualism. Diversity is perceived as an element of strength and not of weakness. In this model, language occupies a central place in the same way as the concepts of diversity, democracy and human rights. In a report by the European Council, Starkey (2002) points out that "[t]he nation is only one possible community (imagined) in which one can exert one's citizenship" (p. 7).

The promotion of linguistic diversity and the preservation of cultural wealth is associated with changing conceptions of citizenship and of shifting political philosophies. It is certainly for similar reasons that Amazigh-speakers, especially in Algeria, remain the best advocates for maintaining the French language; an approach that places the movement in direct opposition to the advocates of Arabism. As long as the Amazigh language issue remains confined to political and cultural considerations and linked to the question of national identity, political considerations will remain in the foreground, at the expense of pedagogical ones.

Comparative Perspectives

The experiences of INALCO and IRCAM, in France and Morocco respectively, remain indicative of the larger power politics involved in determining the position of Amazigh in the linguistic landscape, and particularly in the field of education. Contrasting these two experiences helps us show how the politics of indigenous Maghrebi languages play out in different geo-cultural spaces – within the Maghreb and in the diaspora – and how they shape the role schools play in mediating representations of the nation and articulations of citizenship.

The INALCO Experience in France

In the Maghreb, the teaching of Amazigh is marred by vehement ideological debates concerned with the primacy of Arabic. In France, Amazigh is considered a language of 'foreigners'.[11] Its teaching could therefore theoretically provide an opportunity to address scientific, linguistic, didactic and pedagogic issues which are not otherwise addressed in the Maghreb.

The teaching of Amazigh in France started at the School of Oriental Languages in Paris as early as 1915. This explains why the National Institute of Oriental Languages and Civilizations (INALCO) has long been regarded as the main training centre for the Amazigh language in the world, before other institutions were set up in Morocco and Algeria.

One could also expect that, in France, the teaching of Amazigh would remain largely disconnected from political sensitivities. Notwithstanding, the controversies surrounding the introduction of Amazigh courses in a Parisian high school by the French government in 2004 shows that this was not the case. Salem Chaker (2005) spoke of "attempting to control Algerian politics" in France. In that sense, the teaching of Amazigh in metropolitan France intersects with political alignments prevalent among Maghrebi communities.

If Berber claims in France do not have the historical and demographic weight they have in Morocco and Algeria, they offset this weakness by the strength of the freedom they enjoy in Europe. However, it is the status of Amazigh that shows more clearly the progress made by this language in France. Like the Arabic dialects, in 1999, the Amazigh language was recognized as a "language of France" by the European Charter for Regional or Minority Languages, thus enjoying the same status as regional languages, such as Breton and Occitan. Yet, France, which signed the Charter, did not ratify it because its Constitutional Council declared the Charter to stand in contradiction to Article 2 of the French Constitution, which states "The language of the Republic shall be French." Almost the same problem of legitimacy faces the Amazigh language in the Maghreb. In both contexts, Amazigh speakers strive to achieve the status of a recognized language that can be taught and formally supported.

Learning the Amazigh language in France is free. It is integrated into the educational system only at the baccalaureate level (high school), as an optional subject. Two limitations characterize this course. First, the offering of Amazigh is confined to the Academies of Paris and Aix-Marseille, which are the only two academic regions offering the subject. Then comes the exam itself; it has no binding character because no instruction is provided. INALCO remains the only official institution that provides such training.

The involvement of INALCO in the teaching of Amazigh is recent. It dates back to 1993. Since that year, the institution has received hundreds of registration files each year. This is far from being a success when one considers that the Berber population in France consists of about 1–1.5 million people. Nevertheless, the number of candidates who chose to take the baccalaureate 'Berber' exam has experienced a remarkable increase. In Paris, there were 30 candidates in 1978. In 2004, there were 2,250 candidates. This strong demand qualifies Amazigh as the language most in demand for these exams after the regional languages of France (Chaker, 1997). The teaching of Amazigh suffers as a result of the lack of teachers, examiners and resources.[12] To remedy to this situation, since 1995 the Berber exams have been in written rather than oral format.

Paradoxically, the teaching of the Amazigh language in France was gradually consolidated, as a formal offering, while it had no place in its indigenous space— the Maghreb. Notwithstanding, INALCO hardly deals with pedagogical methods and their adequacy. Managing the increasing number of students forces the Institute to limit its mission to the organization of exams and to the correction of tests. Furthermore, INALCO suffers from lack of means. Chaker (1997) reports the difficulties facing the teaching of Amazigh in France as follows:

> The exams are organized each year in very difficult conditions, not to say deplorable: No prior preparation of students, no real agenda and rating standards, lack of examiners … In fact, these oral tests work only thanks to the motivation and the semi-volunteering of a certain number of teachers, advanced INALCO students, and leaders of Berber associations who have devoted themselves to ensure [that these exams] take place.
>
> (Chaker, 1997, p. 6)

On another register, one cannot discount the possibility that the interest of young Berbers in the Amazigh language could be just pragmatic, reflecting a candidate's desire to obtain additional marks to boost their baccalaureate results.

In sum, the teaching of Amazigh in France is overtaken by political considerations. One could add to this the consequences brought about by the lack of resources and political will to improve its standing. It could be argued that these problems do not leave much time for INALCO to establish a genuine experience in the teaching of the language.

The IRCAM Experience in Morocco

The Royal Institute for Amazigh Culture (IRCAM), established by the Ajdir Decree in October 2001, is not the first institution of its kind to be set up in independent Morocco. In October 1978, the government submitted to parliament a draft law stipulating the establishment of the Institute for Research in the Amazigh Language. This project, which was voted unanimously by the Education Committee of the

Moroccan parliament, has never been submitted to a vote in a plenary session. Two years passed, until October 1980, before King Hassan II appointed a national commission chaired by Mahjoubi Ahardane to study the matter.[13] In the absence of political resolve, the commission did not succeed in advancing discussions on the matter (Ouazzi, 2000).

Enjoying the status of a consultative body, attached directly to the Royal Cabinet, IRCAM is endowed with important human and material resources. On the political level, this institution reflects the formal recognition of the Amazigh dimension of Morocco and therefore the multilingual character of Moroccan society. In practical terms, IRCAM's mission includes the design and implementation of scientific and technical means to promote the Amazigh language and culture. It is entrusted with the task of setting up, accompanying and evaluating the language planning of Amazigh. In other words, IRCAM is mandated to enhance the status of this language and expand its corpus. The areas of intervention are quite numerous and interlinked: linguistic (language standardization), didactic (textbooks, establishment of schools and their distribution), sociolinguistic (functions of languages in contact, fields of use) and legal (legislative texts).

The codification of Amazigh spelling is among the major challenges that this institution has been called upon to address. Three options present themselves to that end, reflecting the weight of the components of the Moroccan linguistic landscape: the Arabic alphabet, the Latin alphabet and the Tifinagh alphabet.[14] The choice among the three options is basically political and ideological. Supporters of the Arabic option put forward arguments associated with the limited cost of the operation and the large number of speakers in Morocco as well as in the other Arab countries who may have access to this language. Advocates of the Latin alphabet emphasized its international character and its technical efficiency, particularly in the field of the new information technologies and communication (Ben Maïssa, 2002). Proponents of the Tifinagh alphabet argued that this alphabet is the trace of the Amazigh origin (a national record). In their view, choosing a different alphabet (Arabic or Latin) would absorb the language and forcefully integrate it in a language and civilization that is not its own (Akhayyat, 2003). After several meetings, in January 2003, the IRCAM board voted in support of the adoption of the Tifinagh alphabet.[15] This choice highlights the confluence of the plurality of linguistic and cultural heritage of the country and emphasizes the importance of Amazigh in the Moroccan national identity.

In the field of education, during the academic year 2003–2004, IRCAM introduced the Amazigh language in 317 schools spread across different regions of Morocco.[16] This initiative was undertaken in collaboration with the Ministry of Education. This included the participation of native teachers trained in the Amazigh language, literature and culture; the setting up of appropriate teacher training programs; and the design and development of textbooks and dictionaries. This collaboration has continued, through the Regional Academies of Education and Training and their Provincial Delegations. Many efforts were invested in this experience by extending it to other schools and by organizing a number of pedagogic and didactic activities (training sessions, workshops, study days) for teachers, supervisors and administrators of educational institutions. Table 12.1

Table 12.1   The teaching of the Amazigh language in the Doukkala-Abda region (Morocco)

	Schools	Classes	Students	Teachers	Inspectors
2003–4	3	7	245	5	–
2007–8	66	137	4287	79	5

provides information on the teaching of the Amazigh language in Doukkala-Abda, one of Morocco's sixteen regions.[17]

Besides education, other areas were also affected by the rehabilitation and promotion of the Amazigh language through joint commissions of IRCAM with other agencies. This mainly involves the Ministry of Communications with regard to the significant integration of this language in the media landscape (the launching of an Amazigh Channel, the production and broadcasting of films, plays, documentaries, songs) and the Higher Institute of Information and Communication in the training of journalists (audiovisual and written press) (Boukous, 2006; Antara, 2007).

For a number of activists of the Amazigh movement, IRCAM remains the only public institution for the promotion of the Amazigh language and culture. As such, it has not fulfilled all the tasks for which it was created and has done little to make the State honor all its commitments, particularly in the educational field (generalization of Amazigh teaching) and the audiovisual field (Antara, 2007). For Amazigh speakers, the State cannot continue to ignore the linguistic and cultural demands that are becoming increasingly numerous.

Conclusion

The teaching of the Amazigh language is, primarily, a political question. This reflects the long struggle waged by the Amazigh movement to access a legitimate space of expression, by right, which would not be perceived by the State as a political threat. Under such conditions, the pedagogic and institutional considerations within which the teaching of Amazigh is undertaken operate within the field of power politics and within the larger problematic of what constitutes a legitimate citizenship.

It is clear that the two institutions, IRCAM and INALCO, share similarities as well as differences. Their main common feature is undoubtedly the political dimension associated with the teaching of Amazigh. Both in France and in the Maghreb, cultural identity and the legitimacy of belonging to a community/nation is always on the agenda. However, INALCO's mission is limited, by its statute, exclusively to educational issues while IRCAM is more than a simple institution of the Amazigh language. It is in charge of all aspects of the Amazigh culture whose language is of course the most prominent feature.

The teaching of the Amazigh language remains, both in the Maghreb and in France, a question of recognition and of equality with the dominant national language. It emphasizes the centrality of linguistic and cultural diversity within competing conceptions of citizenship. As such, the controversies over the teaching of the Amazigh language are indicative of the larger debates over the underpinnings of the nation-state and the sources of its political legitimation. In that sense, language policies, and their pedagogic articulations within schools and higher education institutions cannot be detached from the larger power politics within which they operate.

In France, the Amazigh language has a favorable democratic political environment but not in the Maghreb. There is also the example of other minority languages such as Breton, which has managed to have an advanced status. Finally, considerable work has been done by the EU (the European Charter for Regional or Minority Languages) for the defense of minority languages, including Amazigh. All this indicates a difference in the claims of the Amazigh in France compared with the Maghreb.

It is obvious that the accommodation of the Amazigh language in Maghrebi schools will not only recognize a large section of the population as a legitimate part of the polity, it will also offer an opportunity for the school to make a significant contribution in terms of inscribing in society new models of citizenship in which the difference of the 'Other' is perceived as new horizons in relation to which the 'nation' can be imagined and reconfigured in a more inclusive manner.

Acknowledgements

We thank our colleague, Professor Ahmadou Bouyimani, for all his work and efforts in translating this chapter from French.

Notes

1　This reference to a 'Berber' language, while widespread in the past, is increasingly abandoned. It is perceived as a pejorative connotation for the Imazighen people. However, many researchers, including Salem Chaker, continue to use the term 'Berber' in a sense they consider neutral.

2　"The Tuareg are a nomadic, camel-owning people, who traditionally roamed across the Sahara from Mauritania to western Sudan. Although originally the Tuareg were a Berber group from North Africa (their language, Tamashek, has Berber roots), who migrated to the desert after the Arab-Islamic invasion of the 7th and 11th century" (Ham, Bainbridge, Bewer & Carillet, 2006, p. 78).

3　France ruled Algeria as a colony from 1830 to 1956. Tunisia and Morocco were French Protectorates, from 1883 to 1962 and from 1912 to 1956, respectively.

4　Considered as one of the major figures of the Amazigh cause in Algeria, Lounès Matoub, a young singer, was assassinated on 25 June 1998. According to the official version, the Islamist groups are responsible for his assassination. Amazigh activists rather point the finger at the government.

5　"In April 2001, a gendarme shot dead a young Kabylian while in custody, and a social explosion burst out with unprecedented violence. ... These incidents have come to be known as 'Black Spring'" (Baldauf & Kaplan, 2007, p. 81).

6　The Revolution Day of the King and the People is celebrated on 20 August.

7　Many observers consider this speech as an official reaction to events that occurred in May 1994 in Goulmima and in which officers of the Association Tilili had brandished banners written in Tifinagh characters. The march was banned and members were arrested and tried.

8   This decision will be implemented with the reform of the education system as described in the Charter of Education and Training. No official evaluation of the teaching of Amazigh language has been published to date.
9   It is the Government headed by Abderrahmane Youssoufi, a former opponent of the régime of Hassan II. This government, which took office on 14 March 1998, was formed by a coalition of parties known as the 'Koutla': Socialist Union of Popular Forces (USFP), The Istiqlal (*Independence*) Party (PI), the Popular Democratic Action Oganization (OADP), the party of Progress and Socialism (PPS) and the following parties: National Rally of Independents (RNI), Popular National Movement (MNP), Democratic Forces Front (FFD) and the Social Democratic Party (PSD).
10   No English version of the official text of this Charter is available. The quotes used in the chapter have been translated by the authors based on the original French document.
11   Chaker (1997) estimated the number of Amazigh speakers in France at between 1 and 1.5 million people. Two-thirds are of Algerian origin and one-third are of Moroccan origin.
12   In the Tamazgha report (2007), the authors describe the conditions in which these exams are taken. Among the problems often mentioned, we find: lack of training and competent examiners, lack of resources, no student preparation, absence of real programs and marking standards.
13   Minister of State and Head of the Popular Movement party known as "Amazigh". We are referring here to the Ahmed Ousman government which came into office on October 10, 1977.
14   The Tifinagh alphabet dates back to the 16th century BCE. It stands now as a variant referred to as 'neo-Tifinagh' (Chaker, 2007).
15   The distribution of the votes is indicative. There were 18 votes in support of the Tifinagh alphabet, 8 in support of the Latin alphabet and none in support of the Arabic alphabet (Zakari, 2004).
16   We refer to Ministerial Statement No. 133 on the teaching of Amazigh (a circular issued by the Ministry of Education in September 2007).
17   Data provided by the Regional Academy of Education and Training (Doukkala-Abda). Our university (Chouaïb Doukkali) is located in this region, in El Jadida city. We do not have data for other regions.

References

Akhayyat, B. (2003). Tadrisu al-lughati al-amāzighiyyati [The teaching of Amazigh language]. *Fi al-masʾala al-amāzighiyya: Qadāya wa ārā' [On the Amazigh question: Issues and opinions]* (1), 31–39. (In Arabic.)

'Antara, M. (2007). Al-maʿhadu al-malaki lit-thaqāfa al-amāzighiyya. Siyāq ʿan-nachʾati, aladāʾu wa taqyimu [The Royal Institute for Amazigh Culture: Its founding and Operation]. *Wijhāt nadhar [Perspectives]* 31, 40–47. (In Arabic.)

Bainbridge, J., Bewer, T., Carillet., J.-B., and Ham, A (2006). *West Africa*. London, Lonely Planet.

Baldauf, R, & Kaplan, R. (2007). *Language planning and policy in Africa: Algeria, Côte d'Ivoire, Nigeria and Tunisia*. Bristol, Multilingual Matters.

Ben Maïssa, A. (2002). Biʾayyati abajidiyyatin yajibu an naktuba? Almasʾalatu al-amāzighiyyatu fi al-maghrib [Which alphabet should we write with? The Amazigh question in the Maghreb]. *Nawāfidh [Windows]* 17–18, 147–156. (In Arabic.)

Boukous, A. (1979). Le profil sociolinguistique du Maroc. *Bulletin économique et social du Maroc* 140, 5–31.

Boukous, A. (1995). *Société, langues et cultures au Maroc, enjeux symboliques* (Série Essais et études 8). Rabat, Publication de la Faculté des Lettres.

Boukous, A. (2006). Editorial. Inymsin n usinag [News]. *Bulletin d'information de l'IRCAM* 5-6. (In Amazigh.)

Chaker, S. (1997). *Enseignement des langues d'origine et immigration nord-africaine en Europe: langue maternelle ou langue d'Etat?* Paris: Inalco.

Chaker, S. (2005). Le berbère au Bac et dans le secondaire: mise au point (provisoire). http://www.tamazgha.fr/Berbere-au-Bac-Session-2006-corrige-du-sujet-kabyle,1646.html

Chaker, S. (2007). Langue et littérature berbères. *Clio* 1–10. http://www.clio.fr/bibliotheque/langue_et_litterature_berberes.asp

Commission Spéciale Education-Formation (2000). *Texte de la charte nationale d'éducation et de formation.* Rabat: Commission Spéciale Education-Formation. http://www.enssup.gov.ma/dajesp/loi/charte.pdf

Elmedlaoui, M. (2007). Langue maternelle, musique, identité et stabilité psychosociale : rapport entre gestion et recherche. *La Vérité* Mai 26–30, 33–34.

Ouazzi, H. (2000). *Nach'atu al-harakati at-taqāfiyyati al-amāzighiyyati bil-maghribi* [*The emergence of the Amazigh cultural movement in the Maghrib*]. Rabat: Imprimerie Al Ma'ārif al-jadida. (In Arabic.)

Ruiter, J. J. (2006). *Les jeunes marocains et leurs langues.* Paris: l'Harmattan.

Starkey, H. (2002). *Citoyenneté démocratique, langues, diversité et droits de l'homme.* Strasbourg: Conseil de l'Europe.

Tamazgha (2007). Droits linguistiques et culturels des Berbères en France. Rapport alternatif au Comité des droits économiques, sociaux et culturels. Nations Unies. Conseil Economique et Social. Pacte international relatif aux droits économiques, sociaux et culturels. Pré-session de la 38ème session du Comité pour les droits économiques, sociaux et culturels. Geneva, 21–25 May.

Zakari, O. (2004). Al-judhuru al-tārikhiyyatu li-tachakkuli al-tarkibati al-bachāriyyati al-maghribiyyati [The historical origins of the population composition of the Maghrib]. In Benabdallaoui, M. (Ed.) *Al-amāzighiyya.* Casablanca: Publications Forum de la citoyenneté. (In Arabic.)

13   Educational Provision and *Spatial Dis-[O]rientation* Among Pastoralist Communities in the Middle East and North Africa

Steven Dinero

The provision of formal educational services to pastoral nomadic communities in the Middle East and North Africa (MENA) has been a centerpiece of state formation and consolidation, most especially since World War II and the decolonization of the region. Arab bedouin, Berbers, and other nomadic pastoral communities living throughout the area have been the subject of widespread educational programs, most being implemented throughout the 1950s and 1960s.

Regardless of location, nearly all such initiatives include some common elements and shared assumptions. For example, it is assumed by state education policy makers that political, economic and social structures make education for nomads "problematic" (Chatty, 2006: 212–13), and a "conundrum" (Dyer, 2001: 315), a challenge that governments can and must face and overcome. An overall assumption underlying this argument is the "universal value" of education (Krätli & Dyer, 2006: 11), which can and should be accessible to all, regardless of background, geographic residence, and the like.

The discourse which presents formal education in this context also suggests that it is incumbent upon the state to educate its citizenry (Krätli & Dyer, 2006: 9). This is an innovation in the history of humankind, which in the past left the socialization of a community's youth to parents, extended family and the tribe – but not, under any circumstances, to an interfering or potentially contradictory and imposing value system associated with the socially constructed state apparatus. The inevitable clash between the interests of individual needs and rights and the interests of nomadic communities (Meir, 1992: 7), stems from a *functional* conflict between the family's ability to socialize conformity amongst its members, and the desire of the state to perpetuate a discourse premised upon individual desires, needs and goals.

It is difficult to separate the formal education discourse so prevalent throughout the MENA region with that of "modernization." Many state planners have long held the presumption that nomadism was part of an evolutionary arc (Meir, 1987); thus, formal education might be used as the vehicle to help serve as a bridging mechanism to foster the movement away from the "traditional" system of economy and society, moving progressively forward towards a system of "development" (Krätli, 2000: 6) and a "better way of life." Although it is an unfounded assertion to assume that all nomadic peoples are by definition "poor," many educational programs have been posited based upon the assumption that pastoralism will naturally die away given its declining viability and relevance as an archaic and irrational economic system, and that options and alternatives will likely be limited without formal education.

However, the existence of pastoral nomadism in the Middle East is not solely due to its economic value, but also dictates and is dictated by social, political, cultural and other forces. While environmental aspects contribute to the perpetuation of pastoral economies, they do not dictate their adaptation without the simultaneous existence of certain social and other economically-oriented determinants (Aronson, 1981: 45). Social structures such as marriage directly affect pastoral technologies and economies. The manner in which flocks are distributed to newly married sons (Swidler, 1973: 31), for example, or the way in which land rights are redistributed following the death of a family leader determine, and are determined by, the nomadic lifestyle. Similarly, the flow of goods from outside of and within a community, as well as the balance of power among tribe members, are two key social principles inherent to the actions of nomadic groups.

The point to be emphasized here is that environmental factors, while certainly the initial impetus for the development of pastoral nomadic systems, are today but one facet of a larger picture of pastoral nomadic adaptation. Certain cultural traits of communities defined by their spatial mobility, such as the development of small, homogenous, well-defined co-liable groups with specific rules of behavior and social interaction, reveal the extent to which nomadism has shaped, and is shaped by, the social interactions found in tribal societies pursuing a livelihood in harsh geographic environments (Rapaport, 1978: 219). The retention of flocks, for example, is undertaken not only for economic purposes, but also for sacrifices and other celebratory events (Marx, 1967: 95). Thus, despite its apparent obsolescence from a "rational" economic standpoint, pastoral nomadism continues to the present day in places where agriculture might more easily and successfully be carried out given modern technologies and new ideals (Bruins, 1986: 55).

Moreover, one of the defining characteristics of such communities is the centrality of territory in economic and social exchange. This in turn leads to a very strong attachment to *the land*, for it provides the primary resources of such populations in terms of water, pasturage, fuel for fires, materials for clothing and shelter, and fields for crops. The centrality of land in indigenous cultures typically lends to a mutual respect for, and communal control of, this most precious source of resources.

It is well recognized that, unlike Western societies which tend to view land as commoditized property (i.e. real estate), pastoral nomadic societies view land as inalienable, and a trust to be handed down from generation to generation. But nomads nonetheless have a sense of territoriality, albeit which is by definition geographically extensive, and particularly valued for its pasturage potential. This nomadic sense of territory or region, though not as specifically defined in terms of borders or boundaries as delimited in the West (Meir, 1992: 13), has strong economic, historic and cultural connections.

When schooling has been extended to most nomadic communities in the MENA region over the past century, its introduction has been undertaken in order to encourage the abandonment of pastoralism as an economic and social system

(Dyer, 2001: 317). It is difficult to find examples of education provision that do not exist concomitant with sedentarization initiatives; education by definition promotes sedentarization – and, it should be added, sedentarization processes, in theory, abet and promote successful educational service provision.

Conflicts over land ownership have been at the center of many if not all such resettlement initiatives (e.g. Bocco, 2000: 200; Lavie & Young, 1984: 38; Meninger, 1993). By implementing seemingly benevolent social development programs, states have sought to resolve these conflicts in their favor. Education has thereby served multiple uses to the state, acting as a mechanism of control, assimilation, encapsulation, and ultimately, sedentarization. As such, the modernity enterprise furthered by these programs rests upon a spatially defined set of preconditions that, as will be seen below, are potentially oppressive, racist and more.

The *Dis-[O]rientation* of Nomadic Peoples: Education's Role in the Creation of a "Third Space"

The use of educational service provision for pastoral nomads as a tool for state building in the MENA region must be viewed through the lens of what may be termed economic, social, and cultural *dis-[O]rientation*, that is, a set of processes which is imposed concomitant with spatial conquest, reorganization and reconfiguration. I see this process as embodying more than a "*disorienting*" of the communities in the traditional sense of the word; rather, "*dis-[O]rientation*" as I use it here should be viewed as an active effort on the part of the state to create policies intended to "modernize"/"develop" these "traditional" communities, and to take them "out of the Orient," as it were. Thus, these goals are interconnected, but rely upon the process of uprooting and resettling/sedentarizing the region's nomads upon lands which, unlike historic grazing lands, are geographically constrained, rational, and easily monitored and controlled by state authorities.

Such policies directly follow well-established patterns which have been documented throughout the literature with regard to the relationship between spatiality, identity, and the colonial/post-colonial agenda. While identity may be defined as a fluid set of constructs, for example, Gandana notes that the literature is clear in its contention that "identity must be placed in the context of history, culture and power ... Nor can it be detached from the existing resources that contribute to shaping who we might become ... It is something that is always 'in process', changing, constructed in many different ways, though its 'operation' is limited within boundaries. The boundaries here ... may be in the forms of geographical areas, political or religious perspectives or cultural and linguistic traditions" (2008: 144). Saldanha further argues with regard to Massey's extensive discussions on the connections of space, identity and culture that it is "logically impossible to think of history without space" (2008: 2087) – or, extending beyond this, it is similarly difficult if not impossible to consider culture, identity, and a people without considering that all of these are (or once were) bound up within a spatial context.

The role of territory in identity building is crucial, and thus the loss of land and loss of identity are concomitant processes (Yiftachel, 2003: 26). For to despatialize is to dis-[O]rient; a community effectively becomes decontextualized, shifting away from the known and from that which makes it who/what it is. In the case of involuntary migratory movements, there is no doubt that relocation is also a form of *dislocation*, an "unsettling" experience which, at the communal level, may lead to doubt about "who we are" or "where we belong" (Gandana, 2008: 143).

In the MENA region, pastoral nomadic communities have experienced a particularly dis-[O]rienting experience, as the de-territorialization of their communities has occurred within the broader "power-geometry" context of the colonial/state-building initiative (Massey, 2005: 64). As Yiftachel (2003) contends, the struggle for control of the land for the purposes of state-building is one of unequal power dynamics, and of centralized political control within discriminatory social structures. As he notes, "the issues of land, land use, and spatial planning have been absolutely central to the mechanisms of control over indigenous minorities in ethnocratic states" (2003: 25).

The role of the construction and control of space, of "making" spaces and places is "essential to social development, social control, and empowerment in any social order" (Harvey, 1996: 265). While Massey offers arguments which assert that culture, identity, and history should not be viewed as concepts which are spatially bound (2005: 67), it is clear that social control is actualized by spatial ordering. Such values serve to validate the status quo, or for that matter, to rationalize the creation of a new reality and to repeatedly seek to press for the affirmation of its existence or legitimacy. Thus, *a government which wishes to impose a new social order must impose a new spatial order* (Harvey, 1996: 230) – a task to which formal education provision is ideally suited.

Further, in the process of creating an "other" space (Saldanha, 2008: 2087), state planners and policy makers have created spaces of "Otherness," that is, marginalized spaces of which and in which the Otherizing of the region's pastoral nomads was not an accidental outcome per se, but indeed a planned intent. Gandana (2008) notes that Bhabha speaks of the creation of the "Other" through the colonial enterprise who, unlike Edward Said's binary opposite of the developed Westerner, is the "hybrid" (see also Dinero *et. al.*, 2006), who is "in-between" cultures (Gandana, 2008: 145) or, one could say, while being *a part* of many cultures, and *apart* from them all.

And yet this definition is not complete. This space of ambivalence (Gandana, 2008: 146) can be considered hypothetical but, in the present case, is an actual territory of conflict, resistance, and dis-[O]rientation for nomadic peoples in the post-colonial resettled environment. As Massey puts it (2005: 71):

> Places, rather than being locations of coherence, [have] become the foci of the meeting and the nonmeeting of the previously unrelated and thus integral to the generation of novelty. The spatial in its role of bringing distinct temporarilities into new configurations, of time itself, as being not about the unfolding of some internalised story (some already-established identities) – the self-producing story of Europe – but about interaction and *the process of constitution of* identities – the reformulated notion of (the multiplicities of) colonisation.

Saldanha (2008) sees such enviroments in Foucaultian terms, in which such environments are Heterotopia or "third spaces," a lacuna of *neither here nor there*, spaces in the present instance of a lost landscape demarked by familiar icons (pasturage, temporary mobile dwellings, herds), replaced with an imposed iconography in which the school building is centralized and a dominant aspect of the newly evolving landscape (Dinero, 2004: 403), a place wherein modes of learning and knowing are enacted upon a geographically concentrated terrain of unfamiliarity and uncertainty. "Heterotopia are not quite spaces of transition – the chasm they represent can never be closed up – but they are spaces of deferral, spaces where ideas and practices that represent the good life can come into being, from nowhere, even if they never actually achieve what they set out to achieve ..." (Kevin Hetherington as quoted in Saldanha, 2008: 2091).

In this regard then, the de-spatialized experiences of the formally nomadic communities of the MENA region can easily be situated in the "third spaces" of the "Other." They are neither here nor there, located in the interstices of a globalizing world which, while deceptively seamless, are riddled with Heterotopic cracks. Connections to the land, based upon water and pasture resources stemming back centuries, gave these communities a sense of common interests, common goals, common behaviors, and with these, a common destiny hailing back millennia (Cole, 2003: 239). As this connection is severed – socially, economically and geographically – so too are these attributes challenged.

In the following section, I look at ways in which different MENA regional governments have addressed formal educational provision to pastoral nomads. By assessing schooling/education in different areas of the region, a state of heteronomy can be discerned, as the logistical provision of the service, as well as the ideas and values found therein, effectively help to create a space where the familiar is rendered obsolete or irrelevant, and yet the newly introduced ideas of the formal classroom are difficult to access, integrate and incorporate into a logical and rational whole.

Although a number of examples of educational programs have been introduced throughout the region during the twentieth century which well illustrate the dynamics of nomad de-territorialization and dis-[O]rientation described above, I limit my examples to two of the best known and most controversial. The case of the Qashqa'i tribe of Iran reveals ways in which the provision of education has been used as an effective tool of displacement and disempowerment of this ethnic/linguistic minority group, relying upon state co-optation of the community leadership as one of its key advantages. As for the bedouin of the Negev, Israel, the case exemplifies every aspect of a state using educational policy to *dis-[O]rient*, including forced geographic displacement, economic policies of proletarianization, and a political agenda of encapsulation, in this instance manifested by efforts to "de-Palestinianize" these Arabs while simultaneously "Israelizing" them through the use of the resettlement/education initiative.

Education as an Agent of *Dis-[O]rientation* in Pastoral Communities of the MENA Region

One of the earliest educational initiatives that served to construct a "third space" for its nomads can be found in the case of the Qashqa'i tribe in Iran. The tribal tent school initiative for this tribe, a Shi'i, Turkish-speaking, ethnic minority in Iran, was first implemented from 1929 to 1941. Parents began sending children to school with the belief, if not fear, that pastoralism was no longer viable, and that schooling would prepare children for a non-pastoral lifestyle (Shahbazi, 2001a: 56). And yet, by 1942 following the Shah's abdication a year earlier, some were able to resume limited pastoral nomadic activities (Shahbazi, 2001b: 106).

By the late 1950s, a state-supported literacy program was implemented (Shahbazi, 2001b: 98). Initially, only elementary schools were provided, with secondary schools added in the late 1960s (Kratli, 2000: 20). Mohammad Bahmanbaigi was the spearhead of the government initiative starting in the late 1950s (Shahbazi, 2006: 177). Himself a Qashqa'i who had been engaged by the government to work in its educational program, Bahmanbaigi had risen to prominence as one of the most famous and educated tribesmen of his community. As the government put forward its educational agenda, his goal was primarily one of developing and increasing literacy within the tribe. Virtually all of the literature points to his central role in this endeavor throughout the 1960s and 1970s.

An emphasis on co-education (male/female), albeit highly valued and encouraged in the West, challenged Qashqa'i norms and attitudes. And yet, following Bhabha's hybridization model, "traditional" Qashqa'i identity also was encouraged, and made a part of the teacher training, in theory allowing educators to encourage "their students to practice their culture." In practice, what this entailed was that through this literacy program, students were able to read and write *about* subjects pertaining to their own culture and history. Like artifacts of a bygone nomadic era (Dinero, 2002: 84), such elements in the curriculum helped foster and concretize a sense of peoplehood from a nostalgic perspective, yet also reified their obsolescence in the modern period, furthering students' understanding of the need to now move in a "professional direction" (Shahbazi, 2006: 179–83). In essence then, an effort was made to convert "Qashqa'iness" into a conceptual set of ideas and a curricular topic of study rather than an actual identity, something separate from oneself, freestanding and distinct.

Similarly, the dis-[O]rientation of the Qashqa'i community included a spatial element of geographic dislocation as well. In the early years of the program (1930s) especially, the government instituted a "brutal policy" of forced sedentarization (Barker, 1981: 143). Barker argues that much of what motivated the initiative was the idea in Iran at the time that the black tent was the "epitome" of ignorance and backwardness, and that what informed the creation of the tent schools was a sense that the nomads were "wild, unfortunate, hungry" and worthy of mercy (Barker, 1981: 147).

Thus, he contends, the tent schools did not succeed in the early years, particularly because the itinerant schoolteachers were not able to tolerate the "hardships" of nomadic life (Barker, 1981: 152). He concedes too that over time the educational initiative began to succeed, mostly because the program "was built on and around tribal traditions, timetables, and values. The schools made deep appeals to tribal pride and encouraged in the students the image of the 'new tribal warrior,' whose shield was a book, whose bullets were chalk, and whose enemy was whatever kept the warrior from attaining a dignified position in the emerging Iran" (Barker, 1981: 154).

Indeed, many educated Qashqa'i today strive to bring other Qashqa'i into the post-nomadic, "modern" era. They are highly assimilated and co-opted, and now work in concert with the state apparatus, using "their own culture [and] some of the techniques and discursive practices that state officials and the intelligentsia" employ (Shahbazi, 2001a: 116).

As a result, some observers view the tent school initiative as part and parcel of a neo-colonial enterprise complicit with western policies and perspectives (Shahshahani, 1995: 148). As nomadism wanes throughout the country, most certainly a result of this government-sponsored educational initiative, education for Iran's pastoral peoples rests upon a strongly nationalistic curriculum, which in Shahshahani's estimation (1995) has only served as a "humiliation" to those who actually still follow a nomadic lifestyle, "prais[ing] urban ways of life, the climax of which [is] the American lifestyle" (1995: 153).

Largely settled within the state of modern Iran, few of the estimated million plus Qashqa'i now rely primarily upon pastoral nomadic activity. Land reform and nationalization, in concert with the Shah's and later Ayatollah's efforts to unify the state through an aggressive educational program, have served to alter virtually every aspect of Qashqa'i social and economic behavior and activity.

These changes have not come easily or without ramifications. As self-sustaining herding has declined, wage-labor employment has not effectively filled the vacuum. Among the Koohi sub-tribe, for example, only 40 percent of those aged 6 years and above have been identified as formally employed (FAO, 2004). The power exercised by traditional leaders is also on the decline, a result of changes in the role and value of herds and herding as the primary form of economic prowess and success. In turn, such weakened roles are reflected in a variety of aspects of Qashqa'i social life. Use of illegal drugs by these former nomads, especially among the youth, is now apparent, another reflection of cultural dysfunction during a period of societal flux.

A similarly aggressive and far-reaching government policy can be found in the case of the bedouin of the Negev Desert, Israel (Arabic, *an-Naqab*). The Jewish conquest and colonization of Arab Palestine and the initiative to forcibly concentrate and sedentarize the bedouin community into planned towns while using educational service provision as a central pillar of that program directly parallels the experiences found in Iran and throughout the MENA region. Given this context, it should come as little surprise that the provision and use of educational services is highly controversial and politicized.

The "Compulsory Education Law" was created soon after the creation of the state of Israel in 1948, though early on few bedouin students actually attended school and initially the state made little effort to enforce the ruling (Abu-Saad, 1997: 25–6; Abu-Saad, 2006: 147). During the early years after Israel's War of Independence, state control and protection of its borders was considered paramount. This was due to the fact that the bedouin community was part of the Palestinian minority now under Israeli sovereignty; the ambivalence created by the ability and willingness of the state to provide the bedouin with services, as well as the community's readiness to accept what the state was offering as the process of forced sedentarization and land confiscation was carried out, has its roots in this early period.

By the mid-1950s, roughly 17 percent of the school-aged population was actually enrolled, though this figure refers only to boys. A drop-out rate of 37 percent before graduation (Abu-Rubiyya *et al.*, 1996: 2) led to a very low level of bedouin education "success" overall. Only after the *seig* (Hebrew, *"restricted area"*), a reservation-like space within which the bedouin had been confined since Israeli independence, was removed and a planned town program was initiated in the late 1960s (which concentrated the bedouin into still smaller areas) did enrollment gradually begin to rise (Abu-Rubiyya *et al.*, 1996: 3).

Dropping out of school is one concern, but other issues concerning education in the bedouin community also play a role. Statistics reveal that only 60 percent of the regional teachers are Negev bedouin, the rest hailing from the more urbane north (Galilee), where there tends to be a surplus of teachers (Abu-Saad, 1995: 156; Human Rights Watch, 2001: 113). Most bedouin elementary school teachers were men in the past though this is slowly changing; predictably, female teachers tend to come from outside the Negev (Abu-Rubiyya *et al.*, 1996: 4). Yet this presents some issues as well, especially when single Arab women living far from home and teaching in bedouin culture are not fully comfortable with the situation (Abu-Saad & Isralovitch, 1992: 778). Also, a high proportion of the teachers who have taught in the bedouin schools, historically, were uncertified (Abu-Rubiyya *et al.*, 1996: 17). This lack of role models is of course problematic and cyclical, as very few see the value in pursuing education as an attractive, viable career option (Al-Farona, 2007).

Thus, by 1995 only 6 percent of all bedouin high school students who took the national matriculation exam passed, compared with 22 percent in the rest of the Arab sector, and 40 percent in the Jewish sector (Katz *et al.*, 1998: 5). The figure saw considerable improvement by 2002, with 26 percent of bedouin students matriculating. And yet, that same year, 34 percent matriculated in the rest of the Arab sector, and 52 percent in the Jewish sector, directly impacting their access to higher education and job opportunities (Abu-Rabi'a, 2006: 877).

Predictably, observers argue that problems in bedouin education, including high drop-out rates and low scores on national tests, are due to bedouin culture (Meir, 1997: 176) rather than to the innumerable ways in which the bedouin educational system is inadequate and inferior to the Jewish one. Alternatively, Abu-Saad is one of very few scholars who has documented the ways in which bedouin education is jeopardized not, as many argue, because of culture, traditional mindsets and the like, but rather, due to the purposeful neglect and unequal treatment of Arabs in Israel in general, and of the bedouin in particular. He notes, for example the disproportionate distribution of funding, teaching hours, professional resources and facilities which are inequitably distributed between these systems (1995: 150).

And yet, despite such inadequacies, all indices today indicate that most of the bedouin of the Negev (male and female alike) who reside in the resettled town environment are clearly accessing the accoutrements of formal education (see Dinero, forthcoming). Indeed, it may be argued that these bedouin may be some of the most highly educated in the entire MENA region, at least as measured from a statistical perspective.

Still, critics are quick to point out that despite these advances, the bedouin resettlement villages and cities of the Negev also experience the highest rates of poverty of any other communities, Jewish or Arab, in the entire State of Israel. The overall unemployment rate in the first seven planned communities is 35 percent; in the local Jewish communities nearby the rate is 12 percent (Dinero, forthcoming). Many bedouin who are employed – often regardless of their levels of education – occupy low-wage, "blue collar," positions. Incipient drug use, family violence, and a variety of struggles both internal and in relation to state efforts to further confiscate tribal lands are all chronic difficulties of daily Negev bedouin life.

Longitudinal research (Dinero, forthcoming) suggests that as the bedouin residents are more formally versed in the Israeli educational system, they are not merely learning basic literacy and numeracy. Rather, the data suggests that today's Negev bedouin, as he or she becomes educated in the classroom setting, is also becoming all the more aware of the social, political and economic inadequacies and injustices which are a part of daily bedouin life in Israel. The more they learn, the more they realize just how much the bedouin community is truly lacking access to economic and social resources and political empowerment relative to its surroundings in the rest of Israel, the Middle East and beyond. Thus, one primary aspect of this more highly educated, post-nomadic, "hybridized" Negev bedouin is the manner in which exposure to new ideas and modes of perceiving and knowing, framed by and through the formal educational initiatives of the "third space," has served to radicalize their developing identities within a globalizing core/Western/Israeli/dominant cultural context.

Conclusions: Separating Educational Initiatives from the *Dis-[O]rientation* Discourse

The processes of de-territorialization amongst pastoral nomadic communities concomitant with socio-economic assimilation, "modernization" and the development of a de-nomadized proletariat class all segue well with formal educational policy in the Middle East and North Africa over the past century. As such, the provision and use of this service has proven inherently conflictual; states struggle to foster the development of a more easily controlled and rationalized populace, and pastoral nomads enter a "third space" which, while facilitating a state of rootless hybridity, often fails to completely satisfy communal desires and needs. It may be contended that these spaces in many ways represent the failure of states to succeed in their assimilationist goals, as identity formation is flexible and resilient, reconstituting in new patterns and forms in the re-spatialized, urban environment (Abu-Saad, 2008: 1722).

That said, one can find examples of curricula which are centered upon the "familiar" – that is, which are neither urban-centric nor antithetical to nomadic values and lifeways but which also acknowledge global developments and technological change. These are not only more appropriate for such unique communities but also, in the long run, are more likely to foster retention and more positive, successful results.

Such an initiative has been implemented in one of Israel's planned bedouin towns, Segev Shalom/Shqeb. There, a primary school has been developed which uses a unique curriculum, "The Desert as an Open Laboratory for Science Study." The school combines the study, application and appreciation of traditional bedouin knowledge and values with the fields of environmental science and sustainability (*Ha'aretz*, 2005). Through field excursions, laboratory experiments, and a variety of in- and out-side classroom activities, the school encourages students to draw upon a variety of knowledges, ideas, experiences, and understandings of the natural environment and their role within it. As the school headmaster explains the ideology behind the school's curriculum, "our culture is like the roots of a tree. If we turn to Western ideas, but don't have these roots deep into the ground, then there are problems. There is nothing wrong with some of these Western things, so long as we keep our bedouin values. But we have to pick and choose, and this is hard, especially for the young" (Jirjawi, 2007).

This raises a key question however, which is whether the formal education discourse, which in the final analysis has long been designed to facilitate change at any cost, does not deserve re-evaluation in the pastoral nomadic context. By definition, what is inherent and directly embedded into virtually every educational initiative in Middle Eastern and North African pastoral communities over the last century is the underlying assumption that formal education aids in cultural assimilation and is "directly antagonistic to nomadic values" (Dyer, 2001: 325).

Thus, by assuming that informal education is inadequate, and that the scientific method, modern technology, literacy and numeracy are all essential and invaluable (Ezeomah, 1990: 15), Western thought has been elevated to a level which supersedes all other forms of knowing (Krätli, 2000: 12) and, by default, renders other ways of interacting with and understanding the world irrelevant. But as the Segev Shalom school approach exemplifies, traditional knowledge and Western ways can be incorporated and integrated, recognized as equally valid, not only because of their especially effective pedagogical power, but further, because such approaches *both* resonate well with today's highly hybridized post-nomadic student (*Ha'aretz*, 2005). And yet, while the state may overcome logistical challenges through new technologies and other delivery techniques, the ability to provide a service which is perceived as relevant and non-threatening is the greatest challenge of all, most especially when that provision is directly connected with the loss of territory, and the economic and social modes of interaction which are embedded within it.

As Lancaster and Lancaster (2006) poignantly conclude, many young people from nomadic cultures throughout the Middle East and North Africa today are now highly literate, numerate, and formally trained. Yet for these post-nomadic pastoralists, this gain has come with little perceived benefit but rather, with the sense that they have lost a great deal in the process, as they now lack traditional knowledge of their cultural heritage, and are increasingly dependent upon the state for economic development and support. They may be more educated in the sciences, for example, than their relatives and friends, but their sisters and brothers who are less educated seem somehow to be happier, and more fulfilled (2006: 345).

Clearly, such seemingly counter-intuitive outcomes must be situated within the maze of contradictions, conflicts, uncertainty, instability – and above all, *dis-[O]rientation* – that typifies the "third space" post-nomads now call home. While teachers, parents and students alike all must negotiate across and within this newly formed territory in the decades ahead as they strive to succeed in meeting the economic demands and strains of an ever-globalizing post-colonial Middle East, they do so at the behest of state actors and policy makers who, in the early twenty-first century, continue to expropriate land and resettle these pastoral populations, often with little regard for where and how these communities wish to live. So long as state policies are designed to marginalize these populations and denigrate their citizens' equal rights, effective education provision will be jeopardized.

And yet, as the Negev case also suggests, pastoral peoples are pushing back and seeking to stake new claims in a post-global world. For it is the very bedouin who have been educated in Israel's schools who now are leading the resistance movement to fight for minority rights in Israel, for an end to land expropriation, for a recognition of the spontaneous, unplanned settlements, and so on (Abu-Saad, 2008: 1741–2). Their non-violent participation in the democratic process suggests the possibility of new political and economic opportunities and upward mobility in the future re-spatialization of the post-nomadic MENA region.

In such a context, regional governments would be wise to rethink spatial policy and its implications. As these populations continue to grow exponentially, it would be shortsighted to do otherwise.

References

Abu-Rabiʿa, A. (2006). A century of education: Bedouin contestation within formal education in Israel. In D. Chatty (Ed.), *Nomadic Societies in the Middle East and North Africa: Entering the 21st Century* (pp. 865–82). Leiden & Boston, MA: Brill.

Abu-Rubiyya, S., al-Athauna, F., & al-Bador, S. (1996). Survey of Bedouin schools in the Negev. Adva Survey available at www.adva.org/trans.html. Accessed January 18, 2006.

Abu-Saad, I. (2008). Spatial transformation and indigenous resistance: The urbanization of the Palestinian Bedouin in Southern Israel. *American Behavioral Scientist,* 51(12), 1, 713–54.

Abu-Saad, I. (2006). Bedouin Arabs in Israel: Education, political control and social control. In C. Dyer (Ed.), *The Education of Nomadic Peoples: Current Issues, Future Prospects.* (pp. 141–58). New York: Berghahn Books.

Abu-Saad, I. (1997). The education of Israel's Beduin: Background and prospects. *Israel Studies,* 2(2), 21–39.

Abu-Saad, I. (1995). Bedouin arab education in the context of radical social change: What is the future? *Compare: A Journal of Comparative Education,* 25(2), 149–60.

Abu-Saad, I. & Isralowitz, R. E. (1992). Teachers' job satisfaction in transitional society within the Bedouin Arab schools of the Negev. *Journal of Social Psychology*, 132(6), 771–81.

Al-Farona, M. (2007). Headmaster, Segev Shalom Elementary School. Personal communication, February 19.

Aronson, D. (1981). Development for nomadic pastoralists: Who benefits? In J.G. Galaty, G. D. Aronson & P. C. Salzman (Eds.), *The Future of Pastoral Peoples: Proceedings of a Conference Held in Nairobi, Kenya, 4–8 August, 1980* (pp. 42–51). Ottawa: International Development Research Centre.

Barker, P. (1981). Tent schools of the Qashqa'i: A paradox of local initiative and state control. In M. E. Bonine & N. R. Keddie (Eds.), *Modern Iran: The Dialectics of Continuity and Change* (pp. 139–58). Albany, NY: SUNY Press.

Bocco, R. (2000). International organizations and the settlement of nomads in the Arab Middle East, 1950–1990. In M. Mundy & B. Musallam (Eds.), *The Transformation of Nomadic Society in the Arab East* (pp. 197–217). Cambridge: Cambridge University Press.

Bruins, H. J. (1986). *Desert Environment and Agriculture in the Central Negev and Kadesh-Barnea During Historical Times*. Nijkerk: Midbar Foundation.

Chatty, D. (2006). Boarding schools for mobile peoples: The Harasiis in the Sultanate of Oman. In C. Dyer (Ed.), *The Education of Nomadic Peoples: Current Issues, Future Prospects* (pp. 212–30). New York and Oxford: Berghahn Books.

Cole, D. P. (2003). Where have the Bedouin gone? *Anthropological Quarterly*, 76(2), 235–67.

Dinero, S. C. (forthcoming). *Settling for Less: The Planned Resettlement of Israel's Negev Bedouin*. Oxford and New York: Berghahn Books

Dinero, S. C. (2004). The politics of education provision in rural Native Alaska: The case of Yukon Village. *Race Ethnicity and Education*, 7(4), 399–417.

Dinero, S. C. (2002). Image is everything: The development of the Negev Bedouin as a tourist attraction. *Nomadic Peoples*, 6(1), 69–94.

Dinero, S. C., McGee, T., Bhagat, P. S., & Mariotz, E. (2006). Website development and Alaska Native identities: Hunting for meaning in cyberspace. *International Journal of Technology, Knowledge and Society*, 2(1), 79–90.

Dyer, C. (2001). Nomads and Education for All: Education for development or domestication. *Comparative Education*, 37(2), 315–27.

Ezeomah, C. (1990). *Educating Nomads for Self-actualization and Development*. Geneva: International Bureau of Education, UNESCO.

FAO Centre for Sustainable Development, Iran, for the Rural Institutions and Participation Service. (2004). The role of local institutions in reducing vulnerability to recurrent natural disasters and in sustainable livelihoods development: Case study, the role of Qashqai nomadic communities in reducing vulnerability to recurrent drought and sustainable livelihoods development in Iran. Available at http://www.fao.org/docrep/007/ae089e/ae089e02.htm. Accessed January 13, 2009.

Gandana, I. (2008). Exploring third spaces: Negotiating identities and cultural differences. *International Journal of Diversity in Organisations, Communities and Nations*, 7(6), 143–50.

Ha'aretz (2005) A learning oasis in the desert. March 27.

Harvey, D. (1996). *Justice, Nature & the Geography of Difference*. Malden, MA and Oxford: Blackwell.

Human Rights Watch (2001). *Second Class: Discrimination against Palestinian Arab children in Israel's schools*. Human Rights Watch Position Paper. New York: Human Rights Watch.

Jirjawi, A. (2007). Headmaster, Segev Shalom Elementary School. Personal communication, February 7.

Katz, Y., *et al.* (1998). Excerpts from 'The Investigatory Committee on the Bedouin Educational System in the Negev' ['The Katz Report']. Available at w3.bgu.ac.il/bedouin/katz-excerpts.htm. Accessed January 18, 2006.

Krätli, S. (2000). *Education Provision to Nomadic Pastoralists: A Literature Review.* Washington, DC: World Bank.

Krätli, S., & Dyer, C. (2006). Education and development for nomads: The issues and the evidence. In C. Dyer (Ed.), *The Education of Nomadic Peoples: Current Issues, Future Prospects* (pp. 8–34). New York: Berghahn Books.

Lancaster, W., & Lancaster, F. (2006). Integration into modernity: Some tribal rural societies in the Bilad Ash-Sham. In D. Chatty (Ed.), *Nomadic Societies in the Middle East and North Africa: Entering the 21st Century* (pp. 335–69). Leiden: Brill.

Lavie, S., & Young, W. (1984). Bedouin in limbo: Egyptian and Israeli development policies in southern Sinai. *Antipode, 16*(2), 33–44.

Marx, E. (1967). *Bedouin of the Negev.* New York: Frederick A. Praeger Press.

Massey, D. (2005). *For Space.* Thousand Oaks, CA: Sage.

Meir, A. (1997). *As Nomadism Ends: The Israeli Bedouin of the Negev.* Boulder, CO: Westview Press.

Meir, A. (1992). Territoriality among the Negev Bedouin: From nomadism to semi-urbanism. Paper presented at the Conference on Tribal and Peasant Pastoralism, Pavia, Italy.

Meir, A. (1987). Comparative vital statistics along the pastoral nomadism–sedentarism continuum. *Human Ecology, 15*(1), 91–107.

Meninger, D. (1993). Bedouin on the periphery of the frontier: the mobile water tank and overgrazing. Paper presented at Ben-Gurion University Conference on "Regional Development: The Challenge of the Frontier," Ein Boqeq, Israel.

Rapaport, A. (1978). Nomadism as a man–environment system. *Environment and Behavior, 10*(2), 214–46.

Saldanha, A. (2008). Heterotopia and structuralism. *Environment and Planning, 40,* 2080–96.

Shahbazi, M. (2006). The Qashqa'i, formal education and indigenous educators. In C. Dyer (Ed.), *The Education of Nomadic Peoples: Current Issues, Future Prospects* (pp. 175–92). New York: Berghahn Books.

Shahbazi, M. (2001a). The Qashqa'i nomads of Iran (Part I): Formal education. *Nomadic Peoples, 5*(1), 37–64.

Shahbazi, M. (2001b). The Qashqa'i nomads of Iran (Part II): State-supported literacy and ethnic identity. *Nomadic Peoples, 6*(1), 95–123.

Shahshahani, S. (1995). Tribal schools of Iran: sedentarization through education. *Nomadic Peoples, 36/37,* 145–56.

Swidler, W. W. (1973). Adaptive processes regulating nomad-sedentary interaction in the Middle East. In C. Nelson (Ed.), *The Desert and the Sown: Nomads in the Wider Society* (pp. 23–41). Institute of International Studies Research Series 21. Berkeley, CA: University of California.

Yiftachel, O. (2003). Bedouin Arabs and the Israeli settler state: Land policies and indigenous resistance. In D. Champagne & I. Abu-Saad (Eds.), *The Future of Indigenous Peoples: Strategies for Survival and Development.* Los Angeles, CA: UCLA American Indian Studies Center.

14 Citizenship, Difference, and the Schooling of Muslim Children in Malta

Louise Chircop

Introduction

Malta, a small island-state in the middle of the Mediterranean, represents an 'in between' country. A member of the European Union, its roots are nonetheless embedded in North African soil. Located on the periphery of the European Union, it is geographically nearer to North Africa than to many of the European countries its inhabitants try to emulate. It can be figuratively said that the Maltese people are very much like Janus. One face, representing the present and future, looks in awe towards Europe. The other face glares at North Africa, watching its past. Sometimes referred to as the island of 'Catholic Arabs', Malta was conquered by the Arabs from Tunisia in 870, and was once fully Muslim (Wettinger, 1986). Arab rule came to an end 220 years later, when Count Roger captured Malta, although Islam remained on the Maltese islands for much longer. According to Guido de Marco (2007), former President of Malta, 'the island can act as a bridge between the north and south of the region [the Mediterranean]' (p. 204). More recently, Sultana (2009) pointed out that,

> our [Maltese] history shows that what we have done best is to act as a bulwark to keep 'non-Europeans' – whoever these are – (and Islam) out of Europe – a vocation that, might I add, we ironically seem to have revived with a vengeance when, following our entry into the EU in 2004, we became a vital outpost in helping the EU secure its borders through collaborating on Frontex operations. (p. 12)

There seems to be a deliberate attempt by the Maltese to distance, or rather detach, themselves from their Arab heritage. For instance, Dr Ugo Mifsud Bonnici (1989), then Education Minister and later President of the Republic, in his address to the National Congress on the Maltese cultural identity, went to great lengths to explain that Maltese culture is European. He pointed out that Malta is formed by Catholic values just like the rest of Europe. In that sense, our culture defines our identity. A very important aspect of Maltese culture is without doubt religion: 'Our moral culture gives great value to gentlemanly behaviour as well as to charity … it is a European Culture, in the sense that Europe, like us, was formed on Catholic values' (p. xiii). Dr Mifsud Bonnici seems to imply that gentlemanly behaviour is the monopoly of European culture, more so since its roots lie in Catholic values. There is a tacit insinuation that those who are not European are boorish, since they are not Christians. Thus, Christianity and Catholicism are depicted as being part and parcel of the Maltese identity irrespective of the fact that many nowadays are not practising Catholics. According to the Sunday Mass Attendance Census of 2005, only 52.6 per cent of Maltese Catholics attend Mass on Sunday (Discern, 2006). Many more people follow other religions.

The Republic of Malta had 410,000 inhabitants in 2008. According to its National Statistics Office, 95 per cent of the inhabitants are Catholics. Various government and media reports suggest that in 2007, there were also about 3,000 Muslims, 500 Jehovah's Witnesses,[1] some 200 Coptic Christians and very small communities of Greek Orthodox, Church of England, Church of Scotland, Hindus and Jews, among others (Vassallo, 2009).

When speaking about the Maltese language, Dr Mifsud Bonnici added, 'We speak a language which we kept and enriched, but from which we removed [*neħħejna*] excessively harsh sounds' (p. xiii). It is clear that the harsh sounds referred to are the guttural sounds of some Arabic phonemes. Interestingly, he used the word '*neħħejna*' (removed), as if this was done consciously, a deliberate attempt to distance Malta from its Arab heritage in order to take on its European identity.

Dr Mifsud Bonnici's approach is well reflected in more recent statements of other Maltese politicians. For instance, Edward Fenech Adami, President of Malta in 2004–2009, frequently alluded to the Christian identity of the Maltese. In a speech delivered on the occasion of Republic Day in 2007, he stated that, 'We should acknowledge and feel proud that Maltese society still treasures Christian moral principles that have nurtured our identity, we have to make sure that we pass on these values to future generations'.[2] Thus, there is the assumption that to be a 'good' Maltese citizen one has to be Christian. Linking citizenship with Christian identity can be considered as a discourse of exclusion in relation to Maltese citizens who are not Christian. It conflates citizenship and religious affiliation, while the latter is not the same for all Maltese.

Furthermore, the large number of undocumented African migrants reaching Maltese shores has provoked a discourse of invasion and Islamisation, regardless of the fact that many migrants are in fact Christians. The main political parties exacerbate this negative discourse[3] by riding on the crest of people's negative attitudes towards immigrants in order to gain votes for the forthcoming European Parliament elections (Debono, 2009). Many regard the presence of Africans and Muslims as a threat to Maltese identity, as John Spiteri (2009), a member of Azzjoni Nazzjonali and candidate for the European Parliament, wrote in his blog that "Flooding Europe with immigrants ... helps destroy the culture and identities of the member states".

Thus immigration is seen as a threat to Maltese identity and there is a call, especially from right-wing parties, such as Azzjoni Nazzjonali and Imperium Ewropa, as well as from exponents of both the Labour and Nationalist parties, to preserve Maltese identity. The immigration issue is merging with other issues such as national culture, identity and rights to create a discourse of exclusion.

A number of Maltese people have tried hard to believe that they cannot be anything but European and Christian to the core.[4] Through the curriculum and their choice of textbooks, politicians, religious leaders and education authorities have done their utmost to depict the Arab Muslim as our enemy, positing that we have nothing in common with our North African neighbours, '... conveniently forgetting to tell us that linguistically, culturally, genetically and even religiously, we had absorbed our so-called "adversaries" right into the core of our being' (Sultana, 2009, p. 15).

The ambivalent identity of the Maltese is further accentuated by the fact that while Malta professes to be 'European' it lacks the lay traditions of most European states. The hegemony of the Catholic Church is such that politicians are afraid to take a more progressive stance in areas such as education, health, and civil rights. For instance, Savona-Ventura (1995) notes how the Church influenced the Government in suspending the service of Intrauterine Contraceptive Device (IUCD) insertion in the state's family planning centres (p. 31). Also, as of 1995, the Maltese state and the Vatican reached an agreement which stipulates that if a marriage is celebrated according to the Catholic rite, it is recognised and has the same effect as a civil marriage (Marriage Act, 1975, 21(1)). One must also note that the Catholic religion is mentioned in the Constitution as the state religion.

In this chapter I argue that the underpinnings of a Maltese homogeneous identity, as outlined above, have created a chasm between those who are included 'within' Maltese society and those who are considered as 'outsiders' to it. This chapter illustrates how the concept of citizenship is culturalised, that is, woven together with culture and religion in ways that define citizen rights in exclusive terms. The chapter examines this problematic as it is reflected in schools. The chapter shows how Maltese minority groups, in this case Muslims, are regarded as the 'Other', because they do not fit the perception of what a Maltese citizen stands for.[5]

Citizenship, Difference and Equality

For critics of multicultural citizenship, the discourse linking citizenship and cultural difference is often regarded as an oxymoron (see Lister, 1998; Volpp, 2007; Antonopoulos and Cos-Montiel, 2007). Citizenship is built on the notion that every citizen should be treated in an equal manner; 'equal' as equivalent to undifferentiated and sameness. For them, a 'neutral' or culture-free citizenship reflects a concept of equality understood as universal and transcends the bounds of social differences. French conceptions of citizenship may perhaps best illustrate this approach. Conversely, for proponents of a multicultural citizenship, such a treatment would automatically exclude all those who are different in one way or another (culturally, religiously, ethnically), and thus do not fit in this universalist paradigm. For them, a 'politics of difference', which recognises and acknowledges differences (Young, 1990; Kymlicka and Norman, 2000), is *a sine qua non* for social justice to prevail. Conceptions of multiculturalism prevalent in Canada may perhaps best illustrate this approach.

Many advocates of assimilationist policies insist that culture cannot form part of the equation of citizenship. For them, citizenship should be formed on the republican model in which an individual's rights are the topmost priority. They thus contend that by granting all citizens the same rights citizens have the same opportunities. They assume that justice will prevail because laws exist. Moreover, critics of minority rights argue that, 'justice require[s] state institutions to be "colour-blind"' (Kymlicka and Norman, 2000, p. 3). However, Volpp (2007) insists that there is no such thing as a culture-free citizenship. He draws on the example of the French Republican model to highlight the fallacy about France's *laïcité* (secularism). He contends that the French Republican tradition is 'marked by a Christianity that appears not visible to the French' (p. 596). Parekh (2006) also concludes that:

> No European society or political system is secular in the sense in which liberals use the term ... The views of human nature and history that inform much of the European political thought and practice, many of its current laws and practices, and even such trivial things as treating Sunday and Christmas as public holidays, are all further examples of the continuing influence of Christianity. (p. 189)

Thus, for critics of a republican model, dominant groups universalise cultural and religious practices, presenting them as 'normal' and 'ordinary' and ignore their exclusionary effects on the 'Other'. Young (1990) is also very critical of this presumed impartiality. She maintains that,

> ... claims to impartiality feed cultural imperialism by allowing the particular experience and perspective of privileged groups to parade as universal ... [and] ... the conviction that bureaucrats and experts can exercise their decisionmaking power in an impartial manner legitimates authoritarian hierarchy. (p. 10)

Such a view resonates with that of Connolly for whom 'no culturally constituted constellation of identities ever deserves to define itself simply as natural, complete or inclusive' (cited by McLaren, 1997, p. 12).

The imposition of constraints on some groups may be 'embedded in unquestioned norms, habits, and symbols, in the assumptions underlying institutional rules and the collective consequences of following those rules' (Young, 1990, p. 41). This is what Volpp means when he points out that cultureless citizenship is an impossible quest because it is impossible for one to totally divest oneself of one's identity and the end product of policies and rules would ultimately reflect the general consensus. Thus, the claim to cultureless citizenship can be regarded as a process through which citizens are assimilated into a presumed 'universal' culture. Wieviorka (2004) argues that assimilation 'requires not only that cultural specificities be invisible or excluded from the public sphere, but further that they disappear altogether in the melting pot, or crucible of the nation and therefore in the dominant identity of society' (p. 293). As an illustration, Volpp (2007) invokes the headscarf debate in France. He notes that this debate is perceived 'as the battle between a culture-free citizenship and a culturally-laden other' (p. 571).

Such a principle of citizenship expects the state to show neutrality towards cultural and ethnic difference. Therefore it is presumed that the state is neutral because it does not support or show preference to any culture. Modood (2007) contests this idea and, drawing on the work of William Kymlicka, considers that state neutrality is virtually impossible because '[m]ost polities will have a history in which one or more dominant cultural, linguistic or religious groups have fashioned institutions and conventions to suit themselves' (p. 25). Thus, a state which expects the citizens who do not fall within the mould provided by it, to fit in, 'is to treat them as second class citizens and to disadvantage them in all sorts of ways' (p. 25). With regard to claims of a culture-free citizenship in France, Poulter (1997) remarks that its underpinning political discourse requires minority groups 'to surrender the distinctive characteristics of their separate identities and blend into wider society' (p. 46). Rosaldo (1989) calls this 'cultural stripping' where citizens become transparent to the state (see also McLaren, 1997, p. 522). The invisibility resulting from cultural stripping is then transformed into social inequalities on the basis of region, religion and ethnicity and the exclusion of minorities from the public sphere. Dürr, Michaelowa and Vollenweider (2008) consider this to be 'hollow citizenship' because, 'political equality is absent either because of flaws in democratic institutions or because of deficits in democratic politics' (2008, p. 4).

The Maltese context provides a similar, yet different, scenario to that of France. It is similar in its presentation of one accepted idea of identity and citizenship. Its difference lies in strong ties between the state and the Catholic Church. Thus, it can be considered as neither a secular, nor a 'culture-free' state compared with the French republican model. In fact, the Christianisation of Maltese identity is opposed to the notion of a cultureless citizenship as articulated in France. It is, however, just as hegemonic, as it assumes a single identity founded on European, Christian values. This dominant culture maintains its position of power through its institutions, such as the educational system. Thus, those who do not subscribe to such an identity are deemed 'outsiders': 'they may feel that, even though they would appear to have a strong *prima facie* claim to a national identity, the way in which this identity is socially constructed serves to exclude them from belonging to it' (Bond, 2006, p. 611).

The problematic associated with the intersections of culture and citizenship has two major implications with regard to the equitable provision of public education in a diverse society. First, as noted by Lynch and Baker (2005), 'While equalizing access and participation are key equality objectives, we need a more holistic and integrated approach to achievement of equality in education, if we are to make schools truly egalitarian institutions' (p. 132). These authors suggest that it is important to acknowledge the relationship between education and socio-cultural, political, economic and affective systems that exist in society if equality in education is to be achieved. They put forward the concept of 'equality of condition' to indicate that equalising 'people's "real options", ... involves the *equal enabling and empowerment of individuals*' (p. 132, italics in original). Their conclusion resonates well with Tiedt and Tiedt (1999) who emphasize that, in a diverse and multicultural society, it is crucial to devise '… an inclusion/teaching process that engages all students in developing a strong sense of self-esteem, discovering empathy for persons of diverse cultural backgrounds and experiencing equitable opportunities to achieve their fullest potential'. Secondly, citizenship is not approached as merely a status that grants an individual a set of rights but also as a 'feeling intertwined with a sense of identity and therefore a sense of belonging' (Grech, 2005, p. 3).

In the present chapter, I dwell on the schooling of Muslim children and youth in Malta, as a case in point to explore the intersections between citizenship, cultural difference and schooling in Malta. I am particularly interested in exploring how, in this particular national context, curricula, texts and pedagogical practices intersect and re-inscribe in schools exclusive hegemonic and dominant forms of identity.

Muslims in Malta

In 2007, of around 3,000 Muslim residing in Malta, less than 200 were born in the country.[6] A parliamentary document further suggests that there are 400 Muslim students attending state schools,[7] out of a total school population (K-12) of around 38,028 (Ministry of Education, 2008, p. 355).[8]

The number of Muslims in Malta is increasing due to naturalisation. Muslims who do not hold Maltese citizenship originate from different countries forming a multicultural and multiethnic group, with Islam as its common denominator. The Constitution endorses Muslims' right to practise their faith as is stated in Chapter IV Article 32 (b), and therefore Islam and every other religion are formally on equal par with the Catholic faith.

For many Maltese, Muslim is synonymous with Arab and, apart from being the object of contempt, the word 'Arab' is often used to homogenise the Muslim community into one single 'race', irrespective of ethnic and cultural differences. This contempt towards Arabs and Muslims has its roots both in recent and distant historical events because, as Briscoe (2006) points out, 'A socio-political context is always the product of history' (p. 1). For example, the Great Siege of 1565, in which the Maltese and the Knights Hospitallers[9] kept the Ottoman Turks away, and thus 'saved' the people from re-Islamisation, is granted an important position in the construction of Maltese 'collective memory'.

More recent events also contribute to this uneasiness and ill-feeling towards Arabs. In the 1970s, Malta's Prime Minister of the day, Duminku Mintoff (1955–1958 and 1971–1984), strengthened ties with Libya in order to bring investment to the country. Thus came about the introduction of Arabic in secondary schools – a compulsory subject resisted by students, teachers and administrators. The opposition criticised Mintoff's policies. The resistance shown by the students in schools reflected a discourse against Arabs that was developing, which Sciriha (2001) captured in her study:

> Only 1% of respondents who attend a state school study [Arabic]. This tiny percentage is testimony to a gradual build-up of negative sentiments that the Maltese in general have regarding Arabs … To the Maltese, the Arabs do not

represent 'the enemy', but despite the increasing contact with them and the knowledge that they are more prosperous because of their oil-rich economies, the notion Arabic is still somewhat scorned at, particularly in certain Maltese circles … In truth, the Maltese did not want to be even remotely associated with their wealthy neighbours. (pp. 28–29)

The negative reaction towards Arabic was expressed by Josef, a Maltese Muslim parent, in the following words:

Arabic had a stigma as well, apart from the political reasons behind it, 'Why study Arabic? What do we need it for?' Then you had one side of the political spectrum[10] that used to call Arabs '*tal-ḥabbażiż*' and that wasn't fair either. All that is happening now has its roots in those times. That is, all this is built upon and reflects, at the end of the day, that the Maltese have a superiority complex towards the Arabs and an inferiority complex towards the Europeans. This is a mistake. This is the paradox, the extremes in Maltese society – that we think that the Italians and the British are better than us. Then we think that we are better than the Arabs – which isn't the case in either.

Negative attitudes towards Muslims and Arabs are very alive today, and one still hears parents threatening their children that if they do not behave well an Arab will come and kidnap them ('*Ara jiġi xi Għarbi u jieħdok*'). The stigma towards Arabs and Muslims has meant that some of them feel oppressed, more so by the religious hegemony that exists. One parent, Maria, a Catholic woman married to a Muslim said:

You know how the Maltese are. How they regard Arabs and Muslims. My husband and I discussed this issue and decided that we should see what's best for our son. And as we are in Malta we decided that it would be better to raise him as Catholic.

Maria, who has been subjected to racist comments and sustained a violent attack because of her marriage, presents an example of the difficulties Muslims encounter in Maltese society. As parents, Maria and her husband feel that their son would not be considered as equal to other Maltese citizens if he were brought up as a Muslim. Therefore, one way in which they could deal with stigma is to deny their son a part of his identity because it is easier to be accepted when one conforms to society's expectations. What Maria's family experiences resonates with the experience of British Muslims who are also pressured to compromise their religious identities to feel accepted (Modood & Ahmad, 2007, p. 201). In the Maltese context, Muslims might find it doubly difficult to assert their religious identity because the Catholic religion permeates every aspect of social life (see Mayo, 2001, p. 180).

Curricular Spaces and Constituting the Subaltern 'Other'

The Maltese state is bound by law to provide schools wherein, according to the Education Act 1988, students can 'receive education and instruction without any distinction of age, sex, belief or economic means' (Part 1, Sec. 3). This clause implies that every student is regarded as equal to his or her peers and the educational experience provided by the state ensures the full development of all students. On the other hand the same law also stipulates that:

> It shall be the duty of the Minister to provide for the education and teaching of the Catholic religion in State schools and to establish the curriculum for the education and teaching of that religion in those schools according to the dispositions in this regard of the Bishops in Ordinary of these Islands.
>
> (Part IV, Sec. 47 (2))

Therefore, the Catholic Church is given exclusive power on what is taught in schools with regards to religious knowledge. Despite the increasing number of Muslim students who attend state schools there has been little, if any, effort to engage the curriculum and educational practices in more inclusive ways.

In the late 1990s, the Ministry of Education launched a curriculum review process, leading up to the implementation of a new National Minimum Curriculum (NMC) (Ministry of Education, 1999). Borg (2006)—one of the key persons on the Committee entrusted with the reform—notes that when the review committee tried to ensure that the new curriculum reflected the multicultural and multi-faith presence in Malta, there was a strong negative reaction by the Catholic Church, which felt the exclusive space traditionally allocated to Catholic religious instruction was being compromised. The Minister of Education at the time backed the Church, pointing out the 'constitutional and contractual obligations on the government to respect Malta's Catholic identity' (cited in Borg, 2006, p. 63). The attempt to introduce a more inclusive curriculum was thus successfully foiled.

While those who do not follow the Catholic faith are not forced to attend these religious lessons, the state does not offer any other alternative to cater for their needs. This poses a problem on two counts: first, the state is retracting from its pledge to provide all children with education that develops their whole personality, and in this sense, Muslim parents who wish their children to receive a more holistic education have no choice but to send them to Mariam Albatool School ('Maria, the Holiest Woman School'), the only Islamic school currently operating in Malta.[11] Moreover, when the state is securing the teaching of only one religion, it may actually be hindering the access of non-Catholic students to its schools and thus posing indirect barriers to their right to an equal public education. The Imam serving the Muslim community commented on the issue saying:

> Every child has a right to education including religious and spiritual education … therefore, first and foremost it is a right and secondly it is very important. Muslims and those who practice other religions have the same right because

you cannot discriminate between one pupil and another. Muslim students in state schools have a right to learn their religion.

Taken from this perspective, Malta's education system does not promote 'equality of condition' (Lynch & Baker, 2005). Effectively, during religion lessons, students who are not Catholic may either withdraw from the classroom or do something else, such as homework.[12] 'Opting out' of religious education lessons ultimately constitutes these students as fundamentally the different 'Other' among us. In that sense, if one builds on Tiedt and Tiedt (1999), the organisation of the curricular space does not reflect a concern for inclusiveness in relation to social diversity. In fact, one could argue that having to leave the classroom during religious education classes does not promote respect for diversity and quality education for all, let alone education in a multicultural setting (p. 18). Teachers and administrators are aware that such practices do not influence students positively, when referring to Muslim students:

> They do not attend. In fact, it is as if these children, especially those whose religion is different, they become marginalized ... religious feasts, Christmas. They are marginalized.

Another teacher acknowledged that the lack of inclusive curricular spaces within schools bring about exclusion, pointing out the fact that Muslim children are expected to withdraw from religious activities with the ensuing repercussions on their education:

> I think that these children are receiving an education fraught with interruptions, not holistic education. You have taken them out of class because of mass, because it is the feast of Our Lady of Sorrows, because it is Christmastime, because it is Easter time; ... Every time these children go out of the class you are putting them at a disadvantage because then, when it is time to return they have to readjust and focus to continue with the lessons. This means that these children are losing much more, not only are they losing out on a subject upon which no choice is available, but then they are losing out when it is time to concentrate on maths, English and the other subjects ... In my opinion this system is erroneously conceived and wrong because you would have lost the children by the time you try to integrate them in the day-to-day programme ... We are always talking about child centred [education] that every child is different and thus we should respect him or her and provide him or her with the best education possible. All this is deemed irrelevant as it is far from the truth.

By avoiding the question of religious pluralism, the state reproduces inequalities associated with the relative location of different social groups in society. Schools operate as hegemonic apparatuses that reproduce epistemic frameworks that view Maltese citizenship through a particular cultural prism.

Curricular Spaces and the Enactment of 'Hollow' Citizenship

Borg and Mayo (2001) observe that the 'celebration of differences' projected in the NMC is contradictory to the 'totalising statement that students are to "acquire knowledge and information" in "the religion of the Maltese people"' (p. 81). Such a statement implies that every Maltese person follows the same religion, ignoring the fact that Muslims, Jehovah's Witnesses, and other religious groups are also part of the 'Maltese' polity. Thus, as Borg and Mayo observe, 'the Maltese people are … conceived of as an undifferentiated mass, a unitary subject, with one belief system' (p. 81). By defining Maltese people as those following one particular religion, one is automatically excluding the possibility of identifying oneself as Maltese and Muslim. One interviewee referred to this discourse of equating identity with religion:

> There is the impression that if you are Muslim, you are not Maltese and if you are Maltese, it's because you acquired the passport. The idea that there are Maltese Muslims, or converts, like I am; but there are also Maltese who have one foreign parent who lives in Malta (now whether he has obtained citizenship or else he is still foreigner) and one Maltese parent. Now, these are Muslims and like the majority of the children in the school, they are hundred percent Maltese, they were born in Malta, they are Maltese citizens, they speak Maltese and in the morning they sing the National Anthem, but they are Muslims.

By conflating one's religious identity, culture, and the attributes of citizenship, the curriculum creates a divide between citizenship and identity in an exclusionary manner because, within this rationality, being Catholic seems to be a pre-condition of citizenship. Therefore, while Muslim students might 'enjoy' universal rights (such as entitlement to free education) because they are Maltese born and thus 'insiders', the curriculum marks them as 'outsiders' because they are culturally different. Thus, in spite of the 'celebration of diversity' encouraged by the curriculum, the privileged position of the Catholic church contributes to the existing inequalities of respect and recognition towards Muslims, thus reducing this principle to a 'ritual performance' (McLaren, 1999).

Moreover the way in which Maltese state schools project their mission and role – their institutional identity as Catholic – challenges Muslim students in terms of developing their religious and civic identities. Some educators who were interviewed considered the teaching of only the Catholic religion as discriminatory. One head of school said:

> If we say that we are a democratic country, I would say that they have every right to learn Islam. It is a human right. Why shouldn't it be granted to them if they are living in the same country, attending the same school? Why not?

According to Amor (2001), 'Religious education is a contributing factor to the shaping up of one's identity' (para. 37). Therefore, while Muslim parents do not condemn state schools for not offering their children the Muslim perspective of life, they feel that their children are entitled to an education that conforms to their beliefs, despite being a minority. In fact, all the parents who sent their children to Mariam Albatool School mentioned the importance of learning Islam and being brought up in an Islamic culture. Many Muslim parents said that they did not have much contact with other Muslims in everyday life, as their extended family and neighbours, for example were not Muslim. Therefore Mariam Albatool School was the only space apart from home where children could be nurtured in an Islamic culture. Josef said in relation to his son's education:

> I want him to learn religion – learn Islam. Therefore, it is a natural choice, apart from the fact that I believe that at the school at the Islamic Centre my son is brought up in an Islamic culture. That is, not only will he learn Islam from the Qur'ān but will grow up in an Islamic culture – he'll behave as Muslim, because Islam is not simply a religion but a way of life.

Josef's statement captures parents' concern with regard to their children's religious education. All Muslim parents who were interviewed supported the idea of sending their children to Mariam Albatool School. Some of them, however, did not do so because they could not afford the fees. Some parents said that if the state included Islamic religious education as part of the public curriculum, they would consider sending their children to a state school. They would do so because the latter is much cheaper compared to a private school. However, parents believed that Mariam Albatool School would be the ideal choice because it is the only school with an Islamic ethos. They did not agree with the idea that attending a Muslim school would mark their children as 'different'. Notwithstanding, the tensions underpinning the role of Mariam Albatool School can be felt in the way the school is narrated by different members of the community. For instance, the Imam in charge of Mariam Albatool School stated that one of the aims of the school is for Muslims not to be isolated from Maltese society but '… to mix and to integrate in society while maintaining their own identity. We also want to promote a sense of belonging to the country, a sense of loyalty and citizenship' (Schembri, 2004). In contradistinction, Hana echoed other Muslim parents when she said that in view of the small number of Muslim students in state schools,

> [students] may find they are subject to more peer pressure than children already are … it's massively strong, especially in high school. So we wanted to make sure that our children have the opportunity to make Muslim friends, not exclusively Muslim friends, but we wanted to make sure that they could make Muslim friends. And the best way we thought they could do this, because we couldn't make sure they have Muslim friends in their immediate neighbourhood, was to go to a Muslim school. That way, they would have friends who understand about fasting, they understand that we don't celebrate Christmas and we do celebrate Eid and all the other things … [that] dating isn't acceptable, and things like that.

'Cultural safety' is an important consideration for parents of Muslim children. In that sense, Mariam Albatool School operates at the juncture of disrupted narratives of citizenship and belonging.

Peer Pressure and Racism

Parents of Muslim children were concerned with prejudice and racism. One Muslim parent said:

> I think that here in Malta, if people see you're a Muslim then they think that you're an Arab or a Libyan. And so you get this prejudice against you unfortunately and not just because of your religion but because of your race. And I think that most people don't have to look at what is different. If you are happy and comfortable in your environment and you're in the majority, there's no reason for you to have any understanding.

This statement is indicative of the embeddedness of hegemonic power relations in daily life. It is also indicative of an approach which considers the 'different' as carrying the full burden and cost of assimilation as minority. Not least, it captures processes of racialisation, in which people's cultural backgrounds are locked into fixed racial attributes. This is also recognised by some teachers working in public schools. One head of school said that sometimes teachers attributed a child's action to his or her 'race'. For example, when a student presents what is perceived a untidy work she heard teachers comment that the student did so, '*Ghax dak missieru Gharbi*', which translates into English as 'Because his father is an Arab'. According to Tator and Henry (2000) such a discourse 'is not just a symptom or sign of the presence of racism but rather it essentially constructs, reproduces and transmits the racist beliefs and actions of the White majority' (para. 1). The interviewed head of school was very concerned because she said that such an attitude would hinder these children from learning and maximising their potential. She added that when teachers were not open and accepting of other cultures and religions they were bound to be racist.

Social Texts and Textbooks

Muslim children, especially those who have Arab lineage, find it difficult to belong and feel accepted in mainstream public schools in Malta. A head of a public school interviewed recognised that very often students who have an Arab surname are marginalised. Parents are conscious of the prejudice that exists against Arabs and Muslims and are concerned that this might affect their children's self-image. Marcon, a young parent who converted to Islam years ago, said that at Mariam Albatool School her daughter 'will be safe from these misconceptions. She will not need to equate herself with others in terms of worth'. Moreover, several interviewees pointed out that Maltese literature and history books were replete with anti-Arab and anti-Muslim sentiments. These further promote a negative self-image in Muslim children and youth and also influence the perceptions of those who are not Muslim. For instance, the Form 1 history textbook 'Ġrajjiet *Malta (L-Ewwel Ktieb)*' (1976), incidentally written by a priest, and which has not been revised since its introduction 30 years ago, can be considered as one of the more problematic textbooks for its portrayal of Arabs:

> [Arabs are] nothing but Bedouins, that is, people who roam around aimlessly and live on the desert sand …

The text is littered with terms such as 'Mawmettani'[13] and conveys the implicit message that Arabs are vindictive because:

> … they destroyed a Maltese temple, probably because some of our forefathers broke the agreement …

State Support for an Islamic school in Malta – A Right?

The debate about minority rights has a fairly recent history in Maltese society. The first group to contest the hegemony of universality was the National Commission for Persons with Disability. Very recently, the Malta Gay Rights Movement lobbied for legislation in favour of same-sex unions, among other matters. As far as this debate is concerned, the Muslim community has remained very much in the background and has not made its demands publicly as have other organised groups. However, representatives of the community met with state officials to discuss the funding of Mariam Albatool School. The Imam said:

> We applied and spoke a number of times. The government did not say no, but said that there is no budget allotted. Our problem is that the authorities are considering our school as an independent school, a private school and they treat our school as the other independent schools which do not receive state subsidy. But our school is different. Those schools do not provide anything different from state or church schools. But we offer subjects that are not taught in state schools and so we are doing the state's job.

Apparently, the state recognises the Muslim community and in some ways it seems to be aware of its particular needs. For example, it allows ritual slaughter and has granted permission for the building of a 500-grave cemetery. On the other hand, where educational matters are concerned, the state does not grant any special rights to Muslims as a community. The head of Mariam Albatool School explained that the school administration has unsuccessfully petitioned the state for at least partial funding. The school is considered as a non-governmental organisation (NGO), meaning that the state does recognise its important role in the Muslim community. However, while the government can decide to pay the salary of the public officer on secondment with NGOs, for some reason the head of Mariam Albatool School has always been paid exclusively by the school. It is also pertinent to point out that while the state finances the salaries of the teaching staff in Catholic church schools,[14] Mariam Albatool School pays its teachers' salaries. The church–state agreement bound church schools not to charge fees, although parents are expected to give a donation every year. On the other hand Mariam Albatool School has to charge fees in order to keep its doors open. While Mariam Albatool School is essentially a faith school, the government considers it as an independent private school and thus parents are entitled to a tax rebate.

The Muslim community is petitioning the state to acknowledge their different educational needs. They ask to be granted the means that would enable all Muslim parents who wish to send their children to an Islamic school to do so without having to shoulder the financial burden. In this regard, Mariam Albatool's Imam said that it is important that the state finances the school, because by doing so the state would be considering Muslims as part of Maltese society. Funding the Islamic school would help promote respect and cooperation.

In financing the school, the state would thus acknowledge the position of Muslims within Maltese society as a legitimate part of the polity. Demands for state funding for Mariam Albatool School as a 'minority right' might not materialise for a variety of reasons. Politicians, who depend on electoral votes, are bound to be influenced by the reaction of the public to these demands. Considering the prejudice that exists against Muslims,[15] there is a strong possibility that this request might not be granted. The number of Maltese Muslims is relatively insignificant in the context of political representation and thus it might be difficult for them to garner support for particular rights.

Interestingly, when a non-Muslim parents' foundation petitioned the government to build a school at L-Imselliet, a piece of pristine, rural land on the outskirts of Mgarr (west of Malta Island) which was also outside the development zone, the government ultimately gave in (Balzan, 2006). Ostensibly, it is interesting to dwell on the government's reaction compared with Mariam Albatool School. In both instances, the argument for the right of children to education was put forward, but while the government gave in to the parents' foundation it has not yet given heed to the Muslims' request for funding. Clearly, the government showed more concern for the interests of the majority, which according to Karayanni (2007) 'is an inevitable reality in democratic societies' (p. 42). Thus it can be argued that such liberal approaches to democracy result, often, in a flawed and morally undemocratic process regarding resource allocation.

Whether members of the growing Muslim community should or should not be entitled to 'minority rights' is a matter for debate, if one draws on the broader literature. Loobuyck (2005), citing Kymlicka's (1996) arguments about minority rights, states that group differentiated rights 'are based upon the idea that justice between groups requires that the members of different groups be accorded different rights' (p. 115). Kymlicka and Norman (2000) contend that as difference-blind institutions implicitly lean towards the interests of the majority, 'the adoption of certain minority rights … helps to remedy the disadvantages that minorities suffer within difference-blind institutions and in doing so promotes fairness' (p. 4). Kymlicka (1996) also explains that special rights 'can be seen as putting the various groups on a more equal footing by reducing the extent to which the smaller group is vulnerable to the larger' (pp. 36–37). Based on this point of view, Maltese

Muslims should be entitled to rights, such as the right to free Islamic education, which put them on par with the rest of the Maltese citizens.

Not all agree about the need to grant Muslims differentiated minority rights, however. Tariq Ramadan, a prominent Muslim activist and philosopher, regards the idea of 'minority thinking' as an anathema to integration. In an interview he granted to Bechler (2004) he stated that if one does not go beyond this 'us' versus 'them' mentality, one would be assuming that difference is the beginning and the end. Ramadan reiterates that the four principles[16] of Islamic identity go with any cultural dress and thus Muslims have a lot in common with their non-Muslim fellow citizens and therefore being a Muslim does not make one a minority:

> When you live in the European landscape and come to understand its social fabric, you are not a minority citizen. You are, simply, a citizen ... When I call for social justice to remove racism and discrimination from European societies, I am invoking majority not minority values ... There is no such thing as a minority answer and a different majority answer. We have to speak as citizens. (p. 3)

Thus, if one draws on Ramadan's logic to inform educational policy in Malta, the state should not differentiate between one being a member of a minority or majority group and their entitlement to attend equitable schools. Rather, the state should seek to transform schools into inclusive, pluralist and ethically oriented institutions, which operate in such ways as to offer 'equality of condition' (Lynch & Baker, 2005) to all. Equally, Muslims in Malta should seek to promote and enhance values of equality and equity in Malta as primordial values, and as part and parcel of their engagement and commitments as citizens.

Conclusion

State schools in Malta are far removed from the egalitarian institutions described by Lynch and Baker (2005). In a pluralist and diverse society education is crucial for social cohesion. The extent to which schools respect diversity and accommodate different student needs sends out a strong message about the values that society places on diversity and on belonging. These messages, in turn, influence students' attitudes towards diversity. The Maltese curriculum, imbued as it is with Catholic influence and its presentation of a homogeneous Maltese identity, supports 'tribalism' and nationalistic solidarity through fostering negative attitudes towards others (Hull, 2000).

The state expects Muslim students to fit in a system which, in fact, alienates them. The curriculum, in its presentation of citizenship through a Eurocentric and Christian worldview does not leave space for those whose religious identities differ from the mainstream but are nevertheless Maltese citizens. Muslim students, as well as other non-Catholics, have to bear the brunt of an inadequate curriculum that roots for the celebration of diversity on paper and insists on conformity in practice. In encouraging students to conform, the curriculum reinforces the prestige and dominance of one particular culture and set of exclusive normative behaviours that underpin Maltese citizenship.

Justice in education requires a curriculum that is representative and inclusive of the diversity that exists within the schools and society. For example, the curriculum empowers students when it allows them to identify themselves as Maltese albeit with different religious identities without making differences more prominent than commonalities (Cockrell, Placier, Cockrell, & Middleton, 1999); when it combats racism and islamophobia; and when it offers a curriculum that allows for critical education rather than encourage exclusion and the articulation of a fragmented citizenship.

Notes

1 http://www.state.gov/g/drl/rls/irf/2003/24422.htm
2 Address by H.E. Dr Edward Fenech Adami, President of Malta, on the occasion of Republic Day – Grand Council Chamber, The Palace, Valletta Thursday, 13 December 2007.
3 As an example see 'Voting rights for migrants "a red line" issue' at http://www.timesofmalta.com/articles/view/20090423/local/voting-rights-for-migrants-a-red-line-issue.
4 As an example follow comments on http://baheyeldin.com/writings/culture/arab-heritage-in-malta.html?page=2, some of which were made by a prospective European Parliament candidate.
5 The data presented here is part of a post-graduate research project, in which around 20 Muslim parents, their religious leader, teachers and school administrators from different sectors of the educational spectrum were interviewed.
6 http://www.state.gov/g/drl/rls/irf/2003/24422.htm
7 Parliamentary Question 2724, Sitting 38, 06/10/08.
8 http://www.pq.gov.mt/PQweb.nsf/5ab326fbcb184092c1256877002c4f19/c1256e7b00 3e1c2dc12574da00476c6b?OpenDocument
9 The Knights, also known as the Sovereign Military Hospitaller Order of St John of Jerusalem, of Rhodes and of Malta, were given Malta by Charles V of Spain in 1530. The Knights remained in Malta for 268 years until it was captured by Napoleon in 1798.
10 Until the end of World War II the Nationalist Party was culturally and politically affiliated to Italy to the extent that some of the members wanted Malta to integrate with the Italian state. Historically they represented the cleric-professional classes and opposed British rule.
11 The translation of the school's name was provided by the Imam. Mariam Albatool School offers an environment that is free from religious prejudice and from negative Muslim and Arab stereotyping. The school offers a curriculum similar to the one mandated by the NMC and at the same time it acknowledges and respects the beliefs and needs of its Muslim students. In this school citizenship is not entwined with Catholic religious identity and therefore students grow in the knowledge that one can be Muslim and a good Maltese citizen at the same time. In this sense, one could argue that it ensures a certain 'equality of condition' (Lynch and Baker, 2005). The school is open only to those who can afford to pay school fees. At present there are 105 Maltese students attending Mariam Albatool school (Parliamentary Question 2725, Sitting 38, 06/10/08). It also includes students whose parents are working in Malta but who do not hold Maltese citizenship.
12 It is stipulated that primary school teachers have to provide daily half-hour religion lessons. In secondary schools the time is reduced by one hour.

13 The term 'Mawmettani' is a corruption of the Italian 'Moameddo'. It connotes the worshippers of Muhammad. Muslims do not subscribe to this term, said Mario Farrugia-Borg, Daeyah (a person who invites people to embrace Islam) at the Islamic centre. He explained that they are not worshippers of Muhammad. Islam means submission to the will of God, and thus Muslims do not follow anyone other than God. He said that this term is normally used by those who seek to degrade Islam.

14 The agreement between the government of Malta and the Vatican with regard to the funding of church schools came about after the 1983 agreement between the two parties on the devolution of church property. The definitive agreement between the two parties was signed in 1991.

15 See http://www.timesofmalta.com/articles/view/20090502/local/muslims-gather-in-prayer-along-sliema-front as an example. The newspaper report was about Muslims praying in Sliema. Many of the talkback commentators considered those who were praying at Sliema as 'foreigners' because of the colour of their skin and because they were Muslims, and thus they were considered outsiders and certainly not welcome in Malta.

16 The four principles he mentions are: grace, practice and spirituality; religion (understanding the text and the context); education and transmission; action and participation.

References

Amor, A. (2001). *The role of religious education in the pursuit of tolerance and non-discrimination.* Study prepared for the International Consultative Conference on School Education in relation with Freedom of Religion and Belief, Tolerance and Non-discrimination (Madrid, 23–25 November 2001). Retrieved April 8, 2008, from http://www.unhchr.ch/html/menu2/7/b/cfedu-basicdoc.htm.

Antonopoulos, R. & Cos-Montiel, F. (2007). *State, difference and diversity: Toward a path of expanded democracy and gender equality.* Working Paper No. 493, The Levy Economics Institute. Retrieved May 11, 2008 from http://papers.ssrn.com/sol3/papers.cfm?abstract_id=975685.

Balzan, S. (2006). Editorial. *maltatoday.* May 14. Retrieved on April 15, 2009 from http://www.maltatoday.com.mt/2006/05/14/editorial.html.

Bechler, R. (2004). A bridge across fear: An interview with Tariq Ramadan. *openDemocracy*, July 15, pp. 1–11. Retrieved May 14, 2008 from http://www.opendemocracy.net/node/2006/pdf.

Bond, R. (2006). Belonging and becoming: National identity and exclusion. *Sociology*, 40(4), 609–626.

Borg, C. (2006). Catholic hegemony in Malta: State schools as sites of cultural reproduction. In Clayton, T. (Ed) *Rethinking hegemony* (pp. 59–78). Melbourne: James Nicholas.

Borg, C. & Mayo, P. (2001). Social difference, cultural arbitrary and identity: An analysis of a new national curriculum document in a non-secular environment. *International Studies in Sociology of Education*, 11(1), 71–89.

Briscoe, F.M. (2006). Reproduction of racialized hierarchies: Ethnic identities in the discourse of educational leadership. *Journal for Critical Education Policy Studies*, 4(1), Retrieved on May 17, 2007 from http://www.jceps.com/?pageID= article&articleID=60.

Cockrell, K.S., Placier, P.L., Cockrell, D.H. & Middleton, J. (1999). Coming to terms with 'diversity' and 'multiculturalism' in teacher education: Learning about our students, changing our practice. *Teaching and Teacher Education*, 15, 351–366.

Debono, J. (2009). A case of sink or swim. *maltatoday on Sunday.* Retrieved on May 28, 2009 from maltatoday.com.mt/2009/05/03/t10.html.

256 Louise Chircop

De Marco, G., (2007). *Politics of persuasion*. Malta: Allied Publications.

Discern (2006). Sunday mass attendance census, 2005: Preliminary Report. Retrieved on May 28, 2009 from http://discern-malta.org/pdf_files/census_2005.pdf.

Dürr, J., Michaelowa, K. & Vollenweider, J. (2008). *Poverty reduction strategies, democratization and the role of the World Bank*. Working paper 39. Zurich: Centre for Comparative and International Studies.

Grech, L. (2005). Education for democratic citizenship and its implications on educational assessment practices. *The Times* October 14 and October 21.

Hull, J.M. (2000). Religionism and religious education. In Leicester, M., Modgil, C., & Modgil, S. (Eds.) *Education, culture and values: Spiritual and religious education, Vol. 5*, (pp. 75–85). London: Falmer Press.

Karayanni, M.M. (2007). Multiculture me no more! Multicultural qualifications and the Palestinian-Arab minority of Israel. *Diogenes*, 54(3), 39–58.

Kymlicka, W. (1996) *Multicultural citizenship: A liberal theory of minority rights*. Oxford University Press.

Kymlicka, W. & Norman, W. (2000). Citizenship in culturally diverse societies. In Kymlicka, W. and Norman, W. (Eds.) *Citizens in diverse societies*. Oxford Scholarship Online Monographs. Retrieved May 5, 2008 from http://fds.oup.com/www.oup.co.uk/pdf/0-19-829644-4.pdf.

Lister, R. (1998). Citizenship and difference: Towards a differentiated universalism. *European Journal of Social Theory*, 1(1), 71–90.

Loobuyck, P. (2005). Liberal multiculturalism: A defence of liberal multicultural measures without minority rights. *Ethnicities*, 5(1), 108–135.

Lynch, K. & Baker, J. (2005). Equality in education: An equality of condition perspective. *Theory and Research in Education*, 3(2), 131–164.

Mayo, P. (2001). Globalisation, postcolonialism and identity: The role of education in the Mediterranean region. In Švob-Đokić (Ed.) *Redefining cultural identities: The multicultural contexts of the central European and Mediterranean regions*. Joint Publications Series No.3. Zagreb: Culturelink.

McLaren, P. (1999). *Schooling as a ritual performance: Towards a political economy of educational symbols and gestures*. Lanham, MD: Rowman and Littlefield.

McLaren, P. (1997). Multiculturalism and the postmodern critique: Toward a pedagogy of resistance and transformation. In Halsey, A.H., Lauder, H., Brown, P. & Stuart Wells, A. (Eds.) *Education: Culture, economy, society*. Oxford: Oxford University Press.

Mifsud Bonnici, U. (1989). L-identità kulturali ta' Malta. In Cortis, T. (Ed). *L-Identità kulturali ta' Malta*. Malta: Department of Information. (In Maltese.)

Ministry of Education (1999). *Creating the future together: National Minimum Curriculum*. Floriana, Malta: Ministry of Education.

Ministry of Education (2008). Annual Report of Government Departments, Malta: Ministry of Education, Culture, Youth and Sport. Retrieved on May 20, 2008 from http://www.education.gov.mt/ministry/doc/pdf/annual_reports/en/Annual_Report_2008.pdf.

Modood, T. (2007). *Multiculturalism*. Cambridge: Polity Press.

Modood, T. & Ahmad, F. (2007). British Muslim perspectives on multiculturalism. *Theory, Culture, Society*, 24(2), 187–213.

Parekh, B. (2006). Europe, liberalism and the 'Muslim question'. In Modood, T., Triandafyllidou, A. & Zapata-Barrero, R. (Eds.) *Multiculturalism, Muslims and Citizenship* (pp. 179–203). London: Routledge.

Poulter, S. (1997). Muslim headscarves in school: Contrasting legal approaches in England and France. *Oxford Journal of Legal Studies*, 17(1), 43–74.

Rosaldo, R. (1989). *Culture and truth: The reworking of social analysis.* Boston, MA: Beacon

Savona-Ventura, C. (1995). The influence of the Roman Catholic Church on midwifery practices in Malta. *Medical History*, 39, 18–34.

Schembri, K. (2004). Lifting the veil. *maltatoday.* September 26. Retrieved March 13, 2006 from http://www.maltatoday.com.mt/2004/09/26/interview.html.

Sciriha, L. (2001). Trilingualism in Malta: Social and educational perspectives. *International Journal of Bilingual Education and Bilingualism*, 4(1), 23–37.

Spiteri, J. (2009). *Immigrant vote.* Retrieved on May 31, 2009 from http://www.timesofmalta.com/mepelections/blogs/john-spiteri/20090508/immigrant-vote.

Sultana, R.G. (2009). Looking back before moving forward: Building on 15 years of comparative educational research in the Mediterranean. *Mediterranean Journal of Educational Studies*, 13(2), 9–25.

Tator, C. & Henry, F. (2000). The role and practice of racialized discourse in culture and cultural production. *Journal of Canadian Studies*, 35(3), 120–137.

Tiedt, P.L. & Tiedt, I.M. (1999). *Multicultural teaching: A handbook of activities, information and resources.* London: Allyn and Bacon.

Vassallo, H. (2009). A map of faith in Malta. *maltatoday midweek.* April 8. Retrieved May 28, 2009 from http://www.maltatoday.com.mt/2009/04/08/t5.html.

Volpp, L (2007). The culture of citizenship. *Theoretical Inquiries in Law*, 8(2), 571–601.

Wettinger, G. (1986). The Arabs in Malta. In *Malta: Studies of its Heritage and History*, pp. 87–104. Malta: Mid-Med Bank.

Wieviorka, M. (2004). The making of differences. *International Sociology*, 19(3), 281–297.

Young, I.M. (1990). *Justice and the politics of difference.* Princeton, NJ: Princeton University.

Part IV
Knowledge Imaginaries

15 Nationalism, Islamic Political Activism, and Religious Education in the Arab Region

Rukhsana Zia

Introduction

Terrorist events around the world, specifically since 9/11, have consolidated the perception of 'a militant Islam' and Islamic 'militancy' (Pew, 2003). Coupled with the media coverage of the Israel–Palestine conflict, the image of Muslims in the media in general (Said, 1997 [1981]; Hoyer, 2004) and images of Arab Muslims more particularly, are presented as intimidating. This sense of intimidation has led many politicians, religious leaders, scholars and educational professionals to raise concerns over the ways formal schooling in Muslim societies inculcates values in students, particularly in relation to Islamic education. Like schools in many other countries, 'religious education' (*tarbiya diniyya*), sometimes also referred to as 'moral education', is a component of school curricula across the Arab region. It is generally perceived to be the main content area responsible for inculcating cultural values among pupils, though this curricular component does not have a monopoly over the realm of values (Doumato and Starrett, 2007).

This chapter focuses on the sociopolitical underpinnings of religious education in the Arab region, and how curricula are constructed within schools. The chapter also comparatively examines the emphases placed on religious studies in the curricular organization of public schools in Arab and other countries.

Positioning the Arab States Region

The Arab States region formally comprises 22 countries.[1] The Arabic language represents a shared cultural tradition across the region. Arabs emerged on the world historical stage in the seventh century with the Prophet Muhammad and the emergence of Islam from the Arabian Peninsula. The 'Muslim explosion' (Ahmed, 1999) after the Prophet's death saw Islam spread to South and South-East Asia, southern Spain and Eastern Europe, North Africa and, by the eighteenth century, to the Americas. This melding of Arab and the non-Arab cultures, among others, contributed to the emergence of diverse articulations of Islam (Eickelman, 1989; An-Na'im, 1999; Gregorian, 2001). It also facilitated the emergence of an Islamic civilization that reached its apex between the seventh and tenth centuries. Periodic conflicts between Arabs and Europeans took place during this period. The balance of power started to shift in the seventeenth century and culminated in the nineteenth century with the European colonization of most of the Arab world, apart from Saudi Arabia. Current borders of the Arab nation-states were often drawn by European imperial powers during the nineteenth and twentieth centuries.

The population of the Arab region is presently estimated at 300 million. The majority of the population shares a common religion, Islam in its diverse traditions. The region is marked by cultural, social, economic, ethnic and political diversity, and includes social groups affiliated to different religious and cultural traditions. Despite significant intra-regional variations, the Arab countries are mostly developing economies, where poverty and unemployment (particularly among youth) is widespread (Ali and Elbadawi, 2002). The majority of Arab societies share the malaise affecting any developing region, and development progress has been uneven both between and within countries. The Human Development Index (HDI) of the Arab region tends to be lower than the world average (Arab Human Development Report, 2002), suggesting a low quality of life of the citizens of these countries. Scarcity of water and arable land are two major resource constraints in the region. Most of the Arab states are in the World Bank's 'Water Poverty' line. The high fertility rate in the region (2% annual growth rate compared with 1.4% in the less-developed world as a whole), coupled with a high concentration of young adults, presents great growth challenges in Arab countries. It also increases these societies' vulnerability to civil conflict (Cincotta, Engelman and Anastasion, 2003). Over the years, political and military interference by Western powers across the Arab region have also compounded matters.

At present the educational indicators of most countries in the Arab region as a whole appear to be quite low compared with the other seven regions of the world. Some countries are advancing well on their Education for All (EFA) targets (Bahrain, Kuwait, Lebanon, Jordan, and Qatar) (UNESCO, EFA Global Monitoring Report, 2005). However, the Arab region has the second lowest Gross Enrolment Ratio (GER) for pre-primary and primary classes (18% and 97% respectively). Though retention rates for the region are generally high (94%), some countries, such as Yemen and Sudan, have very low participation rates due to lack of schools, unfriendly schools, war, or poverty. Participation in secondary and tertiary education has improved since 1998, except in Djibouti, Mauritania, Morocco, Sudan, and Yemen (UNESCO, EFA Global Monitoring Report, 2005). The region has the largest gender disparity, particularly in primary and adult literacy rates. Gender disparities in higher education are also visible. Compared with other regions, the Arab countries allocate a greater proportion of the total public expenditure to education. For instance, more than half the countries with data available allocated 20% of public expenditure to education in 2006 (UNESCO, EFA Global Monitoring Report, 2009).

Like other developing countries struggling with the expansion of schooling, the region is faced with the dilemma of providing both more education and higher quality education. Students from rural and disadvantaged socio-economic backgrounds are particularly vulnerable in terms of learning achievement. In fact, the UNDP-sponsored *Arab Human Development Report* (2002) states that the quality of education has deteriorated specifically with regard to knowledge acquisition and analytical and creative skills.

Contexts of Islamic Education

To understand the tensions and challenges that underpin Islamic education in the Arab region, it is important to clarify how Islamic world views, and their mobilization, are closely tied to political agendas and political movements, either located in the Arab region or within the Muslim world. Religious education stands at the juncture of competing forces. As the case studies edited by Doumato and Starrett (2007) show, states use their own brand of Islamic world views to justify and legitimize their régimes and their ideological underpinnings. At the same time, different groups within countries might use Islamic symbolism to legitimize political action in their political resistance and in articulating social, political and economic agendas (Dessouki, 1982, p. 4). There are myriad variations regarding what 'Muslims', Islam and Islamic ideology/world views stand for, with as many variations in schooling, all termed equally Islamic.[2] Given this plurality of meanings, repeated calls have been made across the Muslim world to emphasize the need for a holistic Islamic world view which is consonant and consistent with changing global contexts (Al-Zeera, 2001; Osman, n.d.; Zaman, 2006). It should be noted that various types of Islamic ideologies do not warrant, in themselves, an anti-Western or an anti-modern bias, nor do they promote militancy. The anti-American (rather than 'anti-Western') sentiments currently associated with an Islamic identity across the Arab region have more to do with the politics of geopolitical intervention than with any particular religious ideology. Tessler (2003) observes that, "anti-Americanism is for the most part a response to perceptions and judgment regarding US foreign policy" (p. 180). Others offer competing explanations to account for the rise of political Islam, like the weakness of 'non-Islamist parties' (Herb, 2005).

In all this, what is still missing is a detailed analysis of appeals to particular forms of religious education launched by militant Islamic groups and movements. It is not my intention to engage in this analysis here for reasons of space. How knowledge is classified as 'Islamic' versus 'non-Islamic' (Barazangi, 1995, p. 406) or, how Islam is interpreted and Islamic ideology is structured into the school curriculum (as the latter includes other subject matters taught alongside it), is of equal concern, though it is not considered for reasons of space. This said, it is worth observing that there are differences in how Islamic teachings are interpreted by Muslims, within different religious traditions, schools of thought, societies, cultures, and even in distinct regions of the world. It is safe to conclude that the language of textual Islam can be interpreted in ways that espouse adherence to rights, obligations and duties to oneself and to others and in ways that resonate with the contexts imposed by a globalized world (Bayat, 2007). And yet, the major difference lies in the superimposition of the spiritual dimension as the primary motive (Zia, 2003). In other words, in Islamic education, the justification for these rights, obligations, duties to oneself and others, is solely derived from the religious context in Islam.

Less discussed in relation to Islamic education are the ways in which Arab nationalism and political Islam affect the curricular articulations of religious education. Both Arab nationalism and politically active Islamic groups are quite recent phenomena, primarily results of nineteenth and twentieth century geo-political transformations. Before engaging this aspect of the questions at hand, it is worth recalling what Emerson (1960) stated almost five decades ago. He noted that for a full-scale analysis of Arab nationalism, "it would be necessary to evaluate the whole record of Arab experience, including such matters as the tribal, sectarian, and other divisions, the effects of Ottoman rule, the machinations of the European powers, and the role of Islam and of the Arab language and culture" (p. 126).

Arab nationalism first arose in the nineteenth century as a reaction not to Western rule but to the Ottoman Empire, a Muslim political entity whose head, along with his title of Caliph, was also considered as a head of state and successor of the Prophet Muhammad (Kramer, 1993). Arab nationalism has been on the rise since the early twentieth century on the basic premise that the peoples and countries that now comprise the Arab region are one ethnic 'nation', bound together by their common linguistic, cultural, and historical heritage. Pan-Arabism, a related concept, not only asserts the singularity of the 'Arab Nation', but calls for the creation of a single Arab State. Thus, whilst all Pan-Arabists are Arab nationalists, not all Arab nationalists are Pan-Arabists.

Colonization proved a watershed for the Muslim world (Al-e-Ahmed, 1980) in general and for the Arab world in particular. Arab nationalism prospered on anti-imperialist struggles and slogans. Antipathy to Western imperialism translated into a hostility not only to the policies of the West but also to its institutions. In a bid to realize the dream to regain the lost splendor of earlier times, nationalists employed a powerful argument: the Arabs were once a great people while the twentieth century belongs to the Western world; a world of technology, science, and cultural advancements associated with modernity. To catch up with the West, so the argument went, Arabs must forgo the old ways and take the route of modernity. But Arab nationalism had to face the results of the Arab defeat at the hands of Israel in 1948 and in 1967 and the consequences and ramifications of the Gulf War of 1991and the US-led occupation of Iraq since 2003. These events continue to divide the political agendas of Arab countries and peoples. Country-specific nationalisms, each with its own brand of 'Islamic world view', came into play in the social, economic, educational arenas of the different countries. Hence, state and sub-state identities compete with Arab nationalism, including identities rooted in radical conceptions of Islam (Khadduri, 1998, p. 45).

Arab nationalism was forged primarily on the basis of a shared ethnicity, not religion, even though some (such as Michel 'Aflaq, a foundational figure in Pan-Arab thought) contended that the power of Islam was revived in the form of Arab nationalism (Aflaq, 1963, p. 55). However, paralleled by Islamism as a movement, from the eighteenth century onward, Arab nationalism had to compete with various organizations and reformers who emerged in the region, like elsewhere in the Muslim world, with the aim of safeguarding 'Muslim identity against Westernization' (Zia, 2006, p. 121).[3] The purpose of these reformers was to promote an Islamic world view for a spectrum of political, economic, governmental, and social causes, including in the field of education. By the late 1980s, Pan-Arabism and Arab nationalism were eclipsed by politically engaged Islamic movements. Talks about an alliance between Arab nationalists and Islamists ensued. Some questioned if the champions of Islam already existing in the form of well-organized and disciplined mass movements were interested in an alliance with the 'discredited stragglers of Arab nationalism', as one participant at a roundtable of Arab nationalist intellectuals stated regarding the possibility of nationalist-Islamist rapprochement (*Al-Mustaqbal al-'Arabi*, 1992).

The US–UK's war to topple the Iraqi (Pan-Arabist) régime and the occupation of Iraq in 2003 brought about further waning of Arab nationalism. In the war's aftermath, the United States, some Arab states, and Israel moved to translate that victory over Arab nationalism into a new regional order. While economic constraints and fiscal crises may have pushed many Arab states to rethink Arab nationalism (Al-Khuli, 1992; Dawisha, 2008), the war on Iraq represents its ultimate undoing. Clearly, in the vacuum created by an emasculated Arab nationalism, politically engaged Islamic movements are becoming more pronounced and visible as components of Arab identity, thus repositioning large segments within Arab societies as an ethnic group nested within the larger Islamic *umma*, or community of believers.

The rise of political Islam in Arab countries represents a mixture of nationalistic resentment against foreign domination (anti-imperialism), economic discontent, and the challenges in maintaining established religious values and beliefs as part of the organization of the community (Munsen, 2003). Some analysts have detected the emergence of a 'new' kind of Arabism – a spiritual and political bond that is evolving independently of state institutions, particularly among Arab intellectual elites (Telhami, 1999, pp. 55–59), while others question its effectiveness (Dawisha, 2003). There are others who point to the emergence of an overarching political nexus of countries beyond the confines of the region and within differing Islamic world views (Mweiri and Staffell, 2009, pp. 63–74). The emergence of 'moderate Islam and Islamic movements' is taking place in some Arab countries (e.g. Justice and Development Party in Morocco; *Isláh* or *Wasat* parties in Kuwait, Yemen and Jordan, quoted by Masmoudi, 2004). Yet, if Islamic education found itself at the juncture of the competing forces of Arabism and political Islam, it has also been affected by the significant variations of normative frameworks in Arab countries – state laws, *Shari'a* and local customs. This raises difficulties in defining a consensual position on various issues within a country, impacting *inter alia* the options available to citizens to enjoy the right to their identity.

In sum, when discussing social, educational, cultural or legal aspects pertaining to the Arab region, grouping all Arab states on the basis of religion alone is extremely problematic, to say the least. It is clear that for Muslims across the Arab region, the Islamic identity and the Arab identity are intertwined and rooted in political and military events and political configurations of power, which have affected the Arab region especially so since the past century. How these dynamics, rooted both in Arab nationalism and Islamic political activism, impact educational policies, curricular contents and the organization of schools remains a matter that has not been given due attention by researchers, policy makers and scholars working on education in the Arab region.

Religious Education and the Arab Nation-State

In his book, *Putting Islam to Work*, Starrett (1998) convincingly shows how Islamic world views have been 'functionalized', that is, how they were put "consciously to work for various types of social and political purposes" (p. 10), either by the state or by political movements. As part of this process, the curriculum of Islamic education shifted from an inclusive approach, to the transmission of politically constructed notions of a fragmented religious education, as shown in the recent studies edited by Doumato and Starrett (2007) in their book, *Teaching Islam*. In the present section I delve into this process, its ramifications and implications for religious education in the Arab region.

With the colonization of the Arab region, secular educational institutions were established and promoted, to the point of currently superseding the old-established institutions of the *madrasas* and colleges (Makdisi, 1981; Eickelman, 1985). Ideas introduced by colonizers regarding a separation between the state and religion were viewed by many Muslims as a heresy. For opponents of this view, this was the beginning of the disconnection between the two systems of education, the public and the religious, despite attempts on the part of the state to control both.

With the spread of modern education, religious institutions (like the *kuttāb* or *madrasa*) have been affected in many ways in terms of their pedagogies and structures, but they did not disappear. Some were integrated into national school systems, serving as the basis for public schools (Tibawi, 1979). In other national contexts, religious institutions abandoned the pursuit of modern sciences and secular subjects, thus cutting the masses from the acquisition of secular areas of knowledge. In some other instances, still, these institutions tend to cater for the poor who cannot afford the fees of Western-style schools, as the study of Tawil (2007) suggests. Yet, as Boyle (2004) also shows with regard to Morocco, Qur'anic schools have adapted, "borrow[ing] liberally from public school methodologies", and co-existing alongside them. Thus, it is incorrect to view veteran religious institutions of education in Arab and Muslim societies as having 'disappeared' with the spread of modern national systems of schooling and as public school systems emerged to become the norm. Rather, their accommodation, adaptation and multifaceted engagements with their environments are indicative of the changes and transformations religious education institutions underwent within different national and sub-regional contexts, both within and beyond the Arab region (see, e.g. Heffner, 2007, p. 3; Eickelman, 1985). In a pioneering review of Islamic education in the Arab states, Tibawi (1979) observed already three decades ago:

> Viewed from the vantage point of the present, Islamic education is a shadow of its past. Its modernization has in the end led to its complete transformation. The modern systems have not simply supplemented it as was intended by the early modernists; they have in fact supplanted it, even though not always by the conscious effort of the modernists. Indeed, some of these still pay more than lip service to the Islamic educational tradition as may be observed in certain state constitutions, in national laws and also in the curricula. But there

is no mistaking the radical shift in educational thought and practice from religious to national orientation. (p. 197)

Within the larger context of competing political agendas and ideological currents across the Arab region, some have observed that political Islam has gained a 'pronounced role' (Massialas and Jarrar, 1991, p. 174) in determining educational policy and planning in the public schooling system of Arab countries. Moreover, political changes in the Arab countries have narrowed, over the years, the concept of Islamic education. Some have argued that the increasing 'Islamization' of the state, and of its educational system, is probably used as a ploy by some Muslim (and Arab in this case) governments to divert the attention of the masses from such allegations as increasing corruption, inept governance, mismanagement and worsening economic conditions, to name but a few reasons (Zia, 2003).

Religious Education and School Curricula[4]

All Arab countries, for which data is available, offer Islamic religious education as a part of their school curricula, with the exception of Lebanon, which offers 'Civic Education' instead. In comparing time allocation to religious education across grade levels, one finds that religious education is taught with greater frequency towards the end of primary education and the beginning of secondary education, while relative time allotments for this subject decline, on average, at secondary level. At the primary school level it is 10–20 percent of the total time spent in the classrooms, and at secondary level it varies between 4 and 11 percent.

All countries providing data explicitly state that Islamic attitudes and orientations are part of their educational policy objectives, and that Islamic education remains part of the core curriculum through the secondary level. A few countries have a separate compulsory subject-matter regarding Qur'ān recitation along with religious education. Over the period 1985–2000, the prominence and relative emphasis on religious education in Muslim countries has declined (Zia, 2006), specifically for Arab countries.

The data I analyzed (Zia, 2006) also clearly show that, since 1985 religious education has been and continues to be an extremely important subject area in the primary and secondary school curriculum of all Arab States. In non-Arab Muslim countries, by contrast, religious education was taught less frequently in the 1980s and its prevalence declined over recent decades. In terms of decline in the time allocated in the official curriculum to religious education, the differences, while smaller, show the drop in time allocation was higher in Arab countries. With respect to moral and spiritual education, a different pattern emerges. Arab countries foster the spiritual and moral development of young children almost exclusively through religiously framed subjects (that is, teach *through* and *for* religion rather than *about* religion) while schools in most non-Arab Muslim countries tend to transmit value-laden contents via two subject areas: moral education and religious education (Zia, 2006).

In terms of comparison between Arab and non-Arab countries, it has been shown that the time allocated to religious education and, in the case of the latter, to moral education, is very similar, with the former being allocated on average one percent more time than the latter (Zia, 2006). Since 1985 a decline is visible in the time allotted to religious and moral education in both groups of countries, Arab and non-Arab. It seems that variations between countries, Arab and non-Arab, have shifted over time. In 1985, among all Muslim countries, Saudi Arabia alloted the greatest amount of curricular time, 30 percent. Among non-Arab countries Luxembourg topped the list with 18 percent. By 2006–2007, however, Saudi Arabia stood at 14 percent, while the country with the largest percentage of curricular time devoted to religious education in the Arab region is now Yemen with 20 percent. In the non-Arab group, Israel allocated the largest time to religious education which, according to UNESCO data collected in 2000 stood at 18 percent (Zia, 2006) at the primary level and 14 percent at the secondary level (WDE, 2006–2007). Here, it is worth reiterating that official curricular time allocated to religious and/or moral education is not indicative of the content, much less the quality, of the classroom teaching and subsequent student learning.

Tentative Conclusions

In this chapter I explored the ideological and political forces impacting religious education in the Arab region. The chapter supports the conclusions of previous studies, which indicate that what it means to be a Muslim varies significantly across national contexts (Doumato and Starrett, 2007). There exist different 'Islams' practiced locally within a variety of countries (Sadaalah, 2004, p. 37). As a result, Islamic education assumes many forms and institutional locations, in different political and cultural contexts and in historical periods (Eickelman, 1985, p. 59; Kadi and Billeh, 2007). Moreover, "each curriculum's representation of Islam is unique" and affected by the country's "policy interest" (Doumato and Starrett, 2007, p. 5).

The two main parallel streams of education system prevalent in the Arab region –the *madrasa* and the public school – are institutionally converging, with the *madrasa* increasingly offering, where available, secular/modern education, while the curriculum in the public school system is being Islamized. Care is needed to rethink the role of the *madrasa* in modern-day schooling. The challenges facing any 'integration' of religious education within a secular system of education remains particularly complex and nested within multi-layered dynamics, local, national and global. Further studies are needed to understand the differences between the two 'streams', how they are situated in relation to each other in different countries, and what models of integration are possible, if at all.

Religious education is not an unusually overwhelming part of the curriculum in Arab countries. Time allocation for religious education has been on the decline over the past two decades. Perhaps the impact of religious schooling in Arab countries is 'overstated' (generally poor enrolment in formal schooling, while a large percentage of the population remains out of formal schools; *madrasa* education remains marginal). More attention therefore needs to be given to other in-school factors like the content of religious education, quality of teachers and teaching methods, as well as to out-of-school contextual realities, exploring how they enact the curriculum and what it stands for in different national contexts.

There are many concerns that lie beyond the scope of this chapter and which need to be extensively investigated. Religious and other ideologies need to be studied beyond their textual and discursive manifestations if we are to understand how these texts are actually interpreted, enacted and lived. Particular attention should be granted to the effects of these interpretative processes on the organization of the school and the articulation of curricular modules. More generally, it would be of interest to study how ideologies operating within schools – whether in Arab, Western or other school systems – shape the global orientations and inclusiveness of learners, and in which directions. Such a comparative study – which requires a concerted international effort – will clarify the multifaceted impacts of national, regional and global transformations on students in ways which allow us to consider processes of divergence and convergence between countries in terms of the role played by religious and other political ideologies, rather than exclusively contemplate only one side of the equation.

Notes

1 The countries listed as members of the Arab region are: Algeria, Bahrain, the Comoros, Djibouti, Egypt, Iraq, Jordan, Kuwait, Lebanon, Libya, Mauritania, Morocco, Oman, Qatar, Saudi Arabia, Somalia, Sudan, Syria, Tunisia, United Arab Emirates, and Yemen. UNESCO's regional grouping also includes Malta which has been removed from this list. The EFA Global Monitoring Report (2005) does not include Somalia but includes Palestine, which though not enjoying the status of State is included in this chapter where applicable.

2 For a detailed discussion of the various Islamic orientations and their implications for an understanding of Islamic education, refer to Sadaalah (2004). In her chapter, Sadaalah reviews the positions and approaches prevalent among four main 'orientations' she identifies: secularist, traditionalist, modernist/liberal, and fundamentalist, with the latter offering a distinction between 'mainstream' and 'radical' orientations. See also the detailed discussion by Zaman (2007) with regard to conceptions of Islam and education within distinct traditions and within higher education institutions.

3 For instance, one could refer (among many others) to the influential role played by Sayyid Qutb (1906–1966), who articulated the social and political role of Islam in the contemporary world in his work and activism, in ways that have informed the orientations of politically engaged Islamic movements. See Musallam (1993).

4 In the present section   I analyze official curricular data, collected by UNESCO International Bureau of Education (IBE) for two time-periods, 1985 and 2000. Data refer to instructional time allocated to religious education within the overall organization of public school curricula. The data are taken from one of my earlier publications (Zia, 2006) and from the World Data on Education (WDE) (UNESCO IBE, 2007) for 2006–2007. WDE contains the profiles of 161 education systems and has been updated, mainly using the National Reports on the Development of Education presented at the 47th session of the International Conference on Education (Geneva, September 2004), supplemented with information from a wide range of official sources and recent reports.

References

'Aflaq, M. (1963). *Fi sabil al-ba'th* [*For the Ba'th*]. Beirut: Dar al-Tali'a. (In Arabic.)

Ahmed, A.S. (1999). *Islam Today: A Short Introduction to the Muslim World*. London: I.B. Tauris Publishers.

Al-e-Ahmed, J. (1980). *Occidentosis: The Plague of the West*. Chicago, IL: Mizan Publications.

Ali, A.A. & Elbadawi, I.A. (2002). Poverty in the Arab world: the role of inequality and growth, in *Human Capital: Population Economics in the Middle East*, (ed.) I. Serageldin, pp. 62–95. London: I.B. Tauris.

Al-Khuli, L. (1992). 'Arab? Na'am wa-lakin sharq awsatiyin aydan! [Arabs? Yes, but Middle Eastern too!]. *Al-Hayat*, London, May 20. (In Arabic.)

Al-Mustaqbal al-'Arabi [*The Arab Furture*] (July 1992). 161, pp. 96–119. .

Al-Zeera, Z. (2001). *Wholeness and Holiness in Education: an Islamic Perspective*. Herndon: International Institute of Islamic Thought.

An-Na'im, A.A. (1999). Political Islam in national politics and international relations, in *The Desecularization of the World: Resurgent Religion and World Politics*, (ed.) P.L. Berger, pp. 103–121. Grand Rapids, MI: William B. Eerdman.

Arab Human Development Report (2002). *Creating Opportunities for Future Generations*. New York: United Nations Development Programme, Arab Fund for Economic and Social Development.

Barazangi, N.H. (1995). Religious education, in *Oxford Encyclopedia of the Modern Islamic World* (ed.) J.L. Esposito, pp. 406–411. Vol. 1. New York: Oxford University Press.

Bayat, A. (2007). *Making Islam Democratic: Social Movements and the Post-Islamic Turn*. Stanford, CA: Stanford University Press.

Boyle, H.N. (2004). Modernization of education and Kur'anic adaptation in Morocco, in *Muslim Educational Strategies in a Global Context*, (eds) H. Daun & G. Walford . Leiden: Brill Academic.

Cincotta, R., Engelman, R. & Anastasion, D. (2003). *The Security Demographic: Population and Civil Conflict after the Cold War*. Washington, DC: Population Action International.

Dawisha, A. (2003). *Rise and Fall of Arab Nationalism*. Princeton. NJ: Princeton University Press.

Dawisha, A. (2008). *Arab Nationalism in the Twentieth Century: From Triumph to Despair*. Princeton, NJ: Princeton University Press.

Dessouki, A.E.H. (Ed.) (1982). *Islamic Resurgence in the Arab World*. New York: Praeger.

Doumato, E.A. & Starret G. (Eds.) (2007). *Teaching Islam: Textbooks and Religion in the Middle East*. Boulder, CO: Lynne Reinner.

Eickelman, D. (1985). *Knowledge and Power in Morocco*. Princeton, NJ: Princeton University Press.

Eickelman, D. (1989). *The Middle East. An Anthropological Approach*. Second edition. Englewood Cliffs, NJ: Prentice Hall.

Emerson, R. (1960). *From Empire to Nation: The Rise to Self-Assertion of Asian and African Peoples*. Cambridge: Harvard University Press.

Gregorian, V. (2001). *A Mosaic, Not a Monolith!* New York: Carnegie Corporation of New York.

Heffner, R.W. (2007). Introduction: The culture, politics, and future of Muslim education, in *Schooling Islam: The Culture and Politics of Modern Muslim Education*, (ed.) R.W. Hefner and M.Q. Zaman, pp. 1–39. Princeton: Princeton University Press.

Herb, M. (2005). Islamist movements and the problem of democracy in the Arab world. Paper presented at the Annual Meeting of the Middle East Studies Association.

Hoover, Dennis R. (2004). Is Evangelicalism itching for a civilization fight?, *The Brandywine Review of Fath & International Affairs*, Spring, pp. 11–16.

Kadi, W. & Billeh, V. (2007). *Islam and Education: Myths and Truths*. Chicago, IL: University of Chicago Press.

Khadduri, W. (1998). Al-qawmiya al-'Arabiya wad-dimuqratiya: Muraja'a naqdiya [Arab nationalism and democracy: A critical review]. *Al-Mustaqbal al-'Arabi* [*The Arab Future*], February.

Kramer, M. (1993). Arab nationalism: mistaken identity, *Daedalus*, Summer, pp. 171–206.

Makdisi, G. (1981). *The Rise of Colleges: Institutions of Learning in Islam and the West.* Edinburgh: Edinburgh University Press.

Masmoudi, R.A. (2004). Political Islam and the future of democracy in the Middle East. www.theamericanmuslim.org/tam.php/features/articles/political_islam_and_the_ future_of_democracy_in_the_middle_east/

Massialas, B.G. & Jarrar, S.A. (1991). *Arab Education in Transition: A Source Book.* New York: Garlands Publishing.

Munsen, H. (2003). Islam, nationalism and resentment of foreign domination, *Middle East Policy*, X, 2, pp. 40–53.

Musallam, A. (1993). Sayyid Qutb and social justice, *Journal of Islamic Studies*, 4, 1, pp. 52–70.

Mweiri, M. & Staffell, S. (2009). Talking with religion: lessons from Iran, Turkey and Pakistan, *Middle East Policy*, 16, 1, pp. 63–74.

Osman, F. (n.d.). Why a new Muslim World View. Accessed April 2009 at www.usc.edu/ schools/college/crcc/private/cmje/pluralism_issues/Fathi_Osman

Pew Research Center (2000). Pew Forum on Religion and Public Life: Survery on Americation Attitudes Toward Island, July, at www.pewforum.com.

Sadaalah, S. (2004). Islamic orientations and education, in *Educational Strategies Among Muslims in the Context of Globalization: Some National Case Studies*, (eds) H. Daun & G. Walford, pp. 27–61. Leiden and Boston: Brill Academic.

Said, E. (1997). *Covering Islam: How the Media and the Experts Determine How We See the Rest of the World* (revised edition). New York: Vintage Books.

Starrett, G. (1998). *Putting Islam to Work: Education, Politics, and Religious Transformation in Egypt.* Berkeley, CA: California Press.

Tawil, S. (2007). Qur'anic education and social change in Northern Morocco: perspectives from Chefchaouen, in *Islam and Education: Myths and Truths*, (eds) W. Kadi & V. Billeh. Chicago IL: University of Chicago Press.

Telhami, S. (1999). Power, legitimacy and peace-making in Arab conditions: the new Arabism, in *Ethnic Conflict and International Politics in the Middle East*, (ed.) L. Binder. Gainesville, FL: University Press of Florida.

Tessler, M. (2003). Arab and Muslim political attitudes: stereotypes and evidence from survey research, *International Studies Perspective*, 1, 175 180.

Tibawi, A.L. (1979). *Islamic Education: Its Traditions and Modernization into the Arab National Systems.* London: Luzac.

UNESCO EFA Global Monitoring Report (2005). *Education for All: The Quality Imperative.* Paris: UNESCO Publishing.

UNESCO EFA Global Monitoring Report (2009). *Overcoming Inequality: Why Governance Matters.* Paris: UNESCO Publishing.

UNESCO IBE (2007). *World Data on Education 2007/07* (sixth edition). Geneva: International Bureau of Education.

Zaman, A. (2006). Developing an Islamic world view: An essential component of an Islamic education, *Lahore Journal of Policy Studies*, 1, 1, 2007.

Zaman, M.Q. (2007). Epilogue: Competing conceptions of Islamic education, in *Schooling Islam: The Culture and Politics of Modern Muslim Education*, pp. 242–268. Princeton: Princeton University Press.

Zia, R. (2003). Religion and education in Pakistan: An overview, in *Prospects*, XXXIII, 2, pp. 165–178.

Zia, R. (2006). Transmission of values in Muslim countries: religious education and moral development in school curricula, in *School Knowledge in Comparative and Historical Perspective: Changing Curricula in Primary and Secondary Education*, (eds) Aaron Benavot and Cecilia Braslavsky, pp. 119–134. Comparative Education Research Centre, University of Hong Kong: Springer.

16 Higher Education and Differentiation Based on Knowledge

Algeria's Aborted Dream

Hocine Khelfaoui

Following its independence from France, in 1962, Algeria's society was characterized by a low level of economic, social and cultural differentiation. As a result, how the social space would be restructured, and which system of values the new structure would be based on, remained open questions. As a result of over a century of levelling down by the colonial system, the social structure, in which the social space is constituted of agents holding different types of capital (economic, academic), needed to be rebuilt. In the absence of other forms of capital, access to education and to scholastic knowledge imposed itself as the constitutive element of this value system and the only legitimate factor of social differentiation.

In a context where the state controls all economic and social activities, higher education appears as the pathway to the highly distinctive positions of public administration. Higher education is thus a core social, cultural and political stake. Its social status reaches its peak, and academic degrees are almost assimilated to nobility titles. Higher education becomes a space that reflects the knowledge/power relationship, in which the correlation between the social status of knowledge and its relationship to power are highlighted. In the present chapter I unpack this relationship. First, I outline the theoretical framework and define the concepts of knowledge and power. In the second part, I analyze the social and political conditions in which the knowledge/power relationship was established within universities following Algeria's independence. In the third part, I examine the implications of this analysis for the relationship between knowledge and power in Algerian society.

The Knowledge/Power Relationship

It is useful to start by defining the articulation of knowledge and power. The two are always interdependent and never foreign to each other. However, in the Algerian context, there occurs an intense struggle for differentiation through knowledge. This intensifies the role of the university as the primary space of knowledge production and transmission. As a source of symbolic capital and a factor of differentiation and promotion, knowledge only had one "competitor", that of one's individual record of engagement in the war which led to Algeria's national liberation. This record could be conceived of as a "revolutionary" (*thawri*) form of symbolic capital. For those who hold the Power associated with the State (hereafter designated as Power), and whose legitimacy is based on the Revolution, the symbolism of knowledge is perceived as evocative of their own deficit and as a threat to their legitimacy. Moreover, the deficit is acutely felt at the highest rungs of Power since, as Gilbert Meynier (2003) has shown, the educational level of individuals with a revolutionary record decreases as one approaches the top of the political pyramid.

Nevertheless, knowledge and power should not be irreducibly opposed. Nor is it meant that knowledge can only bloom if power is excluded from the field of higher education. As noted by Foucault, the point is not to pretend "that knowledge can only exist where power relations are suspended and that knowledge can develop only outside its injunctions, its demands and its interests" (Foucault, 1979a: 27). Rather, it is the interaction between knowledge and power, as well as the capacity of knowledge to disrupt power struggles that incite power to seek legitimacy in knowledge or, failing that, to control it. The dichotomy opposing knowledge as a source of liberation versus power as a source of confinement must also be avoided. Foucault reminds us that, "It's not a question of emancipating truth from every system of power – which would be a chimera, because truth is already itself power – but of detaching the power of truth from the forms of hegemony (social, economic and cultural) within which it operates" (Foucault, 1979b: 47). This resonates well with a somewhat different articulation put forth by Bourdieu (1996) who notes, "The field of power is organized according to a chiasmatic structure" (p. 270), characterized by a multifaceted hierarchy of intersecting forms of economic and cultural capital and which determines the configuration of the field of power. Within this context, Power invests in knowledge in a way that "allows power to constitute knowledge and [in a way] that allows knowledge to constitute objects for power to grasp" (Labbé, 1991: 91). Knowledge is thus politically constructed, being primarily defined by its relationship to a given social and historic context. In the case of Algeria, the context is an almost undifferentiated society, where knowledge appears as an essential factor of differentiation, hence becoming a stake in power struggles and an instrument of domination.

Higher Education and its Restructuring of State and Society

Following the independence of Algeria in 1962, higher education was called to contribute to the resolution of two major difficulties related to the legacy of colonization, which remain unresolved to this day. First, higher education had to provide the State with scientific and technical legitimacy. Second, it needed to reorganize society on the basis of knowledge, as the egalitarianism and the socialist orientation of the period excluded distinction on the basis of economic capital.

"Revolution" and "knowledge" were the only two remaining sources of legitimacy following independence. "Revolution" could be claimed by anyone. "Revolutionary" legitimacy (*shar'iya thawriya*)[1] represented at the time a strong national symbol, yet of little differentiating potential since it belonged to no one. The motto "One hero: the people" was written on walls throughout the city. The sacrifices required by the liberation struggle now made it urgent to get over the "colonial situation" (Balandier, 2001), as the causes and purposes of the Revolution were still very much alive in the collective conscience. "Revolutionary legitimacy" was a necessary, albeit insufficient, condition that needed to be complemented with knowledge-based legitimacy.

Few could claim legitimacy based on knowledge, yet all members of society aspired to it. Both the State and parents invested extensive material resources and emotions in education. The fledgling State and its institutions could not only seek their legitimacy in the symbolism of the "Revolution." They also needed the legitimacy conferred by "knowledge" (*'ilm*). Thus, knowledge acquired an essentially utilitarian function: knowledge would be the tool that would pull the new generation out of their parents' living conditions. As the core venue of knowledge creation, production/reproduction and transmission, higher education was experienced as the gateway *par excellence* to the most valued positions of society, those that simultaneously led to Power and owed to Power. The State and society shared this utilitarian vision of knowledge, in which knowledge is viewed not as a source of liberation and creativity but rather as an "ideological and institutional construction" (Touraine, 1992: 167).

Institutions of higher education (institutes and universities) had an important role to play to overcome the above-mentioned challenges. They were largely responsible for bestowing on the State a scientific and technical legitimacy, providing the necessary professionals, and structuring society on the basis of knowledge. Here, the State is defined by its institutions. The latter are identical to those of democratic countries as far as their formal structure is concerned, yet they exercise power in completely different ways. Consequently, there is a significant difference between State and Power; a difference that is largely downplayed in Algeria. The country faced an institutional and professional void after the war. The construction of the State, of the scientific and technical professions, and of society had to occur at the same time, supporting each other as they organized themselves. Everything proceeded as though higher education was to become the space through which both the State and society can be structured.

Colonial Legacy and the Foundation of Algerian Higher Education

At the time of its independence, Algeria found itself confronted with a deep void as far as higher education was concerned. The colonial legacy was insignificant, both in terms of student population (only about 500 students were registered) and infrastructure (only one university, in Algiers). From a scientific standpoint, the university had been exclusively responding to the needs of colonization and European settlers (Colonna & Brahimi, 1976). The colonial university was socially isolated in Algeria. It represented nothing but a counter-model. The occupier, when leaving, did not provide the country with a new generation of scientists ready to take over the country's institutions. It even made sure to burn the sole university library (Abdi, 1985).[2]

The newborn State quickly obliterated the few institutions left by the colonial system by multiplying its own initiatives, including the construction of universities, schools, and institutions. To staff these institutions, it massively recruited professors from all over the world (e.g. France, Canada, USSR, India, Arab countries). The colonial university was denied the possibility to significantly influence the future of higher education in Algeria. Intensive training programs (that begun during the war) and infrastructure building took over, following a radically different model. Consequently, in terms of both scientific content and programs, Algerian higher education owed little of its eventual successes and failures to the colonial system. The only exception is the continued use of the French language, the effects of which cannot be ignored. Algerian higher education is an entirely new creation, its teachings and scientific orientations building neither on established colonial institutions, nor on pre-existing university traditions.

While owing little to the colonial scientific legacy, the Algerian field of higher education is considerably influenced by the configuration of the social and political spaces which were deeply transformed by colonization. First, the Algerian university has inherited the worst aspects of its predecessor: the high degree of dependency of the university on political power. The colonial university depended on colonial Power, and the Algerian university now depended on political Power from 1962 onward. Thus, the colonial legacy lives more in the knowledge/power relationship than in the field of knowledge itself. Second, the social structure inherited from the colonial period, notably the low level of literacy and of economic, social and cultural differentiation, paradoxically contributed to increase the value attached to education in general and to higher education in particular. Algerians, who had long been denied access to knowledge, now demanded schooling, and believed in education as a decisive factor of social promotion. Political power could not simply ignore their request. Here again, higher education proved to be influenced by the social structure inherited from the colonial period more than by the latter's scientific content and institutions.

Wavering Between "Occidentalism" and "Localism"

Despite avoiding borrowing from the colonial model, Algerian higher education adopts the main characteristics of the dominant "Western" model, more specifically its French variant. This model is presumed "universal" and the only path to modernity. Beyond the desirability of Western modernity, many factors have contributed to the imposition of this model as a reference: the domination of the French language, the massive resort to foreign cooperation, and the influence, within the State, of Saint-Simonianism (including the "industrialist" movement), imbued with "scientism" (Wallerstein, 2006). The foundational discourse of the *Instituts technologiques* (Techological Institutes) (1969) and of the *Réforme de l'enseignement supérieur* (Reform of Higher Education) (1971) assigns universities the mission to adapt to the "economic, social and cultural realities of Algerian society." Notwithstanding, scientific and pedagogical practices are largely inspired by universalistic notions of higher education and knowledge. This remains currently the case (Kadri, 1991). But in the end, because one can only access universality through a local door, Algerian higher education remains in a wavering state, incapable of accessing either one.

The social meaning attributed to knowledge also favored this orientation. Knowledge is perceived as a crisis-solving tool, as a way to exit the "colonial situation" of generalized poverty and illiteracy. The urgency of the social demand is such that it obscures the questions of culture, language and authenticity, reducing them to political slogans. The urgency also benefited the French language, pushing Arabic back into the confines of the régime's propaganda apparatus. The urgency of the situation was further accompanied by apologetic conceptions of "progress" and "modernity." Seen as universal attributes, which Algerians needed to appropriate, this meant transcending traditions and local customs. The latter two were seen largely as antithetical to "social progress," a key idea of the national independence movement. As a result, while Arabic and French were instrumentalized by political elites, after 1962 they were not the object of specific social demands. French was simply there and occupied a dominant position in the administrative and economic sectors. Even Arabic-speaking and Islam-adhering families preferred to send their children to French schools, considered more likely to lead to a prosperous future. Following this utilitarian view of higher education, many segments in society did not mind, as the Chinese proverb goes, "the colour of the cat, as long as it catches the mouse."

Thus, the Arabization of teaching remained a claim driven by culture and identity. It was not perceived as a condition for the appropriation of knowledge. It remained a political slogan with no practical implications. Arabization became a factor of political division rather than the hearth of an identity under construction. It increasingly belonged to a sort of double-talk without true scientific and cultural consistency. It contributed more to the impoverishment of the university than to the "assimilation to the self" (Schwartz, 1991: 173) of modern knowledge and techniques. Torn between two linguistic and cultural universes, neither of which it mastered, the university took a hybrid shape, composed of ill-assorted linguistic elements out of tune with each other. With the exception of a few historically and geographically localized nuances resulting from "institutional effects" (Cousin, 1999), this configuration remains the dominant model and reflects the co-existence of political trends belonging to the two linguistic spheres. As a result of an arbitrary that is more political than cultural (Bourdieu & Passeron, 1990), the university's ambivalence reflects two levels of power struggles, first, between the social and political groups represented within the university; and second, between these groups and the caesarist Power that maintains them in a state of conflict without allowing one or the other to win. The ambivalence of the university thus perpetuates the conditions of production and reproduction of a dual society (Guérid, 2007), the division of which contributes to maintaining the arbitration and arbitrary of the political field.

Under such conditions, the State and its institutions become organized around the supremacy of Power but, beyond this "red line," it leaves it to constituting groups to struggle for their different functions (economic, social, cultural, ...) and to target different social categories. Thus, religious education essentially targets Arabized, disadvantaged, and mainly rural groups. Technological and professional education targets middle and lower-middle classes which are for the most part urban. Finally, academic education is aimed at upper-middle and higher social classes with political ambitions (Haddab, 1980; Khelfaoui, 2000). This arbitrated freedom gives way, for instance, to many partitioned sub-systems constituted of higher education institutions dedicated to professional, religious or academic education broadly defined. The diversity of cultural and social orientations reflects the conglomerate of political movements co-existing within Power. These sub-systems take the shape of playing fields which are strictly bound and delimited by Power.

For all that, knowledge and power never stray far away from each other. Whether it is present or absent, knowledge weighs on the position of agents in the social space, even if Power remains the ultimate determinant. The need for knowledge as a factor of legitimacy explains post-independence policies guaranteeing veterans' access to higher education regardless of academic requirements. It also explains how, in the 1990s, political supporters were recruited among degree holders. Political parties bragged to the media about the rate of academics among their candidates. In order to access economic capital (here defined as distributed oil rent), individuals needed to hold (usually illegitimately) symbolic forms of capital embedded in either the title of "revolutionary" or "academic." This was possible as long as they accepted the "rules of the game" imposed by Power, and as long as they showed proof of their acceptance of those rules, turning their back on the ethics implied by their original title, replacing it with political loyalty. It is in the context of such a tense and reluctant knowledge/power relationship that higher education has been structured and destructured since Algeria's independence.

The next section examines this process of structuration/destructuration and its articulations over three distinct historic periods.

Rise, Autonomy, and Decline of the Higher Education Field

Higher education in Algeria evolved over three separate historic periods. The first period corresponds to the foundational moment, during which institutions were created and the various social groups involved in higher education were constituted (faculty members, administrators, students). The second period, after the effervescence of the foundational moment, is characterized by stability and increasing autonomy. It is a period of adjustment and regulation during which the components of the field of higher education and of the broader social field attempted to negotiate a new relationship with the political field. The third period breaks with the stability and autonomy process as the field's regulation grows more authoritarian, and academics' working conditions deteriorate. Following Bourdieu and Passeron (1990: 90), the last two periods can be described as "organic" and "critical," respectively.

Rise and Autonomy of the Field of Higher Education

The first period starts in 1962 and ends during the 1970s. The State plays a foundational and demiurge role in the emergence of multiple institutions of higher education, with specific attention paid to the scientific and technical professions (Henni, 1990). Many of the highly-educated professions, notably engineering, were constituted during this phase, covering a wide range of specializations. This expansion resulted from State intervention rather than from the logic of the economic field, setting Algeria apart from industrialized countries in which industrial initiatives led to the creation of those professions (Shinn, 1980). As the country lacked industrial infrastructure, the economic field itself was too weak to influence the orientation of higher education without the intervention of the political field (the State). A network of technological institutes was created by the economic sector, but the latter largely relied on the labor of State bureaucracy to simultaneously address the network's economic goals and the need for social stratification. Furthermore, as the State monopolized the economy, there was practically no independent economic demand. Yet, a strong social demand for knowledge existed, relayed and materialized by a State still imbued with independence-seeking nationalism. This is how most of the infrastructure and institutions of higher education were constructed during this period, as dozens of universities, *écoles supérieures* and institutes were established.

The second period is characterized by the progressive rise, from the end of the 1970s until the beginning of the 1990s, of a relatively autonomous field of higher education. Its emergence concomitantly resulted from the formation of new professional groups and from the "liberalization" that followed the crisis of the late 1980s. As significant numbers of new professionals were trained, the social space adopted a new consistency. The field of higher education took shape as universities were built, and as professors were trained, replacing foreign *coopérants* ("cooperation volunteers" usually from France). The same process is at play in the economic field, with the training of engineers and managers, and in other professional fields (e.g. journalism, law). This movement through which social groups are constituted leads to changes in power struggles between the political field and the various professional fields. Henceforth, Power no longer enjoys absolute control over educational and economic policies, which it has to negotiate with newly constituted social groups. For the first time, the relationship between the field of higher education and the economic field ceases to be centrally defined and mediated by Power, and the social playing field is occupied by agents other than those designated by Power to represent it. Confronted with the struggle for autonomy of professional and social groups, Power momentarily retreats.

On the ground, the autonomy of the field of higher education takes the shape of a twofold process. First, it gains ownership of its scientific and pedagogical activities. Programs and contents were less likely to be centrally prescribed, compared with the first period. Second, higher education progressively establishes direct connections with other professional fields, bypassing the bureaucracy, the arm of Power in the State's basic institutions. The many acts and bylaws that regulated economic and social life in the 1970s and 1980s, while not repealed, are forgotten. Social groups express their interests through informal channels. The faculty body took advantage of this period to structure itself and organize its members in unions and professional organizations. Faculty members thus gained access, on their own and without mediation, to the two spheres which will notably transform their profession: international science and industry.

Local collective action, strikes, and publications in independent newspapers – the latter appearing during the same period due to similar processes, and welcoming academics' concerns – transform the inner workings of higher education institutions and of their relationship with political Power. Training programs are criticized and modified. More flexible and less interventionist structures are created, loosening the grasp of administrative functions over scientific and pedagogical functions. Organizations dedicated to consultation and advising, such as scientific councils, begin their work. Criteria for scientific productivity are introduced into the management of academic careers. The purposes of education, and in particular its social and economic functions, are again discussed. Direct ties are established with the economic and social spheres, often through alumni. For the first time since the "big debates" of 1969 and 1970, which led to the creation of the *Instituts technologiques* and to the *Réforme de l'enseignement supérieur*, the modalities of collaboration between universities and companies were hotly debated. Together, these multifaceted initiatives, arising from all professional fields simultaneously, threatened to significantly loosen the grasp Power previously exercised on society.

Power Again Takes Over Higher Education

The third period begins in the early 1990s. A brutal reorientation occurs on many levels: Power takes over higher education, professions are dismantled, the student population explodes and the life and work conditions of faculty members deteriorate. Going backwards along the path it just travelled during the second period, the field of higher education sees its control move back to the political field, first to the national level and soon to the international level as policy makers decide to jump on the bandwagon of European reforms (Bologna process). Under the combined effects of industrial collapse, structural adjustments and a prolonged civil war, professional groups are weakened and the social field loses the levers of its autonomy (Khelfaoui, 2003). The resulting social, political and intellectual void facilitates the return of a strong central Power. As it regains its position in the centre of the social field, an authoritarian and vindictive Power confronts society in general and academics in particular, while submitting itself to the forces of globalization. New reforms, notably those concerning higher education, are in line with this new perspective: social groups aspiring to autonomy are disciplined and must pay deference to global forces.

The generalized co-optation of upper and intermediate university administrators – rectors and deans, respectively – represents a key mode of control of the field of higher education. The dominant positions within the field are defined and distributed from the outside, following the logic of the political field. In turn, owing their position to Power, administrators use identical co-optation practices to fill the lower rungs of the academic hierarchy. As a result, academic administrators now lacked scientific legitimacy, and are incapable of securing a scientific career (which would have been incompatible with their policing role). Their expectations can only be fulfilled by "importing into the university field properties or powers acquired on other terrains" (Bourdieu, 1988: 87) than those of knowledge. The logic of the political field replaced the logic of the field of higher education, leading to a de-professionalization of the latter, reducing its autonomy to low-stake domains from the perspective of Power.

The resulting exercise of power is complex and, as Foucault suggests, is no longer embodied in an institution or a person. Instead it is located in practices of allegiance, interest, and clan-based solidarity that are tolerated or even encouraged by Power in exchange for favors, because they reproduce Power's own practices. As power becomes centralized, its practices diffuse into other social spheres and penetrate all levels of society. The State is no longer the source or origin of power, but rather a set of practices which often, if not always, contradict the orientation of the State and of its institutions. The latter turn into mere smokescreens. Scientific institutions are now managed not along the lines of rationality claims but in order to support the conditions perceived as necessary for the exercise and perpetuation of Power. The latter is not "everywhere and nowhere" as argued by Foucault, which would mean that its presence is acknowledged and integrated. Rather, it is everywhere, in the Orwellian sense of the word. It is endured more than accepted.

Incapable of mustering legitimacy other than by force, and failing to impose its image of itself on emerging social groups, Power reacts by intensifying humiliating practices, primarily against academics. As soon as they stray from their assigned function – perceived as relays of Power – faculty members are hit with specific measures targeting their professional identity (such as breaches in the basic norms of promotion and sanction, and massive recruitment of students on the basis of political motives) and their dignity (progressively reducing their claims to the level of mere survival income). Rectors tell striking professors that they will "starve them," hounding down academics who refuse to acknowledge their power and whose very existence remind the politically doted of their scientific inadequacy. In his novel *The Watchers* (2002) (*Les Vigiles*, 1991), the assassinated writer Tahar Djaout (1954–1993) illustrated this relationship in a passage where the character who embodies Power, proclaiming himself to be the founder and guardian of the nation, snubs Mahfoudh Lemdjad, a researcher who attempts to patent a new type of loom rooted in traditional knowledge. The "watcher" despises Lemdjad who, to him, is nothing but the inventor of an old woman's loom.

The Deconsecration of Knowledge

After having been perceived as an essential factor of social distinction in the 1960s and 1970s, knowledge lost its status and scientific professionals were pushed back to the lowest of social categories. While knowledge previously sustained, among social agents, the double belief that they could reach the truth and move toward progress (Kuty, 1991: 11), it now only meagerly contributes to ascending social strategies. Dominant social categories maintain their investments in higher education as a mode of distribution of titles certifying the acquisition of knowledge, but they primarily do so to legitimize a social position previously gained through other means.

Because the political field dominates all domains and all levels of society, the field of higher education depends on Power both materially and financially, yet paradoxically becomes closer to it. The incapacity of higher education's agents to mobilize means of distinction within their own field promotes practices that operate as indispensable means of access to society's dominant positions and which favor proximity to the political field. A social representation of knowledge, associating power and knowledge, arises from this proximity. The resulting "cultural model," which follows Touraine's categorization, transforms the functions of higher education. Knowledge is no longer a tool supporting change. Instead, it supports and comforts the established political order.

By marginalizing the scientific and technical professions, Algeria's political elites have successfully "deconsecrated" knowledge as well as the institutions and social groups that are its wardens and providers. In so doing, Power denies itself a source of scientific and economic legitimacy. The only way to make up for this deficit is a return to the Revolution. The Revolution is appropriated by the holders of Power, thus excluding the social categories that do not support Power. Elevated to the status of a myth and somehow dissociated from society, the Revolution now occupies the position that takes on the ideological function ascribed to scientism during the first two periods. Using self-proclaimed official organizations that belong to the "revolutionary family,"[3] Power turned the Revolution into an exclusive factor of distinction, an inherited nobility title of divine right. Revolution is reified and separated from its original motives and purposes. Failing to pay deference to the Revolution is no longer an act of "shame," moving instead to the realm of the taboo, of the "sacred" (Douglas, 2005).

Conclusion

At the end of almost five decades of independence, Algeria's society finds itself stratified and differentiated. Its social structure is profoundly transformed and a new value system has taken shape. However, against the hopes of the early days following independence, education and knowledge play a marginal, perhaps even subordinate, role in the emergence of the new value system.

As Power excludes knowledge as a means of access to society's dominant positions, knowledge ceases to work as a factor of distinction and promotion. Knowledge is deconsecrated and produces disaffection towards education. Power refuses that social groups, organized around scientific and technical knowledge, regulate Power's relationship with society, in view of loosening its totalitarian grasp on it and dissolving its only source of strength. The autonomization process of universities and industry that started during the first two periods revealed social, political and economic stakes that threatened the knowledge/power relationship. Socially, the autonomization process embodied a counter-model and an alternative to Power's practices because it infuses into social relations a rationality that is different from that of Power. Economically, this process appeared as a threat against new political alliances arising from the transfer of oil rents, from investment toward speculation. To interrupt the autonomization process, Power dismantled all social groups which threatened its durability, starting with academics, scientists, engineers and entrepreneurs.

Consequently, the two forms of capital – economic and cultural – that constitute the most efficient factors of differentiation in advanced societies (Bourdieu, 1998) – play an exclusively marginal role in the structuration of power in the Algerian social space. Agents and groups are distributed in the social field according to their proximity to Power. The initial processes of knowledge- and work-based differentiation are replaced with a rentier system of differentiation based on oil-generated income, corruption, utilitarian uses of history, and, if all else fails, armed force. The university becomes nothing but a means of subjugation. Its subjugated agents are nothing but an emanation of power. In this process, Power subtly combines "traditions," "charisma," and smokescreens of "legality," and becomes increasingly dependent on global rather than local forces. While Power may have succeeded in maintaining its domain, academics have failed in maintaining theirs. They are not in a position to carry out a scientific perspective grounded in local culture and contexts, which is, at the same time, attuned to universal forms of knowledge.

Acknowledgment

Thank you to Brigitte Gemme from translating this chapter from French.

Notes

1 The Algerian political discourse is ripe with this expression. However, one never encounters the idea of a scientific legitimacy. Knowledge is slanted as a means of economic emancipation, never as a source of political legitimacy. The latter, as we will see later in this chapter, is reserved to "revolutionaries."
2 The University Library fire remains under-documented and under-studied, victim of a "memoricide". See, the following historical bulletin notices: <http://bbf.enssib.fr/consulter/bbf-1962-07-0375-001>,<http://bbf.enssib.fr/consulter/bbf-1962-11-0549-001>. For a more recent account, refer to <http://www.ihtp.cnrs.fr/spip.php%3Farticle335&lang=fr.html>. For a visualization of the fire, refer to the following link: <http://www.ina.fr/economie-et-societe/education-et-enseignement/video/CAF90005878/incendie-a-la-faculte-d-alger.fr.html>.
3 Among these organizations, one can find associations of war veterans, of children of the martyrs of the war of liberation, and of children of veterans.

References

Abdi, A. (1985). *La reconstitution de la bibliothèque universitaire après l'incendie du 7 Juin 1962*. Université d'Alger: Mémoire de bibiothéconomie.
Balandier, G. (2001). La situation coloniale: Approche théorique. *Cahiers Internationaux de Sociologie*, 110 (1), 9–29.
Bourdieu, P. (1988). *Homo Academicus*. Stanford, CA: Stanford University Press.
Bourdieu, P. (1996). *The State Nobility: Elite Schools in the Field of Power* (L.C. Clough, Trans.). Stanford, CA: Stanford University Press.
Bourdieu, P. (1998). *Practical Reason: On the Theory of Action*. Stanford, CA: Stanford University Press.
Bourdieu, P. & Passeron, J.-C. (1990). *Reproduction in Education, Society, and Culture*. Thousand Oaks, CA: Sage.
Colonna, F. & Brahimi, H. (1976). Du bon usage de la science coloniale. *Cahiers Jussieu* (collection 10/18), 2, 221–241.
Cousin, O. (1999). *L'Efficacité des Collèges: Sociologie de l'Effet d'Établissement*. Paris: PUF.
Djaout, T. (2002). *The Watchers* (Marjolijn de Jager, Trans.). St Paul, MN: Ruminator Books.
Douglas, M. (2005). *Purity and Danger: An Analysis of the Concept of Pollution and Taboo*. London, New York: Routledge.

Foucault, M. (1979a). *Discipline and Punish: The Birth of the Prison*. New York: Vintage Books.

Foucault, Michel (1979b). *Michel Foucault: Power, Truth, Strategy*. Edited by Meaghan Morris and Paul Patton. Sydney: Feral Publications.

Guérid, D. (2007). Algérie: dualité de la société et dualité de l'élite. Les origines historiques. In O. Lardjane (Ed.), *Élites et Société en Algérie et en Égypte* (pp. 50–67). Algiers: Casbah.

Haddab, M. (1980). *Éducation et Changements Socio-culturels. Les Moniteurs de l'Enseignement Élémentaires en Algérie*. Algiers/Paris: Centre de recherches et d'études sur les sociétés méditerranéennes/Office des Publications universitaires/CNRS.

Henni, A. (1990). *L'Option Scientifique et Technique en Algérie*. Algiers: OPU.

Kadri, A. (1991). De l'université coloniale à l'université nationale: instrumentalisation et "idéologisation" de l'institution. *Peuples Méditerranéens*, 54–55 (2), 151–174.

Khelfaoui, H. (2000). *Les Ingénieurs dans le Système Éducatif: L'Aventure des Instituts Technologiques Algériens*. Paris: Publisud.

Khelfaoui, H. (2003) Le champ universitaire algérien, entre pouvoirs politiques et champ économique. *Actes de la Recherche en Sciences Sociales*, 148, 34–46.

Kuty, O. (1991). La problématique de la création des valeurs dans la sociologie contemporaine des professions de première ligne. *Sciences Sociales et Santé*, 9 (2), 5–30.

Labbé, S. (1991). *Récit de Vie dans la Problématique Savoir-Pouvoir*. Montreal: UQAM.

Meynier, G. (2003). Les cadres du FLN/ALN, 1954–1962. In N. Sraïeb (Ed.), *Anciennes et Nouvelles Élites du Maghreb* (pp. 209–227). Algiers, Tunis and Aix-en-Provence: IRENAM, Inas-Cérès-Edis.

Schwartz, Y. (1991). La dimension anthropologique de la technique et ses défis. In J. Perrin (Ed.), *Construire une Science des Techniques* (pp. 87–109), Limonest: L'Interdisciplinaire Technologie(s).

Shinn, T. (1980). *Savoir Scientifique et Pouvoir Social. L'École Polytechnique – 1794–1914*. Paris: Presses de la fondation nationale des sciences politiques.

Touraine, A. (1992). *Critique de la Modernité*. Paris: Fayard.

Wallerstein, I. (2006). *European Universalism: The Rhetoric of Power*. New York: New Press.

17 Going International

The Politics of Educational Reform in Egypt

Iman Farag

Knowledge: Between the Global and the Local

In the nineteenth century, the French thinker Ernest Renan (1823-1892), used the expression 'Latin Averroïsm' to describe and qualify western philosophical doctrines of the thirteenth century that came to know the Aristotelian legacy through Muslim scholars and philosophers. In his seminal work, *Thinking in the Middle Ages* [*Penser au Moyen Âge*], the philosopher Alain de Libera, adds that 'Latin Averroïsm' constituted a kind of intellectual movement around the Sorbonne and contributed significantly to the shaping of the role of the Sorbonne's intellectuals. Indicatively, in its time, what has come to be known as 'Latin Averroïsm' was rather known as 'Arabism'. De Libera insists that this was not an East versus West encounter, or a unilateral transfer of knowledge. It rather illustrates the fact that intellectuals in Medieval societies in Europe and the Muslim world were sharing debates across religious divides, around questions of faith and reason (de Libera, 1991. See also Le Goff, 1985).[1]

More recently, Benjamen Fortna locates late Ottoman educational experiences in a global context, showing similarities to France, Czarist Russia, China, and Japan (Fortna, 2002). It was around the 1820s that the ruler of an Ottoman province—Egypt—sent groups of students to learn abroad. He also opened the door to foreign experts and scientists. A recent chapter in what seems to be a continuous dynamic was recently written when a conference was held in Cairo to discuss and praise the role of foreign academia in the Egyptian university.[2] Such a transfer of knowledge and scientists is closely related to European colonialism and to cosmopolitanism, with their paradoxical and complex relationship. This interaction was not limited to East/West encounters and did not concern only secular knowledge and modern institutions. If 'international students' are considered to be one of the main features of higher education internationalization, one should mention earlier forms. Indeed, prestigious institutions devoted to the study of religious sciences, such as the millennial Al-Azhar mosque in Egypt (founded in 972), were quite used to 'international students' hailing from as far as Java or Senegal. Such student mobility needs to be considered within the framework of an 'Islamic universalism'.

We assume that knowledge and its dissemination was always shared and transmitted across borders, gaining new dimensions and interpretations, with every move over space and time. Learners and masters also moved across borders, carrying books, tools and ideas. They were able to argue, to agree, to disagree and to communicate. In this respect, revising early forms of globalization, either imperial or colonial, leads to reconsidering internationalization of knowledge as a new phenomena. However, one should note that the invention of nation-states has definitely affected the relationship between qualification and occupation, and hence the transfer of knowledge: 'Latin Averroïsm', or 'Arabism' as it was known, did not need accreditation, and neither did Indonesian Azhari scholars need to qualify for the job market. This does not mean that early forms of knowledge were free from all types of legitimation. However, the modern conception of degrees and qualifications, which is closely related to a specific political power, has its effects on knowledge transfer in contemporary times.

This historical backdrop raises several questions about the ongoing internationalization of education and higher education. What is new about it? Does privatization constitute the bedrock for internationalization? Is it the expression of the allegedly universal shift from Phase 1, autonomous knowledge for the sake of knowledge, to Phase 2, 'knowledge for the market' (Gibbons *et al.*, 1994)? Is such a shift, whose description has been popularized by Michael Gibbons, and whose implementation has been endorsed by international organizations, a simple and innocent description, or is it a doctrinal prescription? Who 'should learn to pay', to quote the title of Colclough's (1991) visionary article … and to learn what? Is it always relevant to constitute 'global educational policies' as an autonomous research area, disconnected from ongoing forms of exchange? Who is able and willing to compete on the international level? How far can education go in claiming to be an 'international social system', where the interplay between knowledge and power takes place within and beyond nation states? What does the internationalization of education and higher education mean outside the US and 'fortress Europe'? Assuming that the educational question addresses political, cultural, as well as social resources, how should one conceive its internationalization? How are global agendas translated into indigenous languages? How should we analyze the translation of presumably global norms into local practices?

The Egyptian case provides some insights into these questions. Egypt has a highly centralized educational system, and historically, education was central to the project of nation-state building. Social as well as technological progress, social and gender equity, as well as citizenship could only be achieved through education. An Egyptian model was diffused among some other Arab countries. Today such a model is depicted as being on the verge of collapse, its high degree of success bearing the seeds of its own failure. As in other countries of the world, new goals are defined and implemented for Egypt, paraded under the banner of the 'knowledge society', often relying on foreign agencies and credit. Such reforms generate resistance, adaptation, as well as clients and neo-experts (Mazawi, 2007).

In what follows, we will propose the hypothesis that one of the strategies adopted to play the internationalization game is the adoption of a common language. We will first examine Egyptian educational reform projects inspired by a global agenda, and how these serve as a vehicle for new discourses, notions and concepts. We will then examine, more specifically, the Egyptian debate about the ranking of universities. Finally, we will address the issues of evaluation and quality assessment and their dissemination through 'new' institutions as well as 'old' techniques of power.

Debating Reforms

By the end of December 2008, Egypt was witnessing a new phase in the endless debate that started about ten years earlier concerning a draft law meant to improve the regulations governing higher education establishments. Further details about the proposed law were given either by State authorities, or by opponents—chief among them being members of the 9th March Movement for the Autonomy of Universities, a movement made up of academics.[3] An active and influential minority made up of professors from all public universities was able to unite and to express its interests and views in an organized manner, thus forming a protest group. *9th March* is concerned both by the material conditions under which academics have to work, as well as by the intellectual and political environment which restricts the autonomy of the university, and which hampers professional ethics. The *9th March* movement managed to impose itself as a player in the social field, engaging in tough discussions with the Minister of Higher Education and Scientific Research about the draft law—by all accounts, quite an exceptional feat for oppositional movements in Egypt. What is new about this?

Let us first look at what is at stake. Significantly, under the title 'philosophy underpinning the project', an emphasis is placed by the draft law on new worldwide changes as imposed by globalization, on the redefinition of the socio-political orientation of Egypt's political system, on the dynamics of social mobility related to higher education, on the necessity for quality assurance and for new procedures and criteria for evaluation. Under this same title of 'philosophy', the draft law emphasizes international competition, arguing that the General Agreement for Trade and Services makes the changes in higher education unavoidable.

At the forefront of these major changes we find the dissociation between the ownership of higher education establishments, their governance and their financing (Mazawi, 2005). The connection of these three elements should not be considered as a given. The reform project also refers to 'civil society organizations and stakeholders'. These are described as being those who express the aspirations of society, and who are concerned with the attainment of excellence through competition. These actors, in the view of the project, can be involved in several fields of action, including participation in managing universities through being members of boards of trustees and of quality assessment agencies. They can also be involved in supporting graduates, in providing financial as well as moral support, and, significantly, through contributing to the definition of research priorities. Finally, the project emphasizes the need for higher education institutions to be managed as autonomous units when it comes to finance. These units would be expected to provide services to students ('clients') according to established quality standards, and on the basis of the real costs of the educational services provided. In this respect, free higher education is transformed into a negotiable relationship between the student and the State; it is no longer a systematic commitment of public institutions towards students.[4]

If one had to compare this draft law with previous declarations of intentions that linked education (including higher education)[5] to nation-state building and engineered social change, one would conclude that it is the exact opposite to the 'ideological' or 'utopian' documents of the Nasserist era (1954–1970). The latter, in contrast to the new draft law, stress free higher education as a social and political right, and as a way of alleviating class differentiation and of correcting social injustices inherited from the past. Above all, the older documents related education to 'dignity'—a symbolic dimension which still finds resonance in Egyptian society, and which then complemented rather than clashed with the practical goals of economic and technological development. If the draft law now sounds familiar and 'realistic', it is very simply due to the fact that the package echoes a worldwide recipe: Egypt, or rather its ruling elite class, considers itself as one of the countries that must follow the universal trajectory of educational reforms, and that such a destination is best reached with the support of foreign agency funding and expertise.

In this respect, several 'scripts' (Meyer and Rowan, 1977 cited by Musselin, 2008) or normative prescriptions are circulating in the institutional environment of universities, enunciating legitimate propositions, standards and norms. Following the 'right' script constitutes the proof that a country is on the 'right' way and that its rulers are willing to adapt societal realities to what seems to be rational and modern norms. As with all reforms in general, and educational reforms in particular, narratives count as much as implementation of action on the ground. We should also take into consideration the unintended effects of such narratives.

Musselin (2008) identifies five scripts in relation to higher education. All of these are in fact interrelated, and all involve modifications in the role of the State. The latter cannot be cornered into making the choice between the two binary opposites of disengagement on the one hand, and involvement on the other. If the name of the game is to alleviate the financial burden of higher education on public resources, and to dispatch social responsibility among a plurality of actors, the State is more likely to intervene as a regulator, even if it is not a provider—or the sole provider—of higher education services. A second perspective is to rebuild universities as corporations. This raises the question of the multiple definitions of university autonomy and the limits of this claim under authoritarian situations. In such contexts, academic freedom is more than free expression within or outside the campus. It has to do with patron/client relations between academia and political authority. Besides, to conceive universities as corporate entities introduces a new layer of analysis if one is to take seriously the dissemination of governance as an analytical tool or, perhaps, as a set of arrangements. As autonomous from the State, universities as corporate entities should, paradoxically, consolidate partnership with the so-called 'stakeholders'. Here too definitions of who the 'stakeholder' is vary, ranging from student unions to external auditors, evaluators and financiers. The assumption is that universities should cease to function as ivory towers, with their scientific concerns being guided by stakeholder views. Chief among such stakeholders are those actors able to provide the institution with a financial boost, thus giving a fillip to the production of useful academic knowledge. Privatization thus intervenes as a core element, ranging from the establishment of private universities to the introduction of privatized logics within public ones. Finally, and as a fifth script, norms and standards of universities are expected to have a trans-national dimension, allowing the accreditation of degrees and international students.

Needless to say, these scripts are always interpellating local conditions: they work with, on and around national histories and political constraints, in relation to the allocation of private and public resources, and in response to social expectations. The translation of scripts into practices remains specific and localized. What seems important is the way they are diffused and generalized and become self-evident assumptions within a huge variety of régimes and societies. This is at least the case of higher education in Egypt: public universities suffer from a rapid devaluation. Apart from the rise of the phenomenon of private universities, invariably under the umbrella of the State, privatized departments are being established within public universities. For all practical purposes, the autonomy of universities is defined by—and limited to—the ability of the respective institutions to raise funds, in a context where the administrative or managerial hierarchy gains more power over academia. Finally, along with the constant devaluation of national degrees, there are paradoxical attempts to conform to formal international standards—a phenomenon we will consider in some detail in the last section of this chapter.

Common Language

As is usually expected when the *de facto* is heavily orienting the *de jure*, the Egyptian draft law we have been referring to is already applied even if it is still under discussion,[6] at least inasmuch as some of its broad orientations are concerned. Such is the remarkable consistency with the ongoing international script that this 'Egyptian' draft could be Syrian, Indonesian, or indeed French. It constitutes the perfect example of what may be considered as educational reform in a global era. The dissemination of the recipe through different channels to different societies from the North and the South constitutes a veritable field of investigation.[7] In Egypt, such orientations may have been enforced by the fact that major educational reform programs relied on loans and credits from international organizations, primarily the World Bank. But how is all of this working?

The Egypt Higher Education Enhancement Project (HEEP) plays in important role in reshaping the structure of higher education. This is due to the enormous amount of financial investment involved, and to the scope of HEEP, which concerns almost all the components of a huge higher education system. HEEP's influence is also due to the fact that it is often presented as a success story. The project is made up of six components, which collectively address the areas that have been identified as requiring attention if higher education is to be enhanced. These components include [1] The Faculty/Staff and Leadership Development Project (FLDP); [2] the Information and Communication Technology Project (ICTP); [3] the Quality Assurance and Accreditation Project (QAAP); [4] the Faculty of Education Project (FOEP); [5] the Egyptian Technical Colleges Project (ETCP); and [6] the Higher Education Enhancement Project Fund (HEEPF).[8]

It is important to point out that other World Bank projects, using much the same labels, and similarly packaged under the broad referential umbrella of the 'knowledge society', were designed and financed for the higher education sectors in several countries, including Argentina, Slovenia, China, Mozambique, Sri Lanka, and Bangladesh. Here the copy blueprint hypothesis is quite simplistic and the parallels deserve analysis.[9]

But here too narratives count. In February 2000, a two-day 'First National Conference for Higher Education Enhancement' attended by 1,000 participants endorsed a plan for reform. Twenty-five key sectors were targeted, and these were later reduced to twelve, and then further collapsed within six priority projects. Within two years, these projects were financed by a World Bank loan of USD 13,000,000. The end of 2008 marks the end of Phase 1, bringing with it the 8th World Bank supervision mission to Cairo. As with the launch of the project, a national conference is to close HEEP's first phase. The second phase should follow soon after.

Experts and evaluators will have to assess the outcomes of the project, to conceive and formulate the rationale for an eventual second phase, as well as the financial resources required. HEEP critics have already qualified the project as disconnected from reality: they claim that it is illusive, and that it ignores the central structural problem of higher education in Egypt, namely the scarcity of public expenditures on universities.[10] Others underlined and denounced favoritism and corruption, while still others criticized the allocation of the financial resources within the HEEP.[11] Some university staff expressed their disappointment at the way some welcome innovations have been translated into mere bureaucratic and routine procedures when implemented (Kamal, Guindy, and Abu Bakr, n.d.).

As for the 'storytelling perspective', one should note that while starting and ending with a national conference, the HEEP raises several questions about its design and the kind of coordination fostered between grantees and donors. Here is the defensive answer of the highest official in charge: "These allegations are false," he said. "Our vision was elaborated in 2000. It was the outcome of years of work and it was attended by all the experts. We prepared a global document, and conceived a strategic plan for higher education enhancement. We needed financial support and had an agreement with the World Bank. This occurred *after* the strategic 2000 plan was endorsed."[12]

In terms of 'political ritual', the signing of the agreement with the World Bank following the national conference blessing is, in itself, meaningful. Does chronology matter as long as a common language facilitates comprehension? According to some university professors, the proposed regulations linking the wage increase for academics with new forms of professional evaluation were the direct outcome of a foreign expert's mission to Cairo. In principle, wages for academics are regulated by the relevant university laws. According to these professors, the shift to a new system on the initiative of the Minister of Higher Education and Scientific Research operating under pressure from external actors, is not only a violation of the law but also an attempt to force a legislative framework against the will of the academic corps. Here too, as elsewhere,[13] local pressures exercised over university staff are more consequential than 'foreign pressures': we are here referring not only to a set of regulations but rather to a kit of ready-made notions, where 'evaluation' occupies the central place.

The 'hidden agenda'/'black box' explanatory framework is neither sufficient nor satisfactory here, especially when agendas are not hidden. Several studies (*inter alia*, Koschtall, 2005) show that the links between receivers and donors are much more complicated than the usual paradigm of pure imposition: donors need to donate while receivers are seeking financial resources. There is room for negotiation, both parties have shared as well as competing views, and both are able to formulate justifications referring to public interest. Also the set of actors engaged in such transactions vary from one situation to another, even when bundled under the unifying label of 'stakeholders'. The set of actors is often constructed and transformed through the negotiation process. The constitution of negotiators as 'partners'—and vice versa—is not only a prerequisite, but merely one of the outcomes of the negotiation process. Besides, equally important as common interests—if not more—is the common language that enables the formulation of agendas, even if the use of a common language does not exclude misinterpretations or, should we say, multi-interpretations. For instance, a key issue such as 'university autonomy' can be interpreted primarily as the ability and flexibility of universities as corporate entities to adapt to the market. Another conceptualization of autonomy may emphasize political constraints imposed by authoritarian régimes, while a third one could target collegial leadership within universities and the respective power of academia and the administration.

Given this variety of considerations, in what sense can a reform project constitute the vehicle of a common language? The HEEP covered the six key projects previously mentioned, and all the public higher education systems; it mobilized thousands of civil servants, university professors and casual personnel. It entailed innumerable working hours, not to mention committees, meetings, travel, wages, training, paperwork, labelled stationery, software, and equipment. Intensive use of ICT was reflected in dozens of websites and networks. Permanent units and bureaucratic structures were created to replace the old ones. HEEP in fact provides us with an excellent opportunity to draw up an anthropology of educational reform in a globalized world. It is through a whole set of practices and actors and more or less shared knowledge that HEEP comforts the 'common language' hypothesis. However, a common language does not mean a common concern.

From Cairo to Shanghai: Ranking as a Global Norm

Even if their contents are familiar, it seems that fashionable words acquire an inner legitimacy. I would like to argue that the uses of an acknowledged vocabulary may be an illustration of voluntary consent to hegemony. The global ranking of universities is a significant example. One can wonder why they are becoming a matter of universal interest, even in less-developed countries which are far from being concerned by international competition and by attracting international students. But who said that losers do not want to be part of the game? The journey to Cairo of the Shanghai ranking of world universities provides an example of the diffusion of a common language.

In 2003, Shanghai Jiao Tong University's Institute of Higher Education published an Academic Ranking of Word Universities for the first time (Liu, 2009). According to the methodology used in 2008:

> the ranking list includes every institution that has any Nobel Laureates, Fields Medals, and Highly-Cited Researchers. In addition, major universities of every country with a significant amount of articles indexed by Science Citation Index-Expanded (SCIE) and Social Science Citation Index (SSCI) are also included. In total, more than one thousand institutions have been actually ranked in each of the five broad subject fields: Natural Sciences and Mathematics, Engineering/Technology and Computer Sciences, Life and Agriculture Sciences, Clinical Medicine and Pharmacy and Social Sciences. Arts and humanities are not ranked because of the technical difficulties in finding internationally comparable indicators with reliable data. Psychology/ Psychiatry is not included in the ranking because of its multi-disciplinary characteristics.
>
> (Shanghai Jiao Tong University, 2008)

It is worth noting that the Shanghai ranking is based on web research, a fact that does not in itself deny the validity of the exercise, but imposes the usual limitations associated with all data provided by such virtual sources. This is particularly true for Arab universities. It is assumed that science speaks one language and relying on the English language is an evident bias of the ranking. Furthermore, some critics underline the fact that the Shanghai ranking was originally conceived to allow comparisons among Chinese, Japanese and American universities. Outside this original scale and when applied to other universities of the world, the methodology turns out to be irrelevant. We should add to this other questions concerning periodicity, including the validity of an annual ranking, and what this is actually measuring given that science and short term hardly correspond. Finally, the national structures of higher education and scientific research vary considerably. According to the designed ranking, whole sectors of scientific research outside universities are left out even if they contribute to defining the scientific profile of the universities. Additionally, the ranking fails to take into account the historically specific conditions under which universities were constructed in different parts of the world: in post-colonial situations, for instance, their aims may be different and knowledge diffusion may not lead to research.

In spite of its simplicity, or rather *because* of it—purporting as it does to represent a universal model of the university—the Shanghai ranking has become a point of reference. It was more or less contested, yet reproduced, in Europe, Africa and the Muslim world. To reproduce the worldwide exercise on the regional level poses questions about scale, comparability and relevance. In a way, moving to these levels means that these factors matter and that they were not taken in account in a universal ranking. History still acts in the present moment, and global cultural references have not abolished local references. As we shall see when we consider the political usage made of the results, there are always rankings in the rankings, in the sense that *ad hoc* effective classifications have their own plural logics. As with all kinds of ranking, reducing several elements to a unique quantified value transforms the latter into a substance: the ranking of a given university tells nothing about specific performances by discipline, even if the data is available. What counts is the announcement effect. Here again come the eventual discrepancies between the so-called objective measurements and their social usages. As with all kinds of ranking, the same outcome may be qualified as accurate and precise or used as a vague and rough indicator. As with all kinds of ranking, this same outcome could also count twice as a result and as the starting point for a chain of intended and unintended consequences.[14]

Apart from the accuracy and the elaboration of the index, there remains a question of *raison d'être*. What would be the purposes behind the ranking of world universities? And how would this account for the specificities of the context of Arab universities?

If we attempt to grasp the essence of an international ranking, the key elements would be the following: a global higher education market, open to competition, where students/clients have to be advised before making their choices, where the flow of endowments and funds is disputed among universities, and finally where national frontiers do not count any more—at least for the first ranked 500 universities. Even if the indicators are doubtful, the ranking effect stimulates competition, universities are mobilized to up-grade themselves in the interest of sciences and consumers. Both are expressed in a single value: rank. We will not discuss here the assumptions underpinning this logic, i.e. the existence of a perfect market.

However, when it comes to a worldwide ranking of universities, one should first ask about the inner logic of a cognitive and social practice. If one has to take the anthropologist Marcel Mauss (1872–1950) seriously, ranking should be considered and analyzed as a way among others to organize the world and to make sense of it. In this respect, the spectrum should be enlarged: 'rankimania' concerns not only universities, but also democracy, transparency, social capital, human development and so on.

The socio-political usages of the Shanghai ranking pose a supplementary and problematic question: is this ranking about universities, about nations, or about both? How is it working in the matrix of what are, presumably, knowledge 'free markets', big money concerns, transnational communities of scientists, 'scientific nationalism' and nationalism?

The same goes for the Egyptian debate about the Shanghai ranking perceived to be unbiased, quantifiable, universal, Asian (read, 'not western'), and depoliticized. It is for this mix of reasons that the ranking is considered to be objective and relevant. Add to this the fact that the Shanghai ranking reveals what we already know: the poor condition of Egyptian universities. If it is so, why is it that Cairo University's ranking is polemical and dealt with as a surprising result, and is it a good or a bad surprise?

In 2005 there were no Egyptian universities in the top 500. In 2006, Cairo University (as representing Egypt?) shared the rank 401–500 with some 200 universities. In 2007, its rank was 403–510. It disappeared again in 2008. Yearly measurements of academic performance seem as frequent as stock market calculations while changes are grossly limited.

The inclusion of Cairo University seems due to the fact that three Nobel prize graduates of the University were taken in account. It barely needs to be pointed out that the success of the Nobel prize laureates for Literature (Naguib Mahfouz) or Peace (Yasser Arafat and Mohamed El Baradei) have probably very little to do with Cairo University's credentials. Arafat studied engineering and one may wonder if authors like Mahfouz acquire universal recognition *despite* the institution they belong to, rather than thanks to them. In any case, such is the logic underpinning the ranking.

Now it is quite ambiguous to determine if the surprise was good or bad. Through Cairo University, Egypt was present in the list of the world's 'top 500 universities', which starts with Harvard. But it occupies the bottom of the top. Is this promising or disappointing? Interestingly, one of the outcomes is that Egyptian universities are investing in promoting their scientific reputation through their websites, and emphasizing the pages that appear in English. Symbol ranking turns to be an objective in itself.

What seems to be at stake here is Egypt's reputation, as made by one of its public universities. However, it bears asking the question: how is this university evaluated? There is little sense in comparing Cairo University with Harvard— indeed, commentators had in mind the few lucky (South) African universities that made it into the list. There was, however, another way to read the Shanghai ranking: when noting the Israeli universities that rank among the top 500, Egyptian commentators turn to define themselves as 'we Arabs', deploring, in so doing, the degradation of Arab universities and the inability of Arab countries to face Israeli supremacy. The Shanghai ranking interpellates and appeals to other rankings. In the *Times Higher Education* one Arab country—Egypt (again)—is in a less bad position. The situation changes radically when it comes to the Pakistani ranking of Muslim universities across the world; it is difficult to accept that Gulf universities precede the famous and oldest reference, Cairo University, given that Egypt has been the most prolific disseminator of knowledge across the Arab region, not to mention that it is also the exporter of a model of the university, largely framed by Cairo University's historical excellence.

As has just been demonstrated, there are several ways to evaluate a single value. There are also several ways to make sense of these values as well. As a global norm, the Shanghai ranking is mobilized as a perfectly legitimate reference by different actors striving to establish their competing views. Such mobilization is considered to be even more *à propos* given that it coincided with an important memorial event, the Cairo University centennial. All the observers magnified the golden past, contrasting it with the present state of affairs. While some of the commentators were emphasizing the liberal philanthropic foundation of the Egyptian university, others relied on its present ranking to argue that scientific excellence and innovation should primarily be the responsibility of the State. From the point of view of the champions of the political autonomy of universities, the ranking of Cairo University quite simply represents the result of authoritarian rule that prevents innovation and creates, moreover, a suitable environment for academic corruption. Over and above all else, for these militants there remained the burning issue that global norms were challenging 'national pride'.

Who Shall Evaluate the Evaluators?

We finally examine a third aspect of the spread of a common language. In Egypt as in other parts of the world, a set of notions and practices have been recently developed as a core notion: these are quite heterogeneous, except that they are more or less linked to evaluation. Here too the 'Egyptianization' of international norms has been active in a variety of ways.

As with the ranking of universities, evaluation presumes competition and grading, and presupposes criteria and authority. When it comes to knowledge producers, receivers and transmitters, evaluation reminds us of a whole gamut of recurrent practices, ranging from examinations to peer appraisal. In all cases the assumption is that evaluators are entitled to assume such a position, thanks to their competence and their experience, which give them both credibility and legitimacy. They belong to the same world as those who are being evaluated, and share the same values. So far there is nothing new in that, except that internationalization promotes a new vocabulary as well as new institutional arrangements. Both the vocabulary and the arrangements seem to express the idea that the 'conventional' rules of the game ought not to be in play any more, and this goes for all the components of the educational system, be they teachers, university staff, degrees, curricula, as well as schools and universities. At all these levels, terms like 'accreditation', 'quality assessment', and 'benchmarking' seem to refer to a unique process which is 'evaluation', while evaluators are no longer masters or peers, but rather external managers. They are supposedly more competent, more objective, less corrupt and, moreover, less marked by professional *habitus* and corporatist interest—factors often considered to be the culprits that prevent positive change. Implementing external evaluation presumes a preliminary phase, namely internal evaluation. This aims to involve 'knowledge workers' in their self-reform, establishing so-called horizontal relationships between the two parties. Taken together, these two steps are expected to guarantee objectivity. The latter is often expressed in quantified results.

How do these factors relate to each other? In Egypt, the quality assessment trend in education plays a central role in the indigenization of the global agenda. It has an impact both on the norms embraced, and on the institutions created to express these norms. It moreover concerns not just the higher education sector, but the pre-university education sector as well. The year 2007 witnessed the creation of the National Authority for Quality Assurance and Accreditation of Education (NAQAAE).[15] Within the framework of HEEP mentioned earlier, a Quality Assurance and Accreditation Project (QAAP) aimed to implement the national agency and to prepare the higher education establishments for the new prerequisites. Here also, and as stated before concerning universities ranking, the aim is to allow a kind of control on educational services and to guarantee equivalence between degrees. Quality assessment and certification in the realm of education is equally sustained by the idea of an open education market, where students/consumers make their choice.

It is worth mentioning that when this system emerged in the United Sates in the first years of the 20th century, the idea was to protect students (El Khawas, 2001). As Evans (2000) notes, "Education was among the functions not specifically expressed as a federal responsibility ... Education in the US primarily has been a local, state or private function, not a federal one. Against this backdrop emerged a system of accreditation as a form of self-regulation of higher education" (p. 12). Almost a century after the emergence of independent agencies, their numerous promoters—including UNESCO, World Bank, and the OECD—succeeded in spreading the concept. Such independent evaluation agencies can be private, national or regional. An example of the latter can be found across Europe, with the Bologna process facilitating the development of a coherent and unified system for European citizens moving from one EU member state to another.

NAQAAE, on its part, is an autonomous body reporting to Egypt's Prime Minister and the Parliament. As is to be expected, the Egyptian 'national authority' follows the trans-national recipe. However local debates and micro-effects deserve attention. They remind us of the way international norms are modified when translated to specific contexts.

NAQAAE's sphere of competence covers the entire education and higher education system, including al-Azhar and the technical education sector. Accreditation of more than 50,000 establishments is to be done periodically every five years: the ritual of the reviewers' visit has been established, and when NAQAAE paid its first visit to a school, it was reported by the media as a kind of national celebration. As for higher education, NAQAAE is still organizing the accreditation protocols.

In Egypt, there are national curricula and national textbooks. Pre-university education is mainly public. The education system is highly centralized, with the vast majority of students relying on the public school system. The State determines budgets, credentials, targeted enrolment rates, classrooms size, public examinations, and even school building design. The State, as a political authority, used to be the principal if not the sole accreditation agency. In such a context, what would/could the aims of NAQAAE be? Who should be accredited by whom?

In the first place, independent evaluation and accreditation agencies seem to give substance to the notion of educational establishments as independent units. This seems to be both a pre-condition and an outcome. We are therefore far from the logic of national reform. We are also entering into another logic when it comes to the delegation of competence and expertise. Independent evaluation and accreditation agencies seem to usurp the competence of over a million civil servants employed by the Ministry of Education, who were previously entitled to inspect, to define excellence, and to up-grade and to sanction. This is certainly what at least a good number of schoolteachers and inspectors seem to have felt. Conflicts of interests and views did occur, but these were not between schools and evaluators as much as between officials of the Ministry and the NAQAAE. We should add that in Egypt, as in other countries, evaluation through (or for) accreditation is based on a harsh and under-analyzed distinction between institutional capacities and educational effectiveness. It seems that such a distinction misses precisely the point, when it comes to mass education. Most importantly and as noted by several observers, the accreditation of schools, as independent establishments, could mean another type of allocation of public resources. It may constitute the prelude for restrictions on free education but consequences are still uncertain. According to a university professor quoted by a newspaper, quality, assurance and accreditation issues may be compared to "a blind man searching for an imaginary black cat in a dark room."[16]

Conclusion

We started this investigation by referring to the internationalization of knowledge in the Middle Ages. Our aim was to characterize knowledge transfer in contemporary times. Seeking knowledge about knowledge, we have tried to identify and analyze the adoption of a globalized agenda for educational reform in Egypt. Our hypothesis was that the adoption of a common language operates as a way to cope with internationalization. It was examined first by referring to a draft law concerning higher education organization and the way it fits with international agencies' recommendations and ongoing reform project. We then identified the main features of the Egyptian debate over the ranking of universities, and the political usage made of this exercise. Quality assessment and accreditation trends were finally examined via the creation of an independent authority. In the three examples, it seems clear that change is related to the adoption of a global agenda. However it seems equally clear that a relatively indigenized recipe is applied, producing its own dynamics, unintended effects and resistance.

Neither pure imposition nor conspiracy can explain the adoption of the global agenda in a country like Egypt. Available funds can surely create the opportunity, but common language adoption is both a precondition and an outcome. And 'being part of the world' as an argument and a legitimate political aspiration should be taken seriously.

There remains the question about the social costs, the priorities and an eventual division of work on the global level and its effects on the spread of knowledge. The interrelation between power and knowledge is not uneven in itself. Its neoliberal actualization has to be questioned.

Looking back again to the nineteenth-century educational reforms, and the similarities between empires in this respect: one may wonder about the contemporary global educational agenda. Fast forward two centuries, and the question is: what kind of new world order should we expect?

Notes

1 Recently this whole debate was raised again when Sylvain Gouguenheim argued that Arabs transmitted nothing and that Christian Europe found its own ways to Greek philosophy (Gouguenheim, 2008). Refer to the counter-critique by Büttgen et al., 2009. Refer to Lebjowicz, 2009.
2 'Foreigners in Egyptian Universities', Cairo, March 2009—a conference organized by the Supreme Council for Culture and Cairo University Centre for Scientific Heritage.

3 On this movement, see El Sadda, H., 'Resistance as a prerequisite for reform', *Al-Ahram Weekly*, 21–27 September 2006.
4 *Al-Badil* daily newspaper 17 December 2008. (In Arabic.)
5 One may wonder if the construction Education vs. Higher Education could be challenged. For the moment, 'Education for All' and 'knowledge society' are two separate realms.
6 This is particularly true for the creative public/private mix. Providing that they can pay the required fees, students may have access to 'departments of excellence' in some public universities.
7 It is worth observing the division of labour between different agencies, and the 'style' in which they carry out their work (e.g. UNESCO versus World Bank).
8 See the HEEPF website at http://www.heepf.org.eg
9 There are possibly parallels here with the use of foreign expertise in the field of agricultural politics (Mitchell, 2002).
10 *Al-Masry Al-Youm*, daily newspaper, 10 March 2009 (special issue on 9th March Mouvement).
11 *Al-Ahram*, daily newspaper, 12 December 2006.
12 *Al-Masry Al-Youm*, daily newspaper, 10 March 2009 (special issue on 9th March Mouvement).
13 As in other parts of the world, even the industrialized one, there is a striking consistency between agendas and between opposition movements as well, even when higher education 'objective' conditions are different.
14 For instance, one of the allegations for the re-structuring of research and higher education in France was the negative ranking that the universities obtained on the Shanghai scale. At the same time, authorities expressed their interest in having the universities ranked on a European scale, perceived as more valid. A report by the French Senate recommended caution, suggesting that there should not be a sole reliance on the Shanghai ranking when evaluating French universities (Bourdin, 2008).
15 http://www.naqaae.org/pre/
16 *Al-Ahram* daily newspaper, 7 April 2009.

References

Bourdin, J. (2008). *Challenging higher education rankings. An information report.* Paris: Senate Delegation for Planning. (In French.)
Büttgen, Ph. *et al.* (Eds) (2009). *Les Grecs, les Arabes et nous. Enquête sur l'islamophobie savante.* Paris: Fayard.
Colclough, C. (1991). Who should learn to pay? An assessment of neoliberal approach to education policy. In C. Colclough and J. Manor (Eds.) *States or market? Neo-liberalism and the development policy debate.* Oxford: Clarendon Press.
El-Khawas, E. (2001). Accreditation in the United States: Origins, development and future prospects. Retrieved May 30, 2009 from http://unesdoc.unesco.org/images/0,012/001292/129295e.pdf
Evans, P. P. (2000). Accreditation in the United States: Achieving quality in education. Third European Symposium of Public Health, Zurich, Switzerland, Feb. 3–4, 2000.
Fortna, B. (2002). *Imperial classroom: Islam, the state, and education in the Late Ottoman Empire.* New York: Oxford University Press.
Gibbons, M., Limoges, C., Novotny, H., Schwartwman, S., Scott, P., & Trow, M. (1994). *The new production of knowledge: The dynamics of science and research in contemporary societies.* London: Sage.

Gouguenheim, S. (2008). *Aristotle at Saint Michel's Monastery: The Greek roots of Christian Europe*. Paris: Seuil. (In French.)

Kamal, H., Guindy, G., and Abu Bakr, R. (n.d.). Note on the quality assessment unit, Faculty of Arts. http://www.march9online.net/ (In Arabic.)

Koschtall, F. (2005). Democracy reversed. The public policies arena in Egypt and Morocco. 8th Congress of the French Association for Political Sciences. Retrieved May 30, 2009 from http://sites.univ-lyon2.fr/congres-afsp/article.php3?id_article=194. (In French.)

Le Goff, J. (1985). *Intellectuals in the Middle Ages*. Paris: Seuil. (In French.)

Lejbowicz, M. (Ed.) (2009). *L'Islam médiéval en terres chrétiennes: Science et théologie*. Paris: Presses Universitaires du Septentrion.

de Libera, A. (1991). *Thinking in the Middle Ages*. Paris: Seuil. (In French.)

Liu, N. C. (2009). The story of academic rankings. *International Higher Education, 54* (Winter). Retrieved May 30, 2009 from http://www.bc.edu/bc_org/avp/soe/cihe/newsletter/Number54/p2_Liu.htm

Mazawi, A. E. (2005). Contrasting perspectives on higher education governance in the Arab States. *Higher Education: Handbook of Theory and Research, 20*, 133–189.

Mazawi, A. E. (2007). 'Knowledge society' or work as 'spectacle'? Education for work and the prospects of social transformation in Arab societies. In L. Farrel & T. Fenwick (Eds.) *Educating the global workforce: Knowledge, knowledge work and knowledge workers* (pp. 251–267). London: Routledge.

Meyer, J., and Rowan, B. (1977). Institutionalized organizations: Formal structure as myth and ceremony. *American Journal of Sociology, 83*(2), 340–363.

Mitchell, T. (2002). *Rule of experts: Egypt, techno-politics, modernity*. Berkeley, CA: University of California Press.

Musselin, C. (2008). Higher education: Towards an international market? *Critique Internationale, 39* (April–June), 13–24 (In French.)

Shanghai Jiao Tong University. (2008). Academic ranking of world universities. Retrieved May 30, 2009 from http://www.arwu.org/

Newspapers

Al-Ahram Weekly
Al-Ahram
Al-Badil
Al-Masry Al-Youm

18 Arab Youth, Education, and Satellite Broadcasting

Imad N. K. Karam

Introduction

This chapter explores the complex intersections between Arab youth, satellite broadcasting and informal education in the Arab region, with particular focus on the extent to which youth favourite television programmes act as sources of cultural and moral education. Informal education is a lifelong process within which the individual acquires attitudes, values, skills and knowledge from his/her closest surroundings including family, work, leisure, and the mass media (Guseva and Kravale, 2006). In this chapter, informal education refers to the learning and acquisition of knowledge, information, values, behaviour and lifestyles associated with young people's interaction with and experience of satellite television.

Contrary to arguments in the Arab public discourse[1] that youth's exposure to satellite television, and especially entertainment programmes, is 'corrupting' and at best 'bad education', this chapter argues that satellite broadcasting is an important source of informal education for youth. It provides them with opportunities to learn and enhance their knowledge about many issues whether political, social, economic, or cultural, and thus, contributes to their intellectual enrichment, personal development and self-esteem. The Arab public discourse, which is dominated by the elder generation, is filled with warnings that youth consumption of television is passive in nature, and that young people are merely absorbing materials they are offered (Amin, 2000; Abaza, 2001; Al-Fawi, 2001; Jum'a and Al-Shawāf, 2005). Concerns revolve around issues which might affect the formation of their identity in a negative way – in particular relating to what is seen as economic affluence, moral permissiveness, corruption, and a reduced sense of Arab cultural identity.

However, this chapter argues that youth responses to television involve interpreting what they see, not just absorbing the contents offered. In this, I agree with Giddens (1993) that "TV watching, even of trivial programmes, is not an inherently low-level intellectual activity; that young people 'read' programmes by relating them to other systems of meaning in their everyday lives" (p. 451). The chapter reveals that youths acknowledge the influence satellite television has on their lifestyle, values, and behaviour, and consider it is necessary for their education and personal development. This is seen either as a positive force (wanting to emulate) or negative (rejection of what is portrayed on screen). Either way, the data collected show a conscious rather than passive viewing, which leads to the conclusion that youth are an active audience, critically assessing the programmes on offer. They also contend that programmes provide them with access to information and experiences that can contribute to their learning and therefore help build their value-system and lifestyle in general, even more than do the school or the home.

In the developing world youth is a stage of life that has only recently begun to receive focused attention, mainly because of high demographic rates in this sector of the population, and consequently the latter's political importance (Lloyd, 2005: 1). The use and meaning of the terms 'young people' and 'youth' vary around the world, depending on political, economic and socio-cultural context. Also, sociologists and psychologists have different opinions in determining the characteristics of this stage and its length. Yet, it is generally agreed to be the stage where the most significant changes in youths' interests, social behaviour and tendency to freedom and individuality occur (Al-Askary, 2001). In this chapter, individuals aged between 16 and 27 years old have been interviewed to probe youth engagement with media in Arab society.

The study of the role of the media in youth education is not devoid of problems. The complexity of the process involved in media consumption makes it more difficult to methodologically measure the effect of media on youth education. Neither large-scale surveys nor detailed experiments replicate or reflect that actual experience of viewing and reading (Street, 2001: 93). It is also very difficult to separate the influence of media from all other social, psychological and educational factors involved in the formation of personality. It is my view that inadequacies inherent in audience studies analysis are due to the fact that media stimuli routinely interact with other social stimuli. Disentangling these multiple influences is extremely difficult and as a result clear evidence of direct media influence is difficult to obtain (Croteau and Hoynes, 2000: 242), still less to quantify.

By employing qualitative techniques, this chapter is moving away from inherently inadequate approaches which measure and quantify media effects in an attempt to disentangle different media influences, towards an ethnography of discourse, of attitudes, and opinions as well as perceptions of youth audiences. Popular media texts such as entertainment programming (reality TV shows, soap operas, movies, music, etc.) were initially approached by researchers throughout the 1980s and early 1990s (cf. Ang, 1991; Hobson, 1982; Morley, 1980) as sites in which ideological discourses around class, gender, race and power were produced, organized and negotiated (Tincknell and Raghuram, 2002: 200). In doing so, the agency involved in the sense-making processes that audiences bring to their understanding of textual meaning was emphasized. Thus, audiences were seen as active agents, not passive subjects, in their consumption and enjoyment of popular texts, and the process of understanding was one of negotiation rather than imposition (ibid.).

To explore selective aspects of the above issues, research was undertaken between 2005 and 2008 amongst a cross-section of Arab youth in Jordan, Egypt, United Arab Emirates and Palestine. The main method of data collection was focus group interviews. Twelve focus group interviews (totalling 86 participants in mixed and non-mixed gender groups and numbering on average seven participants in each) were conducted with young Arabs in the focal countries. This is both an ample and still a manageable size for qualitative research. While representativeness is not an objective in qualitative research, when making a generalization about Arab youth it is important to aim for a fair representation of variation within the Arab population. Therefore, care was taken to choose equal numbers from both sexes, as well as informants from a mixture of socio-economic groups, such as the seven young people from the poorer Cairene neighbourhood of Manshiet Nasser.[2] Participants were randomly selected by using the snowballing technique. The chapter offers some analyses of the discourses underlying the aspirations of Arab youth and their views on media and education.

Arab Youth and Satellite Viewing

'Our youth are wandering in life without finding anyone to hear them. They are surrounded by orders and lists of forbidden things from all directions. They have no clear channels to express themselves and how they feel. They feel excluded from decision-making and dialogue. Information channels are also limited for them.

(Bibars, 2004)

In the Arab world concern has been growing for some time over the current conditions and future of Arab youth who are being marginalized and alienated by economic and social changes and seduced by external values such as Western pop culture. In her study of Saudi youth, Yamani (2000) addressed the complexity of the situation, arguing that youth suffer a sense of incoherence and dislocation: "The new generation has grown up in a complex, confusing and rapidly changing world. They have to operate in a globalized economy, but want the certainties of a localized culture" (p. 51). Similarly, Meijer (2000) argues that Arab youth are torn between trying to keep up with modernization and global culture on the one hand and being seen as 'Western' on the other hand.

Arab youth constitute the largest segment of society in the Arab world due to falling infant mortality and high fertility, making them proportionally the largest cohort in Arab history (Al-Ghaffar, 2005). But although demographically the most important group, they experience particular disadvantages in the Arab world because of their position in a strongly traditional and patriarchal system. Furthermore, their weak social status is exacerbated by economic reliance on older generations through high unemployment rates.[3] These factors make 'normal aspirations' such as marrying and setting-up a home, near impossible. In view of their minimal social, political, and economic participation, it is hardly surprising that many reports indicate a growing sense of alienation felt by Arab youth in direct correlation to their declining social, economic and political chances (Meijer, 2000; Al-Askary, 2001; Bibars, 2004). They are a highly marginalized section of society and, although everybody talks about them and readily gives them advice, no one appears willing or able to allow them a 'voice'. This includes the media, which youths look up to as a forum of self-expression and a voice.

The mass media are the most important agents for the public diffusion of knowledge, yet Arab countries have lower information media to population ratios (number of newspapers, radio and televisions per 1,000 people) compared with the world average (UNDP, 2004). In most Arab countries, the media operate in an environment that sharply restricts freedom of expression and opinion. Most media institutions are state owned, particularly radio and television. However, over the last decade or so some private satellite channels have started to contest the monopoly of state channels over the broadcast media. The most important characteristics of this new medium are its ability to reach audiences beyond national boundaries and also that it broadcasts in Arabic, thereby addressing the largest segment of the Arab audience (ibid.).

The increasing influence of satellite television is probably the single most important development in the Arab media of the past fifteen years. Virtually every household now possesses a TV set and most Arab homes receive satellite broadcasting (Karam, 2005: 975). Satellite broadcasting, moreover, is central to youths' lives and provides many necessary information services as well as offering possibilities for self-learning, self-enlightenment and entertainment. But it has also triggered a moral panic and provided a focus for the usual fears about youth with ample material for concern. This is not only because the new medium crosses national boundaries and has the ability to carry programmes that are not controlled by national authorities, but also because it has proved to be pervasive and very popular amongst audiences.

Concern about the negative impact of the media on young people has a very long history. Buckingham (1998) cites the Greek philosopher Plato as proposing to ban dramatic poets from his ideal republic "for fear that their stories about the immoral antics of the gods would influence impressionable young minds". In a similar vein today, young viewers are seen to be inherently vulnerable to television which has the "... irresistible ability to 'brainwash' and 'narcotize' them, drawing them away from other, more worthwhile activities and influences" (p. 133). Arab public discourse is replete with such sentiments that exemplify Buckingham's theory: young people's relationship with television is perceived as a "fundamentally negative and damaging element in their lives" (p. 132). Al-Shuaibi[4] (2006) for example argues that Arab satellite broadcasting is "making coordinated attempts to eclipse its cultural programming and contribute to the deterioration of public taste by showing mindless plays, distasteful songs and trivial talk shows" (p. 154). Nonetheless, Arab satellite broadcasting offers the potential to be a powerful and uncensored (or at least not State-controlled) channel of informal education for youths. Therefore, how satellite television speaks to and about them is of manifest importance. The special significance of the relationship between Arab satellite broadcasting and Arab youth lies in two other factors. Firstly, Arab youth spend many hours per day watching television, most of it beamed by satellite (Fakhro, 2006). This is because they have plenty of free time because they are either jobless or still at school.

Moreover, due to Arab society cultural norms, youth – and especially girls – tend to be home-based. Secondly, Arab youth tend to be less resistant to messages received via satellite channels than they are to messages coming from state television, school or from the family (Fakhro, 2006; Karam, 2007). This is linked to the fact that many youths feel that they have no voice at home, at school or on state television and therefore are negative towards them and find the messages coming from them didactic and out of touch with their reality. This will be further explored in the subsequent sections.

Like young people elsewhere, Arab youth are exposed to and consume many types of media from traditional sources such as newspapers, magazines, radio and national television, to less traditional forms of media and communications such as satellite television, mobile phones and the Internet. While, the Internet penetration rate is still very low in the Arab world (Internet World Stats, 2008),[5] Arab satellite broadcasting seems to be the most popular among young viewers. Arab youth appear to spend a high proportion of their free time – outside school or work obligations – watching Arab satellite broadcasts (Karam, 2007). My research among 16–27 year-olds in Egypt, Jordan, the United Arab Emirates and Palestine reveals that 97 per cent of young people watch television – many for several hours a day. Over half of the respondents to my questionnaire said they watched television for up to three hours a day during a typical school or work day;[6] 17 per cent said they watched four to six hours a day; 7 per cent said they watched television for more than six hours a day. Fewer than a quarter (24 per cent) said they watched television for less than one hour a day.

Youth viewing time is nevertheless considered excessive by education specialists and raises concerns. Fakhro (2006), for example, warns that students who spend more time per day watching television than in the classroom will not practise the methods that the school teaches them. Rather, they will "practice the superficial and hasty methods that the audio-visual media tend to inculcate" (p. 144). However, this apparent 'clash' as expressed so often in Arab discourse[7] between the 'accepted' formal avenues of education and the 'unaccepted' informal avenues of learning, is in reality far less noticeable upon deeper examination. The anti-entertainment discourses are indicative of a moral panic and a crisis of culture and values. Satellite technology, naturally, represents a facet of modernity and therefore figures at a deeper level in discussions pertaining to the Arab present and future cultural identity. It has become a target figure in the 'crisis of culture' which certain commentators associate with the "structural economic and … political hegemony of the Arab world by the Western world" (Abu-Rabi', 2004: xvi).

Some educators fear that exposure to foreign symbols through satellite television could weaken allegiance to and eventually replace existing (identity) symbols. This assumption has been expressed in political, educational, cultural, and religious circles in all Arab countries. Most of the critics of Arab satellite television refer to the increasing number of youth who consume 'Western' media (as well as Western food and clothes) as being 'Western' or becoming 'Westernized'. Either way, the concept of a stagnant identity is all the more unreasonable to maintain in the light of today's multi-cultural exchanges (Hall, 1997). Identity, as Parekh (1997) notes, is never entirely coherent "since a culture evolves over time, is a precipitate of diverse influences, and has no co-ordinating authority" (p. 166). In this regard, what Fakhro and others do not mention are the reasons why Arab youth feel the need to spend most of their viewing time watching television and what they derive from it. The young people interviewed contend that their main intention is to get away from their daily burdens through watching entertainment programmes (Karam, 2007). However, they seem to find it also educative in general, and especially when it comes to learning about other people's experiences and cultures.

The Media as a Venue for Informal Education

The role of the media as a venue for informal education for young people is an aspect which has so far largely been neglected in our understanding of education and youth in the Arab region. Most of the research into the relationship between media and education in the Arab world has focused on the clash or contradiction between the two fields (see for example Fakhro, 2006). With the spread of satellite broadcasting in the Arab region, the role of television as a vehicle for public information and education has been increasing. Al-Shuaibi (2006) recognizes that television has become "the undisputed school for public education ... open around the clock" (p. 153). Likewise, Al-Shiryan (2006) notes that the mass media in the United States, in its totality, is the most important means of conveying and spreading culture, and that it has "replaced the school, church and family in influencing people, teaching them modes of behaviour and the norms that support or justify this behaviour" (p. 151).

However, this aspect of the media is looked at with a critical and concerned eye in the Arab world. Al-Shuaibi (2006) warns that:

> Television ... can help either to support existing value systems or to shatter cultural and value barriers. This fact imposes a massive responsibility on the media, not only in educating children and youngsters, but in educating society as a whole. (p. 153)

In a conference in 2005 in Abu Dhabi organized by the Emirates Centre for Strategic Studies and Research, Bahrain's former Minister of Education, Dr Ali Mohammed Fakhro, warned that "media values are standing against education values"; that "what is emphasized through the media can eventually turn into culture".[8] Dr Fakhro expressed concern that satellite channels are creating new role-models who are mainly 'artists and sporties'. Naturally, the mass media, especially television, are often associated with entertainment, which is seen as rather marginal to most people's lives. Giddens (1993) argues that such a view is quite misleading since even entertainment on television has a wide-ranging influence over people's experience. "This is not just because they affect our attitudes in specific ways, but because they are the *means of access* to the knowledge on which many social activities depend" (Giddens, 1993: 446).

This power of the media to shape young people's minds and value systems is recognized in the Arab public discourse, but in a negative way. For example, Jum'a and Al-Shawwāf (2005) believe that, "TV has the power to build and equally destroy youth as it invades the minds and thoughts of the youth and influences their beliefs, morals, values, and principles, thus potentially implanting an alien culture". The authors of "Youth: the problems and the solutions", also argue that "there is a psychological struggle in youth between the original values (*al-qiyam al-asīlah*) that come from school and society and the cheap values (*al-qiyam al-hābitah*) that come from the media and television in particular" (p. 192). The nefarious results of TV in the authors' opinions are manifold but those of a sexual nature are the most elaborated on, such that: "Satellite television has done more damage in five years than terrestrial television has in 30 years" (p. 329). Yet, what critics seem to consider less frequently when it comes to satellite broadcasting is its potential for positive change and opportunities to make young people aware of social issues that affect them and to educate them about their rights and responsibilities (Geary *et al.*, 2005). Moreover, it is very important that we examine why youth find satellite television attractive and what gratification and benefits they derive from its content.

Most Arab youth seem to be watching television primarily for entertainment purposes rather than for direct information or knowledge (formal education). They seem to watch with the intent of entertaining themselves and any subsequent educational benefit is therefore unintentional. Entertainment programmes such as movies, drama, talk shows, and reality TV, carry inherited values and thus have the ability to influence young people's behaviour and lifestyles. When probed deeper in the focus groups, most youths showed themselves to be active viewers and demonstrated a sense of self-awareness in relation to the programmes they watched as well as their analysis. The questionnaire results show that 65.7 per cent of the respondents watch television for entertainment and for passing time/"escaping reality"; 21.3 per cent cited direct information or knowledge; and only 13 per cent cited both entertainment and information as their main reason for watching television. Similar results were reflected in the kinds of programmes watched by males and females: 27.1 per cent of the respondents said that movies were the programmes they watched most on television; 19.8 per cent watched mostly news; 41.1 per cent enjoyed 'music and singing' and other programmes while only about 12 per cent cited religious programmes as their favourites.

Moreover, news featured more prominently in Jordanian and Palestinian youth viewing than in the Emirates and Egypt where youths expressed a lack of interest in the news. They clarified that they flick to the news to get the headlines and maybe the main news and then return to entertainment. They may come back to the news at the head of the hour, but most of their viewing time is spent watching entertainment channels. In the Emirates, youths talked of being bored with the news and showed more interest in entertainment, while in Egypt they talked of having enough (negative) news at home and more news will "suffocate" them. For example, in a focus group discussion in Egypt, Ahmed (19 m.) said: "We already feel depressed and watching the news, which is all about killing, will make us even more so."[9] In another group, in Egypt, Shady (20 m.) explained youth's lack of interest in the news in the following words: "It is because we sometimes feel suffocated. We escape from and try to avoid news programmes as they give us the sense that we are suffocating."[10]

In the Emirates, young people talked of being 'pushed away' from politics. When asked why young people seem uninterested in news and current affairs, I was told repeatedly that the reason lies in the lack of freedom of speech. Mustafa (19 m.), one of the participants, explained: "when young people watch news, which is largely about the killing of fellow Arabs, they feel involved. Yet, when they try to protest, they get harassed by the authorities". He added:

> We do not have the freedom of expression to demonstrate freely to support the Palestinians or to protest against the war in Iraq. For example, in this country when the [Palestinian] intifada broke out and we all went on a demonstration, the guys who were in the first rows of the demonstration were taken in by the intelligence service … We cannot even talk politics in cafés.[11]

Some felt helpless and hopeless that their situation would ever change or the possibility that political leaders would do anything about it. It is because they see existing leaders as part of the problem rather than the solution that their feelings tend towards frustration or indifference. Ibrahim (20 m.) said:

> If we feel that there is any hope, then we would follow the news and get involved, but there is no hope. So, whether we watch or not watch it is not going to make a difference. So, when hope is lost, we start looking for entertainment.[12]

Clearly, this sense of restriction in public sphere participation is leading to a lack of interest in politics and public affairs. Similar feelings were shared by participants in another focus group who expressed it as follows:

> The problem is that the youth have no influence on politics in their own country and society; I mean they are not allowed to be influential or make a difference. They are only allowed to watch and observe rather than participate in politics. And since you will be seeing the same scene time and again, you get tired and fed up, so you stop watching. So, if youth had the kind of influence we are talking about, for example, if young people could talk freely to rulers or any other officials, then everything would be different. (Hassan, 18 m.)

> No one is interested in attracting young people to politics. On the contrary they push you away from it. And if you do talk politics, then you may be in trouble. But they occupy you with singing and music. They give you what you like: nice and sexy girls. And if you vote on a TV programme you may win. (Zakaria, 20 m.)

This lack of interest in the news is also linked to many of the youths feeling that they have had enough. Participants in the focus groups noted that their lives are serious enough already without trying to look for more serious matters from television. Entertainment, they said, gave them the chance to forget about their problems. Nada (18 f.), from a middle-class family in Cairo, said in a group discussion in Egypt that television helped her to 'escape from her problems'. She explained: "Had it not been for TV, my problems would stare me in the face all the time. TV gives me the chance to break away from my problems."[13] Youth concerns and problems revolve around issues such as looking for jobs, challenges in the relationship with parents and family, difficulties to get married, etc.

Television and Youth Concerns

Many of the youth interviewed felt that television does not help them address or deal with the problems and concerns which they face. Heba (19 f.) said that there were no television channels that aimed at addressing young people's problems.[14] Ali (27 m.), who works for Jordanian television, said that television does sometimes talk about young people's problems, but is never able to offer solutions.[15] Rita (20 f.) said that there were certain TV programmes that dealt with youth and which represent young people, but there were no channels that are exclusively about or for youths.[16]

Some participants even disapproved of programmes supposedly aimed at young people, expressing a concern with regards to the corruption of morals. Farah (21 m.) felt that youth's television programmes were either corrupting or irrelevant:

> There are many young people's programmes that are corrupting, but still very popular among youth, but there is not a single programme that is at the same time not corrupting and still attracts me. They say this programme is for young people: nonsense, I cannot see it, it is very irritating; it's like my grandfather is talking to me ... there is not even one programme that seriously debates young people's problems; well there are some, but they approach the issue from the viewpoint of the elderly not of young people.[17]

Saba (24 f.) agrees that the supposed programmes for young people are in effect for the elderly: "Even programmes like *Sirah wa Infitāhāt*[18] are not about young people though they have aired two or three episodes on youth issues". Saba went on to say:

> Even when they invite a psychiatrist to respond to young people's problems, I sometimes wish I could be there to tell him how wrong he is. This doctor does not know anything about what's going through a young person's head, but is rather psychoanalysing himself.[19]

Hana (21 f.) agreed and said that there were no TV programmes that deal with the real concerns of young people.[20] However, other participants disagreed and argued that *Sirah wa Infitāhāt* was very useful to young people (see quote from Nidal in the subsequent section). In Egypt, Randa (22 f.) complained about the lack of TV shows that invite politicians and allow the public to interact with them: "I never saw a programme where young people talk to political leaders. There was once a programme here in Egypt where students were questioning [former US secretary of State] Colin Powell through a video conference link. This was the only time I actually saw young people questioning a political leader."[21]

Dina (18 f.) said that all political programmes and economic programmes on television only involve older people: "I never saw a political programme with young people sitting talking and discussing".[22] Hesa (19 f.) added that young people are noticeably absent when the topic is political: "you do not see young people on a political programme – unless they have been involved in some sort of crisis – then they'd have to interview that person".

Rana (22 f.) felt that young people are excluded from decision-making and their opinion is rarely asked for: "They do not consider it's worth knowing our opinion on everything that is going on." Rana added that no single opinion was authoritative. She explained: "They only want to take the opinion of leaders – people who can have an effect on society, culture or the economy. The opinion of average working class people are hardly seen or heard on television, except in surveys. An average working class person can be seen on television only if he has done something significant like murdering his wife or child."[23]

However, not all the comments about Arab television programmes made by focus group members were negative. Some expressed that they were able to relate positively to some of the programmes in relation to their daily lives, and in particular emotional and spiritual needs. Kader (20 m.) from the Emirates commented that, "TV has programmes and shows that cover all topics and there are TV series that deal with relationships and help address young people's emotional problems".[24] An 18-year-old female from Jordan commented in the questionnaire: "Young people watch TV to kill time, but there are shows that help solve young people's emotional problems." Similarly, another 18-year-old female from Egypt wrote: "Sometimes, television helps to escape from problems. On the other hand it gives solutions in an indirect way." This suggests a learning process whereby the youth find drama and talk shows helpful in suggesting ways of dealing with certain issues. Maha (22 f.) from the Emirates thought the onus was on young people to take advantage of the assistance offered: "when watched, social talk shows do give suggestions to young people on how to solve problems they face, but unfortunately teenage youth prefer singing shows".[25]

Although many young people complained that television was not particularly helpful in addressing their concerns and offering them a voice, the interviews revealed that some found in certain television programmes a forum in which to explore emotions, and in particular, to learn about human relationships, a facet which is neglected by formal education which focuses on 'factual' learning.

Television as a Source of Cultural Education

Entertainment programmes which are heavily criticized as alien corrupting forces are considered by youth to be an essential source of cultural education. Most of those interviewed felt that television played an important role as a tool of self-learning and education. When asked if they believed that watching TV influenced their lives in general, the majority of the questionnaire respondents in the different countries (60–70 per cent) felt that this was the case. Moreover, a higher percentage of youth respondents in each country believed that television influences youth behaviour and culture.

These quantitative findings were confirmed in the focus groups: a majority of Arab youths affirmed television's influence on their personal development, culture and behaviour. Noticeably within these groups, there was a tendency to believe that younger youths were more susceptible to television's influence than themselves. For example, only 62.9 per cent of Emiratis acknowledged that TV influenced their lives, and yet almost all of that same group (96.2 per cent) also agreed that TV influences youth in general.

A further structured question revealed a majority positive outlook for TV's role in learning about other societies and cultures. Over 80 per cent of the respondents felt that what they watched on TV helped them learn more about other societies and cultures. This greater access and exposure to other societies and cultures which we witness among contemporary youth, has in part been instigated and facilitated by satellite television. More than ever, Arab youth feel the need to connect with the outside world and also to follow youth elsewhere in the Arab region through a common pan-Arab output. Many of the young people interviewed felt that television provides them with an opportunity to learn about other peoples, cultures and societies. In a focus group in Jordan, Musa (22 m.) commented that satellite television taught what other Arab cities look like: "The extensive coverage of the recent events in Lebanon, for example, made us learn about what the streets of Beirut look like." Musa added that satellite television "made us learn more about countries like Afghanistan. We started learning and seeing things about countries we had never seen or heard of."[26]

In another focus group discussion in Jordan, Ahmed (25 m.) commented that television was very useful and it was the "biggest blessing our people and society could have had". He argued that television "brings to you the whole world while you are sitting in the comfort of your living room". [27] In the same group, Nidal (25 m.), added that some television programmes are relevant to young people's lives:

> There are many programmes that have tackled young people's concerns and issues such as Zafen Kouyoumdjian's *Sirah wa Infitāhāt*. The show discusses issues particularly pertinent or of interest to young people such as drugs and marriage. *Zafen* once discussed the issue of tattoos. Some people believe tattoos deform the body, others view them as a nice thing, and others have a moral issue with them and disapprove of them. Programmes on drugs are also useful for young people: What are the effects of taking drugs? What does it do to your family? Where could you end up?

In another focus group interview in Jordan, Nada (21 f.) said that a number of TV serials mirrored real and existing social issues and could therefore help to address real-life problems.[28] Jumana (21 f.), a Palestinian female studying in Jordan, agreed with Nada adding that social issues were represented on TV: "Recently they started paying attention to social problems: marriage, divorce, HIV, cancer and even smoking, in a bid to try and raise awareness with the society as a whole and to make people aware of new developments and hazards." She added that "even political programmes try to raise your awareness of politics through political talk shows and programmes ... they offer more than just the news".[29]

It was also argued that entertainment-type programmes which are most heavily criticized in public discourses have more wide-ranging benefits. Some participants found that drama taught them about their own history. For example, participants in a focus group in Palestine and another in the Emirates mentioned a drama *Al-taghriba al-filistīniya*[30] as a show that educated them on how life was in Palestine before the 1948 War. Rola (21 f.) said in a focus group in Jordan that she finds television helpful in teaching her about fashion so that she can even design her own clothes.[31] Nidal (25 m.) said in another focus group in Jordan that singing shows were not all negative: "after all *Super Star* and *Star Academy* are about young people who have an aspiration".[32]

Clearly youths consider their consumption of entertainment as a form of self-learning and education. They learn through entertainment about important issues that they may not necessarily find satisfactory information about or answers to through other avenues. Such issues include the relationship between the sexes and with their parents, drugs, HIV and crime.

Satellite Broadcasting and Moral Education

Another aspect of Arab satellite broadcasting that was received positively in the discussions was religious programming, which is a recent phenomenon and one widely perceived as successful both by young and older viewers alike. Basma (2006) describes religious broadcasting as one the fastest growing programming segments in the Arab World: "And it appears that the battle for hearts and minds is only heating up" (p. 28). Basma quotes market research by Arab Advisors Group which concluded that "piety now shares the spotlight with pop culture as both religious and music video channels grew at a rate of 60 per cent last year".

Religious programmes as a source of moral education were frequently cited by participants in the present study as useful. Many of them referred to religious programmes as the 'main good thing that comes out of Arab TV'. Saleh (18 m.) in the Emirates, said: "Television is generally good and bad. In our case, it is more of the bad than the good. The main good thing I believe is the religious programming."[33]

In Jordan, when asked about good TV programmes for youth, Nada (21 f.) referred to the TV shows of Islamic preacher 'Amr Khaled: "There are good youth programmes such as 'Amr Khaled's: Even though he discusses youth issues from a religious angle, still he's got a good way of addressing youth and dealing with the issues."[34] Nada's comment was corroborated by Sama in Egypt who said that "'Amr Khaled's *Ahbābi* show solves many of our problems. It discusses issues in a good, morally acceptable and youthful way. Many youngsters have been greatly influenced by him."[35]

Ahmed (28 m.), in a focus group in Jordan, said the Iqra' channel[36] was "very good at addressing youth and their issues in addition to the Jordanian Channel 3 which is a youth channel".[37] In the Emirates, Sami (18 m.) said that "there are Sheikhs like 'Amr Khaled and Tareq Alsuwaidan who are knowledgeable and humble. They would like to help heal the society."[38] Dina (18 f.) from Egypt said that she learnt a lot when watching a religious show by 'Amr Khaled about relations between kids and their parents that has helped her in her own relationship with her mother.[39]

Many of the research participants clearly find that the religious programmes have a moral education role. Yet, while television seems to play such a role, enabling them to learn about their own and others' cultures and societies, it is not as effective in providing them with a venue to express themselves, and voice their concerns and aspirations.

Conclusion

The relationship between the fields of education and the media in the Arab world is presented by Arab educators, writers and commentators mainly as one of tension and discord. Many of them are quick to blame popular entertainment programmes on satellite television for many educational and social ills. This position presents education and entertainment as binary opposites, when, as this chapter has shown, the boundaries between them are difficult to establish. The role of the media as a venue for informal education for young people is an aspect which clearly needs to be revisited rather than dismissed as negative.

The Arab public discourse on media, which is dominated by the elder generation, is filled with warnings for youths and especially regarding their consumption of television. These discourses are often not informed by research and/or on close contact with youth. As the chapter has shown, satellite broadcasting is an important source of learning that contributes, in many different ways, to the personal development and intellectual enrichment of Arab youth in as much as it captures their frustrations and aspirations. The criticisms of youth exposure to satellite television are an expression of fear or concern; a sense of moral panic on the part of many educators. This presupposes that the consequences of television for education, culture and identity are straightforward and that young people are merely passively absorbing materials that are offered. It is important that Arab educators reassess their assumptions about youth and the media consumption. In this, they need to take into account youth voices, their needs and aspirations, their self-representation and their view of how the media represents them.

Moreover, the criticisms against satellite television reflect the power inequities and the patriarchal structure of Arab societies where the older generation are keen on keeping control over youth. The school, alongside the family, has traditionally been the centre of social life in the Arab world, where values are transmitted and identities constructed. However, this role has been weakened by the emergence of popular satellite television. The evolution of communications satellite in the Arab World has enabled a large proportion of young Arabs to access and learn about certain aspects of other people's societies and cultures (including other Arab) to an unprecedented scale. Therefore, the current generation of Arab youth is arguably more exposed to other cultures than any previous generation.

This chapter has revealed the multifaceted dimensions of Arab satellite broadcasting in relation to young people's self-learning opportunities. The interviews clearly indicate that television is perceived as a venue of education by youth while being underestimated or seen negatively by many experts. Youths acknowledge the influence satellite television has on their lifestyle, values, and behaviour, and consider it is necessary for their education and personal development. Although they watch primarily for entertainment rather than directly for education or knowledge, when considering what they derive out of this process, television operates as an important source that shapes their knowledge, values and perceptions. The impact of television, and especially entertainment, therefore, goes beyond escapism and into the realm of self-learning and the acquisition of values, behaviour and lifestyles.

The over-riding concern of those youths interviewed, however, is the wish to explore television as one of the avenues of self-expression, learning and education. They would like television to address their 'problems' – that is their location within the broader socio-political contexts in which they act – in ways that involve them and provides solutions. Many felt that satellite television did not help them address or deal with their problems and concerns. To date, Arab satellite broadcasting has largely ignored youth problems, especially those directly related to government, politics and social issues, such as unemployment and under-representation of youth in politics and public affairs. More than a decade and a half after the emergence of this phenomenon, programmes that allow young people to represent themselves to each other and to decision-makers are still lacking. Arab satellite channels have through entertainment programming assured for themselves a strong youth following but in fact, as this research reveals, these same youths look for quality factual programmes that would educate and inform while entertaining.

The views expressed in this chapter have been selected from a cross-section of young people and they clearly indicate that Arab satellite television is playing a significant role as an agent for the public diffusion of knowledge and information. What is striking though is how homogenous in their views the young people from the different countries and different socio-economic background were. Differences between youths in the rich Gulf and the poor of Egypt or those in conflict areas such as Lebanon and Palestine are as wide as the differences between those countries. However, when it came to questions regarding Arab satellite television offerings, the generational gap, Arab society and governments, they seemed to be strikingly converging in their attitudes and aspirations.

Finally, this chapter has opened many avenues for further research which are left unexplored. For example, how does satellite television act as a facilitator of the emergence of 'youth culture' – which is strongly associated in the Arab public discourse with elements of 'Westernization'? What, if any, is the relationship between media informal education and the construction of 'youth culture'? I propose that future research deepens and extends understanding of Arab youth culture in relation to informal and lifelong learning through media, and its relationship with local and global dynamics.

Notes

1 The use of 'public discourse' in this chapter refers to arguments, comments, and opinions expressed in Arab public debates, whether published in books, newspapers, magazines or TV shows.

2 Manshiet Nasser is situated on the rocky slopes of the Mugattam range of hills which form the eastern physical boundary to the city of Cairo. It occupies a space of 1.5 square kilometres predominantly for residential use (Tekçe, Oldham & Shorter, 1993).

3 The overall unemployment rate in the Arab world reached 20 per cent in 2003, of which 60 per cent was among youths. (Source: Middle East News Agency. '20 per cent increase in unemployment in Arab region', 11 July, 2005 [Available in Arabic online at http://www.menareport.com/ar/business/231310.)

4 Director of the Security Awareness Department and Media Advisor of the Community Service Department for Dubai police.

5 Although it is steadily increasing, Internet penetration remains modest in the Arab world. According to the Internet World Stats latest figures, Internet penetration in the Arab countries is 14.22 per cent of the total population, and for the Middle East is 23.3 per cent, which includes Israel (74 per cent) and Iran (34.9 per cent). In comparison, the penetration rate in the European Union area is 60.7 per cent (Internet World Stats).

6 In comparison, the 2007 Television Bureau of Advertising (not-for-profit trade association of America's broadcast television industry) statistics show that American youth spend on average a similar average of 3.21 hours per day watching television.

7 See for example Amin, 2000; Taweela, 2002; Elmessiri, 2005; Jum'a and Al-Shawwāf, 2005.

8 The use of the term 'culture' in this chapter refers to 'the entire or total way of life of people, including a shared social heritage, visions of social reality, value orientations, beliefs, customs, norms, traditions, skills, and the like' (Barakat, 1993: 41).

9 Focus Group (5) Cairo, Egypt March 2005.

10 Focus Group (2) Cairo, Egypt March 2005.

11 Focus Group interview (2), United Arab Emirates, January 2005.

12 Focus Group interview (1), United Arab Emirates, January 2005.

13 Focus Group interview with Egyptian youth (1), August 2004.

14 Focus Group interview (1), Jordan, March, 2005.

15 ibid.

16 ibid.

17 Focus group interview (2), Jordan, March, 2005.

18 Started in November 1999, *Sirah wa Infitāhāt* is a leading Arab talk show on Future Television, Lebanon, hosted by Zaven Kouyoumdjian. According to his website [http://www.zavenonline.com], the chat show is the 'first peak time talk show to speak to the hearts and minds of the young adult audience in the Arab world, bringing people from all over the Arab world to recount their personal experiences and express their innermost feelings on live TV, and bringing society face to face with its taboos and values'.

19 Focus Group interview (2), Jordan, March, 2005.

20 ibid.

21 Focus Group (4), Egypt, February, 2005.

22 ibid.

23 ibid.

24 Focus Group interview (3), United Arab Emirates, January 2005.

25 Focus Group interview (3), United Arab Emirates, January 2005.

26 Focus Group interview (1), Jordan, March, 2005.

27 Focus Group interview (2), Jordan, March, 2005.

28 Focus Group interview (1), Jordan, March, 2005.

29 Focus Group interview (1), Jordan, March, 2005.

30 *Al-taghriba al-filistīniya* is a joint Syrian–Jordanian drama production. The drama centres around the suffering of a Palestinian family during the British Mandate on Palestine in the 1930s and later under the Jewish militias until the 1960s.

31 Focus Group interview (1), Jordan, March, 2005.

32 Focus Group interview (2), Jordan, March, 2005.

33 Focus Group interview 3, United Arab Emirates, January 2005.

34 Focus Group interview (2), Jordan, March 2005.

35 Focus Group (3), Egypt, February, 2005.

36 Iqra', set up in 1998, is the first Arab Islamic satellite channel (Amin, 2000). The Saudi-funded channel is the most popular religious channel according to the website of the Arabic news channel *Al-'Arabiya*. [Competition between the religious channels over veiled female celebrities, *Al-'Arabiya* website: http://www.alarabiya.net/Articles/2006/04/11/22764.html

37 Focus Group interview (1), Jordan, March, 2005.

38 Focus Group interview (2), United Arab Emirates, January 2005.

39 Focus Group (4), Egypt, February, 2005.

References

Abaza, M. (2001). Shopping Malls, Consumer Culture and the Reshaping of Public Space in Egypt. *Theory, Culture & Society*, 18(5): 97–122.

Abu-Rabi', I. (2004). *Contemporary Arab Thought: Studies in Post-1967 Arab Intellectual History*. London: Pluto Press.

Al-Askary, S. (2001). Al-Shabāb al-'arabī wa malāmih thawrah jadīdah [Arab Youth and the Features of a New Revolution]. *Al-'Arabi Magazine,* July, 512. (In Arabic.)

Al-Fawi, A. (2001). Arab Culture in the Age of Globalization. *Al-Ahram Daily*, February 22.

Al-Ghaffar, A. (2005). *Al-shabāb wa sūq al-'amal fi mamlakat Al-Bahrain* [*Youth and the Labor Market in the Kingdom of Bahrain*]. Jam'iyat al-'amal al-watani al-dimukrāti. (In Arabic.)

Al-Shiryan, D. (2006). The Media as a Component of National Culture. In Emirates Center for Strategic Studies and Research (Ed.) *Arab Media in the Information Age* (pp. 149–152). Abu Dhabi: Emirates Center for Strategic Studies and Research.

Al-Shuaibi, A. (2006). The Role of Media: Between Education and Entertainment. In Emirates Center for Strategic Studies and Research (Ed.) *Arab Media in the Information Age* (pp. 153–160). Abu Dhabi: Emirates Center for Strategic Studies and Research.

Amin, G. (2000). *Whatever Happened to the Egyptians: Changes in Egyptian Society from 1950 to the Present*. Cairo: AUC Press.

Ang, I. (1991). *Desperately Seeking the Audience*. London and New York: Routledge.

Barakat, H. (1993). *The Arab World, Society, Culture and State*. Berkeley, CA: University of California Press.

Barakat, H. (2004). *Al-hawiyya: azmat al-hadāthah wa-al-wa'ī al-taqlīdī* [*Identity: The Crisis of Modernity and Traditional Consciousness*]. Beirut: Riyad El-Rayyes Books.

Basma, A. (2006). Religious Broadcasters Avoid Confrontation. *Middle East Broadcasters Journal*, June–July, 27–28.

Bibars, I. (2004). Al-Shabāb wa al wa'i al-siyāsī. [Youth and Political Awareness]. *Al-Ahram Daily,* January 13. (In Arabic.)

Buckingham, D. (1998). Children and Television: A Critical Overview of the Research. In Dickinson, R., Harindranath, R., and Linné, O. (Eds.) *Approaches to Audiences: A Reader*. London: Arnold.

Croteau, D. and Hoynes, W. (2000). *Media Society: Industries, Images, and Audiences* (2nd edn). Thousand Oaks, CA: Pine Forge Press.

Fakhro, A. (2006). Impact of Media on Education: Reality and Ambition. In Emirates Center for Strategic Studies and Research (Ed.) *Arab Media in the Information Age* (pp. 139–148). Abu Dhabi: Emirates Center for Strategic Studies and Research.

Geary, C., Mahler, H., Finger, W. and Shears, K. (2005). Using Global Media to Reach Youth. *Youth Issues Paper, 5.* Family Health International.

Giddens, A. (1993). *Sociology* (2nd edn). London, Polity Press.

Guseva, V. and Kravale, M. (2006) Informal Education of Youth and Inclusive Environment. *Acta Pedagogica Vilnensia,* 16, 40–45.

Hall, S. (1997). The Centrality of Culture: Notes on the Cultural Revolutions of Our Time. In Thompson, K. (Ed.) *Media and Cultural Regulation.* London: Sage Publications.

Internet World Stats. (2009) World Internet Users. Retrieved April 20, 2009 from http://www.internetworldstats.com/stats9.htm.

Jum'a, A. and al-Shawwāf, I. (2005). *Al-shabāb: mushqilāt wa hulūl* [*Youth: Problems and Solutions*] Damascus: Al-Yamāmah. (In Arabic.)

Karam, I. (2005). Book Review, Lila Abu Lughod, *Dramas of Nationhood: The Politics of Television in Egypt. Ethnic and Racial Studies,* 28, 5, 974–975.

Karam, I. (2007). Satellite Television: A Breathing Space for Arab Youth? In Sakr, N. (Ed.) *Arab Media and Political Renewal.* London: I.B. Tauris.

Lloyd, C. (Ed.). (2005). *Growing Up Global: The Changing Transitions to Adulthood in Developing Countries.* Washington, DC: National Academies Press.

Meijer, R. (Ed.). (2000). *Alienation or Integration of Arab Youth: Between Family, State and Street.* Richmond: Curzon.

Parekh, B. (1997). National Culture and Multiculturalism. In Thompson, K. (Ed.) *Media and Cultural Regulation.* London: Sage Publications.

Street, J. (2001). *Mass Media, Politics and Democracy.* London: Palgrave.

Tekçe, B., Oldham, L., & Shorter, F.C.D. (1993). *A Place to Live: Families and Child Health in a Cairo Neighborhood.* Cairo: American University in Cairo Press.

Tincknell, E. and Raghuram, P. (2002). Big Brother: Reconfiguring the 'Active' Audience of Cultural Studies? *European Journal of Cultural Studies,* 5, 199–215.

UNDP. (2004). *Arab Human Development Report 2003: Building a Knowledge Society.* New York: UNDP.

Yamani, M. (2000). *Changed Identities: The Challenge of the New Generation in Saudi Arabia.* London: Royal Institute of International Affairs.

Part V

Geopolitical Predicaments

19 American Dreams of Reinventing the 'Orient'

Digital Democracy and Arab Youth Cultures in a Regional Perspective

Omar El-Khairy

> When it comes to the Arabs, I must admit to an incurable romanticism.
>
> Raphael Patai (1973: i)

Penetrating Native Spaces

The histories of foreign influence in the Middle East have come to be dominated by numerous military interventions. The dominance of hard power has helped mask the equally influential role that 'softer' forms have had on shaping local cultures and societies. The construction of the 'Orient', as what Edward Said called a 'living tableau of queerness', has been ripped from the pages of Goethe, Flaubert and Renan, and is now presented through a new mixture of government, NGO, philanthropic and private flows (Said, 1988: 103). This chapter, therefore, attempts to construct an alternative genealogy of interventions in the Arab region by putting non-militaristic and diplomatic techniques at the heart of the story of influences to shape the character of the contemporary Middle East. The particular role of educational support and training, which is often sold as a benign and benevolent practice, has historically been central to such cultural strategies. This is evident from the growing influence of foreign universities in the Middle East during British and French colonial rule, to the development of philanthropic funds, Fulbright scholarships and the restructuring and re-facultisation of university departments under the auspices of the United States – whose influence in the region has come to replace that of the former colonisers in the post-Cold War era. Moreover, such processes have been considerably affected by today's era of globalisation, with its increasing spread of North American universities across the globe and the more general trend of the privatisation of higher education. These global processes are having a considerable impact on present trends in the development of higher education in the Middle East.

'America's Lost its Groove, But We're America Right!'

British sociologist Anthony Giddens argues that, 'globalisation has something to do with the thesis that we now all live in one world' (Giddens, 1999: 7); a phenomenon he characterises by fundamental changes in the world economy, the communications revolution and global trade in physical commodities, information and currency. Giddens and other theorists are right to stress that the era of the nation-state is over, or at the very least moving towards a slow death. Under contemporary globalisation nations are undoubtedly losing elements of the sovereignty they once took for granted, just as politicians and officials are losing much of their capability to directly influence events. Nevertheless, the problem with such characterisations lies in the predominately triumphant tone of the literature, which promises both an alternative and an improved global political arrangement. Such a celebratory climate has led some to conclude that globalisation is creating a genuinely democratic 'global civil society', carried along by a mixture of economic, technological and cultural imperatives (Kaldor, 2003). Their 'runaway world', however, cannot be so easily described as a series of uncontrollable changes. This would not only serve to ignore histories of colonialism and imperialism that were so crucial to its formation, particularly across the 'developing world', but would also occlude certain institutionalised processes that are carrying forward some of these global transformations today.

A closely related concern is that popular accounts of contemporary globalisation seem inadequate in addressing the ways in which these processes have more specifically provided the infrastructure for America's global hegemony. Thomas Friedman's idea of globalisation as inducing a 'flatter world' is interwoven with the perceived trend that middle classes across the world are increasingly producing and consuming like Americans (Friedman, 2007). However, what goes missing in this narrative is that this 'new society' of complete mobilisation combines in productive union the features of the welfare state and the warfare state – a project of global economic integration as 'benevolent supremacy'. Such an endeavour is not a traditional colonial project, but rather a pursuit of hegemony through policies of modernisation and development. Globalisation can thus be described as submerging the effects of imperialism into cultural ecumenism or economic fatalism, and of making transnational relationships of power appear both neutral and necessary; in other words the naturalisation of the schemata of neo-liberal thought.

If You Can Have It, Why Can't They?

Antonio Gramsci's writings on Fordism and Americanism offer an important insight into the political and cultural significance of contemporary globalisation and its relationship to those processes characterised as 'Americanisation'.[1] This institutionalised Fordism, in turn, had far-reaching and long lasting geopolitical consequences by enabling the US to provide the economic dynamism necessary to spark the reconstruction of the immediate postwar years along with the more recent spread of its military industrial complex. This proved particularly effective as the Cold War acted to legitimate US interventions that protected and extended transnational business interests under the hegemonic banner of protecting the 'free world' from Communism, as well as promoting an ideology of free choice and consumer sovereignty. Importantly, the value system appropriate for the successful transition to capitalist modernisation was the culture-ideology of consumerism.

This is where the nexus between Americanisation, capitalist consumerism and globalisation can be articulated – at the 'vanishing point of modernity' (Anderson, 2002: 24).[2] Not only has the 'American dream' been central to the project of global capitalism, but as Leslie Sklair argues, the reformation of capitalism can be seen as the Americanisation of capitalism, and the culture-ideology of consumerism its rationale (Sklair, 1991). This nexus is how the cultural ideological sphere, particularly since the 'communications revolution' of the 1980s, conspires with the logics of political imperialism and economic neo-imperialism.

This political-economic project is therefore driven by the symbolic, as well as material violence of the globalisation of the themes of American social doxa. All the carriers and importers of cultural products are thus facilitating the actual globalisation of American problems. Cultural imperialism has always rested on the power to universalise particularisms linked to a singular historical tradition by causing them to be misrecognised. Complex and controversial realities of a particular historical society are now tacitly constituted as a model for every other and a yardstick for all things. Pierre Bourdieu and Loïc Wacquant highlight the conceptual 'import–export' of America's cultural industry – 'those mystified mystifiers who can transport unknowingly the hidden, and often accursed, portion of the cultural products which they put into circulation' (Bourdieu & Wacquant, 1999: 47).

The logic of post-modern consumer capitalism, and in particular the globalisation of American lifestyle choices, increasingly attempts to create the world in its own image and thereby redefine political and social reality. The social lives of things are increasingly becoming the primary front to this post-modern political economy wherein there is an increased interdependence between public and private interests (Appadurai, 1988). The key to its success is to drive aspirational values. This branded form of edutainment attempts a synergy between various formats to individualise and personalise its message and products for informed consumers. This is particularly reflected in the new target demographic of such techniques. The intended audience of this info-war is no longer the educated elite or business and professional echelons of society, but rather youth, attempting to cut across racial, class and other socio-economic differences and discipline through the democratic medium of popular technology. Jared Cohen, the young rising star within the US State Department, highlights this unity between public and private interests by stating that, 'the civil liberties young people have found online for organizing a good time have become the same freedoms that they now leverage for dissent and action' (Cohen, 2008b).

However, the problem remains that most discussions on the subject of American global power continue to be framed within the unsatisfactory paradigm of 'hard' and 'soft' power (Nye, 1990). Within this framework, the relationship between military, financial and cultural power remains characterised in simple linear terms of one-to-one relations. Most debates in the current global climate question whether or not a decline in America's previously hegemonic financial and military global standing could be offset by its cultural standing, or whether it will simply lead to the dethroning of the US as the sole global superpower. However, such deliberations are proving inappropriate for better understanding our particular geopolitical nomos and seeing that states are no longer unitary actors. They are unable to capture the complexities of contemporary statecraft and its various modalities of power, particularly those networks that circumvent the constricted logic of the state and its increasingly weakening boundaries.

In this context, the latest buzzword to come out of US foreign policy circles is that of 'smart' power – seen as a more synergetic integration of hard power with its 'softer' counterpart.[3] The idea of smart power makes it clear that violence is not only still a viable option, but also a necessary one. However, what it also attempts to articulate is that the choice of legitimate targets and combatants is no longer simply righteous, but also culturally informed. This strategic readjustment in US foreign policy thinking reminds us that the last words scrawled by Kurtz in his pamphlet on 'civilising the savages' – to 'exterminate all the brutes' – are still alive with us today. The 'horror' for Kurtz at the end of Conrad's novella is invoked in the increasing realisation amongst US government and military officials that there can ultimately be no military solutions to political wars (Conrad, 1973).

Why Do They Hate Us? Why Do They Hate Each Other?

This post-9/11 landscape has also encouraged renewed debate on the particular place of public diplomacy, more specifically a new cultural diplomacy, in this developing environment of 'human security'. The assumption is that with this security agenda the resulting policies will be diametrically opposed to the projection of soft power. However, what these discussions fail to recognise is that culture has always been central to the long-term success and stability of colonial projects. One of Edward Said's decisive contributions was to show that the colonial project was not reducible to a simple military–economic system, but was also underpinned by a discursive infrastructure and whole apparatus of knowledge whose violence was as much epistemic as it was physical. Colonial prose, that is to say the symbolic forms and representations underpinning the imperial project, has always attempted to reify the mind and culture of its subjects in order to justify its actions (Said, 1998). Since the attacks on the Twin Towers and the Pentagon, civilisationalist and culturalist interpretations to explain away politics have taken on a new lease of life. This can be seen in the particular attention given to Samuel Huntington's thesis on the 'clash of civilisations'. Huntington opened his original essay on the matter by saying that world politics was entering a new phase. Whereas in the recent past world conflicts have been confined to ideological camps, this new style of politics he discerned would be between different civilisations. 'The great divisions among humankind and the dominating source of conflict will be cultural. The clash of civilisations will dominate global politics' (Huntington, 1993: 1).

Culture remains reified in much of the literature that attempts to make sense of the political developments in our post-Cold War world. Within this framework, 'terrorists' and their sympathisers are constructed as extremists motivated by a pre-modern irrational zeal and thereby seen as pursuing agendas untranslatable by any modern paradigm. The world, therefore, continues to be imagined in Manichean terms of mullahs and malls and religious absolutism and market determinism.

In such a world only two possible political futures can be imagined. The first is one characterised as a *Jihād* of sorts – a 'retribalisation' of large parts of the planet by war and bloodshed in which culture is pitted against culture. The second is what Benjamin Barber calls 'McWorld', which is borne in on us by integration and uniformity that 'mesmerises the world with fast music, fast computers and fast food, pressing nations into one commercially homogenous global network' (Barber, 1996: 4). The tendencies of the forces of '*Jihād*' and the forces of 'McWorld' are seen to operate with equal strength and in strictly opposite directions: the one driven by parochial hatreds that re-create ancient subnational and ethnic borders from within, the other by universalising markets that attempt to make national borders porous from without. For Barber and others, this is global democracy's moment to seek out indigenous democratic impulses. Or as Barber puts it, 'there is always a desire for self-government, always some expression of participation, accountability, consent, and representation, even in traditional hierarchical societies. These need to be identified, tapped, modified, and incorporated into new democratic practices with an indigenous flavour' (Barber, 1996: 209).

Speaking on Huntington's work, the late Edward Said highlighted that, 'much of the tremendous interest subsequently taken in Huntington's essay I think derives from its timing, rather than exclusively from what it says ... there have been several intellectual and political attempts since the end of the Cold War to map the emerging world situation. And this includes Francis Fukayama's thesis on the end of history, which no-one talks about. So, the end of Fukayama really and the thesis put about during the later days of the Bush administration, the theory of the so-called New World order' (Said, 1996). In his lecture, Said noted Huntington's reliance on the thinking of Orientalists, particularly that of Bernard Lewis. In his 1990 article, *Roots of Muslim Rage*, Lewis argued that, 'it should by now be clear that we are facing a mood and a movement in Islam far transcending the level of issues and policies and the governments that pursue them this is no less than a clash of civilisations' (Lewis, 1990). For Said, such thinking was intended as a manual in the art of maintaining a wartime status in the minds of Americans and others. This post-9/11 talk resonates clearly with earlier forms of colonial Manichaeism, which saw the world as divided in two – modern and pre-modern. The key difference being is that moderns make their culture, they can distinguish between the good and the bad in the culture, and progress by building on the good. Modern peoples are historical in that sense. Pre-moderns, in contrast, are born into a culture, and are to an extent a victim of that culture, and the only way for them to be salvaged is from the outside through philanthropic or military intervention.

More generally, Mahmoud Mamdani's idea of 'culture talk' not only helps to unpack some of the aforementioned processes, but also places them in a clear historical framework. For Mamdani, 'culture talk' involves a double claim. The first is that pre-modern peoples possess an ahistorical and unchanging culture, like a badge they wear or a collective twitch from which they suffer. The second is that their politics can be decoded as a necessary and direct effect of this unchanging culture (Mamdani, 2005). The inner workings of this 'culture talk' can be seen in the resurrection of the syntax of the 'Arab mind' in the 'war on terror'. The combination of political and cultural identities takes on a particularly disturbing shape in the context of the 'war on terror' and its attempts to re-produce the 'orient'. Raphael Patai's 1973 book, *The Arab Mind*, has received a pseudo-intellectual revival in both diplomatic and military circles as the basis of cultural instruction.[4] However disreputable such thinking may seem, its relevance cannot be downplayed and its consequences have been both real and deadly. Central to the thesis are violence and sex(uality) – Arabs are constructed as a people who only understand force and whose biggest weaknesses are shame and humiliation. Contemporary applications of such thinking can be found in the writing of neo-Orientalists, as well as popular neo-liberal Arab intellectuals such as Fouad Ajami and Kanan Makiya. In a *Guardian* opinion piece, 'Extremism: the loser's revenge', published in 2006, Ian Buruma opens by asking, 'does masturbation lead to suicide bombing?' Buruma argues that there may be a legitimate connection between sexual inadequacy, frustration and deprivation to the pull towards violent Islamic extremism. The loser's revenge, for Buruma, lies in the 'tantalising prospect of having one's pick of the loveliest virgins in paradise' (Buruma, 2006).

Education, Education, Education

It is important to stress that despite the radical shift in terms of how American cultural diplomacy is panning out across the Middle East, it has clear relations to colonial, Cold War and post-colonial encounters in the region, all with their shared ambition of reinventing the 'orient'. As early as 1949, Dr Mortimer Graves, then Executive Director of the American Council of Learned Societies, repeatedly warned that the study of Middle Eastern languages and culture was imperative for the future (Bertelsen, 2007). From the mid-1950s a full arsenal of cultural weapons were deployed by the United States in the Middle East, with the pace of intervention increasing with the threat of Communism and Arab nationalism in the late 1950s and early 1960s. With technological innovation today opening up the possibilities to reach new audiences in novel forms, education continues to serve as a primary form of diplomatic efforts in the region.

The American University of Beirut is one of the oldest and most prestigious American educational institutions in the Arab world and has long played a major role in the political developments of the region. The university highlights the double-edged nature of such policies. Founded by American missionaries in 1866 as the Syrian Protestant College, when Lebanon was part of Syria, the university later received funding from the US government and both the Ford and Rockefeller Foundations. However, by the end of World War II, it was an important intellectual hub for budding Arab nationalists who would later run the affairs of numerous independent Arab states. As early as the late 1940s the Rockefeller Foundation collaborated with the American University of Beirut to expand the Arab Studies Group to include Turkey, Iran, Afghanistan, Pakistan and India. At the time, the *New York Times* noted that, 'the studies group laid down a programme of research and of synthesising available information of value to Americans concerned with problems in the area, notably members of the Government services, or active in education or journalism' (*New York Times*, 1950). The article goes on to say that, 'the overall subject of the studies and writing projects is called the "Making of the Modern Arab mind." This definition was laid down by the Rockefeller Foundation and broken up into individual subjects to be undertaken by the Arab Studies Group.' The cultural brokers of such initiatives are professors and researchers who are 'either Arabs or were born Arabs and have all lived and studied in the West, chiefly in the United States'. The work of Rasmus Bertelsen attempts to build a genealogy of the politics and soft power of British, French and American universities in the Middle East and dispel the image of their neutral projections of perceived universal academic norms (Bertelsen, 2007). The foundation of the American University of Beirut, the Université Saint Joseph and the American University in Cairo were all part of separate attempts to attract and co-opt the indigenous population to Christianity through education and the training of leaders of society. However, there appears to be a significant shift in the reasons behind the contemporary establishing of universities in the Middle East. The powerplay between Jesuits determined to develop universities as part of the educational competition with the Anglo-Saxon Protestant missionaries in Lebanon has been replaced with a new ideological mix of consumer capitalism and American self-interest. American academia has been exceptionally powerful in setting research agendas, choosing topics and methods, determining standards and defining structures of study and career. The American university system, therefore, can be seen as the new Catholic Church of Gramscian hegemony. A central component of American soft power efforts in the Middle East since World War II has been that of education and cultural programmes. Such initiatives included the educational exchanges of the Fulbright Programme, visitor grantees and youth exchanges. John Waterbury, President of the American University of Beirut, suggests that American higher education has more attraction and familiarity to Middle Easterners than any other American institution. In the words of Waterbury, 'the word "American" is to education what "Swiss" is to watches' (Bertelsen, 2009: 7).

The latest trend in educational interventions in the Middle East is closely associated with the attempts to turn the Arabian Gulf into the financial and cultural hub of the region. In the era of globalisation US universities are attempting to extend their influence by setting up outposts across the Middle East. English has been the lingua franca of academia for some time, but it is the American system of higher education that is increasingly the envy of the world. Furthermore, as a particularly potent weapon in the arsenal of American cultural diplomacy, it is becoming an important export as more universities take their programmes overseas. Both the events of 9/11 and the subsequent policy reorientations under the guise of the 'war on terror' have sharpened the focus on the Middle East again. David Skorton, President of Cornell University, argues that, 'higher education is the most important diplomatic asset we have. I believe these programmes can actually reduce friction between countries and cultures' (Lewin, 2008).

At Education City in Doha (Qatar), one can study medicine at Weill Medical College of Cornell University, international affairs at Georgetown, computer science and business at Carnegie Mellon, fine arts at Virginia Commonwealth, engineering at Texas A&M, and soon, journalism at Northwestern. At a time of limited state funding, such projects highlight the increasing codependence between government policies and private interests. The emerging synergy between geopolitical, pedagogic and economic interests is the central concern of this chapter. As Representative Brian Baird, a Washington Democrat and Chairman of the House Science and Technology Subcommittee on Research and Science Education says, 'if the U.S. universities are not doing this, someone else likely will. I think it is better that we be invited in than we be left out' (Bertelsen, 2007). Therefore, these overseas campuses serve a double purpose. They are seen as ventures into tapping new markets and bringing education to new students – a shared vision of building bridges between the Western world and the Arab world.

The cementing of the relationship between US higher education and official public policy came during the most turbulent years of the Cold War. The effects of US military, intelligence and propaganda agencies during this period would come to influence both academic culture and intellectual life (Simpson, 1998). Charles Thorpe, Dean of Carnegie Mellon in Qatar, stresses this by saying that, 'we want our students to be good businessmen and businesswomen, and good computer scientists, but we also want them to be good people, and that requires the full array of liberal education and student affairs. So there is much more going on here than just technical education' (Lewin, 2008). Therefore, the strength of such pedagogic diplomacy lies in its perceived ability to teach Middle Eastern youth how to deal with the Western world, without forcing them into acting like Westerners or changing their personal values. This idea is at the heart of the State Department's new thinking. James Glassman, the new Under Secretary of State for Public Diplomacy, wants to bring people in contact with America, rather than tell them what to think. Both the State Department and Pentagon officials see him as an intellectual cousin of Defense Secretary Robert Gates, who said in his 2008 US Global Leadership Campaign speech that, 'we know we cannot kill or capture our way to victory' (Gates, 2008). Glassman, therefore, has largely shelved the unsuccessful strategy of his predecessor, Karen Hughes, who waged this battle as an advertisement campaign, flooding the unreceptive market with positive messages about the United States.

Diplomacy Version 2.0

It is important to emphasise that public diplomacy is hardly a new paradigm within international politics, but at the same time it has taken on both a new mission statement and reconstituted its 'publics' to better suit our increasingly networked world. The digital divide is becoming increasingly crucial in attempting to understand how this new politics is unfolding. Digital media is beginning to be embraced within policy circles that now believe that with unprecedented global interest, more citizens of the world are having 'digital box seats to watch, hear, and feel the democratic experience' (Cohen, 2008). In a world increasingly connected through user-generated software – Google searches, YouTube videos, Facebook statuses and Twitter updates – the US Department of State believes that it can reinvigorate its 'democratic vision'. Those on the 'wrong side of history' will increasingly be characterised as those on the wrong side of this digital divide. James Glassman argues that, 'even when people are doing the kinds of things that we want them to be doing, if we get too deeply involved it tends to be counterproductive' (Kushner, 2009). The democratic imperative ushered in by this interactive digital culture is having a considerable impact on the shift in technologies associated with this new form of diplomacy. It is no longer interested in the purely passive practices traditionally associated with listening to official government messages through radios and televisions, but rather the user-generated production and consumption of Facebook groups, YouTube videos, Vlogs and short films and music on the mobile phones of today's 'digital natives'. In our 'Facebook Age', US cultural diplomacy can be seen as shifting its techniques, aesthetics and tempo to fit the reorientation from 24/7 news cycles to instantaneous Twitter updates.

Therefore, it could be argued that the emerging shift in US cultural diplomacy is attempting to exploit this very relationship between the transfer of information and the hegemony of our technoaesthetic culture. More specifically, the virtual real that connects this 'tribe' through a network of mobile phones, digital cameras, YouTube videos and Twitter, Facebook and MySpace pages. The global explosion of this audiovisual republic, which includes all the formats shaped around digital moving images, is crucial if this newfound strategy is to achieve any notable success. Furthermore, the virtual public(s) that such developments are attempting to construct, are increasingly being seen as spaces wherein all young people can act as 'diplomats' through 'dormroom diplomacy' to influence communities around them, as well as those they have little or no contact with. This goes to show how American public diplomacy, increasingly characterised as an open communication forum, is being opened up by global mass media and technology. Policy circles are realising that other institutions and online forums circulate as 'America' with more authority than state agencies. However, what this discourse chooses to ignore is the fact that the political aspects of today's prevailing technological rationality lie in 'democratic unfreedom' as a token of technical progress (Rose, 1999).

Despite the increased openness that YouTube, MySpace and other video and music sharing sites have created, they are far from free of the fingerprints of officialdom. Not only have record and film companies set up their own official channels and accounts to offer better quality clips, as well as a forum for advertisements, but governments have also begun to see the potential of reaching vast audiences without the backdrop of propaganda that would have been tagged to the same initiatives had they been attempted through more traditional state mechanisms. So, from Queen Rania of Jordan's popular YouTube channel, to US President Obama's extremely effective use of social networking sites – including the ability to donate your Facebook status to his presidential campaign – ways of communicating to publics have been drastically changed. More specifically, the social networking phenomenon is fast becoming a central battleground for governments, institutions and corporations and their fight for virtual advertising space, new markets and ultimately users' attention.[5] Facebook's founder, Mark Zuckerberg, has promised to continue expanding aggressively around the world. At the last Web 2.0 summit, Zuckerberg suggested that, 'the challenge that we have is to bring people along the whole path, first bring people along to Facebook, and make people comfortable with sharing information online. We got people through this really big hurdle of wanting to put up their full name, picture – their mobile phone number in many cases' (Johnson, 2008). Zuckerberg also noted that the future for social networking technology was limitless. The crucial next step for such sites was the chance to take social networking truly mobile, and thereby take advantage of increasingly popular phone technology.[6]

Jared Cohen is beginning to hold increasing sway on more traditional circles that until now have dictated policy prescriptions. For Cohen, 'the one-sided web 1.0 approach of violent extremists is no match from a web 2.0 (interactive and user-generated) inclined youth demographic keen on expanding their social networks and exploring new media' (Cohen, 2008b). Cohen is attempting to placate more conservative policy makers' fears by highlighting that, unlike the impact of radio and cassette tapes across the developing world in the 1970s, today's media environment is both interactive and user-generated. The technological developments in these new media forms have drastically reshaped our socio-political culture, particularly that of 'democratic propaganda'. Such a digital media that comes with 'rules and regulations that are imposed by companies who will not allow their platforms to be used to kill or to terrorise' is seen to be replacing the more politically unstable cassette tape. Therefore, for Cohen, the diplomatic potential for this new digital media relies heavily on the private sector's continued incentive in putting information technology on the public domain.[7]

Dropping iPods on 'Digital Natives'

Early in 2009, in a meeting room located in Baghdad's Green Zone, Scott Heiferman, chief executive of Meetup.com, and Jason Liebman, chief executive of user-generated video site Howcast, met with Iraqi Deputy Prime Minister Barham Salih. Heiferman and Liebman formed part of a delegation of Silicon Valley and New York-based technology executives, which included Twitter co-founder Jack Dorsey, Blue State Digital's David Nassar, WordPress's Raanan Bar-Cohen, as well as representatives from YouTube, Google and AT&T. The first US State Department 'New Media Technology' Delegation was sent to Iraq to survey the state of technology in the country and to help formulate ideas on how to build its infrastructure from scratch. During the four-day trip, the executives met with General Nasier Abadi, Iraqi Armed Forces' deputy chief of staff; Marc Wall, coordinator for economic transition in Iraq; and Ralph Steen, officer in charge of the national fibre network installation project. Just as importantly, they organised roundtables with students from the University of Technology and the University of Baghdad to discuss how they use Facebook and videos they upload or view on YouTube. For the delegation, the point of the trip was not aimed at bringing 'some American Internet brand into the country', but rather about 'the raw piping for how people connect with each other in ways that just literally do not compute if you have been in the Saddam dark ages for a bunch of decades.' Mr Heiferman continued by saying that, 'this is not bringing McDonald's to Iraq. It is bringing some of the rawest ideas of how technology helps them be more themselves' (Reagan, 2009).

What this latest effort in post-conflict reconstruction and development agendas highlights, is a sharp ideological break from the narrowly conceived political and economic efforts of the past. The long-term aim of the delegation is to explore technological trends and explore the new opportunities that such technological developments hold for achieving American objectives in Iraq. As Mr Heiferman said, 'our whole purpose here is to try to understand the possibilities of investing in Internet infrastructure and having a discussion of the needs that people have. We tried to explain the basic notion of having a private sector, the basic notion of being a democracy, and that the Internet will be increasingly vital if they are going to participate in the larger world' (Reagan, 2009).

The ability of digital technology today to uncouple cultures both temporally and spatially, and then transmit them almost instantaneously across the globe is proving to be a double-edged sword. Our increasingly high-definition world, or what some have come to describe as an 'audiovisual republic', is seen as a world in which 'we are video'.[8] Such literature, which uncritically celebrates the social changes ushered in by this latest technological revolution, is not only thriving, but equally being embraced within influential policy circles. Today's enthusiasts choose to stress the falling prices in digital technology, as well as the plethora of user-generated content that it has ushered. Therefore, the democratisation of the public realm, or more specifically the creation of a new audiovisual interactive sphere, is seen by many to have broken the monopoly over the production and transfer of public information. Such rhetoric, however, relies on a number of unquestioned assumptions. Who exactly is the 'we' that makes up this new virtual public sphere? Who can speak? Who gets heard? And most importantly, who has access? The possibility that our increasing dependence on audiovisual formats is actually creating new hegemonic positions in our public sphere(s) has yet to be satisfactorily explored. Paul Valéry warned us that, 'just as water, gas and electricity are brought into our houses from far off to satisfy our needs in response to a minimal effort, so we shall be supplied with visual or auditory images, which will appear and disappear at a simple movement of the hand, hardly more than a sign' (Benjamin, 1999: 217).

What distinguishes contemporary US cultural diplomacy from its Cold War past is its attempts, particularly in the Muslim and Arab world, to manipulate the relationship between peoples' 'social and recreational activities' and their 'ideological enterprises'. Such initiatives attempt to convert the growing anti-Americanism across the region through the perceived desire amongst youth to 'forget about the society they are living in so long as the music blasts, the fashion is displayed and the interactions are flirtatious'. This is seen to be particularly pertinent to 'Middle Eastern youth culture', wherein young people are attempting 'to put history behind them' and 'continue to break the patterns of violence of their parent's generation' (Cohen, 2008a). With a narrowed target audience/demographic of the 'emerging market(s) of Arab youth', 'urban culture' along with mass consumer technology and communication have become the latest lifestyle weapons of the US Department of State's Bureau of Public Diplomacy and Public Affairs and its current 'counter-radicalisation' agenda of 'breaking the shackles of tradition across the Muslim and Arab world'.[9]

Such consumer technological innovations, alongside unprecedented access to the outside world, have supposedly given these young people not only sources of entertainment and means for communication that their parents never enjoyed, but more importantly it has further allowed them to embrace connectivity that transcends politics, religion and extremism. Cohen and others hope the civil liberties that this technoliterate class of youth have found online for organising good time have become the same freedoms that they are now able to leverage for dissent and action. However, what is interesting to note in much of this problematic discourse is that the definition of 'liberated Arab youth' is predominately defined along the lines of neo-liberal values of individual freedom and Western conceptualisations of what it means to be 'modern' and 'free', rather than in terms of the strict ideological camps of the past. For US cultural diplomacy the winning of their 'hearts and minds' is now intricately intertwined with the phenomenon that has become characterised as the age of 'digital freedom', where the Internet in and of itself constitutes 'their democratic society' and the satellite dish may serve as the 'biggest anti-propaganda tool' (Cohen, 2008a). It is now primarily in a virtual (public) sphere, and through digital means, that the youth of the region are to be emancipated from the rest of the population – autonomy and freedom, be it from American occupation or the internal oppression of police-states, is to be achieved through a democratic mass-communications revolution.[10]

The 'Facebook Age' has brought with it a modern battle over technology. For architects of America's global cultural offensive and proponents of modern technology, its liberating potential supposedly lies in its ability to give Middle Eastern youth the access to know what they are missing out on and what they now see they have been deprived of. Within such a scenario, technology provides disenfranchised youth the ability to dream of another world and another life. Such arguments make tenuous links between global technological diffusion, 'global civil society' and democracy, with its citizens armed with a new modern identity. For such modern initiatives access is evidently no longer a hurdle – satellite television is one of the most prevalent technologies in the Middle East. The issue now lies in changing their preferences, which will be a far more difficult task. The United States Information Agency (USIA) has always been in the export business – of 'telling American's story to the world' through various means. George Creel, a renowned American journalist and eventual head of the US Committee on Public Information (CPI), described such processes as 'a plain publicity proposition, a vast enterprise in salesmanship, the world's greatest adventure in advertising' (Snow, 1998: 16). What US cultural diplomacy in the Middle East is now attempting to achieve is no less than the transformation, as well as to a large extent the de-politicisation, of a new generation. Social justice is not part of this lexicon – in their view, what is most promising is the fact that Palestinian youth are two generations removed from the days when they lived in their homeland (Cohen, 2008a). Orientalist discourses of the 'Arab street' are nothing new, but this 'street' has taken on a very different and dangerous global form in the eyes of the United States government. The demographic target audience, within the Arab world as well as the diaspora, is the under twenty-five age bracket. The fact that well over half the populations of Egypt, Palestine, Syria, Saudi Arabia, Iran and Iraq are under twenty-five years old is often cited by US government, think-tanks and international commercial sources.[11]

Such an approach to culture as hermetically sealed and dehistoricised leads Cohen to see it as a continuing 'puzzling paradox' that 'they [young Hezbollah supporters that he interviewed during his travels] were religious extremists, committed to the establishment of an Islamic republic, the destruction of Israel, and attacks on America. On the other hand, they were typical Lebanese youth: clubbers, bar-hoppers, and lovers of American fast food' (Cohen, 2008a: 41). However, culture and cultural exchange cannot be treated in such a reductive manner. What the State Department and others are now asking is whether or not this new approach to cultural diplomacy will succeed, or if such projects will merely end up as relics of another failed imperial mission. Former Undersecretary of State Charlotte Beers stated on numerous occasions that a 30 per cent conversion rate for Muslims would represent a sales curve any corporation would envy (De Grazia, 2002). It is clearly too early to judge, but what is evident is that US cultural diplomatic efforts have learnt from the failures of their earlier formalised processes of 'cultural diffusion' in the region and are starting to invest more time and money in these new techniques and technologies. They have understood that Arab audiences cannot be simply conceived of as passive consumers and objects of American desire. Therefore, with 'youth' as the new demographic target, there is an increased effort to manipulate their participation as independent agents in this globalised consumer capitalist culture. Rather than stressing the obvious failures of officially sponsored programmes such as *Al-Hurra* or *Radio Sawa*, one should be more concerned with the increasing shift to more fluid and ambivalent exporters of America's culture industry and social doxa, which will undoubtedly be more successful than its predecessors.

If there is a clear ideology at play in today's shift in US cultural diplomacy it functions exactly at this intersection of mass communication and incommunicability of shared experience. It is this very space that is now celebrated by many as increasingly democratic. Cultural consumers are told that they have never been more independent of the stranglehold of industries, and for the first time they are free to make their own choices. However, what is insidiously left out of this picture is the intentional destruction of vital sources of shared experiences and convivial culture that such techniques necessitate. The logic of the 'war on terror' and our post-9/11 global landscape have forced policy makers to construct Middle Eastern youth as part of a 'target demographic', a social group that needs to be constructed as ideal 'citizen-consumers' for the new mix of government and private sector initiatives in the region. What this chapter highlights is that the increasing synergy between geopolitical, pedagogic and economic interests needs to be severed if educational policies in the Middle East are to help create an environment for the production of shared knowledge across racial, class and cultural markers.

Notes

1 Gramsci called attention to the 'long process' of socio-political change through which Fordist capitalism might achieve some measure of institutional stability. The ideological and institutional legitimacy of this new 'ultra-modern form of production

and of working methods' would be embodied in cultural practices and social relations far beyond the workplace. Domestically, Cold War ideology played a crucial role in the stabilisation of Fordist institutions in the United States. A coalition of social forces, with deradicalised industrial labour unions incorporated as junior partners, worked to rebuild the 'free world' along liberal capitalist lines to resist the threat of a presumed Communist menace (Gramsci, 1971: 280).

2   In his editorial piece, 'Force and Consent', Perry Anderson argues that the 'American direction, as opposed to domination of the globe does not, of course, rest simply on an ideological creed. Historically, it has been the attractive power of US models of production and culture that has extended the reach of this hegemony. The two have over time become increasingly unified in the sphere of consumption, to offer a single way of life as a pattern to the world. But analytically they should be kept distinct … so long as this economic lead was maintained America could figure in a world-wide imaginary as the vanishing point of modernity: in the eyes of millions of people overseas, the form of life that traced an ideal shape of their own future. This image was, and is, a function of technological advance' (Anderson, 2002: 24).

3   In her confirmation hearing as the new US Secretary of State in President Obama's administration, Hillary Clinton stressed that, 'we must use what has been called smart power, the full range of tools at our disposal – diplomatic, economic, military, political, legal and cultural – picking the right tool or combination of tools for each situation' (Clinton, 2009 January 13).

4   *The Arab Mind* was revived by Hather-Leigh Press in 2002 and reprinted with an enthusiastic introduction by Norvell De Atkine, former US army colonel and head of Middle East Studies at Fort Bragg. It is one of the most popular and widely read books on 'Arabs' in the US military. At one time, the training departments at the State Department gave away free copies to officials who were to be posted to US embassies in the Middle East. It is also used as a textbook for officers at the JFK Special Warfare School in Fort Bragg (Patai, 2002).

5   Facebook has an estimated 161 million members – with a substantial growth during 2008, from 50 million to 161 million users. MySpace also boasts 118 million users (ComScore, September, 2008).

6   A recent United Nations report reveals that more than half the global population now pay to use a mobile phone. With the drastic expansion in the mobile services available, from instant money transfers to public health advice and Internet access, the end of 2008 saw 4.1 billion mobile subscriptions (1 billion in 2002). Furthermore, also nearly a quarter of the world's 6.7 billion people now use the Internet (11% in 2002 and 23% in 2008). What is particularly important to stress is that these developments are all the more sharp in developing countries, with the fastest growth in the Middle East and Africa. Developing countries now account for about 2/3 of the mobile phones in use (less than half in 2002). The report also notes that over 100,000 phone masts are erected each year, with the number of places with 'no signal' dwindling fast. More than 90% of the global population now has some form of access. It is interesting that these trends coincide with the increasing rush for Coltan (metallic mineral) – essential in the manufacture of electrical components in mobile phones – that is creating widespread conflict across Africa, particularly in the Democratice Republic of Congo. For more on the UN report see <http://www.itu.int/net/home/index.aspx>.

7   The most recent example of this was the *Alliance of Youth Movements Summit 2008* in New York. The summit brought together leaders of youth movements and other prominent government, business, NGO, philanthropist and celebrity figures 'to learn, share and discuss how to change the world by building powerful grassroots movement'. This concoction included strategists of Barack Obama's Presidential Campaign, the Undersecretary of State for Public Diplomacy, the Co-Founder of Facebook and Whoopi Goldberg, as well as non-violent youth organisations from Columbia, Burma, Egypt and Cuba. Moreover, the summit was sponsored by Howcast, a company founded by veterans of Google and YouTube that aims to show consumers 'engaging,

useful how-to videos and guides wherever, whenever they need to learn how'. For more see <http://youthmovements.howcast.com/>.

8 The term first began to appear in think-tank circles. For example, see Bradwell, Hannon & Tims (2008).

9 For more on the US Department of State's Bureau of Public Diplomacy and Public Affairs and its particular 'counter-radicalisation programmes', see <http://www.state.gov/r/>.

10 The year 2009 saw the official launch of Muxlim Pal, which is the first virtual world aimed at the 'Muslim community'. Based on Second Life, Muxlim's online world 'reaches from the prayer mat to the shopping centre'. Mohamed El-Fatatry, founder of Muxlim Pal, says, 'we are not a religious site, we are a site that is focused on the lifestyle' (BBC News, 2008). Already boasting 1.5 million monthly users, El-Fatatry's market research reveals that the site aims to enhance the 'Muslim lifestyle' through virtual beach bars and shopping malls. Muxlim Pal's founder is equally keen to stress that, unlike The Sims, sociality is at the core of the site and thereby hopes to foster understanding among Muslims and non-Muslims alike.

11 For a more detailed breakdown see the International Programmes Centre at the Census Bureau at <http://www.census.gov/ipc/www/idb/>.

References

Anderson, P. (2002). Force and Consent. *New Left Review*, 17: 5–30.

Appaduari, A. (1988). *The Social Life of Things: Commodities in Cultural Perspective.* Cambridge University Press.

Barber, B. (1996). *Jihad vs. McWorld: Terrorism's Challenge to Democracy.* New York: Corgi Books.

BBC News. (2008). Virtual World for Muslims Debuts. December 8. Retrieved from <http://news.bbc.co.uk/1/hi/technology/7768601.stm>.

Benjamin, W. (1999). *Illuminations.* London: Pimlico.

Bertelsen, R. (2007). The Politics and Soft Power of American, British and French Universities in the Middle East. American Political Science Association Annual Meeting.

Bertelsen, R. (2009). Contextual Factors and the Soft Power of American and French Origin Universities in the Middle East. Paper presented at the ISA 50th Annual Convention 'Exploring the Past, Anticipating the Future'.

Bourdieu, P. & Wacquant, L. (1999). On the Cunning of Imperialist Reason. *Theory, Culture & Society*, 16, 1, 41–58.

Bradwell, P., Hannon, C. & Tims, C. (2008). *Video Republic.* London: Demos. Retrieved from <http://www.demos.co.uk/files/Video%20republic%20-%20web.pdf>.

Buck-Morss, S. (1992). Aesthetics and Anaesthetics: Walter Benjamin's Artwork Essay Reconsidered. *October*, 62, 3–41.

Buruma, I. (2006). Extremism: The Loser's Revenge. *The Guardian*, February 25. Retrieved from <http://www.guardian.co.uk/world/2006/feb/25/terrorism.comment>.

Clinton, H. (2009). Secretary of State Nomination Hearing. Washington, DC. Retrieved from <http://www.state.gov/secretary/rm/2009a/01/115196.htm>.

Cohen, J. (2008a). *Children of Jihad: A Young American's Travels Among the Youth of the Middle East.* New York: Gotham Books.

Cohen, J. (2008b). Digital Age has Ushered in an Opportunity for Unprecedented Global Collaboration. *Huffington Post*, December 17. Retrieved from <http://www.huffingtonpost.com/jared-cohen/digital-age-has-ushered-i_b_151698.html>.

Cohen, J. (2008c). Rebutting the Sceptics: Digital Media Is America's Ally. *Huffington Post*, December 24. Retrieved from <http://www.huffingtonpost.com/jared-cohen/rebutting-the-skeptics-di_b_153357.html>.

Commisso, A. (2004). Iraqi Textbook Quality Improvement Program for Primary and Secondary Education Mathematics and Science Textbooks: Review, Training, Printing, and Distribution Process: A Case Study (draft). Paris: UNESCO.

ComScore 2008: <http://www.comscore.com/>

Conrad, J. (1973). *Heart of Darkness*. Harmondsworth: Penguin.

De Grazia, V. (2002). The Nation: The Selling of America, Bush Style. *The New York Times*, August 25. Retrieved from <http://www.nytimes.com/2002/08/25/weekinreview/the-nation-the-selling-of-america-bush-style.html>

Friedman, T. (2007). *The World is Flat: The Globalised World in the Twenty-first Century*. Harmondsworth: Penguin.

Gates, R.M. (2008, July 15). U.S. global leadership campaign. Speech delivered by the Secretary of Defense. Washington, DC: U.S. Department of Defense. Available online at http://www.defenselink.mil/speeches/speech.aspx?speechid=1262.

Giddens, A. (1999). *Runaway World: How Globalisation Is Shaping Our Lives*. London: Profile Books.

Gramsci, A. (1971). *Selections from the Prison Notebooks*. London: Hoare and Smith.

Huntington, S. (1993). The Clash of Civilisations? *Foreign Affairs*, Summer. Retrieved from <http://www.foreignaffairs.com/articles/48950/samuel-p-huntington/the-clash-of-civilizations>

Johnson, B. (2008). Facebook and MySpace Go Head to Head with Their Visions of Future. *The Guardian*, November 8. Retrieved from <http://www.guardian.co.uk/technology/2008/nov/08/facebook-myspace-social-networking-ipod>.

Kaldor, M. (2003). *Global Civil Society: An Answer to War*. Cambridge: Polity Press.

Kushner, A. (2009). How to Sell America. *Newsweek*, January 3. Retrieved from <http://www.newsweek.com/id/177682>.

Lewin, T. (2008). Global Classrooms: U.S. Universities Rush to Set Up Outposts Abroad. *The New York Times*, February 10. Retrieved from <http://www.nytimes.com/2008/02/10/education/10global.html>.

Lewis, B. (1990). The Roots of Muslim Rage. *The Atlantic*, September. Retrieved from <http://www.theatlantic.com/doc/199009/muslim-rage>.

Mamdani, M. (2005). *Good Muslim, Bad Muslim: America, the Cold War, and the Roots of Terror*. New York: Three Leaves Publishing.

New York Times (1950). Wider Arab Study Sought to Aid U.S. Editorial. June 11.

Nye, J. (1990). *Bound to Lead: The Changing Nature of American Power*. New York: Basic Books.

Patai, R. (1973). *The Arab Mind*. New York: Charles Scribners and Sons.

Patai, R. (2002). *The Arab Mind*. Revised Edition. New York: Hatherleigh Press.

Reagan, G. (2009). Google Me in Baghdad. *The New York Observer*, April 28. Retrieved from <http://www.observer.com/2009/media/google-me-baghdad?page=1>.

Rose, N. (1999). *Powers of Freedom: Reframing Political Thought*. Cambridge: Cambridge University Press.

Said, E. (1988). *Orientalism*. London: Vintage.

Said, E. (1996). The Myth of the Clash of Civilisations, Public Lecture (Part 1). Amherst, MA: University of Massachusetts. Retrieved from <http://www.youtube.com/watch?v=boBzrqF4vmo>.

Said, E. (1998). *Culture and Imperialism*. London: Vintage.

Simpson, C. (1998). *Universities and Empire: Money and Politics in the Social Sciences During the Cold War*. New York: New Press.

Sklair, L. (1991). *Sociology of the Global System*. London: Harvester.

Snow, N. (1998). *Propaganda, Inc.: Selling America's Culture to the World*. New York: Seven Stories Press.

20 Palestinians, Education, and the Israeli "Industry of Fear"

Nadera Shalhoub-Kevorkian

Introduction

There have been surprisingly few studies on the combined effects of military occupation, racism, the so-called "war on terror" and the industry of fear it raises on access to education and the perpetuation of colonizer/colonized relations. While there may be a dearth of research in this area, these concepts are implicit and integrally associated with education in conflict zones in the Middle East. The theoretical and methodological premise of this chapter is predicated on the belief that it is from the day-to-day life experiences of those who suffer injustice, domination, a perpetual "refugee status" and displacement, that we can begin to conceptualize and understand the difficulties of education in militarized areas (Appadurai, 2006; Bauman, 2003). By focusing on the deprivation of education, as a tool for collective punishment, the present chapter maps and analyzes voices of Palestinians whose right to a safe and secure education continues to be violated, unhindered.

Studying the deprivation of education as a tool for collective punishment is deeply affected by my experience and standpoint – as a Palestinian mother and scholar living in the old city of Jerusalem and who feels the profound pain of how we, Palestinians, merely survive living in such a contested area. Asserting the need for a just and liberatory research approach requires us to listen carefully to those who suffer a history of subjugation, domination, diaspora, and displacement. Being a mother of three daughters who need to challenge the effects of military occupation at every single step and decision they take when building their future, made me realize how one could live an exilic life at home. Moreover, my experience as a Palestinian academic, first teaching at a Palestinian university, then at an Israeli one, made me understand what it means to belong to a privileged group, with the power to decide who has the right to have a right. My location as a Palestinian, mother, academic and activist, and the research shared in this paper, all require me to call on scholars to consider their role, not only in terms of listening to the voices of the muted and silenced, or looking for absolute truths, but also in terms of joining forces with those who seek and work for justice.

The daily terror facing young Palestinians in the West Bank and Gaza Strip when exercising their right to education, challenges claims that education is an apolitical or neutral zone in the midst of conflict. Rather, as I hope to illustrate, disrupting the access of the colonized to education is a primary tool in the hands of the colonizer in perpetuating colonial domination. Consequently, analyzing the systemic unleashing of an industry of fear and organized terror by the Israeli occupation forces, reveals how Palestinian education is literally placed under siege. In that sense, education becomes highly politicized within the larger field of power mediating colonizer–colonized relations. It "racializes" Palestinians by constructing them as people to be "feared". Hence, this "industry of fear" – that is, the colonial mechanisms of racialization – sustains and reproduces modes of racism that ultimately totally subordinate the right to education to "security considerations".

I start the chapter by examining how education is utilized as a tool for oppression in conflict zones, primarily and precisely because it can be used to affect social and political transformation, emancipation, and liberation. In a second stage, I then move to examine the particular case of Israel's deprivation of the Palestinians' right to education by analyzing official statements, policy guidelines, court decisions and the reports of non-governmental organizations (NGOs) that delineate various aspects of this policy and reveal its rationale. In a third stage, I invoke the voices of Palestinian children and youth from my own fieldwork to create spaces for them to bring forward their experiential realities of these Israeli policies and the impacts of such realities on their education. I conclude the chapter by making a number of observations about educational research in zones of military upheaval and their implications for the role of the researcher.

The Right to Education in Conflict Zones

Article 26 of the Universal Declaration of Human Rights states the following: "The right to education is a fundamental human right and basic to human freedom". The International Covenant on Economic, Social and Cultural Rights (ICESCR), ratified by Israel in 1991 (despite its continued violation), underlines the fact that "Education is both a human right in itself and an indispensable means of realizing other human rights".

Despite the above internationally recognized safeguards, the dynamics of violence in contemporary conflict zones increasingly use collective punishment to further oppress disenfranchised populations through limiting their education prospects, among other methods. Military strategists systematically exert control over populations through the production of uncertainty and the creation and manipulation of fear (Nordstrom, 1992; Corradi, Weiss Fagen & Garreton, 1992). Methods of collective punishment such as starving populations, destroying infrastructure, ethnic and social cleansing, deprivation of education, and killings have been used by the Israeli military occupation in historical Palestine (Pappe, 2003, 2007; Khalidi, 2004, 2006; Sultana, 2006; Palestinian Center for Human Rights, 2009a, 2009b; B'Tselem, 2008, 2009) as they have been used in many other conflict zones in Asia, Africa and South America. Under such violent conditions, the very existence of the occupied and colonized community is thought to be a threat to occupying forces. Consequently, when the occupied are being labeled as the source of threat, the war expands to include all social and communal arenas such as homes, schools, hospitals and playgrounds. Under colonization, education becomes a particularly utilitarian tool for oppression and control (Bush & Saltarelli, 2000), as it is often one of the few optimistic avenues left to the colonized to struggle towards emancipation. As the voices of the students quoted in this chapter reveal, colonized subjects fully understand this articulation. They consequently value education as a means to an end towards freedom. Both the value they place on education, as a way to empower themselves through knowledge, as well as the way they use that knowledge to fight oppression, can be heard in their voices, suggesting that children and youth are fully aware of the political contingencies in which their education is being hindered. Thus, any restrictions on the right to education—whether material and/or psychological and less obviously coercive, should be viewed as a warning signal that calls for urgent action from international power holders to prevent further deterioration in the condition of the life of colonized peoples.

Theorists have engaged education as a dialogic process that enables people to acquire collective knowledge they can utilize to create an environment conducive to social change and transformation (Shor 1992; hooks 1994; Freire 2000). Building on Freire's liberation pedagogy, bell hooks discusses her concept of "engaged pedagogy" (1994) as a practice of freedom in which learning becomes action and reflection upon the world in order to change it. During armed conflict, education can operate as an important medium of social and political mobilization. For instance, in apartheid South Africa, which was based on a legalized White supremacy, schools were the most important sites of mobilization against the apartheid system via radical educational pedagogies.

In Palestine, political violence dates back to the early twentieth century when Britain legitimated its military occupation through a mandate obtained from the Society of Nations. Moreover, the occupation of the land by the Zionist movement, under the auspices of the Balfour Declaration, and Palestinian resistance to colonization, were part of an unbalanced power which ultimately resulted in the material creation of an ethnocracy—in this instance, Israel.

Concern for the voices of the oppressed is central for my articulation of a socially and politically engaged research strategy. As part of this methodological approach, my intent is not to focus on "education" as a "lesson taught" to children in school, or to ask whether teaching and classroom "planning" was undertaken under optimal or menaced conditions. Rather, my intention is to approach education by mapping the effects of militarism and racism on the life of the occupied in conflict zones. My ultimate aim is to understand how oppressed adults, children and youth learn to re-think and re-map hidden epistemologies as part of fighting oppression within their cities and towns, neighborhoods, villages, refugee camps, and schools.

The present chapter draws on and juxtaposes two sets of data: The first is the voice of Israeli officials addressing Palestinian education. In addition, it draws on claims raised in some of the petitions submitted to the Israeli courts by Gisha – The Legal Center for Freedom of Movement, and which challenge violations of rights of access to education.[1] The second set of data includes a historical analysis of the attacks on Palestinian education and excerpts of the voices of

Palestinian students sharing their ordeals in circumventing restrictions on their access to education.[2]

The second set of data analyzed here includes narratives and voices that reveal the suffering through the words of Palestinian youth and children's stories. Talking to young Palestinian students in their own environment took me to areas where houses were demolished and to refugee camps. I also talked to children and youth while they were waiting to cross military checkpoints on their way to or back from school, or still at their colleges. This is not an easy task for a Palestinian researcher who is a member of the community under study, particularly when faced with participants' historicization of injustice. One emotionally overwhelming situation I faced occurred during my data collection in Silwan, a Palestinian village only ten minutes walking distance from my Jerusalem house. I was talking to schoolgirls about housing demolition policies and how these policies affect their education due to the displacement and dispossession of their families following the demolition of the house. We were all walking together in the direction of a family that had just lost its home and to whom I wanted to talk. The house was where 16-year-old Mervat and her family lived. Mervat started showing us the rubble of whatever remained of the house, when all of a sudden she saw her history notebook among the débris. She pulled out her notebook and told us: "this is how we study, under the rubble, this is our history under the rubble, and soon – it seems – we will be under the rubble", adding in Arabic, "*wala hada hāsses fīnā*", freely translated as "no one feels us", that is to say: we are invisible, so nobody cares. Talking to people like Mervat following the demolition of her home (in focus groups, face to face, or during individual interviews), not only captures the conditions under which people survive trauma and militarization, but it also allows us, as researchers, to unpack hegemonic maps, feel the profound effects of such victimization and observe the innate power that children and youth mobilize in order to survive such human rights violations. Moreover, accessing such data under military conditions allowed other members of the group of young men and women walking with me to learn about each other's ordeals, acknowledge pains and hardships, share their own techniques of coping, and even plan future supportive actions. This chapter cannot by any stretch of the imagination reveal the magnitude of suffering that unfolds in these traumatized, but extremely rich context-specific studies.

Research undertaken to date in the Occupied Palestinian Territories of the West Bank and Gaza Strip is mired in either theoretical or rhetorical debates. The latter generally attempt to determine who is "telling the truth". The former approach violence and the consequent materiality of war from various "perspectives", be they global, Marxist, feminist, post-colonial, concerns with global capitalism, security, theology or even various combinations of these perspectives. While I am not opposed to applied theoretical scholarship, or to theoretical debates, I advocate a process of listening, through research, to the voices of children that would reveal the complex interconnectedness between militaristic ideologies and the various manifestations of oppression and colonization— the lack of safe and free educational access being the specific concern in this instance. I also feel that the search for an invincible truth is pointless in a field of discourse predicated on a dynamic where one voice can and does supersede the one that went before it.

In an age of constant and global surveillance technology, "truth" is not so much empirical as it is a floating and ever-changing signifier. The best we can do with "truth" is to unpack the mechanisms of oppression within which multiple versions of "truth" are allowed to reside and circulate.

"Security Necessities" or Mis-Education as Collective Punishment

Since June 2006, 1.5 million Palestinians have been trapped in the Gaza Strip, effectively erecting the entire Gaza Strip into a large prison that prevents children, youth and adults, students and workers, and inhabitants from all walks of life from leading a "normal", healthy and dignified life. The effects on education and educational institutions is devastating. According to human rights organizations, and some editorials published in the daily press, such imprisonment is an illegal and straightforward act of collective and undifferentiated punishment, which stands in violation of both international and Israeli law.[3] The Palestinian Civil Affairs Committee pointed out that Gaza Strip residents, and particularly postsecondary students, are effectively banned from leaving the region or traveling for their study, either abroad or even transit to the West Bank in order to attend Palestinian universities there. The then Chair of Israel's Knesset Education Committee, Rabbi Michael Malchior stated (on May 28, 2008) that: "Trapping hundreds of students in Gaza is immoral and unwise." Israeli Supreme Court Justice Elyakim Rubinstein reckoned (on June 2, 2008) that the closure on the Gaza Strip seems "no less harmful to the Israeli interest, because we have to live with the Palestinians in the future, too."

In a letter dated July 7, 2008, the then Israeli Foreign Minister, Tzipi Livni, stated:

> The policy of not permitting exit abroad for students from Gaza is part of the [Israeli] Security Cabinet decision from 19.09.07 which defined Gaza as a hostile entity and placed restrictions on the borders for passage of goods and movement of people from the Strip and to it except for humanitarian cases. As of today, there is no change in this policy. At the same time, after consideration of particular cases, a few exceptions were approved, following, among other things, requests made by international actors.[4]

Livni's letter reveals Israel's official position that education is not a "humanitarian" field of activity. Moreover, defining Gaza as a "hostile entity" necessitates dealing with it as a monolithic block. This entails (a) treating all its inhabitants as "security risk" and (b) placing "restrictions on the borders for passage of goods and movement of people". Any need of any individual Gazan—be it related to health, education, work or other needs—is subsumed under this logic of "security threats" to the Israeli state.

Some cases involving the violation of Palestinians' right to education have reached the courts. One has to question the ability and efficacy of the current Israeli justice system to prevent injustices, replete as it is with prejudices and discriminatory legislation, for instance, as in the case of "family unification".

The variety of such restrictions include, but are not limited to, restrictions that apply to Gaza and West Bank residents: a ban on students from Gaza leaving for study abroad (including discussion of consular escort requirement); a ban on Gaza students studying in Israel and also in the West Bank;[5] restrictions on West Bank students leaving for study abroad based on individual security arguments; restrictions on students living in the West Bank but holding a Gaza Strip identity card which prevents them from returning to the West Bank if they leave it; internal checkpoints located across the West Bank and which block the movement of students to and from educational institutions.

In a response to an Israeli High Court petition on behalf of a Palestinian student from the Gaza Strip who applied to Nottingham University in the UK, the Office of Israel's Attorney General explained: the State will only consider requests to exit the Gaza Strip "if at the time of submitting the application the applicant is in possession of a recognized scholarship." Palestinian students, like Azhar Alboraey (23 years old), who requested access to education but failed to meet the Israeli criteria of "recognized" scholarships granted by institutions in "friendly" countries (primarily Western countries), were not permitted to leave. In response to a petition by Gisha, the Israeli military declined to define what a "recognized" scholarship is.[6] Requests submitted by students who do not hold scholarships or by those seeking to study in non-Western countries have been rejected or ignored by the military. The effect of such violation of students' right to education often ends up discouraging young women and men from applying to colleges and universities, both locally and abroad. Under these circumstances, many were led to change their choices of study to what is available locally, within their immediate vicinity (for more details, see Shalhoub-Kevorkian, 2007b). As for university students, many of them lost their scholarships and/or university places, including students who were granted a Fullbright scholarship.

The following cases illustrate the issues at stake. Mona Bakheet, 28 years old (cited in Gefen, 2008) stated:

> In summer 2007, and after two and a half years of being away, I came to visit my family in Gaza, during my summer break between my studies for my first and my second degree at Illinois University [IU]. I found myself stuck in Gaza, losing the first and the second semester [at IU]. All my future plans collapsed when they imprisoned me in Gaza. The siege is suffocating our soul, our dreams, and is turning the people of Gaza, mainly young children, into hopeless people.

Wael al Dayyah from Gaza was also prohibited by Israel from reaching his university to start his doctoral studies in business administration at Bradford University, UK (Gefen, 2008). He was able to leave later via the Rafah Crossing into Egypt.

Cases submitted to the Israeli High Court of Justice (HCJ) offer additional insights. For instance, in HCJ 12220/05 *Hamdan and others v. Military Commander of the Gaza Strip* and nine related cases, the petitions challenged the Israeli Defense Minister's policy not to allow students from Gaza to study in West

Bank universities. The State's response, issued on 20 March 2007, stated that West Bank universities are considered "greenhouses for growing terrorists", and that the students belong to a risk group that calls for "the elimination of Israel". Therefore, Gaza residents can't study in West Bank academic institutions. The State's response also noted that even if a Gaza Strip student comes to the West Bank for study purposes only, this act of transiting and joining an academic institution is risky to the State of Israel, the supposition being that once the students get there, they will develop an intention to engage in terrorism. The Court upheld this rationale, stating that,

> The Court does not live in a vacuum ... the Court is situated in Jerusalem, and more than once Jerusalem suffered from uncontrolled terrorism. We are aware of the effect of terror and destruction against the State and its citizens. Like any other Israeli, we acknowledge the need to protect the State and its citizens from the harsh attack of terror.
>
> (Hamdan, HCJ 12220/05)

The Court's statement demonstrates the centrality of "security considerations" in its rulings: "the need to protect the State and its citizens". The Court went as far as to state that, "analyzing the existing data shows that the age group 16–35 is the main age group involved in acts of terror". The Court ended up affirming that due to the fact that "the general security policy regarding individuals ages 16–35 is based on the evaluation of risks," students should not be permitted to access their education.

In several individual cases, students from the Gaza Strip asked to study abroad but failed to get a permit. Other cases involve students from the West Bank who asked to study abroad but were restricted from exiting the West Bank through Allenby Bridge,[7] once again due to "security" reasons, unless they signed a document saying that they would not be engaging in "terrorist activity", or only if they committed themselves to remain outside the West Bank for a minimal period of time, generally a year or two. Thus, the fulfillment of the right to education was conditioned by the students accepting restrictions on their movements or by "self-exiling" for a specific period of time.

For example, in the case of Wissam Madhoun's court petition HCJ 07 /4496 from June 2007, the verdict explained that entrance to Israel for Gaza Strip residents is limited to "humanitarian" purposes and that Gaza Strip residents are not permitted to study in Israel because education is not a humanitarian purpose.

In cases when students managed to travel to a different country to acquire an education, some of them were unable to return to their homes, due to Israel's "fear" and/or due to "security" justifications. When students managed to visit their families during vacations, some were prevented from returning to their universities. Moreover, as the case of Marwan Muteir shows, Israel's bureaucracy was used to further exercise control over Palestinians. Marwan, who managed to get a permit to travel and study abroad, was refused an assurance that he would be able to return to the West Bank, his place of residence, because his Israeli-approved identity card listed the Gaza Strip as his place of residence.[8] When accepted to study at prestigious universities outside the West Bank, Palestinian students face difficulties leaving the West Bank and are then further at risk of not being able to get a permit in the future to return to their place of residence, either definitively or for a visit. In the Gaza Strip, Palestinian residents who meet the restrictive criteria of being eligible for study abroad because they were granted prestigious scholarships to the EU and the United States, are required by Israel to be escorted to the border crossing by consular officials from the country "receiving" them, a burden that makes it increasingly unlikely for them to attain an education, turning the journey into an arduous and oppressive path.

Moreover, students from the Gaza Strip without scholarships, or those traveling to countries Israel does not define as "friendly," are not permitted to leave the Gaza Strip because of Israel's "fear" and "security" justifications. Even students who meet the restrictive criteria are often denied permission to leave the Gaza Strip on an individual basis due to unspecified "security reasons" that are usually based on "secret information" that the students or their lawyers cannot review or challenge. Hence, in addition to human rights violations, students are denied the right to due process.

Even when students plan to study within their own areas in the West Bank, their opportunities for acquiring higher education, or high school education, remain limited by military checkpoints, the Israeli-built illegal "separation wall" and other unexpected restrictions such as balloon-borne checkpoints (Shalhoub-Kevorkian, 2009). As it is, the state of higher education within the Gaza Strip is particularly constrained. Not only does Israel constantly attack educational institutions, it also prevents lecturers and academics from abroad, and even from the West Bank, from working and participating in building educational institutions. Israel has also prevented Palestinian academics from traveling abroad to pursue their education or participate in academic activities and conferences. Many medical and para-medical courses are not offered in Gaza, including occupational therapy, speech therapy, dentistry and physiotherapy, in addition to practical anatomy courses. The limitations of the higher education system in the Gaza Strip are due, among other things, to the restrictions on entrance for nonresidents, a policy that Israel has enforced throughout its military occupation. The violation of Palestinian students' right to education, including those who were accepted to Israeli academic institutions, was always justified with appeals to "fear" and "security." Such violations prevent them also from accessing medical care, finding jobs, or securing economic opportunities.

Israeli expressions of power reside in the capacity to dictate who may access an educational institution of her/his choice, and who may not. Hence, in the name of "security" and "fear of a hostile entity", Israel has the power to control the Palestinian "Other", as Livni's letter, cited above, further demonstrates. The implementation of Israel's right to a life "free of fear" and for "security" clarifies who should be protected, and who is a disposable "Other". The question remains whether the notions of "fear" and "security" are sufficient to account for the ways in which the individual and collective right of one group to education may be violated, under the guise of an absolutist security doctrine based on what may be called a "theology of the fearful." Collective punishment, after all, may be conceived in its articulations along Foucault's (1984) notion of "biopower", that is the legalization of the right to dispose of the lives of others and to annihilate them. To exercise such power over the education of Palestinian students is to place Palestinians in the same politico-juridical structure of the camp; as Giorgio Agamben (cited in Mbembe, 2003: 12) explains, it is to exercise control over their spaces, their spatial arrangements, and future development and life, while keeping them continually outside the state of law, in a continuous "state of exception".

The Voices of Palestinian Children

I now invoke the voices of Palestinian children to examine how they face to Israeli military and juridical machinations.

Education is systematically obstructed and educational sites are at times destroyed outright by the Israeli military occupation of the West Bank and Gaza Strip. The Palestinian Monitoring Group (2005) stated that the Israeli military and settler activity has resulted in killings, injuries, and arrests affecting 28 percent of the Palestinian student population, without counting disruptions to school schedules and daily routines. UNICEF (2006) reported that 144 schools in the Occupied Palestinian Territories were disrupted during the 2005–2006 academic year, resulting in disturbance of schooling for 64,712 students and 2,470 teachers. During the week of 26 March 2007 alone, the following incidences involving students were recorded: the Israeli army invaded Jenin University and abducted two young people (Bannoura 2007), Palestinian university students were harassed at a checkpoint (Palestine News Network 2007), and Israeli troops detained Palestinian teachers at a Nablus check point (International Middle East Media Centre 2007).

I undertook two recent studies within this larger context. In these studies, I showed that Palestinian children in the Gaza Strip and the West Bank stressed the role of education in promoting their ability to survive the effects of militarization (Shalhoub-Kevorkian, 2007a, 2008). In these studies, young women repeatedly mentioned their fear of not being able to access educational institutions. Afnan, a 15-year-old student stated:

> All you hear in the news, is about the fears of the occupiers ... they fear us if we walk to school, they fear us if we carry books, they fear women if they are pregnant, they fear our veils, they fear us if we are working together during the olive harvest, they fear our existence, and of course, if we will be educated, and we will tell the world about their atrocities, they would want us dead. Now you understand why I fear their acts? All they want is to imprison us, close our schools, block us from reaching our universities, and for Palestinian youth, educational institutions are the only source of support and solidarity. To summarize it to you, all they want is for us to die, slow death.

Children and young women and men stressed that schooling and university studies are a critical aspect of the fabric of their lives, despite the hardships they undergo. Young women mentioned how fears within their families, due to living with constant uncertainties and in the midst of war, resulted in the early marriages of sisters or cousins. Restrictions are also imposed by the family on women's movements while others are withdrawn from school due to safety reasons or for fears. These fears were expressed in the following way by Nawal, a young woman:

> As much as we dream and hope for better days to come, our lives as women are different from the lives of men. My cousin Samira is a very beautiful girl, but she was very bright in school too. She wanted to finish school and go to the university in Gaza City. But her father's fears and her family's worries about the political situation, and the fact that many men are in the streets and unemployed, made the whole family agree that she was to marry her cousin. She wanted to feel safer, and marriage makes you feel safe, but when I visit her she tells me that she wishes she were still in school. She always tells me to study and finish school, for she feels a sorrow and distress in her heart because she lost her chance to continue her education.

Both girls and boys explained that more often than not, girls suffered more from patriarchal practices imposed on girls in the name of "masculine protection". The militarization of spaces, the deterioration of economic conditions, and the deprivation of safe education reproduces and reinforces patriarchy within Palestinian society, while further encouraging early and child marriage, the imposition of veiling and other modalities of gender discrimination. Moreover, young women suffered more from the constant changes imposed on school schedules because they could not count on any sense of routine. Complaining of these uncertainties, Imad, a 15-year-old schoolboy, stated:

> Since we started studying in one school, some girls lost their education because their parents feared sending them to school during the afternoon, mainly because no one knows when the bombing will start, and if the boy is at school he can manage to hide and protect himself, but with girls it is more complicated. My father is always afraid that someone would hurt or dishonour my sisters, and he needed to ask them to wear the black veil, and also not leave the house after 4:00 p.m.

Children are particularly vulnerable under such circumstances. Their ability to attend school is hindered due to the daily hardships and the constant restrictions on their access to schools. In other instances, the challenges involved furthered their resolve to complete their studies. Anxiety over economic hardships was also apparent in children's perceptions of their ability to study. Their determination to fight back was based on their conviction that promoting their personal growth through education contributes to their freedom. Mona expressed this idea in the following way: "Getting my degree is my weapon against future atrocities; my degree is my passport to freedom." Looking for ways to deal with the daily hardships imposed on Palestinian access to education was also apparent in the interviewees' detailed explanations regarding the support they feel they get from their parents, family members and teachers when they are successful in school.

Their attachment to their school and their feeling of belonging, increased their desire to overcome obstacles facing them on their way to school or university. Manal, a schoolgirl, explained this point in the following way:

> Reaching school under the threat of the bombing and the constant fear is not an easy task, but I never miss my school. I love coming to school. I meet my friend Hidaya and share with her all my secrets; I tell her things that I never share even with my own mother. I love my school, and I worry about it. I always dream that the Jews demolished my school, so I rush every day here to make my eyes see it again and again. I know deep inside me that one day they will destroy it. Last year before the end of the school, I took my uncle's camera and took some pictures of my school. I do not want ever to forget it. I helped paint the eastern wall [of the school], and I love the way it looks now.

Conversations with Palestinian children repeatedly revealed that schools have become a site of opposition for many: by attending school, they refuse to give in to the horrors of life around them and to lose the source of support, love, and belonging, and perhaps most importantly, stability. This was particularly apparent when talking to young women. Young women were anxious about losing their access to their schools and colleges, and to their close friends. They also feared patriarchal oppression following such incapacitation, and the uncertainty and instability it produces. They reiterated their fear of their fathers, uncles or brothers; and explained how losing their right to attend school might empower some of their male family members and give them the chance to exercise control and to discriminate against them. For young girls, schools and teachers were not only sources of empowerment, but also sources and sites of transformation and growth. Salwa explained: "For us, Palestinian women, our teachers and our schools are our life oxygen."

Many children disclosed their close connection with their teachers; some even shared poems they had written in praise of their teachers. They revealed how some of their teachers had become profound symbols of knowledge, care and belonging for them. Muhammad told us:

> When I grow up, I want to be like my teacher Samir. He is so quiet, and very knowledgeable. He is my science teacher, but he knows and analyzes politics in a different way. He knows historical facts; he knows lots of scientists, many philosophers and so much more. He always brings us new books and reads small parts of them [to us]. I think that he was supposed to be a university teacher, but the political situation and the fact that his brother was assassinated made him stay with his family and work closer to them. I really respect the way he teaches, he is so patient with the students, and the way he treats his children, I wish my father were like him. He never hits or screams at any students, but they all fear and respect him.

As many of these narratives reveal, the negative effects of the militarization of education (indeed of their entire lives) have been accompanied by a sense of agency and resistance to such racialized oppression. For example, the counter-hegemonic language present in the children's thoughts and voices was apparent in Hidaya's words. At the very end of a focus group, children were asked whether they would like to add anything. Hidaya seized the opportunity and said:

> How can the world live in peace when we suffer every single minute? I am sure they pay a high price. I am sure. See, every time they hear about our resistance, they feel weak … for they are weak. I believe that I, Hidaya, the very simple person, is much stronger than all of them, otherwise why would they send a tank, big computerized planes and machines to kill me. They fear the Palestinian child, and therefore we must stay strong, love each other, help and support the needy, and be educated. They fear educated people that can speak English and tell the world about their crimes.

The voices of Palestinian youth and children living under constant military upheaval reveals that, for them, schools are sites of belonging, support, resistance, and continuity (Shalhoub-Kevorkian 2007a). Reflecting on their comments, I wondered how long these children could continue and endure the effects of a militarized education.

Conclusion

This chapter illustrates how, what I call the "industry of fear", racializes Palestinians as people to be feared. More specifically, it turns Palestinian students into "security risks." Furthermore, sharing the ordeals and voices of the Palestinian students and juxtaposing them with a review of official Israeli positions and court decisions reveals how this "racialization" sustains modes of racism that subordinate and disrupt the right to education in the name of "security considerations."

Referring to Palestinians' access to education as a "security threat," and always as potential producers of physical danger to Israel, leads to the conclusion that Palestinians are objectified and reinscribed in the space of conflict as "threatening subjects". Such logic constructs a more "ordered" gaze on the racial division between those who have the right to education and security, and those that are considered a "danger" and should be prevented from accessing education as part and parcel of the act of maintaining security. Such tactics, I suggest, should be highlighted, first, because despite their intended totalizing effects, Palestinian children and youth preserve a sense of agency when the educational system is under siege.

Secondly, this chapter underlines the politics of accountability that requires scholars and activists to trace relations of power and penalty. Both the politics of acknowledgment and the politics of accountability suggest that we cannot proceed as researchers unless we examine not only the workings of power but also our complicity, as scholars, in not questioning our understanding beyond the justifications of "security" and "fear," articulated and disseminated, for instance, through the media, official statements, and court decisions.

Thirdly, the chapter emphasizes the need for researchers and scholars to listen carefully to the day-to-day experiences of those living under the canopy of violent conflicts in order to capture the effects of military occupation, and understand how it is raced, classed and gendered. As Mbembe states, "Politics can only be traced as a spiral transgression, as that difference that disorients the very idea of the limit" (Mbembe, 2003: 16). Mbembe's observation expresses the legal insanity or rupture operating between those who have the right to have rights and those who have no such rights and are not allowed to claim any. Such normalized "fear", supported by an absolutist security theology, objectifies individuals and entire communities, as mere labels and categories in a wider "industry of fear" and colonial violence. It thus sets the stage for the victim's ultimate destruction.

Notes

1 Based on Gisha (2008b). This report provides the background of different Israeli policies that restrict access to education in the Occupied Palestinian Territories.
2 Based on fieldwork data collected by Shalhoub-Kevorkian (2008).
3 Based on Gisha (2008c). See also the Hebrew daily, *Ha'aretz*, in its editorial dated 18 May 2009, accessible on the newspaper's website at <http://www.haaretz.co.il/hasite/spages/1086536.html>.
4 Letter included in Gisha's (2008a) report.
5 This includes, for example, the cases of students from the Gaza Strip who study occupational therapy at Bethlehem University in the West Bank, mainly because universities in the Gaza Strip do not teach this specialization. See also, HCJ. 11120/05 *Hamdan v. Southern Military Commander* and related cases, from January 19, 2006.
6 Letter to Gisha quoted in Gisha (2008a).
7 The "Allenby Bridge" crosses the Jordan River and connects Jericho in the West Bank to the Hashemite Kingdom of Jordan. It is currently the designated exit/entry point for Palestinians residing in the West Bank and who are traveling to and from Jordan to the West Bank and/or to Israel.
8 That is the case for many students living in the West Bank but whose address is registered with the Israeli bureaucracy as being in the Gaza Strip.

References

Appadurai, A. (2006). *Fear of Small Numbers: An Essay on the Geography of Anger*. Durham, NC: Duke University Press.
Bannoura, G. (2007). Israeli army invades Jenin University: abducts two youths. Birzeit University Right to Education Campaign and News Centre, Birzeit, West Bank, Palestine, 26 March. Retrieved April 9, 2007, from http://right2edu.birzeit.edu/news/article163
Bauman, Z. (2003). *City of Fear, City of Hope*. London: Goldsmiths College, University of London.
B'Tselem (2008). Access denied: Israeli measures to deny Palestinians access to lands around settlements. Retrieved March 22, 2009, from http://www.btselem.org/english/Publications/Summaries/200809_Access_Denied.asp
B'Tselem (2009). Guidelines for Israel's investigation into Operation Cast Lead: 27 December 2008 – 18 January 2009. Retrieved March 22, 2009, from http://www.btselem.org/Download/200902_Operation_Cast_Lead_Position_paper_Eng.pdf

Bush, K.D. and Saltarelli, D. (2000). The two faces of education in ethnic conflict: Towards a peace building education for children. Florence: UNICEF. Retrieved March 22, 2009, from http://unicef-irc.org/publications/pdf/insight4.pdf

Corradi, J.E., Weiss Fagen, P. and Garreton, M.A. (eds.) (1992). *Fear at the Edge: State Terror and Resistance in Latin America*. Berkeley, CA University of California Press.

Foucault, M. (1984). *The Foucault Reader*, ed. P. Rabinow. New York: Pantheon Books.

Freire, P. (2000). *Pedagogy of the Oppressed*. New York: Continuum.

Gefen, Y. (2008). "Darkening brains". *Ma'ariv*. Retrieved March 22, 2009, from http://www. nrg.co.il/online/1/ART1/780/263.html (In Hebrew.)

Gisha (2008a). Frequently asked questions: Students trapped in Gaza. Retrieved March 15, 2009, from http://www.gisha.org/UserFiles/File/publications_english/Publications %20and%20Reports_English/Frequently_Asked_Questions_November_2008.pdf (In Hebrew.)

Gisha (2008b). Held back: Students trapped in Gaza. Retrieved March 15, 2009, from http:// www.gisha.org/UserFiles/File/Students%20report%20Eng%20-%20Online%20Version. pdf (In Hebrew.)

Gisha (2008c). Gaza closure defined: Collective punishment. Retrieved March 15, 2009, from http://www.gisha.org/UserFiles/File/publications_english/Publications%20 and%20Reports_English/Gaza%20Closure%20Defined%20Eng(1).pdf) (In Hebrew.)

hooks, b. (1994). *Teaching to Transgress: Education as the Practice of Freedom*. New York: Routledge.

Khalidi, R. (2004). *Resurrecting Empire: Western Footprints and America's Perilous Path in the Middle East*. Boston, MA: Beacon Press.

Khalidi, R. (2006). *The Iron Cage: The Story of the Palestinian Struggle for Statehood*. Boston, MA: Beacon Press.

Mbembe, A. (2003). Necropolitics. *Public Culture*, 15(1), 11–40.

Nordstrom, C. (1992). Backyard front. In Nordstrom, C. and Martin, J.A. (eds.), *The Paths to Domination, Resistance and Terror*. Berkeley, CA: University of California Press.

Palestinian Center for Human Rights (2009a). IOF war on the Gaza Strip enters third week. Retrieved March 22, 2009, from http://www.pchrgaza.org/files/PressR/ English/2008/09-2009.html

Palestinian Center for Human Rights (2009b). Israeli Occupation Forces (IOF) have continued their war on the Gaza for the 3rd consecutive week under international silence. Retrieved March 22, 2009, from http://www.pchrgaza.org/files/W_report/ English/2008/pdf/weekly%20report%2002-09.pdf

Pappe, I. (2003). The post-territorial dimension of a future homeland in Israel and Palestine. *Comparative Studies of South Asia, Africa and the Middle East*, 23(1–2), 224–233.

Pappe, I. (2007). *The Ethnic Cleansing of Palestine*. Oxford: Oneworld.

Shalhoub-Kevorkian, N. (2009). *Militarization and Violence against Women in Conflict Zones in the Middle East*. Cambridge: Cambridge University Press.

Shalhoub-Kevorkian, N. (2007a). *Facing the Wall: Palestinian Children and Adolescents Speak About the Israeli Separation Wall*. Jerusalem: World Vision.

Shalhoub-Kevorkian, N. (2007b). *Gender and the Militarization of Education in Palestine*. Jerusalem: Women Studies Center. (In Arabic.)

Shalhoub-Kevorkian, N. (2008). The gendered nature of education under siege: a Palestinian feminist perspective. *International Journal of Lifelong Education*, 27(2), 179–200.

Shor, I. (1992). *Empowering Education: Critical Teaching and Social Change*. Chicago, IL: University of Chicago Press.

Sultana, R.G. (2006). Education in conflict situations: Palestinian children and distance education in Hebron. *Mediterranean Journal of Educational Studies*, 11(1), 49–81.

UNICEF (2006). UNICEF occupied Palestinian territory (oPt) selected statistics. Retrieved April 15, 2007, from http://www.unicef.org/oPt/Gaza_statistics_27_July_2006_Eng.pdf

Websites

Palestine News Network: http://english.pnn.ps/

International Middle East Media Centre: http://imemc.org/

21 War, State Collapse, and the Predicament of Education in Iraq[1]

Nabil Al-Tikriti

Egyptians write, Lebanese publish, Iraqis read. – Arab saying

The venerable saying above has come to apply less in recent years, at least as far as Iraq is concerned. Iraqi writers have published a great deal of new work in the course of the country's post-2003 dislocation; Iraqi textbooks have mostly been published in Jordan since the early 1990s;[2] and Iraqi literacy rates have fallen to levels unseen since the 1960s. Today, the saying might run something like "Iraqis write, Jordanians publish, and no one can read."

Bush administration officials managing the 2003 US invasion and subsequent occupation of Iraq hoped to comprehensively remake the political, economic, cultural, and intellectual face of the country. Consistent with US Secretary of State Condoleezza Rice's "creative chaos" doctrine,[3] American officials first fostered the instant privatization of state assets by allowing mass looting, then enacted a series of reforms intended to reorient Iraq's education system. Concentrating on such interventions as textbook reform, facility restoration, de-Ba'thification, and bilateral university assistance, Coalition Provisional Authority (CPA) officials had hoped to shepherd a new and more amenable Iraq out of the shell of the old. One of the more ambitious announced interventions of U.S. government officials in Iraq's education system involved reforming all levels of curriculum to better coincide with "international standards," – particularly through textbook revision. As it turns out, following the completion of the UNICEF/UNESCO textbook editing projects, Project RISE, and a series of higher education projects, the CPA educational legacy turned out to be remarkably modest.

Educational Evolution, 1920–2003

When a child starts going to school, the book is a window to the world.[4]

Centralized control over textbook production has a long history in modern Iraq, extending even back to the late Ottoman era.[5] Following the hostile takeover and international recognition of the British-installed Iraqi state and Hashemite monarchy, a new curriculum emerged. This curriculum did not evolve without its share of controversy and debate, however. In the 1920s–1930s, Director-General of

Education Sāti' al-Husri (1879–1967) resisted international supervision under the auspices of either British advisors or the League of Nations, arguing that anything produced by such sources would reflect the colonialist outlook of the origin nations.[6] Seeing education as playing a key role in inculcating proper views in the youth, al-Husri was eventually able to combine Arabism and Iraqi nationalism into a coherent curricular vision intended to buttress Hashemite legitimacy.[7]

Following the 1958 revolution, a new course entitled *Social Studies and National Education* [*al-Ijtimā'iyāt wa al-tarbiya al-wataniyya*] debuted. Apparently the forefather of the renowned Ba'thist course, *National Education* [*al-Tarbiya al-wataniyya*], this class entailed "a civics course aimed at socializing students to new (post-Hashemite) political loyalties," and a "highly centralized and politicized undertaking that attempted to expose as many students as possible to the ruling ideology."[8] Outside of this course, most of the Hashemite-era curriculum remained unchanged.

As has been widely noted, Iraq's education sector witnessed dramatic fluctuations in performance over the forty years since the Ba'th party achieved lasting power in the summer of 1968. After significant expansion and improvement from 1968 to the early 1980s, the sector underwent stagnation from then until the early 1990s, a gradual and debilitating decline of standards throughout the early 1990s, and dramatic looting and destruction in the course of the 2003 invasion and occupation. Considering that these destructive events were more recently succeeded by the intense civil war of 2006–07, it should not surprise anyone that the new Government of Iraq has to date remained unable to devote sufficient energies to curriculum reform and education investment.

Throughout the 1960s, the Iraqi state had engaged on an ambitious expansion of primary education, which the Ba'thist government continued.[9] In the first few years after seizing power in the 17–30 July 1968 coup, the Ba'thist government emphasized gradual improvement and continuity within the educational system which they had inherited from prior governments. By that time, the system they inherited reflected a hybrid blend of late Ottoman pedagogical legacies and ethical values, British curricular models, and pan-Arab nationalist political orientations.[10]

Much changed in 1974 following the Eighth Regional (Iraqi) Congress of the Ba'th Party. Marking the political consolidation and social expansion of the Ba'thist venture, at that point the government dedicated the educational system more thoroughly toward political indoctrination and "changed the ideological basis of the educational system from the promotion of a general sense of Iraqi nationalism towards the rhetoric of the Ba'th Party and especially of its leadership."[11] In the course of this Congress, the party announced a far-reaching educational reform initiative, which included "removal of persons of reactionary and bourgeois views from all levels of education, from nursery school to university, [and] the provision of new books and syllabuses [sic] which conform to the principles of the Party and the Revolution."[12] After thus announcing the intention to cleanse educational faculty and staff from anti-Ba'thist elements and revamp all course materials – in a policy move eerily similar to those promulgated in 2003 – the party described its goal of shaping a "new Arab man" who would protect the ideals of its revolution throughout society. This policy directive, rendered state law by Public Law 115 in

1976, marked the beginning of a comprehensive curriculum overhaul which was largely complete by 1981.[13]

The interpretative results of the post-1974 curriculum reform were largely encapsulated in a voluminous team publication entitled *al-'Irāq fī al-tārikh / Iraq in History*.[14] Completed in 1983 and designed as a comprehensive survey of Iraq's role in history, this work provided an advanced ideological guide to collegiate research and writing about Iraq throughout the ages. *Iraq in History* appears to have been a cooperative effort between state and quasi-state actors. Although not issued by a government ministry, several indicators demonstrate the state's and party's involvement in the production process. Most of the chapter contributors were either university faculty or held posts in state cultural institutions. The "Leader-President" Saddam Hussein provided the book's opening quote, itself suggestive of the conflictive nature of historical interpretation: "History is the final product that the will of the *umma* itself decides upon."[15] Finally, the book's introduction explicitly credits Mr Hussein with backing the project upon perceiving the need for a general overview of Iraq's history.[16] At the same time, the preface's author and most public representative of the project, Dr Salih Ahmad al-'Ali, was the president of the well-regarded private and pre-Ba'thist Iraqi Academy of Sciences.

Iraq in History sums up the Ba'thist view of Iraq's history, a view which remains quite resonant to this day within Iraqi society. According to this view, Iraq is an essentially Arab Semitic region which originated human civilization. The Ottomans are treated as one of several non-Arab occupying powers succeeding the 1258 Mongol conquest of Baghdad, rather than as the ruling empire governing parts or all of the regions which became Iraq for over four centuries. The modern country is effectively devoid of sectarian identities, and the Kurds are not seen as possessing any particular characteristics distinct from the Iraqi people as a whole. The work ends with the 1958 revolution, perhaps indicative of the difficulty of enforcing a unitary vision on more recent developments.

In the course of the 1980–88 Iran–Iraq war, a conscious effort to portray Iran as a longstanding enemy was introduced to textbook content.[17] The guiding state-backed book for this issue was *al-Sirā' al-'Irāqī al-Fārsī / The Iraqi–Persian Conflict*.[18] According to this view, Iraq and Iran have always been in conflict, as the primary representatives of and leaders within an eternal Arab-'Ajam ethnic rivalry.[19] As with all historical narratives, this view presented a highly selective view of history, ignoring in this case Kurdish–Iranian linguistic affinities; Iranian–Iraqi Shi'ite religious affinities since the early 16th century; the distinctive histories of several Iraqi minorities; and periods of Iranian–[proto]Iraqi political unity under Sassanid, Ilkhanid, Qaraqoyunlu, Aqqoyunlu, and Safavid rule. Such portrayals remained largely unchanged through 2003, even though the 1980–88 Iran–Iraq war had long since ended. Since eliminating negative portrayals of Iran – as opposed to those of America and Israel – was not included in the USAID-financed reform agenda of 2003–04, such passages were not deleted. Considering the far friendlier relationship between all post-2005 Iraqi governments and the Iranian state, it is likely that such portrayals will eventually be adjusted, although the paradigm has remained in evidence in textbooks published as late as 2008.

One of the key components of state indoctrination was the renowned *al-Tarbiya al-wataniyya / National Education* course. Abolished as Ba'thist propaganda by CPA officials in 2003, this course in some sense continued the post-1958 *Social Studies and National Education* course. Based on a 1999 2nd Intermediate (8th Grade) *al-Tarbiya al-wataniyya* edition, it is clear that this course was designed to inculcate loyalty to the state of Iraq, the Ba'th Party, Arab Nationalism, and Saddam Hussein as the country's "President-Leader." Although the text was based on the original 1981 first edition, certain changes had been made referencing developments since that date – such as to the 1991 *Umm al-ma'ārik* / Mother of All Battles [Gulf War]. Following standard introductory material such as a picture of and quote from Mr Hussein, a picture of the flag, the text of the national anthem, and a list of recognized national and religious holidays, the textbook offered four brief chapters, entitled: "the Arab *Umma,*" "Arab Nationalism," "the Message of the Arab *Umma,*" and "Palestine." Chapter contents were completely infused with Ba'thist ideology, designed to familiarize middle-school students with the basic tenets of the party. The chapter on "Palestine" contextualizes the Arab–Israeli conflict from an Arab nationalist perspective, situating the conflict strictly within an anti-colonial rubric. For example, all chapter headings characterize the conflict as one between "Zionism," "British Imperialism," and the "Arab People." While Ba'thism in the United States has on occasion been compared with Nazism, due to its dual nationalist and socialist ideological program, this textbook characterizes the Arab *umma*'s primary opponent as "racist Zionism."[20] This course is no longer taught in its prior form, and its replacement is said to inculcate a far less militant version of citizenship ideals.[21]

There is some disagreement as to the condition of the education sector by the late 1980s, with some analysts believing that the sector had degraded seriously during the Iran–Iraq war, and others believing that the Iraqi state maintained standards and had hoped to quickly return to "normalcy" once the war ended.[22] Ideologically, educational messaging gradually became marked more by what can best be described as "Saddamization" rather than "Ba'thification." There is some disagreement as to how to separate these two ideological strands, and when this transition was completed. In his analysis of Iraqi collective memory, *Memories of State*, Eric Davis did not generally distinguish between the two, frequently referring to the Iraqi ruling party as the "Takriti Ba'th."[23] Others date this "Saddamization" to President Hussein's 1979 rise to power, while still others believe this process really got under way only in the 1990s, when the régime withdrew within itself under the intense pressures of the sanctions. Upon examining textbooks and state-issued works of historiographic interest, it appears fairly clear that Mr Hussein's personality cult had advanced quite a bit by the early 1980s – and that such messaging was the only aspect of Iraqi historical education that was unambiguously and immediately eliminated following the 2003 invasion and occupation.

Although modern Iraq's educational orientation can be characterized as primarily secular in nature, the definition of this secularism has always been contested. According to Bashkin, the secular approach to education in the mid-1930s emphasized strong bodies, masculinity, military uniforms, a cosmopolitan secularism which downplayed medieval Islamic theories, professionalization and a fetishism of science, and a "new reading of the Islamic past."[24] Although most of these points remain accurate even today, by the 1990s a newfound cultivation of medieval Islamic theories such as the "circle of justice" idea were evident.[25]

As Starrett and Doumato have suggested, most textbooks in the Middle East invent "an original generic Islam that avoids recognition of sectarian differences and is designed to foster a sense of nationalism, promote the legitimacy of the regime in power, or, in some places, provide a counterweight to an immoderate Islamism being disseminated through public discourse."[26] Iraqi textbooks certainly conform to these parameters. Based on a 1998 edition *al-Tarbiya al-Islāmiyya* text, the Ba'thist interpretation of this secular orientation can be characterized as generically Sunni Muslim in orientation.[27] Not very controversial in themselves, the choice of passages for this text indicated a vaguely and somewhat generic Sunni preference. Despite the coming to power since 2005 of Shi'a dominant governments which many commentators have characterized as highly sectarian in nature, such texts have also remained largely unchanged.

Iraqi Kurdish Developments, 1991–2003

In the wake of the 1991 Gulf War, Kurdish parties in Northern Iraq gradually gained de-facto independence under international protection – and Kurdish educators eventually created their own textbook materials. André Mazzawi has pointed to the dearth of studies addressing educators during and after times of conflict, which in Iraq's case has characterized society far more than stability in recent decades. As Mazzawi has suggested, "educators – particularly history teachers – act as 'critical' witnesses in the 'public construction' of memory."[28] Iraqi Kurdistan's teachers in the 1990s played this role in a pivotal fashion, creating educational materials which provided students under their sway with a more radically variant narrative concerning modern Iraqi history than their cohorts in central and southern Iraq.[29]

As Bashkin argued, although the state has long monopolized textbook production and curricular development, teachers and students have always had the ability to "resist and subvert" the systematic inculcation of state values.[30] While the Ministry of Education continuously produced special textbooks designed for "Kurdish study in the autonomous zone,"[31] nothing prevented students from marking up their personal copies – especially after March 1991. One student substituted a 1997 state textbook's statement that "Erbil is in Iraq" with "Erbil is in Iraqi Kurdistan." The same student emphatically crossed out the textbook's statement that "the autonomous region is one of the accomplishments of the 17–30 July Revolution [i.e. Ba'thist government]" – perhaps with the guidance of that class's teacher.[32]

While it is unclear how long such materials were being published and revised, it appears that Kurdish educators had created their own materials by the mid-1990s. Textbook revisions in Kurdish regions evolved from teachers' own initiatives in the early 1990s, with educators initially continuing to use Baghdad's textbooks, then creating their own supplementary materials, and then adopting Kurdish party materials in the mid-1990s. From then until 2002, there were two sets of textbooks, one each designed by the two major Kurdish parties, the Kurdistan Democratic Party (KDP) and the Patriotic Union of Kurdistan (PUK). Since at least 2002, the unified Kurdish Regional Government (KRG) has united its curriculum and is using a common set of textbooks throughout the territories under their control.[33]

One of the earlier Kurdish regional textbooks examined was entitled *al-Tarbiya al-wataniyya*, and effectively continued the Ba'thist tradition of national education – in reverse. The textbook was distributed by a Kurdish NGO named "Save the Children, Kurdistan." The text features a maximalist map of greater Kurdistan, stretching from just north of the Persian Gulf to the Mediterranean, and including Baghdad, Mosul, and other population centers with sizeable Kurdish minorities.[34]

Developments Since 2003

> The world created in ... schoolbooks is essentially a world of fantasy – a fantasy made up by adults as a guide for their children, but inhabited by no one outside the pages of schoolbooks.[35]

Since 2003, Iraq's education sector, like most of the rest of Iraqi society, has struggled to cope with violent dislocation while attempting to continue delivery of services and meet expectations of curricular reform.[36] American assistance to Iraqi primary and secondary education was mainly funneled through two programs: the UNESCO/USAID Textbook Quality Improvement Programme (TQIP) and USAID/CAII's Project RISE.[37]

The TQIP project was a rapidly implemented program financed by USAID, legally sanctioned by UN Security Council Resolution 1483, organized under the administrative umbrella of UNESCO, and implemented by a mixed team of international consultants and Iraqi educators. Curriculum revision goals were logistically modest, but highly sensitive politically. Such goals included removing all photographic and textual references to Saddam Hussein and the Ba'th Party, all hostile references to the United States and Israel, and any references considered hostile to gender equality.[38] TQIP concentrated on the relatively unproblematic mathematics and science texts, leaving primary school social science textbooks to a separate project organized through UNICEF.[39] The UNESCO project ran for a year, from May 2003 to May 2004, and faced a serious obstacle when the international staff were evacuated to Jordan in the wake of the August 2003 Canal Hotel bombing.

The general program objective of the TQIP project was to "provide immediate support for basic education in Iraq by revising, editing, printing, and distributing math and science school textbooks that are gender appropriate, politically neutral, and free from bias."[40] Project participants did not attempt to revise math and science contents or pedagogical methods, as such revisions are far more complicated to implement, requiring years of committee revisions. Instead, the project concentrated on purely political revision.[41] The specific objectives were "reviewing and editing science and mathematics textbooks for primary and secondary schools in Iraq, *according to the textbook revision parameters developed by UNESCO and USAID* [emphasis added]," and "training Iraqi officials on science textbook analysis, review, and revision."[42] Although sanctioned by international bodies, the relative civilizational presumptions of these objectives are self-evident. At the same time, according to one international consultant, the Iraqi educators made all the key decisions once the actual work of revisions began.[43] TQIP met all of its stated goals, and also successfully accomplished several additional goals such as renewing contacts between Iraqi educators that had been severed for as long as 13 years, refurbishing local publishing capacities, and setting up a Ministry data collection system.[44]

According to the UNESCO draft report, the deleted textbook passages consisted of "Ba'thist ideology; Saddam Hussein's cult of personality; discriminatory statements against ethnic, religious, and other groups; politicized information from the previous régime; references that suggest inequality of the sexes; and references encouraging violence." Considering the legal basis of the entire effort, the addition of a seventh requirement that texts be "free from any religious references in order to comply with the American constitution," which "served as a basis for progressive communication between donors and UNESCO principles of universal values", demonstrates the leverage exercised by USAID as the donor institution.[45] An eighth requirement, the elimination of "statements which promoted fighting, for example, against the USA or against Israel" was also mentioned separately.[46] Considering the recent history of tensions and violence between Iraq and these two states, such a requirement should not have appealed to all Iraqi educators. The political nature of the textbook revisions is demonstrated by the facts that some of the revised textbooks were not approved by USAID; and that 26 titles in Turkish and Kurdish were not included in the program at all, and were reprinted without any changes under recovered Oil For Food program funding. The explanation given for not revising such texts referred to the textual changes already introduced in the years prior to the 2003 Anglo-American invasion.[47]

The 2004 UNESCO draft report's "lessons learned" section contained comments suggestive of tensions inherent in such an effort. Notably, "approaches to the work should have been discussed in some depth among UNESCO and USAID agents, in order to avoid delays and misunderstandings" during implementation. Likewise, "one should make sure that Iraqi educators are comfortable with the revision parameters," and "more educational partners should have been involved." The guidelines for revision "were not discussed properly among Iraqi and other education specialists," which eliminated the possibility of Iraqi educators forming their own guidelines at this stage.[48] Finally, in a statement suggesting serious – if unspecified – tensions, the report states that "[t]here has been a real communication gap between the International Advisory Councils and other protagonists."[49] Such conclusions suggest that not all stakeholders were in complete agreement concerning certain aspects of textbook revision, and that minimalist goals were largely a result of occasionally incompatible goals. Tellingly, such critical comments were excised from the official and less informative final project report.

As it turns out, the actual textbook revisions made under the TQIP program appear to have been quite modest, although more significant – and sensitive –

changes were considered. According to the final report, changes were limited to removal of Ba'thist ideology, images of Saddam Hussein, and references suggesting an inequality of the sexes.[50] The draft report also referred to the "eliminated political statements (against the USA and Israel)" in mathematics textbooks. In the final report, however, this reference to the U.S. and Israel was redacted, which would appear to constitute a revision of the revisions report.[51] According to the appendices of both the draft and final reports, however, more sensitive changes such as the elimination of the "*Allahu Akbar*" (God is Great) on the Iraqi flag, "*Bismillah*" (In the Name of God) at the beginning of textbooks, quotations of *hadith* and Qur'anic verses concerning the value of learning, and the district mapping of Iraq were considered but rejected.[52] In each of these cases, the explanation provided for retention of the original format was indicative of various positions held by certain Iraqi and international actors. For example, the reason given for retaining the district mapping of Iraq was that "the district boundaries and their political status will presumably not be changed before a new constitution is released and no foreign territories are included."[53] Although several internationally sanctioned changes were completed, such differences within the TQIP team suggest that some actors had hoped to impose textbook revisions well beyond their limited legal powers under International Humanitarian Law governing military occupation.

The USAID-funded UNICEF initiative to revise social science textbooks at the primary and secondary school level appears to have either never effectively launched, or to have neglected to release a public report. This process was far less transparent than the UNESCO initiative in math and science texts, which was itself not entirely transparent.

Although a detailed examination of textbook changes based on actual pre-2003 and post-invasion textbooks is beyond the scope of this chapter, a brief examination of certain textbooks published between 2005 and 2008 demonstrated that wholesale curriculum reform has yet to be enacted. In addition, a quick comparison of the 1998 and 2007 editions of the 2nd Intermediate *al-Tārikh al-'Arabī wa al-Islāmī / Arab and Islamic History* textbook showed surprisingly modest changes in a text with explicitly historiographic and religious overtones. While textual changes in most cases resulted in the change of a few letters or words, and at most involved adding a paragraph, the changes enacted for the 2007 edition subtly elevated the role of scholars '*ulāmā*' in society, rehabilitated the legacy of medieval Persians, re-emphasized 'Alī b. Abī Tālib, and transformed references away from an "Arab *umma*" towards those of the more traditional Muslim *umma*.[54] Considering ongoing sensitivities involving Iraqi collective memory and social identity, and the violent instability fueled in part by conflict over such identity, it is perhaps not surprising that Iraqi curriculum reform since 2003 remains somewhat modest.

Notes

1 I thank the Georg-Eckert-Institut für internationale Schulbuchforschung (GEI) and the United States Institute of Peace (USIP) for logistical and financial support provided to carry out this research. I especially thank the USIP Baghdad staff member

who persuaded her uncle to purchase several Iraqi textbooks on my behalf at the al-Mutanabi book market (Baghdad) in August 2008. I also wish to thank Hersh Abdula, Samira Alayan-Beck, Elizabeth Cole, Linda Herrera, Phebe Marr, André Mazzawi, Achim Rohde, and Haifa Zengana for information, collaboration, sources, and advice connected to this project.

2 According to UNESCO, 80% of Iraq's textbooks were printed in Jordan in 1991–2003. Angela Commisso, *Iraqi Textbook Quality Improvement Program For Primary and Secondary Education Mathematics and Science Textbooks: Review, Training, Printing and Distribution Process: A Case Study.* UNESCO, April 2004, p. 31.

3 For references to the term 'creative chaos' and its use by neo-cons and Condoleeza Rice, see http://weekly.ahram.org.eg/2005/737/op2.htm and http://www.time.com/time/world/article/0,8599,1219325,00.html

4 Commisso, "Iraqi Textbook Quality Improvement Program…," p. 10.

5 For literature addressing the pre-2003 evolution of Iraq's education system see: Orit Bashkin, "'When Mu'awiya Entered the Curriculum' – Some Comments on the Iraqi Education System in the Interwar Period," *Comparative Education Review* 50:3 (2006): 346–366; Charles Michael Brown, "The Administration of State-Run Primary and Secondary Education in Iraq", 1958–1989, unpublished Master Thesis, University of Utah, 2005; Huda al-Khaizaran, "Traditions of Moral Education in Iraq," *Journal of Moral Education* 36:3 (2007): 321–332; Delwin A. Roy, "The Educational System of Iraq," *Middle Eastern Studies* 29:2 (1993): 167–197.

6 Bashkin, *When Mu'awiya Entered the Curriculum*, 352.

7 Brown, *The Administration of State-Run Primary and Secondary Education in Iraq, 1958–1989*, 17–18.

8 Brown, *The Administration of State-Run Primary and Secondary Education in Iraq, 1958–1989*, 18.

9 Brown, *The Administration of State-Run Primary and Secondary Education in Iraq, 1958–1989*, 18–19, 36.

10 For a detailed study of late Ottoman education, see Benjamin Fortna, *Imperial Classroom: Islam, State, and Education in the Late Ottoman Empire*, New York: Oxford, 2002. For an exploration of the transitional inter-war evolution of this hybrid system, see Bashkin, "When Mu'awiya Entered the Curriculum."

11 Brown, *The Administration of State-Run Primary and Secondary Education in Iraq, 1958–1989*, 35.

12 Brown, *The Administration of State-Run Primary and Secondary Education in Iraq, 1958–1989*, 38. Although all course materials and policies were produced centrally, primary school administration and teacher recruitment was left to provincial representatives of the Ministry of Local Affairs. In the same year, all private and foreign schools were nationalized. Brown, 41, 49.

13 Brown, *The Administration of State-Run Primary and Secondary Education in Iraq, 1958–1989*, 37–40. One example of the gradual nature of such curriculum reform is that in 1975 the Ministry of Education was still issuing a first grade alphabet primer originally authored by Sāti' al-Husri in ca. 1960. Abu Khaldun Sāti' al-Husri, *Mabādi' al-qirā'a al-khaldūniyya, al-alafbā'*, 15th printing, Baghdad: Dar al-hurriya lil-tibā'a, 1975.

14 Salih Ahmad al-'Ali *et al.*, *al-'Irāq fi al-tārikh*, Baghdad: Dar al-hurriya lil-tiba'a, 1983. For a brief survey of this work's ideological intent, see Eric Davis, *Memories of State: Politics, History, and Collective Identity in Modern Iraq*, Berkeley: University of California, 2005, pp. 185–188.

15 "*al-tārikh huwa al-natīja al-nihā'iyya allati tuqariruha al-umma dhātuhā.*" *al-'Irāq fi al-tārikh*, p. III.

16 Salih Ahmad al-'Ali *et al.*, *al-'Irāq fi al-tārikh*, pp. 13–14.

17 Brown, *The Administration of State-Run Primary and Secondary Education in Iraq, 1958–1989*, 72.

18 *al-Sirā' al-'Irāqī al-Fārsī*, Baghdad: Dar al-hurriya lil-tibā'a, 1983. For a brief discussion of this work and the series it was part of, see Eric Davis, *Memories of State*, 184–188.

19 For a detailed summary of negative points made about Iran by Iraqi textbooks prior to 1997, see Talal Atrissi, "The Image of the Iranians in Arab Schoolbooks," in *Arab-Iranian Relations*, Khair El-Din Haseeb, editor, London: I.B. Taurus, 1998, pp. 155–168.

20 Republic of Iraq, Ministry of Education, *al-Tarbiya al-Wataniyya*, Amman: Jordanian Center for Professional Printing, 17th printing, 1999 [1st Printing 1981].

21 I have been unable to locate the textbook intended to replace *al-Tarbiya al-wataniyya*.

22 Brown [*The Administration of State-Run Primary and Secondary Education in Iraq, 1958–1989*] believes that the 1990s sanctions-era degradation has been overstated, with most of the damage done in the 1980s. Roy [*The Educational System of Iraq*] stated in 1993 that an expected return to "normalcy" was imminent.

23 Davis, *Memories of State*.

24 Bashkin, *When Mu'awiya Entered the Curriculum*, 349–352.

25 Republic of Iraq, Ministry of Education, *al-Qirā'a al-'Arabiyya*, 6th printing, Arab Company for the Production and Trade of Papers, 1997 [no location], pp. 104–106.

26 Starrett and Doumato, *Textbook Islam, Nation Building, and the Question of Violence*, 5.

27 Republic of Iraq, Ministry of Education, *al-Tarbiya al-Islāmiyya*, 16th printing, 1998, United Arab Commercial Group.

28 André Mazzawi, "Dis/integrated Orders and the Politics of Recognition: Civil Upheavals, Militarism, and Educators' Lives and Work," *Mediterranean Journal of Educational Studies* 13:2 (2008), 70.

29 As Mazzawi ["Dis/integrated Orders and the Politics of Recognition," p. 72] observed, "when social and political orders collapse in the midst of military and armed conflicts, and state surveillance and regulate power dissipate, educators may become engaged in myriad sites of action, outside the direct regulative power of established accountability regimes."

30 Bashkin, *When Mu'awiya Entered the Curriculum*, 347, 354–364.

31 Although Baghdad may have stopped shipping most textbooks dedicated to the Kurdish autonomous zone after imposing a comprehensive internal blockade on Kurdish militia controlled areas in 1992, such textbooks were still being published and used as late as 1997. GEI possesses a 1997 sixth grade Arabic instructional text designed for use in the Kurdish autonomous zone. It is a sixth edition work, probably dating the original version to 1991. Ministry of Education, *al-Qirā'a al-'Arabiyya*, 1997.

32 Ministry of Education, *al-Qirā'a al-'Arabiyya*, 1997, p. 119.

33 Interviews with Hersh Abdula, Lecturer, Department of History, Sulaymania University, and Aras Abdullah, General Director, Curriculum, KRG Ministry of Education. According to an April 2004 draft UNESCO report [Commisso, "Iraqi Textbook Quality Improvement Program…," p. 45], the KRG Ministry of Education began revising textbooks in 2001. Certain other details concerning the timing and implementation of Kurdish curriculum reform since 1991 remain opaque following these interviews and textbook research.

34 Ministry of Education, The Kurdistan Region of Iraq, *al-Tarbiya al-wataniyya*, 1st edition, Erbil, 1996. This appears to be an Arabic translation of a Kurdish original publication, intended for 6th grade students.

35 Ruth Miller Elson, *Guardians of Tradition: American Schoolbooks of the Nineteenth Century*, University of Nebraska Press, 1964, p. 337, quoted in Gregory Starrett and Eleanor Abdella Doumato, "Textbook Islam, Nation Building, and the Question of Violence," chapter in Eleanor Abdella Doumato and Gregory Starrett, *Teaching Islam: Textbooks and Religion in the Middle East*, Boulder: Lynne Rienner, p. 1.

36 For the general state of Iraqi education since 2003, see: Agustín Velloso de Santisteban, "Sanctions, War, Occupation, and the De-Development of Education in Iraq," *International Review of Education* 51 (2005): 59–71; Jacqueline Ismael, Tareq Y. Ismael, and Raymond William Baker, "Iraq and Human Development: Culture, Education, and the Globalization of Hope," *Arab Studies Quarterly* 26:2 (2004): 49–66; Kenneth

J. Saltman, "Creative Associates International: Corporate Education and 'Democracy Promotion' in Iraq," *The Review of Education, Pedagogy, and Cultural Studies* 28:1 (2006): 25–65; Athena Vongalis-Macrow, "Rebuilding Régimes or Rebuilding Community? Teachers' Agency for Social Reconstruction in Iraq," *Journal of Peace Education* 3:1 (2006): 99–113; Haifa Zangana, "Women and Survival in the Iraqi War Zone," *International Journal of Lifelong Education* 27:2 (2008): 153–168.

37 For critical analyses of Project RISE and other U.S. Government initiatives in Iraqi education since 2003, see Saltman, "Creative Associates International: Corporate Education and 'Democracy Promotion' in Iraq," and Velloso de Santisteban, "Sanctions, War, Occupation, and the De-Development of Education in Iraq."

38 For TQIP project details, see Commisso, "Iraqi Textbook Quality Improvement Program...," and UNESCO, "Textbook Quality Improvement Programme: Support to Basic Education in Iraq," Final Report, March 2005.

39 Commisso, "Iraqi Textbook Quality Improvement Program...," pp. 20–21. The UNICEF project does not appear to have ever released a final report.

40 Commisso, "Iraqi Textbook Quality Improvement Program...," p. 15.

41 Interview with TQIP consultant, December 2008. Commisso, "Iraqi Textbook Quality Improvement Program...," p. 23.

42 Commisso, "Iraqi Textbook Quality Improvement Program...," p. 15.

43 Interview with TQIP consultant, December 2008. This consultant also stated that all Iraqi participants were resident in Iraq prior to the invasion, were happy to see Mr Hussein out of power, worked together well with each other, were representative of all the country's ethnic groups, and had not participated in curriculum review committees under the old régime.

44 Commisso, "Iraqi Textbook Quality Improvement Program...," pp. 16–18.

45 Commisso, "Iraqi Textbook Quality Improvement Program...," p. 23.

46 Commisso, "Iraqi Textbook Quality Improvement Program...," p. 26.

47 Commisso, "Iraqi Textbook Quality Improvement Program...," p. 33.

48 Commisso, "Iraqi Textbook Quality Improvement Program...," pp. 28–30.

49 Commisso, "Iraqi Textbook Quality Improvement Program...," p. 49.

50 UNESCO, "Textbook Quality Improvement Programme: Support to Basic Education in Iraq," Final Report, March 2005, p. 14.

51 Commisso, "Iraqi Textbook Quality Improvement Program...," p. 58, and UNESCO, "Textbook Quality Improvement Programme," p. 37.

52 Commisso, "Iraqi Textbook Quality Improvement Program...," pp. 58–67; and UNESCO, "Textbook Quality Improvement Programme," pp. 37–43.

53 Commisso, "Iraqi Textbook Quality Improvement Program...," p. 58, and UNESCO, "Textbook Quality Improvement Programme," p. 37.

54 Republic of Iraq, Ministry of Education, *Al-Tārikh al-'Arabī wa al-Islāmī*, 11th printing, Jordan: al-Safadi Printing, 1998; Republic of Iraq, Ministry of Education, *Al-Tārikh al-'Arabī wa al-Islāmī*, 20th printing, [Baghdad?]: Nu'man Mustafa Company for Printing, 2007.

22 Representations of Arabs in Iranian Elementary School Textbooks

Golnar Mehran

Introduction

The identification of being Arab in the Iranian psyche depends to a great extent on the definition of the Iranian identity. Who is an Iranian? The answer to this question was relatively easy during the reign of the Pahlavi dynasty (1925–1979). Schoolchildren learned that they were Aryans, proud of their rich pre-Islamic heritage rooted in the glory of the Persian Empire. The sons and daughters of Cyrus the Great, "the King of the Nation" (Lamb 2007: 355) and the author of the "oldest declaration of human rights" (Moradi Ghias Abadi 2007: 8), Iranians belonged to a civilization that once ruled a great proportion of the world. Pre-revolutionary formal education emphasized belonging to the Iranian nation as a source of pride, with clear lines of demarcation from Arabs.

The Islamic Republic of Iran, established in 1979 after the overthrow of the late Shah, presented schoolchildren with a totally different world view. Almost overnight, the children of the revolution were told that it was not the Iranian nation but the Islamic *umma* (community of believers) that was to be their source of pride. Students learned that what mattered was no longer the boundaries of a land called Iran, but a sense of belonging to a vast community called Islam. Iranian-ness was replaced by Muslim-ness. There was no longer a division among Iranians and Arabs based on language and race, but a strong unity founded on a common religion. Paradoxically, however, Iranians continued to separate themselves from the majority of the Muslim *umma* through their faith and language. While undermining Zoroastrianism as the original religion of Iran, and replacing the pre-revolutionary language that pointed to the "Arab conquest of Iran" in the seventh century as the "invitation of Arabs to believe in Islam," the leaders of the Islamic Republic have ensured that Iranians remained distinct by keeping Persian as the formal language and Shi'ism as the state religion.

The pendulum continues to swing in Iranian politics even today, from emphasis on Iranian-ness to Islamic unity, at the center of which is the Arab world. Both voices have been heard in Iran in 2009; solidarity with the Palestinian victims in Gaza during the Israeli bombardments while, at the same time, blaming the late Shah for the loss of one of the "former provinces of Iran", namely Bahrain, were part of the sentiments expressed by Iranian politicians.

The school, as an important agent of socialization, plays a significant role in shaping the minds of the younger generations. It is true that the family, peer group, media, and the Internet present themselves as strong rivals, yet this does not negate the impact of formal education especially during the primary school period. The socialization role of the school has long been recognized by the Islamic Republic of Iran. The post-revolutionary Iranian authorities have used textbooks as key instruments of political and ideological education, charged with teaching the younger generations about the values and attitudes deemed appropriate in the construction of the "new revolutionary society." Textbook content has, therefore, been used to represent the political, social, and cultural values of the régime. Post-revolutionary textbook content has been the focus of various studies addressing such diverse topics as ideology (Shorish 1988, Siavoshi 1995); identity (Higgins 1985); gender roles (Touba 1987, Higgins and Shoar-Ghaffari 1991, Ferdows 1994); nationalism (Ram 2000, Kashani-Sabet 2002); and socialization (Mehran 1989, 2007).

This chapter focuses, more specifically, on constructions of the image of Arabs in elementary school textbooks in Iran. The primary school level (ages 6–10) has been chosen since political education, as an institutional form of political knowledge acquisition, first takes place at the primary level. Realizing that elementary schooling is the first and at times the only exposure of Iranians to formal education, the Islamic Republic has made every effort to disseminate the dominant political ideology through primary school textbooks. The centralization of the Iranian educational system, and the use of standard textbooks throughout the country, despite linguistic, religious, and ethnic diversity, highlights the importance of textbooks.

School Textbooks

The range of textbooks taught at the primary school level include *Persian*, *Religious Studies*, *Qur'ān Instruction*, *Science*, *Mathematics*, and *Social Studies* (Ministry of Education 2006: 155). *Persian* textbooks focus mainly on the formation of the Iranian identity, using the Persian language as the uniting factor among the linguistically diverse population of Iran. *Science* and *Mathematics* books introduce Iranian and non-Iranian Muslims as the world-leading scientists, mathematicians, and philosophers during the Golden Age of the Islamic civilization (c. 700–1300 of the Common Era). *Religious Studies* emphasize Islam and Muslim unity despite differences of opinion among Sunnis and Shi'is regarding the leadership of Muslims following the death of the Prophet Muhammad. Different textbooks are compiled for the "officially recognized" religious minorities in Iran—namely, Zoroastrians, Jews, and Christians (Mehran 2007: 99). Teaching the Qur'ān is the most evident symbol of Islamic unity in Iranian education. The Qur'ān, the teachings of Islam, and the use of the Arabic language as the language of the Qur'ān represent the manifest tie between Iranian Muslims and their Arab counterparts.

Social Studies textbooks have been chosen for their direct role in the transmission of the ruling political and religious ideology. Elementary textbooks begin a process throughout the Iranian educational system in which there is an open and deliberate attempt to politicize and Islamize schoolchildren. The system of education in Iran is highly centralized and both public and private schools use the same government textbooks. There are no alternative, government approved, textbooks on the market and all students study the same textbooks throughout the country. Examinations are also based on the content of the textbooks taught by government-trained teachers. Textbooks are produced by the Office of Planning and Compilation of School Textbooks at the Ministry of Education located in the capital city of Tehran.

The textbook compilers are government trained and officially approved members of the Ministry, comprised of subject specialists, textbook writers, and at times experienced teachers. In some cases, university professors who have worked with the Ministry of Education are consulted or even included in the textbook compilation team. One of the textbooks analyzed in this study, the Grade 3 *Social Studies* book, was written by one of the high ranking members of the Ministry of Education, who later became a member and then Speaker of the Parliament. Different versions of the textbooks have been published since the establishment of the Islamic Republic in 1979 to reflect the changes during the past thirty years. The main themes, however, remain the same: the politicization and Islamization of the young; loyalty to the religio-political leaders of Iran and the principles of the revolution; dislike for the previous régime; and hatred for the ever-present enemy, led by the USA, that threatens the revolution and the Islamic government.

In sum, the textbooks present one point of view; that is, the government's point of view. The emphasis is on the transmission of "state approved" information and the portrayal of what is deemed appropriate by high-ranking members of the Ministry of Education. The stress is on learning government determined "facts," memorizing them and reporting them on their examination papers. There are always a few "questions" posed at the end of each lesson that require answers based on the information imparted in the text. The same is basically true with sections titled "class activity" and "class discussions." Presentation of conflicting views and alternative narratives, as well as discussions and brainstorming sessions to arrive at student opinions are missing in the daily activities of Iranian schools. There is surely a hidden curriculum that questions the status quo, but for the most part, the government narrative is taught, memorized, and repeated by students during exams.

Social Studies textbooks play a special role at the primary school level. They include History, Geography, and Civic Education and the topics are arranged with an aim to transmit the dominant values of the Islamic Republic. Political education occurs in its most open and manifest form in Civics. Given the fact that not all primary school graduates in Iran continue their schooling, educational authorities have condensed and simplified the basic concepts that all schoolchildren are to be introduced to. This task is accomplished in *Social Studies* textbooks, through which the core of socio-political values are transmitted and young Iranians learn about their dual identity as members of the Iranian nation as well as the Muslim *umma*. They are also taught that the ideal citizen is a politicized Shiʻi who is to serve the *velayat-e faqih* (governance of the religious jurisprudent) as a national mission while remaining true to the tenets of Shiʻism. The interplay of nationalism and religion in *Social Studies* textbooks that ask young schoolchildren to play a dual role as Iranians and Muslims, as well as the identification of the "self" and the "other" in terms of Iranian and Arab, makes the focus of this chapter on History, Geography, and Civics textbooks an important endeavor. Furthermore, the study of topics taught at the primary school level is important since this may be the first and only chance for many Iranians to experience formal education aimed at creating the ideal citizens of the Islamic Republic of Iran from the point of view of the ruling leaders.

Aims of the Chapter

The present chapter delves in the textbooks used during the 2008–09 academic year. An in-depth content and pictorial analysis of these elementary school textbooks is conducted to identify the messages conveyed to young children regarding Iranian-ness, Arabs, Muslimhood, and the complex interplay among the three. This study unpacks the image of Arabs in Iranian school textbooks, based on the contention that there is a dialectical relationship between understanding the "self" and the "other" in which the "other" can be identified only in relation to the "self" and never in isolation (Tedesco 1997). Moreover, the search for one's identity is possible through the "concept of the 'other' or the image of the 'other'" (Akkari 2003: 397). This is in line with Tedesco's (1997; see also Mehran 2002) argument that socialization "implies the identification of what is 'different,' or the identification of a borderline" (p. 62), hence the notion of the social construction of "difference". The major distinguishing feature of one who is "different" is that he/she is not perceived to be "like us." As such, the "other" can be identified only in relation to us and never in isolation. At the same time, however, one should be especially sensitive to distortions in the presentation of the "other". Through "reading against the text" in the textual and pictorial analysis of primary school textbooks, one should pay special attention to detecting national, racial, ethnic, gender, and religious constructions and stereotypes. This study thus seeks to identify the "other" by discovering the "self." More specifically, this chapter asks: How do educational authorities instill a separate and independent sense of Iranian identity among the young, given the intricate, often complex relationships between Iranians and Arabs throughout their shared history, bound by a common religion and geographical proximity?

Textbooks and the Question of Representation

To understand the image of Arabs in Iranian textbooks, one needs to unpack the intricate triangle of Iranian-ness, Arab-ness, and Muslim-hood. The main overlap between Iranians and Arabs is indeed Islam. While language and constructed notions of ethnicity distinguish them, religion and a shared history during the Golden Age of the Islamic civilization (*c.* 700–1300 of the Common Era) connect them. Iran's Arab population offers another point of connection, but the fact that most Iranian Arabs are Shi'i may at the same time distinguish them from the predominantly Sunni population in the Arab region. To understand how these points of connection and distinction are articulated in textbooks, one must examine the construction of the Iranian "self" and identify the features of the borderline that is erected between that "self" and the Arab "other".

The Iranian "Self"

Young Iranians first learn about Iranian-ness through pictures and symbols. Mount Damavand, the snow-covered peak of the Alborz mountains and one of the important symbols of Iran, is shown on the cover of the Third Grade *Social Studies* textbook published by the Ministry of Education of the Islamic Republic of Iran in 2008. Mount Damavand reappears on page 44 in its full glory in the same book. The map of Iran can be found on many pages with strong emphasis on the name of the Persian Gulf[1] amid controversies about the name among those who refer to the Arabian Gulf and Iranians, who refer to the Persian Gulf. The emphasis on the name in textbooks coincides with naming many major roads and bridges as the "Ever Persian Gulf" (*Khalij-e Hamisheh Fars*) and publishing stamps with the map of Iran in which the Persian Gulf stands out with a brilliant blue color.

The green, white, and red flag of Iran is also portrayed in another attempt to instill the sense of Iranian-ness in young schoolchildren (pp. 62, 69). Monuments built to celebrate the Iranian heritage and celebrate the memory of great Iranian poets and artists abound in the Third Year *Social Studies* textbook. The tombs of Iranian poets, sufis, scientists, and artists including Hafez in Shiraz (p. 10) as well as Khayyam, Attar, and Kamal al-Molk in Neyshabur (pp. 67, 68) are relevant examples. Other historical monuments closely linked with the Iranian historical identity include the Khaju Bridge and Naqsh-e Jahan Square in Isfahan, both built during the golden period of the Safavid dynasty in the sixteenth century. Pictures of grand museums (pp. 39, 40) and old bazaars (pp. 9, 59) along with pictures of the natural beauties of Iran throughout the Third Grade *Social Studies* textbook are additional attempts to instill a sense of pride in young Iranians.

Schoolchildren view pictures of a highly popular Iranian national hero, Gholam Reza Takhti, who died at a young age at the peak of his athletic career in the 1960s (pp. iv, 56). Takhti remains a symbol of Iranian pride, dignity, and honor, not only for bringing many medals for the country, but also for his courageous acts against the rule of the late Shah and the deep love and respect he had earned among the people. The portrayal of Iranian religio-political leaders is part of the political socialization process that takes place in schools. Pictures of Ayatollah Khomeini as the founder of the Islamic Republic abound.[2] Other pictures include the present religious leader Ayatollah Khamene'i (pp. 1, 37, 59), and prominent religio-political leaders who died or were killed during the early days of the revolution. They include Ayatollah Taleqani (p. 35), and the three martyrs (*shohada*), Raja'i, Beheshti, and Bahonar (p. 34). Chamran, a military leader who was martyred during the 1980–88 Iran–Iraq war, appears on page 35.

The covers of the Fourth Grade *Social Studies* textbooks also portray Mount Damavand as if it is overlooking and protecting the entire country. The back covers illustrate the historical symbols of pre-Islamic Iran, the remainders of an ancient civilization that was attacked many times and eventually conquered by the Arabs in the seventh century. The section on Geography includes the map of Iran, portraying the Persian Gulf in each picture.[3] The maps of ancient and modern Iran also appear in the section on History.[4] It is interesting to note that while Greece, Egypt, Palestine, Syria, Armenia, and India are noted in ancient maps, lands inhabited by Arabs are simply pointed to as *Arab-ha* or Arabs (pp. 89, 101). The History section also includes many pictures and drawings of pre-Islamic Iran, including ancient monuments,[5] statues (pp. 87, 96), coins (pp. 91, 102), and valuable objects (p. 91) showing the glory of the country before the advent of Islam.

A pictorial analysis of the History section reveals a strong sense of Iranian-ness and pride in belonging to an ancient civilization. Drawings and maps illustrate the migration of Aryans to a land to be called Iran or the "land of the Aryans" around four thousand years ago (pp. 86, 87). The maps of ancient Iran cover the lands from India in the east to cities close to Greece in the west (p. 89). Even more impressive are the drawings of the magnificent palaces of Takht-e Jamshid or Persepolis (p. 93); the victory of Iranians in the battle against the Romans (p. 97) and the Roman Emperor kneeling before the King of Iran (p. 102); as well as the surrender of the Roman Emperor carved on a mountain in the province of Fars in Iran (p. 102). The achievements of Iranians before Islam as well as the rise and fall of the Persian Empire in various wars, especially the conquest of Iran by Alexander, are clearly noted in the Fourth Grade History section.

The content analysis of the History section of the Fourth Grade *Social Studies* textbook leads one to the identification of the Iranian "self." What Iranian means appears in the section on the formation of the "land of the Aryans" or Iran (pp. 86–88) which introduces the official religion of pre-Islamic Iran, namely Zoroastrianism, its Holy Book *Avesta*, and three basic principles: Good Thought, Good Words, and Good Behavior (p. 100). The origins of the present day Persian language are presented too (p. 105). Although Zoroastrians comprise a religious minority in Iran today, emphasis on belonging to the Aryan race and speaking Persian are clear lines of demarcation from the Arab "other."

A more contemporary construction of Iranian-ness can be found in Lesson 7 of the Fourth Grade Civic Education section titled the "Iranian Nation." Schoolchildren learn that the people of Iran live as family members in a big house called Iran. The Iranian nation and state has a common flag, national anthem, calendar, and constitution (p. 128). Young children are told that the formal language and script of the Iranian nation is Persian (Farsi) and Noruz (March 21) marks the beginning of the Iranian year (p. 129). Emphasizing "commonality" among Iranians, the Civic Education section underlines the common history of the people of Iran who have lived together throughout the centuries, defending their land and religion, sharing their happiness and sorrow, and having common dreams (p. 129). Schoolchildren also learn that the "Islamic Revolution of Iran" is the symbol of the "unity of the Iranian nation" in their struggle to "free themselves from the hardship of the past" to reach the "common goals" of the future (p. 130). Even more forceful than the written word are the pictures that show young Iranians from different ethnic groups throughout the country wearing their local clothing and holding the Iranian flag; portraying the map of Iran with the flag and the national anthem written within the geographical boundaries of present day

Iran; and showing the familiar symbols of the Iranian New Year, Noruz, celebrated by all Iranians regardless of their religion, language, or ethnicity (pp. 128–129).

Mount Damavand reappears on the covers of the Fifth Grade *Social Studies* textbooks, once again looming high over the land and the nation. The back covers show other symbols of Iranian identity, including the famous Persian carpet and ancient pottery. The portrait of Ferdowsi (935–1020), the epic poet of Iran, is probably the most important symbol of Iranian-ness and the historical struggle to remain Iranian. Ferdowsi kept the Persian language alive following the Arab conquest of the country and despite attempts to Arabize the society.

The 2008 version of the Fifth Grade *Social Studies* textbook includes a note to the teacher in its introductory section. It states that one of the important goals of replacing the book is "to increase the love of the land" among schoolchildren (*Social Studies*, Grade 5 2008: i). One can assume that the compilers may have been faced with two challenges. The first has been posed since the early days of the 1979 revolution, during which educational authorities, appointed by the government based on their commitment (*ta'ahhod*) and loyalty to the Islamic régime, undermined the Iranian identity while overemphasizing Muslimhood and unity with the rest of the Islamic world. It is true that the majority of Iranians are Muslim, but undermining Iranian-ness has created a conflict in the minds of the young who seek a distinct identity as Iranians, not just Muslims in general. The second challenge is posed through access to the Internet and international media in the global era. Globalization and the unprecedented migration of Iranians to other countries have also opened the door to many young Iranians who seek to escape social and cultural isolation and search for new horizons. One cannot assess the impact of either challenge without conducting field research, yet it may be a safe assumption to state that domestic and international challenges have compelled government-appointed educational decision makers to emphasize national identity and seek to increase the sense of love for the homeland.

The Geography section of the Fifth Grade *Social Studies* textbook has a number of illustrations showing the map of Iran and noting the Persian Gulf.[6] The same textbook locates Iran among her neighbors, including a detailed discussion of Iraq (pp. 46–49), which will be analyzed at a later point. The Iranian flag appears again in the History section (pp. 75, 131) along with a number of maps showing the geographical boundaries of the country during the reign of different dynasties and the rule of different invaders including Arabs, Mongols, and Timurids.[7] Four maps (pp. 100–101) are of special importance since they illustrate the boundaries of the first "independent Iranian states" since the Arab conquest of the seventh century. The Tahirids, Saffarids, Samanids, and Al-e Buyeh formed independent states during the reign of the Abbasid dynasty (750–1258). Ironically, Turkish-speaking tribes that "migrated" to Northeastern Iran (p. 102) also formed independent dynasties and ruled Iran for almost five hundred years, among which are the Ghaznavids, Seljukids, and Khwarezmshahs (pp. 102–103). It should be noted that the Turkish-speaking dynasties are not treated as the "other" in the Fifth Grade History section, perhaps because textbook compilers refer to their use of "clever Iranian ministers to run the affairs of the state" (p. 103).

One can see a strong sense of patriotism in the History section of the Fifth Grade *Social Studies* textbook, in which there is a manifest emphasis on "us" versus "them." At this point the "other" is portrayed in terms of the enemy (*doshman*). Primary schoolchildren are at all times confronted by an ever-present enemy that has existed since the Mongol invasion of Iran (thirteenth century). It seems as if the deliberate emphasis on the enemy is intended to create a sense of emergency in defending the homeland (*khak-e mihan*). The enemy throughout the History section ranges from the Mongols, Timurids, Ottoman Turks, Uzbeks, and Afghans to Russia, Britain, France, Israel, and the United States. The above have gained the title of the enemy or foreigners (*biganegan*) either through their invasion and destruction of the homeland or indirect interference in the internal affairs of Iran (pp. 105–128).

It is important to note that the language used regarding the foreigners' threats against the homeland depends upon who the "other" is. For example, the terminology used to describe Mongol and Timurid invasion is "destruction" (*kharabi*), "shedding blood" (*khunrizi*), "putting on fire" (*atashsuzi*), "devastation" (*virani*) and "genocide" (*qatl-e 'am-e mardom-e Iran*) (pp. 106–107). The terms utilized regarding Ottomans and Afghans are the "failure" (*shekast*) of Iranians at war or their "surrender" to the enemy (pp. 110, 112). The Europeans and Americans, however, are considered foreign powers, blamed for their continuous "conspiracy" (*tote'eh*), "interference" (*dekhalat*), and "influence" (*nofuz*).[8] On the other hand, the Arab conquest of Iran is introduced in such terms as "the spread of Islam" (p. 79), "the invitation to Islam" (p. 85), and the fact that during the rule of the second Caliph 'Omar (634–644), "Muslims added many lands to the realm of Islam, including Iran" (p. 88). There are indeed times where such statements as the "attack of Muslims" and the "defeat of the Sassanid dynasty in Iran" are used (p. 89). In the majority of cases, however, "Arab Muslims" (*Mosalmanan-e Arab*) are not considered as foreigners or treated as the enemy.

The situation is different when schoolchildren read about the 1980–88 Iran–Iraq war. An example is a letter written by Iranian pupils to Ayatollah Khomeini in 1981, in which they prayed for victory over the "forces of Saddam and the Ba'thi non-believers (*kafaran*)" (*Social Studies*, Grade 3 2008: 69). The Fifth Grade History section also includes a lesson on the narrative of war. Children are informed that after the victory of the 1979 revolution, "our enemies, especially America, continued their conspiracy against Iran." The textbook further goes on to state that in 1980, the Iraqi army, led by Saddam Hussein (ruled 1979–2003), attacked Iran and imposed a bloody war for eight years against the Islamic Republic. It points out that in this war, many cities and villages in Iran were destroyed and factories, hospitals, and schools were bombarded (*Social Studies*, Grade 5 2008: 132). This lesson includes pictures of the ruins of war as well as school-age boys holding rifles in the battlefield. There are two powerful photographs of the destruction of schools with broken benches and scattered pages of textbooks being picked up by a young boy (pp. 132–133). The pictures are followed by notes explaining that "during the war, the enemy did not have any mercy, even for people's homes and schools which led to the martyrdom (*shahadat*) of a number of schoolchildren."

Young pupils are then told that "now we must follow the path of the martyred (*shahid*) schoolchildren by trying hard and studying a lot" (p. 132).

This lesson conveys two messages. First, Iraq is never introduced as an Arab country and it is never mentioned that there was a war between Arabs and Iranians. In fact, Iraq during the war is treated as a separate entity led by Saddam, without any connection to the Arab world in general. The manifest enemy is presented as Saddam Hussein, who acted within the policy of conspiracy by the hidden enemy, the United States of America. The second message is one of patriotism and love of the homeland. Fifth graders are taught that "the people of our country rose against the enemy and defended the Islamic nation along with the army and the revolutionary guards" (p. 132). The unity of Iranians in defending their motherland is emphasized in such statements as "all of the people, old and young, prepared themselves for the defense of the country after the attack of the Iraqi army against Iran," and "in this war, many of our brave and pious youth were martyred, but they were able to push the forces of the enemy out of our homeland ..." (pp. 132–133). It is interesting to note that while all ages are included, the same is not true with gender or socio-cultural groups. In fact, gender blindness is the general rule as far as the treatment of the Iran–Iraq war is concerned.

The concept of protecting the homeland (*khak-e mihan*) against the aggression of the "foreigners" and the interference of the "enemy" is also emphasized in the Civic Education section of the Fifth Grade *Social Studies* textbook. The map of Iran with a young soldier holding a rifle, ready to protect the homeland, is presented as part of the responsibilities of the government to "protect the independence of the nation" (p. 148). The 1980–88 Iran–Iraq war is, once again, the main theme of Lesson 9 titled "Isar (Altruism) and *Fadakari* (Sacrifice)." Fifth graders are once again reminded that "during the imposed war (*jang-e tahmili*) ... the Iraqi army attacked Iran with the support of America" (p. 162). They learn that the eight-year war witnessed the martyrdom of those who sacrificed themselves to defend the country and confront the "aggressors." The pictures portray armed boys and girls, gathered to fight against the enemy as members of the Students' Mobilization (*basij*) Forces. Teaching children that martyrdom is the highest degree of altruism, the lesson commemorates the memory of a 12-year-old schoolchild, Hossein Fahmideh, who threw himself under the enemy's tank in order to blow it up with a hand-held grenade. His martyrdom marks the Universal Day of the Child in Iran and his story is one read by all schoolchildren as a symbol of altruism and sacrifice during the "holy defense" (*defa'-e moqaddas*) (p. 164).

The narration of war and the portrayal of an ever present enemy throughout the history of Iran may reflect an attempt by the ruling authorities to alert children against any manifest or hidden conspiracy threatening the country and the continuous need for Iranians to unite in order to protect the homeland. It seems that the preservation of the Iranian identity and the reproduction of Iranian-ness are solidified by the presence of an enemy and conspiring foreigners who seek to weaken Iran and challenge her independence. In fact, the "self" is strengthened in the attempt to protect itself against the "other." The existence of "us" is closely connected to the presence of "them." The question that still remains to be answered is whether Arabs represent that "other" and can one put them in the us/them, friend/enemy category.

The Arab "Other"

Who is an Arab? How are Arabs presented in Iranian textbooks? How are Arabness and Muslimhood situated in relation to each other in primary school books?

The first manifestation of Arab-ness is the Arabic language and the name of Allah printed on a frame in the Third Grade *Social Studies* textbook (*Social Studies*, Grade 3 2008: 1). Another example is the use of "*Bismillah*" (In the Name of God) at the beginning of letters (pp. 70–72) as opposed to the Persian-language version "*Beh Nam-e Khoda*" (In the Name of God) (p. 65). The above Arabic words are, of course, the common religious terminology used by Muslims throughout the world. The other example is the date used by Ayatollah Khomeini to sign a letter (p. 72). The year mentioned first is 1402, based on the lunar calendar (*sal-e qamari*) used by Arabs, as opposed to 1360 according to the solar calendar (*sal-e khorshidi*) of Iranians, which is mentioned later in the letter.

Throughout the Third Grade *Social Studies* textbook, Arabic names are mentioned, mainly due to the fact that Iranians have used such names since the advent of Islam in the seventh century. 'Ali, Mahmud, Tahereh, Hashemi (p. 1), Javad (p. 24), Tayyebeh (p. 25), and Zahra (p. 33) are examples of Arabic names used, compared with only two Iranian names, Maryam (p. 1) and Parvin (p. 65) mentioned in the same textbook. In addition, there are the names of religious figures, including the name of the Eighth Shi'i Imam Reza (pp. 7, 54, 55, 56); his sister, Ma'sumeh (p. 21); Imam Mohammad Taqi (p. 70); and the Twelfth Shi'i Imam Mahdi (p. 70). It is also interesting to note that Ayatollah Khomeini's signature on a letter addressed to schoolchildren is written in the Arabic form, namely Ruhollah al-Mousavi al-Khomeini (p. 72) as opposed to the Persian-language form of Ruhollah Mousavi Khomeini. Other examples include the use of Islamic terms in the daily life of Iranians; terms such as Imam (p. i) and Ayatollah (pp. 34–35). It should be noted that the advent of Islam in Iran led to the use of the Arabic script and the mixing of Arabic and Persian words. Persian, however, remains the official language of Iran and the sole language of instruction in schools throughout the country.

The first introduction of the word "Arabs" occurs in the Fourth Grade *Social Studies* textbook in which the general term *Arab-ha*, the Persian language version of Arabs, is used in the History section (*Social Studies*, Grade 4 2008: 89, 101). Later, the term Muslim Arabs (*Arab-ha-ye Mosalman*) (pp. 105, 106), Muslims (*Mosalmanan*), the Army of Islam (*Sepah-e Islam*) (p. 105), and Muslim Soldiers (*Sepahian-e Islam*) (p. 106) are used to refer to the Arabs who conquered Iran in the seventh century. Iranian schoolchildren, however, are soon taught that Arabs were divided into two groups during the early days of Islam: the Muslim Arabs and the Arab non-believers (*kafaran*) and idol worshippers (*bot parastan*) (*Social Studies*, Grade 5 2008: 79–86). The Arabs are thus divided into a good (Muslim) versus an evil (non-believer, idol worshipper) category. The good/evil dichotomy continues in the introduction of Arabs as the advocates of Islam who invited people to practice "brotherhood and freedom" (*Social Studies*, Grade 4 2008: 105), and those who did not act according to "Islamic laws and justice" and believed that "the Arab race is superior to other races" (*Social Studies*, Grade 5 2008: 97). The good/evil category among Arabs continues in the Fifth Grade textbook, mainly through the introduction of the "evil" (Arab) Umayyad and Abbasid rulers who oppressed, imprisoned, poisoned, and killed the "good" (Arab) Shiʻi Imams (pp. 90–99). At first, however, schoolchildren read that Arabs brought nothing but freedom (*azadi*) and brotherhood (*baradari*) for the people of Iran in a lesson titled "The Rise of the Sun of Islam in Iran" (*Social Studies*, Grade 4 2008: 104–105). Using such words as the "invitation to Islam" (p. 104); the "entrance of Islam to Iran;" and the "embracing of Islam by Iranians" (p. 105) teaches children that Iranians converted to Islam willingly due to the oppression and injustice imposed by the Iranian Kings before the Arabs entered the country.

The very same lesson refers to the "attack of Muslim Arabs;" "the conquest of Tisfun," the capital of the (pre-Islamic) Persian Empire; and the "victory" of Muslim soldiers and the "defeat" of the Sassanid army in "war" (p. 105). The duality in the language used to refer to Arabs is clarified when fifth graders read that originally the Prophet Muhammad wrote a letter to the Iranian King Khosrow Parviz, inviting him to embrace Islam. The King's refusal to accept the invitation, his anger and tearing of the letter was followed by Prophet Muhammad's statement that, "In the future, Muslims will conquer the land of the Sassanids" (*Social Studies*, Grade 5 2008: 85). Iran was indeed "conquered" by Arabs and the Sassanid dynasty was "defeated" during the rule of the Arab/Muslim Caliph ʻOmar (pp. 88–89).

Other references to present-day Arab lands include the birthplaces of several prophets. Iranian children read that Noah lived in Beyn al-Nahreyn [between the two rivers] (today's Iraq) (*Social Studies*, Grade 4 2008: 81); Ibrahim (Abraham) was born in Babylon (in present-day Iraq); the birthplace of Moses was Egypt (p. 83); and Jesus was born in Palestine (p. 98). Fourth graders are provided with a map in which the names of pre-Islamic (now Arab) lands appear as the oldest civilizations (p. 79), along with a picture of the pyramids in Egypt introduced as one of the seven wonders of the world (p. 83). The specific word "Arabs" is used only to cover the geographical area of present-day Saudi Arabia (pp. 89, 101). Another historical reference to Arab lands includes a section in the Fifth Grade *Social Studies* textbook. It is noted that during the reign of the Safavid dynasty in Iran in the sixteenth century, Shah Abbas defeated the Ottomans and conquered (the now Iraqi cities of) Baghdad, Karbala, and Najaf (p. 110). The textbook also includes a map of the realm of Iran during the Safavid period (1501–1722), showing the present-day Iraqi cities of Baghdad, Najaf, and Mosul as part of Iran (p. 109). In the Geography section of the Fifth Grade *Social Studies* textbook, a map of what is today known as the Middle East displays the Arab countries of the region, including Iraq, Syria, Lebanon, Jordan, Occupied Palestine (*Felestin-e Eshghali*), Egypt, Saudi Arabia, Yemen, Oman, the United Arab Emirates, Qatar, Bahrain, and Kuwait (p. 27). Palestine is also mentioned in the Third Grade textbook in which Iranian children pray for the day when "all Muslims unite to free Palestine and save Qods from the enemies of Islam" (*Social Studies*, Grade 3 2008: 57).

The content analysis of Iranian textbooks leads one to believe that the Islamic Republic has made every effort to avoid any discussion of actual or potential division between Arabs and Iranians in the political and/or religious spheres by refusing to discuss current affairs with young primary schoolchildren.

Representations of the Islamic Community

While primary school textbooks do not discuss Arab countries in the contemporary period, there is a lot of information regarding Arabs throughout history. The History section of the Fifth Grade *Social Studies* textbook begins with a lesson on the "Advent of Islam." Students read that "Islam rose from the land of Arabia (*Arabestan*)," the people of which lived both in the cities and the desert and led a tribal life (p. 76). At the center of attention is the life and mission of the Prophet Muhammad in Arabia. The titles of the different sections illustrate the main focus of Iranian textbooks: The Infancy and Youth of the Prophet; Prophethood; the Spread of Islam; Secret and Open Invitation (to Islam); Hurting the Prophet and His Followers; Migration to Habasheh (today's Ethiopia); Ceasing Relations with Muslims; the Establishment of Islamic Rule; the Migration of the Prophet; the Prophet's Wars; the Conquest of Mecca; Inviting the Ruling Leaders to Islam; and Death of the Prophet (pp. 76–87).

The friend/enemy dichotomy in the above section focuses on Muslims versus non-believers and idol worshippers. After that, the Fifth Grade textbook focuses on the "Islamic Society after the Prophet," noting the Caliphates of Abu Bakr, 'Omar, 'Osman, and 'Ali. It is at this point that the "difference in opinion" among Muslims regarding the leadership of the Islamic community after the death of Prophet Muhammad is referred to. From this point onward, children read about the Iranian/Shi'i version of Arab history and Arab rule. It is after the account of the Shi'i–Sunni "split" and the discussion about the four Caliphs that Iranian history focuses on the "cruel" rule of the Umayyad and Abbasid dynasties and the "oppression" and "martyrdom" of the Shi'i Imams. An almost exclusive focus is placed on Shi'i Imams in the historical narrative of Arab-Muslim rule with minimum concentration on the achievements of the Golden Age of the Islamic Civilization in every human endeavor possible. Yet one must remember that Shi'ism is very much part of Iranian-ness and historical account of the lives of struggles of Shi'i Imams is integral to the formation of the Iranian-Shi'i identity.

The Shi'i/Sunni dichotomy is delicately treated in the Fifth Grade History section. It is stated that after the death of the Prophet Muhammad, there was a "difference of opinion" regarding who should be the leader of the Muslim community. Children are taught that, "a group regarded 'Ali [Prophet Muhammad's cousin and son-in-law] as the successor, based on what the Prophet had stated. Finally, Abu Bakr was chosen as Caliph. A group of people pledged allegiance (*bey'at*) with Abu Bakr … 'Ali and his followers chose to remain silent to prevent any split among Muslims" (*Social Studies*, Grade 5 2008: 88). Young Iranians are told that 'Ali remained silent during the Caliphate of 'Omar ("when Iran was added to the realm of Islam") and 'Osman. After the murder of 'Osman, "Muslims pleaded with 'Ali to accept the Caliphate" (p. 89).

The Caliphate of 'Ali is filled with war against Mo'aviyyeh—the ruler of Sham (located in today's Syria)—and the *Khavarej* (Outsiders). 'Ali became a "martyr" upon his murder by one of the members of the *Khavarej* on the twenty-first day of the month of Ramadan while he was praying. Iranian fifth graders read that the five-year Caliphate of 'Ali in Kufeh (Iraq) was filled with struggle against his enemies and he was never at peace. During this short and troubled time, however, " 'Ali was able to bring justice to the society and end cruelty and oppression. He was the friend and supporter of the oppressed and orphans, and a true example of courage and faith." 'Ali is introduced as the one who "brought back to life the almost forgotten path of the Prophet and the religion of Islam" (p. 92).

Primary schoolchildren are then informed that the Caliphate of 'Ali was not followed by his sons Imam Hassan and Imam Hossein. Instead Mo'aviyyeh established the Umayyad dynasty and chose his son Yazid as his successor. According to this account, the Second Shi'i Imam Hassan was poisoned during the rule of Mo'aviyyeh, and his brother, Imam Hossein, and his followers were brutally murdered in Karbala (Iraq) by Yazid's army (pp. 94–96). The martyrdom of Imam Hossein on the tenth day of the month of Moharram, known as 'Ashura, is a most important event for Iranian Shi'is. Grand-scale mourning ceremonies are held on 'Ashura throughout the country for Imam Hossein, known among Iranians as *Seyyed al-Shohada*, or the Lord of Martyrs.

The martyrdom of Imam 'Ali and Imam Hossein, the event of Karbala, and 'Ashura are very much part of the Iranian Shi'i identity. It should be noted that the Imams 'Ali and Hossein were Arab religious leaders who fought other Arab leaders in Arab lands with no connection to Iranian history. For Iranians, however, they are exemplary Muslims and true role models whose path is to be followed by all Shi'is, whether they are Iranian or not. There is no Arab/Iranian dichotomy when it comes to Shi'i Imams. The latter are regarded as "perfect human beings" regardless of their country of origin, race, and language. The duality is not an Arab/non-Arab one, but the adoption of Muslim figures as revered religious leaders. Young Iranians are instilled with love for the twelve Shi'i Imams—all Arabs—who struggled against the "oppressive and cruel" rule of the Umayyad and Abbasid rulers—all Arabs.

The fact that solidarity with and sympathy for the Arab Shi'i Imams overshadows the role of Iranians in the history of Islamic civilization is evident in the Iranian account of the Abbasid rule. Children are told that the Abbasid dynasty came to power after defeating the Umayyad rulers with the help of an Iranian military leader named Abu Muslim e Khorasani. In a section titled "The Role of Iranians during the Rule of Bani Abbas," children are informed that Abbasids had "many followers among Iranians" and chose Iranian ministers to help them in the affairs of the state. The Barmakiyan are introduced as one of the famous Iranian families who, along with other Iranian scholars, scientists, and physicians, helped advance knowledge during the reign of the Abbasid dynasty (p. 98). Despite the high status of Iranians in military, literary, and scientific circles, the Abbasid leaders are introduced as oppressors who did not follow the precepts of Islam and killed and imprisoned many during their rule. Most importantly for Iranians, however, stands the cruelty against the Shiʻi population and the martyrdom of Shiʻi Imams at the hands of the Abbasids.

One can clearly see that it is not the nationality or ethnic affiliation of the people that matters for textbook compilers. Rather, it is whether or not the persons referred to sympathized with the Shiʻi Imams. It is evident that the religious identity of Iranians seems to be the determining factor and the dichotomy is not an Arab/Iranian but a Shiʻi/non-Shiʻi one. It should be emphasized that textbooks never categorize the Umayyads and Abbasids as Sunnis; instead they have been identified as rulers who have brought misery to their people, especially to the Shiʻis and their leaders—the Infallible Imams. Textbooks do not focus on the national origin of Iranians, but portray them as the advocates of Shiʻism and the faithful followers of Shiʻi Imams—Arabs who were martyred during the reign of the two powerful Arab Muslim dynasties. Ultimately, children are told that Shiʻi Iranians are waiting for the Hidden Imam Mahdi—the Twelfth and last Shiʻi Imam—who will appear and "save the dispossessed (*mostazʻafan*) from the oppression and domination of the great powers" (*Social Studies*, Grade 5 2008: 134).

Paradoxically, the fact that Iranians played a significant role in the advancement of the Islamic civilization, especially during the Abbasid period, gains secondary importance to the Islamic pride in the fact that the Eighth Shiʻi Imam Reza lived in Iran and is buried in the city of Mashhad. The account of Imam Reza's poisoning ordered by Abbasid Caliph Maʼmun (reigned 813–833) (*Social Studies*, Grade 3 2008: 57) is portrayed as being much more important than taking pride in Iranian scientific and literary achievements during the Golden Age of Islamic rule. This does not negate the importance of instilling a sense of Iranian identity or taking pride in Iranian-ness, as illustrated in the section on the Iranian "self," but it does point to how identities are hierarchically constructed. The 2008 textbooks do not distinguish between Iranian-ness and Arab-ness, but rather between notions of good and evil, friend and enemy. There is no doubt that Shiʻis are considered as "good" and the "enemy" is those who impose war on Iran (like Iraqi ruler Saddam Hussein), not because of being Arab or Sunni, but because of their aggressive and oppressive nature.

Accordingly, in the 2008 version of the primary school textbooks, one does not detect manifest national, racial, ethnic, gender, and religious biases and stereotypes in the process of "reading against the text". This applies equally to the content and to the pictorial analysis. What can be detected is the direct instilling of the values of the Iranian ruling authorities on most accounts, combined with a policy of silence on potentially controversial issues. This does not deny the fact that the narration offered in primary school textbooks is a narration of the Iranian government. While this narration is not neutral or value-free, as is the case with any country's narrative, it is also not disrespectful of the social, cultural, religious, and political values of any nation.

Representations of Iraq

The only Arab country that is discussed in detail in the contemporary period is Iraq. In Lesson 6 of the Fifth Grade Geography section, schoolchildren learn about Iran's neighboring countries and read that "our neighbors" have "their own language, religion, and traditions" (*Social Studies*, Grade 5 2008: 27). Iraq is then introduced as one of Iran's neighboring countries, followed by a description of the country's natural, human, and economic situation. Iraq is introduced as an ancient country and the seat of one of the first human civilizations, located along the two rivers, the Dejleh (Tigris) and Forat (Euphrates) (p. 47). Iraq is presented as the country through which Iran is connected to other Arab nations such as Syria, Jordan, Saudi Arabia, and Kuwait (p. 46). Schoolchildren are taught that the people of Iraq are Muslim and speak Arabic. The picture of the Iraqi flag with the inscription *Allah-o Akbar* (God is Great) is yet another reference to the Muslimhood of Iraqis (p. 49). It is emphasized that "more than half of the Iraqi population is composed of Shi'i Muslims (*Mosalmanan-e Shi'i*)" (p. 47). In fact, textbook compilers emphasize that a number of Shi'i Imams are buried in the Iraqi cities of Najaf, Karbala, Kazemeyn, and Samera. Children read that "every year, many Iranians ... undertake a pilgrimage (*ziyarat*) to these cities" (p. 47). They are then asked to locate the cities in which one can find the holy shrines of the Shi'i Imams. A number of pictures show the holy shrines of the Third Shi'i Imam Hossein in Karbala (p. 47), Imam 'Ali in Najaf (p. 92), and Imams Mousa Kazem and Mohammad Taqi in Kazemeyn (p. 99).

Another reference to Iraq appears in the History section of the Fifth Grade *Social Studies* textbook. Iraq is mentioned as the country where Ayatollah Khomeini lived in exile, from 1963 to 1978, on the orders of the late Shah due to his call for rebellion against the Pahlavi dynasty (p. 130). Later it is noted that Ayatollah Khomeini was forced to leave Iraq in 1978 due to the pressure imposed by the Shah, the United States, and the government of Iraq (p. 131).

All the points mentioned above refer to the commonalities shared by Iraq and Iran. The presentation of the 1980–88 war between Iraq and Iran is a bitter one, however. Fifth graders read that the people of Iraq suffered much hardship under Saddam Hussein, "the oppressive ruler of their country" (p. 49). They are told that Saddam attacked Iran in 1980 and imposed a war against Iran and that he was toppled as part of the United States of America's military occupation of Iraq. The textbook adds that "In the year 1385 [2006], Saddam was hanged by the order of this country's [Iraq's] court, and was thereby punished for his ugly acts" (p. 49).

Once again, Iraq is not introduced as an enemy. At all times, evil is personified as Saddam Hussein, Iraq's ruler. He is presented as the one who caused much suffering for both the Iraqi and Iranian people. Children are not taught to look at Iran–Iraq relations within a good/evil or friend/enemy framework. Instead they learn about the person called Saddam Hussein, whose oppressive rule led to an imposed war against Iran. There is an indirect message that the death of Saddam Hussein marks the end of animosity against Iran, and the relationship between the two countries is now centered upon Iranian pilgrims visiting the holy shrines of Shi'i Imams.

Historicizing Iranian Textbooks

It is important to historicize Iranian textbooks and examine whether the representation of the Arabs has changed over time since the establishment of the Islamic Republic. A review of elementary textbooks used at different points of time shows that political shifts in relations with different governments in the Arab world have not been reflected in the school books at the primary level. Even at the peak of the Iran–Iraq war one finds an emphasis on the "holy defense" (*defa'-e moqaddas*) of the homeland. Textbooks never mention that it was a war between Iranians and Arabs. It was instead referred to as a war imposed (*jang-e tahmili*) by the Ba'thi régime to defeat the 1979 revolution and the newly-established Islamic régime.

The Palestinian cause and the struggle against Zionism is also a persisting theme in Iranian textbooks. Yet the Israeli–Palestinian conflict is never portrayed as a war between Jews and Arabs, but rather as a battle between the "oppressor (*zalem*) and the oppressed (*mazlum*). Such events as the Iraqi attack on Kuwait in the 1990s, close connections between the Iranian government and the Hezbollah forces in the region, and the heated and open debate over the name of the Persian Gulf in recent years have never found a place in Iranian primary textbooks. As far as the elementary school textbooks are concerned, compilers choose to remain silent on controversial issues and remain true to the doctrine of Islamic unity, in spite of political debate, division, and at times hostility among Muslims.

The Muslim "Us"

At present, 99.5 percent of Iran's population is Muslim, the majority of whom are Shi'i (Hakimi 2004: 23). Shi'ism became the official religion of Iran in the sixteenth century by the order of Shah Isma'il, the founder of the Safavid dynasty. According to Soudavar (2002), "in the year 1500, Isma'il the Safavid ... barely twelve years old ... scion of the Sufi sheikhs of Ardebil ..." preached Shi'ism and introduced Imam 'Ali and his eleven (male) descendants as the true successors of the Prophet Muhammad (p. 89). This official decree separated Iran from the majority of the Muslim countries that surrounded her. Most importantly, it made Iran distinct from the Ottomans who were at war with Iran. It may be argued that the Safavid decision to declare Shi'ism as the state religion was a political one to create further schism between Iranians and Ottomans. Whatever the underlying reason may be, Iran became, and still remains, the only Muslim country whose state religion is Shi'ism.

Do the above facts distinguish Iran from the rest of the Middle East? In what follows I map the different aspects of this question. First, one could answer the question in the affirmative, by a yes, because the official language of Iran is Persian, distinguishing her from the neighboring Arabic-speaking nations. Furthermore, the Iranian identity is rooted in the pre-Islamic Persian Empire, constructing a different historical memory from Arabs. In addition, Iran is a Shi'i state in the midst of predominantly Sunni Arab states. Within Iran, Arabs and Sunnis are among the linguistic and religious minority groups in the country whose voices have not been heard for centuries. On the other hand, Shi'ism is part of Islam; being Shi'i is integral to the Iranian identity which is heavily imbued with Shi'i beliefs and traditions. In addition, the Islamic Republic of Iran has, for the last thirty years, made every effort to identify itself as part of the greater Islamic community, the majority of which are Sunni.

The Islamic Republic has used many ways to emphasize the Islamic identity of Iranians and create a bond between Iranians and the rest of the Muslim world. The first act of the post-revolutionary government in 1979 was to change the name of the country from Iran, or the land of the Aryans, to the Islamic Republic of Iran. The Iranian flag retained its colors—green, white, and red—but the lion, the sword, and the rising sun in the middle was changed to a symbol marking the name of Allah, with *Allah-o Akbar* (God is Great) printed in the margins. The national anthem was changed (twice) from emphasis on loyalty to the Shah to the commemoration of the Islamic revolution, Ayatollah Khomeini, and the martyrs. The Constitution was changed to the Constitution of the Islamic Republic of Iran, and the Parliament (*Majles*), formerly known as the National Council (*Shora-ye Melli*), was transformed into the Islamic Council (*Shora-ye Islami*) (*Social Studies*, Grade 5 2008: 142–144).

Furthermore, the popular revolution of 1978–79 is referred to as the Islamic revolution (*Enqelab-e Islami*),[9] the slogans of which were Independence, Freedom, and Islamic Republic (*Esteqlal, Azadi, Jomhuri-ye Islami*) (p. 138). Fifth graders are told that the "Muslim people of Iran … wanted to implement Islamic laws in the country" (p. 139); they "revolted to preserve Islam and gave their lives to implement the orders of Islam and the Qur'ān" (p. 148). According to the Civic Education section of the Fifth Grade *Social Studies* textbook, "more than 98 per cent of Iranians voted for the establishment of an Islamic Republic" in April 1979—two months after the overthrow of the Pahlavi dynasty and the end of royal rule in Iran (p. 140). The Islamic Republic is, in turn, obliged "to protect Islam and implement Islamic laws" (p. 148). Schoolchildren are told that "the law in our country is the law of Islam and our people feel obliged to obey the rules and regulations of Islam" (p. 140).

The Islamic identity of post-revolutionary Iran and the Muslimhood of Iranians is emphasized not only by using such terms as "the Muslim people of Iran" (*Mardom-e Mosalman-e Iran*) (pp. 124, 139) and the "Islamic homeland" (*Mihan-e Islami*) (p. 132), but also "our Islamic society," "our Islamic government," and "our Islamic country" (pp. 146–147). Such an emphasis ignores the existence of non-Muslim Iranians who have lived in this country for centuries. It also fails to take into consideration the pre-Islamic religion of this nation—Zoroastrianism— and the originally Iranian prophet—Zoroaster. The policy of focusing on Islam and connecting Iran to the Muslim world excludes the non-Islamic identity of Iranians who have very much been part of the history of this country. The result may be a new identification of "us" and "them" in which the "self" includes all Muslims regardless of their origin, and the "other" is comprised of non-Muslims even if they are Iranian.

The Muslim identity of the Iranian people is also consolidated by the presence of an enemy that seeks to undermine Islam. Fifth graders read that one of the obligations of individuals living in a Muslim society is to feel "hatred for the enemies of the Islamic society" (p. 151). Instilling such a strong negative sentiment among children may be surprising, but directing attention to the "enemies of Islam" (*doshmanan-e Islam*) is perceived as a useful tool to maintain Islamic unity and solidarity. In a lesson titled "Unity," fifth graders read that if division replaces unity in an Islamic society, "the enemies will easily defeat the Muslims" (p. 154). They are also told that "the people of Iran, with faith in God, continue to struggle against the enemies of Islam" (p. 134). The ever-present enemy in primary school books serves two purposes: one is an attempt to unite Iranians against those who are considered "counter-revolutionary" and "anti-establishment," and the other is to create unity among Muslims in general against "foreigners" and "big powers."

The term Iranian Islamic identity (*hoviyyat-e Irani Islami*) is used by the Islamic Republic to define being Iranian during the post-revolutionary period. The emphasis on the Islamic identity is a deliberate effort to connect Iranians to the greater Muslim community. This is for the most part done in primary school textbooks through pictures of mosques, shrines of Shi'i Imams, verses from the Qur'ān, and statements by the Prophet. Children read that they have a dual identity, a hyphenated national–religious (*melli-mazhabi*) one, in which nationality and religion are bound together. The co-existence of the two is indeed reflected in the post-revolutionary name of the country—Islamic Republic of Iran. In a key sentence, schoolchildren are informed that "the Muslim people of Iran are part of the Iranian nation (*mellat-e Iran*) as well as the Islamic community (*ommat-e Islami*)" (*Social Studies*, Grade 4 2008: 132). As a result, they are obliged to "strengthen their ties to the Muslims of other countries" (p. 132).

The theme of belonging to the Iranian nation as well as the larger Muslim community is the point where the Iranian "self" and the Arab "other" is articulated in the Muslim "us." Islamic unity is noted throughout the textbooks studied. Fourth graders read that all Muslims who live in different countries of the world are members of a "big family" called the Islamic *umma*, the population of which is one billion. They are told that "all Muslims belong to the Islamic *umma* ... and believe in one God, Allah. Their Prophet is Hazrat-e Muhammad, their Holy Book is the Qur'ān, and they all say their prayers facing the same *Qibla*. All Muslims (therefore) have the same God, Prophet, Holy Book, and Qibla" (p. 132). Islamic unity is represented by a picture in which Ka'ba is shown during *Hajj* (pilgrimage); children also read Prophet Muhammad's statement that a Muslim is not a Muslim if he/she does not help another Muslim crying for help (pp. 131–132).

The above indicates that textbook compilers seek to emphasize the Muslimhood of Iranians and avoid pointing to Shi'i or Sunni differences. The statement "most of the people of Iran are Muslim" (*bishtar-e mardom-e Iran mosalmanand*) (p. 129) is a deliberate effort to link Iranians to the rest of the Islamic community, without any reference to the schism that often appears between Iran and the Arab world in the political arena, between Sunnis and Shi'is. Educational authorities have even taken radical steps in portraying Iran as having central importance in the Islamic world. The following are examples of this attempt. In the exercise section of the Fourth Grade *Social Studies* textbook, children are asked "Whether Muslims who live outside of Iran are part of the Islamic *umma*?" (p. 133). In the fifth grade, they read that after the death of Ayatollah Khomeini, Ayatollah Khamene'i was chosen as the leader and the "people of Iran and many of the Muslims of the world pledged allegiance (*bey'at*) to the new leader" (*Social Studies*, Grade 5 2008: 133). The word *bey'at* had formerly been used only in reference to the Arab-Muslim Caliphs, denoting acceptance of the Caliphs' leadership. As such, its use in the Iranian context represents another attempt to link the Shi'is in Iran to the Sunni majority living in the Arab world.

The above example is the climax of the conscious and deliberate effort to minimize the borderline between the Iranian "self" and the Arab "other." The pendulum thus stops to swing from Iranian-ness to Arab-ness and reaches the middle ground in the emphasis on the Iranian Islamic identity and the inevitable link between the Iranian nation and the Muslim community.

Looking back at the theoretical framework offered by Tedesco (1997) regarding the identification of the "self" and the "other," and the United Nations declarations and recommendations (UN 1999), one can come to the following conclusion regarding the presentation of Arabs in Iranian school textbooks. The content analysis of primary school *Social Studies* textbooks in Iran shows that it is difficult to draw a definite borderline between the Iranian "self" and the Arab "other" due to the undeniable historical, religious, and cultural ties that bring Iranians and Arabs together. The analysis also shows that it is difficult to approach Arab–Iranian relations in isolation of the larger geopolitical context in which it unfolds as the two have been closely intertwined since the seventh century.

Concluding Remarks

The present study portrays the paradoxical relationship between Iran and the Arab world as portrayed in elementary school textbooks; a relationship between the Arab conqueror and the once-conquered Iranian who still keeps their historical memory of pre-Islamic greatness, takes pride in their glorious past, and preserves their rich cultural heritage. The Persian Empire was indeed conquered by the Arabs and Zoroastrianism was for the most part replaced by Islam. It is true that Iran was ruled by Arabs for almost two hundred years and was considered part of the Islamic-Arabic civilization, to the extent that a number of scientists, mathematicians, physicians, and philosophers born and raised within the geographical boundaries of Iran are known as Arabs throughout the world.[10] It is also true that the present ruling elite of Iran have made every effort to Islamize the country and emphasize Muslim unity with the Palestinian cause at its center. And yet, it seems that the message transmitted by elementary school textbooks is that Iran may have been conquered physically, but it was never dissolved as a nation in the process. Iranian children learn that time after time the conquered rose from the ashes to conquer the conqueror in the cultural, artistic, literary, and even political domains. Even when it comes to Islam, it took nine centuries—from the Arab conquest of the seventh century to the establishment of the Safavid dynasty in the sixteenth century—for Iranians to establish Shi'ism as the state religion. Shi'ism was distinct from the Sunnism of the Arabs and Ottomans and allowed Iranians to keep their distinct identity.

It may not be correct to call Shi'ism the Iranian version of Islam, given the religious and historical roots of the Sunni–Shi'i split and the significant proportion of Shi'i Arabs and non-Arabs in the Muslim community. Yet, just as with the Persian language, Shi'ism has kept Iranians distinct from Arabs. It has also informed the meaning of Iranian-ness at a time when other non-Arabs adopted the Arabic language. Keeping its distinct identity through every means possible may be the Iranian way of healing from a conquest, the effects of which have been considered both a blessing and a wound. Reproducing the Iranian identity, using Persian as the formal language, choosing Shi'ism as the state religion, and celebrating the pre-Islamic heritage through various ceremonies including the Iranian New Year (Noruz), may have separated the "self" and the "other" without disrespect and lack of tolerance for the Arabs and Arab-ness in general. Such a separation may have motivated the compilers of the post-revolutionary Iranian school textbooks to refuse to let their nationalist spirit and very sense of identity and uniqueness be crushed and disappear, long after the Arab conquerors have left their homeland.

Notes

1　*Social Studies*, Grade 3 2008: 7, 18, 46, 69.
2　*Social Studies*, Grade 3 2008: iii, iv, 1, 59, 71, 72.
3　*Social Studies*, Grade 4, 2008: 1, 6, 8, 24, 26, 30, 37, 43–46, 52, 57, 62, 64, 66.
4　*Social Studies*, Grade 4, 2008: 79, 87, 89, 92, 96, 101.
5　*Social Studies*, Grade 4, 2008: 69, 89, 90, 91, 93, 98, 101, 102.
6　*Social Studies*, Grade 5, 2008: 2, 3, 7, 11, 19, 25, 27, 62.
7　*Social Studies*, Grade 5, 2008: 76, 100, 101, 105, 109, 113, 118.
8　*Social Studies*, Grade 5, 2008: 117–119, 123, 126, 128, 129.
9　*Social Studies*, Grade 5, 2008: 138, 143, 147, 148, 154, 162, 163.
10　Here, it is possible to refer, for instance, to Al-Razi, Al-Majusi (Al-Sharrah 2003: 417), and Ibn Sina (Avicenna) who are referred to as "non-Arab scholars from Persia" (Ihtiyar 2003: 237).

References

Akkari, Abdeljalil (2003). "What is Education's Role?" *Prospects* 33: 397–403.
Al-Sharrah, Yaqoub Ahmed. (2003). "The Arab Tradition of Medical Education and Its Relationship with the European Tradition." *Prospects* 33: 413–425.
Ferdows, Adele (1994). "Gender Roles in Iranian School Textbooks." In Samih K. Farsoun and Mehrdad Mashayekhi (eds.) *Iran: Political Culture in the Islamic Republic*, pp. 325–336. London and New York: Routledge.
Hakimi, Ali (2004). *A General Overview of Education in the Islamic Republic of Iran*. Tehran: Institute for Educational Research, Ministry of Education.
Higgins, Patricia J. (1985). "Changing Perceptions of Iranian Identity in Elementary Textbooks." In Elizabeth W. Fernea (ed.) *Women and the Family in the Middle East: New Voices of Change*, pp. 337–363. Austin, TX: University of Texas Press.
Higgins, Patricia J. and Shoar-Ghaffari, Pirouz (1991). "Sex Role Socialization in Iranian Textbooks." *NWSA Journal* 3: 213–232.
Ihtiyar, Nese (2003). "Islam in German Textbooks: Examples from Geography and History." *Prospects* 33: 427–437.
Kashani-Sabet, Firoozeh (2002). "Culture of Iranianness: The Evolving Polemic of Iranian Nationalism." In Nikki R. Keddie and Rudi Matthee (eds.) *Iran and the Surrounding*

World: Interactions in Culture and Cultural Politics, pp. 162–181. Seattle, WA and London: University of Washington Press.

Lamb, Harold Albert (2007). *Cyrus the Great [Kourosh-e Kabir]* Translated by Reza Zadeh Shafaq. Tehran: Pars Ketab. (In Persian.)

Mehran, Golnar (1989). "Socialization of Schoolchildren in the Islamic Republic of Iran." *Iranian Studies* 22: 35–50.

Mehran, Golnar (2002). "The Presentation of the 'Self' and the 'Other' in Postrevolutionary Iranian School Textbooks." In Nikki R. Keddie and Rudi Matthee (eds.) *Iran and the Surrounding World: Interactions in Culture and Cultural Politics*, pp. 232–253. Seattle, WA and London: University of Washington Press.

Mehran, Golnar (2007). "Religious Education of Muslim and Non-Muslim Schoolchildren in the Islamic Republic of Iran." In Colin Brock and Lila Zia Levers (eds.) *Aspects of Education in the Middle East and North Africa*, pp. 99–125. Oxford: Symposium Books.

Ministry of Education, Islamic Republic of Iran (2006). *Collection of the Ratified Laws of the High Council of Education [Majmu'eh-ye Mosavvabat-e Shora-ye 'Ali-ye Amuzesh va Parvaresh]* Tehran: Madreseh Publications. (In Persian.)

Moradi Ghias Abadi, Reza (2007). *Cylinder of Cyrus [Manshour-e Kourosh]*. Shiraz: Navid-e Shiraz Publications. (In Persian.)

Ram, Haggay (2000). "The Immemorial Iranian Nation? School Textbooks and Historical Memory in Post-Revolutionary Iran." *Nations and Nationalism*, 6(1): 67–90.

Shorish, Mobin M. (1988). "Textbooks in Revolutionary Iran." In Philip G. Altbach and Gail P. Kelly (eds.) *Textbooks in the Third World*, pp. 247–268. New York: Garland.

Siavoshi, Sussan (1995). "Régime Legitimacy and High-School Textbooks." In Saeed Rahnema and Sohrab Behdad (eds.) *Iran After the Revolution: Crisis of an Islamic State*. London: I. B. Tauris.

Social Studies, Grade 3 [Ta'limat-e Ejtema'i, Sevvom-e Dabestan]. (2008). Tehran: Ministry of Education. (In Persian.)

Social Studies, Grade 4 (Civic Education) Ta'limat-e Ejtema'i, Chaharom-e Dabestan (Ta'limat-e Madani). (2008). Tehran: Ministry of Education. (In Persian.)

Social Studies, Grade 4 (Geography) Ta'limat-e Ejtema'i, Chaharom-e Dabestan (Joghrafia). (2008). Tehran: Ministry of Education. (In Persian.)

Social Studies, Grade 4 (History) Ta'limat-e Ejtema'i, Chaharom-e Dabestan (Tarikh). (2008). Tehran: Ministry of Education. (In Persian.)

Social Studies, Grade 5 (Civic Education) Ta'limat-e Ejtema'i, Panjom-e Dabestan (Ta'limat-e Madani). (2008). Tehran: Ministry of Education. (In Persian.)

Social Studies, Grade 5 (Geography) Ta'limat-e Ejtema'i, Panjom-e Dabestan (Joghrafia). (2008). Tehran: Ministry of Education. (In Persian.)

Social Studies, Grade 5 (History) Ta'limat-e Ejtema'i, Panjom-e Dabestan (Tarikh). (2008). Tehran: Ministry of Education. (In Persian.)

Soudavar, Abolala (2002). "The Early Safavids and Their Cultural Interactions with Surrounding States." In Nikki R. Keddie and Rudi Matthee (eds.) *Iran and the Surrounding World: Interactions in Culture and Cultural Politics*, pp. 89–120. Seattle, WA and London: University of Washington Press.

Tedesco, Juan Carlos (1997). *The New Educational Pact: Education, Competitiveness, and Citizenship in Modern Society*. Paris: UNESCO, IBE.

Touba, Jacquiline Rudolph (1987). "Cultural Effects on Sex Role Images in Elementary Schoolbooks in Iran: A Content Analysis after the Revolution." *International Journal of Sociology of the Family*, 17: 143–158.

UN (1999). *The Right to Human Rights Education*. New York and Geneva: Office of the United Nations High Commissioner for Human Rights.

Index

'Arabic surnames prefixed by al- or el- are alphabetized under the element following the particle.' The letters 'n' and 't' in a locator refer to 'note' and 'table,' respectively.

Suher Zaher

'Abd Al-Nasser, Gamal 111n5
'Aflaq, Michel 264
awrāt see music
Abdullah I (King of Jordan) 132
Abdullah II (King of Jordan) 132
abla 126
Abu-Habib, L. 209
Abu-Saad, I. 233
Academic Ranking of World Universities *see* Shanghai ranking
access to education 183-4, 186, 187, 188-9, 190-2, 200, 234, 335, 346; and CESCR 190-2; 'Compulsory Education Law' (Israel) 232; and disabilities 196; and gender 166, 345; and international aid 88; and literacy 187-8, 189t10.2, 231; and national identity 81; and security considerations 340-4, *see also* right to education; student enrollment
access to information 301, 330
access to rehabilitative services 203
accountability: and role of scholars 346; policy in Lebanon 97
Adami, Edward Fenech 240
Adely, Fida xiii, 17, 18, 19, 35
adolescents: in Arab society 124; participation in patriotic rituals 134, *see also* youth
adult authority: and students 122, 124-5
Agadir Charter *see* Amazigh; AMREC
Agamben, Giorgio 343
Agasi, Tikva (née Amal Salih) 164
Ahardane, Mahjoubi 221

Ajami, Fouad 324
Akkari, Abdeljalil xiv, 13-14, 26, 32
Algeria: access to education in 187; Algerian crisis (1991) 79; and discrimination 273; education policies of 45, 69, 217; higher education in 273-4, 275-6, 277, 278-82, 283; language policies of 215, 216-17; literacy in 188, 189t10.2; privatization in 47; public funding in 190; society 273, 282; socio–linguistic tensions 215; state vs. power in 275; student enrollment 46, 188, 189t10.1, 190, *see also* Maghreb; Alghazo, E.M. 203
Allais, S. 63, 64
Alliance israélite universelle (school) 166, 168, 169, *see also* Iraqi schools; schools; *Shammash* (school)
Almozlino, Shoshana Arbeli 171, 172
Alsup, J. 146
Amazigh: identity 217; NGOs 217, *see also* Amazigh language, AMREC
Amazigh language 214-18, 219-20, 221-3, 222t12.1, *see also* language policies; languages
American University in Cairo (AUC) 120, 121, 325
American University of Beirut (AUB) 324-5
Amin, S. 67
Amor, A. 248
AMREC (Moroccan Association for Research and Culture Exchange) 217
anti-Americanism: and geopolitics 263; and Islamic identity 263; and US cultural diplomacy 329
'anti-Arabism': in Lebanon 108, 111n5; and political Islam 265, *see also* Arabism (contemporary)
apartheid 337
Appadurai, A. 12